T0203017

Lecture Notes in Computer Science 11642

Founding Editors

Gerhard Goos
  Karlsruhe Institute of Technology, Karlsruhe, Germany
Juris Hartmanis
  Cornell University, Ithaca, NY, USA

Editorial Board Members

Elisa Bertino
  Purdue University, West Lafayette, IN, USA
Wen Gao
  Peking University, Beijing, China
Bernhard Steffen
  TU Dortmund University, Dortmund, Germany
Gerhard Woeginger
  RWTH Aachen, Aachen, Germany
Moti Yung
  Columbia University, New York, NY, USA

More information about this series at http://www.springer.com/series/7409

Jie Shao · Man Lung Yiu ·
Masashi Toyoda · Dongxiang Zhang ·
Wei Wang · Bin Cui (Eds.)

Web and Big Data

Third International Joint Conference, APWeb-WAIM 2019
Chengdu, China, August 1–3, 2019
Proceedings, Part II

 Springer

Editors
Jie Shao
University of Electronic Science
and Technology of China
Chengdu, China

Masashi Toyoda
The University of Tokyo
Tokyo, Japan

Wei Wang
National University of Singapore
Singapore, Singapore

Man Lung Yiu
Hong Kong Polytechnic University
Hong Kong, China

Dongxiang Zhang
Zhejiang University
Hangzhou, China

Bin Cui
Peking University
Beijing, China

ISSN 0302-9743   ISSN 1611-3349 (electronic)
Lecture Notes in Computer Science
ISBN 978-3-030-26074-3   ISBN 978-3-030-26075-0 (eBook)
https://doi.org/10.1007/978-3-030-26075-0

LNCS Sublibrary: SL3 – Information Systems and Applications, incl. Internet/Web, and HCI

© Springer Nature Switzerland AG 2019
This work is subject to copyright. All rights are reserved by the Publisher, whether the whole or part of the material is concerned, specifically the rights of translation, reprinting, reuse of illustrations, recitation, broadcasting, reproduction on microfilms or in any other physical way, and transmission or information storage and retrieval, electronic adaptation, computer software, or by similar or dissimilar methodology now known or hereafter developed.
The use of general descriptive names, registered names, trademarks, service marks, etc. in this publication does not imply, even in the absence of a specific statement, that such names are exempt from the relevant protective laws and regulations and therefore free for general use.
The publisher, the authors and the editors are safe to assume that the advice and information in this book are believed to be true and accurate at the date of publication. Neither the publisher nor the authors or the editors give a warranty, expressed or implied, with respect to the material contained herein or for any errors or omissions that may have been made. The publisher remains neutral with regard to jurisdictional claims in published maps and institutional affiliations.

This Springer imprint is published by the registered company Springer Nature Switzerland AG
The registered company address is: Gewerbestrasse 11, 6330 Cham, Switzerland

Preface

This volume (LNCS 11641) and its companion volume (LNCS 11642) contain the proceedings of the Third Asia-Pacific Web (APWeb) and Web-Age Information Management (WAIM) Joint Conference on Web and Big Data, called APWeb-WAIM. This joint conference aims at attracting professionals of different communities related to Web and big data who have common interests in interdisciplinary research to share and exchange ideas, experiences, and the underlying techniques and applications, including Web technologies, database systems, information management, software engineering, and big data.

The Third APWeb-WAIM conference was held in Chengdu, China, during August 1–3, 2019. APWeb and WAIM are two separate leading international conferences on research, development, and applications of Web technologies and database systems. Previous APWeb conferences were held in Beijing (1998), Hong Kong (1999), Xi'an (2000), Changsha (2001), Xi'an (2003), Hangzhou (2004), Shanghai (2005), Harbin (2006), Huangshan (2007), Shenyang (2008), Suzhou (2009), Busan (2010), Beijing (2011), Kunming (2012), Sydney (2013), Changsha (2014), Guangzhou (2015), and Suzhou (2016). Previous WAIM conferences were held in Shanghai (2000), Xi'an (2001), Beijing (2002), Chengdu (2003), Dalian (2004), Hangzhou (2005), Hong Kong (2006), Huangshan (2007), Zhangjiajie (2008), Suzhou (2009), Jiuzhaigou (2010), Wuhan (2011), Harbin (2012), Beidaihe (2013), Macau (2014), Qingdao (2015), and Nanchang (2016). Starting in 2017, the two conference committees agreed to launch a joint conference. The First APWeb-WAIM conference was held in Bejing (2017) and the Second APWeb-WAIM conference was held in Macau (2018). With the increased focus on big data, the new joint conference is expected to attract more professionals from different industrial and academic communities, not only from the Asia Pacific countries but also from other continents.

The high-quality program documented in these proceedings would not have been possible without the authors who chose APWeb-WAIM for disseminating their findings. After the double-blind review process (each paper received at least three review reports), out of 180 submissions, the conference accepted 42 regular (23.33%), 17 short research papers, and six demonstrations. The contributed papers address a wide range of topics, such as big data analytics, data and information quality, data mining and application, graph data and social networks, information extraction and retrieval, knowledge graph, machine learning, recommender systems, storage, indexing and physical database design, text analysis and mining. We are deeply thankful to the Program Committee members for lending their time and expertise to the conference. The technical program also included keynotes by Dr. Divesh Srivastava (AT&T Labs-Research, USA), Dr. Xindong Wu (Mininglamp Technology, China), Prof. Christian S. Jensen (Aalborg University, Denmark), and Prof. Guoliang Li (Tsinghua University, China). We are grateful to these distinguished scientists for their invaluable contributions to the conference program.

We thank the general co-chairs (Heng Tao Shen, Kotagiri Ramamohanarao, and Jiliu Zhou) for their guidance and support. Thanks also go to the workshop co-chairs (Jingkuan Song and Xiaofeng Zhu), tutorial co-chairs (Shaojie Qiao and Jiajun Liu), demo co-chairs (Wei Lu and Jizhou Luo), industry co-chairs (Jianjun Chen and Jia Zhu), and publicity co-chairs (Lei Duan, Yoshiharu Ishikawa, Jianxin Li, and Weining Qian).

We hope you enjoy the exciting program of APWeb-WAIM 2019 as documented in these proceedings.

June 2019

Jie Shao
Man Lung Yiu
Masashi Toyoda
Dongxiang Zhang
Wei Wang
Bin Cui

Organization

General Chairs

Heng Tao Shen	University of Electronic Science and Technology of China, China
Kotagiri Ramamohanarao	University of Melbourne, Australia
Jiliu Zhou	Chengdu University of Information Technology, China

Program Committee Chairs

Jie Shao	University of Electronic Science and Technology of China, China
Man Lung Yiu	Hong Kong Polytechnic University, Hong Kong SAR, China
Masashi Toyoda	The University of Tokyo, Japan

Workshop Chairs

Jingkuan Song	University of Electronic Science and Technology of China, China
Xiaofeng Zhu	Massey University, New Zealand

Tutorial Chairs

Shaojie Qiao	Chengdu University of Information Technology, China
Jiajun Liu	Renmin University of China, China

Demo Chairs

Wei Lu	Renmin University of China, China
Jizhou Luo	Harbin Institue of Technology, China

Industry Chairs

Jianjun Chen	Huawei America Research, USA
Jia Zhu	South China Normal University, China

Publication Chairs

Dongxiang Zhang	Zhejiang University, China
Wei Wang	National University of Singapore, Singapore
Bin Cui	Peking University, China

Publicity Chairs

Lei Duan	Sichuan University, China
Yoshiharu Ishikawa	Nagoya University, Japan
Jianxin Li	University of Western Australia, Australia
Weining Qian	East China Normal University, China

Local Arrangements Chairs

Yang Yang	University of Electronic Science and Technology of China, China
Hong Xiao	University of Electronic Science and Technology of China, China

Webmaster

Xiaochen Wang	University of Electronic Science and Technology of China, China

Senior Program Committee

Toshiyuki Amagasa	University of Tsukuba, Japan
Wolf-Tilo Balke	TU Braunschweig, Germany
Xin Luna Dong	Amazon, USA
Mizuho Iwaihara	Waseda University, Japan
Peer Kroger	Ludwig Maximilian University of Munich, Germany
Byung Suk Lee	University of Vermont, USA
Sebastian Link	University of Auckland, New Zealand
Wookey Lee	Inha University, South Korea
Yang-Sae Moon	Kangwon National University, South Korea
Xiaokui Xiao	National University of Singapore, Singapore
Rui Zhang	University of Melbourne, Australia
Shuigeng Zhou	Fudan University, China
Xiangliang Zhang	King Abdullah University of Science and Technology, Saudi Arabia
Xingquan Zhu	Florida Atlantic University, USA

Program Committee

Zhifeng Bao	RMIT University, Australia
Ilaria Bartolini	University of Bologna, Italy
Ladjel Bellatreche	ISAE-ENSMA, France
Zouhaier Brahmia	University of Sfax, Tunisia
Yi Cai	South China University of Technology, China
Tru Cao	Ho Chi Minh City University of Technology, Vietnam

Lisi Chen	Inception Institute of Artificial Intelligence, United Arab Emirates
Tanzima Hashem	Bangladesh University of Engineering and Technology, Bangladesh
Reynold Cheng	University of Hong Kong, Hong Kong SAR, China
Lizhen Cui	Shandong University, China
Jiangtao Cui	Xidian University, China
Alex Delis	University of Athens, Greece
Lei Duan	Sichuan University, China
Amr Ebaid	Purdue University, USA
Ju Fan	Renmin University of China, China
Yaokai Feng	Kyushu University, Japan
Yunjun Gao	Zhejiang University, China
Tingjian Ge	University of Massachusetts, Lowell, USA
Zhiguo Gong	University of Macau, Macau SAR, China
Chenjuan Guo	Aalborg University, Denmark
Jialong Han	Tencent, China
Haibo Hu	Hong Kong Polytechnic University, Hong Kong SAR, China
Jianbin Huang	Xidian University, China
Chih-Chieh Hung	Tamkang University, Taiwan
Dawei Jiang	Zhejiang University, China
Cheqing Jin	East China Normal University, China
Peiquan Jin	University of Science and Technology of China, China
Feifei Li	University of Utah, USA
Tianrui Li	Southwest Jiaotong University, China
Hui Li	Xiamen University, China
Zheng Li	Amazon, USA
Yu Li	Hangzhou Dianzi University, China
Xiang Lian	Kent State University, USA
An Liu	Soochow University, China
Hailong Liu	Northwestern Polytechnical University, China
Guanfeng Liu	Macquarie University, Australia
Hua Lu	Aalborg University, Denmark
Mihai Lupu	Vienna University of Technology, Austria
Zakaria Maamar	Zayed University, United Arab Emirates
Mirco Nanni	ISTI-CNR Pisa, Italy
Sanjay Madria	Missouri University of Science and Technology, USA
P. Krishna Reddy	International Institute of Information Technology, Hyderabad, India
Wee Siong Ng	Institute for Infocomm Research, Singapore
Baoning Niu	Taiyuan University of Technology, China
Hiroaki Ohshima	University of Hyogo, Japan
Yuwei Peng	Wuhan University, China
Jianzhong Qi	University of Melbourne, Australia
Yanghui Rao	Sun Yat-sen University, China

Dimitris Sacharidis	Vienna University of Technology, Austria
Aviv Segev	University of South Alabama, USA
Yingxia Shao	Beijing University of Posts and Telecommunication, China
Junming Shao	University of Electronic Science and Technology of China, China
Derong Shen	Northeastern University, China
Victor Sheng	University of Central Arkansas, USA
Kyuseok Shim	Seoul National University, South Korea
Lidan Shou	Zhejiang University, China
Shaoxu Song	Tsinghua University, China
Yong Tang	South China Normal University, China
Bo Tang	Southern University of Science and Technology, China
Goce Trajcevski	Iowa State University, USA
Leong Hou U.	University of Macau, Macau SAR, China
Kazutoshi Umemoto	University of Tokyo, Japan
Hongzhi Wang	Harbin Institute of Technology, China
Jianguo Wang	University of California, San Diego, USA
Lizhen Wang	Yunnan University, China
Yijie Wang	National University of Defense Technology, China
Xin Wang	Tianjin University, China
Sheng Wang	RMIT University, Australia
Raymond Chi-Wing Wong	Hong Kong University of Science and Technology, Hong Kong SAR, China
Han Su	University of Electronic Science and Technology of China, China
Shengli Wu	Jiangsu University, China
Yanghua Xiao	Fudan University, China
Xike Xie	University of Science and Technology of China, China
Qing Xie	Wuhan University of Technology, China
Jianliang Xu	Hong Kong Baptist University, Hong Kong SAR, China
Xin-Shun Xu	Shandong University, China
Dingyu, Yang	Shanghai Dian Ji University, China
Lianghuai Yang	Zhejiang University of Technology, China
Junjie Yao	East China Normal University, China
Hongzhi Yin	University of Queensland, Australia
Xiaohui Yu	Shandong University, China
Meihui Zhang	Beijing Institute of Technology, China
Xujian Zhao	Southwest University of Science and Technology, China
Jianqiu Xu	Nanjing University of Aeronautics and Astronautics, China
Xiang Zhao	National University of Defence Technology, China
Lei Zhao	Soochow University, China
Xiangmin Zhou	RMIT University, Australia

Feida Zhu   Singapore Management University, Singapore
Zhaonian Zou   Harbin Institute of Technology, China
Lei Zou   Peking University, China
Bolong Zheng   Huazhong University of Science and Technology,
                           China
Kai Zheng   University of Electronic Science and Technology
                           of China, China

Contents – Part II

Machine Learning

Using Sentiment Representation Learning to Enhance Gender Classification
for User Profiling 3
    Yunpei Zheng, Lin Li, Jianwei Zhang, Qing Xie, and Luo Zhong

Exploring Nonnegative and Low-Rank Correlation for Noise-Resistant
Spectral Clustering 12
    Zheng Wang, Cai Na, Zeyu Ma, Si Chen, Lingyun Song, and Yang Yang

FeatureBand: A Feature Selection Method by Combining Early Stopping
and Genetic Local Search.. 27
    Huanran Xue, Jiawei Jiang, Yingxia Shao, and Bin Cui

Supervised Hashing with Recurrent Scaling 42
    Xiyao Fu, Yi Bin, Zheng Wang, Qin Wei, and Si Chen

TRPN: Matrix Factorization Meets Recurrent Neural Network for Temporal
Rating Prediction 57
    Haozhe Zhu, Yanyan Shen, and Xian Zhou

Improved Review Sentiment Analysis with a Syntax-Aware Encoder....... 73
    Jiangfeng Zeng, Ming Yang, Ke Zhou, Xiao Ma, Yangtao Wang,
    Xiaodong Xu, and Zhili Xiao

Who Is the Abnormal User: Anomaly Detection Framework based
on the Graph Convolutional Networks................................ 88
    Zetao Zheng, Jia Zhu, Yong Tang, and Jiabing Du

I-mRMR: Incremental Max-Relevance, and Min-Redundancy
Feature Selection... 103
    Yeliang Xiu, Suyun Zhao, Hong Chen, and Cuiping Li

ST-DCN: A Spatial-Temporal Densely Connected Networks for Crowd
Flow Prediction 111
    Longlong Xu, Xiansheng Chen, Yue Xu, Wei Chen, and Tengjiao Wang

Recommender Systems

Streaming Recommendation Algorithm with User Interest Drift Analysis 121
    Jianzong Chen, Hanlu Li, Qing Xie, Lin Li, and Yongjian Liu

Unified Group Recommendation Towards Multiple Criteria   137
   Yi Wu, Ning Yang, and Huanrui Luo

A Novel Ensemble Approach for Click-Through Rate Prediction Based
on Factorization Machines and Gradient Boosting Decision Trees   152
   Xiaochen Wang, Gang Hu, Haoyang Lin, and Jiayu Sun

Latent Path Connected Space Model for Recommendation   163
   Lang Mei, Jun He, Hongyan Liu, and Xiaoyong Du

Storage, Indexing and Physical Database Design

FreshJoin: An Efficient and Adaptive Algorithm for Set Containment Join . . .   175
   Jizhou Luo, Wei Zhang, Shengfei Shi, Hong Gao, Jianzhong Li,
   Tao Zhang, and Zening Zhou

Apara: Workload-Aware Data Partition and Replication
for Parallel Databases   191
   Xiaolei Zhang, Chunxi Zhang, Yuming Li, Rong Zhang,
   and Aoying Zhou

Which Category Is Better: Benchmarking the RDBMSs and GDBMSs   207
   Pengjie Ding, Yijian Cheng, Wei Lu, Hao Huang, and Xiaoyong Du

Spatial, Temporal and Multimedia Databases

A Meta-Path-Based Recurrent Model for Next POI Prediction with Spatial
and Temporal Contexts   219
   Hengpeng Xu, Peizhi Wu, Jinmao Wei, Zhenglu Yang, and Jun Wang

Discovering Attractive Segments in the User Generated Video Streams   236
   Jie Zhou, Jiangbo Ai, Zheng Wang, Si Chen, and Qin Wei

Spatial Temporal Trajectory Similarity Join   251
   Tangpeng Dan, Changyin Luo, Yanhong Li, Bolong Zheng,
   and Guohui Li

Data Driven Charging Station Placement   260
   Yudi Guo, Junjie Yao, Jiaxiang Huang, and Yijun Chen

An Efficient Top-*k* Spatial Join Query Processing Algorithm
on Big Spatial Data.   268
   Baiyou Qiao, Bing Hu, Xiyu Qiao, Laigang Yao, Junhai Zhu,
   and Gang Wu

Multi-view Based Spatial-Keyword Query Processing for Real Estate   276
   Xi Duan, Liping Wang, and Shiyu Yang

Text Analysis and Mining

PowerMonitor: Aspect Mining and Sentiment Analysis
on Online Reviews   295
  Zhibin Zhao, Lan Yao, Siyuan Wang, and Ge Yu

Transformer and Multi-scale Convolution for Target-Oriented
Sentiment Analysis   310
  Yinxu Pan, Binheng Song, Ningqi Luo, Xiaojun Chen, and Hengbin Cui

A New Feature Selection Algorithm Based on Category Difference
for Text Categorization   322
  Wang Zhang, Chanjuan Chen, Lei Jiang, and Xu Bai

Opinion-Aware Knowledge Embedding for Stance Detection   337
  *Zhenhui Xu, Qiang Li, Wei Chen, Yingbao Cui, Zhen Qiu,
  and Tengjiao Wang*

History-Driven Entity Categorization   349
  Yijun Duan, Adam Jatowt, and Katsumi Tanaka

MBMN: Multivariate Bernoulli Mixture Network for News
Emotion Analysis   365
  Xue Zhao, Ying Zhang, Wenya Guo, and Xiaojie Yuan

Multi-label Text Classification: Select Distinct Semantic Understanding
for Different Labels   380
  *Wei Sun, Xiangying Ran, Xiangyang Luo, Yunlai Xu,
  and Chongjun Wang*

Demos

FMQO: A Federated RDF System Supporting Multi-query Optimization   397
  Qi Ge, Peng Peng, Zhiwei Xu, Lei Zou, and Zheng Qin

DataServiceHatch: Generating and Composing Continuous Data Services. . . .   402
  Guiling Wang, Tongtong Cui, Xiaojiang Zuo, Yao Xu, and Yanbo Han

A Mobile Phone Data Visualization Tool for People Flow Analysis   407
  Liangjian Chen, Siyu Chen, Shengnan Guo, Yue Yang, and Jianqiu Xu

NativeHelper: A Bilingual Sentence Search and Recommendation Engine
for Academic Writing   412
  Weijian Ni, Yujian Sun, Tong Liu, Qingtian Zeng, and Nengfu Xie

PKRS: A Product Knowledge Retrieve System   417
  Taoyi Huang, Yuming Lin, Haibo Tang, You Li, and Huibing Zhang

DataSESec: Security Monitoring for Data Share and Exchange Platform   422
  Guowei Shen, Lu Liu, Qin Wei, Jicheng Lei, and Chun Guo

Author Index   429

Contents – Part I

Big Data Analytic

A Framework for Image Dark Data Assessment   3
  Yu Liu, Yangtao Wang, Ke Zhou, Yujuan Yang, Yifei Liu, Jingkuan Song,
  and Zhili Xiao

Medical Treatment Migration Prediction in Healthcare via Attention-Based
Bidirectional GRU 19
  Lin Cheng, Yongjian Ren, Kun Zhang, and Yuliang Shi

WRL: A Combined Model for Short-Term Load Forecasting 35
  Yuecan Liu, Kun Zhang, Shuai Zhen, Yongming Guan, and Yuliang Shi

Data and Information Quality

DeepAM: Deep Semantic Address Representation for Address Matching 45
  Shuangli Shan, Zhixu Li, Yang Qiang, An Liu, Jiajie Xu,
  and Zhigang Chen

Drawing CoCo Core-Sets from Incomplete Relational Data 61
  Yongnan Liu and Jianzhong Li

Reducing Wrong Labels for Distant Supervision Relation Extraction
with Selective Capsule Network 77
  Zihao Wang, Yong Zhang, and Chunxiao Xing

Data Mining and Application

Coupled Semi-supervised Clustering: Exploring Attribute Correlations
in Heterogeneous Information Networks. 95
  Jianan Zhao, Ding Xiao, Linmei Hu, and Chuan Shi

PrivBUD-Wise: Differentially Private Frequent Itemsets Mining
in High-Dimensional Databases 110
  Jingxin Xu, Kai Han, Pingping Song, Chaoting Xu, and Fei Gui

A Learning Approach for Topic-Aware Influence Maximization 125
  Shan Tian, Ping Zhang, Songsong Mo, Liwei Wang, and Zhiyong Peng

DeepDial: Passage Completion on Dialogs 141
  Nan Hu, Jianyun Zhou, and Xiaojun Wan

A Survival Certification Model Based on Active Learning over Medical
Insurance Data   156
   Yongjian Ren, Kun Zhang, and Yuliang Shi

A Novel Approach for Air Quality Inference and Prediction Based
on DBU-LSTM.   171
   Liang Ge, Aoli Zhou, Junling Liu, and Hang Li

Predictive Role Discovery of Research Teams Using Ordinal
Factorization Machines   187
   Tong Liu, Weijian Ni, Qingtian Zeng, and Nengfu Xie

Deep Learning for Online Display Advertising User Clicks
and Interests Prediction   196
   Zhabiz Gharibshah, Xingquan Zhu, Arthur Hainline,
   and Michael Conway

Graph Data and Social Networks

In Pursuit of Social Capital: Upgrading Social Circle Through
Edge Rewiring   207
   Qian Chen, Hongyi Su, Jiamou Liu, Bo Yan, Hong Zheng, and He Zhao

Distributed Landmark Selection for Lower Bound Estimation of Distances
in Large Graphs   223
   Mingdao Li, Peng Peng, Yang Xu, Hao Xia, and Zheng Qin

AERIAL: An Efficient Randomized Incentive-Based Influence
Maximization Algorithm   240
   Yongyue Sun, Qingyun Wang, and Hongyan Li

Cider: Highly Efficient Processing of Densely Overlapped Communities in
Big Graphs.   255
   Yadi Chen, Wen Bai, Runyuan Chen, Di Wu, Guoqiao Ye,
   and Zhichuan Huang

Time Optimal Profit Maximization in a Social Network.   264
   Yong Liu, Zitu Liu, Shengnan Xie, and Xiaokun Li

Iterative Hypergraph Computation Based
on Hyperedge-Connected Graphs   273
   Kaiqiang Yu, Yu Gu, Shuo Yao, Zhen Song, and Ge Yu

How to Reach: Discovering Multi-resolution Paths
on Large Scale Networks   281
   Zhaokun Zhang, Ning Yang, and Philip S. Yu

Analysis and Management to Hash-Based Graph and Rank 289
 Yangtao Wang, Yu Liu, Yifei Liu, Ke Zhou, Yujuan Yang,
 Jiangfeng Zeng, Xiaodong Xu, and Zhili Xiao

Information Extraction and Retrieval

Two-Encoder Pointer-Generator Network for Summarizing Segments of
Long Articles 299
 Junhao Li and Mizuho Iwaihara

Enhancing Joint Entity and Relation Extraction with Language Modeling
and Hierarchical Attention 314
 Renjun Chi, Bin Wu, Linmei Hu, and Yunlei Zhang

An Unsupervised Learning Approach for NER Based on Online
Encyclopedia 329
 Maolong Li, Qiang Yang, Fuzhen He, Zhixu Li, Pengpeng Zhao,
 Lei Zhao, and Zhigang Chen

Pseudo Topic Analysis for Boosting Pseudo Relevance Feedback 345
 Rong Yan and Guanglai Gao

Knowledge Graph

Leveraging Domain Context for Question Answering over
Knowledge Graph 365
 Peihao Tong, Junjie Yao, Linzi He, and Liang Xu

Leveraging Lexical Semantic Information for Learning Concept-Based
Multiple Embedding Representations for Knowledge Graph Completion 382
 Yashen Wang, Yifeng Liu, Huanhuan Zhang, and Haiyong Xie

Efficient Distributed Knowledge Representation Learning for Large
Knowledge Graphs 398
 Lele Chai, Xin Wang, Baozhu Liu, and Yajun Yang

Coherence and Salience-Based Multi-Document Relationship Mining 414
 Yongpan Sheng and Zenglin Xu

Author Index 431

Machine Learning

Using Sentiment Representation Learning to Enhance Gender Classification for User Profiling

Yunpei Zheng[1], Lin Li[1(✉)], Jianwei Zhang[2], Qing Xie[1], and Luo Zhong[1]

[1] School of Computer Science and Technology, Wuhan University of Technology,
Wuhan 430070, China
`PPgirl87@foxmail.com`, {`cathylilin,felixxq,zhongluo`}`@whut.edu.cn`
[2] Faculty of Science and Engineering, Iwate University, Morioka 0208551, Japan
`zhang@iwate-u.ac.jp`

Abstract. User profiling means exploiting the technology of machine learning to predict attributes of users, such as demographic attributes, hobby attributes, preference attributes, etc. It's a powerful data support of precision marketing. Existing methods mainly study network behavior, personal preferences and post texts to build user profile. Through our data analysis of micro-blog, we find that females show more positive and have richer sentiments than males in online social platform. This difference is very conducive to the distinction between genders. Therefore, we argue that sentiment context is important as well for user profiling. In this paper, we propose to predict one of the demographic labels: gender by exploring micro-blog user posts. Firstly we build a sentiment polarity classifier in advance by training a Long Short-Term Memory (LSTM) model. Next we extract sentiment representations from LSTM middle layer. Lastly we combine sentiment representations with virtual document vectors to train a basic MLP network for gender classification. We conduct experiments on a dataset provided by SMP CUP 2016 in China. Experimental results show that our approach can improve gender classification accuracy by 5.53%, compared with classical MLP gender classification without sentiment context.

Keywords: Gender classification · Neural networks ·
Sentiment representation · User profiling

1 Introduction

User profiling is a labeled user model abstracted from information like user social attributes, lifestyle and consumer behavior. The key work of user profiling is to

This work is supported by the National Social Science Foundation of China (Grant No: 15BGL048), Hubei Provincial Natural Science Foundation of China (Grant No. 2017CFA012) and JSPS KAKENHI Grant Number 19K12230.

© Springer Nature Switzerland AG 2019
J. Shao et al. (Eds.): APWeb-WAIM 2019, LNCS 11642, pp. 3–11, 2019.
https://doi.org/10.1007/978-3-030-26075-0_1

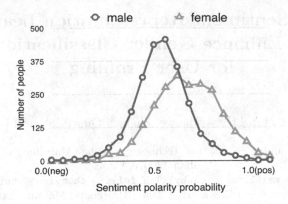

Fig. 1. Sentiment polarity probability difference between male and female.

label users with some highly refined features that can summarize user characteristics through analysis of various user information, in a word, digitizing users. The potential applications of user profiling includes precision marketing, Data statistics, decision support, etc. Gender label supports designing a personalized product. However, in social media, filling basic information is not compulsive. As a result, some labels may be missing or untrue. Therefore, it is necessary to predict the gender of users.

In order to improve the accuracy of gender classification, it is very important to select effective features. After investigating the data, we find there exits sentiment difference between male and female. Through analyzing our sample data, we make a sentiment polarity probability distribution of different gender. We can see from Fig. 1 that, most of the micro-blog posts sent by male are very neutral, while on the whole, female are more positive than male. Experiments conducted by Zhang et al. [21] and Bianchin et al. [1] also confirmed this point.

To the best of our knowledge, there is few researchers who study gender classification by adding sentiment in user profiling. However, there exist two problems: (1) How to get sentiment labels since there is no labelled sentiment information in micro-blog training set. (2) How to effectively represent sentiment information for gender classification. Our main contribution is listed as follows to alleviate the above problems:

- In order to get sentiment labels of micro-blog, we learn sentiment information from commodity reviews. We calculate the similarity between reviews and micro-blog, and select the high similarity data to be source domain. We train a LSTM sentiment classifier on source domain data.
- We input micro-blog posts to the LSTM to get target domain sentiment representations. More specifically, we extract frozen LSTM layer output to be our sentiment representations. Micro-blog post vectors are combined with these sentiment representations to form the final input representations.

Experimental results show that our approach can improve classical gender classification by 5.53%. The rest of this paper is organized as follows: Sect. 2

reviews the related work of user profiling and sentiment analysis, Sect. 3 describes our approach in detail, Sect. 4 validates our proposal by experiment results, and Sect. 5 makes a conclusion of our work and discusses our future work.

2 Related Work

User profiling has attracted many research efforts. Researchers have exploited wide various forms of data for user profiling. Zhang et al. [20] incorporate multiple textual perspectives to classify users. Volkova et al. [12] learn log-linear models using lexical features to infer various traits from user communications in social media. Li et al. [6] explore character and word n-gram as features as well as character and word embeddings for classification. Farnadi et al. [4] merge multiple modalities of user data to predict age, gender, and personality. Multi-view based analysis is another effective way to deal with multiple modal data. [14–16]. Burger et al. [2] conduct experiments on screen name, full name, description, tweets to predict gender. Li et al. [7] infer missing attributes of user profile based on Convolutional Neural Network (CNN). Our work is different from the above research since we consider sentiment analysis in user profiling.

As for sentiment analysis, various researchers have developed effective approaches of sentiment analysis. Li et al. [8] propose a Hierarchical Attention Transfer Network (HATN) for cross-domain sentiment classification. Wang et al. [17] build a RNN-Capsule for sentiment analysis without using any linguistic knowledge on movie reviews and other datasets. Wang et al. [13] investigate a novel task of online dispute detection. Pla et al. [11] develop a sentiment analysis system to detect user political tendency. Sentiment analysis has a lot of applications such as public opinion analysis, political tendency analysis, information prediction. However, there are few researches which apply it to user profiling.

3 Our SRL-MLP Approach

3.1 Framework

This paper utilizes a supervised approach to classify gender of micro-blog users. The framework of our proposed approach is showed in Fig. 2. This framework include three parts. The first part is micro-blog posts preprocess. In this part we input tokenized micro-blog posts to get two types of document representation. The second part is sentiment representation learning. In this part we consider some deep learning models, like Long Short-Term Memory (LSTM) and Convolutional Neural Network (CNN), to get sentiment representation learning model. The third part is gender classification part. In this part, candidate networks for the gender classifier include Multi-Layer Perceptron (MLP), CNN, LSTM, Bidirectional Long Short-Term Memory (BiLSTM), Hierarchical Attention Networks (HAN), etc.

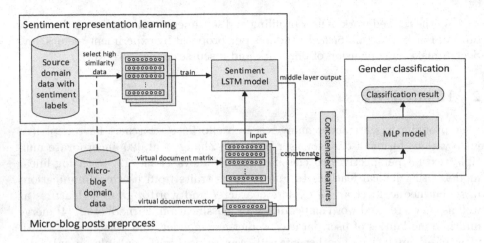

Fig. 2. The framework of our SRL-MLP approach.

3.2 Sentiment Representation Learning

There is no explicit sentiment information in target domain. Inspired by the idea of transfer learning, we utilize labeled data from source domain that are close to target domain. Here we consider online commodity reviews with star rates as related source domain. As a consequence, after getting a model trained by source domain, we can transfer it to target domain to get sentiment representation.

Select High Similarity Data. Pan et al. [10] summarize the basic methods of transfer learning. In general, source domain and target domain have different probability distributions, and they are both unknown. Here we calculate similarity based on instances and select source domain data which have high similarity with target domain data. We train a LSTM sentiment representation learning model on these selected data.

Sentiment Representation. After have trained a LSTM model by selected source domain data, we get a model that can predict sentiment polarity. Yosinski et al. [19] have validated features are transferable in deep neural networks. After inputting micro-blog posts to LSTM model, we can extract sentiment representations in two ways: (1) extract last layer which predicts the sentiment polarity 0(neg)/1(pos); (2) extract middle layer output such as dense or LSTM layer. We conduct experiments on both. However, as sentiment polarity contains less sentiment information, experiments show middle layer output performs better.

3.3 Gender Classification

In Sect. 3.2 we get micro-blog post sentiment representations. There are several ways to concatenate sentiment representations with document representations, such as concatenating them in the MLP input layer, or concatenating sentiment

Table 1. Accuracy of different classifiers.

Classifiers	Accuracy(%)	Classifiers	Accuracy(%)
Logistic regression [12]	67.06	CNN [7]	77.99%
Random forest [3]	72.15	LSTM [5]	73.67
Support vector machine [2]	76.34	BiLSTM [22]	77.35
MLP [4]	**84.20**	HAN [18]	79.26%

representation with MLP dense layer output or else. Experiments show directly concatenating in the input layer works better than dense layer.

The preceding concatenating methods are frozen layer concatenation. Finetune is a method of deep network transfer. It provides auxiliary method for the traditional artificial features extracting method. For finetune, we concatenate LSTM layer of LSTM model with MLP input layer to form a multi-input model. We finetune parts of origin LSTM model when training gender classifier.

4 Experiments

4.1 Dataset and Evaluation Measure

All micro-blog data used in this paper are from SMP (Social Media Processing) CUP 2016[1]. It consists of 3,138 labeled users, and each user has about 100 posts. Since we need to learn the sentiment representation of micro-blog, and there is no label about sentiment in these micro-blog posts. We selected JD commodity review data[2] with pos/neg labels as the source domain data, because reviews have more pronounced sentiment polarities. It contains 10,696 positive reviews and 10,428 negative reviews. We learn the sentiment representation and transfer it to the target domain of micro-blog. All the data and source codes we used in this paper can be found at our github[3].

Our evaluation measure is accuracy which is the ratio of rightly classified number to total test samples number. For evaluating the overall performance of the model, we do 5-fold cross validation, and get their average accuracy.

4.2 Comparison of Different Gender Classifiers

Based on our preliminary experiments on document representation, our document representation is the average of embedding vectors. We try to represent documents using TF-IDF, keywords TF-IDF, LDA, word embedding concatenated with LDA, and word embedding shows the best. Then we try several traditional classifiers and some deep neural network models to get preliminary

---

[1] https://biendata.com/competition/smpcup2016/.
[2] https://kexue.fm/archives/3863.
[3] https://github.com/WUT IDEA/SRI-MLP.

experiment results on gender classification. Results after 5-fold cross validation on 3,138 sample data are showed in Table 1. As a proof-of-concept implementation, we use the simplest, i.e. MLP, as our gender classifier.

4.3   Performance of Our SRL-MLP

Configuring of Our Framework. Our MLP consists of two dense layers and one dropout layer. We compare LSTM and CNN model to determine a sentiment polarity classifiers. In the entire reviews, the accuracy of LSTM model can reach 91.10%, while CNN can only reach 88.75%. Therefore, we learn sentiment representation based on LSTM model. Considering data imbalance, we exploit smote oversampling [9] to generate data. After smote, we can improve the accuracy from 84.20% to 85.89%, that is 1.69%.

Sentiment Representation Learning Results. Since using sentiment polarity features is intuitive, we also conduct experiments of adding sentiment polarity features to enhance gender classification. However, accuracy has been improved by 0.16% only. Therefore we propose our sentiment representation. There are two steps for our sentiment representation learning: (a) select source domain data; (b) extract middle layer.

(a) Select source domain data. In this step we choose different corpus to train our LSTM. We make a accuracy comparison when LSTM sentiment analyzer was trained on (1) only JD reviews; (2) high similarity JD reviews; (3) JD reviews and manually labeled micro-blog posts; (4) high similarity JD reviews and manually labeled micro-blog posts. Their maximum accuracy is shown in Table 2. When source domain data are selected, we use Cosine similarity calculation method,

Table 2. Accuracy(%) of different source domain data and sentiment representation.

Train LSTM model on	Added sentiment representation	Accuracy(%)
entire JD reviews	frozen LSTM layer	88.09
	frozen dense layer	87.98
	finetuned LSTM layer	86.95
high similarity JD reviews	frozen LSTM layer	**89.73**
	frozen dense layer	88.45
	finetuned LSTM layer	87.38
entire JD reviews and manually labeled micro-blog	frozen LSTM layer	88.87
	frozen dense layer	88.13
	finetuned LSTM layer	86.75
high similarity JD reviews and manually labeled micro-blog	frozen LSTM layer	89.31
	frozen dense layer	89.26
	finetuned LSTM layer	87.22

and select the data whose average similarity can exceed 0.25, according to our preliminary parameter study, to be our new source domain data.

(b) Extract middle layer output. In this step we extract middle layer output to be our sentiment representation. We make a sentiment representation comparison between extracting (1) frozen lstm layer; (2) frozen dense layer; (3) finetuned lstm layer.

From Table 2, we can see that after adding sentiment representation, accuracy of gender classification is much improved. Ideally, finetuning will increase more than frozen parameters. But due to small sample size, finetuning does not play a big role, with only increases 1.49% improvement. When training LSTM on high similarity data, and transferring frozen lstm layer sentiment representation, improvement rises from 85.89% to 89.73%, that is 3.84% improvement.

5 Conclusions and Future Work

In this paper, we study user profiling enhanced by sentiment representation. After introducing sentiment representations into MLP, we improve accuracy by 5.53%, from 84.20% to 89.73%. The transferred features are usually rich in expressiveness. This transferability can assist traditional feature extraction, avoiding the time-consuming and complex nature of manual extraction of features.

References

1. Bianchin, M., Angrilli, A.: Gender differences in emotional responses: a psychophysiological study. Physiol. Behav. **105**(4), 925–932 (2012)
2. Burger, J.D., Henderson, J.C., Kim, G., Zarrella, G.: Discriminating gender on Twitter. In: Proceedings of the 2011 Conference on Empirical Methods in Natural Language Processing, EMNLP 2011, John McIntyre Conference Centre, Edinburgh, UK, A meeting of SIGDAT, a Special Interest Group of the ACL, 27–31 July 2011, pp. 1301–1309 (2011)
3. Cheng, Y., Qiao, X., Wang, X., Yu, Q.: Random forest classifier for zero-shot learning based on relative attribute. IEEE Trans. Neural Netw. Learn. Syst. **29**(5), 1662–1674 (2018)
4. Farnadi, G., Tang, J., Cock, M.D., Moens, M.: User profiling through deep multimodal fusion. In: Proceedings of the Eleventh ACM International Conference on Web Search and Data Mining, WSDM 2018, 5–9 February 2018, Marina Del Rey, CA, USA, pp. 171–179 (2018)
5. Hochreiter, S., Schmidhuber, J.: Long short-term memory. Neural Comput. **9**(8), 1735–1780 (1997)
6. Li, W., Dickinson, M.: Gender prediction for chinese social media data. In: Proceedings of the International Conference Recent Advances in Natural Language Processing, RANLP 2017, 2–8 September 2017, Varna, Bulgaria, pp. 438–445 (2017)
7. Li, X., Cao, Y., Shang, Y., Liu, Y., Tan, J., Guo, L.: Inferring user profiles in online social networks based on convolutional neural network. In: Li, G., Ge, Y., Zhang, Z., Jin, Z., Blumenstein, M. (eds.) KSEM 2017. LNCS (LNAI), vol. 10412, pp. 274–286. Springer, Cham (2017). https://doi.org/10.1007/978-3-319-63558-3_23

8. Li, Z., Wei, Y., Zhang, Y., Yang, Q.: Hierarchical attention transfer network for cross-domain sentiment classification. In: Proceedings of the Thirty-Second AAAI Conference on Artificial Intelligence, 2–7 February 2018, New Orleans, Louisiana, USA (2018)
9. Mao, W., Wang, J., Wang, L.: Online sequential classification of imbalanced data by combining extreme learning machine and improved SMOTE algorithm. In: 2015 International Joint Conference on Neural Networks, IJCNN 2015, 12–17 July 2015, Killarney, Ireland (2015)
10. Pan, S.J., Yang, Q.: A survey on transfer learning. IEEE Trans. Knowl. Data Eng. **22**(10), 1345–1359 (2010)
11. Pla, F., Hurtado, L.F.: Political tendency identification in Twitter using sentiment analysis techniques. In: COLING 2014, 25th International Conference on Computational Linguistics, Proceedings of the Conference: Technical Papers, 23–29 August 2014, Dublin, Ireland, pp. 183–192 (2014)
12. Volkova, S., Bachrach, Y., Armstrong, M., Sharma, V.: Inferring latent user properties from texts published in social media. In: Proceedings of the Twenty-Ninth AAAI Conference on Artificial Intelligence, 25–30 January 2015, Austin, Texas, USA, pp. 4296–4297 (2015)
13. Wang, L., Cardie, C.: A piece of my mind: a sentiment analysis approach for online dispute detection. In: Proceedings of the 52nd Annual Meeting of the Association for Computational Linguistics, ACL 2014, 22–27 June 2014, Baltimore, MD, USA, Volume 2: Short Papers, pp. 693–699 (2014)
14. Wang, Y., Lin, X., Wu, L., Zhang, W., Zhang, Q., Huang, X.: Robust subspace clustering for multi-view data by exploiting correlation consensus. IEEE Trans. Image Process. **24**(11), 3939–3949 (2015)
15. Wang, Y., Zhang, W., Wu, L., Lin, X., Zhao, X.: Unsupervised metric fusion over multiview data by graph random walk-based cross-view diffusion. IEEE Trans. Neural Netw. Learn. Syst. **28**(1), 57–70 (2017)
16. Wang, Y., Wu, L., Lin, X., Gao, J.: Multiview spectral clustering via structured low-rank matrix factorization. IEEE Trans. Neural Netw. Learn. Syst. **29**(10), 4833–4843 (2018)
17. Wang, Y., Sun, A., Han, J., Liu, Y., Zhu, X.: Sentiment analysis by capsules. In: Proceedings of the 2018 World Wide Web Conference on World Wide Web, WWW 2018, 23–27 April 2018, Lyon, France, pp. 1165–1174 (2018)
18. Yang, Z., Yang, D., Dyer, C., He, X., Smola, A., Hovy, E.: Hierarchical attention networks for document classification. In: The 2016 Conference of the North American Chapter of the Association for Computational Linguistics: Human Language Technologies, NAACL HLT 2016, 12–17 June 2016, San Diego California, USA, pp. 1480–1489 (2016)
19. Yosinski, J., Clune, J., Bengio, Y., Lipson, H.: How transferable are features in deep neural networks? In: Advances in Neural Information Processing Systems 27: Annual Conference on Neural Information Processing Systems 2014, 8–13 December 2014, Montreal, Quebec, Canada, pp. 3320–3328 (2014)
20. Zhang, D., Li, S., Wang, H., Zhou, G.: User classification with multiple textual perspectives. In: COLING 2016, 26th International Conference on Computational Linguistics, Proceedings of the Conference: Technical Papers, 11–16 December 2016, Osaka, Japan, pp. 2112–2121 (2016)

21. Zhang, Y., Dang, Y., Chen, H.: Research note: examining gender emotional differences in web forum communication. Decis. Support Syst. **55**(3), 851–860 (2013)
22. Zhou, J., Xu, W.: End-to-end learning of semantic role labeling using recurrent neural networks. In: Proceedings of the 53rd Annual Meeting of the Association for Computational Linguistics and the 7th International Joint Conference on Natural Language Processing of the Asian Federation of Natural Language Processing, ACL 2015, Volume 1: Long Papers, 26–31 July 2015, Beijing, China, pp. 1127–1137 (2015)

Exploring Nonnegative and Low-Rank Correlation for Noise-Resistant Spectral Clustering

Zheng Wang[1], Cai Na[2], Zeyu Ma[1], Si Chen[3], Lingyun Song[4],
and Yang Yang[1(✉)]

[1] University of Electronic Science and Technology of China, Chengdu, China
zh_wang@hotmail.com, saviator@163.com, dlyyang@gmail.com
[2] Beijing Institute of Computer Technology and Application, Beijing, China
caliachina@163.com
[3] Information Science Academy, China Electronics Technology Group Corporation,
Beijing, China
[4] Xi'an Jiaotong University, Xi'an, China
xjtusly@163.com

Abstract. Clustering has been extensively explored in pattern recognition and data mining in order to facilitate various applications. Due to the presence of data noise, traditional clustering approaches may become vulnerable and unreliable, thereby degrading clustering performance. In this paper, we propose a robust spectral clustering approach, termed *Non-negative Low-rank Self-reconstruction* (NLS), which simultaneously (a) explores the nonnegative low-rank properties of data correlation as well as (b) adaptively models the structural sparsity of data noise. Specifically, in order to discover the intrinsic correlation among data, we devise a self-reconstruction approach to jointly consider the nonnegativity and low-rank property of data correlation matrix. Meanwhile, we propose to model data noise via a structural norm, i.e., $\ell_{p,2}$-norm, which not only naturally conforms to genuine patterns of data noise in real-world situations, but also provides more adaptivity and flexibility to different noise levels. Extensive experiments on various real-world datasets illustrate the advantage of the proposed robust spectral clustering approach compared to existing clustering methods.

Keywords: Nonnegative · Low-rank · Structural sparsity

1 Introduction

In machine learning and data mining areas, tremendous research endeavors have been dedicated to clustering technique [11] and the corresponding applications [9, 10, 12–14, 20, 23, 28–31], such as image segmentation, gene expression analysis, document analysis, content based image retrieval, image annotation, similarity searches.

© Springer Nature Switzerland AG 2019
J. Shao et al. (Eds.): APWeb-WAIM 2019, LNCS 11642, pp. 12–26, 2019.
https://doi.org/10.1007/978-3-030-26075-0_2

k-means, one of the most classic clustering models, has been practically applied in reality due to its effectiveness and simplicity. The typical procedure of traditional k-means (TKM) clustering algorithm iteratively assigns each data point to its closest cluster and computes a new clustering center. However, the "curse of dimensionality" may degrade the performance of TKM significantly [6]. Several research endeavors have been made to handle this problem by seeking a low-dimensional projection through dimensionality reduction, e.g., PCA, and then performing TKM. To step further, discriminative analysis [6,21,33,34] has been injected into TKM to enhance clustering performance. It has been shown that integrating TKM and LDA into a joint framework is beneficial. In [6,21], TKM and LDA were employed to obtain cluster labels and learn the most discriminative subspace in an alternating way. Ye *et al.* [34] proposed a joint framework, i.e., discriminative k-means (DKM) algorithm to formalize the clustering as a trace maximization problem.

In recent years, spectral analysis [3,5] has been proven to be effective in many applications, especially spectral clustering (SC) [8], which has become one of the most successful clustering methods and it shows more capability in partitioning data with more complicated structures compared to traditional clustering approaches. The underlying reason is that spectral clustering puts more efforts on mining the intrinsic data geometric structures [1,2,17,18,24,26,27,32]. SC has been widely applied and shown their effectiveness in various real-world applications, such as image segmentation [20,35]. The fundamental idea of spectral clustering is that it predicts cluster labels by exploiting the different similarity graphs of data points. Besides NCut and k-way NCut, a new SC algorithm, i.e., local learning based clustering (LLC) [24], was developed according to the assumption that the cluster label of a data point can be determined by its neighbors, and a kernel regression model was used for label prediction. In [32], discriminative information is injected into the construction of the similarity matrix to improve clustering performance. Most of the existing methods heavily rely on such parametric similarity (or correlation) estimation.

Recent years have witnessed the explosion of emerging Web data driven. Such data explosion has been posing more challenges on traditional clustering techniques. On the one hand, due to the fast evolution of Web data, traditional approaches may require expensive cost of parameter tuning process for calculating a proper data similarity matrix and thus become not applicable when confronted with different data types, different data distributions and so on. Besides, most of the existing approaches focus on using local structure rather than global feature, and data correlation is usually calculated independently. The intrinsic nature of data correlation matrix and global structure of data have not been well explored to facilitate the subsequent spectral clustering process. On the other hand, real-world data may be usually contaminated by unpredictable noise and outliers, which can easily make existing method vulnerable.

In this work, we propose a novel approach for robust spectral clustering, termed *Non-negative Low-rank Self-reconstruction* (NLS), to jointly cope with the aforementioned problems. Specifically, NLS aims at jointly (self-) reconstructing a set of data by linearly combining all the data points in the dataset itself. Linear model is possibly the most commonly chosen one due to its ease for use and effectiveness in practice. We first propose to enforce the reconstruction coefficient matrix (i.e., data correlation matrix) to exhibit low-rank property, which not only provides data with a more interpretable representation but also incorporates precious global structural information for identifying data correlation.

Moreover, we deliberately add a nonnegative constraint on the correlation matrix in order to promote the interpretability (i.e., zero indicates no relevance and positive value implies the degree of relevance). The initial motivation of posing the nonnegative constraint on data correlation matrix is to conform with the nonnegative property of data similarity, such as the ones based on Euclidean distance and cosine similarity. In this way, the nonnegative would probably help to characterize the data correlation in a more accurate and interpretable manner, which further boosts the clustering performance. Different from our previous work [32], which posed nonnegative constraint on cluster labels, we use nonnegative constraint to characterize the intrinsic correlation among data.

Furthermore, it is observed that only a (small) proportion of data in a dataset may be corrupted and different sources of data may have different levels of noise. Based on the above observations, we devise a novel noise modelling approach by utilizing an effective $\ell_{p,2}$-norm over noise matrix to characterize noise in a more precise way. The $\ell_{p,2}$-norm is able to produce sample-wise sparsity over noise matrix, thereby leading to automatic identification and modelling of noisy samples. Meanwhile, by varying the value of p, $\ell_{p,2}$-norm can provide more flexibility on controlling levels of noise as well as expand applicable range of our approach.

The contributions of this paper are summarized as follows:

- We propose a novel approach, termed *Non-negative Low-rank Self-reconstruction* (NLS), for facilitating robust spectral clustering. NLS jointly reconstructs data samples in a dataset from themselves, i.e., self-reconstruction, by exploring the intrinsic low-rank nature and nonnegativity of data correlation matrix and precisely modelling sample-wise data noise.
- We devise a nonnegative low-rank approach, which provides data with a more interpretable representation as well as incorporates precious global structural information for identifying data correlation.
- We incorporate an effective $\ell_{p,2}$-norm for characterizing data noise in a more precise way. The $\ell_{p,2}$-norm injects more flexibility to our approach for adapting to different levels of noise and expands applicable range.
- Extensive experiments on multiple real-world datasets illustrate that our proposal outperforms the existing clustering algorithms.

The rest of this paper is organized as follows. Section 2 elaborates the proposed nonnegative low-rank self-reconstruction model. Experiments are reported and analyzed in Sect. 3. In the last, we conclude our work in Sect. 4.

2 The Proposed Approach

In this section, we elaborate the details of the proposed robust spectral clustering approach, including a nonnegative low-rank self-reconstruction process for learning data correlation matrix and a structural noise modelling component for handling noisy data.

Given a set of data points $X = [x_1, x_2, \ldots, x_n] \in \mathbb{R}^{d \times n}$, where each column vector $x_i \in \mathbb{R}^d$ represents a datum and d is the dimensionality of feature space. Ideally, the data in X should not contain any noise. Nonetheless, in real-world scenarios, data would be inevitably contaminated by various unpredictable factors, such as distortion, transmission error, malicious tempering, etc. Intuitively, a reasonable assumption is that only a (small) proportion of data are influenced by noise, i.e., the noise should be sparse. Furthermore, the noise levels in different sources of data may vary significantly, which poses great challenges for precise noise control using a unified model. In this case, the major objective of this work is to devise an effective spectral clustering approach, which is able to capture the genuine correlation among data, identify noisy samples as well as suppress influence of different levels of noise effectively.

2.1 Nonnegative Low-Rank Self-reconstruction

As aforementioned in Sect. 1, we employ linear model for reconstructing data due to its ease for use and effectiveness in practice. Given the data matrix $X = [x_1, x_2, \ldots, x_n] \in \mathbb{R}^{d \times n}$, the i-th datum x_i can be represented as a linear combination of m basis vectors in a dictionary $B = [b_1, b_2, \ldots, b_m] \in \mathbb{R}^{d \times m}$:

$$x_i = Bw_i + \varepsilon_i,$$

where $w_i \in \mathbb{R}^m$ is the reconstruction coefficient of x_i and $\varepsilon_i \in \mathbb{R}^d$ is the noise on x_i. By denoting the linear model in concise matrix form, we have:

$$X = BW + \mathcal{E}, \tag{1}$$

where $W = [w_1, w_2, \ldots, w_n] \in \mathbb{R}^{m \times n}$ is the reconstruction coefficient matrix, which can be regarded as either the new representation of data or the correlation of data in X and the basis in B. $\mathcal{E} = [\varepsilon_1, \varepsilon_2, \ldots, \varepsilon_n] \in \mathbb{R}^{d \times n}$ indicates the noise matrix of all data in X.

In order to infer the data correlation within X, a reasonable way is to exploit X itself as the dictionary to perform (self-)reconstruction as follows:

$$X = XW + \mathcal{E}. \tag{2}$$

In this way, we can regard W as the new representation of X or correlation between data in X and themselves. The i-th column of W, i.e., $w_i = [w_{1i}, w_{2i}, \ldots, w_{ni}]^T \in \mathbb{R}^n$, is the reconstruction coefficient vector of the i-th datum x_i. The coefficient w_{ji} measures the contribution of the j-th datum x_j on the reconstruction of x_i.

In order to model data correlation, one may use sparse constraint (e.g., $\|W\|_1$) [7] for obtain an optimized W. Indeed, it may uncover the local structure of X and achieve the denoising purpose to some extent; nevertheless, such sparse constraint may easily cause the data correlation W ignoring the precious global structural information. Based on this analysis, we propose to employ low-rank constraint, which has been proven to be more proper for characterize the data correlation as well as explore the global information. The general optimization problem is stated as below:

$$\min_{W,\mathcal{E}} \ \text{rank}(W) + \lambda\Omega(\mathcal{E}), \quad \text{s.t. } X = XW + \mathcal{E}, \tag{3}$$

where the first term calculates the rank of W, the second term $\Omega(\mathcal{E})$ enables certain forms of sparsity for modelling data noise, and λ is a balance parameter determining the contribution of these two terms.

It is known that optimizing the rank function is difficult due to its discreteness. To handle this problem, a common way is to relax the rank optimization to a nuclear norm optimization, which is convex. Thus, the problem in Eq. (3) is transformed to

$$\min_{W,\mathcal{E}} \ \|W\|_* + \lambda\Omega(\mathcal{E}), \quad \text{s.t. } X = XW + \mathcal{E}. \tag{4}$$

where $\|\cdot\|_*$ denotes the nuclear norm of a matrix, i.e., the sum of the matrix's singular values.

If we solve the problem in Eq. (4), the optimized W^* would probably be mixing-signed, which makes it difficult to describe data correlation in an interpretable way. Intuitively, given two data points, if they are relevant, in order to quantify the degree of their correlation, we may use a positive value as measurement; otherwise, we use value zero to indicate the fact that they are not relevant. In other words, this intuition implies us that W^* should be nonnegative. It has been shown that nonnegative analysis would probably boost performance [25]. Accordingly, we impose an explicit nonnegative constraint over data correlation matrix W, and the problem is reformulated as

$$\min_{W,\mathcal{E}} \ \|W\|_* + \lambda\Omega(\mathcal{E}), \quad \text{s.t. } X = XW + \mathcal{E} \wedge W \geq 0. \tag{5}$$

In the next part, we will introduce how to precisely characterize data noise $\mathcal{E}$, i.e., specify $\Omega(\mathcal{E})$ to further reinforce the establishment of data correlation.

2.2 Modelling Data Noise

In real-world cases, data would be inevitably contaminated by various types of noise, such as distortion, transmission error, etc. Normally, it is reasonable to assume that only a (small) proportion of data are actually corrupted and the rest are clean. Suppose we use ℓ_1-norm to model data noise as below:

$$\|\mathcal{E}\|_1 = \sum_{j=1}^{d} \sum_{i=1}^{n} |\varepsilon_{ji}|, \tag{6}$$

where ε_{ji} indicates the j-th element of ε_i. Such modelling would probably cause that the identified noise propagated to all the data, thereby negatively influencing other clean samples and further degrading the performance. In order to avoid such noise propagation problem, a more effective way is to intentionally shape noise according to certain reasonable assumption. As aforementioned, noise may only occur in a (small) proportion of data, which inspires us to exploit structural modelling approach, such as $\ell_{1,2}$-norm:

$$\|\mathcal{E}\|_{1,2} = \sum_{i=1}^{n} \|\varepsilon_i\|. \tag{7}$$

As we can see from the definition, $\ell_{1,2}$-norm of $\mathcal{E}$ actually accounts to the ℓ_1-norm of the vector $[\|\varepsilon_1\|, \|\varepsilon_2\|, \dots, \|\varepsilon_n\|]$, which implies that it helps to induce sample-wise sparsity. In other words, some columns of $\mathcal{E}$ shrink to zero.

In order to further increase the flexibility for handling different corrupt levels of data, we propose to generalize of $\ell_{1,2}$-norm to $\ell_{p,2}$-norm:

$$\|\mathcal{E}\|_{p,2} = \sum_{i=1}^{n} \|\varepsilon_i\|^p, \tag{8}$$

where $0 < p < 2$. Note that when p is set to 1, Eq. (8) is identically equivalent to Eq. (7). As p varies, the $\ell_{p,2}$ norm may help to induce different levels of sparsity, which corresponds to different levels of noise intended to be recognized. For instance, when $p \to 2$, the $\ell_{p,2}$ norm tends to become ℓ_2 norm, which will not induce any sparsity, thereby disabling the ability of NLS identifying noisy samples. In contrast, small p would probably induce too much unnecessary sample-wise sparsity, which may force NLS to "over-identify" noisy samples, thereby degrading clustering performance.

Thus, by substituting Eq. (8) into Eq. (5), we have

$$\min_{W, \mathcal{E}} \|W\|_* + \lambda \|\mathcal{E}\|_{p,2}, \quad \text{s.t. } X = XW + \mathcal{E} \wedge W \geq 0. \tag{9}$$

In the next part, we will introduce the optimization details of Eq. (9).

2.3   Optimization

In this subsection, we present an alternating algorithm for optimizing the problem in Eq. (9). We first transform the original problem (9) by adding an additional variable V for facilitating the optimization:

$$\min_{W, \mathcal{E}, V} \|V\|_* + \lambda \|\mathcal{E}\|_{p,2},$$
$$\text{s.t.} \begin{cases} X = XW + \mathcal{E}, \\ W \geq 0, \\ V = W. \end{cases} \tag{10}$$

By utilizing Augmented Lagrange Multiplier (ALM), the above constrained problem can be further changed to the following form:

$$\min_{W,\mathcal{E},V,P,Q} \|V\|_* + \lambda\|\mathcal{E}\|_{p,2} + Tr\left(P^T(X - XW - \mathcal{E})\right) + Tr\left(Q^T(W - V)\right)$$
$$+ \frac{\alpha}{2}\left(\|X - XW - \mathcal{E}\|_F^2 + \|W - V\|_F^2,\right) \quad \text{s.t. } W \geq 0, \tag{11}$$

where $Tr(\cdot)$ is the trace of a matrix. $P \in \mathbb{R}^{d \times n}$ and $Q \in \mathbb{R}^{n \times n}$ are Lagrange multipliers for the two equality constraints, and $\alpha > 0$ is a trade-off parameter. In order to solve the problem (11), we alternatingly update $W, \mathcal{E}, V, P, Q$.

Update V. By fixing $W, \mathcal{E}, P, Q$, we have the following sub-problem:

$$\min_V \|V\|_* - Tr\left(Q^TV\right) + \frac{\alpha}{2}\|W - V\|_F^2, \tag{12}$$

which is equivalent to

$$\min_V \frac{1}{2}\left\|V - \left(W + \frac{Q}{\alpha}\right)\right\|_F^2 + \frac{1}{\alpha}\|V\|_*. \tag{13}$$

The above optimization problem with nuclear norm regularization can be efficiently solved by singular value thresholding [4].

Update W. By fixing $\mathcal{E}, V, P, Q$, the problem (11) is reduced to

$$\min_W Tr\left(-P^TXW + Q^TW\right)$$
$$+ \frac{\alpha}{2}\left(\|X - XW - \mathcal{E}\|_F^2 + \|W - V\|_F^2\right), \tag{14}$$
$$\text{s.t. } W \geq 0,$$

which can be solved by applying the following multiplicative update rule:

$$w_{ij} \leftarrow w_{ij} \times \frac{H_{ij}}{(U\tilde{W})_{ij}}, \tag{15}$$

where $\tilde{W}$ is the outcome in the previous iteration. $U = X^TX + I$ and I is identity matrix of size $n \times n$. $H = (X^TX - X^T\mathcal{E} + V + \frac{1}{\alpha}(X^TP - Q))$.

Update $\mathcal{E}$. Now let us fix W, V, P, Q, then the problem can be transformed to

$$\min_{\mathcal{E}} \frac{\alpha}{2}\|X - XW - \mathcal{E}\|_F^2 - Tr\left(P^T\mathcal{E}\right) + \lambda\|\mathcal{E}\|_{p,2},$$
$$\Leftrightarrow \min_{\mathcal{E}} \frac{1}{2}\left\|\mathcal{E} - (X - XW + \frac{P}{\alpha})\right\|_F^2 + \frac{\lambda}{\alpha}\|\mathcal{E}\|_{p,2}. \tag{16}$$

In order to solve the sub-problem in (16), we first consider the following alternative problem:

$$\min_{\mathcal{E}} \frac{1}{2}\left\|\mathcal{E} - (X - XW + \frac{P}{\alpha})\right\|_F^2 + \frac{\lambda}{\alpha}Tr(\mathcal{E}^TZ\mathcal{E}), \tag{17}$$

where Z is a diagonal matrix, whose i-th diagonal element is computed as

$$Z_{ii} = \frac{p}{2\|\varepsilon_i\|^{2-p}} \tag{18}$$

Note that Z is derived from $\mathcal{E}$ which makes it difficult to directly optimize (17). Hence, we devise an iterative algorithm to handle the problem. To be more specific, in each iteration we alternatingly update Z and $\mathcal{E}$. We first calculate Z with the obtained $\mathcal{E}$ in the previous iteration, then $\mathcal{E}$ is updated via a close-form solution. By fixing Z and setting the derivative of (17) w.r.t. $\mathcal{E}$ to zero, we arrive at

$$\mathcal{E} = (I + \frac{2\lambda}{\alpha}Z)^{-1}(X - XW + \frac{1}{\alpha}P). \tag{19}$$

We can show that by iteratively solving the problem (17), the optimal solution can be obtained for the problem (16). To this end, we present the following lemmas and theorem.

Lemma 1. *Let ε_i be the ith column of the updated $\mathcal{E}$ in previous iteration and $\tilde{\varepsilon}_i$ be the ith column of the variable $\tilde{\mathcal{E}}$ in current iteration, then the following inequality holds:*

$$\|\tilde{\varepsilon}_i\|^p - \frac{p\|\tilde{\varepsilon}_i\|^2}{2\|\varepsilon_i\|^{2-p}} \le \|\varepsilon_i\|^p - \frac{p\|\varepsilon_i\|^2}{2\|\varepsilon_i\|^{2-p}} \tag{20}$$

Proof. Please refer to Appendix for more details.

Lemma 2. *Given $\mathcal{E} = [\varepsilon_1, \varepsilon_2 \dots, \varepsilon_n]$, where ε_i is the ith column of $\mathcal{E}$, then we have the following conclusion:*

$$\sum_{i=1}^{n} \|\tilde{\varepsilon}_i\|^p - \sum_{i=1}^{n} \frac{p\|\tilde{\varepsilon}_i\|^2}{2\|\varepsilon_i\|^{2-p}} \le \sum_{i=1}^{n} \|\varepsilon_i\|^p - \sum_{i=1}^{n} \frac{p\|\varepsilon_i\|^p}{2\|\varepsilon_i\|^{2-p}} \tag{21}$$

Proof. It can be easily seen that by summing up the inequalities over all the columns in $\mathcal{E}$ in Lemma 1 we are able to obtain the conclusion of Lemma 2.

Theorem 1. *At each iteration (line 3–4) of Algorithm 1, the value of the objective function in Eq. (16) monotonically decreases.*

Proof. Please refer to Appendix for more details.

Theorem 1 guarantees the convergence of Algorithm 1.

The algorithm is shown Algorithm 1.

Update P and Q. Given $W, \mathcal{E}, V$, we may update the Lagrange multipliers P and Q as follows:

$$\begin{cases} P \leftarrow P + \alpha(X - XW - \mathcal{E}) \\ Q \leftarrow Q + \alpha(W - V) \end{cases} \tag{22}$$

We summarize the optimization for the problem (11) in Algorithm 2.

Algorithm 1. Algorithm for optimizing the $\ell_{p,2}$-norm regularized problem in Eq. (17).

Input: Data matrix X, correlation matrix W, Lagrange multiplier P, parameters λ, α and p;
Output: $\mathcal{E}$;
1: Initialize $\mathcal{E}$;
2: **repeat**
3:    Compute the diagonal matrix Z according to Eq. (18);
4:    Update $\mathcal{E} = (I + \frac{2\lambda}{\alpha}Z)^{-1}(X - XW + \frac{1}{\alpha}P)$;
5: **until** convergence
6: **return** $\mathcal{E}$;

Algorithm 2. Algorithm for optimizing the problem in Eq. (11).

Input: Data matrix X and parameters λ, p;
Output: W;
1: Initialize $\mathcal{E}, P, Q, W, max_{\alpha} = 10^{10}, \rho = 1.1$;
2: **repeat**
3:    Update V by solving the problem in Eq. (12);
4:    Update W by solving the problem in Eq. (14) with the multiplicative update rule in Eq. (15);
5:    Update $\mathcal{E}$ by running Algorithm 1;
6:    Update P and Q according to Eq. (22);
7:    Update $\alpha = \min(\rho\alpha, max_{\alpha})$;
8: **until** convergence
9: **return** W;

2.4   Overall Spectral Clustering

Given the optimized data correlation matrix W^*, where the element w_{ji}^* indicates the directed relation from the j-th datum to the i-th datum, i.e., the contribution of the j-th datum in the reconstruction process of the i-th datum. Intuitively, it is reasonable to assume that a given datum is only related to a few samples. To this end, we choose to reserve k nearest neighbors in terms of the data correlation and construct the sparse data correlation matrix $\hat{W}^*$, where k is an empirical parameter.

Note that NLS model does not guarantee that $\hat{W}^*$ is symmetric, which implies that in most cases $\hat{w}_{ij}^* \neq \hat{w}_{ji}^*$. In general, most spectral clustering algorithms use symmetric affinity matrix to partition data. Following this convention, we practically add $\hat{W}^*$ and its transpose to guarantee the constructed graph is undirected and the affinity matrix is symmetric, which will facilitate the subsequent typical spectral clustering procedure:

$$A = \frac{\hat{W}^* + (\hat{W}^*)^T}{2}. \tag{23}$$

Finally, we perform spectral clustering by applying eigen-value decomposition on the Laplacian matrix of A and discretizing clustering labels (e.g., spectral rotation or k-means).

3 Experiments

In this section, we evaluate the effectiveness of the proposed NLS spectral clustering algorithm by comparing it to the existing approaches on various datasets.

3.1 Experimental Settings

We evaluate on five datasets, including Jaffe, Umist, Yale, Lenses and Auto. We compare our algorithm to six existing clustering approaches, including k-means clustering (TKM), discriminative k-means (DKM) clustering [34], Spectral Clustering (SC), Normalized Cuts (NCuts) [35], Local Learning Clustering (LLC) [24], CLGR [22] and LRR [15,16]. Besides, we also evaluate three variants of our approach, i.e., LS, LS_1 and NLS_1. LS is the version of our approach NLS without nonnegative constraint. LS_1 and NLS_1 are the corresponding versions of LS and NLS using ℓ_1-norm instead of $\ell_{1,2}$-norm.

For spectral clustering algorithms, we always set $k=5$. We perform the self-tuning algorithm [36] to determine an adaptive bandwidth. For fair comparison, the trade-off parameters in all the comparison algorithms are consistently tuned from the range of $\{10^{-6}, 10^{-4}, 10^{-2}, 10^0, 10^2, 10^4, 10^6\}$; for the parameter p in our approach, we set it in the range of $\{0.25, 0.5, 0.75, 1, 1.25, 1.5, 1.75\}$; and the best results are reported. To reduce statistical variation, each clustering algorithm is run repeatedly for 10 times and the average results are reported.

Following conventional clustering study, we use Accuracy (ACC) and Normalized Mutual Information (NMI) as our evaluation metrics.

3.2 Comparison

In this subsection, we conduct empirical studies on five datasets to show the performance comparison of existing algorithms and our proposed method. The comparison results of ACC and NMI are listed in Tables 1 and 2, respectively. We can derive the following analysis.

- In most cases, NLS_1 achieves better performances than TKM, DKM, SC and NCuts. This phenomenon indicates that jointly exploring nonnegativity and low rank properties of data correlation as well as suppressing data noise can be of benefit for achieving satifactory clustering performance.
- NLS consistently outperforms NLS_1. This observation implies that the structural modelling using $\ell_{p,2}$-norm is able to better capture the genuine distribution of data noise than ℓ_1-norm. NLS exploits $\ell_{p,2}$-norm to "actively" enforce sample-wise sparsity on data noise, thereby accurately identifying and quantifying noisy samples; nonetheless, NLS_1 models data noise using ℓ_1-norm, which tends to "accidentally" propagate noise across all data samples and cause inventible contamination of clean samples.

- NLS always achieves the best performance. Both LLC and CLGR exploit additional knowledge, e.g., discriminative information, to enhance the exploration of data correlation; hence, in most cases they achieve better performance than TKM, DKM, SC, NCuts and LRR. However, compared to our method, they do not fully take any consideration into intrinsic properties of data correlation, namely nonnegativity and low rankness, as well as structural modelling of data noise, which together guarantees a reliable and robust process for data self-reconstruction and the subsequent spectral clustering.

Table 1. Overall ACC performance (%) comparison to the existing algorithms.

	TKM	DKM	SC	NCuts	LLC	CLGR	LRR	NLS_ℓ_1	NLS
Jaffe	73.1 ± 4.6	84.5 ± 0.6	78.5 ± 6.8	84.1 ± 2.0	83.6 ± 5.5	82.6 ± 3.8	91.2 ± 3.9	97.5 ± 0.3	**99.2 ± 0.8**
Umist	38.8 ± 1.0	44.2 ± 0.2	53.3 ± 2.0	51.9 ± 1.3	43.1 ± 0.7	55.0 ± 1.4	68.8 ± 0.5	76.6 ± 0.3	**77.8 ± 0.5**
Yale	38.4 ± 1.1	42.4 ± 0.7	48.9 ± 2.3	47.4 ± 1.8	51.9 ± 2.4	48.3 ± 2.0	46.1 ± 1.4	50.2 ± 0.3	**53.0 ± 0.7**
Lenses	54.6 ± 3.6	66.7 ± 2.0	54.4 ± 5.7	55.8 ± 7.1	55.0 ± 6.7	48.6 ± 7.4	56.0 ± 2.4	60.8 ± 1.9	**68.3 ± 2.9**
Auto	35.1 ± 1.6	39.1 ± 0.1	31.7 ± 1.1	31.6 ± 0.8	37.0 ± 1.1	39.7 ± 0.4	37.7 ± 0.5	38.5 ± 0.2	**41.5 ± 0.4**

Table 2. Overall NMI performance (%) comparison to the existing algorithms.

	TKM	DKM	SC	NCuts	LLC	CLGR	LRR	NLS_ℓ_1	NLS
Jaffe	81.3 ± 2.2	90.1 ± 0.6	84.1 ± 2.7	93.9 ± 1.6	89.5 ± 2.5	92.1 ± 1.1	94.6 ± 2.3	96.9 ± 0.1	**98.7 ± 0.7**
Umist	58.3 ± 0.6	61.8 ± 0.5	74.4 ± 0.8	73.3 ± 0.8	65.8 ± 0.7	76.6 ± 0.8	82.5 ± 0.4	87.6 ± 0.4	**88.5 ± 0.4**
Yale	46.7 ± 0.9	47.7 ± 0.5	54.8 ± 1.2	55.2 ± 1.3	54.9 ± 1.9	53.2 ± 1.4	53.3 ± 1.1	55.4 ± 0.2	**57.7 ± 0.5**
Lenses	26.2 ± 8.9	4.7 ± 0.7	22.1 ± 7.5	32.1 ± 8.0	23.1 ± 7.7	20.9 ± 7.7	29.9 ± 3.1	35.1 ± 3.9	**53.0 ± 3.7**
Auto	15.9 ± 0.6	16.8 ± 0.5	13.5 ± 1.1	13.2 ± 1.2	15.0 ± 0.4	16.9 ± 0.9	15.7 ± 0.4	15.8 ± 0.3	**17.0 ± 0.2**

3.3 Nonnegativity and Noise Modelling

In this part, we evaluate efficacy of the nonnegative constraint and $\ell_{p,2}$-norm for modelling data noise. Specifically, we compare NLS with its variant that uses ℓ_1-norm, denoted as NLS_1. To the end of illustrating the effect of the nonnegative consideration, we also compare NLS and NLS_1 to their counterparts (i.e., LS and LS_1, respectively) that do not pose nonnegative constraint.

The experimental results are reported in Fig. 1. Figure 1(a) and (b) illustrate, respectively, ACC performance and NMI performance of the four comparison algorithms. We can attain the following conclusions:

- NLS and NLS_1 consistently outperform their counterparts, i.e., LS and LS_1, respectively. This fact clearly indicates that the nonnegativity consideration helps to achieve performance improvement. As analyzed before, by explicitly pose nonnegative constraint on data correlation matrix W, we can formulate a better process for jointly reconstructing all data samples, thereby characterizing correlation among data in a more interpretable manner (i.e., value 0 indicates that two data points are not related, and a positive value measures the degree of relationship of two data samples.)

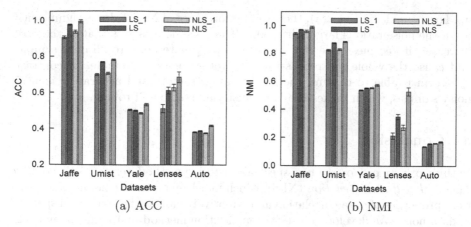

Fig. 1. Effects of nonnegative constraint and data noise modelling. (a) and (b) gives ACC performance and NMI performance, respectively.

– NLS and LS always gain better performance than NLS_1 and LS_1, respectively. Similar to the analysis in Sect. 3.2, such observation reveals the superior efficacy of $\ell_{p,2}$-norm for structurally modelling data noise. Compared to ℓ_1-norm, $\ell_{p,2}$-norm not only captures the genuine noise distribution but also provides sufficient flexible control on different noise levels.

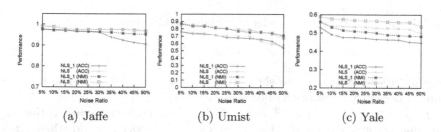

Fig. 2. Robustness of NLS and NLS_1 w.r.t. different ratios of noisy data samples in Jaffe, Umist and Yale datasets.

3.4   Robustness

In this subsection, we test the robustness of the proposed approaches NLS and NLS_1. To this end, we randomly add noise to $\{5\%, 10\%, \ldots, 50\%\}$ of data samples and use the tuned optimal parameter settings for each algorithm. The experimental results on three datasets are listed in Fig. 2. As we can see, in general, as the ratio increases from 5% to 50%, the performance (ACC and NMI) of NLS slightly decreases, which implies that NLS can be tolerant to noise and provide robust clustering ability. Nonetheless, compared to NLS, the stability of NLS_1 resisting the added noise tends to become worse as the proportion of noise goes up. For example, in Fig. 2(a), the ACC performance of NLS_1 drops significantly when the noise ratio is larger than 30%. The possible reason is that as the ratio increases, it becomes easier for ℓ_1-norm to propagate noise to all data samples and cause the whole self-reconstruction process more vulnerable. In contrast, $\ell_{p,2}$-norm is able to capture the global data structure and accurately identify noisy samples, which makes the final clustering stable and robust.

4   Conclusion

In this work, we proposed a new spectral clustering method, termed *Non-negative Low-rank Self-reconstruction* (NLS), which jointly explores the nonnegative low-rank properties of data correlation and adaptively models the structural sparsity of data noise. We developed a self-reconstruction method by taking the nonnegativity and low-rank property of the data correlation matrix into consideration. Furthermore, we employed $\ell_{p,2}$-norm to model data noise, which conforms to the nature of data noise in real-world situation, as well as provides more adaptivity to different noise levels. We reported extensive experiments on various real-world datasets to show the superiority of the proposal. In the future, we intend to explore more reasonable properties of data to better characterize data correlation and enhance the performance of the current proposal.

5   Proof of Lemma 1

Proof. Inspired by [19], we consider the following function

$$f(a) = pa^2 - 2a^p + (2 - p),\tag{24}$$

where $p \in (0, 2)$. We expect to show that when $a > 0$, $f(a) \geq 0$. The first and second order derivatives of the function in Eq. (24) are $f'(a) = 2pa - 2pa^{p-1}$ and $f''(a) = 2p - 2p(p-1)a^{p-2}$, respectively. We can see that $a = 1$ is the only point that satisfies $f'(a) = 0$. Also, when $0 < a < 1$, $f'(a) < 0$ and when $a > 1$, $f'(a) > 0$. This means that $f(a)$ is monotonically decreasing when $0 < a < 1$ and monotonically increasing when $a > 1$. Moreover, we have $f''(1) = 2p(2-p) > 0$. Therefore, for $\forall a > 0$, $f(a) \geq f(1) = 0$.

Then, by substituting $a = \frac{\|\tilde{\varepsilon}_i\|}{\|\varepsilon_i\|}$ into Eq. (24), we obtain the conclusion

$$p\frac{\|\tilde{\varepsilon}_i\|^2}{\|\varepsilon_i\|^2} - 2\frac{\|\tilde{\varepsilon}_i\|^p}{\|\varepsilon_i\|^p} + (2 - p) \geq 0,$$

$$\Leftrightarrow p\|\tilde{\varepsilon}_i\|^2\|\varepsilon_i\|^{p-2} - 2\|\tilde{\varepsilon}_i\|^p + (2 - p)\|\varepsilon_i\|^p \geq 0,$$

$$\Leftrightarrow 2\|\tilde{\varepsilon}_i\|^p - p\|\tilde{\varepsilon}_i\|^2\|\varepsilon_i\|^{p-2} \leq (2 - p)\|\varepsilon_i\|^p,$$

$$\Leftrightarrow \|\tilde{\varepsilon}_i\|^p - \frac{p\|\tilde{\varepsilon}_i\|^2}{2\|\varepsilon_i\|^{2-p}} \leq \|\varepsilon_i\|^p - \frac{p\|\varepsilon_i\|^p}{2\|\varepsilon_i\|^{2-p}}.$$

6   Proof of Theorem 1

Proof. Denote $\mathcal{L}(\mathcal{E}) = \frac{1}{2} \left\| \mathcal{E} - (X - XW + \frac{P}{\alpha}) \right\|_F^2$ and $\lambda' = \lambda/\alpha$. Suppose $\tilde{\mathcal{E}}$ is the optimized solution of the alternative problem (17), then we obtain the following conclusion:

$$\mathcal{L}(\tilde{\mathcal{E}}) + \lambda' Tr(\tilde{\mathcal{E}}^T Z \tilde{\mathcal{E}}) \leq \mathcal{L}(\mathcal{E}) + \lambda' Tr(\mathcal{E}^T Z \mathcal{E})$$

$$\Rightarrow \mathcal{L}(\tilde{\mathcal{E}}) + \lambda' \sum_{i=1}^{n} \|\tilde{\varepsilon}_i\|_p^2 - \lambda'(\sum_{i=1}^{n} \|\tilde{\varepsilon}_i\|_p^2 - \sum_{i=1}^{n} \frac{p\|\tilde{\varepsilon}_i\|^2}{2\|\varepsilon_i\|^{2-p}})$$

$$\leq \mathcal{L}(\mathcal{E}) + \lambda' \sum_{i=1}^{n} \|\varepsilon_i\|_p^2 - \lambda'(\sum_{i=1}^{n} \|\varepsilon_i\|_p^2 - \sum_{i=1}^{n} \frac{p\|\varepsilon_i\|^2}{2\|\varepsilon_i\|^{2-p}}).$$

Given the conclusion of Lemma 2, we finally arrive at

$$\mathcal{L}(\tilde{\mathcal{E}}) + \lambda' \sum_{i=1}^{n} \|\tilde{\varepsilon}_i\|_p^2 \leq \mathcal{L}(\mathcal{E}) + \lambda' \sum_{i=1}^{n} \|\varepsilon_i\|_p^2.$$

Hence, the value of the objective function in Eq. (16) monotonically decreases in each iteration.

References

1. Belkin, M., Niyogi, P.: Laplacian eigenmaps for dimensionality reduction and data representation. Neural Comput. **15**(6), 1373–1396 (2003)
2. Belkin, M., Niyogi, P., Sindhwani, V.: Manifold regularization: a geometric framework for learning from labeled and unlabeled examples. JMLR **7**, 2399–2434 (2006)
3. Borjigin, S.M.Y., Guo, C.H.: Perturbation analysis for the normalized Laplacian matrices in the multiway spectral clustering method. Sci. China Inf. Sci. **57**(11), 112102 (2014)
4. Cai, J.F., Candès, E.J., Shen, Z.: A singular value thresholding algorithm for matrix completion (2008)
5. Chen, L., Xu, D., Tsang, I.H., Li, X.: Spectral embedded hashing for scalable image retrieval. IEEE TCYB **44**(7), 1180–1190 (2014)
6. Ding, C., Li, T.: Adaptive dimension reduction using discriminant analysis and k-means clustering. In: ICML, pp. 521–528 (2007)
7. Elhamifar, E., Vidal, R.: Sparse subspace clustering. In: CVPR (2009)
8. Filippone, M., Camastra, F., Masulli, F., Rovetta, S.: A survey of kernel and spectral methods for clustering. PR **41**(1), 176–190 (2008)
9. Gordon, S., Greenspan, H., Goldberger, J.: Applying the information bottleneck principle to unsupervised clustering of discrete and continuous image representations. In: CVPR, pp. 370–377 (2003)
10. Huang, Q., Wang, T., Tao, D., Li, X.: Biclustering learning of trading rules. IEEE TCYB **45**(10), 2287–2298 (2015)
11. Jain, A., Murty, M., Flynn, P.: Data clustering: a review. ACM Comput. Surv. **31**(3), 264–323 (1999)
12. Jiang, D., Tang, C., Zhang, A.: Cluster analysis for gene expression data: a survey. TKDE **16**(11), 1370–1386 (2004)
13. Li, C., Chang, E., Garcia-Molina, H., Wiederhold, G.: Clustering for approximate similarity search in high-dimensional spaces. TKDE **14**(4), 792–808 (2002)

14. Li, J., Wang, J.: Real-time computerized annotation of pictures. TPAMI **30**(6), 985–1002 (2008)
15. Liu, G., Lin, Z., Yan, S., Sun, J., Yu, Y., Ma, Y.: Robust recovery of subspace structures by low-rank representation. IEEE TPAMI **35**(1), 171–184 (2013)
16. Liu, G., Xu, H., Tang, J., Liu, Q., Yan, S.: A deterministic analysis for LRR. IEEE TPAMI **38**(3), 417–430 (2016)
17. Meng, D., Leung, Y., Xu, Z.: Detecting intrinsic loops underlying data manifold. TKDE **25**(2), 337–347 (2013)
18. Nie, F., Xu, D., Tsang, I., Zhang, C.: Spectral embedded clustering. In: IJCAI, pp. 1181–1186 (2009)
19. Nie, F., Huang, H., Cai, X., Ding, C.H.: Efficient and robust feature selection via joint $\ell 2$, 1-norms minimization. In: NIPS, pp. 1813–1821 (2010)
20. Shi, J., Malik, J.: Normalized cuts and image segmentation. TPAMI **22**(8), 888–905 (2000)
21. De la Torre, F., Kanade, T.: Discriminative cluster analysis. In: ICML, pp. 241–248 (2006)
22. Wang, F., Zhang, C., Li, T.: Clustering with local and global regularization. TKDE **21**(12), 1665–1678 (2009)
23. Wang, X., Zhang, L., Li, X., Ma, W.: Annotating images by mining image search results. TPAMI **30**(11), 1919–1932 (2008)
24. Wu, M., Scholkopf, B.: A local learning approach for clustering. NIPS **19**, 1529–1536 (2007)
25. Xiao, Y., Zhu, Z., Zhao, Y., Wei, Y., Wei, S., Li, X.: Topographic NMF for data representation. IEEE TCYB **44**(10), 1762–1771 (2014)
26. Yang, Y., Shen, H., Nie, F., Ji, R., Zhou, X.: Nonnegative spectral clustering with discriminative regularization. In: AAAI, pp. 555–560 (2011)
27. Yang, Y., Xu, D., Nie, F., Yan, S., Zhuang, Y.: Image clustering using local discriminant models and global integration. TIP **19**(10), 2761–2773 (2010)
28. Yang, Y., Ma, Z., Yang, Y., Nie, F., Shen, H.T.: Multitask spectral clustering by exploring intertask correlation. IEEE Trans. Cybern. **45**(5), 1083–1094 (2015)
29. Yang, Y., Shen, F., Huang, Z., Shen, H.T., Li, X.: Discrete nonnegative spectral clustering. IEEE Trans. Knowl. Data Eng. **29**(9), 1834–1845 (2017)
30. Yang, Y., Shen, F., Huang, Z., Shen, H.T.: A unified framework for discrete spectral clustering. In: IJCAI, pp. 2273–2279 (2016)
31. Yang, Y., Shen, F., Shen, H.T., Li, H., Li, X.: Robust discrete spectral hashing for large-scale image semantic indexing. IEEE Trans. Big Data **1**(4), 162–171 (2015)
32. Yang, Y., Yang, Y., Shen, H.T., Zhang, Y., Du, X., Zhou, X.: Discriminative nonnegative spectral clustering with out-of-sample extension. IEEE TKDE **25**(8), 1760–1771 (2013)
33. Ye, J., Zhao, Z., Liu, H.: Adaptive distance metric learning for clustering. In: CVPR, pp. 1–7 (2007)
34. Ye, J., Zhao, Z., Wu, M.: Discriminative k-means for clustering. NIPS **20**, 1649–1656 (2007)
35. Yu, S., Shi, J.: Multiclass spectral clustering. In: ICCV, pp. 313–319 (2003)
36. Zelnik-Manor, L., Perona, P.: Self-tuning spectral clustering. NIPS **17**, 1601–1608 (2004)

FeatureBand: A Feature Selection Method by Combining Early Stopping and Genetic Local Search

Huanran Xue[1(✉)], Jiawei Jiang[2,3], Yingxia Shao[4], and Bin Cui[1,2]

[1] Center for Data Science, National Engineering Laboratory for Big Data Analysis
and Applications, Peking University,Beijing, China
{xuehuanran,bin.cui}@pku.edu.cn
[2] School of EECS and Key Laboratory of High Confidence Software Technologies
(MOE), Peking University, Beijing, China
blue.jwjiang@pku.edu.cn, jeremyjiang@tencent.com
[3] Tencent Inc., Shenzhen, China
[4] Beijing Key Lab of Intelligent Telecommunications Software and Multimedia,
BUPT, Beijing, China
shaoyx@bupt.edu.cn

Abstract. Feature selection is an important problem in machine learning and data mining. In reality, the wrapper methods are broadly used in feature selection. It treats feature selection as a search problem using a predictor as a black-box. However, most wrapper methods are time-consuming due to the large search space. In this paper, we propose a novel wrapper method, called FeatureBand, for feature selection. We use the early stopping strategy to terminate bad candidate feature subsets and avoid wasting of training time. Further, we use a genetic local search to generate new subsets based on previous ones. These two techniques are combined under an iterative framework in which we gradually allocate more resources for more promising candidate feature subsets. The experimental result shows that FeatureBand achieves a better trade-off between search time and search accuracy. It is 1.45× to 17.6× faster than the state-of-the-art wrapper-based methods without accuracy loss.

Keywords: Feature selection · Early stopping · Genetic local search

1 Introduction

Feature selection (FS) is a key step in the machine learning (ML) and data science applications [17,25]. The selection process keeps the relevant features, and removes irrelevant or redundant features. The main benefits of feature selection are mainly reflected in three aspects—the improvement of predictive performance, cost-effectiveness and better interpretability.

In supervised learning, the purpose of feature selection is to select a subset of features which has the optimal performance on the test set. Given a data set

© Springer Nature Switzerland AG 2019
J. Shao et al. (Eds.): APWeb-WAIM 2019, LNCS 11642, pp. 27–41, 2019.
https://doi.org/10.1007/978-3-030-26075-0_3

$\{(x_1, y_1), ..., (x_N, y_N)\}$, D is the number of features and $U = \{1, 2, ..., D\}$ is the set of possible features, the goal of feature selection is to find an optimal feature subset $F^* = argmax_{F \subset U} J(F)$. Where J is the objective function evaluating the feature subset (e.g. cross validation accuracy).

The classical feature selection methods can be categorized into three types: filter, wrapper and embedded [11]. The wrapper methods use a black-box predictor to evaluate the feature subset on the validation set. The wrapper methods can be formalized as a heuristic search problem. It can find an optimal or suboptimal feature subset given enough time, and generally have the highest accuracy in the three categories of feature selection algorithms. However, the search problem is known as NP-hard [1]. The time complexity of exhaustive search is $O(2^D)$ and it is impractical to enumerate all feature subsets. Due to the high time complexity, the wrapper methods are rarely used in practice. So it is important to reduce the execution time of the wrapper method without the loss of accuracy.

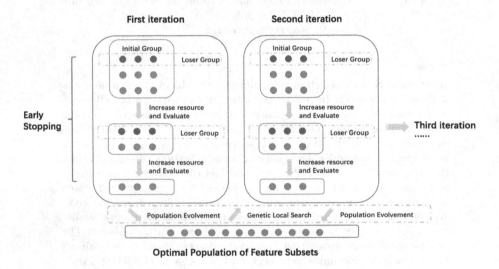

Fig. 1. The framework of FeatureBand.

Since the original wrapper method fails due to the difficulties during the search process, we try to learn lessons from other fields. A common strategy in machine learning tasks is that researchers and engineers often early terminate unpromising trials to save time. For example, early stopping is widely used in tuning hyperparameters for ML algorithms [9,15]. Motivated by this idea, we propose to use **early stopping** mechanism to accelerate the search process. It is not worth using all the trainging resources on such "bad" feature subsets and we use the sub-sampling strategy to evaluate the feature subsets with terminating the training process of the "bad" subsets. In this way, the training resources are used to explore better feature subsets. The basic framework is shown in Fig. 1—(1) allocate a reasonable resource budget to a specific group of feature subsets; (2) evaluate the performance of each feature subset and throw away the worst feature subsets; (3) increase the allocated resource (e.g. number of dataset subsampling) for each remaining feature subset. This process is repeated until the maximal resource is used on the final group of subsets. Next, we use the final "winner" group to update the global population which records the overall best subsets. Then a new initial group of subsets is generated by the global population, and the next selection cycle starts afterwards.

The main contributions of this work can be summarized as follows:

- We use the dynamic early stopping mechanism in the feature selection problem to avoid the wasting of training time on unpromising candidates. The better candidates will get more training resources during the selection process.
- The genetic local search is used to produce the new candidates through the knowledge of the past iterations. The candidates inherited from the "good" candidates will have better performance and this mechanism will speed up the selection process.
- Empirical studies on different types of datasets show the effects of early stopping and genetic local search. Overall, FeatureBand can be 1.45× to 17.6× faster than the baselines while achieving a top-tier accuracy.

This paper is organized as follows. Section 2 introduces the related work of feature selection. Section 3 introduces our method in detail. In the Sect. 4, we empirically compare our method with the state-of-the-art methods on different datasets. We draw a conclusion and propose the future work in Sect. 5.

2   Related Work

2.1   Filter Methods

The filter methods usually use a "scoring function" which gives each feature a score and no ML classifier is used. The scoring functions are mainly based on statistical property or information theory. Then the features are ranked with the scores and the high-ranked features are finally selected. The filter methods are efficient in computation, but the accuracy may not be ideal because the scoring function is hard to choose and it may ignore the relations between features.

The statistics-based methods use various statistical measures to evaluate features, such as t-score and chi-square score [12]. The information-theory-based methods use the information theory criteria to select features. The well-known works include Mutual-Information Maximization [13], conditional mutual information maximization (CMIM) [6], and minimum redundancy maximum relevance (MRMR) [20].

2.2   Wrapper Methods

The wrapper method can be divided into two categories: sequential search and population-based search [4].

Sequential Search. The sequential method selects the optimal feature subset with a sequence. The SFS (sequential forward search) and SBS (sequential backward search) algorithms [18] add the best feature or removes the worst feature one by one. The SFFS (sequential forward floating search) and SBFS [21] algorithms record the subset $X_k, |X_k| = k$, which keeps the current best subset of size k.

Population-based Search. Genetic method is a heuristic algorithm inspired by the natural process of evolution. It is proposed to search a global solution for the optimization problem. The feature selection can also be seen as a combinatorial optimization problem [18]. Each feature subset is a candidate solution of the optimization problem and the subset can be represented as a bitmap, e.g., "11001" means the first, second and fifth features are selected. Other than genetic algorithms, Particle Swarm Algorithm (PSO) [10] is another kind of algorithm aimed at solving the optimization problem of feature selection [8,23,24].

The weak points of sequential search are the low-efficiency and it is impractical to use in the real-world applications. For population-based search, the initial group/swarm in each iteration is initialized at random and the intermediate information is not fully utilized.

2.3   Embedded Methods

The embedded methods can be seen as a trade-off between filter and wrapper methods. The feature selection process is part of the training process with a specified classifier (e.g. Logistic Regression [16] or Linear SVM [22]). The training process seems like wrapper methods. After training, the trained classifier can give each feature a feature importance. Then the relevant features are selected with the feature importance and this process seems like filter methods.

3   FeatureBand

In this section, we first give an overview of FeatureBand, then introduce three main components: genetic local search, early stopping, and population evolvement.

3.1   Overview of FeatureBand

The procedure of our method, FeatureBand, is shown in Algorithm 1. There are two loops in FeatureBand—the inner loop (lines 7–13) and the outer loop (lines 3–15). In the inner loop, the resource for each evaluated feature subset (data sub-sampling) r is increasing and the number of evaluated feature subsets n is decreasing. FeatureBand has the following hyperparameters: r_0 is the initial resource, n_0 is the initial number of evaluated feature subsets, R and T are the maximal resource and maximal iterations respectively, $\eta > 1$ is the early-stopping ratio, and d is the number of selected features predefined by user. The output of the algorithm is an optimal feature subset which has been selected and has the best performance. In the line 2, a population P is created, where P is the current "optimal population" and m is the fixed size of P.

As shown in Algorithm 1, three core components of FeatureBand are genetic local search, early stopping and updating population. We will elaborate each component below.

Algorithm 1. FeatureBand

Input:

r_0: initial number of data subsampling;

n_0: initial number of feature subsets;

R: max resource i.e. the number of instances in dataset;

T: max iteration;

η: early stopping ration;

d: number of selected features which user specifies or **None**;

m: size of global population

Output: F^*

1 $r = r_0, n = n_0$;

2 $P = Null$;

3 // begin the outer loop ;

4 **for** $t = 1 : T$ **do**

5   // genetic local search operation;

6     $S = \text{genetic\_local\_search}(n_0, d, t, P)$;

7   // begin the inner loop ;

8   **while** $r \leq R$ **do**

9        $L = \{ \text{evaluate\_performance}(s, r) : s \in S \}$;

10       $S = \text{get\_top\_subsets}(S, \lfloor n/\eta \rfloor)$;

11       $r \leftarrow r * \eta$;

12       $n \leftarrow \lfloor n/\eta \rfloor$;

13   **end**

14     $\text{population\_evolvement}(S, P)$;

15 **end**

16 $F^* \leftarrow \text{get\_best}(P)$;

17 **return** F^*;

3.2   Genetic Local Search

The mechanism of genetic local search is a strategy that the initial feature subsets are generated from the global optimal group P through the *genetic_local_search* function. The *genetic_local_search* function receives four inputs: n_0, d, t, P, and three hyperparameters: p_m, c, m, and returns a feature subset in which the number of selected features is d. The framework is shown in Algorithm 2.

When the optimal population P is Null, the function returns a random set (lines 2–4). If not, we use the crossover and mutation operations [18] to generate a new set of subsets (lines 5–20). For each time, specifically, we randomly choose two parents p_1 and p_2 of P, and get a new subset ch with crossover and mutation. The two operations are explained as follow.

Algorithm 2. genetic_local_search

Input:
n_0: initial number of feature subsets;
d: number of selected features which user specifies or **None**;
P: the optimal set of feaeture subsets;
p_m: mutation rate;
c: the rate of initial group of subsets inherited from last iteration;

Output: S_0

1 $S_0 = Null$;
2 **if** $P == Null$ **then**
3 | $S_0 = $ random_init(n_0, d);
4 **else**
5 | **for** $i = 1 : cn_0$ **do**
6 | | $p_1 = $ random_select(P);
7 | | $p_2 = $ random_select(P);
8 | | $ch = $ crossover(p_1, p_2);
9 | | // mutation process;
10 | | $p_1 = p_m$;
11 | | $p_0 = \frac{p_m \cdot k}{D-k}$;
12 | | **for** each g in ch **do**
13 | | | $r \leftarrow$ random_number$(0, 1)$;
14 | | | **if** $g == 1$ and $r < p_1$ **then**
15 | | | | $g \leftarrow 0$;
16 | | | **end**
17 | | | **if** $g == 0$ and $r < p_0$ **then**
18 | | | | $g \leftarrow 1$;
19 | | | **end**
20 | | **end**
21 | | //normalize feature numbers;
22 | | **if** d is specified by user **then**
23 | | | **if** $k > d$ **then**
24 | | | | Select $k - d$ 1-bits randomly as l_1;
25 | | | | Convert all the bits in l_1 to 0;
26 | | | **end**
27 | | | **if** $k < d$ **then**
28 | | | | Select $d - k$ 0-bits randomly as l_0;
29 | | | | Convert all the bits in l_0 to 1;
30 | | | **end**
31 | | **end**
32 | | append(S_0, ch);
33 | **end**
34 | $S_0 = S_0 \cup$ random_init$((1 - c)n_0, d)$;
35 **end**
36 **return** S_0;

Crossover process. The feature subset can be represented as a binary string and the crossover operation chooses some cutting points randomly and alternatively copies each segment of two parents and the procedure is shown in Fig. 2. As Fig. 2 shown, two parent subsets are: **10110101, 11100100**, which means the number of all features $D = 8$, and **1** represents the feature is selected, **0** represents the feature is not selected. Then two cutting points are chosen randomly and the child subset gets the first and third parts of the parent1, the second part of the parent2.

Mutation process. The mutation process is shown in lines 10–20, k is the number of 1-bits i.e. number of selected features and D is the number of all features which means $D-k$ is the number of 0-bits. p_0 and p_1 are the mutation probability of 0-bit and 1-bit. As lines 12–20 in Algorithm 2 indicate, for each point in the child subset, we generate a random number r in $(0, 1)$. If $p_i < r$, then convert i to $1 - i$. As Fig. 2 shows, after mutation, the child subset generates the second and sixth, two points to mutate. After mutation, if d is specified by the user, we force the number of selected features to be d exactly. The method is shown in lines 21–32: if the number of selected features $k > d$, select $k - d$ 1-bits randomly and convert the selected 1-bits to 0. When $k < d$, the procedure is similar. At last, the child subset is appended to the S_0. At the end of genetic local search, $(1 - c)n_0$ subsets are initialized randomly for the search ability.

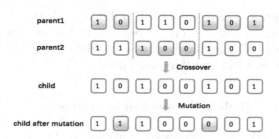

Fig. 2. Crossover process.

3.3   Early Stopping

The early stopping strategy is used in the inner loop. First, at the beginning of the outer loop, the allocated resource r and the number of subsets n are initialized. S is the initialized set of feature subsets to be evaluated and is initialized through *genetic_local_search*. Then, we evaluate the performance of each subset in S. In the setting of FeatureBand, the resource is the number of dataset subsampling. After evaluation, S is partitioned into two groups: the "winner" group and the "loser" group according to the ratio η as shown in Fig. 1. The "loser" group is thrown out. At the end of the inner loop, the resource allocated for each candidate subset increases to $r\eta$ and the number of candidate subsets decreases to $\lfloor n/\eta \rfloor$. This strategy addresses the expensive evaluation problem through throwing away "bad" subsets recursively.

3.4 Population Evolvement

Once finishing one round of the outer loop, the optimal population P is updated. P is a set which keeps the top subsets and generates the initial subsets for each outer loop. In our method, the size of P is fixed and P is updated as below. We first augment P, then sort P according to the evaluation results in a descending order, and choose the top-$|P|$ candidates in line 14. In this way, P always keeps the best $|P|$ subsets.

$$P' \leftarrow P \cup S$$
$$P' \leftarrow sort(P')$$
$$P \leftarrow P'(1:|P|)$$

4 Experiments and Results

In this section, we use four real datasets to evaluate our method and several baselines including filter, embedded and wrapper methods.

4.1 Experimental Setting

Datasets. The datasets are summarized in Table 1. All the datasets are from ASU feature selection website [14]. Madelon is a dataset used in NIPS 2003 Feature Selection Challenge, Basehock is a text dataset, Coil20 is a face image dataset, and Usps is a hand written image dataset.

Table 1. Datasets used in experiments.

Dataset	#instances	#features	#classes
Madelon	2600	500	2
Basehock	1993	4862	2
Coil20	1440	1024	20
Usps	9298	256	10

Baselines. First, we show that our proposed techniques work in FeatureBand. Next, we show that our method has a better performance than the filter and embedded methods including F-test, MI, MRMR, CMIM, CCM and Random Forest [2,6,13,14,20]. Then we present a trade-off between speed and accuracy by comparing with other wrapper methods including SFS, SFFS and genetic algorithm [18,21].

Metrics. The 5-fold cross validation is used to evaluate the algorithms. In each fold of the 5-fold cross validation, the training set (4 folds) is used to select the features, and the remaining 1 fold is used to evaluate the selected features. For wrapper methods, the training set (4 folds) is divided in such a way that the 30% is used as validation set which the accuracy of the validation is the objective function and the remaining 70% is used for training. The classifiers used in the experiments are 3-nearest-neighbor (3-KNN) and logistic regression, following [3,7,26].

Environments. All the experiments are executed on a Ubuntu 14.04 server equipped with 16 cores and 72 GB memory. The algorithms are implemented with Scikit-Learn [19] and Scikit-Feature [14].

Protocol. Since FeatureBand involves several hyperparameters, we set $m = 5, \eta = 3, T = 50, r_0 = 50, n_0 = 500$ in all experiments with manual tuning.

4.2   Effect of Genetic Local Search

In the first part of the experiments, we show the effect of the genetic local search. To achieve this goal, we propose a simplified FeatureBand, namely RandomBand. In RandomBand, the *genetic_local_search* function is actually a random function which means the initial group of feature subsets is initialized at random. The comparison result of the two algorithms on Madelon is shown in Fig. 3.

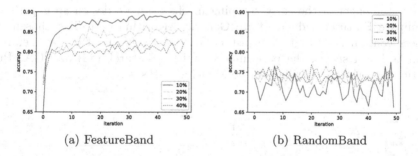

(a) FeatureBand   (b) RandomBand

Fig. 3. FeatureBand versus RandomBand on Madelon dataset. RandomBand only uses Early Stopping without genetic local search. The y-axis is the value of objective function and the x-axis is the iteration number. The classifier is 3-KNN.

The y-axis is the value of the objective function and the x-axis is the iteration number. As the iteration grows, the performing subset found in each outer loop evolves and becomes better, while the performance in RandomBand is nearly random. To give a numerical result, we conduct an experiment to select 10% features from the original features and smooth the objective values with a five-length window. The result is shown in Table 2. As the iteration grows, the average objective value of FeatureBand grows from 78% to 88.90%, but RandomBand is always about 70%. This proves that the genetic local search is effective and the feature subsets generated by "good" parents can probably inherit good features (genes) from its parents.

Table 2. Five-window average objective function value. FeatureBand versus Random-Band, on Madelon dataset

Iteration	FeatureBand	RandomBand
1–5	78.00	71.00
6–10	85.51	73.56
11–15	86.90	70.67
16–20	87.28	70.26
21–25	87.64	70.33
26–30	87.79	72.92
31–35	88.60	70.60
36–40	88.77	69.49
41–45	88.82	70.41
46–50	88.90	72.36

4.3   Effect of Early Stopping

To show the effect of the early stopping mechanism, we design an experiment to compare FeatureBand and Pure Genetic Algorithm [18]. The chosen two datasets contain 2500 and 9280 instances respectively and the classifier is 3-KNN. As Fig. 4 shows, the performance of FB (FeatureBand) and GA (Pure Genetic Algorithm) is similiar on the Madelon dataset.

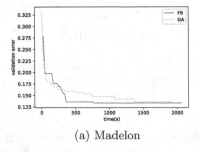
(a) Madelon

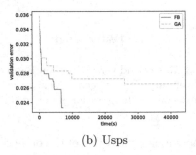
(b) Usps

Fig. 4. Comparison with genetic algorithm.

As Fig. 4 shows, we are actually better. Say we can converge to an error within 500 s, while GA needs about 1500 s. However, when the number of instances becomes larger, the difference is obvious on the Usps dataset. FB can converge to an error of 2.3% within 10000 s, while the error of GA is still 2.7% after 40000 s. The reason is obvious. When the features of dataset become more, the early stopping can save more training time taken on the "bad" subsets. However, GA might consume an unnecessary training process on such "bad" subsets.

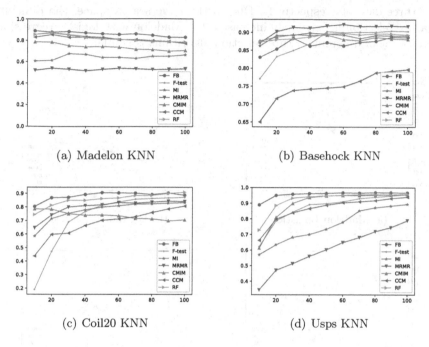

(a) Madelon KNN   (b) Basehock KNN

(c) Coil20 KNN   (d) Usps KNN

Fig. 5. Performance comparison with filter methods with 3-KNN. The y-axis is the average accuracy of 5-fold cross validation, and the x-axis is the number of the selected features from 10 to 100.

4.4   Comparison with Filter and Embedded Methods

In this section, we compare our method with filter and embedded methods and evaluate the methods with 3-KNN and logistic regression. The results show that our method is more accurate than these methods. We use two basic filter methods with ftest and mutual-information [13,14]. These two methods give each feature a score and ignore the relations between the features which are widely used in the machine learning systems, such as scikit-learn [19]. Rather than basic filter methods, we also use the classical state-of-the-art methods, including maximum relevancy minimum redundancy (MRMR) [20], conditional mutual information maximization (CMIM) [6] and conditional covariance minimization (CCM) [5] is the recent work for feature selection. For embedded methods, we use Random Forest [2] as the classifier to extract feature importance and select the features according to the feature importance.

The number of selected features is chosen from $\{10, 20, ..., 100\}$. As Figs. 5 and 6 show, FeatureBand is almost better than other methods on all the datasets. The failing reason on Basehock may be the high dimensionality of Basehock. Suppose we need to select 50 features from 4862 features of Basehock, the solution space of Basehock is 4.88×10^{13}, 3.35×10^{10}, and 4.85×10^{26} larger than other three datasets respectively. Due to the large search space, the difficulty of feature selection is extremely increased. For Madelon with logistic regression, the accuracy of different feature selection algorithms is similar.

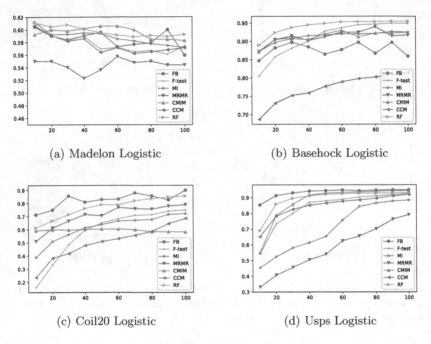

(a) Madelon Logistic   (b) Basehock Logistic

(c) Coil20 Logistic   (d) Usps Logistic

Fig. 6. Performance comparison with filter methods with logistic regression. The y-axis is the average accuracy of 5-fold cross validation, and the x-axis is the number of the selected features from 10 to 100.

4.5   Comparison with Wrapper Methods

Then, we compare FeatureBand with wrapper methods, including SFS, SFFS, and Pure Genetic Algorithm [13, 18]. The result is shown in Tables 3 and 4. We set $d = 50, 100$ and 3-KNN as the classifier. In all 8 experiments, FeatureBand achieves the highest accuracy in 3 experiments. In other experiments, the accuracy of FeatureBand is similar to the best method—at most 4.92% worse. As shown in Table 4, FB is faster than SFS and SFFS by 1.5× to 45×. Overall, FeatureBand can reach an accuracy similar to the best methods with the shortest time.

Table 3. 5-fold accuracy (%) comparison with wrapper methods.

Dataset	d	SFS	SFFS	GA	FB
Madelon	50	**88.58**	88.38	85.62	87.88
	100	**89.38**	88.35	84.77	84.46
Basehock	50	92.33	**93.23**	82.59	90.36
	100	92.88	**93.32**	90.61	90.82
Coil20	50	85.68	85.68	93.39	**94.17**
	100	88.72	90.55	94.34	**95.13**
Usps	50	96.22	96.22	**96.80**	96.75
	100	96.08	95.94	96.71	**97.06**

Table 4. Run time (seconds) comparison with wrapper methods.

Dataset	d	SFS	SFFS	GA	FB
Madelon	50	708	4108	1031	**489**
	100	2747	18204	2696	**1034**
Basehock	50	26515	28350	823	**619**
	100	67435	151442	1558	**1094**
Coil20	50	2388	3046	450	**348**
	100	6168	9506	842	**803**
Usps	50	8457	35327	14664	**3711**
	100	28633	116030	42269	**7093**

4.6 Effects of Feature Dimensionality

To show that the cost of FB is robust to feature dimensionality, Fig. 7 illustrates the run time consumed by FeatureBand and SFS.

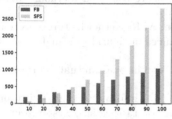
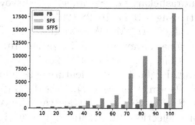

(a) Comparison with SFS.   (b) Comparison with SFS and SFFS.

Fig. 7. Effects of feature dimensionality

When the number of selected features is 10, the run time of SFS and FB is 182 s and 63 s respectively. However, the run time of SFS and FB increases to 2813 s and 1034 s when the number of selected features is 100, while FB is two times faster than SFS. Figure 7 shows the results of FB, SFS and SFFS. Due to the backtracking characteristic of SFFS, the size of the optimal feature subsets is changed during the search process. For this reason, SFFS is most time-consuming when feature dimension is high. At the beginning, the run time of SFFS is at the same level of others. However, it takes 18237 s in the end, which is 17.6 and 6.5 times slower than SFS and FeatureBand respectively.

5 Conclusion

In this work, we proposed a novel method to accelerate the search process of feature selection via early stopping and genetic local search. Our method FeatureBand significantly outperformed filter methods in terms of accuracy. Besides,

FeatureBand was much more efficient than wrapper baselines, and meanwhile achieved a similar accuracy as the state-of-art wrapper methods. Further, the run time of FeatureBand was linear in terms of the selected features, while other wrapper methods were superlinear. In the future, we will extend FeatureBand to distributed environments.

Acknowledgement. This work is supported by NSFC (No. 61832001, 61702015, 61702016, 61572039), the National Key Research and Development Program of China (No. 2018YFB1004403), and PKU-Tencent joint research Lab.

References

1. Amaldi, E., Kann, V.: On the approximability of minimizing nonzero variables or unsatisfied relations in linear systems. Theor. Comput. Sci. **209**(1–2), 237–260 (1998)
2. Breiman, L.: Random forests. Mach. Learn. **45**(1), 5–32 (2001)
3. Brown, G., Pocock, A., Zhao, M.J., Luján, M.: Conditional likelihood maximisation: a unifying framework for information theoretic feature selection. J. Mach. Learn. Res. **13**(Jan), 27–66 (2012)
4. Chandrashekar, G., Sahin, F.: A survey on feature selection methods. Comput. Electr. Eng. **40**(1), 16–28 (2014)
5. Chen, J., Stern, M., Wainwright, M.J., Jordan, M.I.: Kernel feature selection via conditional covariance minimization. In: Advances in Neural Information Processing Systems, pp. 6946–6955 (2017)
6. Fleuret, F.: Fast binary feature selection with conditional mutual information. J. Mach. Learn. Res. **5**(Nov), 1531–1555 (2004)
7. Gao, S., Ver Steeg, G., Galstyan, A.: Variational information maximization for feature selection. In: Advances in Neural Information Processing Systems, pp. 487–495 (2016)
8. Gu, S., Cheng, R., Jin, Y.: Feature selection for high-dimensional classification using a competitive swarm optimizer. Soft Comput. **22**(3), 811–822 (2018)
9. Jamieson, K., Talwalkar, A.: Non-stochastic best arm identification and hyperparameter optimization. In: Artificial Intelligence and Statistics, pp. 240–248 (2016)
10. Kennedy, R.: J. and eberhart, particle swarm optimization. In: Proceedings of IEEE International Conference on Neural Networks IV, vol. 1000 (1995)
11. Kohavi, R., John, G.H.: Wrappers for feature subset selection. Artif. Intell. **97**(1–2), 273–324 (1997)
12. Koller, D., Sahami, M.: Toward optimal feature selection. Technical report, Stanford InfoLab (1996)
13. Lewis, D.D.: Feature selection and feature extraction for text categorization. In: Proceedings of the workshop on Speech and Natural Language, pp. 212–217. Association for Computational Linguistics (1992)
14. Li, J., et al.: Feature selection: a data perspective. ACM Comput. Surv. (CSUR) **50**(6), 94 (2017)
15. Li, L., Jamieson, K., DeSalvo, G., Rostamizadeh, A., Talwalkar, A.: Hyperband: a novel bandit-based approach to hyperparameter optimization. J. Mach. Learn. Res. **18**(1), 6765–6816 (2017)
16. Liao, J., Chin, K.V.: Logistic regression for disease classification using microarray data: model selection in a large p and small n case. Bioinformatics **23**(15), 1945–1951 (2007)

17. Liu, L., Du, X., Zhu, L., Shen, F., Huang, Z.: Learning discrete hashing towards efficient fashion recommendation. Data Sci. Eng. **3**(4), 307–322 (2018). https:// doi.org/10.1007/s41019-018-0079-z
18. Oh, I.S., Lee, J.S., Moon, B.R.: Hybrid genetic algorithms for feature selection. IEEE Trans. Pattern Anal. Mach. Intell. **11**, 1424–1437 (2004)
19. Pedregosa, F., et al.: Scikit-learn: machine learning in python. J. Mach. Learn. Res. **12**(Oct), 2825–2830 (2011)
20. Peng, H., Long, F., Ding, C.: Feature selection based on mutual information criteria of max-dependency, max-relevance, and min-redundancy. IEEE Trans. Pattern Anal. Mach. Intell. **27**(8), 1226–1238 (2005)
21. Pudil, P., Novovičová, J., Kittler, J.: Floating search methods in feature selection. Pattern Recogn. Lett. **15**(11), 1119–1125 (1994)
22. Tan, M., Wang, L., Tsang, I.W.: Learning sparse svm for feature selection on very high dimensional datasets. In: Proceedings of the 27th International Conference on Machine Learning (ICML-10), pp. 1047–1054 (2010)
23. Unler, A., Murat, A.: A discrete particle swarm optimization method for feature selection in binary classification problems. Eur. J. Oper. Res. **206**(3), 528–539 (2010)
24. Xue, B., Zhang, M., Browne, W.N.: Particle swarm optimization for feature selection in classification: a multi-objective approach. IEEE Trans. Cybern. **43**(6), 1656–1671 (2013)
25. Zhang, J., Wang, Q., Yang, Q., Zhou, R., Zhang, Y.: Exploiting multi-category characteristics and unified framework to extract web content. Data Sci. Eng. **3**(2), 101–114 (2018). https://doi.org/10.1007/s41019-018-0067-3
26. Zhou, Y., et al.: Parallel feature selection inspired by group testing. In: Advances in Neural Information Processing Systems, pp. 3554–3562 (2014)

Supervised Hashing with Recurrent Scaling

Xiyao Fu[1,2], Yi Bin[2], Zheng Wang[2(✉)], Qin Wei[1], and Si Chen[3]

[1] Guizhou Provincial Key Laboratory of Public Big Data, Guizhou University,
Guiyang 550025, Guizhou, China
`fu.xiyao.gm@gmail.com, weiq@gzu.edu.cn`
[2] School of Computer Science and Engineering, University of Electronic Science
and Technology of China, Chengdu 611731, Sichuan, China
`yi.bin@hotmail.com, zh_wang@hotmail.com`
[3] Information Science Academy, China Electronics Technology Group Corporation,
Beijing, China
`chensi@cetc.com.cn`

Abstract. Learning to hash is a method that can deal with content-based information retrieval efficiently. Traditional learning to hash methods, however, lack the ability to map the generated hash codes to the high-level semantic space. Attributes, as a kind of higher level of visual data representation compared to features, have the potential ability in deep learning to boost the performance. Utilizing attributes from visual data in deep learning to hash can link every bit of the hash codes and a certain type of attributes, therefore giving the hash code an explicit explanation. This paper presents a novel framework, named Deep Recurrent Scaling Hashing (DRSH), to solve the traditional image retrieval problem. The hash codes generated from DRSH are a combination of the outputs of each step of an enhanced LSTM and features generated from convolutional neural nets and are learned through images' attributes. This RNN is reformed to adjust the decorrelation of data flowing between each cell step, which not only makes the learning phase benefit from the ability of recurrent neural nets to learn with recurrent memory but also enable the availability of each hash bit to preserve distinct information. Experiments show that this framework can achieve appreciable performance on major datasets, and also have the ability to explain the meaning of hash codes based on attributes.

Keywords: Deep hashing · Attribute learning · CBIR

1 Introduction

Since the data on the Internet has a rapid growing speed in both storage and categories in recent years, people are naturally encouraged to seek new ways to fast and efficiently generate the pattern in data. Content-based information retrieval (CBIR), a technique focusing on querying and indexing of a large data

© Springer Nature Switzerland AG 2019
J. Shao et al. (Eds.): APWeb-WAIM 2019, LNCS 11642, pp. 42–56, 2019.
https://doi.org/10.1007/978-3-030-26075-0_4

collection based on visual content, is the key to many multimedia applications including face recognition, action detection, etc. CBIR is able to search and locate in millions of images and videos, which can properly handle the "data explosion" on the Internet.

As a vital method about content-based retrieval on visual data on the Internet, learning to hash has been attracting much more attention in recent years. Through learning the potential data pattern and compressing the learned information in a short range of binary bits, hash codes learning is an essential way to retrieve data on the Internet [3–5, 10, 19, 39, 42–44]. Meanwhile, with the rapid-growing advance in deep learning [13, 14, 20] and certain framework to model the deep learning phase [2, 13], methods which utilize neural network to boost the performance of hashing were proposed as well [3, 9, 17, 24, 25, 35, 36].

Of all the data-dependant learning to hash methods, based on whether using the ground truth labels of the training set in training or not, hashing methods can be divided into supervised or unsupervised type. Usually, supervised methods will gain better performance over unsupervised methods, because the supervised hashing methods probably need a narrower relaxation to get the solution during the optimization step. For instance, iterative quantization combined with canonical correlation analysis (CCA-ITQ) [4] gets obviously higher performance compared with iterative quantization because it uses CCA instead of PCA to choose the available projection from the original data matrix to hash codes space. CCA-ITQ can achieve state-of-the-art performance on current mainstream datasets after combining with deep learning methods which are used to extract features.

On the other hand, the integration of hash learning and deep learning is a crucial question when trying to adjust the deep learning to hash tasks. Recent progress has demonstrated the impressive learning power of different variations of convolutional neural network (CNN) in image classification, object detection, face recognition, and many other vision tasks [21]. The successful applications of CNN in various tasks demonstrate that the features learned by CNN can well capture the underlying semantic structure of images in spite of significant appearance variations. Some deep hashing methods like [9], tried to compute Hamming distance between learned hash codes through a convolutional neural network by computing the similarity between two data points using the ground truth labels. In [3], the recurrent nature of LSTM is used as the encoder for temporal video frames and compute hash codes through the last step output, which was the hidden state been computed through a single fully-connected activation layer. The experiment results showed that the adjustment got boosted performance. However, the nature of strengths for deep neural nets (DNN) to train hash codes is still partially discovered. For example, for a recurrent neural net, we can stretch the learning cycle for hash code learning, and make the DNN adjust the hash bits from the already learned ones.

In this paper, we presented a novel way to adjust the bit-wise learning phase in deep learning procession, named **Deep Recurrent Scaling Hashing** (DRSH). Our method produces a scaling vector in the hash learning process to boost the performance of codes generated from CNN features. In general, deep recurrent scaling hashing consists of the following steps. First, we extract features and attributes of images through deep neural nets. The attributes in training are utilized and computed in this recurrent neural net using the attention mechanism in order to focus on different attributes of an image/image batch at each time step. After extraction we utilize a refined LSTM to approximate the dimensionality reduction and decorrelation between each time step in order to get meaningful scaling vector generated bit-by-bit; then the hash codes for the images are generated through the combination of the output of the RNN and CNN features. The generated hash codes' performance benefits more from both deep features and semantic attributes compared to hash codes merely generated from features. Furthermore, the fusion of features and attributes let the hash codes gain both the ability of index and distinguishable semantic meanings.

2   Related Work

In this section, we provide the background of our work. Such background not only contains direct relation from enlightening methods in learning to hash but also provides possible ways to effectively adjust attributes into deep learning methods.

2.1   Deep Learning to Hash

In recent years there were attempts to combine the generating hash code and the deep learning process. Zhang et al. [3] and Song et al. [7] tried to introduce a new variation of LSTM called Bidirectional LSTM in order to directly generate hash code for retrieving videos. The method consisted of a typical bi-directional LSTM. Through batch normalization [15] and binarizing the output state of the LSTM output, the results were usable hash codes for the video snippet utilized as the input of the LSTM. This strategy can be seen as the primary step to make the deep learning process "simplifies" the data flowing through the LSTM cells.

If we expect multiple data flowing steps between different DNN layers as one learning time for hash codes, the decorrelation between different cells/state is quite important. The learnt result can be of no use or showing no meaningful results if the data flow is not decorrelated. Recent work such as [31,32] shows the attempt to approximate or skip the eigenvalue computation step in traditional decorrelation methods such as CCA [4] and received promising results. Furthermore, proper methods are needed in order to adjust attributes in RNN computation process.

2.2   Multi-instance Learning

Multi-instance learning (MIL) [6] is a method in order to automatically generating image descriptions: visual detectors, language models, and multimodal similarity models learnt directly from a dataset of image captions. The core idea of MIL is the definition and utilization of attributes. Attributes can be seen as a more universal and fundamental description of images and videos compared with features. For example, a cat may have features like "having a tail" and "two-ear", and have attributes like "hairy". Learning through attributes turns out to be more efficient for training a deep neural net.

2.3   Attention Mechanism

As far as utilizing the attributes to boost the performance of attention methods in image/video captioning [1,11,12,16,22,40,41], visual question answering [45,46] and other tasks, Wu et al. [23] tried to not explicitly represent high-level semantic concepts, instead, they sought to directly map from images to text. Aside from available texts they tried to utilize, they also extract attributes from images and used them in the framework. The results showed that by replacing features, the performance on both captioning and VQA received a certain advance.

In order to adopt the attributes learning process in recurrent neural nets to produce the scaling vector, the attributes put in the RNN should not only be able to map the meanings but also vary in focus in different time steps. In recent years, the attention [1,11,12,16,22,40,41] mechanism is a quite popular method in computer vision, e.g. captioning, cross-modal retrieval. Its idea is originally derived from the natural language processing [16]. In general, attention mechanism "guides" the recurrent neural networks to the wanted region of visual data. In [11], the authors provided a "soft" deterministic attention mechanism and a "hard" stochastic attention mechanism. "Soft" attention tried to compute the attention model through basic back-propagation of the neural networks, and "hard" attention mechanism generated the attention vector by the maximum approximate probability of the occurrence of word vectors.

3   DRSH Model

3.1   Problem Definition

Suppose that we have n samples $X = \{x_i\}_{i=1}^{n}$, where $\mathbf{X}$ denotes the entire data point space, and we have the corresponded labels represented in a group of vectors V_f where $V_f = \{f_i\}_{i=1}^{n}$ which are pre-extracted from raw data. The goal is to generate a group of hash codes $B = \{b_i\}_{i=1}^{n} \in \{-1,1\}^{L \times n}$, where the ith hash code b_i has the length of L, that can represent the whole sample set's inner similarity as accurate as possible. Also, in traditional shallow models of hash learning, the whole dataset can be computed one time as the whole. Since the restriction on computer memory in deep methods, we here use batch normalization to approximate, which means n denotes the size of one data batch in training. In order to learn the similarities between them better, we also introduce a group of attributes vectors V_{att} where $V_{att} = \{att_i\}_{i=1}^{n}$. Under this circumstance, the attributes is a group of conceptually connective vectors between features and ground truth labels defined explicitly.

3.2   Framework

The framework we propose is shown in Fig. 1.

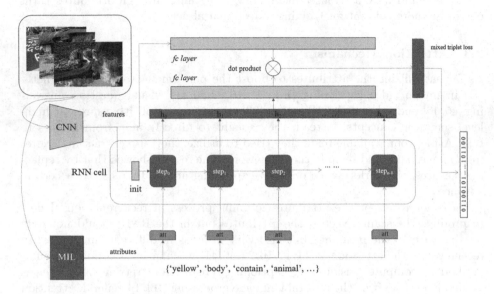

Fig. 1. Overview of the proposed Deep Recurrent Scaling Hashing (DRSH) framework.

This framework can be divided into four parts. The first part uses the convolutional neural nets to extract features and attributes from images in the dataset. Then a refined LSTM is adopted to train the images. The features of the images flowing through RNN cells are used as the initiation. Here the attributes of images are used to form word vector matrices through attention models, which give out the context vectors as the input of the RNN. As the hash code of each image is fixed (the same as RNN steps) and the generation of hash code is bit-wise which means "cell-wise" under the circumstance of recurrent neural nets, one image or images data batch is processed through determined times of RNN cells. Let s be the number of steps a single image/data batch needs to go through. After the RNN finishes the computation of s steps, it generates a series of hidden state $H \in h \times s$ as the raw output of a cell, where h denotes the dimension of hidden state of the LSTM-based RNN. Based on the hidden state series the loss of the framework is computed. At last the hidden state series are processed through a fully connected layer and a sigmoid activation layer, after which they combined with features preprocessed by another fc layer to get the hash codes as the final result. Here the output of the RNN is computed as the "scale" which is discretely put on the output of the fully connected layer computing the features.

In this paper, our novelty is shown in the following aspects. First of all, we try to adjust the deep hashing training phase on a refined version of LSTM. Usually when LSTM or LSTM-based RNN is used in deep hashing, the work aims on video hashing. We also show that training images on LSTM and other variations based on LSTM are also meaningful for the explanation of hash codes. Then soft mechanism is also adopted in the LSTM to give the LSTM option to learn on different "regions" or different "aspect" of on image or images data batch. Such aspect is expected to include certain attributes of the images. Another contribution is on the decorrelation of data between each RNN step. LSTM or other kinds of RNNs are rarely used in deep hashing methods when the dataset is made up of images. If images are trained through raw LSTM and through bit-by-bit generation mechanism, generally it would have poor performance because the original LSTM has the data unit in training all processed at each time step, and moves on to the next one. Since each gate of an LSTM cell processes all the data batch at one time, bit-by-bit generation through different step will not gain meaningful results.

If we expect to utilize the benefit of the LSTM to explain each bit of hash codes and generate them step-by-step and make them useful, we should decor-relate the data at each time step. The traditional way to normalize data, e.g. principal component analysis (PCA), is unavailable on CNN and RNN because the singular value decomposition is required in PCA and eigenvalues of vectors of matrices cannot be derivative. Recent years attempts that aim to simulate the traditional normalization methods appear. Our work gains inspiration from batch normalization and tries to normalize and decorrelate the data flowing between each RNN cell state.

Adjusting Attributes in Recurrent Neural Nets. We would like to adopt the attention mechanism on RNN training which is designed based on LSTM. Before giving out the procession of attention we provide the computation of a traditional LSTM cell. The Long Short Term Memory (LSTM) is a well-designed recurrent neural network. The basic computation process is listed below. Let σ be the sigmoid nonlinearity, the LSTM updates at time step t as h, given inputs at time step t as x_t, previous cell state and hidden state as h_p and c_p, the overall computing procedure are as followed:

$$i_t = \sigma(W_{xi}x_t + W_{hi}h_p + b_i), \qquad (1)$$

$$f_t = \sigma(W_{xf}x_t + W_{hf}h_p + b_f), \qquad (2)$$

$$o_t = \sigma(W_{xo}x_t + W_{ho}h_p + b_o), \qquad (3)$$

$$g_t = tanh(W_{xc}x_t + W_{hc}h_p + b_c), \qquad (4)$$

$$c = f_t \odot c_p + i_t \odot g_t, \qquad (5)$$

$$h = o_t \odot tanh(c_t), \qquad (6)$$

where i_t, f_t, o_t represents the computing procession of input, forget and output state. g_t is the intermediate gates' operation which combines the three states above to compute the gate state. c and h are cell state and hidden state at time step t. All W and b refer to weights and biases specified for the gates to learn.

48   X. Fu et al.

Deep recurrent scaling hashing network utilizes the attention mechanism when preprocessing the input of the RNN. We adopt the **soft attention** mechanism which was first introduced in [26] and frequently used in papers about video and image captioning. This mechanism produces a context vector $\hat{z}_t$ that tell the LSTM the region to aim at during each cell state, which in this case means the "focus" region of an image. The expression of context vector can be written as:

$$\hat{z}_t = \phi(a_i, \alpha_{ti}), \tag{7}$$

where a_i is the ith feature to be captioned. The meaning of α_{ti} is explained below. The goal of captioning is to calculate the list of chances representing all the word in the corpus and choose the one with the biggest odd as the captioned word at time step t, which can be summarized as followed:

$$\log p(y \mid a) = \sum_{t=1}^{T} p(y_i \mid y_1, y_2, ..., y_{i-1}, X), \tag{8}$$

where $\log p(y \mid a)$ denotes the entire caption of one image. Because the captioning process follows the maximum likelihood estimation, the total sum of every log-likelihood of each single captioned word can estimate the entire probability. Under the circumstance of soft attention, given the length of each caption as k (which is also the dimension of the embedding matrix as the raw input of LSTM during captioning), the attention model can be written as:

$$e_{ti} = f_{att}(a_i, h_{t-1}) = V^{\top} \tanh(W_a[a; h_{t-1}]), \tag{9}$$

where e_{ti} represents the attention model, f_{att} denotes the function for computing the model. h_{t-1} is the hidden state of LSTM at time series $t-1$. The computation of α_{ti} can be expressed as:

$$\alpha_{ti} = \frac{\exp(e_i)}{\sum_k \exp(e_{tk})}, \tag{10}$$

where the α_{ti} represents the positive weight in the medium computation process in order to generate the attention weight of the ith feature at time series t. The soft attention adopt the deterministic way of calculating the context vectors, which are computed as:

$$\hat{z}_t = \sum_{i=1}^{L} \alpha_{ti} a_i. \tag{11}$$

As aforementioned, we use word vectors denoted by attributes when computing the attention context vector instead of features. In order to get the attributes in certain regions of one single image, we apply the MIL process on **VGG-16** network, which alter the original computation of $fc8$ layer of VGG-16 with a sigmoid activation layer computing losses through the prediction of bounding boxes. It is there that bounding boxes are divided through bags of words in the training corpus. We utilize a combined-OR version of MIL, which can be expressed as:

$$p(b_i \mid w) = 1 - \prod_{j \in b_i} (1 - p_{ij}^w), \tag{12}$$

where $p(b_i \mid w)$ is the probability of the ith bag of words b_i containing word w, which means one attribute vector here. p_{ij}^w denotes the probability that a given image region j in image i corresponds to word w. Here the term p_{ij}^w is computed through the refined version of VGG-16 mentioned above. The computation of p_{ij}^w is as followed:

$$\frac{1}{1 + \exp\left(-(W^t \varphi(b_{ij}) + B)\right)}, \tag{13}$$

where α represents the fc_7 representation of this particular VGG-16 framework, $\varphi(b_{ij})$ denotes the $fc7$ representation, for image region j in image i, W and B represents the weights of the network associated with word w.

Decorrelation. The original learning phase of LSTM certainly does not consider the possibility of decorrelation between each cell step. In order to adjust LSTM into our learning framework, we need to apply such kind of computation that not only imitate the ways of decorrelation used in classical methods but also would not slow down the computing too much. In this paper, we let the refined LSTM operate deep decorrelation computation through adjusting batch normalization and a specific regularization term in order for decorrelation, meanwhile change the original computation of LSTM operation, as the way of decorrelation. We choose to compute batch normalization on cell state at each step.

Loss Function. We propose a novel loss function, called mixed triplet loss which is designed based on the triplet loss function.

Triplet loss, as a relatively new way to design losses, was proven effective in face recognition, object tracking, image retrieval, and other fields. Its good performance is due to its capability of finding the similarities between potential anchor points and align the similarities in the training procession effectively. The main difference between pairwise and triplet loss is that only pairs of images are compared, whereas the triplet loss encourages a relative distant constraint. Besides, the selection of triplets during training can be tricky. In this paper, we adopt the triplet loss during training with an offline training scheme and semi-hard version of triplet loss computation.

Offline training scheme refers to the randomly choosing strategy of triplets during training. After the anchor point is set, the negative example and the positive example are all randomly selected from the database. Theoretically, triplet mining during training (also named online triplet) will achieve better performance compared with offline training. Such an upgrade can be very useful in comparatively simpler data such as face detection database. However, in this paper, the data we aim to process has multiple labels and enough complexity on a different dimension that the triplet mining after each epoch is not time-efficient and cannot gain much boosting on training results. We show that the triplet loss can reach to convergence at normal speed with proper tuning.

Semi-hard triplet loss is the most popular way to train with triplet loss. Because of the moderate restrictions, it has gained remarkable results on many work [28–30]. The form of this kind of loss is as followed:

$$L_{tri} = Max(0, m - d(I^-, I) + d(I^+, I)), \tag{14}$$

where L_{tri} denotes the triplet loss in the hash code generating phase in our framework, $d(\cdot, \cdot)$ represents the Frobenius norm which computes the distance between anchor points and positive/negative data points and m denotes the margin to restrict the upper bound of the loss term.

The traditional triplet loss, however, meets trouble in our experiment setting. The main reason is that our hash codes not only require the intact learning ability of hash functions but also needs the different bits to discretely learn and learn different parts. Therefore we add a new term after the triplet computation:

$$L_{disc} = \sum_{i=1}^{n} Max(0, m - d(I_i^-, I_i) + d(I_i^+, I_i)), \tag{15}$$

where n is the length of hash codes and m is the margin used to control the bounds of loss. Clearly, it optimizes the discrete learning ability and distinction on every bit of hash code. Then we get the complete form of mixed triplet loss function as:

$$L = L_{tri} + \alpha \times L_{disc}, \tag{16}$$

where α is the super parameter for the discrete triplet loss term.

4   Experiments

4.1   Dataset

We generate the attributes of **COCO** dataset following the method of [12] to train the caffemodel for attribute learning. From [12] we can see that when the training process uses the $top - 10$ attributes of each image and the test process also utilizes the $top - 10$ attributes to compare, the performance is the best compared to other ways of comparison. In order to train the LSTM with attributes in the attention mechanism, we also need to map the attribute vectors to semantic representations. Because of the request of available attributes, the images should have certain complexity and cannot be too low in resolution or the attributes extracted would be too high in deviation. In this case, DRSH cannot be implemented on datasets like **MNIST** and **CIFAR-10** which consist of low-resolution images. We operate our framework using the **NUS-WIDE** and **COCO**[38] dataset.

The NUS-WIDE database contains 269, 648 images collected from Flickr. Of all the images 6 of them occur twice, which makes it a dataset consists of 269642 distinct images. NUS-WIDE is associated with a couple of thousands of ground truth semantic labels, in which each image contains at least one semantic label. We define the true neighbors of a query as the images sharing at least one labels with the query image. We utilize the 21 most frequent labels during the training and testing phase. For each label, 100 images are uniformly sampled for the query set and the remaining images are for the training set. In the whole dataset, there are 89, 527 images that contain at least one label from the 21 most frequent ones. After splitting, the training set has 87, 475 images and the test set contains 2, 052 images.

The COCO dataset is a large-scale object detection, segmentation, and captioning dataset. In this paper we use the 2014 version of the COCO dataset, which contains more than 12k images. We randomly choose ten labels from the total 75, and sample 5000 images for test set. The rest are served as training set.

4.2   Hash Codes Training and Performance

We retrieve the raw images through the urls the dataset provided. The attributes of NUS-WIDE dataset used in training and testing are extracted from the caffemodel which is trained on a refined version of **VGG-16** framework. This framework resembles most of the structure of the VGG-16 network, and alter the last layer of the CNN with a fully-connected layer and a sigmoid activation layer to get attributes from already labeled bounding boxes of images in the dataset. We choose to train the model trained by caffe with the $top10$ most likely attributes of the COCO dataset, and proceed to extract $top10$ attributes from our training datasets, which means that during the LSTM training step the dimension of attention weight α_{ti} is $b \times 10$, where b represents the size of each data batch. Results show that when training after 500, 000 to 600, 000 epochs the attributes generated have the highest mAP, which is the same as precision. In our experiments, we set the input and hidden size of LSTM with 512. The dimension of the context vector is set to 10 as aforementioned. We set the batch size as 10 during training and the super parameter α in the mixed triplet loss as 0.1. We use the **Adam** [37] optimizer to train the framework. In this paper, we utilize **GloVe** [27] vectors to record each image's attributes in order to be computed in the attention model. The attributes matrix used as the input of the attention model is 10×300, where 300 is the length of each GloVe vector. In the experiment, we provide a different kind of preprocessor to initiate the LSTM and the hash code generation training phase. As the attributes of data decide the preference of "focused" attributes of each hash bit generated, the features of images are considered as a base initialization step. Therefore the features are set as the initial cell state and hidden state of the RNN, which went through a single-layered fully connected layer before initialization.

We choose locality sensitive hashing (LSH) [33], ITQ with canonical correlation analysis [4], supervised discrete hashing (SDH) [8], CNNH [9] and Hash-Net [25] as baseline. All methods in the baseline followed the default settings in their papers. Also, we provide the hash codes generated merely through CNN features computed by one fc layer in comparison. All methods compute the features of images extracted from VGG-16 network. The DRSH results from each bit are generated from models saved from 16,000 images to 4 epochs. To evaluate DRSH, we report two mainstream evaluation metrics to measure the performance of the generated hash codes within Hamming radius 2: mean average precision ($mAP@H \leq 2$) and precision score ($Pre@H \leq 2$). The results are shown in Table 1.

Table 1. mAP and precision performances on our method and the benchmark on NUS-WIDE

Precision/mAP	16 bit	32 bit	64 bit	96 bit	128 bit
LSH [33]	0.1940/0.1940	0.1939/0.1924	0.1939/0.1940	0.1938/0.1938	0.1935/0.1947
CCA-ITQ [4]	**0.5282/0.3854**	0.4214/**0.3974**	0.2102/0.3936	0.1395/0.4304	0.1005/0.4438
SDH [8]	0.4069/0.3268	0.4659/0.3590	0.4258/0.3760	0.3199/0.3851	0.1854/0.3855
CNNH [9]	0.4277/0.3046	0.4413/0.3844	0.4158/0.3981	0.4213/0.4117	0.3428/0.4121
HashNet [25]	0.3848/0.3628	0.4150/0.3678	0.4204/0.3745	**0.4254**/0.3801	**0.4190**/0.3962
raw feature	0.2800/0.2527	0.2914/0.2601	0.2312/0.2653	0.2298/0.2661	0.2216/0.2772
DRSH	0.4058/0.3571	**0.4688**/0.3627	**0.4269/0.3955**	0.2201/**0.4789**	0.1476/**0.4991**

Table 2. mAP and precision performances on our method and the benchmark on COCO

Precision/mAP	16 bit	32 bit	64 bit	96 bit	128 bit
LSH [33]	0.1618/0.1619	0.1720/0.1707	0.1684/0.1655	0.1816/0.1848	0.1595/0.1522
CCA-ITQ [4]	**0.3974**/0.3138	0.3254/0.3317	0.1985/0.3461	0.0929/0.3612	0.0705/0.3653
SDH [8]	0.3015/0.3192	0.3858/0.3311	0.3781/0.3726	0.3523/0.4004	0.3214/0.4183
CNNH [9]	0.3892/0.2943	0.4147/0.3422	**0.4367**/0.3628	0.3857/0.3939	0.3316/0.3974
HashNet [25]	0.3317/0.3005	0.3891/0.3231	0.3975/0.3531	**0.3994**/0.3711	**0.3501**/0.3848
raw feature	0.2648/0.2476	0.2703/0.2520	0.2701/0.2618	0.2469/0.2634	0.2014/0.2687
DRSH	0.3627/**0.3364**	**0.4251/0.3485**	0.4269/**0.3757**	0.2812/**0.4081**	0.1996/**0.4163**

We can see from the results that our method, though not peaking on precision, leads most of the mAP performances on different hash code lengths (Table 2). CCA-ITQ is well-performed in lower hash code length but experienced a rapid decline at precision on higher code lengths. Also, in the ablation study, performances of the hash codes generated from raw feature going through a single fc layer are very low consecutively, which means the RNN training on attributes is more than effective.

4.3 The Visualization of Hash Codes

The performance of DRSH shows that it is indeed a valid method to train images in deep hashing. However, proving whether or not the generated hash codes can actually be explained bit-by-bit is also a crucial facet of our work.

In order to prove the availability of explainable in hash codes, we randomly choose a few attributes from the attributes corpus and find the relevant images in the test set from the NUS-WIDE dataset. Those attributes are common in the test set images but not excessive, which in this case we select those attributes that appear more than 300 times but less than 500 times. After filtering there are 14 attributes that satisfy the condition, from which we select 10 attributes[1]. After that, we exclude those which have more than 1 attributes of the 10 in the whole test set. There are 548 images afterward. Then we use each attribute as the single label for those images and visualize their hash codes' distances through t-SNE [34]. The results are shown in Fig. 2.

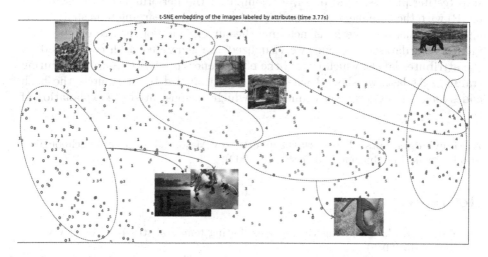

Fig. 2. Overview of the t-SNE visualization with ten attributes as labels on test sets.

The visualization demonstrates that there exists a strong deviation between certain attributes, and each attribute's data point gathers in one or multiple places. For example, the attribute *body* and *picture* are mostly distinct from other attributes. It should be noticed that each attribute usually does not "gather" in one place, which is caused by the level of abstraction of attributes. For instance, although *picture* are one kind of attribute (which is used as the label in the visualization), the images that consist of pictures do not resemble the same description. The highly abstract attributes aim to gather together, though not in one position. Also, some attributes may appear in one gather, which is because of the dataset's inner connection. For example, *building* and *black* are gathered in each cluster, which is caused by usually black buildings shown in the NUS-WIDE dataset. Such concentration also reflects on the images. Although we excluded the images with more than two attributes that are listed on the $top-10$ attribute

---

[1] The attributes (labeled as 0 to 9) are *body, view, background, sky, picture, grass, tree, building, black* and *front.*

labels before, for some images that have more than 10 ground truth attributes they tend to appear in the gatherings. The image retrieved on the top-right corner, for instance, has attributes *grass*, *tree* and *black*.

5   Conclusion

In this paper, we provided a novel framework, called deep recurrent scaling hashing, to train hash codes for image retrieval through a novel recurrent neural network derived from LSTM. In order to show that our method exploited the inputs and generate hash codes with explanations on each bit, we set up a three-step testing process. First of all, we compared the performance (precision and mAP) with the baseline, which consisted of some classic learning to hash methods and some other deep methods including the current state-of-the-art, on currently mainstream datasets. Second, we visualized the generated hash code based on the attributes labels, which proved the effectiveness of attribute learning during training. At last, we showed when images are labeled by attributes, the hash codes have an obvious inner connection, which demonstrated the explanation of them.

Acknowledgements. This work is supported by Major Scientific and Technological Special Project of Guizhou Province (20183002).

References

1. Yao, L., et al.: Describing videos by exploiting temporal structure. In: ICCV, pp. 4507–4515 (2015)
2. Bergstra, J., et al.: Theano: a CPU and GPU math compiler in Python. In: Proceedings of 9th Python in Science Conference, vol. 1, pp. 3–10, June 2010
3. Zhang, H., Wang, M., Hong, R., Chua, T.S.: Play and rewind: optimizing binary representations of videos by self-supervised temporal hashing. In: ACM Multimedia, pp. 781–790, October 2016
4. Gong, Y., Lazebnik, S., Gordo, A., Perronnin, F.: Iterative quantization: a procrustean approach to learning binary codes for large-scale image retrieval. TPAMI **35**(12), 2916–2929 (2013)
5. Liu, W., Wang, J., Ji, R., Jiang, Y.G., Chang, S.F.: Supervised hashing with kernels. In: CVPR, pp. 2074–2081, June 2012
6. Fang, H., et al.: From captions to visual concepts and back. In: CVPR, pp. 1473–1482 (2015)
7. Song, J., Zhang, H., Li, X., Gao, L., Wang, M., Hong, R.: Self-supervised video hashing with hierarchical binary auto-encoder. TIP **27**(7), 3210–3221 (2018)
8. Shen, F., Shen, C., Liu, W., Tao Shen, H.: Supervised discrete hashing. In: CVPR, pp. 37–45 (2015)
9. Xia, R., Pan, Y., Lai, H., Liu, C., Yan, S.: Supervised hashing for image retrieval via image representation learning. In: AAAI, June 2014
10. Weiss, Y., Torralba, A., Fergus, R.: Spectral hashing. In: NIPS, pp. 1753–1760 (2009)

11. Xu, K., et al.: Show, attend and tell: neural image caption generation with visual attention. In: ICML, pp. 2048–2057, June 2015
12. Bin, Y., Yang, Y., Zhou, J., Huang, Z., Shen, H.T.: Adaptively attending to visual attributes and linguistic knowledge for captioning. In: ACM Multimedia, pp. 1345–1353, October 2017
13. Jia, Y.: Caffe: convolutional architecture for fast feature embedding. In: ACM Multimedia, pp. 675–678, November 2014
14. Simonyan, K., Zisserman, A.: Very deep convolutional networks for large-scale image recognition. In: ICLR (2015)
15. Ioffe, S., Szegedy, C.: Batch normalization: accelerating deep network training by reducing internal covariate shift. In: ICLR (2015)
16. Tang, Y., Srivastava, N., Salakhutdinov, R.R.: Learning generative models with visual attention. In: NIPS, pp. 1808–1816 (2014)
17. Zhu, H., Long, M., Wang, J., Cao, Y.: Deep hashing network for efficient similarity retrieval. In: AAAI, March 2016
18. Chua, T.S., Tang, J., Hong, R., Li, H., Luo, Z., Zheng, Y.: NUS-WIDE: a real-world web image database from National University of Singapore. In: ACM CIVR, p. 48, July 2009
19. Gionis, A., Indyk, P., Motwani, R.: Similarity search in high dimensions via hashing. In: VLDB, vol. 99, no. 6, pp. 518–529, September 1999
20. He, K., Zhang, X., Ren, S., Sun, J.: Deep residual learning for image recognition. In: CVPR, pp. 770–778 (2016)
21. Krizhevsky, A., Sutskever, I., Hinton, G.E.: Imagenet classification with deep convolutional neural networks. In: NIPS, pp. 1097–1105 (2012)
22. Yao, T., Pan, Y., Li, Y., Qiu, Z., Mei, T.: Boosting image captioning with attributes. In: ICCV, pp. 4894–4902 (2017)
23. Wu, Q., Shen, C., Wang, P., Dick, A., van den Hengel, A.: Image captioning and visual question answering based on attributes and external knowledge. TPAMI 40(6), 1367–1381 (2018)
24. Liu, H., Wang, R., Shan, S., Chen, X.: Deep supervised hashing for fast image retrieval. In: CVPR, pp. 2064–2072 (2016)
25. Cao, Z., Long, M., Wang, J., Yu, P.S.: Hashnet: deep learning to hash by continuation. In: ICCV, pp. 5608–5617 (2017)
26. Bahdanau, D., Cho, K., Bengio, Y.: Neural machine translation by jointly learning to align and translate. In: ICLR (2014)
27. Pennington, J., Socher, R., Manning, C.: Glove: global vectors for word representation. In: EMNLP, pp. 1532–1543 (2014)
28. Schroff, F., Kalenichenko, D., Philbin, J.: Facenet: a unified embedding for face recognition and clustering. In: CVPR, pp. 815–823 (2015)
29. Cheng, D., Gong, Y., Zhou, S., Wang, J., Zheng, N.: Person re-identification by multi-channel parts-based CNN with improved triplet loss function. In: CVPR, pp. 1335–1344 (2016)
30. Dong, X., Shen, J.: Triplet loss in siamese network for object tracking. In: Ferrari, V., Hebert, M., Sminchisescu, C., Weiss, Y. (eds.) ECCV 2018. LNCS, vol. 11217, pp. 472–488. Springer, Cham (2018). https://doi.org/10.1007/978-3-030-01261-8_28
31. Zhu, X., Zhou, W., Li, H.: Improving deep neural network sparsity through decorrelation regularization. In: IJCAI, pp. 3264–3270 July (2018)

32. Dang, Z., Yi, K.M., Hu, Y., Wang, F., Fua, P., Salzmann, M.: Eigendecomposition-free training of deep networks with zero eigenvalue-based losses. In: Ferrari, V., Hebert, M., Sminchisescu, C., Weiss, Y. (eds.) ECCV 2018. LNCS, vol. 11209, pp. 792–807. Springer, Cham (2018). https://doi.org/10.1007/978-3-030-01228-1_47

33. Indyk, P., Motwani, R., Raghavan, P., Vempala, S.: Locality-preserving hashing in multidimensional spaces. In: STOC, vol. 97, pp. 618–625, May 1997

34. Maaten, L.V.D., Hinton, G.: Visualizing data using t-SNE. JMLR 9(Nov), 2579–2605 (2008)

35. Li, C., et al.: SCRATCH: a scalable discrete matrix factorization hashing for cross-modal retrieval. In: ACM Multimedia (2018)

36. Luo, X., Zhang, P., Huang, Z., Nie, L., Xu, X.: Discrete hashing with multiple supervision. In: TIP, vol. 28, no. 6, pp. 2962–2975, June 2019

37. Kingma, D.P., Ba, J.: Adam: a method for stochastic optimization. In: ICLR (2015)

38. Lin, T., et al.: Microsoft COCO: common objects in context. In: Fleet, D., Pajdla, T., Schiele, B., Tuytelaars, T. (eds.) ECCV 2014. LNCS, vol. 8693, pp. 740–755. Springer, Cham (2014). https://doi.org/10.1007/978-3-319-10602-1_48

39. Hu, M., Yang, Y., Shen, F., Xie, N., Hong, R., Shen, H.T.: Collective reconstructive embeddings for cross-modal hashing. TIP (2019)

40. Yang, Y., et al.: Video captioning with adversarial LSTM. TIP **27**, 5600–5611 (2018)

41. Bin, Y., Yang, Y., Shen, F., Xie, N., Shen, HT., Li, X.: Describing video with attention based bidirectional LSTM. TCYB (2018)

42. Yang, Y., Shen, F., Huang, Z., Shen, HT., Li, X.: Discrete nonnegative spectral clustering. TKDE **29**, 1834–1845 (2017)

43. Yang, Y., Duan, Y., Wang, X., Huang, Z., Xie, N., Shen, H.T.: Hierarchical multi-clue modelling for POI popularity prediction with heterogeneous tourist information. TKDE **31**, 757–768 (2018)

44. Luo, Y., Yang, Y., Shen, F., Huang, Z., Zhou, P., Shen, H.T.: Robust discrete code modeling for supervised hashing. In: PR (2018)

45. Peng, L., et al.: Word-to-region attention network for visual question answering. Multimedia Tools Appl. **78**, 3843–3858 (2018)

46. Zhang, Y., Hare, J., Prügel-Bennett, A.: Learning to count objects in natural images for visual question answering. In: ICLR (2018)

TRPN: Matrix Factorization Meets Recurrent Neural Network for Temporal Rating Prediction

Haozhe Zhu, Yanyan Shen[✉], and Xian Zhou

Department of Computer Science and Engineering, Shanghai Jiao Tong University, Shanghai, China
{zhuhaozhe,shenyy,zhouxian}@sjtu.edu.cn

Abstract. Traditional matrix factorization techniques for recommendation have a basic assumption that user interests will not change over time, which is not consistent with the reality. To this end, temporal user-item interaction sequences are important to capture users' dynamic interests towards more accurate and timely recommendation. Previous works used to capture dynamic interests based on the basic recurrent neural networks. However, they do not distinguish the static interests which reflect user's long-term preferences from temporal interests caused by occasional incidents. They also treat all the user's past temporal interests equally when performing future rating prediction. In this paper, we leverage Probabilistic Matrix Factorization (PMF) to learn both static and temporal interests for users, and design a new filtering layer to adaptively feed the static and temporal user information to RNN at different time step. We also apply item-dependent attention mechanism to discriminate the importance of different temporal interactions. We conduct extensive experiments to evaluate the performance of our proposed temporal rating prediction method named TRPN. The results show that TRPN can achieve higher performance than several state-of-the-art methods.

Keywords: Temporal recommendation · PMF · Recurrent neural network

1 Introduction

In nowadays e-commerce businesses, recommendation plays an important role in exploring personalized user preferences towards numerous items. The core technique used in modern recommender systems is Collaborative Filtering (CF) [19]. Among various CF approaches, Matrix Factorization (MF) based methods [13] are widely adopted due to its superior performance in predicting users' ratings over items. The key idea of MF is to represent users and items with k-dimensional latent feature vectors, which are also referred to as *embeddings*. Given a user embedding and an item embedding, the corresponding rating is computed via the simple inner product operation. To date, most of the existing MF based

© Springer Nature Switzerland AG 2019
J. Shao et al. (Eds.): APWeb-WAIM 2019, LNCS 11642, pp. 57–72, 2019.
https://doi.org/10.1007/978-3-030-26075-0_5

methods [6,7] focus on learning more informative user and item latent features or modeling non-linear feature interactions using neural networks towards higher rating prediction accuracy.

However, in many real-world recommender systems, users are very likely to experience interest drifting. To be more specific, personalized user preferences over items often change with time. For instance, a user who is addicted to action movies may take a liking to love movies during the period of a romantic relationship. Intuitively, capturing such preference dynamics would be beneficial and significant to timely recommendation. However, most of the MF-based recommendation methods are good at capturing user *static* features, but they fail to take the *temporal* effects into account, not even to mention the explicit modeling of user preference dynamics for rating prediction.

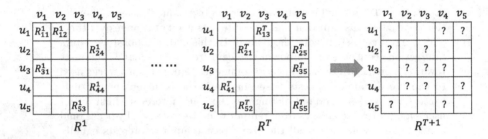

Fig. 1. An example of temporal rating prediction, where we observed some ratings from time $t = 1$ to T, and aim to predict unobserved ratings at time $T + 1$.

In this paper, we aim to study the problem of *temporal rating prediction*, as depicted in Fig. 1. Each historical user-item rating is associated with a timestamp, and by organizing ratings according to the timestamps, we are able to obtain a sequence of rating matrices $R^1, \cdots, R^T$ from time $t = 1$ to T. The goal of this work is to predict the unobserved ratings at time $T + 1$. Some efforts have been devoted to addressing this temporal prediction problem, such as dynamic matrix factorization methods [13,15]. A particular time decay function is introduced to control the effects of historical ratings on the predictions for the next time period. The key limitation of these methods is the difficulty to choose a decay function that has sufficient generalization ability to deal with diverse user preference dynamics. Recent works [9,24] adopted the Recurrent Neural Networks (RNN) to capture the sequential information of temporal user interests. Specifically, they allow each user to have multiple time-dependent embeddings and feed these embeddings to RNN for modeling user preference tendency. However, an important observation is that a user's rating for an item during $T + 1$ is dependent on both his/her static and temporal interests, where the static interests reflect user's intrinsic personality and the temporal ones are typically caused by occasional incidents. None of these RNN-based methods distinguish the two kinds of user interests. Moreover, they treat all the temporal user interests equally for future rating prediction, which may not hold in practice.

To address the above limitations, we develop a novel neural approach for temporal rating prediction (named TRPN) by taking both static and temporal user interests tendency into account. Our contributions can be summarized as follows.

- First, we leverage the Probabilistic Matrix Factorization (PMF) method [18] to learn both static and temporal user interests. The temporal interests are reflected by the ratings made within a short time period (e.g., one week) which can be very sparse. PMF provides a probabilistic view of the observed ratings and is effective to learn user and item embeddings with sparse ratings.
- Second, we model the user interests tendency using RNN, where a new filtering layer is developed to adaptively feed the static and temporal user information to RNN at each time step. We also adopt the attention mechanism [1] to discriminate the importance of different temporal user information for future rating prediction.
- Third, to deliver the final user-item rating at time $T + 1$, we pre-compute two kinds of ratings: one is based on the static user embedding produced by PMF, and the other is based on the user interests tendency learned by the attentive RNN. We introduce a fusion layer to combine two ratings effectively and produce the final rating.
- Finally, we validate our proposed approach on Netflix and MovieLens dataset. The extensive experimental results demonstrate that (1) our approach achieves better performance by taking *temporal* effects into account; (2) our approach outperforms other RNN-based methods by modeling both static and temporal user interests explicitly; (3) the attention mechanism effectively highlights the most important temporal interests.

2   Related Work

Matrix Factorization (MF) for Recommendation. MF and its variants have been studied in many influential works for a long time [4,6,7,14,18,26]. Standard MF first decomposes the observed user-item interaction matrix R into the product of two matrices U and V of lower dimensions. These two matrices represent users and items in a lower dimensional latent space. Then they recover the unobserved values in R by the inner product between corresponding latent vectors in U and V [14]. To address the imbalance problem in dataset, Probabilistic Matrix Factorization [18] scaled linearly with the number of observations by presenting probabilistic algorithms. He et al. [7] weighted the unobserved values based on item popularity to learn MF models from implicit feedback. Neural Collaborative Filtering [6] proposed a Neural Network based MF which learns both linear and non-linear relations from user-item interactions. MF-based methods can also incorporate with additional item information.

Dynamic Modeling in Recommendation. The traditional MF approaches assumed that users' interests almost do not change, which is inconsistent with real scenarios. Koren et al. [13] proposed a temporal extension for MF called

TimeSVD++ to model the temporal bias, but the features are handcrafted and computationally expensive. Incremental MF based approaches [11] dynamically refined the MF models when new interactions come in an online scenario. Gao et al. [5] and Lu et al. [16] manually set time windows. They learned different user/item embeddings in different time windows and added linear constraints between previous embeddings and future embeddings, however, linear combination is not capable of presenting the dependency between previous embeddings and the new ones. TCAM [25] incorporated topic model in recommendation system and considered both user intrinsic interests an temporal contexts in dynamic user modeling. Wang et al. [23] and Wang et al. [21] focused on an online recommendation scenario which requires high-velocity update. TPM [22] introduced topic regions representing both semantic topics and geographical regions in a unified way, thus reducing the prediction space significantly.

Recurrent Neural Network Based Recommendation Models. Recently, many researchers are interested in modeling user temporal interests by recurrent neural network [3,9,20,24]. Hidasi et al. [9] first used Gated Recurrent Unit (GRU) [2] in session-based recommendation. Wu et al. [24] used two Long Short-term Memory Network (LSTM) [10] to model both user and item temporal information respectively, and aimed to predict a rating in future time with these temporal information captured by LSTM. Song et al. [20] fed date in different time granularity into different LSTM to extract both long-term and short-term features. Different from their work, we leverage the PMF model to learn both static and temporal user interests, and model temporal tendency by adaptively feeding the static and temporal user interests to RNN at each time step.

3   Preliminaries

3.1   Definitions and Problem

Let $\mathcal{U} = \{u_1, \cdots, u_M\}$ and $\mathcal{V} = \{v_1, \cdots, v_N\}$ be the sets of users and items, respectively. We consider a set of historical user-item ratings $\{(u, v, s, t)\}$, where each rating represents user $u \in \mathcal{U}$ rated item $v \in \mathcal{V}$ with a score $s \in \mathcal{S}$ at time t. Conceptually, we organize all the observed ratings during time t into an $M \times N$ *temporal rating matrix* R^t.

$$R_{ij}^t = \begin{cases} s, & \text{if } u_i \text{ rated } v_j \text{ with score } s \text{ during time } t \\ 0, & \text{if } u_i \text{ has not yet rated } v_j \end{cases} \tag{1}$$

Without loss of generality, we assume each user rates each item at most once. Hence, the matrices during different time periods do not contain overlapping ratings. In this paper, we consider a sequence of historical rating matrices $R^1, \cdots, R^T$ from time $t = 1$ to $t = T$. Our goal is to predict all the ratings in matrix R^{T+1} during time $t = T + 1$, where the ratings in R^{T+1} are not observed before $T + 1$. We then formally define the temporal rating prediction problem.

Definition 1 (Temporal Rating Prediction). *Given a sequence of rating matrices $R^1, \cdots, R^T$ from time $t = 1$ to $t = T$, we aim to predict the ratings during time $t = T + 1$, i.e., the entries in R^{T+1}.*

In what follows, we describe the probabilistic matrix factorization and recurrent neural network, which are the basic components of our proposed solution.

3.2   Probabilistic Matrix Factorization

Among various CF methods, Matrix Factorization (MF) is undoubtedly one of the most popular methods for recommendation. The key idea of MF is to learn latent representations for both users and items by factorizing an observed rating matrix $R_{M \times N}$ into a user matrix $U_{M \times k}$ and an item matrix $V_{N \times k}$. This is achieved by minimizing the sum squared distance from UV^T to the target matrix R. Let $\mathbf{u}_i$ and $\mathbf{v}_j$ denote the k-dimensional user and item latent vectors in the factorized matrices U and V, respectively. The rating of user u_i over item v_j is then estimated by the inner product of the corresponding latent vectors, i.e., $\mathbf{u}_i^T \mathbf{v}_j$. MF essentially models user-item preferences by combining item factor vectors using user-specific coefficients. This simple linear model suffers from the data sparsity problem in recommendation. That is, the prediction accuracy for users with few ratings is far from satisfactory. To address the problem, the Probabilistic Matrix Factorization (PMF) model [18] incorporates a Gaussian noise when computing user-item ratings. The key idea of PMF is to treat rating prediction as a generative process and define a conditional probability over the observed ratings as follows:

$$p(R|U, V, \sigma^2) = \prod_{i=1}^{M} \prod_{j=1}^{N} [\mathcal{N}(R_{ij} \mid \mathbf{u}_i^T \mathbf{v}_j, \sigma^2)]^{I_{ij}} \tag{2}$$

where $\mathcal{N}(x \mid \mu, \sigma^2)$ is the probability density function of the Gaussian distribution with mean μ and variance σ^2, and I is a binary indicator matrix where the entry I_{ij} equals to 1 if u_i rated v_j and equals to 0 otherwise. PMF also placed zero-mean spherical Gaussian priors on user/item latent vectors:

$$p(U|\sigma_U^2) = \prod_{i=1}^{M} \mathcal{N}(\mathbf{u}_i|0, \sigma_U^2 \mathbf{I}) \qquad p(V|\sigma_V^2) = \prod_{i=1}^{N} \mathcal{N}(\mathbf{v}_j|0, \sigma_V^2 \mathbf{I}) \tag{3}$$

Note that each rating is mapped into the range of $[0, 1]$ via normalization. The goal of PMF is to maximize the log likelihood of the observed ratings based on Eq. (2), which is equivalent to minimizing the sum of squared errors with quadratic regularization norms as follows:

$$E = \frac{1}{2} \sum_{i=1}^{M} \sum_{j=1}^{N} (R_{i,j} - \mathbf{u}_i^T \mathbf{v}_j)^2 I_{ij} + \frac{\lambda_U}{2} \sum_{i=1}^{M} ||\mathbf{u}_i||^2 + \frac{\lambda_V}{2} \sum_{i=1}^{N} ||\mathbf{v}_j||^2 \tag{4}$$

where $|| \bullet ||^2$ denotes L2 norm, $\lambda_U = \sigma^2/\sigma_U^2$, $\lambda_V = \sigma^2/\sigma_V^2$ are hyper-parameters determined by the distribution of dataset to prevent overfitting. For instance, in Netflix dataset, ratings per user are less than ratings per movie, so λ_U should be set a bigger value than λ_V. The above objective function is further optimized by performing gradient descent in U and V, which is efficient with a large number of users and items. While more advanced MF variants [6] adopt neural methods to learn non-linear deep interactions among user and item latent vectors, the training time of PMF is more efficient and scalable to the number of observed ratings.

3.3 Long Short-Term Memory

Long Short-Term Memory (LSTM) is a famous variant of recurrent neural network. It exploits the gating mechanism to capture temporal dependencies in time series effectively, and is capable of solving the gradient vanishing problem in long sequences [10]. The regular LSTM consists of memory cells with self-connections. Each memory cell has a cell state c and a hidden state h that are updated in a recurrent manner. There are three gates associated with each memory cell: input, forget and output gates, which control the information flow of the sequence. Formally, given an input sequence $\{x_1, \cdots, x_T\}$, LSTM maps the input to an output sequence via the following equations:

$$
\begin{aligned}
f_t &= \sigma(W_f[h_{t-1}, x_t] + b_f) \\
i_t &= \sigma(W_i[h_{t-1}, x_t] + b_i) \\
\widetilde{c}_t &= tanh(W_c[h_{t-1}, x_t] + b_c) \\
c_t &= f_t * c_{t-1} + i_t * \widetilde{c}_t \\
o_t &= \sigma(W_o[h_{t-1}, x_t] + b_o) \\
h_t &= o_t * tanh(c_t)
\end{aligned}
\tag{5}
$$

where i, f, o, c are the activation vectors for input gate, forget gate, output gate and cell state, respectively. W terms are weight matrices, b term are bias vectors, $*$ denotes the Hadamard product and σ represents the sigmoid function.

In this paper, we leverage LSTM to capture the sequential information of temporal user interests, while more advanced recurrent neural networks can be incorporated into our solution seamlessly. Without otherwise specified, we use $h_t = LSTM(x_t, h_{t-1})$ to represent the update operations (i.e., Eq. (5)) performed during time step t.

4 Overview

Figure 2 provides an overview of our solution to the temporal rating prediction task, which consists of two major stages: offline learning and online inference. We describe each stage as follows.

– **Offline Learning.** We first combine all the ratings observed from $t = 1$ to $t = T$ into a matrix R^*. We dub R^* as the *global rating matrix*. Apparently, R^* is much denser than individual temporal rating matrix and incorporates user latent features from a more systematic view. A novel attempt of this paper is to consider both temporal user interests and their global representations for temporal rating prediction. The rationale behind is that a user's preference

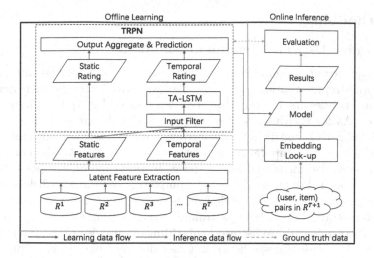

Fig. 2. Temporal rating prediction framework

for an item can be determined by her temporal interests or time-invariant global interests.

Our proposed prediction model applies PMF to learn temporal and global user representations from temporal and global rating matrices, respectively. We assume item representations are time-invariant, which will not evolve over time. We feed user and item latent vectors into LSTM based neural network for learning sequential information at time scale. We further incorporate the attention mechanism to discriminate the importance of global and temporal user interests for rating prediction at $t = T + 1$. In our design, we obtain two ratings for R_{ij}^{T+1}: one is derived by considering the most relevant temporal user interest in the previous time periods, and the other is determined by user's global interest. The two rating scores will be subtly fused to derive the final prediction result.

All the model parameters are learned during this stage. And it is important to notice that the user and item representations are pre-trained based on Eq. (4), where the objective function is dependent on the observed ratings from $t = 1$ to $t = T$. The parameters in the proposed neural network are learned via error backpropagation, where the error function is determined by the ratings during time $T + 1$ in the training set.

– **Online Inference.** In this stage, we try to predict the ratings in matrix R^{T+1}. Consider a user u_i and an item v_j where u_i has not rated v_j before time $T + 1$. We retrieve the learned user and item latent vectors accordingly and feed them into the recurrent neural network model. The output of the model is the predicted rating R_{ij}^{T+1}. Note that, if we want to predict rating R_{ij}^{T+2}, we only need to apply PMF to learn temporal user representations during $T + 1$ and feed them into the recurrent neural network model. The other parameters in our proposed model do not need to be retrained.

5   Methodology

5.1   Learning User and Item Representations

Given a sequence of temporal rating matrices $R^1, \cdots, R^T$, we first aim to learn user and item representations (i.e., *embeddings*) using PMF. As each item representation encodes its inherent features, we denote by $\mathbf{v}_j$ the latent vector for item v_j. As for each user u_i, we compute a global representation $\mathbf{u}_i$ based on the global rating matrix R^*, and further learn time-dependent embeddings $\mathbf{u}_i^1, \cdots, \mathbf{u}_i^T$ based on temporal rating matrices $R^1, \cdots, R^T$. All the embeddings are in the same k-dimensional latent space. Inspired by [8], temporal changes should be smooth. Learning $\mathbf{u}_i^1, \cdots, \mathbf{u}_i^T$ completely separated will lead to dramatic changes and inaccurate result because $R^1, \cdots, R^T$ are extremely sparse. To address this situation, we sample training samples from $t = 1$ to T chronologically. When training $\mathbf{u}_i^t$, we use user embeddings in previous time interval $\mathbf{u}_i^{t-1}$ to initialize. In this learning schema, if a user does not have interaction in time interval t, his embedding $\mathbf{u}_i^t$ will equal to $\mathbf{u}_i^{t-1}$. Only when user has interactions in time interval t, we will further update his embedding in that time interval. Intuitively, $\mathbf{u}_i$ captures the user's static interests, while $\mathbf{u}_i^t$ encodes temporal interests during time t. For instance, a user generally likes action movies but may want to watch comedy movies during festivals.

To learn $\{\mathbf{u}_i\}, \{\mathbf{u}_i^t\}, \{\mathbf{v}_j\}$, we follow the idea of the original PMF and try to optimize the following objective function:

$$
\min_{\{\mathbf{u}_i\},\{\mathbf{v}_j\},\{\mathbf{u}_i^t\}} \sum_{i=1}^{M} \sum_{j=1}^{N} (R_{i,j}^* - \mathbf{u}_i^\top \mathbf{v}_j)^2 I_{ij}
$$

$$
+ \sum_{t=1}^{T} \sum_{i=1}^{M} \sum_{j=1}^{N} (R_{i,j}^t - \mathbf{u}_i^{t\top} \mathbf{v}_j)^2 I_{ij}^t \tag{6}
$$

$$
+ \lambda_U \sum_{i=1}^{M} ||\mathbf{u}_i||^2 + \lambda_V \sum_{j=1}^{N} ||\mathbf{v}_j||^2 + \sum_{t=1}^{T} (\lambda_U^t \sum_{i=1}^{M} ||\mathbf{u}_i^t||^2)
$$

where λ_U and λ_V are set according to the distribution of R^*, $\lambda_U^1, \cdots, \lambda_U^T$ are set according to the distribution of $R^1 \cdots, R^T$. All the temporal and time-invariant embeddings are pre-trained using gradient descent algorithm [17], and will not be updated during the training of the neural network model. Algorithm 1 provides the pseudo-code of our PMF-based representation learning algorithm, which is self-explained. Note that the training process for temporal embeddings $\{\mathbf{u}_i^t\}$ can be viewed as fine tuning the time-invariant embeddings $\{\mathbf{u}_i\}$ by feeding the samples at the t-th time interval.

5.2   Temporal Rating Prediction Network (TRPN)

We now present our neural network model named TRPN for temporal rating prediction based on the learned user and item representations. Specifically, the target of our model is to predict the rating for (u_i, v_j) at time $T + 1$. Figure 3 depicts the detailed model structure.

Algorithm 1. Representation Learning Algorithm

Input: rating matrix before time T $\{R^1 \cdots, R^T\}$
Output: time-invariant embeddings $\{\mathbf{u}_i\}, \{\mathbf{v}_j\}$ and temporal embeddings $\{\mathbf{u}_i^t\}$
1: **for** *epoch* $\in (1, \#$ epochs) **do**
2:   **for** $t \in (1, T)$ **do**
3:     **sample** historical user-item ratings (u, v, s, t) from R^t
4:     **update** time-invariant embeddings $\{\mathbf{u}_i\}, \{\mathbf{v}_j\}$ and temporal embeddings **at current time** $\{\mathbf{u}_i^t\}$ by Equation (6)
5:     $t = t + 1$
6:   **end for**
7: **end for**
8: **return** $\{\mathbf{u}_i\}, \{\mathbf{u}_i^t\}, \{\mathbf{v}_j\}$

Input and Filtering Layer. The core of our model is an LSTM, aiming at capturing temporal dependencies of user interest dynamics. The input at time step t is the concatenation of $\mathbf{u}_i$ and $\mathbf{u}_i^t$, denoted by $\mathbf{u}_i \oplus \mathbf{u}_i^t$. Instead of supplying $\mathbf{u}_i \oplus \mathbf{u}_i^t$ directly to the LSTM, we propose a *filtering layer* to dynamically determine the relative importance of static features against the temporal ones. This is important because temporal user embeddings are derived from sparse temporal rating matrices and can be insufficient to model user interests during a particular time period. The filtering step thus treats each temporal user embedding $\mathbf{u}_i^t$ as a counterpart of the global embedding $\mathbf{u}_i$, by means of learning a weight for each latent dimension in $\mathbf{u}_i^t$. Specifically, we introduce a k-dimensional *filtering vector* $\boldsymbol{\xi}$ which is detached from three factors: $\mathbf{u}_i$, $\mathbf{u}_i^t$ and $\mathbf{v}_j$ via the following function:

$$\boldsymbol{\xi} = \sigma(W_{3k,k}[\mathbf{u}_i \oplus \mathbf{u}_i^t \oplus \mathbf{v}_j]) \tag{7}$$

where σ denotes the *sigmoid* function to limit the values in $\boldsymbol{\xi}$ to $(0, 1)$; k is the dimension of latent space; $[\mathbf{u}_i \oplus \mathbf{u}_i^t \oplus \mathbf{v}_j]$ is the concatenation of three embeddings; $W_{3k,k}$ is a $3k \times k$ transition matrix that can be viewed as the parameters in a fully connected layer. The values in $\boldsymbol{\xi}$ determine the amount of information from $\mathbf{u}_i$ and $\mathbf{u}_i^t$ that can be fed to the LSTM model. In particular, the values reflect the importance of latent features in $\mathbf{u}_i$ for the prediction. Formally, the filtering layer transforms $\mathbf{u}_i \oplus \mathbf{u}_i^t$ into a k-dimensional user representation $\tilde{\mathbf{u}}_i^t$, which is defined as follows:

$$\tilde{\mathbf{u}}_i^t = W_{k,l}[(\boldsymbol{\xi} \odot \mathbf{u}_i) \oplus (\mathbf{1}_k - \boldsymbol{\xi} \odot \mathbf{u}_i^t)] \tag{8}$$

where W term is the weight matrix to be learned and $\mathbf{1}_k$ is an all-one vector.

Attentive Recurrent Layer. This layer adopts the LSTM to capture sequential information in user interest dynamics. By feeding LSTM with $\tilde{\mathbf{u}}_i^t$ at each time step t, we obtain the hidden states $h_1, \cdots, h_T$, where $h_t = LSTM(h_{t-1}, \tilde{\mathbf{u}}_i^t)$. Since user interests at different time periods do not contribute equally to the rating at time $T + 1$, we leverage the attention mechanism to determine the importance of $\tilde{\mathbf{u}}_i^t$ for predicting R_{ij}^{T+1}. Specifically, we derive a weight a^t for $\tilde{\mathbf{u}}_i^t$

based on its relationship to the target item v_j using an attention layer as follows:

$$a^t = \frac{\exp(h_t{}^\top W_{l,k}\mathbf{v}_j)}{\sum_{t=1}^{T}\exp(h_t{}^\top W_{l,k}\mathbf{v}_j)} \tag{9}$$

where W is an $l \times k$ weight matrix to be learned.

After that, we combine all the hidden states with the corresponding weights and compute a user representation $\hat{\mathbf{u}}_i$ via a fully connected layer that encodes item-dependent user interest dynamics. That is:

$$\hat{\mathbf{u}}_i = W_{l,k}(\sum_{t=1}^{T} a^t h_t) \tag{10}$$

Note that $\hat{\mathbf{u}}_i$ is a k-dimensional vector to be aligned with item latent vectors.

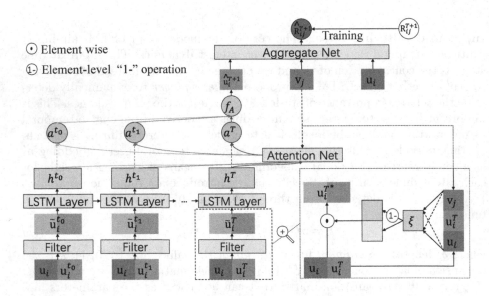

Fig. 3. The overall structure of TRPN

Aggregation and Output Layer. Now that we have two embeddings for user u_i, i.e., $\hat{\mathbf{u}}_i$ and $\mathbf{u_i}$, we can obtain two ratings for R_{ij}^{T+1}: $\hat{\mathbf{u}}_i^\top \mathbf{v}_j$ and $\mathbf{u}_i^\top \mathbf{v}_j$. We compute the final rating R_{ij}^{T+1} via the weighted sum of $\mathbf{u}_i^\top \mathbf{v}_j$ and $\hat{\mathbf{u}}_i^\top \mathbf{v}_j$:

$$\hat{R}_{i,j}^{T+} = c * \hat{\mathbf{u}}_i^\top \mathbf{v}_j + (1-c) * \mathbf{u}_i^\top \mathbf{v}_j \tag{11}$$

The weight c is computed through a fully-connected layer after concatenating the user embeddings with the item embeddings:

$$c = \sigma(W_{2k,1}[\mathbf{u}_i \oplus \mathbf{v}_j]) \tag{12}$$

By doing this, we can treat the static rating $\mathbf{u}_i^\top \mathbf{v}_j$ and the temporal rating $\hat{\mathbf{u}}_i^\top \mathbf{v}_j$ in different ways for final prediction.

5.3   Training and Optimization

The inference process of PMF has already been specified in Sect. 5.1. The optimization objective in TRPN is to find parameters to minimize the squared loss between predicted and actual ratings, which is formally defined as follows.

$$\underset{\Theta}{minimize} \sum_{(i,j,t)\in \Gamma_{train}} (\hat{R}_{ij}^t - R_{ij}^t)^2 + \lambda\Theta^2 \tag{13}$$

where Θ denotes all the parameters to be learned in TRPN, Γ_{train} is the set of ratings in the training set. λ is the L2 regularization term.

6   Experiments

To verify the effectiveness of our proposed method, we conduct experiments to answer the following research questions.

- **RQ1**: Does our proposed TRPN outperform the state-of-the-art methods for temporal rating prediction?
- **RQ2**: Are static and temporal user interests useful for improving the prediction accuracy?
- **RQ3**: Does the attention mechanism highlight the relevant time intervals for enhancing the prediction results?

6.1   Experiment Settings

Table 1. Statistics of the datasets

Dataset	#Users	#Items	Train size	Average #ratings	Sparsity
Netflix 6 months	309.2k	17.7k	28.9M	93.3	0.52%
Netflix full	422.7k	17.7k	97.5M	283.6	1.29%
MovieLens 1M	6039	3704	993.1k	143.9	4.43%

Datasets. We choose two datasets to evaluate the performance of various methods. Table 1 provides the statistics of the two datasets.

- **Netflix dataset** contains 100M rating tuples from December 1999 to December 2005. We test our model on two different time windows with different time periods on this dataset. First we set the time window as a week. The ratings from June 2005 to November 2005 are used for training and ratings in December 2005 are used as test set. In second setting, the time window is set to two months. We use ratings from December 1999 to November 2005 as the training set and the ratings in December 2005 as the test set. We refer to the above two data settings as **Netflix 6 month** and **Netflix full** respectively.

– **MovieLens 1M dataset** contains 1M rating tuples in 35 months. We use the data during first 30 months as training set and the ratings in last 5 months are used as test set.

In preprocessing, we remove the users with less than 10/20 ratings for Netflix 6 months/Netflix full. The items that are not included in training set are excluded from test set.

Comparison methods. We compare our proposed method TRPN with the following baseline methods:

– **PMF** [18] is an effective MF method to predict the ratings.
– **NCF** [6] replaces the inner product operation with a neural network in basic MF models, thus the model can learn from data an arbitrary function which maps user/item embeddings to the corresponding rating.
– **RRN** [24] is a recurrent neural network model to predict ratings by using both user-LSTM and item-LSTM to capture the dynamics in user and item representations.

Implementation Details. To compare with PMF and NCF, we organize all observed historical user-item ratings in the training set into a global rating matrix R^* to learn user/item static embeddings, and leverage static embeddings to predict ratings in the test set.

For training, we adopt Adam optimizer [12] and use mini-batch learning strategy to find optimal parameters. The learning rate is chosen from $\{10^{-2}, 10^{-3}, 10^{-4}\}$ and we set the batch size from $\{64, 128, 256, 512\}$. The number of hidden states in LSTM is chosen from $\{32, 64, 128, 256\}$. The regularization terms in Eq. (13) are selected from $\{10^{-3}, 10^{-2}, 10^{-1}, 10^0\}$. For rating prediction, we consider several input time steps, i.e., $\{4, 8, 12, 16\}$.

Metrics. We use the root mean squared error (RMSE) to measure the performance of all the methods.

$$RMSE = \sqrt{\frac{\sum_{(i,j,t)\in\Gamma_{test}}(\hat{R}_{ij}^t - R_{ij}^t)^2}{N}} \tag{14}$$

where N is the number of ratings in test set. R_{ij}^t and $\hat{R}_{ij}^t$ are the ground-truth and the predicted rating for item i and user j at time t, respectively.

6.2 Results

We first compare our proposed model TRPN with baseline models mentioned above. We then study the sensitivity of different hyper-parameter settings in TRPN. Finally, we discuss the benefits of the attention mechanism.

Performance Comparison (RQ1). To demonstrate the effectiveness of TRPN, we compare it against 3 baseline methods, and the results are shown in Table 2. Among these baselines, PMF and NCF focus on capturing static

Table 2. RMSE on Netflix and MovieLens

	PMF [18]	NCF [6]	RRN [24]	TRPN
Netflix 6 months	0.9363	0.9454	0.9312	**0.9151**
Netflix full	0.9219	0.9216	0.9205	**0.8847**
MovieLens 1M	0.9224	0.9272	0.9235	**0.9197**

interests and ignore the temporal information in the dataset. From Table 2 we can see that NCF is better than PMF on full Netflix dataset, but worse than PMF on 6-month Netflix dataset and MovieLens 1M. This is because there are more parameters in NCF than that in PMF, which makes it more likely to overfit in 6-month Netflix dataset and MovieLens 1M. We also observe that in Table 2, both RRN and TRPN perform better than PMF and NCF on Netflix dataset, which suggests that modeling temporal dynamics in users' interests improves the overall prediction accuracy. Finally, our TRPN outperforms RRN on both datasets. The main strength of our model comes from that we leverage PMF to encode temporal interests at each time step, and fuse temporal and static user interests for all time steps instead of only in the prediction layer. Another differences between TRPN and RRN is that RRN do not use PMF modeling users' embeddings at each time interval and use raw rating vectors as input, we outperform than RRN may also because we first adopt PMF to extract user embeddings so the LSTM-based model can focus on capturing the evolution.

Hyper-parameter Sensitivity (RQ2). To better understand our model and the effects of modeling both static and temporal user interests, we study the sensitivity of TRPN and TRPN-tem (a variant of TRPN which only feeds temporal interests into RNN) with respect to two hyper-parameters, i.e., the length of time steps T and the regularization term λ in Eq. (13). The results are shown in Fig. 4.

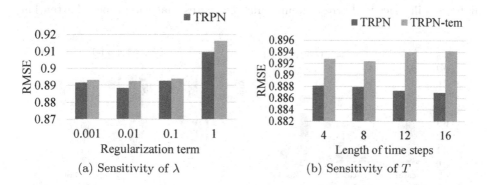

(a) Sensitivity of λ (b) Sensitivity of T

Fig. 4. Hyper-parameter sensitivity

We plot the **RMSE** versus different values of regularization term λ in Fig. 4(a) and we find that TRPN and TRPN-tem achieve the best performances when $\lambda = 0.01$. This suggests that an appropriate value for regularization term can prevent overfitting. Oppositely when the regularization term is too large, the model can also be underfitting.

We also present the **RMSE** results with different lengths of time steps in Fig. 4(b). It can be easily observed that in TRPN-tem, performance begins to deteriorate since $T = 8$. This indicates outdated information is almost irrelevant and may cause a performance degradation. But in TRPN, the performance is getting better when increasing the length of time steps T. This is because we feed both temporal and static user interests in TRPN at each time step and adopt attention mechanism to distinguish irrelevant information.

It is worth mentioning that in both Fig. 4(a) and (b), TRPN performs better than TRPN-tem, which suggests that the fusion of static user interests enhances overall prediction performances.

Attention Analysis (RQ3). We investigate the effects of attention mechanism in our proposed model. By setting $T = 4$, we select three cases and show the attention scores for different time steps in Fig. 5(a). To evaluate the attention scores in TRPN, we compute the *average item similarity* and visualize them in Fig. 5(b). For a rating R_{ij}^{T+1} to be predicted, we calculate the average similarity between v_j and items rated by u_i for previous time steps, i.e.,

$$\frac{\sum_{k \in S_i^t} cos(v_j, v_k)}{N} t = 1, 2, ..., T \tag{15}$$

where S_i^t denotes the items rated by u_i at time t, v_j and v_k are embeddings learned from PMF, $cos(\mathbf{v}_j, \mathbf{v}_k)$ is the cosine similarity between vector $\mathbf{v}_j$ and $\mathbf{v}_k$. PMF method decomposes the observed user-item interaction matrix R into the product of two matrices U, V in latent space and the cosine similarity in the latent space is useful to reflect similarity between users and items. We can observe that in Fig. 5, TRPN gives more attention on those time intervals having higher similarities with target item, which indicates that the proposed attention

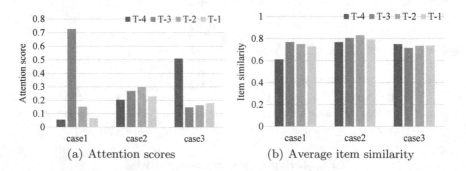

(a) Attention scores   (b) Average item similarity

Fig. 5. Attention visualization

mechanism effectively highlights the relevant time intervals for enhancing overall prediction performance.

7 Conclusion

In this paper, we propose a new neural network method for temporal rating prediction. We leverage PMF to learn both static and temporal user interests and use LSTM units to capture user interest tendency. We introduce a novel filtering layer to adaptively feed temporal and static interests to LSTM units, and an attention mechanism is further employed to highlight the relevant temporal interests when predicting a future rating. The experiments on two datasets demonstrate that (1) our proposed model TRPN outperforms several competitive methods; (2) modeling both static and temporal user interests can improve the overall recommendation accuracy; (3) the attention mechanism effectively highlights the relevant time intervals for enhancing overall prediction performances.

Acknowledgements. This work is supported by the National Key Research and Development Program of China (No. 2018YFC0831604) and NSFC No. 61602297.

References

1. Bahdanau, D., Cho, K., Bengio, Y.: Neural machine translation by jointly learning to align and translate. CoRR abs/1409.0473 (2014)
2. Cho, K., et al.: Learning phrase representations using RNN encoder-decoder for statistical machine translation. In: EMNLP, pp. 1724–1734 (2014)
3. Chung, J., Ahn, S., Bengio, Y.: Hierarchical multiscale recurrent neural networks. CoRR abs/1609.01704 (2016)
4. Du, Y., Xu, C., Tao, D.: Privileged matrix factorization for collaborative filtering. In: IJCAI, pp. 1610–1616 (2017)
5. Gao, L., Wu, J., Zhou, C., Hu, Y.: Collaborative dynamic sparse topic regression with user profile evolution for item recommendation. In: AAAI (2017)
6. He, X., Liao, L., Zhang, H., Nie, L., Hu, X., Chua, T.: Neural collaborative filtering. In: WWW, pp. 173–182 (2017)
7. He, X., Zhang, H., Kan, M., Chua, T.: Fast matrix factorization for online recommendation with implicit feedback. In: SIGIR, pp. 549–558 (2016)
8. He, Y., Li, J., Song, Y., He, M., Peng, H.: Time-evolving text classification with deep neural networks. In: Proceedings of the Twenty-Seventh International Joint Conference on Artificial Intelligence, IJCAI 2018, pp. 2241–2247 (2018)
9. Hidasi, B., Karatzoglou, A., Baltrunas, L., Tikk, D.: Session-based recommendations with recurrent neural networks. CoRR abs/1511.06939 (2015)
10. Hochreiter, S., Schmidhuber, J.: Long short-term memory. Neural Comput. 9(8), 1735–1780 (1997)
11. Huang, X., Wu, L., Chen, E., Zhu, H., Liu, Q., Wang, Y.: Incremental matrix factorization: a linear feature transformation perspective. In: IJCAI (2017)
12. Kingma, D.P., Ba, J.: Adam: A method for stochastic optimization. CoRR abs/1412.6980 (2014)

13. Koren, Y.: Collaborative filtering with temporal dynamics. In: SIGKDD (2009)
14. Koren, Y., Bell, R.M., Volinsky, C.: Matrix factorization techniques for recommender systems. IEEE Comput. **42**(8), 30–37 (2009)
15. Lian, D., Zhang, Z., Ge, Y., Zhang, F., Yuan, N.J., Xie, X.: Regularized content-aware tensor factorization meets temporal-aware location recommendation. In: ICDM, pp. 1029–1034 (2016)
16. Lu, Z., Pan, S.J., Li, Y., Jiang, J., Yang, Q.: Collaborative evolution for user profiling in recommender systems. In: IJCAI, pp. 3804–3810 (2016)
17. Ruder, S.: An overview of gradient descent optimization algorithms. arXiv preprint arXiv:1609.04747 (2016)
18. Salakhutdinov, R., Mnih, A.: Probabilistic matrix factorization. In: NIPS (2007)
19. Sarwar, B.M., Karypis, G., Konstan, J.A., Riedl, J.: Item-based collaborative filtering recommendation algorithms. In: WWW, pp. 285–295 (2001)
20. Song, Y., Elkahky, A.M., He, X.: Multi-rate deep learning for temporal recommendation. In: SIGIR, pp. 909–912 (2016)
21. Wang, Q., Yin, H., Hu, Z., Lian, D., Wang, H., Huang, Z.: Neural memory streaming recommender networks with adversarial training. In: KDD (2018)
22. Wang, W., Yin, H., Du, X., Nguyen, Q.V.H., Zhou, X.: TPM: a temporal personalized model for spatial item recommendation. TIST **9**(6), 61:1–61:25 (2018)
23. Wang, W., Yin, H., Huang, Z., Wang, Q., Du, X., Nguyen, Q.V.H.: Streaming ranking based recommender systems. In: SIGIR, pp. 525–534 (2018)
24. Wu, C., Ahmed, A., Beutel, A., Smola, A.J., Jing, H.: Recurrent recommender networks. In: WSDM, pp. 495–503 (2017)
25. Yin, H., Cui, B., Chen, L., Hu, Z., Zhou, X.: Dynamic user modeling in social media systems. ACM Trans. Inf. Syst. **33**(3), 10:1–10:44 (2015)
26. Zhao, L., Lu, Z., Pan, S.J., Yang, Q.: Matrix factorization+ for movie recommendation. In: IJCAI, pp. 3945–3951 (2016)

Improved Review Sentiment Analysis
with a Syntax-Aware Encoder

Jiangfeng Zeng[1], Ming Yang[2], Ke Zhou[1(✉)], Xiao Ma[3], Yangtao Wang[1],
Xiaodong Xu[1], and Zhili Xiao[4]

[1] Huazhong University of Science and Technology, Wuhan, China
{jfzeng,k.zhou,ytwbruce,xiaodong-xu}@hust.edu.cn
[2] Wuhan cciisoft Co., Ltd., Wuhan, China
mingyangIris@gmail.com
[3] Zhongnan University of Economics and Law, Wuhan, China
cindyma@zuel.edu.cn
[4] Tencent Inc., Shenzhen, China
tomxiao@tencent.com

Abstract. Review sentiment analysis has drawn a lot of active research
interest because of the explosive growth in the amount of available
reviews in our day-to-day activities. The current review sentiment classification work often models each sentence as a sequence of words, thus simply training sequence-structured recurrent neural networks (RNNs) end-
to-end and optimizing via stochastic gradient descent (SGD). However,
such sequence-structured architectures overlook the syntactic hierarchy
among the words in a sentence. As a result, they fail to capture the syntactic properties that would naturally combine words to phrases. In this
paper, we propose to model each sentence of a review with an attention-
based dependency tree-LSTM, where a sentence embedding is obtained
relying on the dependency tree of the sentence as well as the attention
mechanism in the tree structure. Then, we feed all the sentence representations into a sequence-structured long short-term memory network
(LSTM) and exploit attention mechanism to generate the review embedding for final sentiment classification. We evaluate our attention-based
tree-LSTM model on three public datasets, and experimental results turn
out that it outperforms the state-of-the-art baselines.

Keywords: Sentiment analysis · Recurrent neural networks ·
tree-LSTM · Syntax-aware

1 Introduction

As a branch of text-based multimedia analysis, sentiment analysis [20] is a
challenging study of vital importance in natural language processing (NLP).
Recently, more and more attention has been focused on document-level sentiment analysis in the research community these years because of two main reasons: (1) over the past several decades, there has been an explosive growth in

© Springer Nature Switzerland AG 2019
J. Shao et al. (Eds.): APWeb-WAIM 2019, LNCS 11642, pp. 73–87, 2019.
https://doi.org/10.1007/978-3-030-26075-0_6

the amount of reviews from social networks like Twitter, Facebook, Instagram, etc; (2) successfully classifying the review sentiment is crucial to understanding customer preferences and enabling new businesses such as customized recommendation [7].

Existing approaches can be divided into two classes: traditional machine learning models and neural network models. Traditional machine learning methods are dedicated to manually engineering an abundance of useful features like bag-of-words [20], sentiment lexicons [21,23] and social networks [6] to build the classification models. Although traditional methods like Support Vector Machine (SVM) [19] obtained a good performance on this task, they are always blamed for complicated and labor-intensive feature engineering. Since deep learning techniques have been successfully applied to many tasks in both computer vision and natural language processing, some recent studies start to address sentiment classification using well-designed neural networks. Compared with feature based traditional machine learning models, neural networks models have achieved promising results on sentiment analysis for their capability to learn powerful and semantic feature representations from original data without careful handcraft feature engineering [8,11,16,25,26]. Document-level sentiment analysis is a challenging task and far from being solved. Without considering the document structure, cached long short-term memory networks [31] devises a cache mechanism to divide memory into several groups via different forgetting rates, thus enabling the network to capture the overall sentiment information better within a recurrent unit. [2] and [27] realize the vital importance of document hierarchy structure and build hierarchical models to deal with document-level sentiment analysis. To further improve the classification accuracy, attention mechanism is exploited to select important word-level and sentence-level features hierarchically [5,28,33]. In [28], user(product) matrix representation is not well defined because of the data insufficiency in terms of those users(products) with limited reviews. Chen et al. [5] develop NSC+UPA that achieves the state-of-the-art. However, word vectors didn't combine neither user nor product information before attention weights are computed so that the sentence representation misses the opportunity to enrich the sentence semantics with user and product information.

Although these attention based sequence-structured RNNs have shown to significantly improve the sentiment classification results, several prominent researchers push back against this cognition that language is just sequences of words [4,22,34]. In other words, linguistic structure is coming back. Consequently, in this paper, we model each sentence of a review with an attention-based dependency tree-LSTM, where a sentence embedding is obtained relied on the dependency tree of the sentence as well as the attention mechanism in the tree structure. Then, all the sentence representations are fed into a sequence-structured long short-term memory network (LSTM) and the attention mechanism is utilized to generate the review embedding for final sentiment classification. The major contributions of this paper are three-fold:

- We propose an attention-based dependency tree-LSTM to model each sentence, which computes attention based on the dependency parsing tree of a sentence.
- Because of the high computation complexity and the big memory capacity, current tree-LSTM models don't run in batch mode. We implement the attention based tree-LSTM in batch mode, which greatly reduces the training time.
- Experimental results on three open datasets are conducted to demonstrate the effectiveness of our tree-structured model for review sentiment analysis.

The remainder of this paper is organized as follows. First, we present the proposed hierarchical architecture in Sect. 2. Then, Sect. 3 displays extensive experiments conducted to demonstrate the superiority of the proposed architecture. Afterwards, in Sect. 4, we discuss the related works on sentiment analysis. Finally, we draw a conclusion and envision the future in Sect. 5.

2   The Proposed Approach

Let us first formulate the problem of review sentiment classification. We take as input a set of training reviews $D = \{(d_1, y_1), (d_2, y_2), ..., (d_n, y_n)\}$, where d_i is a document-level comment containing more than one sentence and $y_i \in Y$ depicts the sentiment label (e.g., $Y = \{1, 2, 3, 4, 5\}$ means that the rating value is ranged from "one star" to "five star"). Thus, document-level sentiment classification aims at inferring the sentiment label of a review.

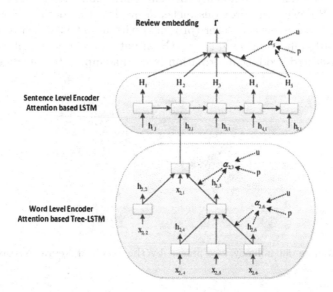

Fig. 1. Overview of the proposed hierarchical architecture for review sentiment analysis.

Considering the hierarchical document structure, we model each review hierarchically as done in [5,33]: word level (from word to sentence) and sentence
level (from sentence to document). In word level, we devise an attention-based
dependency tree-LSTM to encode each sentence of a review. In sentence level, a
sequence-structured LSTM encoder followed by an attention layer is developed
to generate attentive representations for reviews. Note that the attention weights
in both word level and sentence level are computed by using global user preferences and product characteristics as guidance. A high-level illustration of our
proposed approach is shown in Fig. 1. For simplicity and generality, we suppose
that the root of each dependency tree is the first word of each sentence. We then
examine each module detailedly and give intuitions about its formulation.

2.1   Embedding from Word to Sentence

For each sentence of a review, the sentence representation is obtained by modeling the words belonging to the sentence. Suppose that the j-th sentence s_j con-
tains n_j words, and is denoted as $s_j = \{w_{j,1}, w_{j,2}, ..., w_{j,n_j}\}$, where $w_{j,k} \in R^{K_1}$ is
from the pre-trained word embeddings by $word2vec$ [17]. Draw inspirations from
the aspect embedding devised by [30], we vectorize user preferences and product
characteristics as user embedding $u \in R^{L_1}$ for each user and product embedding
$p \in R^{L_2}$ for each product, respectively. Note that user embedding and product
embedding are treated as training parameters like other model parameters. In
addition, we concatenate each word vector $w_{j,k}$ with user vector u and product
vector p as inputs for our attention-based tree-LSTM. For simplicity in notation,
we denote $x_{j,k} = [w_{j,k}; u; p]$. It is worth mentioning that such a concatenation
design contributes a lot to enhancing the sentence semantics with user and product features. However, the previous methods neglect this design. For example,
Tang et al. [28] represent each user (product) with a matrix which is multiplied
with each word embedding $w_{j,k}$ to get the inputs for sentence embeddings. In
[5], neither user and product information is used as inputs to encode sentences.

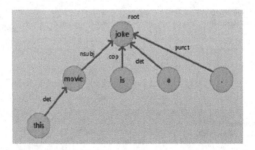

Fig. 2. An example dependency tree parsed by the Stanford Neural Network Dependency Parser.

Evidently, sequence-structured RNNs are increasingly incapable of capturing
long-range dependencies. To make full advantage of the syntactic structure in

each sentence, we employ a tree-LSTM [26] to generate a hidden vector for each word. In detail, we first parse each sentence into a dependency tree or a constituency tree using the Stanford Neural Network Dependency Parser [3]. In this work, we choose the $child - sum$ schema [26] for tree-LSTM to model each sentence. An example dependency tree for the sentence "This movie is a joke." is illustrated in Fig. 2. We can see that an dependency tree is composed of nodes corresponding to words in the sentence and edges representing the syntax relationships between parent node and its child nodes. Note that arrow directions reveal the computing order, that is to say, parent node is computed only after its child nodes have been computed. Then the representation for the root node of the tree is regarded as the sentence representation.

Given a dependency tree of a sentence, we denote $C_{j,k}$ as the set of children for word $w_{j,k}$. Formally, for each input vector $x_{j,k}$, we output a vector $h_{j,k} \in R^{K_2}$, by computing a series of neuron activations for an input gate $g_{j,k}^{(i)}$, several forget gates $g_{j,k,l}^{(f)}$, a memory cell state $g_{j,k}^{(c)}$ and an output gate $g_{j,k}^{(o)}$:

$$\overline{h}_{j,k} = \sum_{w_{j,l} \in C_{j,k}} h_{j,l} \tag{1}$$

$$g_{j,k}^{(i)} = \sigma(W^{(i)} x_{j,k} + U^{(i)} \overline{h}_{j,k} + b^{(i)}) \tag{2}$$

$$g_{j,k,l}^{(f)} = \sigma(W^{(f)} x_{j,k} + U^{(f)} h_{j,l} + b^{(f)}) \tag{3}$$

$$\overline{g}_{j,k}^{(c)} = tanh(W^{(c)} x_{j,k} + U^{(c)} \overline{h}_{j,k} + b^{(c)}) \tag{4}$$

$$g_{j,k}^{(c)} = g_{j,k}^{(i)} \odot \overline{g}_{j,k}^{(c)} + \sum_{w_{j,l} \in C_{j,k}} g_{j,k,l}^{(f)} \odot g_{j,l}^{(c)} \tag{5}$$

$$g_{j,k}^{(o)} = \sigma(W^{(o)} x_{j,k} + U^{(o)} \overline{h}_{j,k} + b^{(o)}) \tag{6}$$

$$h_{j,k} = g_{j,k}^{(o)} \odot tanh(g_{j,k}^{(c)}) \tag{7}$$

where $\odot$ is an element-wise product, and $\Theta^{(tree-lstm)} = \{W^{(i)} \in R^{K_2 \times K_1}, U^{(i)} \in R^{K_2 \times K_2}, b^{(i)} \in R^{K_2}, W^{(f)} \in R^{K_2 \times K_1}, U^{(f)} \in R^{K_2 \times K_2}, b^{(f)} \in R^{K_2}, W^{(c)} \in R^{K_2 \times K_1}, U^{(c)} \in R^{K_2 \times K_2}, b^{(c)} \in R^{K_2}, W^{(o)} \in R^{K_2 \times K_1}, U^{(o)} \in R^{K_2 \times K_2}, b^{(o)} \in R^{K_2}\}$ is the set of parameters for tree-LSTM.

We introduce attention to tree-LSTM based on the dependency tree. In particular, we add attention into both Eqs. 1 and 5. In terms of Eq. 1, to sum up the children hidden vectors is arbitrary. Therefore, we define

$$v_{j,l}^{(s)} = h_{j,l}^T W_2^{(s)} u + h_{j,l}^T W_3^{(s)} p$$

$$\beta_{j,l}^{(s)} = \eta^{(s)} \cdot f(W_1^{(s)} h_{j,l} + b^{(s)}) + v_{j,l}^{(s)}$$

$$\alpha_{j,l} = \frac{\exp(\beta_{j,l}^{(s)})}{\sum_{w_{j,i} \in C_{j,k}} \exp(\beta_{j,i}^{(s)})} \tag{8}$$

where $v_{j,l}^{(s)}$ is a term introduced to indicate the relevance between word hidden vector $h_{j,l}$ and user embedding u, as well as product embedding p. $f(\cdot)$ is a nonlinear function like sigmoid or tanh. $\Theta^{(Att_1)} = \{W_1^{(s)} \in R^{K_2 \times K_2}, W_2^{(s)} \in R^{K_2 \times L_1}, W_3^{(s)} \in R^{K_2 \times L_2}, b^{(s)} \in R^{K_2}, \eta^{(s)} \in R^{K_2}\}$ is the attention network parameters to be learned. Then, by aggregating all the children hidden vectors according to $\alpha_{j,l}$, Eq. 1 can be updated as

$$\overline{h}_{j,k} = \sum_{w_{j,l} \in C_{j,k}} \alpha_{j,l} h_{j,l} \tag{9}$$

Similarly, for Eq. 5, we compute attention weights as

$$\overline{g}_{j,k,l}^{(c)} = g_{j,k,l}^{(f)} \odot g_{j,l}^{(c)}$$
$$v_{j,k,l}^{(t)} = (\overline{g}_{j,k,l}^{(c)})^T W_2^{(t)} u + (\overline{g}_{j,k,l}^{(c)})^T W_3^{(t)} p$$
$$\beta_{j,k,l}^{(t)} = \eta^{(c)} \cdot f(W_1^{(t)} \overline{g}_{j,k,l}^{(c)} + b^{(t)}) + v_{j,k,l}^{(t)} \tag{10}$$
$$\alpha_{j,k,l} = \frac{\exp(\beta_{j,k,l}^{(t)})}{\sum_{w_{j,i} \in C_{j,k}} \exp(\beta_{j,k,i}^{(t)})}$$

where $\Theta^{(Att_2)} = \{W_1^{(t)} \in R^{K_2 \times K_2}, W_2^{(t)} \in R^{K_2 \times L_1}, W_3^{(t)} \in R^{K_2 \times L_2}, b^{(t)} \in R^{K_2}, \eta^{(t)} \in R^{K_2}\}$ is the attention network parameters to be learned. Thus Eq. 5 can be updated as

$$g_{j,k}^{(c)} = g_{j,k}^{(i)} \odot \overline{g}_{j,k}^{(c)} + \sum_{w_{j,l} \in C_{j,k}} \alpha_{j,k,l} \overline{g}_{j,k,l}^{(c)} \tag{11}$$

Finally, we take the output hidden vector of the root of the dependency tree as the ultimate sentence embedding.

2.2 Embedding from Sentence to Document

As shown in Fig. 1, we regard each review as a sequence of sentences. Given the sentence embeddings of a review generated in word level, we develop a sequence-structured LSTM [10], where $\Theta^{lstm} = \{W_{lstm}^{(i)} \in R^{K_2 \times K_2}, U_{lstm}^{(i)} \in R^{K_2 \times K_2}, b_{lstm}^{(i)} \in R^{K_2}, W_{lstm}^{(f)} \in R^{K_2 \times K_2}, U_{lstm}^{(f)} \in R^{K_2 \times K_2}, b_{lstm}^{(f)} \in R^{K_2}, W_{lstm}^{(c)} \in R^{K_2 \times K_2}, U_{lstm}^{(c)} \in R^{K_2 \times K_2}, b_{lstm}^{(c)} \in R^{K_2}, W_{lstm}^{(o)} \in R^{K_2 \times K_2}, U_{lstm}^{(o)} \in R^{K_2 \times K_2}, b_{lstm}^{(o)} \in R^{K_2}\}$. For simplicity in notation, we denote the outputs of LSTM for sentences $\{s_1, s_2, ..., s_m\}$ as $\{H_1, H_2, ..., H_m\}$. Based on this intuition that not all the sentences contribute equally to the semantic meaning of a review, we also exploit attention mechanism to select sentences of significant importance.

Attention weights are computed as follows:

$$v_j^{(r)} = H_j^T W_2^{(r)} u + h_j^T W_3^{(r)} p$$
$$\beta_j^{(r)} = \eta^{(r)} \cdot f(W_1^{(r)} H_j + b^{(r)}) + v_j^{(r)} \qquad (12)$$
$$\alpha_j = \frac{\exp(\beta_j^{(r)})}{\sum_{i=1}^m \exp(\beta_j^{(r)})}$$

where $\Theta^{(Att_3)} = \{W_1^{(r)} \in R^{K_2 \times K_2}, W_2^{(r)} \in R^{K_2 \times L_1}, W_3^{(r)} \in R^{K_2 \times L_2}, b^{(r)} \in R^{K_2}, \eta^{(r)} \in R^{K_2}\}$ is defined as the attention network parameters. Then we aggregate all the sentence hidden vectors according to attention weights α_j and the review embedding is computed by

$$r = \sum_{j=1}^m \alpha_j H_j \qquad (13)$$

2.3   Sentiment Classification

Since review embeddings are hierarchically extracted from the words and sentences, they are high level semantic representations for reviews. Hence, we use them to train our sentiment classifier. We first use a nonlinear layer to project review embedding r into the target space of C classes:

$$\hat{r} = tanh(W_r r + b_r) \qquad (14)$$

where C is the number of sentiment classes, and $\Theta^{(classifier)} = \{W_r \in R^{K_2 \times C}, b_r \in R^C\}$ is the parameters to be learned. Afterwards, a softmax layer is adopted to compute the sentiment distribution:

$$p_c = \frac{\exp(\hat{r}_c)}{\sum_{z=1}^C \exp(\hat{r}_z)} \qquad (15)$$

2.4   Model Training

In our work, we need to optimize all the parameters notated as $\Theta = \{\Theta^{(tree-lstm)}, \Theta^{lstm}, \Theta^{(Att_1)}, \Theta^{(Att_2)}, \Theta^{(Att_3)}, \Theta^{(classifier)}, u, p\}$. Cross entropy with L_2 regularization is defined as the loss function for optimization when training:

$$L = -\sum_{d \in D} \sum_{c=1}^C y_c(d) \cdot \log(p_c(d)) + \lambda L_2(\Theta) \qquad (16)$$

where $y_c(d)$ is the golden sentiment distribution and λ means the coefficient for L_2 regularization.

3 Evaluation

In this section, we present our experiment settings and conduct experiments on the task of document-level review sentiment analysis.

3.1 Experimental Settings

We evaluate the proposed approach on three real-world datasets, i.e., Yelp13, Yelp14 and IMDB, all of which are from [28]. Each record in the datasets is composed of a user ID, a product ID, a review and a rating. We summarize the statistics of our used datasets in Table 1. The Yelp Dataset Challenge produces Yelp 2013 and Yelp 2014 which contain a large number of restaurant reviews labeled with stars ranging from 1 to 5. IMDB contains 84919 movie reviews labeled with stars ranging from 1 to 10. We initialize the word vectors with 200-dimensional *word2vec* [17], and initialize user embedding and product embedding with a 200-dimensional zero vector. During training, word vectors, user embedding and product embedding are all fine-tuned as parameters. We set batch size to be 32, i.e., 32 documents, set L_2-regularization weight to be 0.00001 and initialize learning rate to be 0.05 for AdaDelta.

Table 1. Dataset description

Datasets	#docs	#users	#products	#docs/ user	#docs/ product	#sens/doc	#words/sen
IMDB	84,919	1,310	1,635	64.82	51.94	16.08	24.54
Yelp13	78,966	1,631	1,633	48.42	48.36	10.89	17.38
Yelp14	231,163	4,818	4,194	47.97	55.11	11.41	17.26

3.2 Evaluation Metrics

Two metrics are utilized to evaluate our model. *Accuracy* measures the overall sentiment classification performance, is formalized as:

$$Accuracy = \frac{T}{N} \tag{17}$$

where T is the number of reviews correctly predicted and N is the size of testing dataset. Another metric is $RMSE$, which calculates the divergences between predicted labels and ground truth labels and can be computed as:

$$RMSE = \sqrt{\frac{\sum_{i=1}^{N} (gd_i - pr_i)^2}{N}} \tag{18}$$

where gd_i and pr_i are golden truth label and predicted label respectively.

3.3 Baselines

We list several baseline methods for comparisons with our method as follows.

Majority infers the sentiment category of the test dataset according to the majority sentiment category in training dataset.

Trigram trains a Support Vector Machine with n-gram features, i.e., unigrams, bigrams and trigrams.

TextFeature is an another SVM-based method which is trained using word and character n-grams, sentiment lexicon features, etc.

AvgWordvec builds 200-dimensional word vectors using *word2vec* [17] and averages all the word vectors of each review as final review representation to train a SVM classifier.

SSWE uses sentiment-specific word embeddings generated by [29] to train a SVM classifier.

RNTN+RNN makes use of RNTN [25] to generate sentence embeddings which then are processed by a RNN to produce review representations for final classification.

Paragraph Vector unsupervisedly learns representations for sentences and documents [12].

JMARS is proposed in recommender systems [7]. It combines user information and aspects of a review with collaborative filtering and topic modeling.

UPNN is first to take user and product information into consideration when addressing review sentiment classification. Tang et al. [28] devises user matrix and product matrix which are concatenated with document representation for final sentiment classification.

NSC & **NSC+LA** & **NSC+UPA** are developed by [5], core of which is a sequence-structured LSTM. **NSC** encodes words and sentences of one review in a hierarchical manner, but ignores user and product information. **NSC+LA** use the local attention without using user and product information. While **NSC+UPA** introduces global user preferences and product characteristics as attention guiders over different semantic levels of a document, therefore generating robust and semantic document representations.

3.4 Model Comparisons

We conduct our comparison experiments in two scenarios: with user and product information, denoted as "with U and P", and otherwise denoted as "no U, no P". The classification accuracy and *RMSE* results are shown in Table 2.

From the rows noted by "no U, no P" in Table 2, we can see that our proposed method outperforms almost all of the baselines, which indicates that linguistic structure based neural networks have advantage over sequence-structured neural networks when addressing document-level review sentiment analysis. From the rows noted by "with U and P", we can see that global user preferences and product characteristics play an important role and attention mechanism successfully captures useful semantics related to the user and product which contribute to better training the final sentiment classifier. Evidently, no matter modeling

Table 2. Sentiment classification results of our model against competitor models on IMDB, Yelp13 and Yelp14. Acc(Accuracy) and RMSE are the two used evaluation metrics. Best results in each group are in bold.

Settings	Methods	IMDB		Yelp13		Yelp14	
		Acc	RMSE	Acc	RMSE	Acc	RMSE
no U, no P	Majority	0.196	2.495	0.411	1.060	0.392	1.097
	Trigram	0.399	1.783	0.569	0.814	0.577	0.804
	TextFeature	0.402	1.793	0.556	0.845	0.572	0.800
	AvgWordvec+SVM	0.304	1.985	0.526	0.898	0.530	0.893
	SSWE+SVM	0.312	1.973	0.549	0.849	0.557	0.851
	Paragraph Vector	0.341	1.814	0.554	0.832	0.564	0.802
	RNTN+RNN	0.400	1.764	0.574	0.804	0.582	0.821
	UPNN	0.405	1.629	0.577	0.812	0.585	0.808
	NSC	0.443	1.465	0.627	0.701	**0.637**	**0.686**
	NSC+LA	0.487	1.381	0.631	0.706	0.630	0.715
	Ours	**0.493**	**1.378**	**0.635**	**0.700**	0.634	0.689
with U and P	Trigram+UPF	0.404	1.764	0.570	0.803	0.576	0.789
	TextFeature+UPF	0.402	1.774	0.561	0.822	0.579	0.791
	JMARS	N/A	1.773	N/A	0.985	N/A	0.999
	UPNN	0.435	1.602	0.596	0.784	0.608	0.764
	NSC+UPA	0.533	1.281	**0.650**	**0.692**	0.667	0.654
	Ours+UPA	**0.538**	**1.276**	0.649	0.697	**0.669**	**0.650**

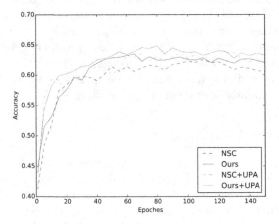

Fig. 3. Convergence speed experiment on Yelp13.

with or without user and product information, our approach is demonstrated to achieve consistent improvements compared with other competitors.

In order to clearly display the advantages of our syntax-aware method over other competitive baselines, we conduct the convergence speed experiment on

Yelp13, results of which are shown in Fig. 3. X-axis is the iteration epochs and Y-axis is the classification accuracy predicted on validation dataset. Note that one epoch in our experiments does not mean to run out the training dataset. Since the datasets used here are too large that We train 3200 random selected reviews one epoch and then validate on our validation dataset, which is also used in the work of [5]. As representatives of the current state-of-the-art sequence-structured methods, the comparison is made between our syntax-aware method and [5]. From Fig. 3, it can be observed that in terms of convergence rate our syntax-aware method beats [5]. The reason why our approach converges faster is that syntactic linguistic features are integrated into review representations and efficiently guides the classifier.

When comparing with other baselines, we have two instructive findings. First, to concatenate each word embedding with user embedding and product embedding as the inputs for neural network models contributes a lot to enriching the sentence semantics with user and product information, which increases the exposure rate of important semantics related to the user and product when computing attention weights. Second, linguistic structure based RNNs are in theory superior to sequence-structured RNNs. But experiment results show that our model based on dependency tree achieves slightly better results than the model proposed in [5]. From the implementation of tree-LSTM, we find that tree-LSTM suffers from the underfitting issue: the same shared compositional function throughout the whole compositional procedure results in the lack of expressive power.

4   Related Works

In essence, sentiment analysis can be thought of as a special kind of text classification. It is obvious that the more effective the extracted features are, the better performance the text classifiers will obtain. Earlier researches on sentiment analysis mostly focus on designing useful handcraft features, which is time-consuming and demands for expert knowledge. For example, Pang et al. [20] exploit machine learning algorithms to train classifiers with bag-of-words. Sentiment lexicons [21,23] are also utilized to improve the classification performance. Cheng et al. [6] mine useful features from social networks. Over the past several years, deep neural networks win a high reputation in substantial applications for automatic representation learning [35]. [11] and [37] represent sentences by using convolutional neural networks (CNNs) to model sentences like images. Recurrent neural networks (RNNs) emerge as methods dedicated to processing sequential data, and have achieved great success in a large number of NLP tasks. Introducing two kinds of syntactic parsing trees, Tai et al. [26] devise tree-structured long-short term memory networks (TreeLSTMs) which work better compared with sequential LSTMs. In the work of Xu et al. [31], cached long short-term memory networks are proposed to solve document-level sentiment classification. Taking into consideration the hierarchical structure of documents, some researchers attempt to model documents hierarchically [2,27]. It has been proved again and again that attention mechanism is beneficial to selecting valuable information and getting rid of useless information for substantial applications including image generation [9,18], machine translation [1,14], image caption [32], natural language inference [24], deep hashing [13,38], etc. Attention mechanism has also been investigated for sentiment analysis [36]. For instance, Yang et al. [33] propose a hierarchical attentive model which can pick out important features in both word-level and sentence-level. [28] and [5] treat the global user preferences and product characteristics as attention guiders and have brought a nice performance gain. Ma et al. [15] try to model multiple objects discussed in one sentence at one time.

In spite of the success of these sequence-structured RNN methods discussed above, the syntactic hierarchy among the words in a sentence is neglected. [34] and [22] show that linguistic structure has obvious benefits for tasks with highly-formalized outputs such as code generation and semantic parsing. Chen et al. [4] improve neural machine translation using a syntax-aware encoder and decoder, and the improvement is greater for longer sentences. As a result, NLP should re-embrace linguistic structure. It's time to announce that linguistic structure is coming back. Motivated by these recent great researches, we design a hierarchical architecture where in word level each sentence of a review is modeled using an attention-based dependency tree-LSTM, and in sentence level an attention-based long short-term memory network (LSTM) is utilized to generate the review embedding for final sentiment classification.

5   Conclusions

With the trend that the demands from people for multimedia analysis is becoming more variant and broad, the Internet-of-Things (IoT) has shown a promising prospect. Motivated by the renaissance of linguistic structure, in this paper, we present a novel hierarchical architecture to deal with review sentiment classification. Taking the dependency parsing tree of sentences, we first encode each sentence of a review using an attention-based dependency tree-LSTM. Then in sentence level, an attention-based LSTM is used to generate the review embedding for final sentiment classification. Finally, we evaluate the architecture on three real-world datasets and verify its superiority over other baselines.

Although tree-structured LSTMs are capable of learning better representations depending on syntactic information than sequential LSTMs, they suffer from the underfitting issue: the same shared compositional function throughout the whole compositional procedure results in the lack of expressive power. In the future, to further improve the sentiment classification performance, we will make our efforts to enhance the expressive power of tree-structured neural networks.

Acknowledgments. This work was supported in part by the National Natural Science Foundation of China under grants No. 61821003 and the National Key Research and Development Program of China under grant No. 2016YFB0800402.

References

1. Bahdanau, D., Cho, K., Bengio, Y.: Neural machine translation by jointly learning to align and translate. CoRR abs/1409.0473 (2014). http://arxiv.org/abs/1409.0473

2. Bhatia, P., Ji, Y., Eisenstein, J.: Better document-level sentiment analysis from RST discourse parsing. In: Proceedings of the 2015 Conference on Empirical Methods in Natural Language Processing, EMNLP 2015, 17–21 September 2015, Lisbon, Portugal, pp. 2212–2218 (2015)

3. Chen, D., Manning, C.D.: A fast and accurate dependency parser using neural networks. In: Proceedings of the 2014 Conference on Empirical Methods in Natural Language Processing, EMNLP 2014, 25–29 October 2014, Doha, Qatar, A meeting of SIGDAT, a Special Interest Group of the ACL, pp. 740–750 (2014)

4. Chen, H., Huang, S., Chiang, D., Chen, J.: Improved neural machine translation with a syntax-aware encoder and decoder. In: Proceedings of the 55th Annual Meeting of the Association for Computational Linguistics, ACL 2017, Vancouver, Canada, 30 July–4 August, vol. 1, pp. 1936–1945 (2017)

5. Chen, H., Sun, M., Tu, C., Lin, Y., Liu, Z.: Neural sentiment classification with user and product attention. In: Proceedings of the 2016 Conference on Empirical Methods in Natural Language Processing, EMNLP 2016, 1–4 November 2016, Austin, Texas, USA, pp. 1650–1659 (2016)

6. Cheng, K., Li, J., Tang, J., Liu, H.: Unsupervised sentiment analysis with signed social networks. In: Proceedings of the Thirty-First AAAI Conference on Artificial Intelligence, 4–9 February 2017, San Francisco, California, USA, pp. 3429–3435 (2017)

7. Diao, Q., Qiu, M., Wu, C., Smola, A.J., Jiang, J., Wang, C.: Jointly modeling aspects, ratings and sentiments for movie recommendation (JMARS). In: The 20th ACM SIGKDD International Conference on Knowledge Discovery and Data Mining, KDD 2014, 24–27 August 2014, New York, NY, USA, pp. 193–202 (2014)

8. Dong, L., Wei, F., Tan, C., Tang, D., Zhou, M., Xu, K.: Adaptive recursive neural network for target-dependent twitter sentiment classification. In: Proceedings of the 52nd Annual Meeting of the Association for Computational Linguistics, ACL 2014, 22–27 June 2014, Baltimore, MD, USA, vol. 2, pp. 49–54 (2014)

9. Gregor, K., Danihelka, I., Graves, A., Rezende, D.J., Wierstra, D.: DRAW: a recurrent neural network for image generation. In: Proceedings of the 32nd International Conference on Machine Learning, ICML 2015, 6–11 July 2015, Lille, France, pp. 1462–1471 (2015)

10. Hochreiter, S., Schmidhuber, J.: Long short-term memory. Neural Comput. **9**(8), 1735–1780 (1997)

11. Kim, Y.: Convolutional neural networks for sentence classification. In: Proceedings of the 2014 Conference on Empirical Methods in Natural Language Processing, EMNLP 2014, 25–29 October 2014, Doha, Qatar, A meeting of SIGDAT, a Special Interest Group of the ACL, pp. 1746–1751 (2014)

12. Le, Q.V., Mikolov, T.: Distributed representations of sentences and documents. In: Proceedings of the 31th International Conference on Machine Learning, ICML 2014, Beijing, China, 21–26 June 2014, pp. 1188–1196 (2014)

13. Liu, Y., et al.: Deep self-taught hashing for image retrieval. IEEE Trans. Cybern. **49**(6), 2229–2241 (2019)

14. Luong, T., Pham, H., Manning, C.D.: Effective approaches to attention-based neural machine translation. In: Proceedings of the 2015 Conference on Empirical Methods in Natural Language Processing, EMNLP 2015, 17–21 September 2015, Lisbon, Portugal, pp. 1412–1421 (2015)

15. Ma, X., Zeng, J., Peng, L., Fortino, G., Zhang, Y.: Modeling multi-aspects within one opinionated sentence simultaneously for aspect-level sentiment analysis. Future Gen. Comput. Syst. **93**, 304–311 (2018)

16. Mikolov, T., Karafiát, M., Burget, L., Cernocký, J., Khudanpur, S.: Recurrent neural network based language model. In: INTERSPEECH 2010, 11th Annual Conference of the International Speech Communication Association, pp. 1045–1048 (2010)

17. Mikolov, T., Sutskever, I., Chen, K., Corrado, G.S., Dean, J.: Distributed representations of words and phrases and their compositionality. In: Advances in Neural Information Processing Systems 26: 27th Annual Conference on Neural Information Processing Systems 2013. Proceedings of a meeting held December 5–8, 2013, Lake Tahoe, Nevada, United States, pp. 3111–3119 (2013)

18. Mnih, V., Heess, N., Graves, A., Kavukcuoglu, K.: Recurrent models of visual attention. In: Advances in Neural Information Processing Systems 27: Annual Conference on Neural Information Processing Systems 2014, 8–13 December 2014, Montreal, Quebec, Canada, pp. 2204–2212 (2014)

19. Mullen, T., Collier, N.: Sentiment analysis using support vector machines with diverse information sources. In: Proceedings of the 2004 Conference on Empirical Methods in Natural Language Processing, EMNLP 2004, A meeting of SIGDAT, a Special Interest Group of the ACL, Held in Conjunction with ACL 2004, 25–26 July 2004, Barcelona, Spain, pp. 412–418 (2004)

20. Pang, B., Lee, L., Vaithyanathan, S.: Thumbs up?: sentiment classification using machine learning techniques. In: Proceedings of the 2002 Conference on Empirical Methods in Natural Language Processing, EMNLP 2002, 6–7 July 2002, Philadelphia, PA, USA, vol. 10, pp. 79–86 (2002)

21. Pérez-Rosas, V., Banea, C., Mihalcea, R.: Learning sentiment lexicons in Spanish. In: Proceedings of the Eighth International Conference on Language Resources and Evaluation, LREC 2012, pp. 3077–3081 (2012)

22. Rabinovich, M., Stern, M., Klein, D.: Abstract syntax networks for code generation and semantic parsing. In: Proceedings of the 55th Annual Meeting of the Association for Computational Linguistics, ACL 2017, 30 July–4 August, Vancouver, Canada, vol. 1, pp. 1139–1149 (2017)

23. Rao, D., Ravichandran, D.: Semi-supervised polarity lexicon induction. In: 12th Conference of the European Chapter of the Association for Computational Linguistics, Proceedings of the Conference, EACL 2009, 30 March–3 April 2009, Athens, Greece, pp. 675–682 (2009)

24. Rocktäschel, T., Grefenstette, E., Hermann, K.M., Kociský, T., Blunsom, P.: Reasoning about entailment with neural attention. CoRR abs/1509.06664 (2015), http://arxiv.org/abs/1509.06664

25. Socher, R., et al.: Recursive deep models for semantic compositionality over a sentiment treebank. In: Proceedings of the 2013 Conference on Empirical Methods in Natural Language Processing, EMNLP 2013, pp. 1631–1642 (2013)

26. Tai, K.S., Socher, R., Manning, C.D.: Improved semantic representations from tree-structured long short-term memory networks. In: Proceedings of the 53rd Annual Meeting of the Association for Computational Linguistics and the 7th International Joint Conference on Natural Language Processing of the Asian Federation of Natural Language Processing, ACL 2015, 26–31 July 2015, Beijing, China, vol. 1, pp. 1556–1566 (2015)
27. Tang, D., Qin, B., Liu, T.: Document modeling with gated recurrent neural network for sentiment classification. In: Proceedings of the 2015 Conference on Empirical Methods in Natural Language Processing, EMNLP 2015, 17–21 September 2015, Lisbon, Portugal, pp. 1422–1432 (2015)
28. Tang, D., Qin, B., Liu, T.: Learning semantic representations of users and products for document level sentiment classification. In: Proceedings of the 53rd Annual Meeting of the Association for Computational Linguistics and the 7th International Joint Conference on Natural Language Processing of the Asian Federation of Natural Language Processing, ACL 2015, 26–31 July 2015, Beijing, China, vol. 1, pp. 1014–1023 (2015)
29. Tang, D., Wei, F., Yang, N., Zhou, M., Liu, T., Qin, B.: Learning sentiment-specific word embedding for Twitter sentiment classification. In: Proceedings of the 52nd Annual Meeting of the Association for Computational Linguistics, ACL 2014, 22–27 June 2014, Baltimore, MD, USA, vol. 1, pp. 1555–1565 (2014)
30. Wang, Y., Huang, M., Zhu, X., Zhao, L.: Attention-based LSTM for aspect-level sentiment classification. In: Proceedings of the 2016 Conference on Empirical Methods in Natural Language Processing, EMNLP 2016, 1–4 November 2016, Austin, Texas, USA, pp. 606–615 (2016)
31. Xu, J., Chen, D., Qiu, X., Huang, X.: Cached long short-term memory neural networks for document-level sentiment classification. In: Proceedings of the 2016 Conference on Empirical Methods in Natural Language Processing, EMNLP 2016, 1–4 November 2016, Austin, Texas, USA, pp. 1660–1669 (2016)
32. Xu, K., et al.: Show, attend and tell: neural image caption generation with visual attention. In: Proceedings of the 32nd International Conference on Machine Learning, ICML 2015, 6–11 July 2015, Lille, France, pp. 2048–2057 (2015)
33. Yang, Z., Yang, D., Dyer, C., He, X., Smola, A.J., Hovy, E.H.: Hierarchical attention networks for document classification. In: NAACL HLT 2016, The 2016 Conference of the North American Chapter of the Association for Computational Linguistics: Human Language Technologies, 12–17 June 2016, San Diego California, USA, pp. 1480–1489 (2016)
34. Yin, P., Neubig, G.: A syntactic neural model for general-purpose code generation. In: Proceedings of the 55th Annual Meeting of the Association for Computational Linguistics, ACL 2017, 30 July–4 August, Vancouver, Canada, vol. 1, pp. 440–450 (2017)
35. Zeng, J., Ma, X., Zhou, K.: CAAE++: improved CAAE for age progression/regression. IEEE Access 6, 66715–66722 (2018)
36. Zeng, J., Ma, X., Zhou, K.: Enhancing attention-based LSTM with position context for aspect-level sentiment classification. IEEE Access 7, 20462–20471 (2019)
37. Zhao, J., Gui, X.: Deep convolution neural networks for Twitter sentiment analysis. IEEE Access (2017)
38. Zhou, K., Zeng, J., Liu, Y., Zou, F.: Deep sentiment hashing for text retrieval in social CIoT. Future Gen. Comput. Syst. 86, 362–371 (2018)

Who Is the Abnormal User: Anomaly Detection Framework based on the Graph Convolutional Networks

Zetao Zheng[1] , Jia Zhu[1](✉), Yong Tang[1] , and Jiabing Du[2]

[1] Data Intelligence Laboratory, School of Computer Science,
South China Normal University, Guangzhou 510630, People's Republic of China
{ztzheng,jzhu,ytang}@m.scnu.edu.cn
[2] FoShan Power Supply Bureau of Guangdong Grid Co.,
FoShan 528000, People's Republic of China
dujiabing@csg.gd.cn

Abstract. Anomaly detection is the identification of items, events or observations which do not conform to an expected pattern in a dataset. It is applicable in a variety of domains, such as intrusion detection, fault detection, medical and public health anomaly monitoring. Existing model usually detects the anomaly according to the data's feature. However, two drawbacks exist if the model only detects anomaly by using the feature. On the one hand, model could not make use of the relationship between users, which contains a large amount of potential information that can strengthen the prediction ability of the model. On the other hand, existing model could not adjust their learning ability automatically with the increasing of the data. To address the issues referred above, we focus on proposing an anomaly detection system based on the Graph Convolutional Networks (GCN). The framework consists of four mechanisms. It can detect the anomalies by using the user features as well as the relationship between users. Experiment result shows that our framework has outstanding performance compared with other state-of-the-art detection models.

Keywords: Graph Convolutional Networks · Anomaly detection · Graph theory

1 Introduction

Anomaly detection is a significant problem that has been researched within diverse research areas and application domains. Anomalies are patterns in data that do not conform to a well-defined notion of normal behavior. Figure 1 illustrates anomalies in a simple two-dimensional dataset. The data has two normal regions called N1 and N2, since most observations lie in these two regions. Points that are sufficiently far away from these regions, for example, points o1 and o2, and points in region O3, are anomalies. The importance of abnormal tests is that

© Springer Nature Switzerland AG 2019
J. Shao et al. (Eds.): APWeb-WAIM 2019, LNCS 11642, pp. 88–102, 2019.
https://doi.org/10.1007/978-3-030-26075-0_7

the anomalies in the data can be transformed into key operational information in a wide variety of application domains. For example, an anomalous traffic pattern in a computer network could mean that a hacked computer is sending out sensitive data to an unauthorized destination. An anomalous MRI image may indicate the presence of malignant tumors. The credit card transaction data anomalies may indicate identity or credit card theft.

Due to the importance of the abnormal detection technology, various anomaly detection techniques have been developed over time. Abnormal detection technology can be divided into three categories: unsupervised anomaly detection, supervised anomaly detection and semi-supervised anomaly detection [5]. Unsupervised anomaly detection techniques detect anomalies in unlabeled test data. Assuming that most instances of the data set are normal, it is an except Unsupervised anomaly detection techniques detect anomalies in an unlabeled test data set under the assumption that the majority of the instances in the data set are normal. It detects anomalies by looking for instances that do not match the rest of the data. Supervised anomaly detection techniques require a data set that has been labeled as "normal" and "abnormal" and involves training a classifier. Semi-supervised anomaly detection techniques construct a model representing normal behavior from a given normal training data set, and then testing the likelihood of a test instance using the model above. However, most of the anomaly detection model rely heavily on the users feature but ignore the relationship between users. It can be vividly illustrated by the Fig. 2. It is a well-known graph dataset: Zachary's club network. Nodes of the same color represent that they belong to the same class. As we can see from the network that nodes in the same class always connected by edges. Besides, with the growing of the data, we require the mode to adjust itself to adopt the increasing of the data. Therefore, we proposed an anomaly detection system based on the Graph Convolutional Networks. Our system can detect the abnormal users by using user features as well as the relationship between users.

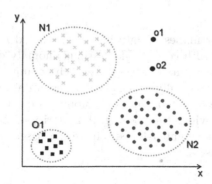

Fig. 1. A simple example of anomalies in a tow-dimensional data set.

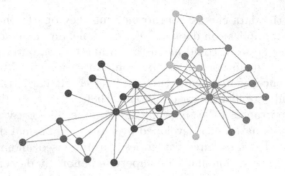

Fig. 2. Zachary's club network.

In general, the significant contributions of our framework can be summarized as follows:

- We first utilize the deep learning model namely Graph Convolutional Networks to detect anomaly for its excellent performance compared with other models.
- We adopt the graph theory and propose a method to transform the original data into a graph that can be fed into GCN, so the potential relation between users can be further utilized.
- We transform the GCN into a model that could predict a single node and applied it to our framework (batch forecast previously).

The rest of the paper is organized as follows: Sect. 2 presents a brief literature review on the issue of anomaly detection techniques and then give a brief introduction to the GCN model. Section 3 presents the details of our framework. Section 4 shows the experiment result and Sect. 5 draw a conclusion on our work.

2   Related Work

Detecting outliers or anomalies in data has been studied in the statistics community as early as the 19th century [4]. Various anomaly detection techniques have been developed over time in several research communities. Many of these techniques have been specifically developed for certain application domains. In this section, we provide a categorization of anomaly detection techniques based on the research area to which they belong. A majority of the techniques can be categorized into nearest neighbor-based, clustering-based, and statistical techniques, classification-based.

2.1   Nearest Neighbor-Based Anomaly Detection

The technique of Nearest neighbor-based anomaly detection are based on the assumption that normal data instances occur in dense neighborhoods while outliers occur far away from their closest neighbors. The Nearest Neighbor-based anomaly detection requires a measurement of distance or similarity between two data instances. Distance (or similarity) between two data instances can be computed in different ways. Euclidean distance is a popular choice to compute continuous attributes. A simple matching coefficient is often used for categorical attributes. For multivariate data instances, distance or similarity is usually computed for each attribute and then combined [7].

Nearest neighbor-based anomaly detection techniques can be roughly divided into two categories:

- techniques that use the instance to its kth nearest neighbor distance as an anomaly score;
- techniques that compute the relative density of each data instance to compute its anomaly score.

Additionally, there are some techniques that detect anomalies in different ways by using the distance between data instances, and we don't elaborate here because of the limitations of the space.

2.2 Clustering Based Anomaly Detection

Clustering [7,8] is used to group similar data instances into clusters. Clustering is primarily an unsupervised technique though semi-supervised clustering [9] has also been explored lately. Clustering-based anomaly detection techniques can be grouped into three categories. The first category of clustering-based techniques relies on the following assumption that normal data instances belong to a cluster in the data, while anomalies do not belong to any cluster. The technique based on this assumption applies a known clustering algorithm to the data set and declares anomaly to any data instances that do not belong to any cluster. There are several clustering algorithms that do not force each data instance to belong to the cluster, such as DBSCAN [10], ROCK [11], and SNN clustering [12] can be used. The second category of clustering-based techniques relies on the assumption that normal data instances lie close to their closest cluster center, while anomalies are far away from their closest cluster center. Techniques based on this assumption consist of two steps. In the first step, the data is clustered using a clustering algorithm. In the second step, for each data instance, its distance to its closest cluster centrt is calculated as its anomaly score.

2.3 Statistical Based Anomaly Detection

The basic principle of any statistical anomaly detection technique is that an anomaly is an observation that is suspected to be partially or completely irrelevant because it is not produced by a hypothetical stochastic model [13]. Statistical anomaly detection techniques are based on the key assumption that normal data instances occur in the high-probability region of the stochastic model and anomalies occur in the low-probability region of the stochastic model. The statistical technique fits the statistical model (usually used for normal behavior) with the given data, and then apply a statistical inference test to determine if an unseen instance belongs to this model or not. Instances that have a low probability of being generated from the learned model, based on the applied test statistic, are declared as anomalies. Both parametric, as well as non-parametric techniques, have been applied to fit a statistical model. While parametric techniques assume the knowledge of the underlying distribution and estimate the parameters from the given data [14], non- parametric techniques do not generally assume knowledge of the underlying distribution [15].

2.4 Classification Based Anomaly Detection

Classification [7,16] is used to learn a model (classifier) from a set of labeled data instances and then, classify a test instance into one of the classes using the learned model. The detection techniques based on classified anomaly work can be divided into two stages. The training phase learns a classifier using the available labeled training data. The testing stage classifies a test instance as normal or anomalous by using the classifier. Classification based anomaly detection techniques operate under the assumption that a classifier can distinguish between normal and abnormal classes in a given feature space. Based on the labels available for the training stage, classification-based anomaly detection techniques can be grouped into two broad categories: multi-class and one- class anomaly detection techniques. The abnormal detection techniques based on multi-class classification assume that the training data contains labeled instances belonging to multiple normal classes [17,18]. Such anomaly detection techniques teach a classifier to distinguish between each normal class and the rest of the classes. See Fig. 3(a) for illustration. A test instance is considered anomalous if it is not classified as normal by any of the classifiers. Some techniques in this subcategory associate a confidence score with the prediction made by the classifier. If none of the classifiers are confident in classifying the test instance as normal, the instance is declared to be anomalous. One-class classification based anomaly detection techniques assumes that all training instances have only one-class label. Such techniques learn a discriminative boundary around the normal instances using a one-class classification algorithm, for example, one-class SVMs [19], one-class Kernel Fisher Discriminants [20,21], as shown in Fig. 3(b). Any test instance that does not fall within the learned boundary is declared as anomalous. Various classification algorithms can be used to build a classifier, such as Bayesian Networks, Support Vector Machines algorithm [22], and neural networks. In the following subsections, we discuss the neural networks based algorithm GCN, the core algorithm we used to detect the anomaly in our framework.

Neural Networks Based Anomaly Detection. Deep learning shows amazing ability in processing speech, image and text, and neural networks have been applied to anomaly detection in multi-class as well as one-class settings. It's a two-step process based on the multi-class anomalies of the neural network. First, input the training data (normal and abnormal) into the neural network,

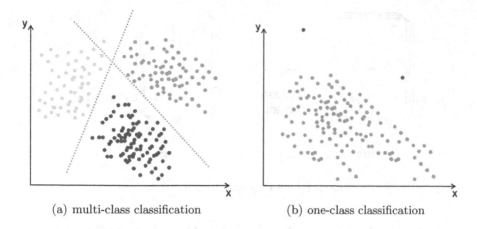

(a) multi-class classification   (b) one-class classification

Fig. 3. Using classification for anomaly detection

Second, each test instance is provided as an input to the neural network and predict which label it belongs to. Kipf [6] proposed a semi-supervised classification model based on the Graph Convolutional Networks, which has excellent performance in node classification compared with other neural networks models.

GCN is a graph representation learning method based on convolution neural network. It uses an efficient layer-wise propagation rule that is based on a first-order approximation of spectral convolutions on graphs. The layer-wise propagation rule have been shown as follow:

$$H^{(l+1)} = \sigma\left(D^{-\frac{1}{2}} A D^{-\frac{1}{2}} H^{(l)} W^{(l)}\right)$$

Here, $A = A + I_N$ is the adjacency matrix of the undirected graph G with added self-connections. I_N is the identity matrix, $D_{ii} = \Sigma_j A_{ij}$ and $W^{(l)}$ is a layer-specific trainable weight matrix. $\sigma(.)$ denotes an activation function, such as the ReLU$(.)$. $H^{(l)} \in \mathbb{R}_N \times D$ is the matrix of activation in the lth layer, $H^{(0)} = X$, X is a matrix of node features.

Having introduced a simple, yet flexible neural network model above for efficient information propagation on graphs, we can return to the problem of anomaly detection. In the following, we consider a two-layer GCN for semi-supervised node classification on a graph with a symmetric adjacency matrix A, we first calculate $A = D^{-\frac{1}{2}} A D^{-\frac{1}{2}}$ in a pre-processing step. Our forward model then takes the simple form:

$$Z = f(X, A) = softmax\left(A\ ReLU\left(AXW^{(0)}\right) W^{(1)}\right)$$

The entire model, a multi-layer GCN for semi-supervised learning, is schematically depicted in Fig. 4 (referring from Kipf [6]).

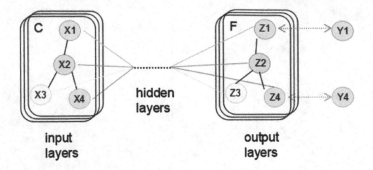

Fig. 4. Graph Convolutional Networks

3   Anomaly Detection Framework Based on GCN

As outlined in the abstract, Our framework can be divided into four parts. Our framework diagram can be shown in Fig. 5. The first step is to construct the original dataset into a format that can be fed into the model. The original data is the user ID and the user's features as shown in Tables 1 and 2. The original data cannot be used as input because the model only accepts the adjacency matrix and feature matrix as input. Compared with the adjacency matrix, it is not a hard thing to construct a feature matrix based on the original data,

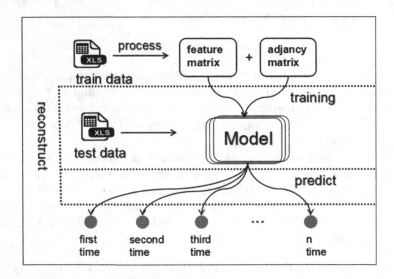

Fig. 5. Framework Schematic Diagram. Component 1 is aimed at converting the original data into a adjacency matrix and feature matrix that can be used as input data. Component 2 is training and saving the model. Component 3 aim at detecting if a user is abnormal. After predict for n times, Component 4 would reconstruct the data and retrain the model.

so we propose a method to find out the relationship between users and we will elaborate on how to construct an adjacency matrix in Sect. 3.2. The second part is the training of the neural network model. The model would be saved, after the training is completed. We save the model structure and the corresponding variables so that we can predict the test set directly without retraining. The third step is to predict an individual test data. Because of the limitation of the input format and output format, we cannot input a single test data like other machine learning models and predict which label the test set belongs to. Therefore, we modified GCN so that it can be used to predict the individual data label. The detail will be described in Sect. 3.4. In the actual industrial production, there will be an artificial error correction module which aims at correcting the wrong prediction label to accumulate more accurate data, which can be used to reconstruct the training data in the next step. In the fourth step, the framework reconstructs the training data set and retrains the model to strengthen the ability of the model to detect anomaly with the growth of data.

3.1 Dataset Describe

In this paper, we use two datasets and all of them are provided by industry. The raw data format is shown in Tables 1 and 2. There are n users in total and each user has m features (where $n = 920$, $m = 141$ in Data1 and $n = 969$, $m = 135$ in Data2). For the sake of user privacy, we only listed some features here. There are three abnormal labels in the Data1 and two abnormal labels in Data2, and the number of abnormal labels can be observed from Table 3.

Table 1. The Data1 records

Userid	Labels	Time	...	Days	Electricity charge
1	1	201704	...	60	267.22
2	2	201707	...	61	132.06
3	1	201705	...	62	1350.24
4	3	201706	...	41	360.59
5	2	201704	...	31	33.48

Table 2. The Data2 records

Userid	Labels	Date	...	Consumption	Charge
1	1	2017/4/6	...	300	186
2	1	2017/2/8	...	184	114.7
3	0	2017/3/9	...	1914	1540.88
4	1	2017/4/2	...	431	360.59
5	0	2017/4/6	...	0	0

Table 3. The abnormal labels status

	Label 1	Label 2	Label 3
Data1	412	131	402
Data2	679	290	–

3.2   Data Preprocessing

There are many problems in the original data, such as missing value, redundancy and irregular data format. Firstly, we removed the features that have a lot of missing values because these features are meaningless, then we processed the data by using binary encoding and one-hot encoding. Finally, we selected 30 features by using the Chi-Square test. The chi-squared test helps you to determine the most significant features among a list of available features by determining the correlation between feature variables and the target variable. The value of the test-statistic is:

$$X^2 = \sum_{i=1}^{n} \frac{(O_i - E_i)^2}{E_i} = N \sum_{i=1}^{n} \frac{(O_i/N - p_i)^2}{p_i}$$

where

- x^2 = Pearson's cumulative test statistic, which asymptotically approaches a X^2 distribution.
- O^2 = the number of observations of type i.
- N = total number of observations
- E_i= the expected (theoretical) count of type i, asserted by the null hypothesis that the fraction of type i in the population is p_i
- n = the number of cells in the table.

the larger the x^2 value, the more informative the corresponding feature is.

3.3   Construct the Graph

As we mentioned earlier, the model only accepts the adjacency matrix and feature matrix as input, so we need to process the data further. We consider each user as a node in the graph. To find out whether there is a connection between the two users, we use the Jaccard similarity coefficient to measure the similarity of the user features.

The Jaccard index [23,24], also known as Jaccard similarity coefficient, is a statistic used for comparing the similarity and diversity of sample sets. The Jaccard coefficient measures the similarity between finite sample sets, and is defined as the size of the intersection divided by the size of the union of the sample sets:

$$J(A, B) = \frac{|A \bigcap B|}{|A \bigcup B|} = \frac{|A \bigcap B|}{|A| + |B| - |A \bigcap B|}$$
$$0 \leq J(A, B) \leq 1$$

The Jaccard index compares features for two sets to see which features are shared and which are distinct. The greater the Jaccard similarity coefficient of the two users, the more shared features the two users have. We assume that there is a relationship between two users if the Jaccard similarity coefficient is greater than 0.65. We calculate the Jaccard index for every user with the others. Finally, each user denotes a node in the graph, and if the Jaccard index is greater than 0.65, we assume there is a edge between two nodes. We display the subgraph which only contains 40 users in Fig. 6.

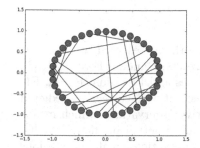

Fig. 6. Part of the constructed graph

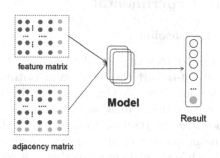

Fig. 7. Predict a single node (Color figure online)

3.4 Single Node Prediction

GCN is a graph that only accepts the adjacency matrix and feature matrix as input. However, in industry, it is often necessary to predict an individual user label. So we need to adapt GCN to predict an individual users.

Our approach is shown in Fig. 7. The black dots on the left represent the feature matrix and the adjacency matrix extracted from the training data set, and the red dots represent the unknown label data. The unknown label data is processed by the same way and added to the tail of the adjacent matrix and the feature matrix of the original training dataset, and a new adjacency matrix and feature matrix are formed, We feed these two new matrices into the model for prediction. And only the tail of the predicted results is taken.

By using the approach we referred above, we can use GCN to predict the label of a individual user.

Table 4. Data1 accuracy comparison with 40% training data

	SVM	Random Forest	Decision Tree	Bayes	**GCN**
Precision	0.19	**0.46**	0.35	0.22	0.37
Recall	0.44	0.20	**0.44**	0.44	0.36
F1-score	0.27	0.16	**0.39**	0.29	0.36

Table 5. Data2 accuracy comparison with 40% training data

	SVM	Random Forest	Decision Tree	Bayes	**GCN**
Precision	0.36	0.57	0.57	0.56	**0.59**
Recall	0.60	0.60	0.60	0.44	**0.60**
F1-score	0.45	0.51	0.51	0.36	**0.59**

4   Experimental

4.1   Baseline

In order to verify the effectiveness of the framework we designed, we use four state-of-the-art classification algorithms, SVM [27–30], Random Forest [31,32], Decision Tree [33,34], Bayes [35–37] as the baselines and Precision, Recall, F1-score as the evaluation criterion. Precision is the ratio of correctly predicted positive observations to the total predicted positive observations, which means the proportion of all correctly predicted results to all actual predicted results. Recall is the ratio of correctly predicted positive observations to all observations in actual class. It represents all correctly predicted results to all results that should be predicted correctly. F1 Score is the weighted average of Precision and Recall. F1 Score might be a better measure to use if we need to seek a balance between Precision and Recall and there is an uneven class distribution. We use 40% of data1 and data2 to train the model respectively. The results are shown in Tables 4 and 5. To further compare against the performance of these model under the situation of data insufficient, we conduct another experiment which uses 20%, 30% of the data for training. The experiment results are shown in Tables 6 and 7.

4.2   Experiment Set

We record the best performance of the baseline methods parameters. For training SVM, we select the $C = 0.2$ which can control the tradeoff between smooth decision boundary and classifying training point correctly; For training DecisionTree, we select max_depth $= 23$, which represents The maximum depth of the tree and min_samples_leaf $= 16$, which means the minimum number of samples required to be at a leaf node. For training Random Forest, except the same parameters as the Decision Tree, Random Forest set n_estimat $= 2$, the number of trees in the forest. For training the BernoulliNB Bayes, the binarize, threshold for binarizing (mapping to booleans) of sample features is set to 1.3 and alpha, an additive Laplace smoothing parameter is set to 0.4.

We train a two-layer GCN by using different proportions of data. We train all models for a maximum of 200 epochs (training iterations) using Adam [25] with a learning rate of 0.01 and we stop training if the validation loss does not decrease for 10 consecutive epochs. We initialize weights using the initialization described in [26] and accordingly (row-)normalize input feature vectors. On the random graph datasets, we use a hidden layer size of 32 units and omit regularization (i.e. neither dropout nor L2 regularization). Finally, we save the model and use it to predict the single node.

4.3 Experiment Result

As shown in Tables 4 and 5, GCN outperforms all baselines on data2. However, the precision is pretty lower than the Random Forest and the Recall and F1-score are pretty lower than the Decision Tree on data1. Moreover, all the baseline methods have got pretty low prediction results. The reason for the results is that, on the one hand, without enough data available for the model training, which leads to the model can not fit the data very well. On the other hand, compared to data 2, data 1 have more categories, however, there is no large amount of data in each category, which makes it difficult for GCN to learn the relationship between users from data 1. Compared with data1, data2 has more data for each category and GCN can learn more relationship between users. Therefore, GCN can have a better performance on data2.

It can be seen from Tables 6 and 7 that, GCN has achieved the best performance on precision metric when using 20% of data as the training set, although it performs ordinary in other metrics. When the training data increased to 30%, the effects of other models have been significantly improved except SVM. And the performance of GCN has also improved although its not as good as Random Forest. In the training of data 2, GCN has also achieved the best performance on precision metric when using 20% of data as the training set. However, when the training data increased to 30%, the effects of other models have improved and the GCN has achieved the best performance in their metrics in all models. The difference between the training effect of two data may be due to the count for each category in the data.

In general, our framework achieves better results than most of the state-of-the-art classification algorithms. Compared with other machine models that only using features, our model makes uses of the potential relationships between the users, which can effectively improve the prediction accuracy.

Table 6. Data1 accuracy comparison on different percentage of training data

	SVM		RF		DT		Bayes		GCN	
	20%	30%	20%	30%	20%	30%	20%	30%	20%	30%
Precision	0.19	0.19	0.19	**0.47**	0.19	0.35	0.19	0.22	**0.25**	0.36
Recall	**0.44**	0.44	0.44	**0.56**	0.44	0.44	0.36	0.44	0.20	0.36
F1-score	**0.27**	0.27	0.27	**0.48**	0.27	0.39	0.25	0.29	0.21	0.36

Table 7. Data2 accuracy comparison on different percentage of training data

	SVM		RF		DT		Bayes		GCN	
	20%	30%	20%	30%	20%	30%	20%	30%	20%	30%
Precision	0.36	0.36	0.52	0.52	0.36	0.57	0.38	0.46	**0.50**	**0.59**
Recall	**0.60**	0.60	0.56	0.56	0.60	**0.60**	0.44	0.40	0.52	**0.60**
F1-score	0.45	0.45	**0.52**	0.52	0.45	0.55	0.40	0.29	0.51	**0.59**

5　Conclusion

In this paper, we proposed an anomaly detection framework based on graph convolutional networks. We first build a graph based on the Jaccard similarity coefficient between each user, and when the similarity is greater than 0.65, we consider there is a connection between the two users. Then the adjacency matrix of the graph and the feature matrix are fed into the model for training. And we designed a way to use this model to predict the label of a single node. The experimental results show that our proposed framework has excellent performance than the other four models.

Acknowledgements. This work was supported by the National Science Foundation of China (No. 61877020, U1811263, 61772211).

References

1. Kumar, V.: Parallel and distributed computing for cybersecurity. IEEE Distrib. Syst. Online **6**, 10 (2005)
2. Spence, C., Parra, L., Sajda, P.: Detection, synthesis and compression in mammographic image analysis with a hierarchical image probability model. In: Proceedings of the IEEE Workshop on Mathematical Methods in Biomedical Image Analysis, p. 3. IEEE Computer Society (2001)
3. Aleskerov, E., Freisleben, B., Rao, B.: CardWatch: a neural network based database mining system for credit card fraud detection. In: Proceedings of the IEEE Conference on Computational Intelligence for Financial Engineering, pp. 220–226 (1997)
4. Edgeworth, F.Y.: On discordant observations. Philos. Mag. **23**(5), 364–375 (1887)
5. Hodge, V., Austin, J.: A survey of outlier detection methodologies. Artif. Intell. Rev. **22**(2), 85–126 (2004)
6. Kipf, T.N., Welling, M.: Semi-supervised classification with graph convolutional networks (2016)
7. Tan, P.-N., Steinbach, M., Kumar, V.: Introduction to Data Mining. Addison-Wesley, Boston (2005)
8. Jain, A.K., Dubes, R.C.: Algorithms for Clustering Data. Prentice-Hall Inc., Upper Saddle River (1998)
9. Basu, S., Bilenko, M., Mooney, R.J.: A probabilistic framework for semi-supervised clustering. In: Proceedings of the 10th ACM SIGKDD International Conference on Knowledge Discovery and Data Mining, pp. 59–68. ACM Press (2004)

10. Ester, M., Kriegel, H.-P., Sander, J., Xu, X.: A density-based algorithm for discovering clusters in large spatial databases with noise. In: Simoudis, E., Han, J., Fayyad, U. (eds.) Proceedings of the 2nd International Conference on Knowledge Discovery and Data Mining, pp. 226–231. AAAI Press (1996)
11. Guha, S., Rastogi, R., Shim, K.: ROCK: a robust clustering algorithm for categorical attributes. Inform. Syst. **25**(5), 345366 (2000)
12. Ertöz, L., Steinbach, M., Kumar, V.: Finding topics in collections of documents: a shared nearest neighbor approach. In: Wu, W., Xiong, H., Shekhar, S. (eds.) Clustering and Information Retrieval. NETA, vol. 11, pp. 83–104. Springer, Boston (2003). https://doi.org/10.1007/978-1-4613-0227-8_3
13. Anscombe, F.J., Guttman, I.: Rejection of outliers. Technometrics **2**(2), 123–147 (1960)
14. Eskin, E., Arnold, A., Prerau, M., Portnoy, L., Stolfo, S.: Ageometric framework for unsupervised anomaly detection. In: Proceedings of the Conference on Applications of Data Mining in Computer Security, pp. 78–100. Kluwer Academics (2002)
15. Desforges, M., Jacob, P., Cooper, J.: Applications of probability density estimation to the detection of abnormal conditions in engineering. In: Proceedings of the Institute of the Mechanical Engineers, vol. 212, pp. 687–703 (1998)
16. Duda, R.O., Hart, P.E., Stork, D.G.: Pattern Classification, 2nd edn. Wiley, Hoboken (2000)
17. Stefano, C., Sansone, C., Vento, M.: To reject or not to reject: that is the question: an answer in the case of neural classifiers. IEEE Trans. Syst. Manag. Cybern. **30**(1), 8494 (2000)
18. Barbara, D., Couto, J., Jajodia, S., Wu, N.: Detecting novel network intrusions using Bayes estimators. In: Proceedings of the 1st SIAM International Conference on Data Mining (2001)
19. Scholkopf, B., Platt, J.C., Shawe-Taylor, J.C., Smola, A.J., Williamson, R.C.: Estimating the support of a high-dimensional distribution. Neural Comput. **13**(7), 14431471 (2001)
20. Roth, V.: Outlier detection with one-class kernel Fisher discriminants. In: Proceedings of the Conference on Advances in Neural Information Processing Systems (NIPS) (2004)
21. Roth, V.: Kernel fisher discriminants for outlier detection. Neural Comput. **18**(4), 942960 (2006)
22. Vapnik, V.N.: The Nature of Statistical Learning Theory. Springer, New York (1995). https://doi.org/10.1007/978-1-4757-2440-0
23. Jaccard, P.: Étude comparative de la distribution florale dans une portion des Alpes et des Jura. Bulletin de la Socit Vaudoise des Sciences Naturelles **37**, 547–579 (1901)
24. Jaccard, P.: The distribution of the flora in the alpine zone. New Phytol. **11**, 37–50 (1912)
25. Kingma, D.P., Ba J.: Adam: a method for stochastic optimization. arXiv preprint arXiv:1412.6980 (2014)
26. Glorot, X., Bengio, Y.: Understanding the difficulty of training deep feedforward neural networks. In: Proceedings of the Thirteenth International Conference on Artificial Intelligence and Statistics, pp. 249–256 (2010)
27. Zhang, T.: Statistical behavior and consistency of classification methods based on convex risk minimization. Ann. Stat. **32**, 56–85 (2004)
28. Smola, A.J., Schlkopf, B.: A tutorial on support vector regression. Stat. Comput. **14**(3), 199–222 (2004)

29. Schlkopf, B., Burges, C.J.C., Smola, A.J. (eds.): Advances in Kernel Methods: Support Vector Learning. MIT Press, Cambridge (1999)
30. Hsu, C.-W., Lin, C.-J.: A comparison of methods for multiclass support vector machines. IEEE Trans. Neural Netw. **13**(2), 415–425 (2002)
31. Rokach, L.: Ensemble-based classifiers. Artif. Intell. Rev. **33**(1–2), 1–39 (2010)
32. Pal, M.: Random forest classifier for remote sensing classification. Int. J. Remote Sens. **26**(1), 217–222 (2005)
33. Myles, A.J., Feudale, R.N., Liu, Y., et al.: An introduction to decision tree modeling. J. Chemom. **18**(6), 275–285 (2004)
34. Murthy, S.K.: Automatic construction of decision trees from data: a multidisciplinary survey. Data Min. Knowl. Disc. **2**(4), 345–389 (1998)
35. Friedman, N., Geiger, D., Goldszmidt, M.: Bayesian network classifiers. Mach. Learn. **29**(2–3), 131–163 (1997)
36. Grossman, D., Domingos, P.: Learning Bayesian network classifiers by maximizing conditional likelihood. In: Proceedings of the Twenty-first International Conference on Machine Learning, p. 46. ACM (2004)
37. Heckerman, D.: A tutorial on learning with Bayesian networks. In: Jordan, M.J. (ed.) Learning in Graphical Models. ASID, vol. 89, pp. 301–354. Springer, Dordrecht (1998). https://doi.org/10.1007/978-94-011-5014-9_11

I-mRMR: Incremental Max-Relevance, and Min-Redundancy Feature Selection

Yeliang Xiu[1], Suyun Zhao[1,2]($\boxtimes$), Hong Chen[1,2], and Cuiping Li[1,2]

[1] Information of School, Renmin University of China,
Beijing, People's Republic of China
zhao.suyun@yahoo.com, 2017104068@ruc.edu.cn
[2] Key Laboratory of Data Engineering and Knowledge Engineering,
Ministry of Education, Beijing, China
http://deke.ruc.edu.cn

Abstract. An incremental method of feature selection based on mutual information, called incremental Max-Relevance, and Min-Redundancy (I-mRMR), is presented. I-mRMR is an incremental version of Max-Relevance, and Min-Redundancy feature selection (mRMR), which is used to handle streaming data or large-scale data. First, Incremental Key Instance Set is proposed which composes of the non-distinguished instances by the historical selected features. Second, an incremental feature selection algorithm is designed in which the incremental key instance set, replacing of all the seen instances so far, is used in the process of adding representative features. Since the Incremental Key Instance Set is far less than the whole instances, the incremental feature selection by using this key set avoids redundant computation and save computation time and space. Finally, the experimental results show that I-mRMR could significantly or even dramatically reduce the time of feature selection with an acceptable classification accuracy.

Keywords: Feature selection · Incremental algorithm ·
Normalized mutual information · Min-Redundancy · Max-Relevance

1 Introduction

Incremental learning is a promising approach to refreshing data mining results, which utilizes previously saved results or data structures to avoid the expense of re-computation [4,13]. The main idea of incremental feature selection is that only part of the data are considered at one time and the results are subsequently combined. Thus incremental feature selection technique makes full use of the historical information, reduce the training scale greatly, and save training time [6,12].

Feature selection based on mutual information has been deeply studied [2, 10,11,14], because mutual information (MI) [8] is a good tool to measure the correlation and redundancy among features. As a pioneer, Battiti [1] proposed

© Springer Nature Switzerland AG 2019
J. Shao et al. (Eds.): APWeb-WAIM 2019, LNCS 11642, pp. 103–110, 2019.
https://doi.org/10.1007/978-3-030-26075-0_8

a greedy selection method called MIFS based on mutual information between inputs and outputs. Considering MIFS does not work well on nonlinear problems, Kwak and Choi [5] proposed an improved feature selection method MIFS-U which is feasible and effective on nonlinear applications. However, both Battiti and Kwak's methods omit the redundancy among features, only relevance among features and labels are considered. Peng et al. [7] then proposed a heuristic "Max-Relevance and Min-Redundancy" framework for feature selection. In [7] it is pointed that mRMR criterion is equal to max-dependency. Furthermore, Estévez and Tesmer [3] proposed an updated feature selection method, called normalized mutual information features selection. However, most of them could only be applied to static data. When new instances are arriving successively, these methods have to be re-computed on the updated datasets.

In this paper, we propose an incremental feature selection algorithm, called I-mRMR. First, Incremental Key Instance Set is proposed which is composed of the instances not distinguished by historical selected features. An incremental algorithm is then proposed based on this Incremental Key Instance Set. Finally, the numerical experiments of I-mRMR shows that I-mRMR makes full use of the historical selected features, reduce the training scale greatly, and save training time.

The remainders of this paper are organized as follows. Section 2 reviews mRMR based on the normalized mutual information. Section 3 introduces the concept of Incremental Key Instance Set and presents the incremental feature selection algorithm, I-mRMR. In Sect. 4, ten UCI datasets are employed to illustrate the effectiveness and efficiency of I-mRMR. Section 5 concludes this paper.

2   Preliminaries

In this section, MI and mRMR are reviewed. For more detailed information about them, please kindly refer to [9].

2.1   Notation Description

Given a set of original instances $U = [x^{(1)}, x^{(2)}, \cdots, x^{(n)}]^T$. Here $U \in R^{(n \times p)}$ is a matrix with n is the number of original instances and p is the number of all features. $x^{(i)} \in R^p$ is a row vector representing the i-th instance in U. S is the index set of selected feature subset. $\overline{S}$ denotes the complementary set of S. x_t is a column vector representing the t-th feature. $x_S^{(i)}$ represents a vector of $x^{(i)}$ under feature subset $S(i = 1, \cdots, n)$, $Y = [y^{(1)}, \cdots .y^{(n)}]^T$ is a column vector representing the label feature in U. Here $y^{(i)}$ is the label for the i-th instance in $U(i = 1, \cdots, n)$.

2.2   Max-Relevance and Min-Redundancy

Max-Relevance is to find the feature x_t that satisfies the following formula:

$$max_{t \in S} D(S), where \quad D = \frac{1}{|S|} \sum_{t \in S} I(Y; x_t) \tag{1}$$

By the Max-Relevance criterion, only the relevance between the features and labels are considered, whereas the relevance among the features is not considered. Thus there may exist great redundancy among the selected features. As a result, it is necessary to make the redundancy among the selected features as small as possible.

$$min_{t \in S} R(S), where \quad R = \frac{1}{|S|^2} \sum_{k,t \in S} I(x_k, x_t) \tag{2}$$

The above two criteria are combined, called "Max-Relevance and Min-Redundancy", and defined as follows.

$$max \ \Phi(D, R), \Phi = D - R \tag{3}$$

Suppose that the feature subset candidate we have selected so far is S_{m-1}, and $m-1$ indicates that $m-1$ features have been selected. And then the feature with the maximum value of $\Phi(D, R)$ is selected. The incremental feature selection algorithm optimizes the following formula:

$$max_{k \in F - S_{m-1}} [I(Y, x_k) - \frac{1}{|S_{m-1}|} \sum_{t \in S_{m-1}} I(x_k, x_t)] \tag{4}$$

2.3   Normalized Mutual Information Feature Selection

The normalized mutual information $NI(x_k, x_t)$ between the feature x_k and the feature x_t is then defined as follows.

$$NI(x_k, x_t) = \frac{I(x_k, x_t)}{min\{H(x_k), H(x_t)\}} \tag{5}$$

Therefore, "Max-Relevance and Min-Redundancy" criterion can be rewritten as follows:

$$max_k [I(Y, x_k) - \frac{1}{|S_{m-1}|} \sum_{t \in S_{m-1}} NI(x_k, x_t)] \tag{6}$$

3   The Proposed Incremental Algorithm

The key idea of our proposed method is to update and maintain the previously selected feature subset by finding the features more representative for discriminating the new instances from its current surrounding.

3.1   Problem Definition

When some new instances, represented by $\Delta U \in R^{m \times p}$ (where m represents the number of newly added instances), are added to U, $y^{(n+j)}$ is the label for the j-th instance in ΔU, $j = 1, \cdots, m$. The selected feature subset S has to be updated from U to $U \cup \Delta U$. The traditional method is directly to recompute the feature selection method on all seen instances $U \cup \Delta U$ to obtain the updated feature subset $S_{U \cup \Delta U}$. It is very time and space consuming and many redundant computations are conducted. Therefore, it is necessary to reduce the amount of computation by using some incremental mechanisms.

3.2   Incremental Key Instance Set

To incrementally update the selected feature subset S, it is necessary to find the features more representative for discriminating the new instances from its current surrounding.

In the following we propose a concept called Incremental Key Instance Set which composes of part of the seen instances so far which are undistinguished by the original features subset S.

Definition 1. *Given U, S, and $\triangle U$, then Incremental Key Instance Set of S, denoted by $\triangle I_S$, is defined as follows.*

$$\triangle I_S = \{x^{(i)} \in U | \exists x^{(n+j)} \ s.t. \ x_S^{(i)} = x_S^{(n+j)}, y^{(i)} \neq y^{(n+j)}\} \cup$$
$$\{x^{(n+j)} \in \triangle U | \exists x^{(i)} \in U \ s.t. \ x_S^{(i)} = x_S^{(n+j)}, y^{(i)} \neq y^{(n+j)}\} \tag{7}$$

Incremental Key Instance Set $\triangle I_S$ composes of such instances which have the same feature values on S but the different labels, which means that the features in S could not distinguish the new instances from its current surrounding and then some new features should be added. $\triangle I_S$ plays the key role to find the new features.

A function that measures the significance of the feature according to the criterion of the "Max-Relevance and Min-Redundancy" is then proposed based on Increment Key Instance Set.

Definition 2. *Given U, Y, F and S, for every $k \in \overline{S}$ and $t \in S$, the significance degree of x_k with respect to Y and S is defined as follows.*

$$Sig(x_k, S, Y) = I(Y, x_k) - \frac{1}{|S|} \sum_{t \in S} NI(x_k, x_t) \tag{8}$$

Computing the significance degrees of $\overline{S}$ on $\triangle I_S$, all the features in $\overline{S}$ are then sorted. Thus the feature with the maximum distinguishing power, i.e. maximum significance degree, is added to S.

3.3   Incremental Feature Selection Algorithm

In this subsection, we present the incremental feature selection algorithm when a set of new instances arriving. I-mRMR is designed in Algorithm 1.

4   Numerical Experiments

In this section, we conduct some numerical experiments to evaluate the proposed algorithm, I-mRMR, on ten datasets from UCI. The Max-Relevance and Min-Redundancy feature selection based on normalized mutual information, denoted by mRMR [3], as the classical non-incremental feature selection algorithm, is compared with I-mRMR.

Algorithm 1: An incremental algorithm for feature selection based on Max-Relevance, and Min-Redundancy (I-mRMR)

Input: $U, F, Y, S, \triangle U, \overline{S}$.

Output: $S_{U \cup \triangle U}$ on $U \cup \triangle U$.

Step 1: Compute $\triangle I_S$.

Step 2: If $|\triangle I_S| = 0$, go to Step 6, else go to Step 4.

Step 3: Compute $I(Y; S), H(Y)$ on $\triangle I_S$.

If $I(Y; S) = H(Y)$, go to Step 6;

Else go to Step 4.

Step 4: While $I(Y; S) \neq H(Y)$ do.

{

For every $k \in \overline{S}$, compute $Sig(x_k, S, Y)$ on $\triangle I_S$;

Select $k^* = arg_k max\{Sig(x_k, S, Y)\}$;

$S \leftarrow S \cup \{k^*\}$, $\overline{S} \leftarrow \overline{S} - \{k^*\}$;

Update $I(Y; S)$ on $\triangle I_S$.

}

Step 5: $S_{U \cup \triangle U} \leftarrow S$.

Step 6: Return $S_{U \cup \triangle U}$.

4.1   Experimental Setup

All the experiments have been conducted on computer with CentOS release 6.5(Final), Westmere E56xx/L56xx/X56xx(Nehalem-C) and 8 GB memory. The programming language is Python. The detail experimental setting are presented as follows.

(1) Since our algorithm is only valid for discrete data, fuzzy-c-means is used to discretize those continuous data sets.

(2) Every dataset is divided into six parts equally, the first part is used as the original data set U, and remaining parts as the newly added dataset $\triangle U$, are added one by one.

(3) All the experimental comparison is demonstrated from three indices: running time, global speedup ratio, local speedup ratio.

Global speedup ratio: $\dfrac{\sum_{streaming\ instances} RT_{mRMR}}{\sum_{streaming\ instances} RT_{I-mRMR}}$

Where RT_{mRMR} denotes the running time of mRMR on the seen instances so far, RT_{I-mRMR} denotes the running time of I-mRMR on the seen instances so far. When the dataset is divided into six parts, $\sum_{streaming\ instances} RT_{mRMR}$ represents the sum of six times running time of mRMR, where each time the dataset is updated when some new instances arriving.

Local speedup ratio: $\dfrac{RT_{mRMR}}{RT_{I-mRMR}}$

When the dataset is divided into six parts, the local speedup ratio is the ratio of the running time of mRMR on the whole dataset to the running time of I-mRMR when the last part arriving.

(4) To show the effectiveness of I-mRMR, SVM and KNN are used to evaluate the classification performance. And 5-fold cross validation is used in classification evaluation.

4.2   Experimental: Evaluation on UCI

To test the performance of I-mRMR, some experimental comparison and analyses are conducted on ten UCI datasets.

Compared with mRMR. In this part, I-mRMR and mRMR are compared. Both of them are feature selection methods based on the normalized mutual information of "Max-Relevance and Min-Redundancy" criterion. One main difference between them is that I-mRMR is an incremental feature selection algorithm, whereas mRMR is a non-incremental feature selection algorithm.

we demonstrate the running time of I-mRMR and mRMR when instances successively arriving and then graph them in Fig. 1.

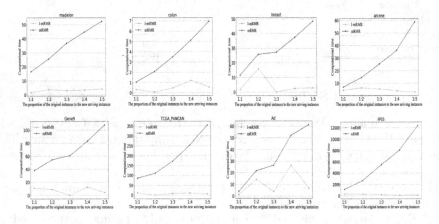

Fig. 1. The running time of I-mRMR and mRMR with instances successively arriving

Figure 1 clearly demonstrates that the running time of I-mRMR changes slightly, whereas the running time of mRMR increases significantly with the instances successively arriving. This shows that I-mRMR works efficiently on streaming instances, whereas mRMR works more and more less-efficiently.

To further illustrate the time superiority of I-mRMR, the global speedup ratio is then presented, seen in Table 1.

Table 1 shows that the total time of mRMR is obviously or even significantly higher than that of I-mRMR, especially on the datasets with high number of instances. This is because when some new instances arriving mRMR has to be recomputed on the whole seen instances so far, which is really time consuming. Furthermore, Table 2 demonstrates the time superiority of I-mRMR from the aspect of local speedup ratio. From Table 2 we observe that I-mRMR is significantly or even dramatically faster than mRMR. This is because I-mRMR only consider part of instances which are not distinguished by the previous selected features, whereas mRMR computes on the whole seen instances so far.

Table 1. The global speedup ratio of mRMR and I-mRMR

Dataset	mRMR	I-mRMR	Global speedup ratio
madelon	184.32 s	32.49 s	5.67
colon	19.08 s	3.79 s	5.03
breast	156.96 s	29.52 s	5.31
arcene	144.37 s	29.73 s	4.85
Gene9	377.17 s	69.47 s	5.43
TCGA_PANCAN	1026.37 s	121.77 s	8.42
Ad	168.14 s	58.17 s	2.89
FPS5	30092 s (8 h 21 m 32 s)	1654 s (27 m 34 s)	18.19
FPS7	35092 s (9 h 44 m 52 s)	4501 s (1 h 25 m 1 s)	7.79
Gisette	103161 s (28 h 39 m 21 s)	10801 s (3 h 1 s)	9.55
Average	17420 s (4 h 50 m 6 s)	1730 s (28 m 50 s)	7.31

Table 2. The local speedup ratio of mRMR and I-mRMR

Dataset	mRMR	I-mRMR	Local speedup ratio
madelon	57.92 s	4.23 s	13.69
colon	19.08 s	0.56	34.07
breast	48.53 s	3.02s	16.06
arcene	58.7 s	3.05 s	19.24
Gene9	107.9 s	4.25 s	25.38
TCGA_PANCAN	355.8 s	16.74 s	21.25
Ad	61.36 s	6.88 s	8.92
FPS5	12392 s (3 h 26 m 32 s)	119 s	104
FPS7	15690 s (4 h 21 m 30 s)	398 s	39.4
Gisettee	30991 s (8 h 36 m 31 s)	105.6 s	293.5
Average	5978 s (1 h 39 m 38 s)	66 s	57.5

5   Conclusions

In this paper, we propose an incremental feature selection algorithm I-mRMR based on max-relevance and min-redundancy criterion. When a new set of instances is arriving, not all seen instances so far are necessary to update the feature selection results. Actually, just an Incremental Key Instance Set, which is composed of the instances undistinguished by historical selected features, is key to update the feature subset. As a result, I-mRMR is designed by using Incremental Key Instance Set, which dramatically improve the efficiency of feature selection on streaming instances. By numerical experiments, we demonstrate that the proposed incremental algorithm is significantly faster than the classical algorithm mRMR not only in the global speedup ratio but also in the local speedup ratio. Furthermore, on the extremely high-dimensional dataset, we experimentally demonstrate that our proposed feature selection algorithm I-mRMR is obviously more efficient than mRMR with an acceptable classification accuracy.

Acknowledgements. This work is supported by National Key Research & Develop Plan (No. 2016YFB1000702, 2018YFB1004401), National Key R&D Program of China(2017YFB1400700), NSFC under the grant No. 61732006, 61532021, 61772536, 61772537, 61702522 and NSSFC (No. 12&ZD220), and the Fundamental Research Funds for the Central Universities, and the Research Funds of Renmin University of China (15XNLQ06). It was partially done when the authors worked in SA Center for Big Data Research in RUC. This Center is funded by a Chinese National 111 Project Attracting. This work is also supported by the Macao Science and Technology Development Fund (081/2015/A3).

References

1. Battiti, R.: Using mutual information for selecting features in supervised neural net learning. IEEE Trans. Neural Netw. **5**(4), 537–550 (1994)
2. Chandrashekar, G., Sahin, F.: A Survey on Feature Selection Methods. Pergamon Press, Inc., Oxford (2014)
3. Estévez, P.A., Tesmer, M., Perez, C.A., Zurada, J.M.: Normalized mutual information feature selection. IEEE Trans. Neural Netw. **20**(2), 189–201 (2009)
4. Guyon, I., Elisseeff, A., Kaelbling, L.P.: An introduction to variable and feature selection. J. Mach. Learn. Res. **3**(6), 1157–1182 (2003)
5. Kwak, N., Choi, C.H.: Input feature selection for classification problems. IEEE Trans. Neural Netw. **13**(1), 143 (2002)
6. Liu, H., Setiono, R.: Incremental feature selection. Appl. Intell. **9**(3), 217–230 (1998). https://doi.org/10.1023/A:1008363719778
7. Peng, H., Long, F., Ding, C.: Feature selection based on mutual information: criteria of max-dependency, max-relevance, and min-redundancy. IEEE Trans. Pattern Anal. Mach. Intell. **27**(8), 1226–1238 (2005)
8. Rossi, F., Lendasse, A., François, D., Wertz, V., Verleysen, M.: Mutual information for the selection of relevant variables in spectrometric nonlinear modelling. Chemom. Intell. Lab. Syst. **80**(2), 215–226 (2006)
9. Schilling, D.L.: Elements of Information Theory. Wiley, Hoboken (2003)
10. Sluga, D., Lotrič, U.: Quadratic mutual information feature selection. Entropy **19**(4), 157 (2017)
11. Vergara, J.R., Estévez, P.A.: A review of feature selection methods based on mutual information. Neural Comput. Appl. **24**(1), 175–186 (2014)
12. Xu, J., Xu, C., Zou, B., Tang, Y.Y., Peng, J., You, X.: New incremental learning algorithm with support vector machines. IEEE Trans. Syst. Man Cybern. Syst. **PP**(99), 1–12 (2018)
13. Ye, J., Li, Q., Xiong, H., Park, H., Janardan, R., Kumar, V.: IDR/QR: an incremental dimension reduction algorithm via QR decomposition. IEEE Trans. Knowl. Data Eng. **17**(9), 1208–1222 (2005)
14. Zhang, Z., Hancock, E.R.: Mutual information criteria for feature selection. In: Pelillo, M., Hancock, E.R. (eds.) SIMBAD 2011. LNCS, vol. 7005, pp. 235–249. Springer, Heidelberg (2011). https://doi.org/10.1007/978-3-642-24471-1_17

ST-DCN: A Spatial-Temporal Densely Connected Networks for Crowd Flow Prediction

Longlong Xu, Xiansheng Chen, Yue Xu, Wei Chen(✉), and Tengjiao Wang

Key Lab of High Confidence Software Technologies (MOE), School of EECS,
Peking University, Beijing 100871, China
{xllsniper,alexchan,xuyueyue,pekingchenwei,tjwang}@pku.edu.cn

Abstract. The accurate prediction of crowd flow is of great significance
for urban traffic management and public safety. Its key challenge lies
in how to model the complex non-linear spatial-temporal dependencies
and other external factors such as holidays and weather conditions. In
this paper, we propose a novel deep-learning-based approach to address
this problem, called Spatial-Temporal Densely Connected Networks (ST-
DCN), which is able to predict both inflow and outflow of crowds in
every region of a city. Specifically, ST-DCN consists of three parts: spatial module, temporal module and external module. The spatial module
is designed with a densely connected convolutional structure to capture
the spatial dependencies at a citywide level. The temporal module is
composed of ConvLSTM units to learn long-term temporal dependencies. We propose an external module consisting of fully connected layers
for modeling the external factors. Then the outputs of these three modules are merged to predict the final crowd flow in each region. ST-DCN
can alleviate the vanishing-gradient problem and strengthen the propagation of spatial features in very deep network. In addition, the spatial
features structure can be maintained throughout the network to avoid
losing implied spatial information of crowd flow. Experimental results on
two real-world datasets demonstrate that ST-DCN achieves significant
improvements over the state-of-the-art methods.

Keywords: Spatial-Temporal · Densely connected · ConvLSTM ·
Crowd flow prediction

1 Introduction

Crowd flow prediction is of great significance for urban traffic management and
public safety. With the advent of big data and mobile internet era, smartphones
and other devices with GPS equipment are gaining increasing popularity. These
devices can be considered as distributed sensors to track the crowd flow, making
it possible to research the patterns of crowd flow at a citywide level. An accurate
prediction of crowd flow is considered to be a great challenge since crowd flow has

© Springer Nature Switzerland AG 2019
J. Shao et al. (Eds.): APWeb-WAIM 2019, LNCS 11642, pp. 111–118, 2019.
https://doi.org/10.1007/978-3-030-26075-0_9

complex non-linear spatial-temporal dependencies and can be affected by various external factors (e.g., holidays, weather conditions and accidents) [12,13].

Classical linear time-series prediction methods such as Auto-Regressive Integrated Moving Average (ARIMA) and its variants are widely used in traffic prediction problem [4,6]. In addition, several researchers have also proposed support vector regression (SVR) model [2] and Kalman filter model [1], etc. However, these methods still fail to capture the complex non-linear spatial-temporal dependencies, and cannot be applied in a large-scale traffic network.

Recently, the success of deep learning for modeling complex non-linearities motivates researchers to apply deep learning techniques on traffic prediction problems. Previous work usually applied Convolutional Neural Network (CNN) to model the spatial dependencies [9]. To model the temporal dependencies, researchers proposed to use Long Short-Term Memory (LSTM) network [11]. Recent studies further combine CNN with LSTM to jointly model both spatial and temporal dependencies [5,10]. However, most of these studies only focus on single or multiple road segments, rather than citywide ones. The state-of-the-art approach [12] designs a CNN-based frame work named ST-ResNet for citywide crowd flow prediction. However, this method simply feeds the flow frames of historical timestamps into different CNN channels to deal with the temporal cues, which is not effective for modeling temporal dependencies.

In this paper, we propose Spatial-Temporal Densely Connected Networks (ST-DCN), a novel deep-learning-based model for citywide crowd flow prediction. In order to capture the spatial dependencies at a citywide level, we design a spatial module which contains shorter connections between each convolutional unit and between each convolutional block. Such structure can alleviate the vanishing-gradient problem and strengthen the propagation of spatial features in very deep network. Specifically, the feature dimensions of spatial module remain constant as the depth of the network increases, so that it can substantially reduce the number of parameters. Then we use Convolutional LSTM (ConvLSTM) [7] units to build the temporal module for learning long-term temporal dependencies, which can maintain the spatial features structure throughout the network to avoid losing implied spatial information of crowd flow. In addition, for modeling the external factors, we further build an external module which consists of fully connected layers. Finally, the external features are fused with the spatial-temporal features to predict the final crowd flow in each and every region of a city.

We evaluate our proposed method on two real-world datasets: taxi trajectory data of Beijing (TaxiBJ) and bike trajectory data of New York City (BikeNYC). Experimental results demonstrate that our proposed method achieves significant improvements over the state-of-the-art methods.

The remainder of this paper is organized as follows. In Sect. 2, the details of our proposed model are described. Section 3 presents the experimental results. Finally, we conclude this paper in Sect. 4.

2   Proposed Model

In this section, we elaborate the details of our proposed Spatial-Temporal Densely Connected Networks (ST-DCN). Figure 1 presents the architecture of ST-DCN.

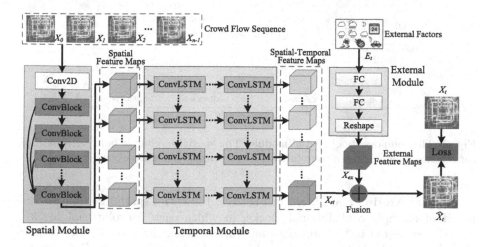

Fig. 1. ST-DCN architecture

2.1   Spatial Module

In order to capture the spatial dependencies at a citywide level, it is necessary to create a deep CNN network [12]. However, too deep network structure is susceptible to the problem of vanishing-gradient and difficult training. To alleviate these problems, we propose a spatial module with densely connected convolutional structure, which can provide implicit deep supervision and improve the information flow between layers.

Convolutional Unit. A convolutional unit consists of two combinations of "ReLU + 2D Convolution", which are connected by a SpatialDropout2D [8] layer, as shown in Fig. 2(a). SpatialDropout2D can randomly drop entire 2D feature maps with a certain probability to prevent overfitting.

Convolutional Block. As shown in Fig. 2(b), a convolutional block consists of multiple convolutional units. Each convolutional unit connects to every other one within a convolutional block, which forms a densely connected network structure. Then the lth unit receives the feature maps of all preceding units (i.e., $[U_{l-1}, U_{l-2}, \ldots, U_0]$) as input:

$$U_l = H_l([U_{l-1} + U_{l-2} + \cdots + U_0]; \theta^l) \tag{1}$$

where $[U_{l-1} + U_{l-2} + \cdots + U_0]$ refers to the summation of the feature maps produced in convolutional unit $l-1, l-2\ldots, 0$. Function H_l is defined as two combinations of "ReLU + 2D Convolution", which connected by a SpatialDropout2D layer. θ^l are all learnable parameters in the lth layer.

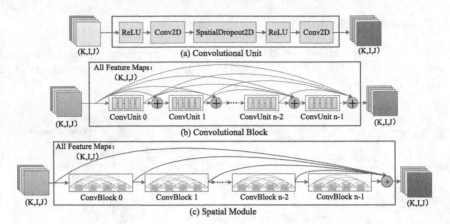

Fig. 2. The components of spatial module. The spatial module is built with multiple convolutional blocks, and a convolutional block consists of multiple convolutional units.

Spatial Module. As shown in Fig. 2(c), the entire spatial module is composed of multiple convolutional blocks, in which each convolutional block is directly connected to the previous one. Furthermore, there are shorter connections between the last convolutional block and all previous ones. For a spatial module with n convolutional blocks, where each convolutional block contains l convolutional units, the output of the spatial module is defined as:

$$E_{sp} = [B_{n-1}^l + B_{n-2}^l + \cdots + B_0^l; n \times \theta^l] \tag{2}$$

where B_i^l is the output of the ith convolutional block (with l convolutional units), $[\cdot]$ is the feature maps summation operation, $n \times \theta^l$ are the learnable parameters in the spatial module (with n convolutional blocks).

2.2 Temporal Module

Different from traditional LSTM, recent work [7] proposed a variant LSTM called convolutional LSTM (ConvLSTM), which is characterized by using convolutions to replace the inner products:

$$
\begin{aligned}
i_t &= \sigma(W_{xi} * X_t + W_{hi} * H_{t-1} + b_i) \\
f_t &= \sigma(W_{xf} * X_t + W_{hf} * H_{t-1} + b_f) \\
o_t &= \sigma(W_{xo} * X_t + W_{ho} * H_{t-1} + b_o) \\
C_t &= f_t \circ C_{t-1} + i_t \circ tanh(W_{xc} * X_t + W_{hc} * H_{t-1} + b_c) \\
H_t &= o_t \circ tanh(C_t)
\end{aligned}
\tag{3}
$$

where X_t is the input at time t, σ is sigmoid function. i_t, f_t, o_t, C_t, H_t are input gate, forget gate, output gate, cell output, hidden state at time t, respectively. Additionally, $\circ$ is the Hadamard product and $*$ denotes the convolution operator. Filter matrices W_* and bias vectors b_* are parameters to be learned.

The key difference is that $*$ is now a convolution, while in a traditional LSTM, it is a matrix multiplication. Therefor, all inputs, cell outputs and hidden states are 3D tensors, which can preserve the spatial features properties.

As shown in the middle part of Fig. 1, the temporal module consists of multiple layers of ConvLSTM, the input is a sequence of crowd flow spatial features produced from the spatial module, and the output is X_{st}, which contains information of both spatial and temporal dependencies of crowd flow.

2.3   External Module

Previous work [12] has explained that crowd flow can be affected by many complex external factors, such as weather conditions and traffic accidents. As illustrated in the top-right part of Fig. 1, the external module contains two fully-connected (FC) layers. We first encode all external factors to a 1D tensor E_t, and feed it into the first FC layer to extract external information. Then, another FC layer is used to map low to high dimensions that have the shape of ($channels \times rows \times cols$). We further reshape the feature into a 3D tensor X_{ex} with the dimensions of ($channels, rows, cols$), which are the same as X_{st}.

2.4   Fusion

Inspired by the fact that spatial-temporal dependencies and external factors affect the prediction in different degrees, we use the parameter-matrix-based fusion method to merge the outputs of temporal module X_{st} and external module X_{ex}. At the tth time interval, the final prediction $\widehat{X}_t$ is defined as:

$$\widehat{X}_t = tanh(W_{st} \circ X_{st} + W_{ex} \circ X_{ex}) \tag{4}$$

where $\circ$ is element-wise multiplication, W_{st} and W_{ex} are the learnable parameters.

In order to jointly train our proposed model, we adopt mean squared error between the predicted flow matrix $\widehat{X}_t$ and the true flow matrix X_t in t^{th} time interval as the loss function.

3   Experiments

In this section, we conduct experiments on two public datasets and analyze the effects of different factors on the performance of our model.

3.1   Datasets and Evaluation Metric

We use two real-world datasets to evaluate our model. TaxiBJ [12] dataset consists of taxi trajectory data and external factors data (i.e., temperature, wind, weather and holidays) of Beijing from 1st Jul. 2013 to 10th Apr. 2016. We choose data from the last four weeks as the testing data. BikeNYC [12] dataset is generated with the New York City bicycle trajectory data from 1st Apr. 2014 to 30th Sept. 2014. The data of the last 10 days are chosen to be the testing data.

We use Root Mean Square Error (RMSE) to evaluate our model. Note that a lower value of RMSE means a better performance.

3.2 Experimental Setup

In our experiments, the convolutions use 32 filters of size 3×3. The batch size is set to 16. The dropout is 0.3, and the learning rate is 0.0001. The sequence length is set to 7. We optimize our network parameters in an end-to-end manner via Adam [3] optimization. We use Keras and Tensorflow to implement our proposed model. All experiments are run on two NVIDIA GTX1080Ti GPUs.

3.3 Experimental Results

Table 1 shows the performance of our proposed model and other baselines on TaxiBJ and BikeNYC datasets.

Table 1. Quantitative comparisons (RMSE) of different methods on TaxiBJ and BikeNYC datasets (smaller is better)

Model		TaxiBJ	BikeNYC
ARIMA		22.78	10.07
VAR		22.88	9.92
ST-LSTM		19.41	7.92
ST-CNN		18.17	7.23
ConvLSTM [7]		17.27	7.03
CNN-ConvLSTM		17.12	6.95
DeepST [13]		18.18	7.43
ST-ResNet [12]		16.69	6.33
	ST-DCN (ours)		
B6-C1	6 ConvBlocks + 1 ConvLSTM layer	15.71	5.89
B6-C2	6 ConvBlocks + 2 ConvLSTM layers	15.68	5.83
B12-C1	12 ConvBlocks + 1 ConvLSTM layer	15.58	5.72
B12-C2	12 ConvBlocks + 2 ConvLSTM layers	**15.40**	**5.61**
C2-noSpatial	without spatial module	16.13	6.12
B12-noTemporal	without temporal module	15.92	6.03
B12-C2-noExternal	without external module	15.51	5.69

Comparison with State-of-the-Art Methods. We first give the comparison with 8 other models on TaxiBJ and BikeNYC datasets, as shown in the

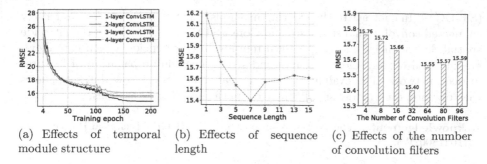

(a) Effects of temporal module structure
(b) Effects of sequence length
(c) Effects of the number of convolution filters

Fig. 3. RMSE with respect to temporal module structure, sequence length and the number of convolution filters on TaxiBJ dataset

upper part of Table 1. On TaxiBJ dataset, ST-DCN makes a great improvement in prediction accuracy. Compared with former best model, its RMSE decreased from 16.69 to 15.40, and achieves a relative improvement of 7.7%. On BikeNYC dataset, ST-DCN also achieves the best performance.

Comparison with Variants of Our Proposed Method. We also compare 7 variants of ST-DCN with different layers and modules on both datasets, as shown in the lower part of Table 1. We can see that ST-DCN with more convolutional blocks and ConvLSTM layers can usually achieve a lower RMSE, and the model with 12 convolutional blocks and 2 ConvLSTM layers (i.e., B12-C2) achieves the best performance.

Effects of Temporal Module Structure. As shown in Fig. 3(a), as the number of ConvLSTM layers increases, the training RMSE of our model decreases, which may be because more recurrent layers have better ability to capture long-term temporal dependencies of crowd flow.

Effects of Sequence Length. As shown in Fig. 3(b), as the sequence length increases, the RMSE shows an overall decreasing trend. However, as the sequence length continues to increase, the performance slightly degrades. One potential reason is that when considering longer sequence length, more parameters need to be learned, making training more difficult.

Effects of the Number of Convolution Filters. As shown in Fig. 3(c), the RMSE continues to decrease as the number of convolution filters increases from 4 to 32. This may be due to the fact that more convolution filters can lead to better modeling capabilities. Furthermore, the RMSE increases slightly as the number increases to 96. This may be because as the number continues to increase, the model will be too complicated, making it more difficult to optimize.

4   Conclusion

In this paper, we study the problem of citywide crowd flow prediction. To incorporate various factors that affect the crowd flow, we propose a novel deep-learning-based model named Spatial-Temporal Densely Connected Networks

(ST-DCN). In contrast to the existing methods, our ST-DCN employs a densely connected convolutional structure and ConvLSTM units to capture the citywide spatial dependencies and longer-term temporal dependencies, which can alleviate the vanishing-gradient problem and strengthen the propagation of features in deep network. The evaluation on two real-world crowd flow datasets shows that our proposed model significantly outperforms all the baselines.

Acknowledgements. The work was supported by State Grid Technical Project (No. 52110418002W).

References

1. Guo, J., Huang, W., Williams, B.M.: Adaptive Kalman filter approach for stochastic short-term traffic flow rate prediction and uncertainty quantification. Transp. Res. Part C: Emerg. Technol. **43**, 50–64 (2014)
2. Hong, W.C.: Application of seasonal SVR with chaotic immune algorithm in traffic flow forecasting. Neural Comput. Appl. **21**(3), 583–593 (2012)
3. Kingma, D.P., Ba, J.: Adam: a method for stochastic optimization. arXiv preprint arXiv:1412.6980 (2014)
4. Lippi, M., Bertini, M., Frasconi, P.: Short-term traffic flow forecasting: an experimental comparison of time-series analysis and supervised learning. IEEE Trans. Intell. Transp. Syst. **14**(2), 871–882 (2013)
5. Lv, Z., Xu, J., Zheng, K., Yin, H., Zhao, P., Zhou, X.: LC-RNN: a deep learning model for traffic speed prediction. In: IJCAI, pp. 3470–3476 (2018)
6. Pan, B., Demiryurek, U., Shahabi, C.: Utilizing real-world transportation data for accurate traffic prediction. In: 2012 IEEE 12th International Conference on Data Mining (ICDM), pp. 595–604. IEEE (2012)
7. Shi, X., Chen, Z., Wang, H., Woo, W.C.: Convolutional LSTM network: a machine learning approach for precipitation nowcasting. In: International Conference on Neural Information Processing Systems, pp. 802–810 (2015)
8. Tompson, J., Goroshin, R., Jain, A., LeCun, Y., Bregler, C.: Efficient object localization using convolutional networks. In: Proceedings of the IEEE Conference on Computer Vision and Pattern Recognition, pp. 648–656 (2015)
9. Xu, Z., Wang, Y., Long, M., Wang, J., KLiss, M.: PredCNN: predictive learning with cascade convolutions. In: IJCAI, pp. 2940–2947 (2018)
10. Yao, H., et al.: Deep multi-view spatial-temporal network for taxi demand prediction. In: Thirty-Second AAAI Conference on Artificial Intelligence (2018)
11. Yu, R., Li, Y., Shahabi, C., Demiryurek, U., Liu, Y.: Deep learning: a generic approach for extreme condition traffic forecasting. In: Proceedings of the 2017 SIAM International Conference on Data Mining, pp. 777–785. SIAM (2017)
12. Zhang, J., Zheng, Y., Qi, D.: Deep spatio-temporal residual networks for citywide crowd flows prediction. In: AAAI, pp. 1655–1661 (2017)
13. Zhang, J., Zheng, Y., Qi, D., Li, R., Yi, X.: DNN-based prediction model for spatio-temporal data. In: Proceedings of the 24th ACM SIGSPATIAL International Conference on Advances in Geographic Information Systems, p. 92. ACM (2016)

Recommender Systems

Streaming Recommendation Algorithm with User Interest Drift Analysis

Jianzong Chen, Hanlu Li, Qing Xie$^{(\boxtimes)}$, Lin Li, and Yongjian Liu

School of Computer Sceince and Technology, Wuhan University of Technology,
Wuhan 430070, China
{chenjianzong,zoelihanlu,felixxq,cathylilin,liuyj}@whut.edu.cn

Abstract. Recommender system is an effective way to solve the problem of information overload, and remarkable progress has been achieved along with the research and applications in both academic and industrial communities. However, the scalability of the conventional recommendation algorithms has been challenged by the exponential growth of the resource data size, and the increasing time span of the data also raises new requirements on the time-awareness of the algorithm. Therefore, a dynamic recommendation model monitoring the user interest drift has become an important task for streaming recommender system. In this paper, an incremental matrix factorization model named streamGBMF is proposed which utilizes the genre information as the resource feature. The proposed model can be updated in real-time according to the streaming data. To achieve the online updating, two kinds of forgetting mechanism are embedded to analyze the users' current interest and preference accurately and timely. To evaluate the performance of our proposed model, the experiments are designed on the popular dataset MovieLens, and different algorithms are compared in streaming environment. The results show that our approach can effectively accelerate the model training process, and the recommendation performance can be improved by real-time user interest drift detection with proposed forgetting mechanisms.

Keywords: Recommender system · Interest drift · Streaming data · Incremental matrix factorization · Online learning

1 Introduction

In recent years, the rapid increasing of the scale and coverage of Internet has introduced the problem of information overload, and it is difficult for the users to discover the most desirable and valuable targets from the massive information

This work is partially supported by National Natural Science Foundation of China (Grant No. 61602353), Natural Science Foundation of Hubei Province (Grant No. 2017CFB505) and the Fundamental Research Funds for the Central Universities (WUT:2019III054GX).

© Springer Nature Switzerland AG 2019
J. Shao et al. (Eds.): APWeb-WAIM 2019, LNCS 11642, pp. 121–136, 2019.
https://doi.org/10.1007/978-3-030-26075-0_10

on the web. Accordingly, the personalized recommender systems are designed to address the information overload problem, and have been successfully applied in e-commerce, social network, movie and POI recommendation [25,26].

Generally, the resource recommendation is to predict the preference of a user on different resource items [1], and the prediction is usually derived from the historical records of the user, including the explicit user rating data and implicit user behavior data. Due to the scalability problem, the memory-based recommendation algorithms cannot handle the exponentially growing web data. Therefore, many model-based algorithms have been proposed to achieve satisfactory recommendation performance, such as matrix factorization model [10] and restricted Boltzmann machines [18].

However, in practical applications, the dramatically increased data volume has brought the following new challenges: (1) Data sparsity. As the explosive growth of the user and resource, the data sparsity problem is severe nowadays, e.g., many resources are purchased but unrated. The recommendation algorithm needs to adapt to the sparse data. (2) Long time span. The time span of the data in practical recommender systems may last for years. Commonly, the users' interest varies in different time period [6], so their preference may change a lot compared with before. Therefore, it is challenging to accurately detect the user interest drift.

Considering the problems and challenges above, we propose a new incremental recommendation model named stream Genre-Based Matrix Factorization (streamGBMF). It aims to adapt to the streaming environment of the practical applications, and capture the user interest drift in an incremental way, so as to estimate the user's current preference and provide accurate recommendations. Primely, we employ Enhanced SVD [7] approach to make prefilling of the sparse resource rating matrix, and design a prefilling approach with popularity penalty by analyzing the effect of the user activity and the resource popularity. Considering the common fitting problem of the conventional incremental matrix factorization models, we propose to extract the feature vectors of the resource items according to their genre information, which are usually annotated by domain experts and widely available in practical applications. During the incremental training process of matrix factorization, partial updating with user feature vector is proposed to avoid increasing the overall fitting error. To capture the user interest drift, many recommendation algorithms bring in the forgetting mechanism, but the users' long term preference or abnormal change are usually discarded. As a result, we propose two new forgetting mechanisms based on streamGBMF to overcome these problems, which are proven in the empirical evaluation.

The organization of this work is as follows: Sect. 2 summarizes some related works. After introducing the notations and the matrix prefilling technique in Sect. 3, we formally describe the streamGBMF model in details in Sect. 4. The empirical study is demonstrated in Sect. 5, and we conclude our work in Sect. 6.

2   Related Works

In this section, we will introduce the most relevant works in literature, and these works can be summarized into the following three topics: matrix prefilling, streaming recommender and user interest drift analysis.

2.1   Matrix Prefilling

Most of the matrix factorization based recommendation algorithms are affected by the high sparsity of resource rating data in practical applications. To address the problem, some research works adopt the matrix prefilling approach. Pan et al. [16] proposed a negative sampling approach to prefill the rating matrix for unobserved data, and the results showed that user-based sampling can achieve best performance. Sun et al. [20] prefilled the missing values of the rating matrix based on the baseline estimation of the users on resource items. Yin et al. [24] designed a social-temparal framework to alleviate the problem of data sparsity. Guan et al. [7] proposed Enhanced SVD (ESVD) algorithm, in which a partial sub-matrix composed by the most active users and popular resources was generated, and the missing values of the sub-matrix were filled by matrix factorization, and kept as prior knowledge for model training.

2.2   Streaming Recommender Systems

For recommender system, the user interactions and feedbacks can be treated as a series of streaming data observed continuously. Therefore, the streaming recommender systems have high requirements for the algorithms in terms of data IO, time and space complexity. Some memory-based streaming recommendation algorithms such as StreamRec [3] and TencenRec [9] propose to recalculate the similarity between the users or resource items according to the streaming data, and it causes the time-consuming online learning, which results in the problem of data overstock. As a result, Subbian et al. [19] proposed to reduce the data in memory by min-hash technique, and optimize the algorithm scalability. Compared to memory-based approaches, model-based algorithms are more popular due to their advantage in scalability. Models in literature [11,17] need to re-train the entire model according to the streaming data, which costs too much time for online updating. Huang et al. [8] designed an incremental matrix factorization to describe the change of implicit feature based on the assumption of linear transformation. However, the overall performance is affected by the sparsity of streaming data. More incremental models proposed to partially update the user or resource feature vectors to meet the online requirement [12,13], but due to the connectivity of user feature and resource feature, partial updating will result in the increase of overall fitting error. Xie et al. [23] proposed an interactive framework to make the dynamic recommendations, but they mainly focused on the recommendation efficiency.

2.3   User Interest Drift Analysis

The user interest will be influenced by the change of aesthetic standard and bursting events [14], and it is important for recommender systems to capture and adapt to these changes. The most straight approach is to "forget" the historical records, so many forgetting mechanisms are proposed in literature. Campos et al. [2] designed a sample selection method, in which a fixed time sliding window was defined. Only the data in the sliding window are considered during the model updating, so it cannot keep the users' long term preference. Ding et al. [6] proposed a sample weighting method, which assigned each data item an exponentially decaying weight according to the time cap. However, this method also ignores the users' long term preference information. To solve this problem, some historical information must be stored in the summarized way, and the "pool" concept was proposed in [5], in which the model kept the sampling of historical records. Wang et al. [22] designed a new Gaussian classification model, which sampled the most informative and useful data from the pool and streaming data. However, the model restricted the resource rating into binary data, and all unobserved data were treated as negative ones, which may introduce errors. Chang et al. [4] assumed that the user and resource feature vectors followed the Brownian motion, and designed a continuous Markov process for each feature vector. Unfortunately, this model has high time complexity. Sun et al. [20] pointed out that seldom people will rate the same resource item for a second time, so there is no sufficient information to determine whether a user keeps his interest in certain items. Considering this, they proposed to cluster the resource items to estimate the user's overall preference on certain resource category. But due to the data sparsity, some dissimilar items were categorized into one cluster, and it influenced the final recommendation results. Matuszyk et al. [14] proposed five different forgetting mechanisms for the incremental matrix factorization model, but the user interest drift cannot be accurately captured. Wang et al. [21] designed the augmented memories to improve model's capability of storing knowledge, and thus user's long-term preference can be preserved.

3   Preprocessing with Matrix Prefilling

In this section, we will introduce the basic notations employed in this paper, and the matrix prefilling process for the rating data. The important notations are listed as follows (Table 1).

The user rating matrix is essential for recommendation algorithm. However, most of the user rating data are sparse in practice. To reduce the sparsity of user rating matrix, we designed a matrix prefilling approach based on ESVD algorithm [7] to primely estimate the missing values of the rating matrix, before the recommendation model training. As demonstrated in Fig. 1, the ESVD algorithm selects the most active users and popular resource items to compose a partial rating sub-matrix, and the missing values of the sub-matrix can be filled by matrix factorization. Since the density of extracted sub-matrix is much higher

Table 1. Notation list

Symbol	Description
M, N, K	number of users, resource items and feature dimension
$U_u(t)$, $V_v(t)$	feature vector of user u and item v at time t respectively
C, c_{uv}	rating matrix after prefilling, and the prefilled rating of user u on item v
p_{uv}, α	popularity penalty in matrix prefilling and its ratio
$r_{uv}(t)$, $\hat{r}_{uv}(t)$	the observed rating and predicted rating of user u on item v at time t
$e_{uv}(t)$, $\hat{e}_{uv}(t)$	the observed emotion and predicted emotion of user u on item v at time t
$R_U(u)$, $R_V(v)$	set of all observed ratings of user u and item v
$R_U^{0:t}(u)$, $R_V^{0:t}(v)$	set of all observed ratings of user u and item v before time t respectively
K_v, I_k	set of genres assigned on item v, and set of items containing genre k
t_r	time stamp of the submission of rating r
$\tau(u)$, $\tau(u, k)$	the time stamp of the last rating of user u and that on genre k
T_{train}, $T_{predict}$	the decay factor in training process and prediction process

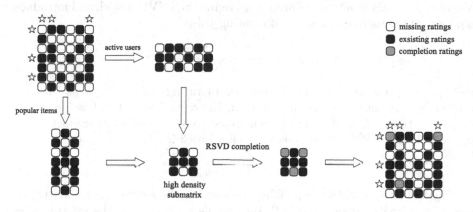

Fig. 1. The procedure of ESVD algorithm.

than the overall rating matrix, the ratings after prefilling can provide higher accuracy, so as to improve the recommendation model training.

To more clearly evaluate the quality of the prefilled ratings, we have conducted a prior experiment, in which the actual rating data are compared with the prefilling values under different sampling rates. We perform this empirical study on MovieLens 1M dataset, and the comparison results are listed in Table 2. Here the mean error (ME) is calculated by Eq. (1), where $Test \cap C$ means the intersection of testing set and the prefilled rating set, and c_{uv} and r_{uv} are the prefilled value and the actual rating value of user u on item v.

$$ME = mean[\sum\nolimits_{r_{uv} \in Test \cap C} (c_{uv} - r_{uv})]. \tag{1}$$

From the Table 2, we can observe that when the sampling rate of active users and popular movies is high, it will result in more filled ratings hitting the

Table 2. The prefilling quality of ESVD results on MovieLens 1M

Sampling rate	# of filled ratings	# of hits in testing set	Hitting rate	ME
5%	17702	1478	8.35%	0.1002
10%	109995	5682	5.17%	0.0524
15%	307727	12385	4.02%	0.0213
20%	629865	20097	3.19%	0.0008

ratings in testing set, but the overall hitting rate will drop dramatically. Lower sampling proportion will naturally cause higher density of the sub-matrix, but the mean error of prefilling will also increase, which means the prefilled ratings are higher than the actual ones. The reason is, for active movie audiences, they usually won't miss any popular movies suiting their tastes, so if they have no ratings on a popular movie, it is likely that they have no interest on this movie. Motivated by this intuition, we propose to refine the ESVD model, and introduce a popularity penalty on each prefilled rating value.

$$p_{uv} = \alpha \frac{|R_U(u)| \cdot |R_V(v)|}{MN}. \tag{2}$$

Here $|R_U(u)|$ and $|R_V(v)|$ are the number of ratings from user u and item v respectively. As indicated in this equation, the refined model will assign higher penalty to those prefilled ratings from more active users and popular movies, i.e., $p_{uv} \propto |R_U^{0:t}(u)| \cdot |R_V^{0:t}(v)|$. Therefore, the final prefilled values will be calculated by

$$c_{uv} = U_u^T V_v - p_{uv} \tag{3}$$

Finally, we can make the prefilling process on the extracted sub-matrix by the refined ESVD model, and both the prefilled ratings and the existing ones will be further applied in the recommendation model training procedure.

4   Design of Streaming Recommendation Algorithm

In this section, we will introduce our proposed streaming recommendation algorithm streamGBMF, and all the description will be demonstrated in the scenario of movie recommendation. The streaming data will be represented by the explicit user rating data, and time factor in our model will be treated as a variable $t \in \mathbb{R}_+$.

4.1   Baseline Estimate

Generally, the rating data are the explicit feedbacks of the user preference, but they are naturally affected by the different evaluation standards of individual users. For example, for a critical user, mark "3" may indicate a neutral comment, but for an easily satisfied user, it may reflect certain negative attitude. In order to eliminate the influence of different evaluation standards, we adopt the baseline estimate approach raised by Koren [10,11] to estimate the actual attitude of the user on specific items.

Formally, the baseline estimate of user u on item v can be defined as

$$b_{uv} = \mu + b_u + b_v, \tag{4}$$

where μ is the mean value of all observed ratings, and b_u and b_v represent the observed rating bias over μ for user u and item v respectively. Exemplified by a movie rating system, b_u reflects the average rating preference of user u and b_v is the overall popularity of movie v. Considering that the evaluation standards of individual users also change over time, the baseline estimate can be refined by involving time factor, and the definition can be revised as

$$b_{uv}(t) = \mu + b_u(t) + b_v(t). \tag{5}$$

Usually speaking, $b_v(t)$ is relatively stable, while $b_u(t)$ is more uncertain because of the users' instant behaviors.

Therefore, let $r_{uv}(t)$ be the observed rating of user u on item v at time t, and we can define the emotional preference of user u on item v based on his rating as

$$e_{uv}(t) = r_{uv}(t) - b_{uv}(t). \tag{6}$$

Obviously, when $e_{uv} > 0$, it represents the positive emotion of the user, i.e., user u likes item v.

The baseline estimate is essential to capture the user interest drift, because the model can more accurately learn the actual preference of the users after eliminating the evaluation standard difference between different users. Therefore, the baseline estimate values will be employed in the model training instead of the rating data.

4.2   User and Item Feature Training

With the refined rating matrix, we can apply the matrix factorization approach to derive the feature vectors of the users and resource items. This process will be performed in the offline manner. The conventional matrix factorization model works to solve the following loss function:

$$\text{loss} = \sum_{r_{uv} \in R} \left(r_{uv} - U_u^T V_v \right)^2 + \lambda(\|U_u\|^2 + \|V_v\|^2). \tag{7}$$

Here λ is regularization parameter to avoid over fitting in optimization, and the feature matrix can be derived by optimizing the loss function.

However, same as other implicit semantic models, the feature vectors derived from the matrix factorization model still has full connectivity in structure, which will result in the increasing fitting error during incremental model updating. At the same time, it is also contradictory to the common sense. For example, the genre of movie "Titanic" should be "Drama", "Romance" and "Adventure", but after an audience watching and rating it, his preference feature about "Comedy", "Animation" and "War" should not be influenced. However, with the fully connected feature structure, all feature values will be updated during the incremental model updating.

Inspired by the intuition above, we believe that the feature vector of each resource item should be relatively steady because of its nature. Every item is highly relevant with only several feature factors, and the feature value V_{vk} can reflect the importance of item v in all items with feature factor k. Therefore, we propose to construct the feature matrix of resource items according to the genre information of them. Considering the time factor, we have

$$V_{vk}(t) = \begin{cases} \dfrac{avg(r_V^{0:t}(v))}{mean\left[\sum_{j \in I_k} avg(r_V^{0:t}(j))\right]}, & v \in I_k \\ 0, & v \notin I_k \end{cases} \tag{8}$$

In practical applications, the genre information is usually annotated by the domain experts, and each item is assigned with at least one kind of genre. For example, the movies can be identified by "Drama" or "Action", and the songs can be described by "Pop" or "Rock". Furthermore, the use of these genre information will make the recommendation results more explicable.

By applying the genre information, the feature structure of the resource feature matrix in our model is no longer fully connected, so as to avoid the aforementioned fitting problem. After generating the resource feature matrix, we can also derive the user feature matrix by minimizing the loss function.

$$loss_U(u) = \sum_{r_{uv} \in R_U(u)} \left[e_{uv} - U_u^T V_v\right]^2 + \lambda \|U_u\|^2. \tag{9}$$

4.3   Model Evolution by Online Learning

When the recommender system receives a new rating data r_{uv}, the recommendation model needs to update the model parameters according to the rating data, so as to capture the instant interest and preference of the user. According to the assumptions in the offline training procedure, the feature vectors of the resource items are derived from their inherent attributes, and more stable than the user feature. Therefore, there is no need to update the resource feature as frequently as the user feature. As explained in Fig. 2, when the system receives a new rating r_{43} (marked as a green square), the model only updates the related user feature U_4, while the item feature V_3 keeps unchanged to avoid increasing the fitting error of r_{13} and r_{53}.

The conventional strategy of user feature updating follows the gradient descent method according to the real-time ratings, which is hard to control the learning rate. Different from the conventional strategy, streamGBMF takes all historical rating data of the target user into account for feature updating, i.e., when a new rating emotion data $e_{uv}(t_r)$ arrives, we have

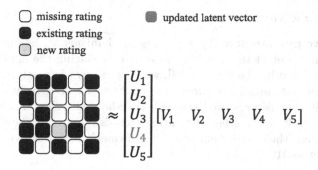

Fig. 2. The incremental updating strategy of streamGBMF.

$$\text{loss}_U(u) = \sum_{r_{uv} \in R_U^{0:t}(u)} [e_{uv}(t_r) - U_u^T V_v]^2 + \lambda \|U_u\|^2. \tag{10}$$

By Eq. (10), the model can effectively integrate the information of historical data and streaming data to update the user feature, so as to avoid the increasing fitting error of the user historical ratings. Moreover, when the difference of the new rating and the prediction is small, the optimization of loss function can converge efficiently. Even if the new rating delivers infrequent information, streamGBMF can still capture the information after several rounds of iteration.

As to the resource feature, our model will perform the regular updating periodically. We divide the time span equally into periods, and the resource feature is fixed in the same period. The scale of time division can adapt to the application scenarios, and in our study, we set the length of each time period as one day.

Considering the streaming dynamics, there will be new registered users and new created resource items continually. For each new user or new item, we need to extend the relevant matrix and initiate their feature vectors. Primely, we assume that the preference of the new user u follows the demography, and his feature vector can be initiated as

$$U_u(t) \sim N(mean(\sum_{i=0}^{M} U_i(t)), \sigma^2). \tag{11}$$

For the new resource item, we initiate its feature vector according to its genre information as follows

$$V_{vk}(t) \sim \begin{cases} N(1, \sigma^2), & v \in I_k \\ 0, & v \notin I_k \end{cases} \tag{12}$$

Here σ aims to control the distribution of the feature initialization of the users and items, and we set it as 0.1 by default in our experiments.

4.4 Forgetting Mechanisms

In this part, we will introduce the forgetting mechanisms applied in our model, which function to detect the user interest drift by reducing the influence of outdated data. Inspired by the work in [14], we propose two forgetting mechanisms based on outliers discarding and time-decay confidence respectively. However, for those users with few records, we have set a threshold and the forgetting mechanisms will not work on the users with rating records fewer than the threshold, so as to avoid losing their important interest information. In our experiment, the threshold is set as 10 by default.

Outliers Discarding. The outliers discarding approach aims to filter the outliers in the rating data. The motivation is, if the model prediction error for a certain rating is much higher than other ratings, it means this rating is inconsistent with the user's common preference, and we should mark it as a rating outlier. Thus the feature training procedure can be further optimized by removing the outliers.

In order to extract all the rating outliers of user u, we can calculate the standard deviation of the model prediction errors for all his ratings, and we mark it as $\mathrm{sd_U}(u)$. For rating r_{uv}, it will be marked as a rating outlier and removed if the condition holds:

$$|\hat{r}_{uv} - r_{uv}| > \beta \cdot \mathrm{sd_U}(u). \tag{13}$$

Here β is applied to control the sensitivity of the forgetting mechanism. Specially, to avoid the mis-dismissal of the information of user interest drift in the streaming data, we only remove the rating outliers in the historical data.

Time-Decay Confidence. The forgetting mechanism based on time-decay confidence will focus on the detection of user interest drift. We summarize the drift into the following two cases: (1) If a user expresses different preference for a genre of resource item at different time spots, how to determine the instant preference of the user on this genre of resource; (2) If a user has no feedback on a genre of resource item for a long time, how to determine the current preference of the user on this genre of resource.

For the first case, it is obvious that the most recent user expression is more important for the recommendation model, and the previous feedbacks should be treated as outdated information. During the model training process, for each rating r_{uv}, we assign it a weight according to the gap between t_r and $\tau_U(u,k)$:

$$w_{train}(r) = \exp\left\{\frac{mean[\sum\limits_{k \in K_v} t_r - \tau_U(u,k)]}{T_{train}}\right\}. \tag{14}$$

The value of $w_{train}(r)$ is limited in $(0,1]$, and the weight will decrease as the enlargement of time gap. The decay parameter T_{train} controls the influence of the outdated data on the model. To this end, we extend the loss function for user feature into:

$$\text{loss}_U(u) = \sum_{r_{uv} \in R_U^{0;t}(u)} w_{\text{train}}(r)[e_{uv}(t_r) - U_u(t)^T V_v(t)]^2 + \lambda \|U_u(t)\|^2. \quad (15)$$

For the second case, we will exemplify our solution by movie rating scenario. Assume a user u gave a high score to the movie "Titanic" years ago. Since "Titanic" is a movie with genre "Romance", the recommendation model will usually determine that this user favors romantic movies. However, he might watch "Titanic" only because of its high popularity and quality, but seldom watch other movies with genre "Romance". The contradiction is, if he really favors romantic movies, he should keep watching other romantic movies of high quality. Generally, a user will keep frequent interaction with those resource items of his interest, until he loses interest. On the contrary, he will avoid the interaction with uninterested items.

Based on the analysis above, we define a factor conf_{uk} to reflect the confidence on the k-th attribute of the user feature vector. If we can determine that the k-th attribute is not related with the user's long-term preference, we will decrease conf_{uk} to reduce its influence on the rating prediction, i.e.,

$$\hat{r}_{uv}(t) = [\text{conf}_{u1}U_{u1}(t), \text{conf}_{u2}U_{u2}(t), \dots, \text{conf}_{uK}U_{uK}(t)]V_v(t) + b_{uv}(t). \quad (16)$$

To verify the influence of time-decay confidence on positive and negative preferences, we have designed three strategies to make the comparison. In Strategy A we will make no decay; in Strategy B we will decay the influence of both positive and negative preference features; in Strategy C we will only decay the influence of positive preference features. The comparison is listed in Table 3. Here $w_{predict}(u, k)$ can be calculated by Eq. (17), and parameter $T_{predict}$ is employed to control the decay of confidence. The influence of different strategies will be demonstrated in the experiment.

$$w_{predict}(u, k) = \exp\left[\frac{\tau_U(u, k) - \tau_U(u)}{T_{predict}}\right]. \quad (17)$$

Table 3. The strategy of time-decay confidence setting

$U_{uk}(t)$	Strategy A	Strategy B	Strategy C
$\geqslant 0$	1	$w_{predict}(u, k)$	$w_{predict}(u, k)$
< 0	1	$w_{predict}(u, k)$	1

5 Experiments

In this section, we will introduce the empirical study to evaluate the effectiveness of our recommendation algorithm, and different forgetting mechanisms will be employed to test the model performance.

5.1 Experiment Setting

The experiments will be carried out on the well-known public movie rating dataset MovieLens 1M, which contains 1000209 rating data on 3952 movies from 6040 users during year 2000 to 2003. All rating scores are integer numbers from 1 to 5, and each user has contributed at least 20 ratings, and each movie has been annotated by at least one genre label.

To simulate the streaming environment, we order all the data by their time stamps, and divide the ordered data according to the following two settings.

- T8: In this setting, we select the first 80% data as the training data, and the remaining 20% data are testing set.
- T9: In this setting, we select the first 90% data as the training data, and the remaining 10% data are testing set.

Based on the settings above, some user records may only appear in the training set or testing set, which increases the difficulty of the prediction. However, this situation widely occurs in the practical applications.

5.2 Comparison Study Design

In our experiments, we will compare the proposed streamGBMF model with other representative time-aware algorithms, which are listed as follows.

- PMF [15]: Probabilistic Matrix Factorization, which is a probabilistic model based on Gaussian observation noise.
- DA-PMF [13]: Dual-Averaging Method for PMF, which updates the model parameters by embedding the streaming data feature during the online learning process.
- timeSVD [11]: a model with time factor which monitors the variety of user rating standard with time.

We apply the popular RMSE (root-mean-square error) to evaluate the performance of our model. For the convenience of comparison study, the common parameters in different models will be assigned the same value. Since there are 18 kinds of genre for the movies in MovieLens 1M dataset, we set the dimension of feature vectors $K = 18$. The parameter λ for regularization is set to 0.1 to avoid the over fitting during the optimization of the loss function. The learning rate is set to 0.01.

5.3 Experiment Results

Comparison Results. The overall comparison results are listed in Table 4. It shows that the proposed streamGBMF achieves the best performance under both T8 and T9 settings, which proves that the streamGBMF model can effectively detect the user interest drift, and improve the recommendation quality.

Table 4. Comparison of different algorithms (RMSE)

Setting	PMF	timeSVD	DA-PMF	streamGBMF
T8	0.997	0.933	0.924	**0.916**
T9	0.909	0.902	0.897	**0.880**

Effect of Prefilling. We also test the effect of matrix prefilling on the recommendation performance in terms of RMSE. Three different prefilling strategies are carried out to make the comparison, and the results are listed in Table 5. The result illustrates that the ESVD model can effectively decrease the data sparsity, so as to improve the recommendation performance. In addition, the ESVD with popularity penalty proposed in this work can further reduce the prediction error, which proves our statement about the relationship between active users and popular movies.

Table 5. The influence of matrix prefilling (RMSE)

Strategy of matrix prefilling	T8	T9
No prefilling	0.9174	0.8828
ESVD	0.9160	0.8811
ESVD with penalty	**0.9155**	**0.8804**

Effect of Forgetting Mechanisms. To evaluate the effect of our proposed forgetting mechanisms, we compare them with the Sensitivity-based Forgetting mechanism [14]. It works to calculate the influence of each new data record on the user feature. If the new record has changed the current user feature dramatically, it will be treated as an outlier and removed. In addition, we also include the results with no forgetting mechanism in the comparison, which are marked as "NoForgetting". As shown in Fig. 3, the effect of Sensitivity-based Forgetting is almost the same as that of "NoForgetting", which means the outlier removing will also lead to the missing of important information in streaming data. The result of "Outliers Discarding" is better than that of "Sensitivity-based Forgetting" because the former only removes the outliers in the historical data, while keeps the user interest drift information in recent streaming data. The "Time-decay Confidence" achieves the best results under both T8 and T9 settings, and it demonstrates that this mechanism can keep the user's long-term preference while capturing his interest drift.

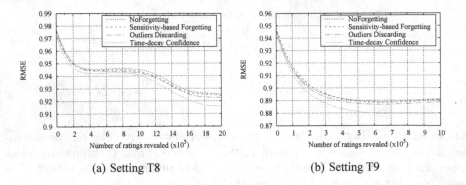

(a) Setting T8   (b) Setting T9

Fig. 3. Comparison of forgetting mechanisms under different settings.

Effect of T_{train}. T_{train} is the decay parameter in the training procedure, and the influence of the outdated data on the model will increase as it rises. Figure 4 records the performance of streamGBMF with different T_{train}. When $T_{train} = 700$, the model can achieve the best results.

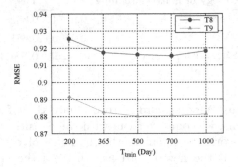

Fig. 4. The effect of T_{train}.

Effect of $T_{predict}$. $T_{predict}$ is the decay parameter in the prediction procedure, and its value reflects the confidence on the fidelity of user feature vectors. Figure 5 demonstrates the comparison of streamGBMF performance with different $T_{predict}$. The results show that, the aforementioned Strategy B is better than Strategy A and Strategy C, and when $T_{predict} = 60$, the model can gain the best results.

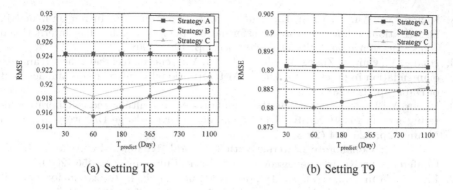

(a) Setting T8   (b) Setting T9

Fig. 5. Results of prediction strategies under different settings.

6   Conclusion

In this paper, we designed a streaming recommendation algorithm to capture the user interest drift, and make dynamic recommendations. We analyzed the relationship between prefilled ratings and user activity and resource popularity, and proposed a matrix prefilling approach with popularity penalty based on ESVD model. With the prefilled rating matrix, we proposed a new incremental matrix factorization model streamGBMF based on resource genre information. Two forgetting mechanisms were designed to reduce the influence of outdated data. The experiment results showed that our proposed approach can achieve better performance on real dataset in comparison study.

References

1. Adomavicius, G., Tuzhilin, A.: Toward the next generation of recommender systems: a survey of the state-of-the-art and possible extensions. IEEE Trans. Knowl. Data Eng. **17**(6), 734–749 (2005)
2. Campos, P.G., Diez, F., Cantador, I.: Time-aware recommender systems: a comprehensive survey and analysis of existing evaluation protocols. User Model. User-Adap. Inter. **24**(1), 67–119 (2014)
3. Chandramouli, B., Levandoski, J.J., Eldawy, A., Mokbel, M.F.: StreamRec: a real-time recommender system. In: The ACM International Conference on Management of Data, pp. 1243–1246 (2011)
4. Chang, S., et al.: Streaming recommender systems. In: The Web Conference, pp. 381–389 (2017)
5. Diazaviles, E., Drumond, L., Schmidtthieme, L., Nejdl, W.: Real-time top-n recommendation in social streams. In: The ACM Conference on Recommender Systems, pp. 59–66 (2012)
6. Ding, Y., Li, X.: Time weight collaborative filtering. In: The 14th ACM International Conference on Information and Knowledge Management, pp. 485–492 (2005)
7. Guan, X., Li, C.T., Guan, Y.: Matrix factorization with rating completion: an enhanced SVD model for collaborative filtering recommender systems. IEEE Access **5**, 27668–27678 (2017)

8. Huang, X., Wu, L., Chen, E., Zhu, H., Liu, Q., Wang, Y.: Incremental matrix factorization: a linear feature transformation perspective. In: The International Joint Conference on Artificial Intelligence, pp. 1901–1908 (2017)
9. Huang, Y., Cui, B., Zhang, W., Jiang, J., Xu, Y.: TencentRec: real-time stream recommendation in practice. In: The ACM International Conference on Management of Data, pp. 227–238 (2015)
10. Koren, Y.: Factorization meets the neighborhood: a multifaceted collaborative filtering model. In: ACM SIGKDD Conference on Knowledge Discovery and Data Mining, pp. 426–434 (2008)
11. Koren, Y.: Collaborative filtering with temporal dynamics. In: ACM SIGKDD Conference on Knowledge Discovery and Data Mining, pp. 447–456 (2009)
12. Lin, C., Wang, L., Tsai, K.: Hybrid real-time matrix factorization for implicit feedback recommendation systems. IEEE Access **6**, 21369–21380 (2018)
13. Ling, G., Yang, H., King, I., Lyu, M.R.: Online learning for collaborative filtering. In: The International Symposium on Neural Networks, pp. 1–8 (2012)
14. Matuszyk, P., Vinagre, J., Spiliopoulou, M., Jorge, A.M., Gama, J.: Forgetting techniques for stream-based matrix factorization in recommender systems. Knowl. Inf. Syst. **55**(2), 275–304 (2018)
15. Mnih, A., Salakhutdinov, R.: Probabilistic matrix factorization. In: The Neural Information Processing Systems Conference, pp. 1257–1264 (2007)
16. Pan, R., et al.: One-class collaborative filtering. In: The IEEE International Conference on Data Mining, pp. 502–511 (2008)
17. Rendle, S., Schmidtthieme, L.: Online-updating regularized kernel matrix factorization models for large-scale recommender systems. In: The ACM Conference on Recommender Systems, pp. 251–258 (2008)
18. Salakhutdinov, R., Mnih, A., Hinton, G.E.: Restricted Boltzmann machines for collaborative filtering. In: The International Conference on Machine Learning, pp. 791–798 (2007)
19. Subbian, K., Aggarwal, C.C., Hegde, K.: Recommendations for streaming data. In: The 25th ACM International Conference on Information and Knowledge Management, pp. 2185–2190 (2016)
20. Sun, B., Dong, L.: Dynamic model adaptive to user interest drift based on cluster and nearest neighbors. IEEE Access **5**, 1682–1691 (2017)
21. Wang, Q., Yin, H., Hu, Z., Lian, D., Wang, H., Huang, Z.: Neural memory streaming recommender networks with adversarial training. In: The 24th ACM SIGKDD Conference on Knowledge Discovery and Data Mining, pp. 2467–2475 (2018)
22. Wang, W., Yin, H., Huang, Z., Wang, Q., Du, X., Nguyen, Q.V.H.: Streaming ranking based recommender systems. In: The International ACM SIGIR Conference on Research and Development in Information Retrieval, pp. 525–534 (2018)
23. Xie, Q., Xiong, F., Han, T., Liu, Y., Li, L., Bao, Z.: Interactive resource recommendation algorithm based on tag information. World Wide Web - Internet Web Inf. Syst. **21**(6), 1655–1673 (2018)
24. Yin, H., Cui, B., Chen, L., Hu, Z., Zhou, X.: Dynamic user modeling in social media systems. ACM Trans. Inf. Syst. **33**(3), 10:1–10:44 (2015)
25. Yin, H., Cui, B., Zhou, X., Wang, W., Huang, Z., Sadiq, S.W.: Joint modeling of user check-in behaviors for real-time point-of-interest recommendation. ACM Trans. Inf. Syst. **35**(2), 11:1–11:44 (2016)
26. Yin, H., Zhou, X., Cui, B., Wang, H., Zheng, K., Nguyen, Q.V.H.: Adapting to user interest drift for poi recommendation. IEEE Trans. Knowl. Data Eng. **28**(10), 2566–2581 (2016)

Unified Group Recommendation Towards Multiple Criteria

Yi Wu, Ning Yang$^{(\boxtimes)}$, and Huanrui Luo

College of Computer Science, Sichuan University, Chengdu, China
wuyihyper.scu@gmail.com, yangning@scu.edu.cn, lolalolalola6363@gmail.com

Abstract. In online social networks, a growing number of people are willing to share their activities with ones who have common interests. This motivates the research on group recommendation, which focuses on the issue of recommending items to a group of users. The existing methods on addressing the problem of grouping users and making recommendations for the formed groups simultaneously, however, often suffer from two defects. The first one is that they separate group partition and group recommendation, which often reduce the overall group satisfaction. The second one is that they tend to pursue a single objective optimum instead of making a balance between multiple objectives.

In this paper, we strive to tackle the key problem of grouping users and making recommendations for the formed groups simultaneously. It is a challenging problem due to the differences between user preferences over items, and how to make a trade-off among their preferences for the recommended items is still the main research point. To address these challenges, we present a Unified Group Recommendation (UGR) model, which intertwines the user grouping and group recommendation in a unified multi-objective optimization process that makes a balance between multiple criteria, including maximizing overall group satisfaction, social relationship density, and overall group fairness. Extensive experiments on two real-world datasets verify the effectiveness of our method.

Keywords: Group partition · Group recommendation ·
Multi-objective optimization

1 Introduction

As more and more people participate in group activities, group recommendation has been playing an important role in online social services, which aims to recommend interesting items to groups of users [13,32,33]. To fulfill group recommendation, two issues have to be overcome, i.e., reasonably partitioning users into groups and setting up an appropriate objective function [24,25,27]. First, the previous work [23] proposes a new framework that first extracts common-interest

This work was supported by the Sci. & Tech. Support Programs of Sichuan Province under Grant 2019YFG0213.

© Springer Nature Switzerland AG 2019
J. Shao et al. (Eds.): APWeb-WAIM 2019, LNCS 11642, pp. 137–151, 2019.
https://doi.org/10.1007/978-3-030-26075-0_11

user subgroups and then generates a recommendation list for each subgroup. After that, the final group recommendation is produced by a novel aggregation function to integrate the recommendation lists of all subgroups. Second, the previous work [16] proposes a Hidden Hierarchical Matrix Factorization (HHMF) method, which learns the hidden hierarchical structure from historical ratings to improve the performance of recommendation, where the group partition based on latent topics is accomplished. Although a few of works on group recommendation have been proposed, the existing methods often suffer from two drawbacks [1,2,31]. First, the existing methods tend to separate the grouping of users from the recommendation, where the recommendations are often made separately after users are partitioned into groups. However, as will be shown later in this paper, the separation of user grouping and recommendation would likely degrade the quality of group recommendation. Second, the existing methods often pursue a single objective when a recommendation is made. In real-world, however, the overall quality of group recommendation arguably depends on a trade-off of group satisfaction [2,6], social closeness of group members [11,12,26], and fairness between group members [22,27,30]. For example, in tourism, considering only group satisfaction may result in a high score for an attraction which is highly liked by the majority of group members but disliked by the others due to their preference disagreement. Such unfairness recommendation may make some users dissatisfied and slighted and spoil their experience. At the same time, assigning tourists who are familiar with each other to the same group would likely bring more enjoyment.

In this paper, we investigate the problem of making group recommendations in the absence of user group information, where three objectives are pursued simultaneously: group satisfaction, social relationship density, and fairness between group members. This is not a trivial task due to the following two challenges.

- **Integrating Group Partition and Recommendation.** As the quality of group recommendation heavily depends on the grouping of users, it is desired to integrate grouping and recommendation instead of separately handling them. However, the problem of user grouping is NP-Hard [2], so it is challenging to design a unified process by which the grouping and recommendation can both reach an acceptable optimal result.
- **Balance between Multiple Criteria.** For our target problem, we need to make group recommendations with respect to multiple criteria including group satisfaction, social relationship density, and fairness. However, it is hard for a solution to satisfy all the objectives simultaneously due to the conflicts between them [9]. Hence we need an appropriate optimal model and an optimization algorithm by which rational group recommendations can be made with a balance between the multiple criteria.

To address these challenges, we propose a novel Unified Group Recommendation (UGR) model. The main idea of UGR is to intertwine the user grouping and group recommendation in a unified multi-objective optimization process. UGR simultaneously generates the optimal user grouping and recommendations with

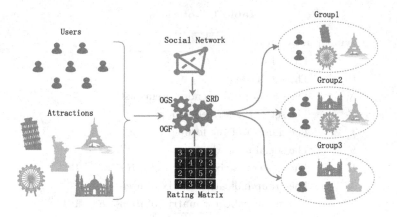

Fig. 1. Illustration of UGR

a fusion of historical ratings and the information extracted from social networks, where a trade-off between multiple criteria including Overall Group Satisfaction (OGS), Social Relationship Density (SRD), and Overall Group Fairness (OGF) is reached. Particularly, to fulfill the multi-objective optimization, we propose a novel alternate optimization algorithm which can facilitate the search of optimal solution via alternately adjusting the user memberships and recommendations at each iteration along the direction of increasing the objective function. Figure 1 shows an illustration of UGR, where tourists are partitioned into some non-overlapping groups and different packages of attractions are recommended to these groups.

The main contributions of this paper can be summarized as follows:

(1) We propose a Unified Group Recommendation (UGR) model that integrates the user grouping and group recommendation with a balance of multiple criteria.
(2) We propose a novel alternate optimization algorithm which facilitates the search of the optimal solution by alternately updating user grouping and recommendations.
(3) Extensive experiments conducted on real-world datasets verify that our approach is superior to the state-of-the-art methods.

In the rest of the paper, we review the related works in Sect. 2. We describe the detailed criteria of group satisfaction, social group density and fairness in Sect. 3. Section 3.2 introduces the problem formulation of group recommendation towards multiple criteria, and a novel alternate optimization algorithm is presented in Sect. 3.3. We analyze the experimental results in Sect. 4. We conclude in Sect. 5. Table 1 summarizes the notations used in this paper.

Table 1. Notations

Symbol	Description
U	The set of users
I	The set of items
K	The size of recommended items list
G	The set of the formed groups
T	The number of the formed groups
S	The social network
R	The rating matrix of user-item, $R \in \mathbb{R}^{|U| \times |I|}$
X	The group indicator matrix of users, $R \in \mathbb{R}^{|U| \times T}$
Y	The group indicator matrix of items, $R \in \mathbb{R}^{|I| \times T}$

2   Related Work

In this section, we briefly review the related work with our research, including collaborative filtering for groups and multi-objective optimization.

2.1   Collaborative Filtering for Groups

Many recommendation approaches are presented based on Collaborative Filtering (CF) [7,14,17,28] which is based on an assumption that a user may be interested in items liked by users who have similar preferences with her. In existing works [3–5], preference aggregation and score aggregation can be applied to group recommendation. When using the preference aggregation approach, preferences of individual users are aggregated into a group profile. Based on the group profile which can be treated as a pseudo user, collaborative filtering determines a ranking for each candidate item. When applying the score aggregation approach in combination with collaborative filtering, ratings can be determined for individual users and then aggregated into a final score for the group via a predefined aggregation strategy.

2.2   Multi-objective Optimization

Various approaches to multi-objective optimization have been proposed [10]. One key feature of multi-objective optimization is that there does not exist a solution that satisfies all the objectives simultaneously. Such problems are solved by a set of trade-off optimal solutions instead of a single optimum solution.

In personalized recommendation tasks, some existing methods [20,29,34] consider multiple objectives. In [34], multiple objectives including accuracy and diversity are considered simultaneously. [29] takes into account accuracy and long tail, and [20] regards spatial, temporal and social information as multiple objectives. They all aim to find a trade-off solution by optimizing a multi-objective function.

3 UGR

3.1 Multiple Criteria

Group Satisfaction. Intuitively, the group satisfaction is determined by the preferences of individuals within a group. The existing works have proposed several strategies to fuse the preferences of group members, such as Least Misery (LM), Maximum (MAX), and Average (AVG) [8]. For the sake of simplicity and convenience, we utilize AVG to aggregate the member preferences to evaluate the group satisfaction, which leads to the following definition:

Definition 1. *Group Satisfaction.* *Given the rating matrix R where R_{ui} represents the rating of item i given by user u, the Group Satisfaction of group g with a recommended item i (denoted as $Sat(g, i)$) is defined as*

$$Sat(g, i) = \frac{1}{|g|} \sum_{u \in g} R_{ui}, \tag{1}$$

where $|g|$ is the number of the members belonging to group g.

Since the historical rating data of users is extremely sparse, the missing entries need to be estimated. The existing works have proposed several effective approaches, such as MF [15], SVD [21], and PMF [19], which all serve our purpose. For convenience, we choose MF to infer the missing entries of a rating matrix.

Social Relationship Density. We propose the following metric called Social Relationship Density to evaluate the social closeness between group members with respect to an item. The higher relationship density of a group indicates that not only there are more friends in the group, but also they have higher collective preference to an item. Given the social network S where an edge $<u, v> \in S$ represents the friendship between users u and v, we can define the Social Relationship Density as follow:

Definition 2. *Social Relationship Density.* *The social relationship density of group g with respect to an item i is defined as*

$$SRD(g, i) = \frac{\sum_{\forall u, v \in g} (R_{ui} + R_{vi}) \mathbb{1}(<u, v> \in S)}{|g|(|g| - 1)}, \tag{2}$$

where $\mathbb{1}(x)$ is the indicator function whose value is 1 if x is true, otherwise 0.

Fairness. The fairness depicts how imbalanced the satisfaction of group members is. The existing work [30] presents several definitions of fairness in different forms, such as Least Misery Fairness, Variance Fairness, and Min-Max Ratio. Variance encourages the group members to achieve close satisfaction between each other, while Least Misery Fairness and Min-Max emphasise the gap between the least and highest satisfaction of group members. Despite the differences of the Fairness in definitions, the intuition of these metrics is to minimize the imbalance of the satisfaction of group members. In this paper, we introduce Variance Fairness [30] as follows:

Definition 3. *Fairness. The fairness of group g on item i is defined as*

$$F(g,i) = 1 - \frac{1}{|g|}\sum_{u\in g}\left|R_{ui} - \frac{1}{|g|}\sum_{v\in g}R_{vi}\right|. \tag{3}$$

The higher the function value, the higher the fairness within a group.

3.2   Optimization Framework

In this section, we formally introduce the optimization framework for the problem of group recommendation towards multiple criteria. We assign weights to each objective and use the weighted sum of different objective functions as a single objective for proximity:

$$
\begin{aligned}
J(X,Y) = &\alpha \sum_{g\in G}\sum_{u\in U}\sum_{i\in I} R_{ui}X_{ug}Y_{ig} \\
&+ \beta \sum_{g\in G}\sum_{u\in U}\sum_{i\in I} \frac{\sum_{v\in U}(R_{ui}+R_{vi})\mathbb{1}(<u,v> \in S)X_{ug}X_{vg}Y_{ig}}{\sum_{v\in U} X_{vg}(\sum_{v\in U} X_{vg}-1)} \\
&+ (\alpha+\beta-1)\sum_{g\in G}\sum_{u\in U}\sum_{i\in I}\left|R_{ui} - \frac{\sum_{v\in U} R_{vi}X_{vg}}{\sum_{v\in U} X_{vg}}\right|X_{ug}Y_{ig},
\end{aligned}
\tag{4}
$$

where three terms of the right side of the Eq. (4) represent the overall group satisfaction, social closeness, and fairness respectively; $X_{ug} \in \{0,1\}$ and $Y_{ig} \in \{0,1\}$ denote whether user u is assigned to group g and item i is recommended to group g.

Problem 1. Given a set of users U, items I, and the rating matrix R, we aim to divide all users into some non-overlapping groups and make recommendations for the formed groups so that the following objective function is maximized. The problem of the user grouping and recommendation can be formulated as follows:

$$
\begin{aligned}
&\arg\max_{X,Y} J(X,Y), \\
&s.t. \sum_{g\in G} X_{ug} = 1, \forall u \in U \\
&\qquad \sum_{i\in I} Y_{ig} = K, \forall g \in G \\
&\qquad X_{ug} \in \{0,1\}, \forall u \in U, g \in G \\
&\qquad Y_{ig} \in \{0,1\}, \forall i \in I, g \in G
\end{aligned}
\tag{5}
$$

Algorithm 1 *Alternate Optimization Algorithm*

Input:
    the user rating matrix R, the set of users U and items I, step size θ,
    the number of groups T, the size of recommended items list for each group K,
    the threshold ϵ, the maximum number of iterations L, parameters α, β.

Output:
    the group indicator matrix of users X, the group indicator matrix of items Y.

1: Initialize $X^{|U| \times T}$, $Y^{|I| \times T}$ with random values between 0 and 1;
2: Initialize $\mathcal{X}^{|U| \times T}$, $\mathcal{Y}^{|I| \times T}$ with random values between 0 and 1;
3: Set $l = 0$;
4: Calculate the initial value of objective function J^0 according to Equation (4);
5: Initialize $\Delta J^l = J^0$;
6: **while** $l < L$ and $\Delta J^l > \epsilon$ **do**
7:    **for** each user u **do**
8:       **for** each group g **do**
9:          Calculate the gradient $\partial_{X_{ug}} J$;
10:       **end for**
11:    **end for**
12:    $X = \min\left(\max\left(X + \theta * \partial_X J, 0\right), 1\right)$;
13:    **for** each group g **do**
14:       Calculate the top-K items for group g: $R(g, K)$;
15:       Assign them to $Y[:, g]$: $Y_{vg} = 1, \forall v \in R(g, K)$;
16:    **end for**
17:    $++l$;
18:    Calculate the l-th iteration of objective function J^l according to Equation (4);
19:    $\Delta J^l = J^l - J^{l-1}$;
20: **end while**
21: **for** each user u **do**
22:    Search the group index p of maximum value in $[X_{u1}, \cdots, X_{ut}]$;
23:    $\mathcal{X}_{up} = 1$;
24: **end for**
25: $X = \mathcal{X}$;
26: **for** each group g **do**
27:    Search the item indices $\mathcal{I}$ of top-K items in $[Y_{1g}, \cdots, Y_{kg}]$;
28:    $\mathcal{Y}_{ig} = 1, \forall i \in \mathcal{I}$;
29: **end for**
30: $Y = \mathcal{Y}$;

The main idea of the formula above is to repeat group partition process and group recommendation process until no user can get higher increase on the objective function by adjust the two processes.

3.3 Algorithm

In this section, we present an alternate optimization algorithm in Algorithm 1. Algorithm 1 gives the procedures of UGR, where a local optima of J is obtained through an iterative process of gradient descent. In detail, the initialization process is in the lines 1 to 5, followed by an alternate optimization process. First, we adjust user memberships according to the gradient. Second, the recommended packages are updated based on the current group partition. The two processed above are repeated until the objective function converges. Due to the entries of two optimized indicator matrices are non-integral value, we clarify the membership of users and the final recommendation results. For each user, she is assigned to the group corresponding to the maximum value. For each group, top-K items are chosen as recommendations.

Our proposed alternate optimization algorithm solves the constrained optimization problem. It first solves the problem with gradient descent and then maps the solution back into the feasible set if the solution is beyond the feasible set. In addition, the integer programming with discrete variables is usually NP-Hard and difficult to solve with an optimal solution. So, during optimization, we need to relax the binary constraint of integer variables to the range of 0 to 1.

4   Experiment

In this section, we conduct extensive experiments with the aim at answering the following two questions:

- **Q1** Does our proposed UGR method outperform the state-of-the-art group recommendation methods?
- **Q2** Is the multi-objective optimization helpful for improving the overall recommendation accuracy?

In what follows, we first present the experimental settings, and then describe the details of the experiments.

4.1   Experimental Settings

Dataset Description. Our experiments are conducted on two publicly accessible datasets: Filmtrust[1], CiaoDVD (See footnote 1). Figure 2 shows that the number of users follows a heavy-tailed distribution over the number of their rated items, which indicates the two datasets are nature. The characteristics of two datasets are summarized in Table 2. The ratings in CiaoDVD range from 1 to 5, and Filmtrust takes values from 0.5 to 4.

Table 2. The statistics of datasets

Dataset	#Users	#Items	#Interactions	#Trusts	#Density
Filmtrust	1508	2071	35497	1853	1.14%
CiaoDVD	17615	16121	72665	40133	0.03%

---

[1] https://www.librec.net/datasets.html.

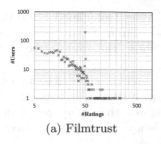

(a) Filmtrust

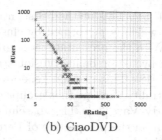

(b) CiaoDVD

Fig. 2. Overviews of datasets

Evaluation Metrics. To evaluate the performance of the group recommendation, we divide data into three parts, where 60% of the data are used for training, 20% of the data are used for validating, and 20% for testing. The performance of a ranking list is judged by $F1$ and *Normalized Discounted Cumulative Gain* (*NDCG*) [30].

Due to the conflict between precision and recall, we consider to reflect the overall performance of the recommendation by a single value. Therefore, we use $F1@K$ to evaluate our model:

$$Precision@K = \frac{\sum_{i=1}^{K} rel_i}{K}, Recall@K = \frac{\sum_{i=1}^{K} rel_i}{|y_u^{test}|}, \qquad (6)$$

$$F1@K = 2 \cdot \frac{Precision@K \cdot Recall@K}{Precision@K + Recall@K}, \qquad (7)$$

where $rel_i = 1$ if the item at rank i in the top-K recommendation list is in the test set, and 0 otherwise. y_u^{test} represents the items rated by user u in the test set.

However, $F1@K$ can not fully reflect the accuracy of recommendation because it does not take positions of hits in the ranking list into consideration. To address this problem, we adopt $NDCG@K$, which assigns higher scores to hits at top ranks:

$$DCG@K = \sum_{i=1}^{K} \frac{2^{rel_i} - 1}{log_2(i+1)}, NDCG@K = \frac{DCG@K}{IDCG@K} \qquad (8)$$

The notion $IDCG$ means the maximum DCG through ideal ranking list. For both metrics, larger values indicate better performance. In the evaluation, we compute both metrics for each user in the test set and report the average score. Without special mention, we set K to 10 for two metrics.

Baselines. To justify the effectiveness of our method, we compare it with six baselines:

GRSE [1]. This method first proposes a formal semantics which accounts for item relevance to a group and preference consensus among group members.

LGM [31]. This method first introduces latent factor model into the group partition which is performed by clustering user latent factor vectors generated by MF. With the presentations of group members, the group presentations are produced by the predefined fusion strategies.

CGF [18]. This method generates groups and recommendations using network centrality concept that groups of users with similar preferences.

Greedy-Var [30]. This baseline investigates the group recommendation problem from the perspective of Pareto Efficiency, which tries to maximize the group satisfaction and the fairness simultaneously.

UGR-F. This is a variant of our UGR model by removing the criterion of relationship density. UGR-F is used for demonstrating the improvements by fusing social information.

UGR-R. This is another variant of our UGR model by omitting the criterion of fairness, which is used to verify that considering fairness in group recommendation leads to better performance.

Hyper-Parameter Setting. For hyper-parameter tuning, we determine α and β in Eq. (4) by the grid search in the range of [0,1] with a fixed step size of 0.1 on the validation set. We observe that $F1@K$ and $NDCG@K$ over the both two real-world datasets achieve the maximum when $\alpha=0.7$ and $\beta=0.2$, therefore we choose the value 0.7, 0.2, and 0.1 as the weights of three criteria respectively in the following experiments. Without special mention following, the learning rate is set to 0.05.

4.2 Performance Comparison (Q1)

We first compare the recommendation performance of all methods on two real-world datasets with respect to both metrics, and then investigate the convergence of our methods.

Overall Comparison. We first compare the recommendation performance of all methods under different number of groups and then investigate the effect of package size on recommendation performance.

The performance comparison of all methods under different package sizes is presented in Fig. 3. The conclusions are threefold:

Firstly, our methods show significant improvements over other baselines. Specifically, both UGR-F and Greedy-Var take the satisfaction and fairness into consideration, but the improvement of UGR-F over Greedy-Var is significant. This verifies the effectiveness of integrating user grouping and recommendation into a same optimization process.

Secondly, compared to UGR-F and UGR-R, UGR obtains a relative improvement, which demonstrates that considering the fairness and relationship closeness within a group leads to better recommendation accuracy. It is an surprising discovery since fairness and relationship closeness are not directly related to recommendation accuracy. The reason is that fairness can alleviate the imbalance

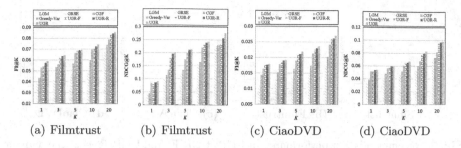

(a) Filmtrust   (b) Filmtrust   (c) CiaoDVD   (d) CiaoDVD

Fig. 3. Performance comparison of $F1@10$ and $NDCG@10$ *w.r.t* the package size on datasets of Filmtrust and CiaoDVD.

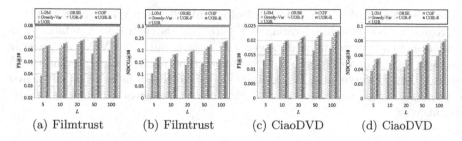

(a) Filmtrust   (b) Filmtrust   (c) CiaoDVD   (d) CiaoDVD

Fig. 4. Performance comparison of $F1@10$ and $NDCG@10$ *w.r.t* the number of formed groups on datasets of Filmtrust and CiaoDVD.

between satisfactions of users and the users who are less satisfied can get more items they like so that the overall recommendation accuracy increases. As such, considering assigning users with friendships or trusts to the same group also can make up for the imbalance between satisfactions of users. For example, an attraction with an amusement park intends to be chosen by a family with children because adults often make compromises for their children, which indicates that decision-making is influenced by relationships between group members.

Figure 4 shows the performance of all methods with respect to the number of formed groups via user grouping. From the two figures, we have following observations:

Firstly, our model UGR and its two simplified variants obtain better performance for group recommendation tasks. The reason is that the multi-objective optimization can effectively improve the recommendation accuracy and fusing user grouping and recommendation facilitates the search of optimal solution.

Secondly, as the number of formed groups increases, the recommendation accuracy keeps rising. The reason is that group members in a smaller group often have more decision-making power than those in a larger group, therefore the items chosen by the smaller group are more likely to satisfy their preferences. To see why the experimental results are reasonable, one can imagine that recommendation accuracy is optimal when all formed groups have only one user who needs to consider only her own tastes.

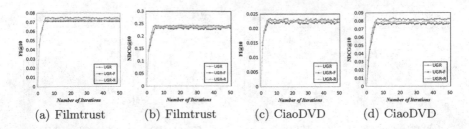

(a) Filmtrust	(b) Filmtrust	(c) CiaoDVD	(d) CiaoDVD

Fig. 5. Recommendation performance of UGR, UGR-F, and UGR-R *w.r.t* the number of iterations on Filmtrust and CiaoDVD

Convergence. In this part, we empirically study the convergence of our method UGR and its two simplified variants. Figure 5 shows the recommendation performance at each iteration on datasets of Filmtrust and CiaoDVD. First, we can see that, with more iterations, the recommendation performance gets improved. Second, they converge quite fast and the most effective updates occur in the first 5 iterations, which indicates the efficiency of our framework of multi-objective optimization.

4.3   Is the Multi-objective Optimization Helpful? (Q2)

The overall performance comparison shows that UGR obtains the best results on two typical metrics, demonstrating the effectiveness of the multi-objective optimization for the group recommendation tasks. To further understand and analyse the effectiveness of components of UGR in contributing to the improvements of recommendation accuracy, we perform some ablation studies.

Fairness Effectiveness Study. In this subsection, we investigate the effectiveness of fairness by controlling the weights on satisfaction and fairness.

Figure 6 shows the results of the simplified variant UGR-F. As α rises, both two metrics gradually get improved, while they slightly decrease when α is over 0.8. This indicates that fusing fairness leads to better performance, but maximizing fairness alone tends to decrease the performance of recommendation. For example, when we recommend commonly disliked items to a group, the fairness is high but the overall group satisfaction is low.

Relationship Closeness Effectiveness Study. UGR-R which removes the fairness effect is used to study the effectiveness of relationship closeness.

The results of the simplified variant UGR-R on two real-world datasets are presented in Fig. 7. The performance of UGR-R rises first and then decreases with the increase of the weight on relationship closeness. This reveals that relationship closeness has a positive impact on the performance of our model, while we do not obtain the best results when relationship closeness among group users is maximized alone.

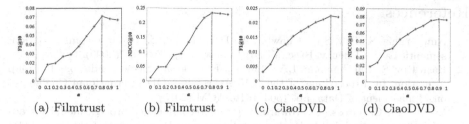

Fig. 6. Performance of UGR-F for each α on datasets of Filmtrust and CiaoDVD.

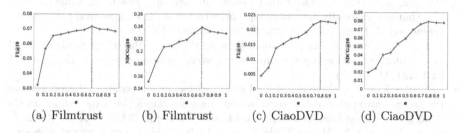

Fig. 7. Performance of UGR-R for each α on datasets of Filmtrust and CiaoDVD.

5   Conclusion

In this paper, we address the group recommendation problem from the perspective of multi-objective optimization. We propose a novel Unified Group Recommendation model for group recommendation. Specifically, given n users, m items, the model assigns these users into l non-overlapping groups and respectively chooses k items with highest scores from candidate items as recommendations for each group. Different from existing works which separate group partition and recommendation, we integrate them into an optimization process and then alternatively adjust the group partition and recommendation by our proposed alternate optimization algorithm. Extensive experiments have been made on two real-world datasets. UGR consistently outperforms the state-of-the-art group recommendation models on two typical metrics. Moreover, we perform deep analyses of the components in UGR, which proves the effectiveness of our model.

By referring to existing methods of group recommendation, we adopt three criteria for designing the objective function. The reason is that we pay more attention to whether the performance can obtain the improvements by integrating group partition and recommendation. In the future, we will incorporate more criteria and additional contextual information to further improve the performance of our model.

References

1. Amer-Yahia, S., Roy, S.B., Chawlat, A., Das, G., Yu, C.: Group recommendation: semantics and efficiency. Proc. VLDB Endow. **2**(1), 754–765 (2009)
2. Basu Roy, S., Lakshmanan, L.V., Liu, R.: From group recommendations to group formation. In: Proceedings of the 2015 ACM SIGMOD International Conference on Management of Data, pp. 1603–1616. ACM (2015)
3. Beckmann, C., Gross, T.: Towards a group recommender process model for ad-hoc groups and on-demand recommendations. In: Proceedings of the 16th ACM International Conference on Supporting Group Work, pp. 329–330. ACM (2010)
4. Boratto, L., Carta, S.: The rating prediction task in a group recommender system that automatically detects groups: architectures, algorithms, and performance evaluation. J. Intell. Inf. Syst. **45**(2), 221–245 (2015)
5. Boratto, L., Carta, S., Fenu, G.: Investigating the role of the rating prediction task in granularity-based group recommender systems and big data scenarios. Inf. Sci. **378**, 424–443 (2017)
6. Carvalho, L.A.M.C., Macedo, H.T.: Users' satisfaction in recommendation systems for groups: an approach based on noncooperative games. In: Proceedings of the 22nd International Conference on World Wide Web, pp. 951–958. ACM (2013)
7. Chen, C., Zheng, X., Wang, Y., Hong, F., Lin, Z., et al.: Context-aware collaborative topic regression with social matrix factorization for recommender systems. In AAAI, pp. 9–15 (2014)
8. De Pessemier, T., Dooms, S., Martens, L.: Comparison of group recommendation algorithms. Multimedia Tools Appl. **72**(3), 2497–2541 (2014)
9. Deb, K.: Multi-objective optimization. In: Burke, E., Kendall, G. (eds.) Search Methodologies, pp. 403–449. Springer, Boston (2014). https://doi.org/10.1007/978-1-4614-6940-7_15
10. Deb, K., Sindhya, K., Hakanen, J.: Multi-objective optimization. In: Decision Sciences: Theory and Practice (2016)
11. Fang, G., Su, L., Jiang, D., Wu, L.: Group recommendation systems based on external social-trust networks. In: Wireless Communications and Mobile Computing (2018)
12. Guo, C., Li, B., Tian, X.: Flickr group recommendation using rich social media information. Neurocomputing **204**, 8–16 (2016)
13. Guo, Z., Tang, C., Tang, H., Fu, Y., Niu, W.: A novel group recommendation mechanism from the perspective of preference distribution. IEEE Access **6**, 5865–5878 (2018)
14. Konstan, J.A., Miller, B.N., Maltz, D., Herlocker, J.L., Gordon, L.R., Riedl, J.: Grouplens: applying collaborative filtering to usenet news. Commun. ACM **40**(3), 77–87 (1997)
15. Koren, Y., Bell, R., Volinsky, C.: Matrix factorization techniques for recommender systems. Computer **8**, 30–37 (2009)
16. Li, H., Liu, Y., Qian, Y., Mamoulis, N., Tu, W., Cheung, D.W.: HHMF: hidden hierarchical matrix factorization for recommender systems. In: Data Mining and Knowledge Discovery (2019)
17. Linden, G., Smith, B., York, J.: Amazon.com recommendations: item-to-item collaborative filtering. IEEE Internet Comput. **1**, 76–80 (2003)
18. Mahyar, H., Ghalebi K, E., Morshedi, S.M., Khalili, S., Grosu, R., Movaghar, A.: Centrality-based group formation in group recommender systems. In: Proceedings of the 26th International Conference on World Wide Web Companion, pp. 1187–1196. International World Wide Web Conferences Steering Committee (2017)

19. Mnih, A., Salakhutdinov, R.R.: Probabilistic matrix factorization. In: Advances in Neural Information Processing Systems, pp. 1257–1264 (2008)
20. Özsoy, M.G., Polat, F., Alhajj, R.: Multi-objective optimization based location and social network aware recommendation. In: 2014 International Conference on Collaborative Computing: Networking, Applications and Worksharing (CollaborateCom), pp. 233–242. IEEE (2014)
21. Polat, H., Du, W.: SVD-based collaborative filtering with privacy. In: Proceedings of the 2005 ACM Symposium on Applied Computing, pp. 791–795. ACM (2005)
22. Qi, S., Mamoulis, N., Pitoura, E., Tsaparas, P.: Recommending packages to groups. In: 2016 IEEE 16th International Conference on Data Mining (ICDM), pp. 449–458. IEEE (2016)
23. Qin, D., Zhou, X., Chen, L., Huang, G., Zhang, Y.: Dynamic connection-based social group recommendation. IEEE Trans. Knowl. Data Eng. **PP**, 1 (2018)
24. Ribeiro, M.T., Lacerda, A., Veloso, A., Ziviani, N.: Pareto-efficient hybridization for multi-objective recommender systems. In: Proceedings of the Sixth ACM Conference on Recommender Systems, pp. 19–26. ACM (2012)
25. Rodriguez, M., Posse, C., Zhang, E.: Multiple objective optimization in recommender systems. In: Proceedings of the Sixth ACM Conference on Recommender Systems, pp. 11–18. ACM (2012)
26. Salehi-Abari, A., Boutilier, C.: Preference-oriented social networks: group recommendation and inference. In: Proceedings of the 9th ACM Conference on Recommender Systems, pp. 35–42. ACM (2015)
27. Serbos, D., Qi, S., Mamoulis, N., Pitoura, E., Tsaparas, P.: Fairness in package-to-group recommendations. In: Proceedings of the 26th International Conference on World Wide Web, pp. 371–379. International World Wide Web Conferences Steering Committee (2017)
28. Su, X., Khoshgoftaar, T.M.: A survey of collaborative filtering techniques. In: Advances in Artificial Intelligence (2009)
29. Wang, S., Gong, M., Li, H., Yang, J.: Multi-objective optimization for long tail recommendation. Knowl.-Based Syst. **104**, 145–155 (2016)
30. Lin, X., Zhang, M., Zhang, Y., Gu, Z., Liu, Y., Ma, S.: Fairness-aware group recommendation with pareto-efficiency. In: Proceedings of the Eleventh ACM Conference on Recommender Systems, pp. 107–115. ACM (2017)
31. Zeng, X., Wu, B., Shi, J., Liu, C., Guo, Q.: Parallelization of latent group model for group recommendation algorithm. In: IEEE International Conference on Data Science in Cyberspace (DSC), pp. 80–89. IEEE (2016)
32. Zhao, J., Liu, K., Tang, F.: A group recommendation strategy based on user's interaction behavior. In: 2017 IEEE 2nd Information Technology, Networking, Electronic and Automation Control Conference (ITNEC), pp. 1170–1174. IEEE (2017)
33. Zhu, Q., Wang, S., Cheng, B., Sun, Q., Yang, F., Chang, R.N.: Context-aware group recommendation for point-of-interests. IEEE Access **6**, 12129–12144 (2018)
34. Zuo, Y., Gong, M., Zeng, J., Ma, L., Jiao, L.: Personalized recommendation based on evolutionary multi-objective optimization [research frontier]. IEEE Comput. Intell. Mag. **10**(1), 52–62 (2015)

A Novel Ensemble Approach for Click-Through Rate Prediction Based on Factorization Machines and Gradient Boosting Decision Trees

Xiaochen Wang$^{(\boxtimes)}$, Gang Hu, Haoyang Lin, and Jiayu Sun

Center for Future Media, School of Computer Science and Engineering,
University of Electronic Science and Technology of China, Chengdu 611731, China
{wangxiaochen,hugang,haoyanglin,jiayusun}@std.uestc.edu.cn

Abstract. Click-Through Rate (CTR) prediction is a significant technique in the field of computational advertising, its accuracy directly affects companies profits and user experience. Achieving great ability of generalization by learning complicated feature interactions behind user behaviors is critical in improving CTR for recommender systems. Factorization Machines (FM) is a hot recommender method for efficiently modeling features' second-order interactions. Nevertheless, FM cannot capture the nonlinear and complex modes implied in the real-world data while it models feature in a linear way and just uses the second-order feature interactions. In this paper, we propose a model named GFM, which is an ensemble learning of FM and Gradient Boosting Decision Trees (GBDT) for recommendations. We use FM to model linear features and second-order feature interactions and use GBDT to model the side information for transforming the raw features to cross-combined features. In addition, we import the attention mechanism to calculate users' latent attention on different features. To illustrate the performance of GFM, we conduct experiments on two real-world datasets, including a movie dataset and a music dataset, the results show that our model is effective in providing accurate recommendations.

Keywords: Factorization Machines ·
Gradient Boosting Decision Trees · CTR prediction · Attention

1 Introduction

In the era of big data, we face the challenge of information load, recommender algorithm is an excellent solution for helping users getting useful information when their needs are not clear and it has been applied in many user-oriented companies such as Amazon and Facebook. Recommender systems are designed to predict how much a user will be interested in an unconsumed item, which drive sales for online businesses and enhance the user experience. Recommender

© Springer Nature Switzerland AG 2019
J. Shao et al. (Eds.): APWeb-WAIM 2019, LNCS 11642, pp. 152–162, 2019.
https://doi.org/10.1007/978-3-030-26075-0_12

systems, especially CTR prediction models, have been widely used by various kinds of companies, they can make profits for companies and make the user get a better experience. It was reported that recommendations accounted for about 60% video clicks in YouTube [8].

In modern recommender systems, FM [24] is a great solution for efficiently modeling features' second-order interactions which are proved to be powerful in enhancing recommender systems' performance [4,28]. Due to FM's strong generalization ability, many variants [10,13,21,31] of this algorithm have been proposed. For example, Guo et al. proposed DeepFM [10] combining deep neural networks and FM to learn the linear and nonlinear inherent structure from click data. However, FM models feature in a linear way and just uses the second-order feature interactions, it is not enough for capturing the nonlinear and complex modes implied in the real-world data. GBDT is widely used in the area of advertisements without identifications of users and items, it can learn nonlinear features by itself and does not depend on previous feature engineering including cross combination and feature normalization. It also has some variants, for example, Chen et al. proposed an optimized distributed gradient boosting library called XGBoost [6], which solved many data science problems in a fast and accurate way. Ke et al. proposed a gradient boosting framework that used tree-based learning algorithms called LightGBM [17], which could achieve faster training speed and higher efficiency. We can often see their shadow in machine learning competitions such as Kaggle and Tianchi.

Recently, whether in the industry or machine learning competitions, individual models are usually assembled and training together to achieve better predictive performance. For example, Google proposed the Wide&Deep structure that learned linear features using the Logistic Regression(LR) and captured the nonlinear feature interactions using the deep neural network. Inspired by the Tree-enhanced Embedding Model proposed by Wang et al. [30], we replace the Matrix Factorization (MF) [19] part with FM because of its ignorance of feature interactions. In this paper, we creatively incorporate FM, GBDT and attention mechanism [5], in order to model feature in the linear and nonlinear way at the same time.

The rest of the paper is organized as follows: after introducing some related work in Sect. 2, we discuss our proposed method in Sect. 3. Then we compare performance with some baselines on two real-world datasets in Sect. 4. Finally, Sect. 5 concludes our work.

2   Related Work

In recent years, deep learning methods have got much attention in the research of the recommender system. For the past few years, due to the amount of data and the dimension of features have become bigger and bigger and the rapid development of GPU, machine learning has made great developments and breakthroughs. Because of the popularity and the excellent performance of machine learning and deep neural networks, most CTR prediction models have applied it and the structure of CTR prediction models has evolved from shallow to deep.

As a pioneer work, NNLM [3] learns the embedding of each word, aiming to decrease the difficulty of dimension in language modeling, it has inspired many CTR prediction models based on latent factors, such as MF and FM. Deep&Crossing and Wide&Deep import multilayer perceptron to learn high-order feature interactions, which enhances the generalization ability of the CTR prediction model. DeepFM import FM as the Wide module in Wide&Deep, it uses the FM module to learn the embedding of sparse features and uses the multilayer perceptron module to learn the high-order interactions of features automatically, this kind of model can reduce the manual feature engineering work greatly.

In many machine learning competitions, the ensemble learning approaches have achieved good results. For example, the gradient boosting library called XGBoost has won the championship in many competitions of Kaggle. In this work, considering FM's great generalization ability and GBDT's ability to extract cross-combined features, we explore the ensemble learning of FM and GBDT. In addition, we import the attention mechanism to learn each user's degree of attention on each cross-combined feature extracted by GBDT. The key idea of the attention mechanism [5,27] is to learn to assign different attentive weights for different features: the higher the weight, the greater the contribution of the corresponding feature to the final result. The attention mechanism has been widely applied in CTR prediction models, such as DIN [34] and DIEN [33] proposed by Alibaba, it enhances those models' performance.

3   Our Approach

In this section, we introduce our proposed GFM model. In order to work out FM's lack of extracting cross-combined features, we import GBDT for nonlinear feature transformation. In addition, we import the attention mechanism to make the model more personalized, it can obtain each user's degree of attention on different characteristics of the user and the item.

3.1   Model Designs

Design 1. GBDT is easy to exploit decision rules and model the side information. Therefore, we can use it to capture cross-combined features. Figure 1 shows the architecture of the hybrid model (GBDT plus LR) [12]. As can be seen, real-valued input features can be transformed into cross-combined features easily. In addition, the initial idea of attention mechanism is based on the fact that different parts of a model make different contributions to the final prediction. In the field of the recommender system, we can also take it for granted that features contribute differently to a user's degree of interest on an item. We incorporate attention mechanism with cross-combined features extracted by GBDT and estimate the target as:

$$\widehat{y}_G(\mathbf{V}_{ui}) = \sum_{\mathbf{v}_l \in \mathbf{V}_{ui}} w_l \cdot \mathbf{v}_l \qquad (1)$$

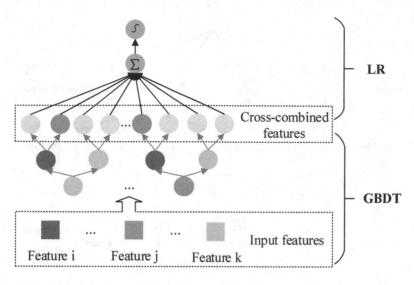

Fig. 1. Hybrid model architecture (GBDT plus LR). It feeds the cross-combined features generated by GBDT part into the LR part.

Corresponding to Fig. 1, $\mathbf{V}_{ui}$ includes all vectors of cross-combined features of a specified user u and a specified item i, which are generated by the GBDT part, and w_l is a trainable parameter denoting the attentive weight of the l-th cross-combined feature vector while $\mathbf{v}_l$ is the embedding of l-th cross-combined feature vector. Importantly, w_l is personalized to be only dependent on identifications of users. The value of w_l can demonstrate the importance of l-th cross-combined feature in the user's mind, it can make the model more personalized.

Design 2. FM was originally proposed for the collaborative recommendation [20,24,26]. Figure 2 presents the structure of FM. Given the real-valued vector of a specified user and a specified item, FM estimates the target by modeling linear features and second-order feature interactions between each pair of features:

$$\widehat{y}_{FM}(\mathbf{X}_{ui}) = w_0 + \sum_{j=1}^{n} w_j \cdot x_j + \sum_{j=1}^{n} \sum_{k=j+1}^{n} \mathbf{v}_j^T \mathbf{v}_k \cdot x_j x_k \tag{2}$$

where X_{ui} is a real-valued vector which contains all feature vectors of a specified user u and a specified item i, w_0 is the global bias, w_j represents the strength of the j-th variable and n is the number of features. The $\mathbf{v}_j^T \mathbf{v}_k$ represents the second-order interaction between the j-th and k-th variable, where $\mathbf{v}_j \in \mathbb{R}^m$ is the embedding vector of the j-th feature and m denotes the dimension of feature $\mathbf{v}_j$. Note that only non-zero features are considered, so we should filter the zero values when we design the model.

Different from MF that only learns the latent factors of users and items, FM can work with real-valued feature vector and learn features' interactions. FM

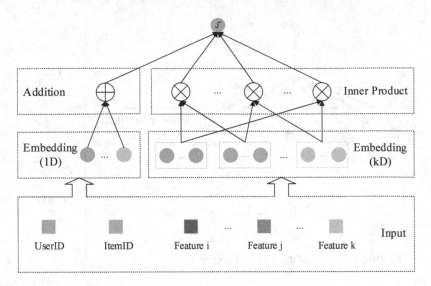

Fig. 2. The architecture of FM. It effectively uses second-order feature interactions.

is one of the most popular and effective embedding-based models for learning from sparse data and it has been successfully applied to many predictive tasks [15, 22, 23] such as computational advertising.

Design 3. Finally, we combine the outputs of models in Design 1 and Design 2:

$$\widehat{y}_{GFM} = sigmoid(\widehat{y}_G(\mathbf{V}_{ui}) + \widehat{y}_{FM}(\mathbf{X}_{ui})) \tag{3}$$

where $\widehat{y}_G$ and $\widehat{y}_{FM}$ represent the outputs of models in Design 1 and Design 2 respectively, and *sigmoid* is a threshold function frequently used in neural networks. The combination of GBDT and attention mechanism can boost the accuracy of model performance because of the lack of capturing cross-combined features in FM. Figure 3 shows the architecture of our proposed GFM model, which is an ensemble learning of GBDT and FM. In addition, we import $L2$ regularization on embeddings of features, which can well prevent overfitting and improve the model's capacity of generalization to unseen data.

3.2 Loss Function

To learn the GFM model, we should specify an objective function to be optimized. As we deal with the problem of CTR prediction, each target is a binary value 1 or 0, so we can regard the learning of GFM model as a binary classification task. We minimize the cross-entropy [32] loss defined as follows:

$$L = -\frac{1}{N}\sum_{i=1}^{N} y_{GFM} \cdot log(\widehat{y}_{GFM}) + (1 - y_{GFM}) \cdot (1 - log(\widehat{y}_{GFM})) \tag{4}$$

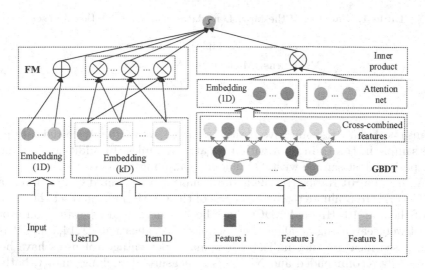

Fig. 3. Overview of our GFM model. We use the GBDT and attention mechanism to extract and process the cross-combined features.

where N is the number of users, y and $\widehat{y}$ represent the true value and the predicted value respectively. Since GFM consists of two cascaded models, both of them are trained to optimize the loss. We first train the GBDT, which greedily fits additive trees on the whole training data. After obtaining the cross-combined features from GBDT, we optimize the GFM model using Adam optimization [18].

4 Experiments

4.1 Datasets and Evaluation Protocol

We conducted experiments on two publicly accessible datasets: the MovieLens[1] and the KKBox[2], both of which have some extra information (e.g., user demographics and item attributes). Table 1 shows some statistical information about the MovieLens dataset and the KKBox dataset. Since we conducted some preprocessing on both two datasets including non-numeric data conversion and sampling negative samples, we directly used the processed data for training and evaluation. For evaluation, we adopted the leave-one-out protocol [25], which only reserved one sample of each user for testing and used other samples as the train data. For MovieLens 1M dataset, we selected the latest consumption as the test data for each user. For KKBox dataset, we only reserved users' consumed items and randomly hold out a sample of each user while most of the non-consumed items in the original data are in users' local library and user likes or liked it.

---

[1] https://grouplens.org/datasets/movielens/latest.
[2] https://www.kaggle.com/c/kkbox-churn-prediction-challenge.

Table 1. Statistics of the MovieLens dataset and the KKBox dataset.

Dataset	Samples	Users	Items
MovieLens 1M	1000209	6040	3952
KKBox	1569159	8216	9201

Because both datasets only have positive samples, we randomly paired each positive sample in the train data with 4 negative samples. In addition, we paired each positive test sample with 99 randomly sampling negative samples.

We use the Hit Ratio (HR) [9] and Normalized Discounted Cumulative Gain (NDCG) [11] to evaluate the performance of the GFM model and set the threshold of them at 10. HR and NDCG have been widely used as evaluation protocols of web search engine algorithms or related applications [1,14,16]. HR is a recall-based measure that indicates how many percentages of users have been successfully recommended and NDCG is a measure of ranking quality, both of which are highly correlated with accuracy. We compute the average scores of all users. Formally, the definitions of HR@10 and NDCG@10 are as follows:

$$HR@10 = \frac{\sum_{i=1}^{N} H(u)}{N} \qquad (5)$$

$$NDCG@10 = \frac{\sum_{i=1}^{N} \frac{log2}{log(p(u)+2)}}{N} \qquad (6)$$

For $HR@10$, u is a specified user, N is the number of users and $H(u)$ is a binary value which means whether the positive sample of u is in the recommendations if we recommend 10 items to the user u. For $NDCG@10$, u and N have the same meaning as $HR@10$, and $p(u)$ is the position of the positive sample in the recommendation list of the user u.

4.2 Baselines

We compared GFM to the following item recommender methods:

GBDT + LR. It is a hybrid model which combines GBDT with LR. In this model, the one-hot encoded [2,28] categorical variables are used as inputs. The output of each decision tree is deemed as a categorical input feature to a linear classifier. GBDT can generate powerful cross-combined features. This method can provide explanations easily at the same time.

Wide&Deep. Wide&Deep is composed of LR and deep neural networks. The LR part models feature in a linear way. The deep neural networks part first concatenates embeddings of different features, then employs a multilayer perceptron to model high-order feature interactions. It aims at acquiring the ability of memorization and generalization at the same time.

MF. MF is a simple but effective embedding-based model for collaborative filtering, the key of which is to learn the embedding of each user and each item. It's very popular since it has been proposed in the Netflix Prize Challenge.

FM. FM is a great solution for efficiently modeling features' second-order interactions, and its linear complexity attracts much attention of advertisements companies. FM possesses outstanding performance on personalized tag recommendation and context-aware prediction. We have introduced the architecture of FM in the previous section.

DeepFM. DeepFM combines FM with deep neural networks. The FM part can learn second-order feature interactions via factorized interaction parameters and the deep neural networks part can learn high-order feature interactions by its complex nonlinear architecture, but this method has a great number of hyper-parameters.

4.3 Parameter Settings

For the purpose of fair comparisons, we learned all of them by employing Adam optimization to minimize the cross-entropy loss (Eq. (4)). To avoid overfitting, we traverse the L2 regularization parameter in the set [0.001, 0.0015, ..., 0.02] and we go through the dropout [29] ratio for the neural network models in the set [0.1, 0.3, 0.5, 0.7] for each embedding-based method. Figure 4 shows the performance of all compared embedding-based methods on two real-world datasets, and we choose the embedding size in the set [8, 16, 32, 64]. For the models containing GBDT, we set the number of trees to 100 and the maximum depth of trees to 4.

Table 2. Performance comparison of Hit@10 ang NDCG@10 Scores (%) at embedding size 64 on MovieLens 1M and KKBox datasets.

Method	MovieLens 1M		KKBox	
	HR@10	NDCG@10	HR@10	NDCG@10
GBDT + LR [12]	38.05	21.14	40.74	25.61
Wide&Deep [7]	68.60	41.23	75.32	53.06
MF [19]	69.81	42.08	75.80	53.10
FM [24]	70.48	42.20	76.02	54.01
DeepFM [10]	69.75	41.83	76.99	54.16
GFM	**70.73**	**42.51**	**77.46**	**54.68**

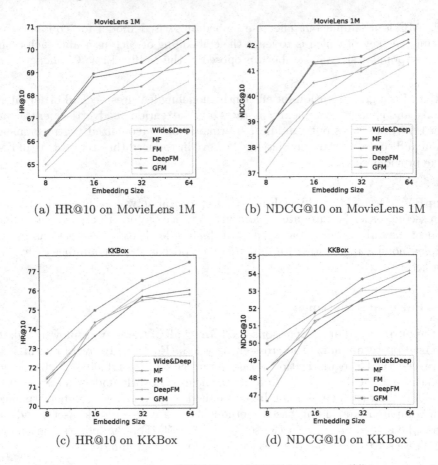

Fig. 4. Performance comparison of HR@10 and NDCG@10 Scores (%) between embedding size {8, 16, 32, 64} on MovieLens 1M and KKBox datasets.

4.4 Performance Comparison

We first make comparisons between our model and other item recommender approaches. Table 2 illustrates the performance of HR@10 and NDCG@10 at embedding size 64 on all compared approaches. Benefited from features' second-order interactions and cross-combined features' modeling, our method achieves equal or even better scores of HR@10 and NDCG@10 than other approaches. As shown in Fig. 4, GFM's improvement on KKBox dataset is better because it has richer side information than Movielens 1M dataset. It indicates that the cross-combined features extracted from GBDT can enhance our model's performance.

5   Conclusion

In this paper, we propose the GFM network to address the problem of CTR prediction in recommender systems. We use FM as the backbone to model linear features and second-order feature interactions, which greatly enhance the latent representation of features. In addition, we use the GBDT and attention mechanism to exploit cross-combined features. Although our approach is simple and easy for implementation, extensive experiments on two real-world datasets show that we have achieved promising performance in terms of accuracy.

Acknowledgments. This work is supported by National Natural Science Foundation of China (grants No. 61672133 and No. 61832001).

References

1. Bai, B., et al.: Learning to rank with (a lot of) word features. Inf. Retr. **13**(3), 291–314 (2010)
2. Bayer, I., He, X., Kanagal, B., Rendle, S.: A generic coordinate descent framework for learning from implicit feedback. In: WWW, pp. 1341–1350. ACM (2017)
3. Bengio, Y., Ducharme, R., Vincent, P., Janvin, C.: A neural probabilistic language model. J. Mach. Learn. Res. **3**, 1137–1155 (2003). http://jmlr.org/papers/v3/bengio03a.html
4. Blondel, M., Ishihata, M., Fujino, A., Ueda, N.: Polynomial networks and factorization machines: new insights and efficient training algorithms. In: ICML. JMLR Workshop and Conference Proceedings, vol. 48, pp. 850–858. JMLR.org (2016)
5. Chen, J., Zhang, H., He, X., Nie, L., Liu, W., Chua, T.: Attentive collaborative filtering: multimedia recommendation with item- and component-level attention. In: SIGIR, pp. 335–344. ACM (2017)
6. Chen, T., Guestrin, C.: XGBoost: a scalable tree boosting system. In: Krishnapuram, B., Shah, M., Smola, A.J., Aggarwal, C.C., Shen, D., Rastogi, R. (eds.) Proceedings of the 22nd ACM SIGKDD International Conference on Knowledge Discovery and Data Mining, San Francisco, CA, USA, 13–17 August 2016, pp. 785–794. ACM (2016). https://doi.org/10.1145/2939672.2939785
7. Cheng, H., et al.: Wide & deep learning for recommender systems. In: DLRS@RecSys, pp. 7–10. ACM (2016)
8. Davidson, J., et al.: The Youtube video recommendation system. In: RecSys, pp. 293–296. ACM (2010)
9. Deshpande, M., Karypis, G.: Item-based top-N recommendation algorithms. ACM Trans. Inf. Syst. **22**(1), 143–177 (2004)
10. Guo, H., Tang, R., Ye, Y., Li, Z., He, X.: DeepFM: a factorization-machine based neural network for CTR prediction. In: IJCAI, pp. 1725–1731. IJCAI.org (2017)
11. He, X., Chen, T., Kan, M., Chen, X.: TriRank: review-aware explainable recommendation by modeling aspects. In: CIKM, pp. 1661–1670. ACM (2015)
12. He, X., et al.: Practical lessons from predicting clicks on ads at Facebook. In: ADKDD@KDD, pp. 5:1–5:9. ACM (2014)
13. Hong, L., Doumith, A.S., Davison, B.D.: Co-factorization machines: modeling user interests and predicting individual decisions in Twitter. In: WSDM, pp. 557–566. ACM (2013)
14. Hong, R., Yang, Y., Wang, M., Hua, X.: Learning visual semantic relationships for efficient visual retrieval. IEEE Trans. Big Data **1**(4), 152–161 (2015)
15. Juan, Y., Zhuang, Y., Chin, W., Lin, C.: Field-aware factorization machines for CTR prediction. In: Sen, S., Geyer, W., Freyne, J., Castells, P. (eds.) Proceedings of the 10th ACM Conference on Recommender Systems, Boston, MA, USA, 15–19 September 2016, pp. 43–50. ACM (2016). https://doi.org/10.1145/2959100.2959134

16. Kabbur, S., Ning, X., Karypis, G.: FISM: factored item similarity models for top-n recommender systems. In: KDD, pp. 659–667. ACM (2013)
17. Ke, G., et al.: LightGBM: a highly efficient gradient boosting decision tree. In: NIPS, pp. 3149–3157 (2017)
18. Kingma, D.P., Ba, J.: Adam: a method for stochastic optimization. CoRR abs/1412.6980 (2014). http://arxiv.org/abs/1412.6980
19. Koren, Y., Bell, R.: Advances in collaborative filtering. In: Ricci, F., Rokach, L., Shapira, B. (eds.) Recommender Systems Handbook, pp. 77–118. Springer, Boston, MA (2015). https://doi.org/10.1007/978-1-4899-7637-6_3
20. Liu, D.C., et al.: Related pins at pinterest: the evolution of a real-world recommender system. In: WWW (Companion Volume), pp. 583–592. ACM (2017)
21. Oentaryo, R.J., Lim, E., Low, J., Lo, D., Finegold, M.: Predicting response in mobile advertising with hierarchical importance-aware factorization machine. In: WSDM, pp. 123–132. ACM (2014)
22. Petroni, F., Corro, L.D., Gemulla, R.: CORE: context-aware open relation extraction with factorization machines. In: Màrquez, L., Callison-Burch, C., Su, J., Pighin, D., Marton, Y. (eds.) Proceedings of the 2015 Conference on Empirical Methods in Natural Language Processing, EMNLP 2015, Lisbon, Portugal, 17–21 September 2015, pp. 1763–1773. The Association for Computational Linguistics (2015). http://aclweb.org/anthology/D/D15/D15-1204.pdf
23. Qiang, R., Liang, F., Yang, J.: Exploiting ranking factorization machines for microblog retrieval. In: He, Q., Iyengar, A., Nejdl, W., Pei, J., Rastogi, R. (eds.) 22nd ACM International Conference on Information and Knowledge Management, CIKM 2013, San Francisco, CA, USA, 27 October–1 November 2013, pp. 1783–1788. ACM (2013). https://doi.org/10.1145/2505515.2505648
24. Rendle, S.: Factorization machines. In: ICDM, pp. 995–1000. IEEE Computer Society (2010)
25. Rendle, S., Freudenthaler, C., Gantner, Z., Schmidt-Thieme, L.: BPR: Bayesian personalized ranking from implicit feedback. In: UAI, pp. 452–461. AUAI Press (2009)
26. Rendle, S., Gantner, Z., Freudenthaler, C., Schmidt-Thieme, L.: Fast context-aware recommendations with factorization machines. In: SIGIR, pp. 635–644. ACM (2011)
27. Rush, A.M., Chopra, S., Weston, J.: A neural attention model for abstractive sentence summarization. In: EMNLP, pp. 379–389. The Association for Computational Linguistics (2015)
28. Shan, Y., Hoens, T.R., Jiao, J., Wang, H., Yu, D., Mao, J.C.: Deep crossing: web-scale modeling without manually crafted combinatorial features. In: KDD, pp. 255–262. ACM (2016)
29. Srivastava, N., Hinton, G.E., Krizhevsky, A., Sutskever, I., Salakhutdinov, R.: Dropout: a simple way to prevent neural networks from overfitting. J. Mach. Learn. Res. **15**(1), 1929–1958 (2014)
30. Wang, X., He, X., Feng, F., Nie, L., Chua, T.: TEM: tree-enhanced embedding model for explainable recommendation. In: WWW, pp. 1543–1552. ACM (2018)
31. Xiao, J., Ye, H., He, X., Zhang, H., Wu, F., Chua, T.: Attentional factorization machines: learning the weight of feature interactions via attention networks. In: IJCAI, pp. 3119–3125. IJCAI.org (2017)
32. Xu, Z., Xia, M.: Hesitant fuzzy entropy and cross-entropy and their use in multi-attribute decision-making. Int. J. Intell. Syst. **27**(9), 799–822 (2012)
33. Zhou, G., et al.: Deep interest evolution network for click-through rate prediction. CoRR abs/1809.03672 (2018)
34. Zhou, G., et al.: Deep interest network for click-through rate prediction. In: KDD, pp. 1059–1068. ACM (2018)

Latent Path Connected Space Model for Recommendation

Lang Mei[1], Jun He[1(✉)], Hongyan Liu[2], and Xiaoyong Du[1]

[1] Key Laboratory of DEKE (MOE), School of Information,
Renmin University of China, Beijing, China
{meilang2013,hejun,duyong}@ruc.edu.cn
[2] School of Economics and Management, Tsinghua University, Beijing, China
liuhy@sem.tsinghua.edu.cn

Abstract. Matrix Factorization (MF) is a latent factor model, which
has been one of the most popular techniques for recommendation systems. Performance of MF-based recommender models degrades as the
sparseness of user-item rating data increases. MF-based models map each
user and each item into a low dimensional space, where either of them is
represented by a point in the space. While a point is a concise and simple representation of a user's preference or an item's characteristics, it is
hard to learn the precise position of the point, especially when the data is
very sparse. In this paper we propose an alternative latent space model,
Latent Path Connected Space model (LSpacc), to address this issue. In
this model, users and items are both represented by path connected space
described by different latent dimensions and spatial intersection between
user space and item space reflects their matching degree. Extensive evaluations on four real-world datasets show that our approach outperforms
the Matrix Factorization model on rating prediction task especially when
the rating data is extremely sparse.

Keywords: Path connected space · Matrix factorization ·
Spatial intersection · Recommendation

1 Introduction

Recommender System (RS) has become one of the most popular and important
components for online business. RS is designed to automatically find the most
relevant items (i.e. movies, products, music, news etc.) from a large candidate
collection, and then generate personalized recommendation lists for users. For
companies, RS can be used to promote their products and enhance user experiences. For users, RS can be utilized to filter products which suit them, and save
their time on picking products from a large corpus. Due to the significance of
RS, many recommender models have been developed in the past decade.

RS usually predicts users' preferences based on historical interaction between
users and items such as ratings, and some auxiliary information such as textual,

© Springer Nature Switzerland AG 2019
J. Shao et al. (Eds.): APWeb-WAIM 2019, LNCS 11642, pp. 163–172, 2019.
https://doi.org/10.1007/978-3-030-26075-0_13

temporal and spatial data. Recommendation system based on explicit rating information usually transforms the problem into rating prediction task, focusing on estimating scores (e.g., 1–5) users give to items. However, the user-item rating matrix is usually very sparse, making most recommendation models such as MF not satisfying.

Matrix factorization (MF) is a widely adopted recommendation model, showing superior performance over memory-based models in many cases [1,2]. Many variants based on matrix factorization such as weighted regularized matrix factorization [3] and probabilistic matrix factorization [4] have been proposed. MF-based models utilize user-item rating matrix (or user-item interaction matrix) and map each user and each item into a low dimensional space, where a user or an item is represented by a point in the space. The matching degree between a user and an item is approximated by inner product of their latent vectors. While a point is a concise and simple representation of a user's preference or an item's characteristics, it is hard to learn the precise position of the point, especially when the data is very sparse. In order to mitigate this issue, existing researches usually use auxiliary information such as textual, social networks, temporal and spatial data to alleviate the problem [7–10,13]. In this paper, we aim to develop an alternative way to model the recommendation task based only on the user-item interaction matrix.

The main contributions of our paper are summarized as follows:

- We propose a novel recommendation model, Latent Path Connected Space model (LSpace), in which users and items are both represented as path connected space and spatial intersection reflects their matching degree.
- We conduct extensive experiments on four real-world datasets, and results show that our proposed model outperforms the Matrix Factorization model on rating prediction task, especially when the rating data is extremely sparse.

2 Related Work

Matrix factorization has been one of the most effective models for recommendation. Many studies aim to improve MF and propose variants for rating prediction. For instance, Koren et al. [11] introduced biases to model specific features of users and items. Salakhutdinov et al. [4,12] extended MF to a probabilistic graphical model. Recently, approaches based on auxiliary information have been developed to utilize textual, social networks, temporal and spatial data. Specifically, Wang et al. proposed collaborative topic regression model (CTR) which combines Latent Dirichlet Allocation (LDA) and collaborative filtering [9]. Kim et al. [14] proposed Convolutional Matrix Factorization (ConvMF) which integrates convolutional neural network (CNN) and matrix factorization to fully capture the document information. These models further developed MF and alleviated the sparsity problem.

However, as aforementioned, most existing methods still aim to overcome the sparsity problem based on matrix factorization rather than consider other alternative models to rely only on user-item interactions. Despite the success of MF, the performance of MF may be constrained by the latent vector representation and the simple prediction through inner product of latent vectors [5,6]. In real applications, users and items are usually described by many correlated aspects. If we treat users and items as points, we oversimplify the representation and make the learning task hard in some circumstances such as severe sparsity.

3   Preliminaries

Suppose we have N users, M items and a rating matrix $R \in \mathbb{R}^{N \times M}$. Let R_{ij} indicates the rating of user i to item j. Usually, most of entries in R are unknown and the aim of recommender models is to predict ratings for unknown entries.

For convenience, Table 1 summarizes the notations used in this paper.

Table 1. Notations

Notations	Description
K	Dimensionality of path connected space
N	Number of users
M	Number of items
$R, \hat{R}$	Rating matrix, predicted rating matrix
U, V	Set of latent models of users and items
u_i, v_j	Latent models of user i and item j
γ	Mapping factor

In MF, user i and item j are represented as K-dimensional vectors, $u_i \in \mathbb{R}^K$ and $v_j \in \mathbb{R}^K$. The rating R_{ij} is approximated by the inner product of latent vectors of user i and item j, $R_{ij} \approx u_i^T v_j$. Generally, to train this latent model, Mean Square Error (MSE) is used as a loss function L, and the latent vectors are learned by minimizing the loss function L:

$$L(U, V) = \sum_{i=1}^{N} \sum_{j=1}^{M} I_{ij} \left(R_{ij} - \hat{R}_{ij} \right)^2 = \sum_{i=1}^{N} \sum_{j=1}^{M} I_{ij} \left(R_{ij} - u_i^T v_j \right)^2 \tag{1}$$

Where I_{ij} indicates if user i rates item j.

4   Latent Path Connected Space Model

In this section, we provide details of the proposed model, Latent Path Connected Space model (LSpace). We first introduce the definition of path connected space, and explain how to simplify the structure of path connected space. Then, we propose to use spatial intersection to measure the matching degree between users and items. Finally, we give the loss function of the model.

4.1 Path Connected Space

Path connected space [17] is a type of topological space in which for any two points x_1, x_2 there always exists a path from x_1 to x_2. Analogously, if we represent users and items as path connected space described by different dimensions of aspects, the relation between any two aspects can be maintained. For example, a movie can be described by many aspects, such as music, dialogue and plot. A movie's music is usually consistent with plot, and the plot is usually consistent with its dialogue. Through the representation of path connected space, we consider the relevance between different aspects of a user or an item. If we know the shape of the space, we can represent it by parameters. For instance, in a three-dimensional situation, a user or item can be represented as an ellipsoid. A point (x, y, z) in the ellipsoid can be described by the following equation:

$$\frac{(x - x_0)^2}{a^2} + \frac{(y - y_0)^2}{b^2} + \frac{(z - z_0)^2}{c^2} \leq 1 \tag{2}$$

Where x_0, y_0, z_0 are the coordinates of the center of the ellipsoid, a, b, c are radius of the dimensions x, y and z. The parameters of space can be defined as:

$$< (x_0, a), (y_0, b), (z_0, c) > \tag{3}$$

For instance, Fig. 1 shows the ellipsoid with parameters $\langle (0, 3), (0, 2), (0, 1) \rangle$. However, if the shape of space is too complex, it will be difficult to describe it with finite parameters. Therefore, we simplify the shape to be a rectangular space which can cover the original space as much as possible. For example, A three-dimensional rectangular space can be used to approximate the ellipsoid as shown in Fig. 1.

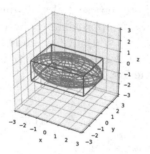

Fig. 1. Ellipsoid space and three-dimensional rectangular space.

The rectangular space can be described with parameters which contain lower and upper bounds of each dimension. Specifically, in K-dimensional situation, a user u_i or an item v_j can be represented as a rectangular space with parameters:

$$u_i = < \left(u_{i1}^{low}, u_{i1}^{up} \right), \left(u_{i2}^{low}, u_{i2}^{up} \right), ..., \left(u_{iK}^{low}, u_{iK}^{up} \right) > \tag{4}$$

$$v_j = < \left(v_{j1}^{low}, v_{j1}^{up} \right), \left(v_{j2}^{low}, v_{j2}^{up} \right), ..., \left(v_{j2}^{low}, v_{jK}^{up} \right) > \tag{5}$$

In the rectangular space of a user, each latent dimension represents one aspect of the user's preference, while in the rectangular space of an item, each latent dimension represents how the item performs in the corresponding aspect.

4.2   Spatial Intersection

If both users and items are modeled as rectangular space, how to measure their matching is important for making recommendation. We propose to use spatial intersection to reflects their matching degree. Spatial intersection of two spaces means the overlapping area of them. The overlapping of the user's space and the item's space indicate the matching of user's preference with the item. For instance, suppose two dimensions of the latent space are genre and actor, if a user prefers comedy movies and actor Charlie Chaplin, a movie is performed by Charlie Chaplin, then the user and movie share the same subspace about Charlie Chaplin. The bigger the overlapping, the higher the matching.

The spatial intersection between user i and item j is denoted as $u_i \cap v_j$, which defines their common subspace. The spatial intersection between user i and item j is defined by Eqs. (6) and (7):

$$u_i \cap v_j = < \delta \left(u_{i1}^{low}, v_{j1}^{low}, u_{i1}^{up}, v_{j1}^{up} \right), \delta \left(u_{i2}^{low}, v_{j2}^{low}, u_{i2}^{up}, v_{j2}^{up} \right),$$
$$..., \delta \left(u_{iK}^{low}, v_{jK}^{low}, u_{iK}^{up}, v_{jK}^{up} \right) > \tag{6}$$

$$\delta \left(u_{ik}^{low}, v_{jk}^{low}, u_{ik}^{up}, v_{jk}^{up} \right) =$$
$$\begin{cases} \phi, if \min \left(u_{ik}^{up}, v_{jk}^{up} \right) - \max \left(u_{ik}^{low}, v_{jk}^{low} \right) < 0 \\ \left(\max \left(u_{ik}^{low}, v_{jk}^{low} \right), \min \left(u_{ik}^{up}, v_{jk}^{up} \right) \right), otherwise \end{cases} \tag{7}$$

Where ϕ indicates empty interval. For instance, Fig. 2 shows the calculation process of spatial intersection $u_i \cap v_j$ in a two-dimensional situation.

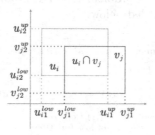

Fig. 2. The calculation of spatial intersection $u_i \cap v_j$ in a two-dimensional space.

The matching degree can be measure by the size of the spatial intersection $|u_i \cap v_j|$ normalized by the size of spatial union $|u_i \cup v_j|$.

$$\frac{|u_i \cap v_j|}{|u_i \cup v_j|} \quad \frac{|u_i \cap v_j|}{|u_i| + |v_j| - |u_i||v_j|} \tag{8}$$

The size of spatial intersection $u_i \cap v_j$, spatial union $u_i \cup v_j$, K-dimensional rectangular space of user i and item j are calculated based on Eqs. (9) to (11).

$$|u_i| = \prod_{k=1}^{K} \left(u_{ik}^{up} - u_{ik}^{low} \right) \tag{9}$$

$$|v_j| = \prod_{k=1}^{K} \left(v_{jk}^{up} - v_{jk}^{low} \right) \tag{10}$$

$$|u_i \cap v_j| = \prod_{k=1}^{K} \max \left(\min \left(u_{ik}^{up}, v_{jk}^{up} \right) - \max \left(u_{ik}^{low}, v_{jk}^{low} \right), 0 \right) \tag{11}$$

The size of the space is defined based on Peano–Jordan measure [15], which is an extension of the notion of size.

If rating range is not in [0,1], we need a mapping function $f(\cdot)$ between normalized spatial intersection $\frac{|u_i \cap v_j|}{|u_i \cup v_j|} \in [0,1]$ and rating $\hat{R}_{ij}$.

$$\hat{R}_{ij} = f \left(\frac{|u_i \cap v_j|}{|u_i \cup v_j|} \right) \tag{12}$$

In our experiment, we use a factor γ to conduct the mapping:

$$\hat{R}_{ij} = \gamma \frac{|u_i \cap v_j|}{|u_i \cup v_j|} \tag{13}$$

4.3 Learning of the Model

In order to compare with Matrix Factorization model, we adopt the widely used squared loss which is the same as used in Matrix Factorization, which is:

$$L(U, V) = \sum_{i=1}^{N} \sum_{j=1}^{M} I_{ij} \left(R_{ij} - \hat{R}_{ij} \right)^2 = \sum_{i=1}^{N} \sum_{j=1}^{M} I_{ij} \left(R_{ij} - \gamma \frac{|u_i \cap v_j|}{|u_i \cup v_j|} \right)^2 \tag{14}$$

Where $U = \{u_i\}_{i=1,...,N}$, $V = \{v_j\}_{j=1,...,M}$.

We solve the optimization problem through gradient descent. The learning algorithm of LSpace is provided below.

Algorithm. LSpace

Input : number of users N, number of items M, rating matrix $R \in \mathbb{R}^{N \times M}$, mapping factor γ, dimension K
Output : U, V
Major steps :
Initialize parameters $U = \{u_i\}_{i=1,...,N}$, $V = \{v_j\}_{j=1,...,M}$ with normal distribution
While not convergence **do**
    Sample minibatch T records (i, j, R_{ij}) from R
    Update U, V by gradient descent of loss function:
$$\sum_{T} \left(R_{ij} - \gamma \frac{|u_i \cap v_j|}{|u_i \cup v_j|} \right)^2$$

---

5   Experiments

To evaluate the performance of the proposed model, we conducted experiments on four real datasets.

5.1   Experiment Setting

We evaluate the performance of our model on rating prediction task using the following datasets:

- **Movielens Datasets.** Movielens-100K and Movielens-1M are widely used in recommendation research. They include historical interactions of users and movies.
- **Amazon Datasets.** We use 2 parts of Amazon data: Amazon Video and Amazon Music. They include historical interactions among users, videos and music.

For convenience, Table 2 summarizes the statistics of the four datasets. Among the datasets, the two Amazon datasets are much more sparser than the Movielens datasets, and Amazon Music has higher sparsity than Amazon Video.

Table 2. Statistics of datasets.

Datasets	Users	Items	Ratings	Density
Movielens-100K	943	1682	100000	6.30%
Movielens-1M	6040	3706	1000209	4.47%
Amazon Video	426922	23965	583933	0.005%
Amazon Music	478235	266414	836006	0.0006%

We optimize our model using Adam optimizer [16] and use mini-batch of size 256. We randomly split each dataset into a training set (80%) and a test set (20%). We compare our model with the Matrix Factorization model. For a fair comparison, we set the same value of dimensions K for these two models and adjust its value from 5 to 10. The performance is measured by root mean square error (RMSE) and mean absolute error (MAE).

5.2   Experimental Results

The comparison is shown in Tables 3, 4, 5, 6, 7 and 8. From these tables we find that for the two Movielens datasets, the performance of our model LSpace is closed to MF, with small improvement. While for the two Amazon datasets, our model performs much better than MF. As the Amazon datasets have much higher sparsity than the other two datasets, we can conclude that our model shows great superiority to MF when the dataset becomes sparse. The reason is that when the data is very sparse, it is hard to learn the accurate position of each user and item in MF model. While using our model, we can estimate a range of values for each dimension, which is easier than learning a particular value.

Table 3. Experiment results with dimension $K = 5$

K = 5	RMSE			MAE		
	LSpace	MF	Improvement	LSpace	MF	Improvement
Movielens-100K	**0.9551**	0.9766	2.20%	**0.7593**	0.7645	0.68%
Movielens-1M	**0.8870**	0.9194	3.52%	**0.7051**	0.7224	2.39%
Amazon Video	**1.7741**	4.5371	60.90%	**1.3599**	3.6418	62.66%
Amazon Music	**2.6272**	4.7680	44.90%	**1.9718**	3.8983	49.42%

Table 4. Experiment results with dimension $K = 6$

K = 6	RMSE			MAE		
	LPCSM	MF	Improvement	LPCSM	MF	Improvement
Movielens-100K	**0.9566**	0.9794	2.33%	**0.7615**	0.7640	0.33%
Movielens-1M	**0.8873**	0.9107	2.57%	**0.7016**	0.7137	1.70%
Amazon Video	**1.8378**	4.4518	58.72%	**1.4269**	3.6123	60.50%
Amazon Music	**2.6875**	4.6111	41.72%	**2.0337**	3.7887	46.32%

Table 5. Experiment results with dimension $K = 7$

K = 7	RMSE			MAE		
	LPCSM	MF	Improvement	LPCSM	MF	Improvement
Movielens-100K	**0.9585**	0.9739	1.58%	**0.7617**	0.7655	0.50%
Movielens-1M	**0.8887**	0.9204	3.44%	**0.7037**	0.7213	2.44%
Amazon Video	**1.8948**	4.2955	55.89%	**1.4596**	3.5103	58.42%
Amazon Music	**2.7475**	4.5409	39.49%	**2.1031**	3.7731	44.26%

Table 6. Experiment results with dimension $K = 8$

K = 8	RMSE			MAE		
	LPCSM	MF	Improvement	LPCSM	MF	Improvement
Movielens-100K	**0.9642**	0.9847	2.08%	**0.7642**	0.7721	1.02%
Movielens-1M	**0.8898**	0.9177	3.04%	**0.7016**	0.7179	2.27%
Amazon Video	**1.9292**	4.1240	53.22%	**1.4950**	3.3900	55.90%
Amazon Music	**2.7906**	4.5680	38.91%	**2.1684**	3.8726	44.01%

Table 7. Experiment results with dimension $K = 9$

K = 9	RMSE			MAE		
	LPCSM	MF	Improvement	LPCSM	MF	Improvement
Movielens-100K	**0.9666**	0.9728	0.64%	0.7681	**0.7638**	−0.56%
Movielens-1M	**0.8920**	0.9147	2.48%	**0.7054**	0.7156	1.43%
Amazon Video	**1.9737**	4.0574	51.36%	**1.5452**	3.4179	54.79%
Amazon Music	**2.8336**	4.5286	37.43%	**2.2309**	3.8445	41.97%

Table 8. Experiment results with dimension $K = 10$

K = 10	RMSE			MAE		
	LPCSM	MF	Improvement	LPCSM	MF	Improvement
Movielens-100K	**0.9680**	0.9914	2.36%	**0.7695**	0.7780	1.09%
Movielens-1M	**0.8932**	0.9222	3.14%	**0.7069**	0.7206	1.90%
Amazon Video	**1.9833**	4.1007	51.64%	**1.5416**	3.4333	55.10%
Amazon Music	**2.8541**	4.4707	36.16%	**2.1978**	3.8225	42.50%

6 Conclusions and Future Works

In this paper we propose a new recommendation model, Latent Path Connected Space model (LSpace). In this model, users and items are represented as path connected space, instead of a point as used in matrix factorization model. We propose to use spatial intersection to reflect the matching degree between user and item. Experiments conducted on four real-world datasets show that our approach outperforms the Matrix Factorization model on rating prediction task, especially when the rating data is extremely sparse.

In the future, we can extend the model to deal with implicit feedback. We can also study how to use auxiliary information such as textual, social networks, temporal and spatial data to further improve the performance of recommendation.

Acknowledgment. This work was supported in part by National Natural Science Foundation of China under grant No. U1711262, 71771131, 71490724 and the MOE Project of Key Research Institute of Humanities and Social Sciences at Universities with grant No.17JJD630006.

References

1. Deshpande, M., Karypis, G.: Item-based top-n recommendation algorithms. ACM Trans. Inf. Syst. **22**(1), 143–177 (2004)
2. Herlocker, J.L., Konstan, J.A., Borchers, A., Riedl, J.: An algorithmic framework for performing collaborative filtering. In: Proceedings of the 22nd Annual International ACM SIGIR Conference on Research and Development in Information Retrieval, SIGIR (1999)

3. Hu, Y., Koren, Y., Volinsky, C.: Collaborative filtering for implicit feedback datasets. In: ICDM (2008)
4. Salakhutdinov, R., Mnih, A.: Probabilistic matrix factorization. In: Proceedings of the 20th International Conference on Neural Information Processing Systems, NIPS (2007)
5. He, X., Liao, L., Zhang, H., Nie, L., Hu, X., Chua, T.-S.: Neural collaborative filtering. In: International World Wide Web Conferences Steering Committee, WWW (2017)
6. Shi, Y., Larson, M., Hanjalic, A.: Collaborative filtering beyond the user-item matrix: a survey of the state of the art and future challenges. ACM Comput. Surv. **47**(1), 3 (2014)
7. Ling, G., Lyu, M.R., King, I.: Ratings meet reviews, a combined approach to recommend. In: Proceedings of the 8th ACM Conference on Recommender Systems, RecSys (2014)
8. McAuley, J., Leskovec, J.: Hidden factors and hidden topics, understanding rating dimensions with review text. In: Proceedings of the 7th ACM Conference on Recommender Systems, RecSys (2013)
9. Wang, C., Blei, D.M.: Collaborative topic modeling for recommending scientific articles. In: Proceedings of the 17th ACM SIGKDD International Conference on Knowledge Discovery and Data Mining, KDD (2011)
10. Wang, H., Wang, N., Yeung, D.-Y.: Collaborative deep learning for recommender systems. In: Proceedings of the 21th ACM SIGKDD International Conference on Knowledge Discovery and Data Mining, KDD (2015)
11. Koren, Y., Bell, R., Volinsky, C.: Matrix factorization techniques for recommender systems. Computer **42**(8), 30–37 (2009)
12. Salakhutdinov, R., Mnih, A.: Bayesian probabilistic matrix factorization using Markov chain Monte Carlo. In: Proceedings of the 25th International Conference on Machine Learning. ACM (2008)
13. Purushotham, S., Liu, Y. Kuo, C.-C.J.: Collaborative topic regression with social matrix factorization for recommendation systems. In: Proceedings of the 29th International Conference on Machine Learning, ICML (2012)
14. Kim, D., Park, C., Oh, J., Lee, S., Yu, H.: Convolutional matrix factorization for document context-aware recommendation. In: Proceedings of the 8th ACM Conference on Recommender Systems, RecSys (2016)
15. https://en.wikipedia.org/wiki/Jordan_measure
16. Kingma, D., Ba, J.: Adam: a method for stochastic optimization. arXiv preprint arXiv:1412.6980 (2014)
17. https://en.wikipedia.org/wiki/Connected_space#Path_connectedness

Storage, Indexing and Physical Database Design

FreshJoin: An Efficient and Adaptive Algorithm for Set Containment Join

Jizhou Luo$^{(\boxtimes)}$, Wei Zhang, Shengfei Shi, Hong Gao, Jianzhong Li,
Tao Zhang, and Zening Zhou

School of Computer Science and Technology, Harbin Institute of Technology,
Heilongjiang, China
{luojizhou,weizhang,shengfei,honggao,lijzh}@hit.edu.cn
zorseti@qq.com, 1666274344@qq.com

Abstract. This paper revisits set containment join (SCJ), which has many fundamental applications in commercial and scientific fields. To improve the performance further, this paper proposes a new adaptive parameter-free in-memory algorithm for SCJ, named as FreshJoin. It accomplishes this by exploiting two flat indices, which record three kinds of signatures (*i.e.,* the two least frequent elements and a hash signature). Experiments on 16 real-life datasets show that FreshJoin usually reduces more than 50% of space costs while remains as competitive as the state-of-the-art algorithms in running time.

Keywords: Set containment join · Frequency hash · Join algorithm

1 Introduction

Sets are ubiquitous and widely used in databases, where data are processed and analyzed. For example, a set-valued attribute of a tuple may record the prerequisites of a course, or the labels of a digital image, or the tokens in an email, and so on. With this comes a large body of research interests on efficient algorithms for fundamental operations on such attributes such as containment joins [1–10], containment queries (*e.g.,* [11]), and similarity joins (*e.g.,* [12]).

This paper focuses on set containment join (SCJ). That is, given two relations $\mathcal{R}$ and $\mathcal{S}$ with a set-valued attribute *set* each, to find all pairs $\langle r, s \rangle \in \mathcal{R} \times \mathcal{S}$ such that $r.set \subseteq s.set$. For instance, in the online course selection system, each course has a set of prerequisites and each student has a set of courses he/she has learned. Let e_i denote a course. Figure 1(a) illustrates prerequisites of courses in $\mathcal{R}$ and Fig. 1(b) shows learnt courses for each student in $\mathcal{S}$. Naturally, a student s can choose a course r only if s has studied all prerequisites of r (*i.e.,* $r.set \subseteq s.set$). By executing SCJ $\mathcal{R} \bowtie_{\subseteq} \mathcal{S}$, the system can forecast all potential course selections and make arrangement for each course correspondingly.

The early SCJ algorithms [6–10] are mainly disk-based. And, their performances are mainly bounded by their underlying in-memory processing strategies [3]. Recently, researchers turned to study in-memory algorithms [1–5], due

© Springer Nature Switzerland AG 2019
J. Shao et al. (Eds.): APWeb-WAIM 2019, LNCS 11642, pp. 175–190, 2019.
https://doi.org/10.1007/978-3-030-26075-0_14

id	set	id	set	id	set
r_1	$\{e_1,e_3,e_4,e_6\}$	s_1	$\{e_1,e_3,e_5,e_6,e_9,e_{11}\}$	s_7	$\{e_4,e_6,e_7,e_{10},e_{11}\}$
r_2	$\{e_1,e_3,e_9,e_{10}\}$	s_2	$\{e_2,e_4,e_5,e_9,e_{10},e_{11}\}$	s_8	$\{e_4,e_7,e_8,e_{10},e_{11}\}$
r_3	$\{e_3,e_5,e_9\}$	s_3	$\{e_2,e_5,e_7,e_9,e_{10},e_{11}\}$	s_9	$\{e_5,e_6,e_8,e_9,e_{10},e_{11}\}$
r_4	$\{e_3,e_7,e_8,e_{11}\}$	s_4	$\{e_3,e_7,e_8,e_9,e_{10},e_{11}\}$	s_{10}	$\{e_6,e_7,e_8,e_{10},e_{11}\}$
r_5	$\{e_5,e_7,e_9,e_{10}\}$	s_5	$\{e_3,e_8,e_9,e_{10},e_{11}\}$	s_{11}	$\{e_6,e_8,e_9,e_{10},e_{11}\}$
r_6	$\{e_5,e_8,e_{10},e_{11}\}$	s_6	$\{e_4,e_5,e_6,e_7,e_8,e_9\}$	s_{12}	$\{e_7,e_8,e_9,e_{10},e_{11}\}$
r_7	$\{e_7,e_8,e_9\}$		The fequency of e_i equals i for $i=1,2,...,11$		

(a) A sample relation $\mathcal{R}$ (b) A sample relation $\mathcal{S}$

Fig. 1. Two relations for running examples

to the improvement of modern hardware and the popularity of distributed computing infrastructures. Such algorithms are either signature baaed or prefix-tree based. Signature-based algorithms (e.g., SHJ [10], PSJ [9], APSJ [7] and PTSJ [3]) encode each set as a hash signature, and use bitwise operation on signatures as a filter to check possible containment. The main challenge there is how to find potential signature pairs that may pass through the filter. The usual way is to, for each signature from $\mathcal{R}$, enumerate all potential signatures from $\mathcal{S}$, which incurs high CPU cost and works well only on short signatures although special structures such as PATRICIA TRIE [3] can be used to alleviate this defect to some extent. While, prefix-tree-based algorithms (*e.g.*, Pretti [5], Pretti+ [3], LIMIT [4], Piejoin [2], ttjoin [1]) achieve high speeds by exploiting prefix tree(s) to share the intersection operations (of inverted lists) among any tuples $r \in \mathcal{R}$ which have common prefixes. However, prefix trees need high space cost. In fact, when the average set size is large, the space for prefix trees is several times of space for the data itself. Although the space cost can be sharply reduced by limiting the height of the tree (*e.g.*, LIMIT [4], ttjoin [1]), or storing the tree as several arrays (*e.g.*, Piejoin [2]), or compressing the non-branching nodes into single nodes (Pretti+ [3]), these algorithms do not perform well on all datasets because their performance depend on some empirical parameters (*e.g.*, the height of prefix trees) or other factors which are hardly adaptive to datasets themselves.

In the big-data era, it is important to make SCJ-algorithms well-scaled in both space cost and running time. To do so, this paper proposes a new parameter-free adaptive algorithm, named as **frequency-hash join** or FreshJoin in short, to evaluate SCJ efficiently. FreshJoin gives up prefix trees totally to reduce space cost. Instead, it uses two flat indices to record three kinds of signatures. The first is the hash signatures (*i.e.*, bitmaps) of sets in both $\mathcal{R}$ and $\mathcal{S}$, and the second (third *resp.*) is the (2nd *resp.*) least frequent elements of sets in $\mathcal{R}$. These signatures are well organized in the new index structure such that (1) FreshJoin can use the bitwise filter (like in SHJ [10] and PTSJ [3]) but without enumerating the hash codes; and (2) FreshJoin can exploit the hash signatures to reduce as many as possible tuple pairs fed into the bitwise filter. This guarantees that FreshJoin evaluates SCJ efficiently. Besides, FreshJoin performs SCJ adaptively according to the statistics of the datasets by allowing the lengths of hash codes to change adaptively. Compared with the state-of-the-art SCJ algorithms, FreshJoin usually keeps as competitive as its counterparts in running time and reduces even more than 50% of space cost. In the worst case, it remains as competitive as its counterparts in both space costs and running time. Our theoretical analysis provides a rule to distinguish the worst case from other cases.

Our main contributions include: (1) We propose a parameter-free adaptive algorithm to evaluate SCJ efficiently, (2) We propose a sparse asymmetric inverted index to make three kinds of signatures work coordinately and economically, (3) We propose a new hash function to estimate the signature length adaptively by partitioning the elements into three groups according to their frequencies, and (4) We conduct experiments on 16 real-life representative datasets and find that our algorithm is adaptive, well scaled, efficient and effective.

The remainder is organized as follows. Section 2 is preliminaries. Section 3 describes the framework of FreshJoin algorithm. The hash function and the signature length are discussed in Sect. 4. Section 5 reports experimental results. Section 6 summaries the related work, followed by the conclusion in Sect. 7.

2 Preliminaries

This section introduces basic concepts and definitions (summarized in Table 1).

Table 1. The summary of notations

Notation	Definition
$\mathcal{U}; \lvert \mathcal{U} \rvert$	Universe set; size of universe set
$r, \mathcal{R}; s, \mathcal{S}$	A tuple, a set-valued relation
$\lvert \mathcal{R} \rvert; \lvert \mathcal{S} \rvert$	Number of tuples in a set-valued relation
$f_{\mathcal{S}}(e_i)$	Frequency of element e_i in $\mathcal{S}$
$I_{\mathcal{R}}(e_i)$	Inverted list of element e_i for tuples in $\mathcal{R}$
$I_{\mathcal{S}}(e_i)$	Inverted list of element e_i for tuples in $\mathcal{S}$
$sig_{\mathcal{R}}(r_j)$	Hash code of a set $r_j.set$ for $r_j \in \mathcal{R}$
$sig_{\mathcal{S}}(s_j)$	Hash code of a set $s_j.set$ for $s_j \in \mathcal{S}$
$e_j^{(r)}; e_j^{(s)}$	j-th element in $r.set$, $s.set$ for $r \in \mathcal{R}$, $s \in \mathcal{S}$
$l_{avg}(\mathcal{S})$	Average size of sets $s.set$ for $s \in \mathcal{S}$
$\sigma_{\mathcal{S}}$	Standard deviation of all $\lvert s.set \rvert$ for $s \in \mathcal{S}$
M	$e_M \in \mathcal{U}$ is the first mid frequency element
H	$e_H \in \mathcal{U}$ is the first high frequency element
w_{sig}	Length of hash code, in unit of 64-bit integer
M'	$b_0 \sim b_{M'-1}$ in signature is for low frequency
H'	$b_{M'} \sim b_{H'-1}$ in signature is for low frequency

We assume a discrete universe set, denoted as $\mathcal{U}$, consisting of a linearly ordered list of elements $e_1, e_2, \cdots, e_n$. Thus, each set can be viewed as a subsequence of $\mathcal{U}$. It is easy to figure out an algorithm verify to verify whether a set A is a subset of a set B in $O(|A| + |B|)$ time.

Set-valued relations associate each tuple with a set from $\mathcal{U}$. The schemas of set-valued relations are represented as $\mathbb{R} = (\mathbb{A}_1, \cdots, \mathbb{A}_p, SET)$, where $\mathbb{A}_i$ is an attribute with domain Ω_i for $i = 1, \cdots, p$ and SET is an attribute with domain $2^{\mathcal{U}}$. A tuple r over schema $\mathbb{R}$ is a finite collection that contains for each $\mathbb{A}_i$ a value $v_i \in \Omega_i$ and for SET a set $r.set$ from the universe $\mathcal{U}$. The i-th element of $r.set$ is denoted as $e_i^{(r)}$ without any ambiguity. A set-valued relation $\mathcal{R}$ over schema $\mathbb{R}$ is a finite collection of tuples over $\mathbb{R}$. The size of $\mathcal{R}$, denoted as $|\mathcal{R}|$, is the number of tuples in $\mathcal{R}$.

Definition 1 (Set Containment Join). *Given two set-valued relations $\mathcal{R}$ and $\mathcal{S}$, the set containment join (or SCJ in short) between $\mathcal{R}$ and $\mathcal{S}$, denoted as $\mathcal{R} \bowtie_{\subseteq} \mathcal{S}$, is to find all tuple-pairs $\langle r, s \rangle \in \mathcal{R} \times \mathcal{S}$ such that $r.set \subseteq s.set$. That is $\mathcal{R} \bowtie_{\subseteq} \mathcal{S} = \{\langle r, s \rangle | r \in \mathcal{R}, s \in \mathcal{S}, r.set \subseteq s.set\}$.*

Example 1. For $\mathcal{R}$ and $\mathcal{S}$ in Fig. 1, the result of set containment join $\mathcal{R} \bowtie_{\subseteq} \mathcal{S}$ is $\{\langle r_3, s_1 \rangle, \langle r_4, s_4 \rangle, \langle r_5, s_3 \rangle, \langle r_6, s_9 \rangle, \langle r_7, s_4 \rangle, \langle r_7, s_6 \rangle, \langle r_7, s_{12} \rangle\}$.

Further, we assume $\mathcal{R}$ and $\mathcal{S}$ share a common universe set $\mathcal{U}$, and all elements in $\mathcal{U}$ are sorted in ascending order of their frequencies, which is defined below.

Definition 2 (frequency of element). *Given $\mathcal{R}$ and $\mathcal{S}$ of SCJ $\mathcal{R} \bowtie_{\subseteq} \mathcal{S}$, the $\mathcal{S}$-frequency (or frequency in short) of each $e_i \in \mathcal{U}$, denoted as $f_{\mathcal{S}}(e_i)$, is the number of tuples $s \in \mathcal{S}$ such that $e_i \in s.set$. That is $f_{\mathcal{S}}(e_i) = |\{s | s \in \mathcal{S}, e_i \in s.set\}|$.*

Example 2. For $\mathcal{R}$ and $\mathcal{S}$ in Fig. 1, $\mathcal{U} = \{e_1, e_2, \cdots, e_{11}\}$, $f_{\mathcal{S}}(e_i) = i$ for $i = 1, 2, ..., 11$, and $\mathcal{U}$ are sorted in ascending order of frequencies.

Based on the sorted universe, tuples in both input relations of SCJ can be sorted further by the data loading procedure in *lexicographical order* of their sets. Most SCJ algorithms (*e.g.*, Pretti [5], Pretti+ [3], LIMIT [4], Piejoin [2] and ttjoin [1]) benefit from this by accelerating both the creation of prefix tree and the joining procedure. This paper also assume the input relations be sorted in this way. For instance, $\mathcal{R}$ (Fig. 1(a)) and $\mathcal{S}$ (Fig. 1(b)) are sorted.

A naive SCJ algorithm applies procedure verify on each pair $\langle r, s \rangle \in \mathcal{R} \times \mathcal{S}$, and results in $O(|\mathcal{R}| \cdot |\mathcal{S}| \cdot l_{avg}(\mathcal{S}))$ time. Hash signatures can be used to accelerate this algorithm by adding a bitwise filter before applying verify.

Hash signatures of sets are bitmaps of length $w_{sig} \cdot 64$. They are used to represent or approximate sets in w_{sig} 64-bit integers. In SCJ, it suffices to set one bit in the signature for each element of the set. A function $hash$ is applied to map each element to an integer in $[0, w_{sig} * 64 - 1]$. Thus, the signature $sig(set)$ of a set set can be computed by successively setting $hash(e_i)$-th bit for each $e_i \in set$. Such signatures are all SCJ-friendly, *i.e.*, $set_1 \subseteq set_2 \Rightarrow sig(set_1) \& sig(set_2) = sig(set_1)$ (& is the bitwise AND operation). Via this fact, it is easy to implement a bitwise filter bitwiseFilter which is helpful for SCJ algorithms.

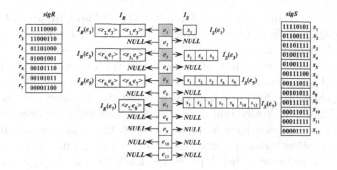

Fig. 2. freshIndex of sample relations in Fig. 1

Example 3. Here is a toy hash function h, which generates 8-bit SCJ-friendly signatures for data in Fig. 1. $h(e_1) = 0$. $h(e_2) = h(e_3) = 1$. $h(e_4) = h(e_5) = 2$. $h(e_6) = 3$. $h(e_7) = h(e_8) = 4$. $h(e_9) = 5$. $h(e_{10}) = 6$ and $h(e_{11}) = 7$. Since $r_6 = \{e_5, e_8, e_{10}, e_{11}\}$, only the 3rd, 5th, 7th and 8th bit of $sig(r_6)$ are 1s, *i.e.*, $sig(r_6) = 00101011$. Similarly, $sig(s_9) = 00111111$ and $sig(s_{10}) = 00011011$. Since $sig(r_6)\&sig(s_9) = sig(r_6)$, $\langle r_6, s_9 \rangle$ may be in $\mathcal{R} \bowtie_\subseteq \mathcal{S}$. While $sig(r_6)\&sig(s_{10}) \neq sig(r_6)$, $\langle r_6, s_{10} \rangle \notin \mathcal{R} \bowtie_\subseteq \mathcal{S}$.

Via the hash signatures and the bitwise filter, SCJ can be evaluated by the filter-and-refine framework, which enumerates all $s \in \mathcal{S}$ probably satisfying $sig(r)\&sig(s) = sig(r)$ for each $r \in \mathcal{R}$ and calls verify $\langle r, s \rangle$ only for pairs passing through the filter. Unlike the approaches adopted in SHJ [10] and PTSJ [3], this paper uses smart mechanisms to avoid such enumerations by establishing connections from hash signatures of $r \in \mathcal{R}$ to hash signatures of such $s \in \mathcal{S}$.

3   Framework of Freshjoin

We first describe our index structure, discuss its creation and space cost (Sect. 3.1). Then, we present FreshJoin algorithm, state its correctness and analyze its complexity (Sect. 3.2). The detail of the hash function is postponed to next section, except that the signature length w_{sig} is assumed.

3.1   The Index and Its Creation

The FreshJoin algorithm uses 3 kinds of signatures. The first is the hash codes associated with tuples in both $\mathcal{R}$ and $\mathcal{S}$. The second is the least frequent element in set $r.set$ for each $r \in \mathcal{R}$. And, the 3rd is 2nd least frequent elements in set $r.set$ for each $r \in \mathcal{R}$. To make these signatures work coordinately, they are well organized into two kinds of flat index structures, *i.e.*, arrays and inverted indices.

The Structure of freshIndex. Two arrays $sig_{\mathcal{R}}$ and $sig_{\mathcal{S}}$ are used to index hash codes for $\mathcal{R}$ and $\mathcal{S}$ respectively. Each unit of the arrays stores w_{sig} 64-bit integers, and can be accessed via the IDs of tuples in $\mathcal{R}$ or $\mathcal{S}$.

A sparse inverted index $I_\mathcal{R}$ is used to index the 2nd and 3rd kind of signatures for tuples in $\mathcal{R}$. Each $e \in \mathcal{U}$ has an inverted list $I_\mathcal{R}(e)$ in $I_\mathcal{R}$. Each item in $I_\mathcal{R}(e)$ is a pair $\langle i, e' \rangle$, which means that $r_i \in \mathcal{R}$ and e (e' reps.) is the (2nd resp.) least frequent element in $r_i.set$. All items in each list are sorted such that items with a same second component are stored contiguously. In this way, all tuples r with $r.set$ having the same 2nd least frequent element can be processed by FreshJoin in a batched manner. Notice that, each $r \in \mathcal{R}$ is indexed only once in $I_\mathcal{R}$. Since sets may share a common least frequent element, many $I_\mathcal{R}(e)$s may be null.

Besides, an other sparse inverted index $I_\mathcal{S}$ is used to index the tuples in $\mathcal{S}$. Each $e \in \mathcal{U}$ has an inverted list $I_\mathcal{S}(e)$ in $I_\mathcal{S}$. Each item in $I_\mathcal{S}(e)$ is a tuple ID i, which means that $s_i \in \mathcal{S}$ and $e \in s_i.set$. Each list $I_\mathcal{S}(e)$ is sorted in an ascending order of its items. In this way, the time cost of computing the intersection of two inverted lists is proportional to the sum of their lengths. Especially, if $e \in \mathcal{U}$ is not the 2nd or 3rd type of signatures for any tuple $r \in \mathcal{R}$, then $I_\mathcal{S}(e)$ is null.

Example 4. Figure 2 illustrates the index structure with data in Fig. 1. Array $sig_\mathcal{R}$ ($sig_\mathcal{S}$ resp.) stores hash signatures of tuples in $\mathcal{R}$ ($\mathcal{S}$ resp.), which are generated via the toy hash function in Example 3. In $I_\mathcal{R}$, $I_\mathcal{R}(e_1)$ contains two items $\langle r_1, e_3 \rangle$ and $\langle r_2, e_3 \rangle$, since only sets of $r_1, r_2 \in \mathcal{R}$ have e_1 as their least frequent elements. $I_\mathcal{R}(e_2)$ is null, since $\mathcal{R}$ has no tuple with e_2 as its least frequent elements. Other lists in $I_\mathcal{R}$ is similar. While in $I_\mathcal{S}$, $I_\mathcal{S}(e)$ is non-null only if $I_\mathcal{R}(e)$ is not null. For instance, $I_\mathcal{S}(e_3)$ contains three items, because $I_\mathcal{R}(e_3)$ is not null and only the sets of $s_1, s_4, s_5 \in \mathcal{S}$ contains e_3. Although e_{11} is the most frequent element, $I_\mathcal{S}(e_{11})$ is null because $I_\mathcal{R}(e_{11})$ is null.

The Creation of freshIndex. The idea to create freshIndex is rather simple. Both $\mathcal{R}$ and $\mathcal{S}$ are sorted lexicographically first, which guarantees a natural order on inverted lists in both $I_\mathcal{R}$ and $I_\mathcal{S}$. Then, $\mathcal{R}$ is indexed and elements in $\mathcal{U}$ are marked. Finally, the $\mathcal{S}$ is indexed according to the marked elements.

Algorithm 1 implements the ideas above. It indexes $\mathcal{R}$ in Line 1–9 and indexes $\mathcal{S}$ in Line 10–15. When $\mathcal{R}$ is indexed, it is sorted first (Line 1), and then each $r_i \in \mathcal{R}$ is indexed (Line 2–9). For r_i, the hash code of $r_i.set$ is obtained by invoking hashAset (see Sect. 4) and stored in the array unit $sig_\mathcal{R}(r_i)$ (Line 3). After that, r_i is indexed in $I_\mathcal{R}$ (Line 4–9). If $|r_i.set| = 1$, then item $\langle r_i.ID, - \rangle$ is appended to $I_\mathcal{R}(e_1^{(r_i)})$ (Line 5) and $e_1^{(r_i)}$ is marked (Line 6). Otherwise, item $\langle r_i.ID, e_2^{(r_i)} \rangle$ is appended to $I_\mathcal{R}(e_1^{(r_i)})$ (Line 8), and both $e_1^{(r_i)}$ and $e_2^{(r_i)}$ are marked (Line 9). When $\mathcal{S}$ is indexed, it is also sorted first (Line 10), and then each $s_i \in \mathcal{S}$ is indexed (Line 11–15). The hash code of $s_i.set$ is obtained and stored in $sig_\mathcal{S}(s_i)$ (Line 12). After that, the ID of s_i is added into some inverted lists according to the elements in $s_i.set$ are marked or not (Line 14–15).

Analysis. It is straightforward to verify that the output of Algorithm 1 is the expected index structure. The time complexity of Algorithm 1 is postponed to Sect. 4 till the procedure hashAset is clear. Now, we answer questions below. Can the design of the sparse inverted indices really save any space? And, why does $I_\mathcal{R}(e)$ use only the least frequent elements?

Algorithm 1. freshIndex $(\mathcal{R},\mathcal{S})$

Input: two set-valued relations $\mathcal{R}$ and $\mathcal{S}$
Output: fresh index of set containment join $\mathcal{R} \bowtie_{\subseteq} \mathcal{S}$

1 sort all tuples in $\mathcal{R}$ lexicographically as $r_1, \cdots, r_{|\mathcal{R}|}$;
2 **for** $i \leftarrow 1$ to $|\mathcal{R}|$ **do**
3      $sig_{\mathcal{R}}(r_i) \leftarrow$ hashAset$(r_i.set)$;   // see sec. 4
4   **if** $|r_i.set| = 1$ **then**
5   add $\langle r_i.ID, - \rangle$ to the end of $I_{\mathcal{R}}(e_1^{(r_i)})$;
6   mark $e_1^{(r_i)}$;
7   **else**
8   add $\langle r_i.ID, e_2^{(r_i)} \rangle$ to the end of $I_{\mathcal{R}}(e_1^{(r_i)})$;
9   mark both $e_1^{(r_i)}$ and $e_2^{(r_i)}$;
10 sort all tuples in $\mathcal{S}$ lexicographically as $s_1, \cdots, s_{|\mathcal{S}|}$;
11 **for** $i \leftarrow 1$ to $|\mathcal{S}|$ **do**
12     $sig_{\mathcal{S}}(s_i) \leftarrow$ hashAset$(s_i.set)$;   // see sec. 4
13   **for** $j \leftarrow 1$ to $|s_i.set|$ **do**
14   **if** $e_j^{(s_i)}$ is *marked* **then**
15   add $s_i.ID$ to the end of $I_{\mathcal{S}}(e_j^{(s_i)})$;

The first question can be answered with the conclusions below, whose proof can be found in our technique report [13].

Lemma 1. *Assume each set r.set ($r \in \mathcal{R}$) be sampled from $\mathcal{U}$ uniformly and independently, then at most $0.9 \cdot |\mathcal{R}|$ elements in $\mathcal{U}$ are marked by Algorithm 1.*

Theorem 1. *The freshIndex of relations $\mathcal{R}$ and $\mathcal{S}$ needs $O((2 + w_{sig}) \cdot |\mathcal{R}| + \lceil \frac{\min(|\mathcal{U}|, 0.9|\mathcal{R}|)}{|\mathcal{U}|} \cdot l_{avg}(\mathcal{S}) + w_{sig}\rceil \cdot |\mathcal{S}|)$ space.*

Remark. Notice that $\frac{\min(|U|, 0.9|\mathcal{R}|)}{|\mathcal{U}|} \leq 1$. Theorem 1 tells us that: (1) when $|\mathcal{R}| \leq |\mathcal{U}|$, freshIndex really saves space; (2) When $|\mathcal{R}| >> |\mathcal{U}|$, freshIndex is a usual inverted index and can not save space; (3) When both w_{sig} and $l_{avg}(\mathcal{S})$ are constants, freshIndex only needs linear space. These conclusions explain well the experimental results in Sect. 5.

For the second question, we have the theorem below (see technique report [13] for its proof). It tells us that $\cap_{e \in r.set} I_{\mathcal{S}}(e)$ can be well approximated even if $k = \frac{\ln|\mathcal{S}|}{\ln|\mathcal{U}| - \ln l_{avg}(\mathcal{S})}$ inverted lists are considered. In fact, $k \geq 3$ only if $|\mathcal{S}| >> |\mathcal{U}|^3$, and $k < 3$ holds for most practical datasets. This positively motivates us to adopt two least frequent elements in $I_{\mathcal{R}}$ and leave intersection of two inverted lists to the bitwise filter.

Theorem 2. *Assume each s.set ($s \in \mathcal{S}$) be sampled from $\mathcal{U}$ uniformly and independently with average length $l_{avg}(\mathcal{S})$, then $E(|\cap_{i=1}^{k} I_{\mathcal{S}}(e_i)|) = (\frac{l_{avg}(\mathcal{S})}{|\mathcal{U}|})^k \cdot |\mathcal{S}|$ for $\forall e_1, ..., e_k \in \mathcal{U}$. Moreover, if $k = \frac{\ln|\mathcal{S}|}{\ln|\mathcal{U}| - \ln l_{avg}(\mathcal{S})}$, then $E(|\cap_{i=1}^{k} I_{\mathcal{S}}(e_i)|) = 1$ for $\forall e_1, ..., e_k \subset \mathcal{U}$.*

3.2   The Join Algorithm

The basic idea of FreshJoin is similar to that of SHJ [10]. That is to use bitwise operations on hash signatures of sets to prune away as many as possible set-pairs whose subset relationships need not to be verified, because bitwise filter is much more economic than the verification. FreshJoin accomplishes this more efficiently by applying appropriately the three kinds of signatures indexed in freshIndex. On the one hand, it uses the 2nd type of signatures of tuples in $\mathcal{R}$ (*i.e.*, the least frequent elements) to locate the hash-code-pairs, which are fed into the bitwise filter, by only joining tuples indexed in $I_{\mathcal{R}}(e)$ and $I_{\mathcal{S}}(e)$ for the same es. This is feasible because any set $s.set$ ($s \in \mathcal{S}$) with $s.set \supseteq r.set$ ($r \in \mathcal{R}$) must contain the least frequent element in $r.set$. On the other hand, since $I_{\mathcal{S}}(e)$ may be very long and comparisons between tuple IDs are often more economic than bitwise filter, FreshJoin exploits the 3rd type of signatures of tuples in $\mathcal{R}$ to reduce the number of hash-signature-pairs by computing the intersection of $I_{\mathcal{S}}(e)$ and $I_{\mathcal{S}}(e')$, where e's are the second component of indexed items in $I_{\mathcal{R}}(e)$.

Algorithm 2 implements the ideas above. First, it calls freshIndex to build index (Line 1), and initializes the output set J (Line 2). Then, it processes each pair $\langle I_{\mathcal{R}}(e_i), I_{\mathcal{S}}(e_i) \rangle$ of inverted lists sequentially (Line 3–14). Null inverted lists are skipped over (Line 4). Indexed items in each non-null list $I_{\mathcal{R}}(e_i)$ are processed one by one (Line 7–14). For each item $\langle j, e_u \rangle \in I_{\mathcal{R}}(e_i)$, it determines whether $I_{\mathcal{S}}(e_i) \cap I_{\mathcal{S}}(e_u)$ needs to be computed, according to whether e_u has been encountered or not. If yes, it does not compute the intersection and skips over Line 8–10. Otherwise, it computes the intersection (Line 9) and traces the new encountered 2nd least frequent element (Line 10). Next, for each remaining tuple ID $k \in List$, it accesses the arrays $\langle sig_{\mathcal{R}}, sig_{\mathcal{S}} \rangle$ to obtain a hash-signature-pair, and feeds each such pair into the bitwise filter (Line 13). Finally, the surviving pairs $\langle r_j, s_k \rangle$ are verified and added into J if $r_j.set \subseteq s_k.set$ (Line 14).

Example 5. Consider SCJ with data in Fig. 1 and the index in Fig. 2. $I_{\mathcal{R}}(e_i)$ and $I_{\mathcal{S}}(e_i)$ are joined for each e_i. When e_1 is considered, since $\langle r_1, e_3 \rangle \in I_{\mathcal{R}}(e_1)$, $I_{\mathcal{S}}(e_1) \cap I_{\mathcal{S}}(e_3) = List = \{s_1\}$ is computed. Since $sig_{\mathcal{R}}(r_1) \& sig_{\mathcal{S}}(s_1) = sig_{\mathcal{R}}(r_1)$, pair $\langle r_1, s_1 \rangle$ is verified and output. For $\langle r_2, e_3 \rangle \in I_{\mathcal{R}}(e_1)$, since it contains the same e_3 as $\langle r_1, e_3 \rangle$, the intersection is not recomputed. Thus, $List$ is still $\{s_1\}$. Since $sig_{\mathcal{R}}(r_2) \& sig_{\mathcal{S}}(s_1) \neq sig_{\mathcal{R}}(r_2)$, pair $\langle r_2, s_1 \rangle$ is pruned away. After all lists are dealt similarly, the result shown in Example 1 is obtained.

Correctness. We assert that the output J of Algorithm 2 is exactly $\mathcal{R} \bowtie_{\subseteq} \mathcal{S}$. It is obvious that $J \subseteq \mathcal{R} \bowtie_{\subseteq} \mathcal{S}$, because $r.set \subseteq s.set$ is verified in Line 14 for any $\langle r, s \rangle \in J$. Reversely, if $\langle r, s \rangle \in \mathcal{R} \bowtie_{\subseteq} \mathcal{S}$, We show $\langle r, s \rangle \in J$ as follows. Without loss of generality, assume $|r.set| \geq 2$. First of all, $\langle r.ID, e_2^{(r)} \rangle$ is indexed in list $I_{\mathcal{R}}(e_1^{(r)})$, according to Algorithm 1. Of course, both $e_1^{(r)}$ and $e_2^{(r)}$ are marked. Now that $r.set \subseteq s.set$, we have $e_1^{(r)} \in s.set$ and $e_2^{(r)} \in s.set$. Moreover, $s.ID$ is indexed in both $I_{\mathcal{S}}(e_1^{(r)})$ and $I_{\mathcal{S}}(e_2^{(r)})$, according to Line 13–15 of Algorithm 1. Therefore, $s.ID$ appears in $List = I_{\mathcal{S}}(e_1^{(r)}) \cap I_{\mathcal{S}}(e_2^{(r)})$ when item $\langle r.ID, e_2^{(r)} \rangle$ is processed in Line 7–14 of Algorithm 2. Since $r.sct \subseteq s.set$ and the signature is

---

Algorithm 2. freshjoin $(\mathcal{R}, \mathcal{S})$

Input: two set-valued relations $\mathcal{R}$ and $\mathcal{S}$
Output: the result set J of $\mathcal{R} \bowtie_{\subseteq} \mathcal{S}$

1 $I_{\mathcal{R}}, sig_{\mathcal{R}}, I_{\mathcal{S}}, sig_{\mathcal{S}} \leftarrow$ freshIndex $(\mathcal{R}, \mathcal{S})$;
2 $J \leftarrow \emptyset$;
3 **for** $i \leftarrow 1$ to $|\mathcal{U}|$ **do**
4   If $I_{\mathcal{R}}(e_i) = NULL$ **then** continue;
5       $e \leftarrow -$;
6       $List \leftarrow I_{\mathcal{S}}(e_i)$;
7   **foreach** $\langle j, e_u \rangle \in I_{\mathcal{R}}(e_i)$ **do**
8   **if** $e \neq e_u$ **then**
9               $List \leftarrow I_{\mathcal{S}}(e_i) \cap I_{\mathcal{S}}(e_u)$;
10              $e \leftarrow e_u$;
11   **foreach** $k \in List$ **do**
12   If $sig_{\mathcal{R}}(r_j) \& sig_{\mathcal{S}}(s_k) \neq sig_{\mathcal{S}}(r_j)$ **then**
13   continue;
14   If $verify(r_j, s_k)$ **then** $J \leftarrow J \cup \{\langle r_j, s_k \rangle\}$;
15 **return** J;

SCJ-friendly, $\langle r, s \rangle$ passes through the bitwise filter (Line 12) and containment verification (Line 14). Thus, $\langle r, s \rangle \in J$.

Complexity. We ignore the verification in Line 14 and obtain the theorem below, whose proof can be found in our technique report [13].

Theorem 3. *Except the costs of verification in Line 14, Algorithm 2 needs extra cost of* $O(|\mathcal{U}| \log |\mathcal{U}| + (|\mathcal{R}| + |\mathcal{S}|) l_{avg}(\mathcal{S})) + O(\frac{|\mathcal{R}| \cdot |\mathcal{S}| \cdot l_{avg}(S)}{|\mathcal{U}|} \cdot (1 + \frac{|\mathcal{S}| \cdot l_{avg}(S) \cdot w_{sig}}{|\mathcal{U}|^2}))$.

Remark. The former item in Theorem 3 is the total cost to index both input relations, and the latter item is the total cost to perform SCJ. It tells us when FreshJoin performs SCJ efficiently and when inefficiently, which explains well the experimental results in Sect. 5. In fact, the joining procedure takes (1) nearly constant time when $|\mathcal{U}| >> |\mathcal{R}| \cdot |\mathcal{S}|$; (2) $O(l_{avg}(\mathcal{S}))$ time when $|\mathcal{U}| \approx |\mathcal{R}| \cdot |\mathcal{S}|$; (3) $O(|\mathcal{R}| \cdot l_{avg}(S))$ time when $|\mathcal{S}| \approx |\mathcal{U}|$; (4) $O(|\mathcal{R}|)$ time when $|\mathcal{S}| \cdot l_{avg}(S) \approx |\mathcal{U}|$; (5) $O(|\mathcal{S}| \cdot l_{avg}(S) \cdot (1 + \frac{|\mathcal{S}| \cdot l_{avg}(S) \cdot w_{sig}}{|\mathcal{U}|^2}))$ time when $|\mathcal{R}| \approx |\mathcal{U}|$; and (6) even $O(|\mathcal{R}| \cdot |\mathcal{S}|^2)$ time when $|\mathcal{U}|$ is very small (comparing to both $|\mathcal{S}|$ and $|\mathcal{R}|$), which is the worst case of FreshJoin.

4 Hash Signatures of Sets

This section discusses the hash signatures for all sets. We first presents basic ideas and the framework of our method, then proposes a new hash function, and finally discusses the length w_{sig} with the hash function.

Framework of the Hash Method. The hash method distinguishes three kinds of elements in $\mathcal{U}$, i.e., low (mid and high) frequency elements. To make the method adaptive to any datasets, the definitions of these elements should not depend on any distribution of the frequencies. We adopt a constant α and consider the accumulated frequencies. Let $total = \sum_{i=1}^{|\mathcal{U}|} f_S(e_i)$. If integers M, H satisfy $\sum_{i=1}^{M-1} f_S(e_i) \leq \alpha \cdot total$, $\sum_{i=1}^{M} f_S(e_i) > \alpha \cdot total$, $\sum_{i=1}^{H-1} f_S(e_i) \leq (1-\alpha) \cdot total$, $\sum_{i=1}^{H} f_S(e_i) > (1-\alpha) \cdot total$, then all $e_1, ..., e_{M-1}$ are called as low frequency elements, all $e_M, ..., e_{H-1}$ are called as mid frequency elements, and all $e_H, ..., e_{|\mathcal{U}|}$ are called as high frequency elements.

This paper fixes $\alpha = 0.25$ and leaves it for future work to determine α according to the datasets. Thus, if the frequencies follow a zipfian distribution, then the first $|\mathcal{U}|^{3/4}$ elements are low frequency ones, and the last $|\mathcal{U}|^{1/4}$ elements are high frequency ones. For example, for datasets in Fig. 1, e_1, e_2, e_3, e_4, e_5 are low frequency elements, e_{10}, e_{11} are high frequency elements.

The main ideas of our hash method come from the fact that elements with different frequencies are all important to the bitwise filter but for different reasons. In fact, low frequency elements appear in fewer sets, and have sound effects to differ a few sets containing them from many sets not containing them. Similarly, high frequency elements appear in more sets, and have sound effects to differ few sets not containing them from many sets containing them. By contrast, the mid frequency elements also have sound effects to differ many sets containing them from many sets not containing them. Thus, none of these three parts can be ignored, but should be exploited independently.

To do so, all bits in the hash signatures are also partitioned into three parts by two integers M' and H', where $0 < M' < H' < w_{sig} \times 64$. All of $b_0, b_1, \cdots, b_{M'-1}$ are used for low frequency elements. Similarly, $b_{M'}, b_{M'+1}, \cdots, b_{H'-1}$ are used for mid frequency elements, and $b_{H'}, b_{H'+1}, \cdots, b_{w_{sig}*64-1}$ are used for high frequency elements. Each bit in each part is used to present whether one or more related elements appear in the given set or not. The mapping between elements and corresponding bits are determined by a hash function named freHash (see next paragraph). It is easy to describe these ideas with an algorithm hashAset, which is omitted here for the lack of space.

A New Hash Function. Generally speaking, any hash function can map an e_i to a bit b_j. For example, $h(i) = i$ or $h(i) = i\%N$ for a suitable N, and so on. On the one hand, such functions are helpless in finding a suitable w_{sig} which should be adaptive to input relations. For example, PTSJ [3] just adopted $w_{sig} = \min\{\frac{1}{2}l_{avg}(S), |\mathcal{U}|, 256\}$ heuristically. On the other hand, such functions just take the input i as a usual integer and ignore its important aspect, *i.e.*, i is the inverted rank of e_i's frequency.

Instead, we use a customized hash function, named as freHash. It also distinguishes low (mid and high) frequency elements. The smaller i is, a lower frequency e_i has and fewer such elements should share a common bit. Similarly, The bigger i is, a higher frequency e_i has and fewer such elements should share a common bit. Here comes the formal definition of freHash. It is clear that, taking binary representation of i as input, an algorithm can computes freHash (i) in $O(\log i)$ time.

									73	81	97	99									
							128		72	80	96	98									
						65	67	69	71	75	83	85	101	105	113						
						64	66	68	70	74	82	84	100	104	112						
					33	35	37	41	49	51	77	79	89	103	107	115					
					32	34	36	40	48	50	76	78	88	102	106	114					
			9	17	19	21	25	39	43	45	53	57	87	91	93	109	117	121			
			8	16	18	20	24	38	42	44	52	56	86	90	92	108	116	120			
	3	5	7	11	13	15	23	27	29	31	47	55	59	61	63	95	111	119	123	125	127
1	2	4	6	10	12	14	22	26	28	30	46	54	58	60	62	94	110	118	122	124	126
$h(x)$ 0	1	2	3	4	5	6	7	8	9	10	11	12	13	14	15	16	17	18	19	20	21

Fig. 3. Illustration of freHash (Color figure online)

Definition 3. *If $i > 0$ be an integer and $i = \sum_{k=0}^{\lfloor log_2 i \rfloor} a_k \cdot 2^k$ for $a_k \in \{0,1\}$, then define* freHash $(i) = \sum_{k=0}^{\lfloor log_2 i \rfloor} a_k \cdot k$.

For example, since $23 = 2^0 + 2^1 + 2^2 + 2^4$, freHash $(23) = 1 + 2 + 4 = 7$. Similarly, since $106 = 2^1 + 2^3 + 2^5 + 2^6$, freHash $(106) = 1 + 3 + 5 + 6 = 15$.

Figure 3 presents freHash (i) for all $1 \le i \le 128$. Clearly, as expected, freHash roughly implements the ideas above *i.e.*, fewer elements with both low and high frequencies have same hash values and more elements with mid frequencies have same values. Moreover, this trend continues when i is in other domains. For instance, in Fig. 3, lower left part under the red dashed line is for $1 \le i \le 32$, and lower left part under the blue dashed line is for $1 \le i \le 70$.

According to Definition 3, we know freHash $(i) = \sum_{k=0, a_k \in \{0,1\}}^{\lfloor log_2 i \rfloor} a_k \cdot k \le \frac{\lfloor log_2 i \rfloor (\lfloor log_2 i \rfloor + 1)}{2}$.

Definition 4. *Let $m_{fh}(n)$ be $\frac{\lfloor log_2 n \rfloor (\lfloor log_2 n \rfloor + 1)}{2}$ for $n > 0$.*

Property 1. For any $1 \le i \le n$, freHash $(i) \le m_{fh}(n)$.

This means that freHash (i) increases at a rate of logarithmic square and provides a good tool to compute a proper w_{sig} which is adaptive to the datasets.

The Length and Partition of the Hash Signatures. Now, we are ready to discuss the signature length w_{sig} and the values M', H' which partition each hash signature into three parts.

w_{sig} is taken as the minimum of three values (*i.e.*, $w_{sig} = \min\{w_1, w_2, w_3\}$), which give upper bounds of w_{sig} from different points of view. The first value w_1 gives an upper bound according to the actual needs of freHash. According to Definition 3, e_i is a low (mid or high *resp.*) frequency element if $i < M$ ($M \le i < H$ or $H \le i$, resp.). Thus, the input of freHash for low (mid and high) frequency elements are upper bounded by M, $H - M$ and $|\mathcal{U}| - H + 1$ respectively. According to Property 1, hash signatures for low (mid and high) frequency elements need $m_{fh}(M-1)+1$, $m_{fh}(H-M)+1$, and $m_{fh}(|\mathcal{U}|-H+1)+1$ bits, respectively. Thus, the sum of them is the total length of signatures. Thus, we have

$$len(M, H, |\mathcal{U}|) = m_{fh}(M - 1) + m_{fh}(H - M) + m_{fh}(|\mathcal{U}| - H + 1)$$

$$w_1 = \lceil \frac{1}{04} \cdot (len(M, H, |\mathcal{U}|) + 3) \rceil \tag{1}$$

The second value w_2 upper-bounds w_{sig} according to the average size $l_{avg}(S)$ and the standard deviation σ_S. View the size of each set as a random variable and apply Chebyshev inequality, we know that $Pr(|s.set| > l_{avg}(S) + 2 \cdot \sigma_S) < 0.25$. That is, more than 75% of sets contain at most $l_{avg}(S) + 2 \cdot \sigma_S$ elements. Thus, we can distinguish these sets from each other by using $l_{avg}(S) + 2 \cdot \sigma_S$ bit-signature and allowing each bit be reused by different elements. Thus we have

$$w_2 = \lceil \frac{1}{64} \cdot (l_{avg}(S) + 2 \cdot \sigma_S) \rceil \tag{2}$$

The third value w_3 gives an upper bound according to $|\mathcal{U}|$. Each set can be differed from all others if we use single bit for each element of $\mathcal{U}$. Thus, we have

$$w_3 = \lceil \frac{1}{64} \cdot |\mathcal{U}| \rceil \tag{3}$$

After w_{sig} is determined, all $64 \cdot w_{sig}$ bits in hash signatures can be partitioned, via integers M' and H', into three parts such that the number of bits in each part is proportional to the actual needs of freHash in mapping elements in each part into bits of the signatures. Thus, we have

$$M' = \lceil 64 w_{sig} \cdot \frac{m_{fh}(M-1)+1}{len(M,H,|\mathcal{U}|)+3} \rceil \tag{4}$$

$$H' = \lceil 64 w_{sig} \cdot \frac{m_{fh}(M-1)+m_{fh}(H-M)+2}{len(M,H,|\mathcal{U}|)+3} \rceil \tag{5}$$

Remark. After M, H, M', H' is determined, the mapping from e_i to b_j can be stored in an array, which makes the average running time of hashAset be $O(l_{avg}(S))$. Therefore, the total time to index both datasets, *i.e.*, the cost of Line 1 of Algorithm 2, is $O(|\mathcal{U}| \log |\mathcal{U}| + (|\mathcal{R}| + |\mathcal{S}|)l_{avg}(S))$.

5   Experimental Results

This section empirically checks the adaptivity and compares the space cost and the running time of FreshJoin with other 6 algorithms on 16 real datasets (more experimental results can be found in our technique report [13]). Both experiments are conducted with single thread on Inspur Server with Intel Xecon 128x2.3 GHz CPU and 3TB RAM running CentOS7 Linux. All algorithms were implemented in C++ and complied with O3 flag. Among these, Pretti, Pretti+, PieJoin, and FreshJoin are parameter free. For both ttjoin and Limit, we set k changes from 1 to 10 on each dataset, and choose the smallest running time as results. For PTSJ, we followed the strategy proposed by the authors to take $\min\{|\mathcal{U}|, \frac{1}{2} \cdot l_{avg}(S), 256\} \times 64$ as the signature length (in bits). As shown in [1,2], the order of elements in sets had a huge impact for Limit, PieJoin and pretti+. Thus, we also followed their empirical conclusion to apply infrequent sort order for Limit, PieJoin, and Pretti, and frequent order for pretti+. For ttjoin, the infrequent order is applied on $\mathcal{R}$, and the frequent order is applied on $\mathcal{S}$. While for

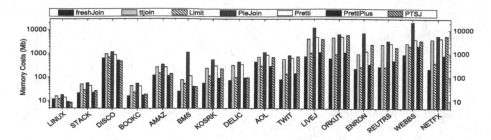

Fig. 4. The memory costs of different algorithms

FreshJoin, the infrequent order is applied on both inputs. As in literatures, all algorithms were run to join each selected dataset with itself.

We adopt 16 real-life datasets selected from different domains with various data properties. The description of these datasets can be found in [1].

For adaptivity (see Table 2), We find that the lengths of hash signatures, the partitions of both elements in $\mathcal{U}$ and the signatures are all adaptive to the datasets themselves.

For memory usage (see Fig. 4), we find that FreshJoin almost always uses least main memory, except on Linux and AOL which is the worst cases of FreshJoin according to the remark at the end of Sect. 3.1 but the costs of FreshJoin are still competitive to the costs of other algorithms. Moreover, FreshJoin saves nearly 50% space of LIMIT and Pretti+ and more than 70% of ttjoin and PTSJ on datasets such as Twitter, LiveJournal, OrKut, Enron, Reuters, Webbase, NetFlix, while keeps competitive on other datasets. This behavior verified the space efficiency of our sparse index structures and the cost analysis in Theorem 1.

For processing time (see Fig. 5), we find that (1) FreshJoin is faster than all other algorithms on more than half of datasets, which benefits from the efficient index structure and the joining procedure of FreshJoin. (2) FreshJoin is a little bit slower (but still competitive to) than some of ttjoin, PieJoin, Pretti, Pretti+, Limit or even PTSJ on some datasets, where $|\mathcal{U}| \ll |\mathcal{S}|$ holds. According to Theorem 3, these are the worst cases for FreshJoin. (3) FreshJoin is always faster than PTSJ, except on the worst case of BMS. These observations verified the effective and efficiency of our adaptive algorithm and the correctness of our analysis of the time complexity of FreshJoin. Therefore, Theorem 3 provides us a rule to choose FreshJoin from the existing set containment algorithms.

More experimental results can be found in our technique report [13].

6   Related Work

Bulk comparison of sets has many practical applications in various domains such as graph analytical tasks, query optimization, OLAP and data mining [3]. Therefore, people have studied extensively the theory and engineering of different operations involving set comparison such as containment queries (*e.g.*, [11]), similarity joins (*e.g.*, [12], equality joins [6] and containment joins [1–10].

Table 2. Characteristic of real datasets

Dataset	Abbrev.	$|\mathcal{S}|$	$l_{avg}(\mathcal{S})$	$|\mathcal{U}|$	M	H	w_{sig}	M'	H'
Linux [1]	LINUX	337,509	1.78	42,045	41,448	42,015	1	43	52
Stack [1]	STACK	545,196	2.39	96,680	81,551	95,585	1	31	51
Discogs [1]	DISCO	7,991,155	2.40	7,949,791	4,682,322	7,840,873	1	26	50
Bookcrossing [1]	BOOKC	337,578	3.40	105,091	98,953	104,894	1	35	56
Amazon [1]	AMAZ	1,231,019	4.67	2,146,277	1,436,024	2,133,860	1	28	52
BMS [4]	BMS	515,597	6.53	1,657	1550	1650	1	43	56
Kosarak [4]	KOSRK	990,002	8.10	41,270	39,789	41,263	1	42	56
Delicious [1]	DELIC	666,841	11.87	685,563	647,962	685,362	1	36	56
AOL [1]	AOL	657,427	26.09	10,154,742	4,287,838	10,115,374	1	26	52
Twitter [3]	TWIT	456,626	32.53	370,341	338582	369740	1	34	55
LiveJournal [1]	LIVEJ	3,201,203	35.08	7,489,296	7,456,367	7,488,933	1	41	56
OrKut [3]	ORKUT	3,072,589	38.14	3,072,626	1,962,178	2,932,062	1	25	47
Reuters	REUTRS	283,911	213.34	781,265	404,447	706,074	2	46	92
Webbase [3]	WEBBS	168,704	2,976	6,142,611	5,881,138	6,121,663	2	63	101
Enron [1]	ENRON	516,782	111.49	435,261	430,538	435,085	3	116	171
Netflix [4]	NETFX	17,770	5,654	480,189	340,724	460,135	4	106	190

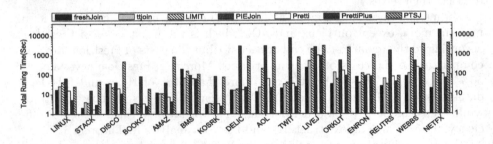

Fig. 5. The total running time of different algorithms

Early work on SCJ mainly focused on disk-based algorithms [6–10]. Although these algorithms have proven quite effective, their performance is bounded by their underlying in-memory processing strategies [3]. For example, PSJ [9] and APSJ [7] share the same in-memory processing strategy with SHJ [10]. To keep up with ever-increasing data volumes and modern hardware trends, recent work turned to develop next generation in-memory SCJ algorithms [1–5], which are either signature-based or prefix-tree based.

All signature-based algorithms (e.g., SHJ [10], PSJ [9], APSJ [7] and PTSJ [3]) follow the filter-and-refine framework in Sect. 2. They use fixed-length bitmaps as signatures to approximate sets, and adopt bitwise operation on the signatures as a filter to prune away as many as possible tuple-pairs whose sets do not have subset relationship. All these existing algorithms take different empirical values as the lengths of bitmaps, and use traditional rand function or element modulo bitmap length as hash functions. This makes them hardly adaptive to datasets automatically. Instead, they care about how to find potential signatures pairs that may pass through the bitwise filter. The usual way is to, for each signature from $\mathcal{R}$, enumerate all potential signatures from $\mathcal{S}$, which incurs high CPU costs and works only on short signatures although special structures such as PATRICIA TRIE [3] can be used to alleviate this defect to some extent. However, FreshJoin computes the signature length adaptively and totally avoids enumerating signatures via the new index.

Most prefix-tree-based algorithms (Pretti [5], Pretti+ [3], LIMIT [4], Piejoin [2]) build a prefix tree $T_{\mathcal{R}}$ and create an inverted index I on $\mathcal{S}$. Then, they traverse $T_{\mathcal{R}}$ in depth-first manner to visit each set $r.set (r \in \mathcal{R})$, compute the intersection $\cap_{e_i \in r} I_{\mathcal{S}}(e_i)$ at the same time, and output $\langle r, s \rangle$ for each s in the intersection. Since common prefix of different sets is represented as a common path in prefix tree, thus many partial results of the intersection can be shared by many tuples in $\mathcal{R}$. Notice that, prefix tree are space-costly and traverses of deep paths in the tree are time-costly. So many optimization techniques are adopted. For example, LIMIT [4] limited the height of tree empirically, Pretti+ [3] compressed the prefix tree by merging these non-branching nodes along each path into single nodes, and Piejoin [2] transforms the prefix trees into linear arrays via preorder coding.

The state-of-the-art algorithm ttjoin [1] are based on both signatures and prefix trees. It takes k-least frequent elements of sets in $\mathcal{R}$ as their signatures and indexes signatures in a prefix tree $T_{\mathcal{R}}$. Besides, all sets in $\mathcal{S}$ are indexed in an other prefix tree $T_{\mathcal{S}}$. Then, ttjoin traverses $T_{\mathcal{S}}$ depth-firstly to visit each set s of $\mathcal{S}$. When each node n of $T_{\mathcal{S}}$ is visited, ttjoin obtains the label e of n and checks whether e is the least frequent element of a set in $\mathcal{R}$ by traversing $T_{\mathcal{R}}$ in depth-first manner. Again, the empirical parameter k makes ttjoin not adaptive to datasets automatically. Besides, the prefix tree $T_{\mathcal{S}}$ is space costly.

7   Conclusion

This paper revisits the set containment join and proposes a parameter-free join algorithm. It exploits the frequencies of elements to partition the universe set into low, mid, and high frequency elements, and maps them separately into different parts of the hash-signatures via a new hash function, which also provides a tool to adaptively estimate the length of hash signatures. The hash signatures are well organized into a index. The time and space complexities of the algorithm are analyzed. Experiments on 16 real-life datasets indicate that the proposed algorithm is adaptive and efficient.

References

1. Yang, J., Zhang, W., Yang, S., Zhang, Y., Lin, X.: TT-join: efficient set containment join. In: Proceedings of ICDE 2017, pp. 509–520 (2017)
2. Kunkel, A., Rheinländer, A., Schiefer, C., Helmer, S., Bouros, P., Leser, U.: Piejoin: towards parallel set containment joins. In: Baumann, P., Manolescu-Goujot, I., Trani, L. (eds.) SSDBM 2016, pp. 11–22 (2016)

3. Luo, Y., Fletcher, G., Hidders, J., De Bra, P.: Efficient and scalable trie-based algorithms for computing set containment relations. In: Gehrke, J., Lehner, W., Shim, K., et al. (eds.) ICDE 2015, pp. 303–314 (2015)
4. Bouros, P., Mamoulis, N., Ge, S., Terrovitis, M.: Set containment join revisited. Knowl. Inf. Syst. **49**, 1–28 (2015)
5. Jampani, R., Pudi, V.: Using prefix-trees for efficiently computing set joins. In: Zhou, L., Ooi, B.C., Meng, X. (eds.) DASFAA 2005. LNCS, vol. 3453, pp. 761–772. Springer, Heidelberg (2005). https://doi.org/10.1007/11408079_69
6. Mamoulis, N.: Efficient processing of joins on set-valued attributes. In: Halevy, A., Ives, Z., Doan, A. (eds.) SIGMOD 2003, pp. 157–168 (2003)
7. Melnik, S., Molina, H.: Adaptive algorithms for set containment joins. ACM Trans. Database Syst. **28**(1), 56–99 (2003)
8. Melnik, S., Garcia-Molina, H.: Divide-and-conquer algorithm for computing set containment joins. In: Jensen, C.S., et al. (eds.) EDBT 2002. LNCS, vol. 2287, pp. 427–444. Springer, Heidelberg (2002). https://doi.org/10.1007/3-540-45876-X_28
9. Ramasamy, K., Patel, J., Naughton, J., Kaushik, R.: Set containment joins: the good, the bad and the ugly. In: Abbadi, A., Brodie, M., Chakravarthy, S., et al. (eds.) VLDB 2000, pp. 386–395 (2000)
10. Helmer, S., Moerkotte, G.: Evaluation of main memory join algorithms for joins with set comparison predicates. In: Jarke, M., Carey, J., Dittrich, R., et al. (eds.) VLDB 1997, pp. 386–395 (1997)
11. Zhu, E., Nargesian, F., Pu, K., Miller, R.: LSH ensemble: internet scale domain search. Proc. VLDB Endow. **9**(12), 1185–1196 (2016)
12. Mann, W., Augsten, N., Bouros, P.: An empirical evaluation of set similarity join techniques. Proc. VLDB Endow. **9**(9), 636–647 (2016)
13. Luo, J., Gao, H., Li, J., et al.: Techique report on Freshjoin an adaptive algorithm for set containment join. https://doi.org/10.13140/RG.2.2.32373.63207

Apara: Workload-Aware Data Partition and Replication for Parallel Databases

Xiaolei Zhang[2], Chunxi Zhang[2], Yuming Li[2], Rong Zhang[1,2(✉)], and Aoying Zhou[2]

[1] International Research Center of Trustworthy Software,
Shanghai Key Laboratory of Trustworthy Computing,
East China Normal University, Shanghai, China
[2] School of Data Science and Engineering,
East China Normal University, Shanghai, China
`xiaoleizhang.ecnu@gmail.com`, {`cxzhang,liyuming`}`@stu.ecnu.edu.cn`,
{`rzhang,ayzhou`}`@dase.ecnu.edu.cn`

Abstract. Data partition and replication mechanisms directly determine query execution patterns in parallel database systems, which have a great impact on system performance. Recently, there have been some workload-aware data storage techniques, but they suffer from problems of narrow support to complex workloads or large requirements for storage. In order to enable the support for complex analytical workloads over massive distributed database systems, we design and implement a workload-aware data partition and replication tool, called *Apara*. We design two heuristic algorithms and define two cost models for effective data partition calculation and efficient replication usages. We run a set of experiments to compare and demonstrate the performance between *Apara* and the other representative work. The results show that *Apara* consistently outperforms the primary solutions on TPC-H workloads.

Keywords: Distributed database · Workload-aware storage ·
Partition · Replication

1 Introduction

As the explosion of data and severe requirement of massive query processing ability, parallel database systems and parallel data processing platforms are developed. Generally, they horizontally partition large amounts of data to distributed nodes in order to provide parallel data processing capabilities for analytical queries. One of the major challenges when horizontally partition data is to achieve low data transferring for executing analytical queries [4,9,14,20]. Data partition and replication are the main technology to reduce the processing cost for those analytical workloads, which shall guarantee process parallelization and data locality. The traditional approach splits each table on some key, using hash or range partition. Hash partition is good for the point query, and range partition

© Springer Nature Switzerland AG 2019
J. Shao et al. (Eds.): APWeb-WAIM 2019, LNCS 11642, pp. 191–206, 2019.
https://doi.org/10.1007/978-3-030-26075-0_15

makes data within a given range of the partition key in the same partition. This helps queries that have selection predicates involving the key go faster, but does not affect the performance of queries without the split key attribute. we demonstrate the critical impact of remote data transferring on query performance in Fig. 1. The test workload is Q_3 in benchmark TPC-H [17], shown in Fig. 2. This experiment is conducted on Greenplum which is deployed on 9 nodes equipped with the Gigabit network (more details presented in Sect. 5). Traditional hash partition based on primary keys or randomly selected attributes have much worse performance compared to our Apara. *Apara* can significantly improve the query performance by 82.2% compared to key-based partition scheme.

Traditionally, hash or range partitioning to data can improve the performance of queries involving the key in selection predicates. For join operators, queries will benefit by co-partition technology on the join attributes. However this method may not be suitable for complex scheme, which can only be used to a subsets of tables sharing the join keys. Oracle [4] proposes a reference partition method REF, and it co-partitions a table by another table that is referenced by an outgoing foreign key. It can avoid duplicating the partition key columns and improve the data integrity. But it cannot be used to optimize the network transmission in distributed environment. Predicate-based reference partition method PREF [20] is a partition scheme that allows to co-partition tables based on given join predicates. However, if there is a deep cascading reference relationship in the schema, substantial data redundancy will be stored in child tables. AdaptDB [9] is a work of adaptive data partition. But it has a strong assumption that reading a remote disk is similar as a local disk and it is unrealistic currently.

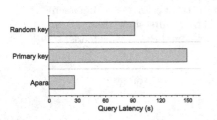

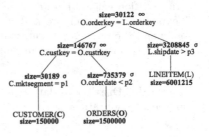

Fig. 1. Query latencies with different partition schemes

Fig. 2. Q3 in TPC-H

In this page, we propose *Apara*, a workload-aware distributed partition and replication tool enabling data distribution effectively and efficiently for parallel database systems. With the input of target application workloads and corresponding database schema, *Apara* can find an appropriate storage mode tailored for the application by near-optimal algorithms. In summary, we make the following major technical contributions:

– We propose a workload-aware data partition tool *Apara* with data partition and replication mechanisms for complex analytical workloads. It is the first work to optimize the data transfer cost for production environment, which can support the complicated workload with the multiple TPC-H style queries.

– We design two near-optimal algorithms which are greedy algorithm and genetic algorithm for partition configuration generation with detailed analysis for the efficiency of our algorithms. We define two cost models, which consider data transferring cost and data replication cost, respectively. It is the first work to limit data redundancy in considering optimizing query processing performance.

– We present extensive experimental results to show that *Apara* has excellent performance on TPC-H workloads and outperforms the other methods.

The rest of this paper is organized as follows. Section 2 describes the overview of Apara. Section 3 presents the methods designed for data partition. Section 4 shows the details of the cost models for both network and replication. Section 5 gives an experimental study. Section 6 describes some related work and Sect. 7 concludes the paper.

2   Overview of Apara

In this paper we provide an workload-Aware data PArtition and ReplicAgtion tool (Apara for short) for complex join processing with the purpose of finding the optimal partition strategy for each table. Apara can be used as a peripheral tool or embedded in the storage layer as a part of the physical design of the database.

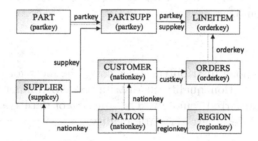

Fig. 3. Schema reference in TPC-H

2.1   Preliminary and Definition

Through the paper, we take the analytical queries in TPC-H as example. The reference relationship and a simplified partition schema among tables are drawn in Fig. 3. The solid arrow line stands for the reference relationship among tables and dotted line is an example of partition configuration. We can see that if table **ORDERS** is hash partitioned on its primary key *orderkey*, then table **LINEITEM** can be co-partitioned using the outgoing foreign key *fk* to

ORDERS. Apara uses hash partition method by default for tables to ensure that the data distributed to each node is roughly balanced. In order to make the description easy, we use capital letter S, W and T to represent schema, workload set and tables. We use A and a to represent attribute set and any single attribute respectively.

Definition 1. *Partition Attribute Set A^T: For table T, there are m join attributes $\{a_k\}$ $(0 \le k \le m-1)$. We call these m attributes partition attribute set for T, represented as A^T.*

One table may join with several other tables having m join attributes, but there is only one attribute a, $a \in A^T$ for partition. For example, in Fig. 3, **NATION** joins with **SUPPLIER**, **CUSTOMER** and **REGION**. Then $A^{NATION} = \{nationkey, regionkey\}$.

Definition 2. *Partition Configuration P : P is a collection of pairs like $<T, a>$, where for table T, it selects attribute $a, a \in A^T$ as its partition attribute. If we have n tables, then $|P| = n$.*

Definition 3. *Problem Definition: Given a schema S involved in workload W, find a good partition P for W such that network transferring $C(P)$ is minimized,i.e.,*

$$arg_p min \qquad C(P)$$
$$subject\ to \quad select\ a\ for\ T,$$
$$\forall\ a \in A^T, \forall\ T \in S.$$

Apara is designed to find a partition configuration P defined in Definition 2, which can help to reduce data transferring cost in distributed environment defined in Definition 3.

2.2   Cost Model

Data transferring among distributed nodes costs the most for distributed query processing. Data partition quality in distributed environment determines the amount of data transferred remotely. The amount of data transferred between nodes is then used to evaluate the data locality.

$$cost_D^P(W) = \sum_{q_i \in W} Cost_D^P(q_i) \tag{1}$$

Where $cost_D^P(W)$ is the total cost of data transferring for workload W under partition configuration P and $Cost_D^P(q_i)$ is the cost for query q_i decided by its involved join operations.

For a cluster with M nodes, the data transferring cost for $T_A \bowtie T_B$ is calculated as follows:

$$Cost_D^{T_A \bowtie T_B} = \begin{cases} 0, & if\ co-partition \\ min(S_A, S_B) \times \frac{M-1}{M}, & if\ shuffle\ join \\ min(S_A, S_B) \times (M-1), & if\ copy-based \end{cases} \tag{2}$$

Where S_A and S_B are the data of T_A and T_B that takes part in the join operation. For co-partition, there is no additional data transferring. If we take shuffle join, we should shuffle the data of small table in one node to all other $(M-1)$ nodes. Supposing S_A is the smaller one and each node stores $\frac{1}{M}$ parts of S_A, when shuffle starts, the shuffling data size of each node is $\overline{D}_{shuffle} = \frac{M-1}{M} \times \frac{|S_A|}{M}$ and the total shuffling size is then $D_{shuffle} = \overline{D}_{shuffle} \times M = \frac{M-1}{M} \times |S_A|$. If table is small enough, we can just copy it to the other $M-1$ nodes.

2.3   Apara Architecture

Apara is designed sensitive to the changes in underlying workloads by enabling the distributed database system to partition and replicate data for improving the join performance. Figure 4 shows the main components of Apara. Inputs to Apara are the database schema and historical query workloads expressed as the query trees. We provide three different tunning algorithms for data distribution, which are optimal partition, greedy partition and genetic partition algorithms. The partition strategy is evaluated by our cost models, which consider data transferring without replication cost (Network-based Cost) and data transferring with replication cost (Network and Replication Cost) respectively. Finally the partition and replication configuration are generated.

From the input database schema, we can get all the table information, e.g. table name and table size. The historical executed query workloads are abstracted as query trees. Each query tree generally involves multiple join operations. Each join operation in the tree has the information about the two join tables, the join attributes, the filter conditions, filter ratio of each table, and the size of join intermediate result set. An example of query tree is shown in Fig. 2, where the number is the data size.

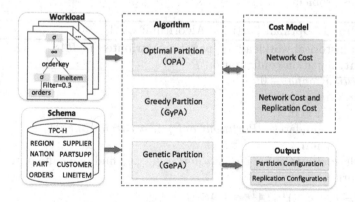

Fig. 4. Overview of Apara architecture

The Optimal Partition module **OPA** tries a traversal search method to find the optimal data partition strategy. But when the number of tables involved with join operations in W is large, it is impossible to traverse all possible candidate partitions because this is a NP-hard problem. So we design new heuristic search strategies to solve this problem. Greedy Partition algorithm **GyPA** is designed by the guide of the data transferring cost among all joins in W, and the Genetic Partition algorithm **GePA** is designed to seek the potential optimal data partition configuration by mapping data partition problem to genetic evolution of nature species. Besides data partition, replication is another way for enhancing data locality. However, copying all the data to the nodes involving with them is obviously unreasonable, because it will generate a lot of redundancy. Then the number of copies and redundant usage of storage resources should be controllable.

3   Workload-Aware Partitioning Algorithm

3.1   Optimal Partition Algorithm *OPA*

The simplest search algorithm is to traverse all partition candidates and then select the partition configuration P with the least transfer cost as shown in Algorithm 1, where we have n tables for partition and each table has its own partition attributes in *PAS*. Line 4–11 is the recursive code for finding all the partition candidates in *allPartitionConfig*. After having all the partition candidates, Line 12 computes the data transferring cost $Cost_D^P$ of every partition configuration P and Line 13 selects the partition with the least cost as the optimal partition configuration. There are N tables involved in join operations with $|P| = N$. The number of average potential partition key of each table is M. Then the time complexity of the traversal search is $O(M^N)$. Clearly when there are many tables in the workload, the search space will be too large to traversing all the partition candidates in limited time. Therefore, we design following heuristic algorithms to solve this problem.

Algorithm 1. Optimal Partition Algorithm: *OPA*

Input: historical workload W, partitionAttributeSets *PAS*
Output: partition configuration P
1 *allPartitionConfig* $\leftarrow \emptyset$;
2 *partitionConfig* $\leftarrow \emptyset$;
3 $n = |PAS|$, i = 0;
4 getAllParCandidate(*allPartitionConfig*, i, *partitionConfig*){
5 **if** $i == n$ **then**
6 | add(*partitionConfig*, *allPartitionConfig*); % find one candidate
7 | return ;
8 **for** $(j = 0; j < |A^{T_i}|, A^{T_i} \in PAS; j++)$ **do**
9 | select one partition attribute $a_j^{T_i} \in A^{T_i}$ into *partitionConfig*;
10 | getAllParCandidate(*allPartitionConfig*, i++, *partitionConfig*);
11 }
12 computer $Cost_D^P, P \in allPartitionConfig$ for each partition candidate;
13 return *partitionConfig* with the least cost;

3.2   Greedy Algorithm for Partitioning *GyPA*

For join between two tables in distributed environment, the network transferring cost will be different according to the selected partition attributes and the join attributes. Generally there are five kinds of join options summarized in Table 1, which are left table shuffle(**LS**), right table shuffle(**RS**), co-partition(**CP**), left table shuffle plus right table shuffle(**LSRS**), table copy(**TC**). Let's take a look at the join segment *"select * from NATION,REGION where NATION.regionkey = REGION.regionkey"* for example, involving table NATION (size = 15) and REGION (size = 5) with join attribute *regionkey*. Selecting different partition attributes, the join costs are different as calculated in Eq. 2, with $M = 5$ as the number of involved distributed nodes:

1. The partition attribute is *regionkey* for both NATION and REGION. Two tables can be co-partitioned with minimal cost *0*;
2. The partition attributes for NATION and REGION are *nationkey* and *regionkey*, respectively. If we perform a shuffle join in NATION according to *regionkey* attribute, the cost of shuffle join **RS** is $\frac{M-1}{M} * |Nation| = \frac{4}{5} \times 15 = 12$. However, if we broadcast REGION to all other nodes, the **TC** broadcast cost is $(M - 1) \times |Region| = 4 \times 5 = 20$. Shuffle join is preferred in this case.
3. The partition attributes of NATION and REGION are *regionkey* and any non-key attribute, e.g. *name*, respectively. If we perform **LS** shuffle join in REGION according to *regionkey*, the cost is $\frac{M-1}{M} \times |Region| = \frac{4}{5} \times 5 = 4$. However, when NATION is broadcast to all other nodes, the **TC** broadcast cost is $(M - 1) \times |Nation| = 4 \times 15 = 60$. Obviously, we should shuffle REGION table instead of copying the NATION table.
4. Neither of the partition attribute of NATION or REGION is the join attribute, e.g. *nationkey* for NATION and *name* for REGION. If we perform **LSRS** shuffle join both in REGION and NATION according to *regionkey* attribute, the cost is $\frac{M-1}{M} \times |Nation| + \frac{M-1}{M} \times |Region| = \frac{4}{5} \times 15 + \frac{4}{5} \times 5 = 16$. If one of the two tables is broadcast to the other nodes, the **TC** cost is $min((M - 1) * |Nation|(M - 1) * |Region|) = min(60, 20) = 20$. Obviously, we should copy REGION table instead of shuffling the two tables.

Table 1. Example Cost Table for R, S and T (where '−1' is the unavailable partition)

(a) Initial Table

cost \\ join	LS	**RS**	CP	LSRS	TC
R.c2, S.c2	4	12	0	-1	5
S.c2, T.c2	12	**32**	**0**	-1	15

(b) Updated Table

cost \\ join	LS	RS	CP	LSRS	TC
R.c2, S.c2	4	-1	0	-1	5
S.c2, T.c2	-1	-1	-1	-1	-1

Join cost can be calculated in advance using query trees and database schema. In order to reduce the cost during SQL execution as much as possible, we should try to filter the expensive join ways as early as possible. So the greedy strategy **GyPA** is to fill the join cost table shown in Table 1, avoid the costly join strategy and select the least cost join method as far as possible.

Algorithm 2 gives the pseudo-code for our greedy algorithm. In Table 1, we have three tables **R**, **S**, and **T**; we have two joins $j_1 = R \underset{R.c_2=S.c_2}{\bowtie} S$ and $j_2 = S \underset{T.c_2=S.c_2}{\bowtie} T$. We first initialize the join cost table *JoinTable* in Line 3, shown in Table 1(a). For the join tables, we iterate (Line 4–8) to find the partition attributes for them. First, we decide the table for checking by finding the largest join cost in the *JoinTable*, which is the worst partition on key $c2$. In Table 1(a), the max cost is 32 by **RS** for j_2. For j_2, partition method **CP** can have the least cost 0. We can then update the *partitionConfig* by adding pairs $<S, c2>$ and $<T, c2>$ as in Line 7. For the selected partition attributes, we recalculate and update *JoinTable* and get a new one shown in Table 1(b) as in Line 8. In distributed environment, we may need to partition the other tables, which are not involved in any joins and are then tackled by hashing acquiescently on their primary key in Line 9. Notice that we select the attribute in partition table instead of the shuffle table to update *partitionConfig*. For example, if LS generates the least cost, the second table and its partition attribute pair is selected to join *partitionConfig*. If CP generates the least cost, both table and partition attribute pairs should be inserted to *partitionConfig*.

Algorithm 2. Greedy Algorithm for Partition: *GyPA*

Input: historical workload W, schema S
Output: partition configuration P
1 *partitionConfig* $\leftarrow \emptyset$;
2 *JoinTable* $\leftarrow \emptyset$;
3 fillJoinTable(*JoinTable*, W, S);
4 **while** *!isAllUpdate()* **do**
5 | $Key = $ getMaxCost(*JoinTable*);
6 | $Key = $ getMinCostByKey(*JoinTable*, Key);
7 | add Key to *partitionConfig*;
8 | update(*JoinTable*);
9 process the other tables;
10 return *partitionConfig*;

Supposing the size of *JoinTable* is n. In cost computing phase, we need traverse all the lines of *JoinTable*, so the time complexity is $O(n)$. When we locate the maximum cost and do updation to *JoinTable*, we may update all the other lines of the table, and the time complexity is $O(n^2)$. So the time complexity of *GyPA* is $O(k*n^2)$, where k is the number of tables involved with joins. But in fact, the method always makes the best choice in current view which is a local optimal solution and does not consider global optimization.

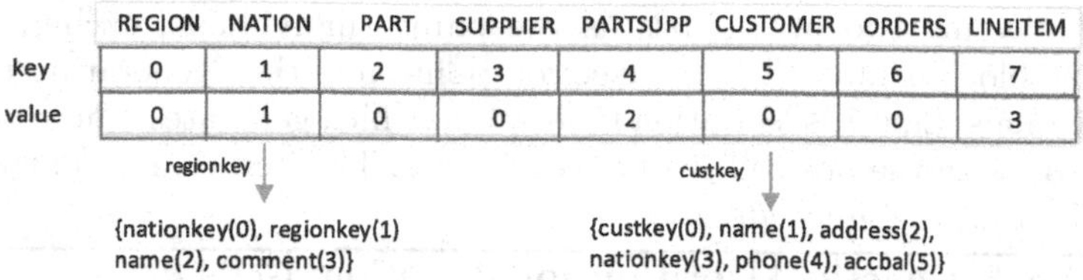

	REGION	NATION	PART	SUPPLIER	PARTSUPP	CUSTOMER	ORDERS	LINEITEM
key	0	1	2	3	4	5	6	7
value	0	1	0	0	2	0	0	3

regionkey

{nationkey(0), regionkey(1) name(2), comment(3)}

custkey

{custkey(0), name(1), address(2), nationkey(3), phone(4), accbal(5)}

Fig. 5. Example individual for TPC-H

3.3 Genetic Algorithm for Partitioning *GePA*

We design a new heuristic algorithm based on the traditional genetic algorithm [19] shown in Algorithm 3 to find a global optimal partition configuration. First, we do individual encoding and population initialization in Line 2, where each individual corresponds to a partition configuration and the genotype of individual is the partition attribute selected for each table. Individual is represented as an array. We represent the individual for TPC-H as an eight-size array, indexed from 0 to 7 for the eight tables (key part). The value for each item is the index of the selected partition attribute, shown in Fig. 5. For example, NATION has four join key candidates, which are *nationkey, regionkey, name, comment*. The value for NATION is *1*, representing *nationkey* selected as its partition key. So Fig. 5 gives an example individual value as {01002003}. The number of individuals defined in the initial population is left as an adjustable parameter according to the scale of the problem. The given initial population size in this paper is 10.

Definition 4. *Selection Probability: Supposing the population size is N and one optional partition configuration is P_i, the Selection Probability of $P_i = \frac{Cost_D^i}{\sum_{i \in N} Cost_D^i}$.*

In the context of our work, the size of data transferring under each partition configuration is the indicator to measure the quality of individuals. We take the size of data transferring as the fitness function for gene evolution, which is also known as the evaluation function and used to select the superior and eliminate the inferior ones in population. The larger the data transferring $Cost_D$, the worse the individual fitness and the more likely to be eliminated. Choosing good partition configurations from the population and eliminating bad ones is executed in each round of iteration shown in Line 4–8 in Algorithm 3. We implement Roulette Selection for gene evolution. Roulette Selection does gene evolution based on Selection Probability defined in Definition 4, which reflects the ratio of the fitness of P_i to the total individual fitness of the entire population. The higher the P_i, the higher the probability of being selected as a bad individual. Line 6 is Crossover Operation, which can generate new partition configurations by randomly exchanging some genes of two individual in the population according to the crossover mode. CrossOne, also known as simple crossover, refers to the random setting of an intersection point in the individual gene string, then randomly selecting two individuals as the parent individuals, exchanging the part of gene block behind their intersection point, and then generating two new child individuals. Line 7 is Variation Operation, which generates a new partition configuration with the possibility of gene changes. The iteration is controlled by predefined parameter *iterNum*.

Algorithm 3. Genetic Algorithm for Partition: *GePA*

Input: historical workload W, schema S, iterationNumber *iterNum*
Output: partition configuration P

1 *partitionConfig* ← ∅;
2 PL = initPopulartion(W, S);
3 *iter* = 0;
4 **while** *iter* < *iterNum* **do**
5   rouletteSelection (PL);
6   crossOne(PL);
7   *partitionConfig* = variation(PL);
8   *iter*++;
9 return *partitionConfig*;

In Algorithm 3, new individuals are generated and the population is updated through CrossOver, Selection, and Variation steps. By continuous iterating, the partition configuration with higher cost is eliminated, and finally the optimal data partition configuration is obtained. Supposing the number of individual in population is N, the time complexity of the selection phase is $O(N * o(N))$, where o(N) is the time complexity for computing individual fitness, the time complexity of the crossover phase is $O(N/2)$ and the variation phase is $O(N)$. So the average time complexity is $O(iterNum * N * o(N))$.

4   Replication-Based Partition Algorithms

Distributed data replication can avoid data transferring with the cost of extra storage [20]. Full redundancy is infeasible especially for big data and we should find an appropriate replication strategy to minimize the data transferring cost with respect to a specified storage space.

4.1   Mixed Cost Model

A good replication strategy can effectively reduce the data transferring of distributed joins and utilize less data redundancy meanwhile. We construct a new cost model by weighting the cost of both data transferring and data redundancy:

$$Cost_{D,C}^{P}(W) = \alpha \times Cost_{D}^{P}(W) + \beta \times Cost_{C}(W) \, , \ \alpha + \beta = 1 \qquad (3)$$

Where $Cost_{D,C}^{P}(W)$ is the cost considering both data transferring $Cost_{D}^{P}(W)$ as in Eq. 2 and data replication $Cost_{C}(W)$, with respective to workload W, partition strategy P and replication strategy C. α and β are weight parameters to specify the importance of data transferring and the data storage.

4.2   Greedy Algorithm Based on Data Replication

Intuitively, data that is frequently joined remotely needs to be replicated, which can be obtained in advance by analyzing workload W and schema S. Since we may have redundant storage limitations, we evaluate data replication usefulness by Eq. 4.

$$Cost_U = \frac{Cost_D}{Cost_C} \tag{4}$$

Where $Cost_U$ is per unit data transferring cost with respect to redundancy. The higher the value, the more useful the data.

We do some modification to GePA in Sect. 3.2 for considering data replication. Running Algorithm 2, it generates the partition configuration without replications. We then calculate *unit network cost* for all the data blocks involved in all the filter conditions, which are sorted in descending order. With respect to the pre-specified space for replications, we greedily select useful data for replication.

4.3   Genetic Algorithm Based on Mixed Cost Model

We improve our genetic algorithm Algorithm 3 by combining the replication strategy. We replace the fitness function by $Cost_{D,C}^{P}(W)$. We extend the individual chromosome to two parts which are the original *partition* feature and current *replication* feature, as shown in Fig. 6. We add all the filters in workloads to the array as the *replication* feature, which generates potential replication data candidates. If the value for the item in replication feature is set to 1, it means data for this filter condition is preferred for replicating. The main idea of CrossOver, Selection, and Variation is roughly similar to Algorithm 3 and will not be repeated here.

Fig. 6. Extended individual

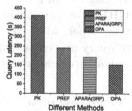

Fig. 7. Total runtime of all TPC-H queries

5   Evaluation

Apara is an assistant module for any database administrators with suggestions about partition configuration and replication strategy. We then run experiments in an open source database called GreenPlumDB [6]. We deploy GreenPlum (v.4.3) on an cluster which includes a master node and other 9 segment nodes. Each node contains two segments. For each table the data is partitioned according to the partition key by Hashing acquiescently and then divided among the segment nodes. Each machine has two 2.00 GHz 6-Core Intel(R) Xeon(R) E5-2620 processes, 120G RAM and 3.6 T local storage. The machine is running on CentOS 6.5.

We select complex workloads in TPC-H [17] for our experiments, which have 22 query templates containing more than sixty join operations. We use IPtraf [8] to collect the information of data transferring among network. Default database size is 20 GB (SF = 20) and the default replication space is set to 2GB on each node. Processing efficiency is evaluated by query latency, which is the total running time of the set of test workloads. In order to reduce cache influence, we run each set of experiments five times and take the average latency.

For comparison, we implement PK (primary key-based partition) and the idea in PREF [20] which is the latest work for locality aware query processing. In our design, we evaluate OPA, GRP (GyPA algorithm), GEP (GePA algorithm), GRPR (GyPA with replication), and GEPR(GePA with replication) in detail.

5.1   Comparison with PREF

In Fig. 7, we compare our method Apara implementing GRP with PREF [20], OPA and PK methods. We can find that Apara is better than PREF without any replication. Though OPA is the best one, its running time is unacceptable for its full traversal, which is infeasible for realistic applications when involving many tables. PREF is implemented with data replication if there is any reference relationship among tables. For Apara, if our partition uses replication, e.g., GRPR, we can get much better performance, which will be shown in the following paper. Moreover, PREF is implemented together with the modification to query processing module. So it is difficult to be applied. So next, we run experiments to compare different algorithms in Apara to show the performance.

5.2   Overview of the Performance Improvement

We compare the algorithms in Apara in Fig. 8(a). The query latency of GRP outperforms PK by 51.21%, GEP outperforms PK by 68.93%. When using replication, GRPR and GEPR can improve better, which are 71.11% and 73.54% compared to PK respectively. Figure 8(b) compares the network transfer cost with different segment nodes from 1 to 8. As we know, disk access and network transfer account for the majority time of query processing. In order to show the effect of network transfer, we set the $effective\_cache\_size$ of GreenPlum to 30GB, which are huge enough to avoid disk access. IPtraf collects network transfer size for all the workloads. When there is only 1 nodes, no data transfer occurs. It is easy to see that with replication we can reduce network transfer cost, which are *GRPR* and *REPR*. *Genetic−based* methods are generally better than *Greedy − based* methods.

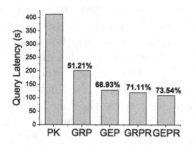 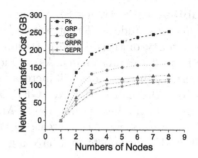

(a) Query Latency for Different Methods (b) The Network Transfer Cost

Fig. 8. Overview of the performance improvement

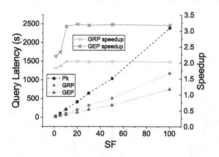 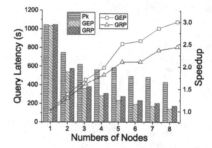

Fig. 9. Query latency with data size

Fig. 10. Query latency with network size

Since GRPR and GEPR are based on GRP and GEP with pre-specified storage spaces, which make better performance, the scalability of both GRPR and GEPR are decided by GRP and GEP. So we only demonstrate the scalability of GRP and GEP in the following paper.

5.3   Algorithm Scalability

Scalability to Data Size: Figure 9 shows the query latency of GRP and GEP with different scale factors (SF = 1, 5, 10, 20, 30, 50, 100). We also calculate the speedup of GRP, GEP compared to PK. For the growth of data size will increase data transfer among nodes, query latency grows up for all three methods. But GEP wins the best scalability.

Speedup is increasing until SF = 10. This happens because of the bottleneck of system resources. When SF is greater than 10, CPU utility consumes almost 100% and it becomes the bottleneck. Then the latency caused by resource competition is more obvious than network transferring.

Scalability to Network Size: Figure 10 compares the query latency of GRP, GEP and PK under different Network size. When the number of node is 1, the query latency of these three partition configuration is almost the same, since there is no data transferring. As we increase the number of nodes, though data transferring among nodes will increase, parallel distributed query processing will improve performance. However GEP can effectively reduce more network cost. So GEP gets the best performance. Moreover, we can see the speedup ratio in Fig. 10 increases with the increase of nodes, so our algorithms can work well in distributed environment and have a good scalability.

Scalability to Complex Workloads: Figure 11 shows the query latency under different numbers of queries, which are selected randomly from the 22 TPC-H workloads. It compares the performance of GRP, GEP and PK. We can see that Apara's algorithms can still achieve better performance when we have larger number of workloads.

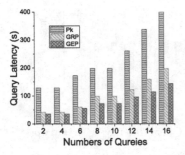 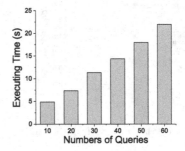

Fig. 11. Query latency with workload size

Fig. 12. Apara execution time with workload size

5.4   Apara Efficiency

Figure 12 shows the total execution time of Apara tool to get all the partition configuration suggestions for our four algorithms, which are GRP, GEP, GRPR and GEPR. Execution time of Apara approximatively linearly increases with the growth of queries selected randomly from TPC-H. Apara can get all the partition and replication configurations in a short time period, which makes it applicable for production environment.

6   Related Work

In order to avoid expensive remote join operations, data partition and replication are the feasible options for improving query performance [3,15]. Data partition can be used for both OLTP workloads [2,12,13] but also for OLAP workloads. Horizontally partition is commonly used in traditionally databases area [18]. Co-partition large tables can effectively avoid remote join operations [5]. However, in complex schemata with increasing number of tables, not all tables can be co-partitioned. Oracle [4] introduces a method REF to partition tables by reference relationships. However, this method simply partitions tables by foreign keys and does not consider the other relationships in join operators. Predicate-based reference partition [20] PREF is a partition scheme that allows to co-partition sets of tables based on given set of join predicates. However, if a referenced table in the PREF scheme contains duplicates, the referencing table will inherit those duplications as well, which may lead to a large size of redundancy. AdaptDB [9] and Amoeba [16] propose the adaptive partition mechanisms. Amoeba is designed for reducing remote disk access considering all filters conditions instead of joins. AdaptDB extends it by supporting optimization for data access in join operations, but it still has strong assumptions which is that remote disk access is the same as local disk access. There are some other work [1,11] designed based on revising query execution plans which is not applicable for production environment. Navathe [10] and HYRISE [7] are two vertical partition methods which focus on disk-based systems and main-memory resident data processing systems, respectively. Apara will consider to add vertical partition for data distribution in future.

7   Conclusion

In this paper, we present Apara, a workload-aware storage distribution guidance tool for complex OLAP workloads with the purpose to reduce the network cost and improve query performance in distributed environment. We firstly discuss the optimal partition algorithm, which is time consuming for large size of applications. Then we present two heuristic algorithms to find the potential optimal solutions. Finally, we consider to use pre-specified replication into our cost model and use it in our heuristic algorithms to further improve the performance of Apara. Our experiments show that Apara works well for complex workloads in distributed environment.

Acknowledgment. We are supported by National Key Projects (No. 2018YFB100-3404) and National Science Foundation of China (No. 61572194).

References

1. Agrawal, S., Narasayya, V., Yang, B.: Integrating vertical and horizontal partitioning into automated physical database design. In: SIGMOD (2004)
2. Curino, C., Jones, E., et al.: Schism: a workload-driven approach to database replication and partitioning. In: VLDB (2010)
3. DeWitt, D.J., Ghandeharizadeh, S., et al.: The gamma database machine project. In: TKDE (1990)
4. Eadon, G., Chong, E.I., et al.: Supporting table partitioning by reference in oracle. In: SIGMOD (2008)
5. Fushimi, S., Kitsuregawa, M., Tanaka, H.: An overview of the system software of a parallel relational database machine grace. In: VLDB (1986)
6. GreenPlumDB. https://greenplum.org/
7. Grund, M., Krüger, J., et al.: Hyrise: a main memory hybrid storage engine. In: VLDB (2010)
8. Iptraf. http://iptraf.seul.org/
9. Lu, Y., Shanbhag, A., et al.: AdaptDB: adaptive partitioning for distributed joins. In: VLDB (2017)
10. Navathe, S., Ceri, S., et al.: Vertical partitioning algorithms for database design. In: TODS (1984)
11. Nehme, R., Bruno, N.: Automated partitioning design in parallel database systems. In: SIGMOD (2011)
12. Pavlo, A., Curino, C., Zdonik, S.: Skew-aware automatic database partitioning in shared-nothing, parallel OLTP systems. In: SIGMOD (2012)
13. Quamar, A., Kumar, K.A., Deshpande, A.: SWORD: scalable workload-aware data placement for transactional workloads. In: EDBT (2013)
14. Rodiger, W., Muhlbauer, T., et al.: Locality-sensitive operators for parallel main-memory database clusters. In: ICDE (2014)
15. Sacca, D., Wiederhold, G.: Database partitioning in a cluster of processors. In: TODS (1985)
16. Shanbhag, A., Jindal, A., et al.: A robust partitioning scheme for ad-hoc query workloads. In: SoCC (2017)
17. TPC-H. http://www.tpc.org/tpch/
18. Waas, F.M.: Beyond conventional data warehousing—massively parallel data processing with greenplum database. In: BIITE (2008)
19. Whitley, D.: A genetic algorithm tutorial. Stat. Comput. 4(2), 65–85 (1994)
20. Zamanian, E., Binnig, C., Salama, A.: Locality-aware partitioning in parallel database systems. In: SIGMOD (2015)

Which Category Is Better: Benchmarking the RDBMSs and GDBMSs

Pengjie Ding[1]([✉]), Yijian Cheng[1]([✉]), Wei Lu[1]([✉]), Hao Huang[2]([✉]),
and Xiaoyong Du[1]([✉])

[1] School of Information and DEKE, MOE,
Renmin University of China, Beijing, China
{pengjie,yijiancheng,lu-wei,duyong}@ruc.edu.cn
[2] School of Computer Science, Wuhan University, Wuhan, China
haohuang@whu.edu.cn

Abstract. Relational database management systems (RDBMSs) have been a common option to manage structured data over the past decades. In recent years, with the prevalence of big data applications, vast unstructured and semi-structured data are generated, deeply challenging the relational model used in RDBMSs. For this reason, a wide spectrum of NoSQL databases are developed for managing unstructured, semi-structured or structured data. For example, graph database management systems (GDBMSs) are commonly used as an important category of NoSQL databases, to manage sophisticated graph data as well as relational data. Nonetheless, as claimed in existing literatures, both RDBMSs and GDBMSs are capable of managing graph data and relational data, the boundaries of them still remain unclear. In this paper, we propose a unified benchmark for RDBMSs and GDBMSs, to evaluate them under the same metrics, and report which category is better in different application scenarios. We conduct extensive experiments over the unified benchmark, and report our findings: (1) RDBMSs are significantly faster for aggregations and order by operations, (2) GDBMSs are shown to be superior for projection, multi-table join and deep recursive operations, (3) GDBMSs and RDBMSs are comparable for two-table join and shallow recursive operations.

Keywords: RDBMSs · GDBMSs · Benchmark

1 Introduction

E.F. Codd introduced the relational data model with relations to represent data, with relational algebra and relational calculus to operate data, and relational integrity constraint to control the consistency and completeness of data. Since then, various RDBMSs have been developed with standard SQL to support data definition, data manipulation, and data control operations.

© Springer Nature Switzerland AG 2019
J. Shao et al. (Eds.): APWeb-WAIM 2019, LNCS 11642, pp. 207–215, 2019.
https://doi.org/10.1007/978-3-030-26075-0_16

In recent years, graphs have been shown increasingly important to big data applications such as social network analysis, spatio-temporal analysis and navigation, and consumer analytics, as it is able to capture complex relationships and data dependencies.

Thus far, great controversies have been raised for the comparison between RDBMSs and GDBMSs: which category is better.

To clearly answer this question, we propose a unified benchmark for both RDBMSs and GDBMSs. First, to address the issue that RDBMSs and GDBMSs have different data models, we propose a relation-to-graph mapping scheme, under which, relational data are able to be transformed to graph data. In this way, we use TPC-H [1], which is a commonly accepted benchmark in RDBMSs, and extend it to evaluate GDBMSs. Similarly, we propose a graph-to-relation mapping scheme, under which, graph data are able to be transformed to relational data. We use LDBC [2], which is commonly used in GDBMSs, and extend it to evaluate RDBMSs. Second, to address the issue that RDBMSs and GDBMSs have different query languages, we transform all 22 SQL queries in TPC-H to graph queries, and transform 5 graph queries into SQL queries. Moreover, Finally, we select PostreSQL, a popular open source RDBMS, as the representative of RDBMSs and Neo4j, ArangoDB as two representatives of GDBMSs. We conduct extensive experiment evaluations by comparing the above two categories of representative systems over TPC-H and LDBC under the metrics, including query processing time, memory utilization ratio, and CPU utilization ratio.

In summary, our contributions are as follows.

- We propose a unified benchmark for both RDBMSs and GDBMSs to evaluate them under the same datasets as well as the same metrics.
- We propose a graph-to-relation inter-mapping scheme under which, graph data and relational data are inter-transformed. We rewrite all SQL queries in TPC-H to graph queries and rewrite all graph queries in LDBC to SQL queries.
- We conduct extensive experimental evaluations for existing popular RDBMSs and GDBMSs over both standard TPC-H and LDBC, and report our findings in details.

The remainder of this paper is organized as follows. We review the related work in Sect. 2, and elaborate our unified benchmark in Sect. 3, following which we report experimental results and our findings in Sect. 4, before concluding the paper in Sect. 5.

2   Related Work

Our work is related to both RDBMSs benchmark and GDBMSs benchmark.

RDBMSs Benchmark. As the mainstream commercial database systems, there exist rich RDBMSs benchmarks. Among them, the most well accepted are the TPC series. TPC-C [3] is an on-line transaction processing (OLTP) benchmark, which involves a mix of five concurrent transactions of different types and complexity. It models order management and extracts the workload. TPC-H is a decision support benchmark which models business procurement, whose datasets consist of 8 tables representing general business procedure. The 22 queries and the data populating the database have been designed to evaluate the capacity of handling critical business questions. TPC-DS [4] is also a decision support benchmark which models several generally applicable aspects of a decision support system, including 24 tables, and 99 randomly replaceable SQL queries. It focuses on emerging technologies, such as Big Data systems, to execute the benchmark.

GDBMSs Benchmark. Unlike RDBMSs benchmarks which are proposed by authoritative organization, GDBMSs benchmarks come from some database companies. NoSQL Performance Benchmark [5] is proposed by ArangoDB [6], with its prime target to compare the performance among MongoDB, PostgreSQL, OrientDB, ArangoDB and Neo4j under the metrics including read/write performance test, memory utilization ratio. GDBMSs Benchmark [7] is created by TigerGraph [8], mainly examines the data loading and query performance of TigerGraph, Neo4j, Amazon Neptune [9], JanusGraph [10], and ArangoDB. The LDBC Graphalytics benchmark [2] is an industrial-grade benchmark for graph analysis platforms. It consists of several typical graph algorithms, standard datasets, data generators and reference outputs, enabling the objective comparison of graph analysis platforms.

3   A Unified Benchmark for RDBMSs and GDBMSs

In this section, we unify RDBMSs benchmark and GDBMSs benchmark. In particular, we utilize the standard RDBMSs benchmark, TPC-H, and extend it to evaluate the performance for GDBMSs. Similarly, we utilize a widely used GDBMSs benchmark, LDBC, and extend it to evaluate the performance for RDBMSs. By doing this, we evaluate RDBMSs and GDBMSs on the same datasets with the same query workloads under the same metrics.

3.1   Data Generation

Data Generation Schemes. Since RDBMSs and GDBMSs have different data models, we need to develop a data inter-transformation scheme between relational data and graph data. To transform relational data to graph data, we propose a relation-to-graph mapping scheme. In this scheme, we generate one-to-one mapping between tuples from entity tables and vertices in the graph model, and use the foreign keys of relational data model to build edges from pairwise tuples.

Similarly, to transform graph data to relational data, we propose a graph-to-relation mapping scheme as well. In this scheme, we simply store the directed edges as triples, which are maintained in a relation with three attributes, namely *fromVertex, edgeLabel, toVertex.* As mentioned before, we utilize LDBC as the graph benchmark.

Datasets to Be Used. In TPC-H benchmark, the relational datasets are generated using the TPC-H data generator with different sizes, ranging from 50 MB to 1 GB. In LDBC benchmark, we transform the graph datasets to relational datasets based on the graph-to-relation mapping scheme.

3.2 Query Workload

Our unified benchmark includes three categories of query workloads. The first category is named as atomic relational queries. It consists of four operations, include *Projection, Aggregation, Join* and *Order by.* We build this category of query load to evaluate and compare the capacity of processing typical atomic operations between RDBMSs and GDBMSs.

The second category is named as TPC-H query workloads. It consists of 22 queries from TPC-H, which are designed to exercise system functionalities in complex business analysis applications.

The third category is named as Graph query workloads, which includes 5 graph algorithms from LDBC Benchmark considered to be representative for graph analysis.

Atomic Relational Queries. Atomic relational queries consist of four basic relational operations in RDBMSs, which are *Projection, Aggregation, Join* and *Order by.*

TPC-H Query Workloads. [11,12] list many query languages for graph databases and show expressive power and complexity of graph query languages. Therefore, we can convert all of the 22 queries of TPC-H using graph query language, specifically, *Cypher* for Neo4j and *AQL* for ArangoDB. The 22 queries include plenty of relational operations, such as *Group by, Order by, Aggregation, Join,* and *Subquery.* Every graph query is completely equivalent to its original TPC-H query, for eliminating query's effect on the experiment results.

Graph Query Workload. We re-implement five graph algorithms using SQL statements. For recursive algorithms, taking *BFS* (Breadth-First Search) [13] for example (shown in Algorithm 3), we use *with [recursive]* [14] clause to do the transformation by referring to *SQL'99* [15,16].

3.3 Metrics

We measure the performance of RDMBSs and GDBMSs under query processing time, memory usage ratio and CPU usage ratio. We run each graph and SQL query for five times, and all the metrics are computed on average.

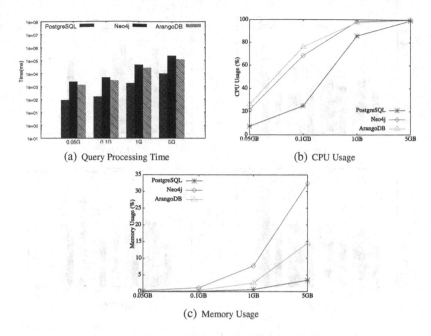

(a) Query Processing Time   (b) CPU Usage

(c) Memory Usage

Fig. 1. Relational operation test

4   Experiments

In this section, we first introduce the experimental setup in terms of design of experiments which consists of two parts, namely, the comparisons for relational operations and for graph algorithms. Then, we report and interpret the experimental results, based on which we elucidate a summarization about the most applicable scenarios for the relational and graph databases.

4.1   Experimental Setup

Design of Experiments: The goal of our unified benchmark is to objectively compare relational databases and graph databases. To this end, we design types of experiments to carry out a comprehensive evaluation on databases.

Performance Comparison for Relational Operations: We evaluate the performance of each database when processing general TPC-H queries and some extra evaluation queries. For TPC-H queries, we execute 22 queries on three databases: PostgreSQL as a representative for RDBMSs, Neo4j represent GDBMSs, and ArangoDB as a typical system for multi-model NoSQL database which includes graph data models. 22 queries are executed on each of them, and meanwhile the processing time, CPU usage and main memory usage are recorded. Mean values are calculated for the processing results of the 22 queries to measure the general capacity of handling business-oriented ad-hoc queries and concurrent data

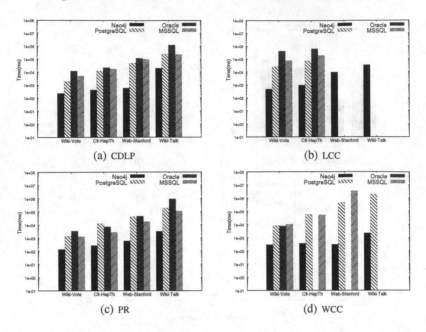

Fig. 2. Testing 4 graph algorithms over 4 datasets

modifications for 3 databases. The evaluation for TPC-H queries only measures general capacity for business oriented scenarios, yet every query in TPC-H consists of many atomic operations such as *Projection, Aggregation, Join* and so on. Four extra queries have been designed to measure the performance of processing 4 typical atomic operations:*Projection, Join, Aggregation* and *Order by.*

Performance Comparison for Graph Algorithms: For graph algorithms, we execute 5 graph algorithms we have introduced in Sect. 3 on four databases: Neo4j as representative for GDBMSs; Oracle, PostgreSQL and Microsoft SQL Server as 3 typical RDBMSs. Every graph algorithm is executed on 4 databases and the processing time is recorded for each database.

4.2   Experimental Results and Analysis

In this section, we report the experimental results analyze the results by highlighting our most critical findings.

Relational Operation Test. We carry out relational operation test on three databases, namely, PostgreSQL, Neo4j and ArangoDB. Figure 1(a) illustrates the average processing time of the whole 22 TPC-H queries in each databases with different sizes of datasets. From the figure, we can observe that the processing time in Neo4j and ArangoDB is significantly longer than that in PostgreSQL, although Neo4j is widely used as a by industry. Figure 1(b) and (c) depict the average CPU usage rate and main memory usage rate, respectively. From the figures, we can observe that PostgreSQL also outperforms the other two tested databases in terms of CPU and main memory usages. Compared with Neo4j, ArangoDB consumes relatively less CPU but more main memory.

Besides, we also carry out an experiment to evaluate the processing time of 4 typical atomic operations (i.e., *Projection, Join, Aggregation, and Order by*) in RDBMSs. We observed that GDBMSs excel in *Projection* and *Join* operations but have disadvantages in *Aggregation* and *Order by* operations. Note that with the increase of data scale, time consumption of PostgreSQL on *Projection* and *Join* enlarge sharply while Neo4j and ArangoDB increase smoothly. Meanwhile, for *Aggregation* and *Order by* operations, there are much higher difference regarding time consumption when data scale increases between RDBMSs and GDBMSs.

From experiments and analysis above, we can find that both RDBMSs and GDBMSs have their merits of dealing with relational operations. Whereas in business oriented scenarios such as TPC-H workload, GDBMSs can not have a desirable performance due to their storage system. According to our extra experiments, the problem can be solved by creating indexes on properties properly and change the schema for graph data transferred from relational databases, for schema of GDBMSs is flexible and adjustable. To be specific, by creating indexes on properties that constantly retrieved and avoid adding too many properties in node via extracting some properties and creating as node, GDBMSs can also have a satisfying performance for relational application scenarios.

Graph Algorithm Evaluation. We carry out graph algorithm evaluation over four real graphs. Figure 2 illustrate the performance of the five algorithms (mentioned in Sect. 3) over four directed graphs we've introduced in the part of datasets, namely, Wiki-Vote, Cit-HepTh, Web-Stanford and Wiki-Talk. We omitted the result for a graph algorithm if it fails to finish in 1 h. In addition, the variable *level* represents the depth of recursive operations for *BFS* algorithm.

As shown in Fig. 2, we can observe that as expected, Neo4j has the best efficiency performance on these four real graphs.

While Oracle and MSSQL fail to process *LCC* and *WCC* algorithms in large dataset in one hour, since *LCC* and *WCC* have massive sophisticated operations, including *Distinct, Aggregation, and Exists* operations which are time-consuming. Specifically, we find the intermediate results reach at a scale of ten billions for our *M* size dataset when we execute *LCC* algorithm. *WCC* algorithm traverses all nodes using *for ... in* loops, each of which involves several iterations to process *Join, Insert, Exists* operations. The number of iterations is an important factor in determining the performance. Departing from *WCC* algorithm which has multi-levels recursive join operation, *CDLP* and *PR* simply find adjacent nodes for every node and loop several times according to a user-defined parameter. Moreover, as graph datasets scale from *S* to *XL*, the time consumption increases for *PR* and *CDLP*.

5   Conclusion

Both RDBMSs and GDBMSs hava capacity of managing relational data and graph data, making the boundaries of them unclear. To clearly answer the question, we have proposed a unified benchmark referring to existing benchmarks for RDBMSs and GDBMSs, which consist of relational workloads and graph algorithms, to evaluate databases on the same datasets under the same metrics, and tested which category is better in different application scenarios. We have implemented a inter-transfer between SQL and graph query languages for querying and importing data in RDBMSs and GDBMSs, respectively. We have conducted extensive experimental evaluations for existing popular RDBMSs and GDBMSs over both standard TPC-H and LDBC, and reported our findings in details. We can conclude that RDBMSs have advantages on processing *Aggregation* and *Order by* operations, while GDBMSs have a desirable performance for *Projection*, multi-table *Join* and deep recursive operations, GDBMSs and RDBMSs are comparable for two-table join and shallow recursive operations. As future work, we will study the optimization on property storage management.

References

1. TPC-H (2012). http://www.tpc.org/tpc_documents_current_versions/pdf/tpc-h_v2.17.1.pdf
2. Iosup, A., et al.: LDBC graphalytics: a benchmark for large-scale graph analysis on parallel and distributed platforms. Proc. VLDB Endow. **9**(13), 1317–1328 (2016). https://doi.org/10.14778/3007263.3007270
3. TPC.TPC-C, February 2010. http://www.tpc.org/tpc_documents_current_versions/pdf/tpc-c_v5.11.0.pdf
4. TPC.TPC-DS, November 2015. http://www.tpc.org/tpc_documents_current_versions/pdf/tpc-ds_v2.1.0.pdf
5. https://www.arangodb.com/2018/02/nosql-performance-benchmark-2018-mongodb-postgresql-orientdb-neo4j-arangodb
6. https://www.arangodb.com
7. https://info.tigergraph.com/benchmark
8. https://www.tigergraph.com
9. https://aws.amazon.com/neptune
10. Janusgraph distributed graph database (2017). http://janusgraph.org
11. Wood, P.T.: Query languages for graph databases. SIGMOD Rec. **41**(1), 50–60 (2012). https://doi.org/10.1145/2206869.2206879
12. Barceló Baeza, P.: Querying graph databases. In: Proceedings of the 32nd ACM SIGMOD-SIGACT-SIGAI Symposium on Principles of Database Systems, ser. PODS 2013, pp. 175–188. ACM, New York (2013). http://doi.acm.org/10.1145/2463664.2465216
13. Cormen, T.H., Leiserson, C.E., Rivest, R.L., Stein, C.: Introduction to Algorithms, 3rd edn. The MIT Press, Cambridge (2009)
14. Ordonez, C.: Optimizing recursive queries in SQL. In: Proceedings of the 2005 ACM SIGMOD International Conference on Management of Data, ser. SIGMOD 2005, pp. 834–839. ACM, New York (2005). http://doi.acm.org/10.1145/1066157.1066260

15. Melton, J., Simon, A.: SQL:1999: Understanding Relational Language Components. Morgan Kaufmann Publishers Inc., San Francisco (2001)
16. Finkelstein, I.M.S.J., Mattos, N., Pirahesh, H.: Expressing recursive queries in SQL. ISO-IEC JTC1/SC21 WG3 DBL MCI, X3H2-96-075 (1996)

Spatial, Temporal and Multimedia Databases

A Meta-Path-Based Recurrent Model for Next POI Prediction with Spatial and Temporal Contexts

Hengpeng Xu[1], Peizhi Wu[1], Jinmao Wei[1(✉)], Zhenglu Yang[1(✉)], and Jun Wang[2]

[1] College of Computer Science, Nankai University, Tianjin, China
{xuhengpeng,wupz}@mail.nankai.edu.cn,
{weijm,yangzl}@nankai.edu.cn
[2] College of Mathematics and Statistics Science, Ludong University, Shandong, China
junwang@mail.nankai.edu.cn

Abstract. Predicting next point of interest (POI) of users in location-based social networks has become an increasingly significant requirement, because of its potential benefits for individuals and businesses. Recently, various recurrent neural network architectures have incorporated contextual information associated with users' sequence of check-ins to capture their dynamic preferences. However, these architectures are limited because they only take the sequential order of check-ins into account and face difficulties in remembering long-range dependencies. In this work, we resort to the heterogeneous of information network (HIN) to address these issues. Specifically, a novel attentional meta-path-based recurrent neural network is proposed, dubbed ST-HIN. ST-HIN predicts the next POI of users from their spatial–temporal incomplete historical check-in sequences, and uses the multi-modal recurrent neural network to capture the complex transition relationship. Furthermore, a meta-path attention embedding module is devised to capture the mutual influence between the users' meta-path-based global information in HIN and the dynamic status of their current mobility. The results of extensive experiments performed on real-world datasets demonstrate the effectiveness of our proposed model.

Keywords: POI prediction · Meta-path · Recurrent model · Spatial context

1 Introduction

At present, users in location-based social networks (LBSNs), such as Foursquare and Gowalla, can share their location with their friends anytime in the form of check-ins, thereby generating a huge amount of spatial and temporal context data. Spatial and temporal contexts reflect the essential factors of "where" and "when" for a certain event. Exploring these contexts is critical in predicting

© Springer Nature Switzerland AG 2019
J. Shao et al. (Eds.): APWeb-WAIM 2019, LNCS 11642, pp. 219–235, 2019.
https://doi.org/10.1007/978-3-030-26075-0_17

the next point of interest (POI) of users, which is a challenging yet important research topic in analyzing LBSNs.

Classical methods, such as matrix factorization (MF) [10], have been widely used in recommending a personalized ranked list of POIs to users. MF-based approaches mainly model the users' locations preferences by using historical user–location interaction records. Various types of context data have also become increasingly available in online services. The extant MF approaches leverage these contextual data to improve their recommendations [11,12,34]. However, predicting the next location of users requires not only calculating the users' location preferences but also modeling the sequential transition regularities from check-in data given the strong sequential dependency of users' mobility patterns [5,14]. To tackle this issue, the Markov model and its variations estimate the probability of future action by building a transition matrix for locations according to their past trajectories, representative as the FPMC-based models [1,3]. Since these models linearly combine all of the embedded Markov chains and constraints, they require a strong independence assumption among different factors, which is nearly impossible in practice. Moreover, these models predict the next location of users based only on their latest check-in data and ignore the influences of short- and long-term sequence contexts.

Various deep neural network-based approaches have recently become popular in POI recommendation due to their inherent ability to model complex non-linearities in data [17,28,30]. Among the NN-based methods, the Recurrent Neural Network (RNN) has been widely used to extend the MF-based approaches and to capture the users' short-term dynamic preferences over time from their historical behaviors sequences. The RNN-based recommendation approaches typically feed users' check-in sequences into the recurrent models and use their hidden states to represent the users' dynamic preferences, and some of them further endeavor to incorporate the contextual information [14,17]. These sequential models emphasize the short-range dependencies among sequence nodes, inducing two major weaknesses: (1) disregarding the critical spatial and temporal correlations, which are essential for mitigating data sparsity existing in the majority of deep learning models; and (2) only taking the sequential orders of check-in into account and thereby facing difficulty of remembering long-range dependencies.

As a promising modeling method, the heterogeneous of information network (HIN), has been successfully applied in recommendation systems [6,32], due to its superiority of modeling rich auxiliary data and links [9,23]. A meta-path, which indicates the relations among connecting objects pairs in HIN, can effectively explore the structure of HIN and capture the rich semantics for recommendation [25]. Figure 1 represents the user LBSN information in the form of HIN, which includes different types of nodes (a.k.a. entities), such as users (U), locations (L), regions (R), and category (C). These entities are connected by different types of relations. For instance, the "user-location-user" meta-path indicates two users co-visiting the same locations, while the "location-category-location" meta-path denotes two locations belonging to the same category. The indirect interactions between users and locations based on different meta-paths can be considered as diverse types of global information.

We benefit from this diversity representation ability of HIN in this work, to recommend the next POI for users by comprehensively analyzing their spatial-temporal incomplete check-in history. Two major limitations of HIN are tackled in this work. First, the existing HIN-based methods assume that the personal preferences of users are stable, disregarding the dynamic spatial-temporal variations across different geographical regions. Second, these methods characterize two-way user–item interactions and seldom exploit and explore the mutual influence between the global information on the meta-path and the users' sequential behaviors over different spatial-temporal contexts.

To address these issues, we leverage the rich meta-path global information in HIN in a highly principled manner. Our objectives are to (1) learn explicit representations for meta-path-based global information to better describe users and items, (2) characterize the mutual influence among three-way interactions $<user, location, metapath>$ that correspond to different spatial and temporal contexts, and (3) predict next POI by jointly utilizing the users' dynamic latent state and the global user and location latent representation that is enhanced via meta-path embedding.

Accordingly, we propose ST-HIN, an attentional RNN model, to predict the next POI based on the lengthy and sparse users' check-in data. ST-HIN utilizes a multi-modal RNN to capture the multiple spatial and temporal factors that govern the transition regularities of human mobility. In the multi-modal RNN, we convert the sparse features (e.g., user ID, location ID, and category ID) into dense representations, which are more complete and expressive. Afterward, we feed the dense representations into a RNN to model long-range and complex dependencies in a trajectory sequence. ST-HIN embeds users' mobility transition patterns (i.e., the multiple factors that govern the human mobility) to capture their personalized dynamic movement preferences, and explores the meta-path-based rich semantic information via a meta-path attention embedding module, which is jointly trained to generate the global meta-path-based context highly correlated with the users' current mobility status. The contributions of our study are summarized as follows:

- We propose a novel meta-path-based next POI prediction model called ST-HIN, which is a deep learning architecture to model global information and sequential relations. ST-HIN combines two types of regularities in a principled way, namely, human mobility transition regularity and meta-path-based semantics, over the objects in HIN. To the best of our knowledge, this work is the first to utilize the deep learning network to simultaneously combine these two important regularities for the next POI.
- We design two attention mechanisms that are tailored to cooperate with the recurrent module. The first is to directly embed meta-path-based information into independent latent vectors and improve the meta-path embedding by using the co-attention mechanism. The second is to interact the users'

global meta-path-based context embedding with the users' current status and generate the most related context for POI prediction.
- We conduct extensive experiments on real-world datasets. The experiment results demonstrate that our model outperforms the state-of-the-art recommendation approaches by a considerable margin.

2 Related Work

In this section, we review the previous studies on spatial and temporal recommendation and HIN-based recommendation methods.

2.1 Spatial and Temporal Recommendation

Factorization-based methods, such as Matrix Factoring (MF) [18], Bayesian personalized ranking (BPR) [21], and factorization machines [12], have been widely used in recommendation systems. These models assume that those users with similar check-in POIs share the same preferences, and therefore more likely to check-in similar POIs. The key idea of these models is to factorize the users-item matrix into two latent matrices that represent users and items characteristics. Recently, deep learning has achieved much success in learning effective representations. Some deep learning models have also been integrated into collaborative filtering models to learn a deep item or user representation from its associated side information for recommendation [4,26]. For example, Wang et al. proposed a hierarchical Bayesian model that utilizes stacked denoising auto-encoders to achieve deep representation learning for the item information and applies collaborative filtering for the user-item matrix. However, this model cannot address user cold–start problems, assumes that personal preferences are stable, and ignores their spatial and temporal dynamics over geographical regions.

Given that MF methods usually suffer from the cold-start problem, many studies have attempted to leverage additional information for recommendation [1,14,16,33]. Previous studies have shown that, incorporating spatial and temporal contexts associated with the users' historical check-in data is critical for enhancing next POI prediction performance. Many studies have leveraged spatial and temporal features to boost prediction performance. We categorize these approaches into three groups, namely, pattern-, model-, and neural-network-based approaches. Pattern-based approaches mine the mobility patterns from movement data. In [2,33] the scatter plot of each user's check-in (e.g., longitude and latitude) is captured by a fixed distribution. However, this approach cannot generate latent representations for the time bins that never or seldom appear in the training data. Markov model and its variants are representative model-based methods [1,3] that estimate the probability of a future action by building a transition matrix for locations according to their past trajectories. Cheng et al. [3] and Chen et al. [1] proposed recommendation models based on personalized Markov chain (FPMC) [22] by factorizing the probability transition. Given that FPMC-based models linearly combine all embedded Markov chains and constraints, they require a strong independence assumption among different factors, which is nearly impossible in practice. Recently, RNNs have been applied in POI recommendation tasks because of its effectiveness in various sequential applications, such as natural language processing, speech recognition, and GPS trajectory modeling Liu et al. [17] proposed ST-RNN to model local temporal and spatial contexts by extending RNNs with time- and distance-specific transition matrices. Liao et al. [14] proposed a multi-task, context-aware RNN that leverages spatial activity in activity and location prediction. When modeling sequential data, RNN assumes that the temporal dependency changes monotonously along with the positions in a sequence, thereby suggesting that compared with the previous element, the recent element in a sequence usually plays a more significant role in prediction. The most recent elements also have similar or even more complex effects on the users' next choice compared with the previous element.

2.2 HIN Based Recommendation

The network structure of HIN illustrates the object types and links that describe the different relations among objects [6,27]. The indirect interactions between users and locations based on different meta-paths can be regarded as types of global information that are adopted in recommender systems to model the global mutual influence between the meta-path and user-item pair. HIN-based recommendation methods can be roughly categorized into two types. The first type usually applies transformation on path-based similarity to enhance the representations of users and items. Yu et al. [32] take advantage of the meta-path-based latent features which captured by utilizing the different types of object relationships in heterogeneous information network and propose a personalized recommendation framework for implicit feedback dataset. Shi et al. [24] incorporated meta-path based user similarity to flexibly integrate heterogeneous information for personalized recommendation. However, most of HIN based methods rely on path based similarity, which may not fully characterize users' and items latent preferences on HINs for recommendation. As a comparison, the second type leverages path based semantic relations over HIN to extract the structure feature and has been successfully applied in recommendation [13].

3 Preliminaries

This section initially defines the research problem and then presents the proposed ST-HIN model in detail along with its learning procedure.

3.1 Problem Definition

Our objective is to predict where a user will go to next at a specific time t given historical check-in records of a users. Given the category set $A = \{a^1, a^1, ..., a^{|A|}\}$, user set $U = \{u^1, u^2, ..., u^{|U|}\}$, location set $L = \{l^1, l^2, ..., l^{|L|}\}$ and region set

$R = \{r^1, r^2, ...r^{|R|}\}$, the check-in data can be defined as a quintuple $s = (u, l, a, r, t)$, which indicates that user u visits location l whose geographical position is located in region r and category is a at time t. Following [8], we set up a lookup layer to transform the one-hot representations of users and items into low-dimensional dense vectors in a process called embedding. The lookup layers correspond to two parameter matrices $P \in \mathbb{R}^{|U| \times D}$ and $Q \in \mathbb{R}^{|L| \times D}$, which store the latent factors for users and items, respectively. Here, D denotes the dimension size of the user and item embedding, whereas $|U|$ and $|L|$ denote the number of users and items, respectively. With these notations, our problem can be formulated as: our goal is to predict the user u's next location l_n based on the next check-in time t_n and the users' historical check-in sequence $S = \{s_1^u, s_2^u, ...s_n^u\}$.

Definition 1 *Heterogenous Information Networks* [25]. An HIN is defined as a directed graph over multiple types of nodes $\mathfrak{I}$ and links $\mathfrak{R}$. In HIN, the network structure is proposed to describe the mete structure. As illustrated the left part of Fig. 1, our proposed model contains four types of objects and four types of links or relations. Apart from the user and POI objects as well as the user-POI relations that represent the historical check-in data of users, the other types of data in this model include:

- **Category nodes:** In LBSNs, POIs are organized by hierarchical category trees that provide a semantic classification of various POIs. Each top-level category is classified into different subcategories. We infuse the categories at the lowest level as our category nodes.
- **Region nodes:** A user typically correlates with several regions. For instance, a delivery man correlates with the delivery-region-based residential areas, his address, and the shopping regions. These regions are mutually affected and spatially dependent, whereas their check-in numbers are positively correlated, that is, a user frequently visits a certain region and its nearby areas. We apply k-means clustering to cluster the POIs and assign each POI with a region ID.
- **POI-Category relations:** Given that each POI corresponds to a lowest-level node of the category tree, we assign each POI to its corresponding category in the lowest level of the hierarchy category tree.
- **POI-Region relation:** We calculate the Euclidean distance between the POI geographical coordinate and the center of the identified regions and then connect each POI to its nearest region.
- **User–user relation:** Users are connected to one another based on their friendship relations on the LBSN. By using these relations, the potential interaction among these users is considered in the POI recommendation. In HIN, two objects or nodes can be connected via different semantic paths or meta-paths.

Definition 2 *Meta-path.* A meta-path ρ takes the form of $\mathfrak{I}_1 \xrightarrow{\mathfrak{R}_1} \mathfrak{I}_2 \xrightarrow{\mathfrak{R}_2} ... \xrightarrow{\mathfrak{R}_l} \mathfrak{I}_l$, which describes a composite relation $\mathfrak{R}_1 \circ \mathfrak{R}_1 \circ ... \circ \mathfrak{R}_l$ between $\mathfrak{I}_1$ and $\mathfrak{I}_l$, where $\circ$ denotes the composition operator on relations.

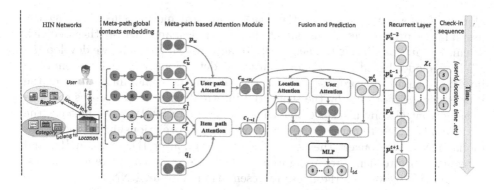

Fig. 1. Main architecture of ST-HIN

Given a meta-path ρ, there exists multiple specific paths under a meta-path that are called path instances, which are denoted by ρ. As we have illustrated above, a meta-path that connects a user with an item in HIN can reveal the users' global semantic preferences for user–item interactions.

Definition 3 *Meta-path based Global context.* Given a user u and an item i, the meta-path-based context is defined as an aggregate set of path instances under the considered meta-paths that connect the two nodes in the HIN.

3.2 Overview

As a powerful-sequence modeling tool, the RNN can capture a long range of sequential information. However, when the sequence is too long, its performance will degrade rapidly. Therefore, directly applying RNN to solve the user mobility prediction problem is intuitive yet inefficient. Some challenges other than the long-term nature mentioned above can lead to RNN failure. One of these challenges is posed by data quality. In general, missing data can confuse and induce the RNN to learn the wrong transition information. Meanwhile, sparse data makes it difficult to train the model for each individual. In sum, the RNN faces the problem of data sparsity and complex transitions, which prevent this model from achieving high accuracy in predicting human mobility.

As a newly emerging research direction, HIN, which comprises multiple types of nodes and links, can utilize rich auxiliary data to learn their rich relations and has been successfully applied in recommendation systems [9,23]. Specifically, meta-path, which refers to a sequence that indicates the relations among connecting object pairs in HIN, has been widely used to effectively explore the structure of HIN and to capture rich semantics for recommendation [25].

Based on the above observations, we propose ST-HIN, an attentional meta-path-based RNN that predicts the next POI from spatial–temporal incomplete historical check-in sequences. Our goal is to build a framework for simultaneously extracting user dynamic preferences over locations, embedding meta-path-based global information, quantifying the spatio-temporal mutual effects among the users' latent preferences, items' latent characteristics, and meta-path-based rich semantics, and predicting the next POI. To accomplish this goal, we develop the ST-HIN model based on the aforementioned definitions. Figure 1 presents the intuition behind our proposed model, that is, the next mobility status of the user is decided not only by the sequential information from this user's check-in behavior but also by his/her global characteristics. In ST-HIN, we first use the multi-modal RNN to capture the complex transition relationship. In the multi-modal RNN, we convert the sparse features (e.g., user ID, location ID, and category ID) into dense representations, which are more complete and expressive. Afterward, we feed the dense representations into an RNN to capture the complex user mobility transition patterns. Through user embedding, ST-HIN performs a personalized POI prediction while training a single model for all users to learn and share the same mobility patterns. Besides, the region and time representation involved in the multi-modal embedding layer enable the RNN to model the spatial and temporal dependent nature.

Another key component of ST-HIN is the meta-path attention embedding module, which captures the mutual influence between the user meta-path-based global information in HIN and the users' current mobility status. The meta-path global-path-based attention module initially performs meta-path embedding by using co-attention mechanisms. Afterward, the global meta-path-based context embedding of the user interacts with this user's dynamic mobility state to generate the most related context. By combining this context with the user's current mobility status, we can predict this user's mobility based on not only the sequential relation but also the meta-path-based global information.

4 The Proposed Model

Figure 1 presents the ST-HIN architecture, which comprises three major components, namely, feature embedding, recurrent model and path-based attention, and prediction.

4.1 Feature Embedding

A feature can be divided into the meta-path-based feature and the check-in sequence feature. Our goal is to utilize the meta-path based global information to learn the users' and items' global effective representations; the objects with other types are of less interest in our task. Here, we only select those meta-paths that start with the user or item type. These paths are likely to generate meta-path sequences with different types of nodes by using abovementioned method. We also remove those nodes which types differ from the starting type. We eventually obtain a final sequence that only includes those nodes which types are similar to the starting type. We transform those node sequences that are constructed by using meta-paths with heterogeneous types into node sequences that use the homogeneous neighborhood. We embed those nodes with the same type in the same space, thereby addressing the challenge in representing all heterogeneous objects in a unified space. Inspired by the recent advancements in network embedding [7,19],we adopt the representation learning method to extract and represent the useful information of HINs for recommendation. Specifically, we utilize the deepwalk [19] method to achieve meta-path embedding.

User mobility patterns are governed by multiple factors, including user preference and check-in time. Therefore, we design a multi-modal embedding module that jointly embeds the spatiotemporal and personal features into dense representations to help model complex transitions. In practice, all available features of one trajectory point, including time, location, and user ID, can be numbered. These numbered features are translated into one-hot vectors and inputted into the multi-modal embedding module. Compared with the limited one-hot representation, the dense representation can better capture a precise semantic spatiotemporal relationship. As another advantage, this dense representation is always lower dimension, thereby facilitating the follow-up computation.

4.2 Recurrent Module

The sequential encode module takes the check-in sequence embedding χt as its input and keeps the intermediate outputs of each step as candidate vectors. The RNN reserves all spatial and temporal information and can extract the users' complex sequential information from historical check-in records. This module relies on the follow-up meta-path-based attention module in generating the global meta-path-based context that is highly correlated with the users' current mobility status.

We obtain the latent vector s_i^t as the input to LSTM. Meanwhile, as output, we use p_u^t, which denotes the latent embedding of the current mobility status from the check-in sequences of user u at time t: $p_u^t = LSTM(p_u^{t-1}, \chi_t)$. We then use transformation matrix $W_o \in R^{D*D}$ to transform the output of LSTM into user dynamic-preferences latent vectors over time, where D denotes the latent-vector dimension of a location and user.

Attention for Meta-Path Based Context. Intuitively, the meta-path-based global information provides important semantic information that reflects the users' or items' global preferences to a certain extent. Therefore, the involved user and item are likely to be affected by this type of information. The same meta-path may also generate different influences on the same user across different spatial and temporal contexts, and each user tends to develop different preferences over the meta-paths.

Based on these discussions, if we can improve the embedding of users, locations, and meta-paths in a mutually enhancing manner, then we can develop a highly effective representation learning method. Inspired by the recent advancements in the attention mechanism for computer vision and natural language processing [20,29], we propose a novel co-attention mechanism to achieve this

goal. Given that different meta-paths may show varying semantics in an interaction, we learn the interaction-specific attention weights over the meta-paths
that are conditioned on the involved user and location.

Given the user embedding $\mathbf{p}_u$, and the user-specific meta-path-based-context
embedding c_u^ρ for meta-path ρ, we adopt the following two-layer architecture to
implement the attention mechanism:

$$\alpha_{u,\rho}^{(1)} = f(\mathbf{W}_u^{(1)} \mathbf{p}_u + \mathbf{W}_\rho^{(1)} \mathbf{c_u}^\rho + \mathbf{b}^{(1)}), \tag{1}$$

$$\alpha_{u,\rho}^{(2)} = f(\mathbf{W}^{(2)\top} \alpha_{u,\rho}^{(1)} + b^{(2)}), \tag{2}$$

where $\mathbf{W}_*^{(1)}$ and $\mathbf{b}^{(1)}$ denote the weight matrix and the bias vector for the first
layer, whereas, the $\mathbf{W}^{(2)}$ and $b^{(2)}$ denote the weight vector and bias for the
second layer. $f(\cdot)$ is set according to the ReLU function.

The final meta-path weights are obtained as follows by normalizing the above
attentive scores over all meta-paths by using the softmax function:

$$\alpha_{u,\rho} = \frac{\exp(\alpha_{u,\rho}^{(2)})}{\sum_{\rho' \in \mathcal{M}_u} \exp(\alpha_{u,\rho'}^{(2)})}, \tag{3}$$

which can be interpreted as the contribution of the meta-path ρ to the interaction between u. After obtaining the meta-path attention scores $\alpha_{u,\rho}$, the new
embedding for the aggregate meta-path context can be given as the following
weighted sum:

$$\mathbf{c}_u = \sum_{\rho \in \mathcal{M}_u} \alpha_{u,\rho} \cdot \mathbf{c_u}^\rho. \tag{4}$$

The meta-path-based context embedding c_l^ρ for location l has the same neural
network structure as mentioned above for user l.

Setting the Fusion Function. By using the previously mentioned fusion function, we obtain the global meta-based-context representations c_u and c_l, which
correspond to user u and location l, respectively, and the latent representations
of user dynamic mobility status p_u^t.

Given the meta-path-based representation of users and items, the user
dynamic mobility status that connects them provides an important interaction
context that is likely to affect the original representations of users and locations.
Therefore, we use a single-layer network to compute the attention vectors β_u
and β_l for user u and item l, respectively, as follows:

$$\beta_u^t = f(\mathbf{W}_u \mathbf{p}_u + p_u^t \mathbf{W}_{u \to u} \mathbf{c}_{u \to u} + \mathbf{b}_u), \tag{5}$$

$$\beta_l^t = f(\mathbf{W}_l' \mathbf{q}_l + p_u^t \mathbf{W}_{l \to l}' \mathbf{c}_{l \to l} + \mathbf{b}_l'), \tag{6}$$

where $\mathbf{W}_*$ and $\mathbf{b}_u$ denote the spatial and temporal transition matrices and the
bias vector for the user attention layer, whereas $\mathbf{W}_*'$ and $\mathbf{b}_i'$ denote the weight
matrix and bias vector for the item attention layer. $f(\cdot)$ is set according to the

ReLU function. The final representations of the user and item are computed by using an element-wise product "$\odot$" with the attention vectors

$$\tilde{\mathbf{p}}_u^t = \boldsymbol{\beta}_u \odot \mathbf{p}_u^t, \tag{7}$$
$$\tilde{\mathbf{q}}_l^t = \boldsymbol{\beta}_i \odot \mathbf{q}_l^t. \tag{8}$$

The attention vectors $\boldsymbol{\beta}_u$ and $\boldsymbol{\beta}_i$ are used to improve the original user and item embeddings that are conditioned on the current mobility status from the recurrent layer. By combining the two parts of attention components, our model improves the original representations for users, items, and the meta-path-based context in a mutually enhancing manner. To the best of our knowledge, only few HIN-based recommendation methods are able to learn explicit representations for meta-paths, especially in an interaction-specific manner.

4.3 Prediction

The prediction module combines the context from different modules to complete the prediction task. Here, we use one concatenated layer to combine the meta-path global context information and the users' sequence mobility pattern with spatial and temporal contexts. In practice, the latent vectors from the recurrent, meta-path-based attention, and embedding modules are combined into a new vector. Afterward, we feed this new vector into the fully connected layers to further predict the next POI. The training goal is minimizing the divergence between the predicted distribution and the true distribution. Thus, we adopt the training loss as the entropy loss.

5 Experiments

5.1 Experimental Setup

We apply our model on public Foursquare check-in datasets collected from two big cities, namely, New York (NYC) and Tokyo (TKY) [30], for the period covering April 2012 to February 2013. The overall statistics are shown in Table 1. In following experiments. For each user, we take the first 80% check-ins as the training set, the following 10% as the evaluation set, and the last 10% as the validation set for the hyperparameters study.

Metrics. We evaluate the performance of the model and the baselines by using three criteria. The first criterion, namely, the accuracy of top K (Acc@K), refers to the percentage of accurate predictions for a list of predictions with length K. The second criterion, the mean average precision of top K (MAP@K), is widely used as an evaluation criterion for ranking tasks. The third criterion, namely, the negative loglikelihood (NLL), measures the likelihood between the predicted and true distributions. To make our results more convincing, we repeat each experiment 10 times and use the average metrics for a comparison.

Baselines. We compare the ST-HIN model with the following baselines:

Table 1. Statistics of the two datasets. The last column reports the selected meta-paths in each dataset.

Datasets	Relations (A-B)	#A	#B	#A-B	Meta-paths
NYC	User-POI	1,083	38,333	227,420	ULRLU
	POI-Category	38,333	240	38,333	ULU
	POI-Region	38,333	120	38,333	ULCLU
TKY	User-POI	2,293	61,858	573,703	LUL
	POI-Category	61,858	240	61,858	LRL
	POI-Region	61,858	120	61,858	LCL

- **MF:** A naive methods that outputs the most frequent locations of user u at time t as prediction.
- **Context-aware hybrid (CAH):** This model [15] initially uses the category to indicate the activity purpose of users to combine the sequential and temporal influences and then predicts the future locations of these users based on the inferred activity.
- **Spatial temporal RNN (ST-RNN):** ST-RNN [17] extends RNNs with time- and distance-specific transition matrices to model the local temporal and spatial contexts, respectively.
- **Semantics-Enriched Recurrent Models (SERM):** SERM [31] is an LSTM model that takes category semantics and spatial–temporal contexts as inputs for location prediction.
- **LGrec:** As an HIN-based method, LGRrec [9] proposes a deep neural network model that learns the relation representations between users and items ad captures the meta-path-based interactions by optimizing a multi-label classification problem.
- **Multi-Task RNN (MCARNN):** MCARNN [14] introduces spatial category topics as latent factors that capture the users' category and location preferences and then them for predicting their next POI.
- **ST-HIN$_{noAtt}$:** A variant of ST-HIN, ST-HIN$_{noAtt}$ has no co-attention mechanisms for characterizing the meta-path-based global information that is used to predict the next POI.
- **ST-HIN$_{noGlo}$:** A variant of ST-HIN, ST-HIN$_{noGlo}$ has no meta-path-based global information for predicting the next POI.
- **ST-HIN:** The proposed model utilizes meta-path-based global information to capture the users' global preferences over locations and to learn the mutual influence of these users' personal and global preferences.

Experimental Results. The performance of the aforementioned approaches on two benchmarks are evaluated by using Acc@K, NLL, and MAP@K as metrics as illustrated in Table 2. We observe that ST-HIN remarkably outperforms all the other methods for NYC (+15% improvement in terms of top-1 accuracy over the best candidate method, namely, MCARNN) and TKY (+12% improvement in terms of top-1 accuracy over MCARNN). Given the lack of supervised

Table 2. Results of effectiveness experiments on four datasets.

Models	NYC					TKY				
	Acc@1	Acc@10	Acc@20	NLL	MAP@100	Acc@1	Acc@10	Acc@20	NLL	MAP@100
MF	0.0774	0.1788	0.1957	8.3399	0.4005	0.1021	0.2041	0.2536	6.6641	0.60181
CAH	0.1328	0.3521	0.4179	7.0680	0.5331	0.1728	0.3877	0.4551	5.9137	0.6662
ST-RNN	0.1663	0.4126	0.4671	6.7701	0.5632	0.2033	0.4904	0.5703	5.5774	0.7033
SERM	0.1480	0.3731	0.4386	7.0104	0.5395	0.1796	0.4271	0.4862	5.8377	0.6726
LGrec	0.1852	0.4315	0.4805	6.4516	0.5774	0.2182	0.5405	0.6136	5.4871	0.7358
MCARNN	0.2011	0.4601	0.5198	6.2961	0.6092	0.2829	0.5807	0.6391	5.0057	0.7452
ST-HIN$_{noAttrn}$	0.2116	0.4675	0.5191	6.2412	0.5923	0.2941	0.5923	0.6421	4.9250	0.7484
ST-HIN$_{noGlo}$	0.1793	0.4223	0.4786	6.538	0.5684	0.2077	0.5314	0.5803	5.514	0.7125
ST-HIN	**0.2322**	**0.4784**	**0.5229**	**6.1213**	**0.6317**	**0.3321**	**0.6124**	**0.6654**	**4.852**	**0.7821**

information, MF, as a naive method, shows an unpromising performance on both datasets. CAH is a two-stage method that utilizes the inherent influence between the sequential dependency and temporal regularity of individual mobility patterns to determine the users' preferences over locations. SERM, ST-RNN and MCARNN are three RNN models that predict location based on check-in data. However, these models are unable to capture the users' long-range or global preferences based on long-range check-in history data and ignore the rich semantics among the objects in HIN, including category, region, user, and POIs. LGrec is a state-of-the-art HIN-based recommendation method that utilizes local and global information in HIN for top-N recommendation. However, LGrec cannot capture the dynamic changes in the users' preferences over time and ignores the spatial and temporal contexts in POI prediction. Therefore, the proposed ST-HIN significantly outperforms these state-of-the-art methods. Specifically, in location prediction, ST-HIN shows a 12% performance improvement on the NYC dataset and a 15% performance improvement on the TKY dataset.

The proposed model is also superior to its variants ST-HIN$_{noAtt}$ and ST-HIN$_{noGlo}$ with the sequence ST-HIN > ST$_{noAtten}$ >ST-HIN$_{noGlo}$. Therefore, the global HIN-based context information and meta-path-based attention mechanism work well in our proposed model, whereas the global HIN-based contexts play a critical role in performance improvements in most cases. The excellent prediction of ability the meta-path-based recurrent model equipped with the attention mechanism can be attributed to two reasons. First, the importance of each meta-path should depend on a specific interaction instead of being treated equal corresponding to different users and dynamic mobility pattern status for one same users. Second, the meta-paths provide important global context for the interaction between users and items, which in turn has a potential influence on the learned representations of users and items.

Impact of Different Meta-Paths. In this section, we further analyze the impact of different meta-paths on the POI prediction performance. We gradually incorporate these meta-paths into the proposed ST-HIN model and observe the POI prediction performance change. We start incorporate meta-paths from user type ,and then item type. In Fig. 2, we can observe that generally the POI

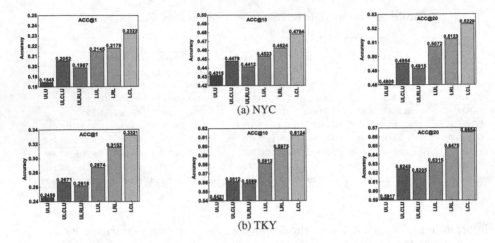

(a) NYC

(b) TKY

Fig. 2. Performance change of ST-HIN when gradually incorporating meta-paths

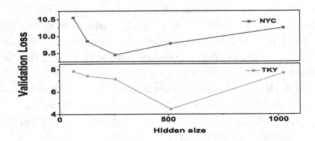

Fig. 3. Effect of the hidden size

prediction performance improves (i.e., the value of acc@K becoming larger) with the incorporation of more meta-paths. However, the performance does not always maintain growth with more meta-paths, and the performance down slightly. The reason is that some meta-paths may contain noise or conflict information with existing ones. Meanwhile, meta-paths seem to have different effects on the POI prediction performance. Particularly, we can find that, adding LUL and ULCLU, ST-HIN has a significantly performances boost in both datasets.

Parameters Study. We examine the effect of the balance parameter and the dimension of embeddings on the performance for our proposed model. Figure 3 shows our model achieves the best performance when $d = 256$, thereby suggesting that the dimension of embeddings cannot be set too small or too large. The size of the hidden state determines the capacity of RNN. Figure 3 compares the performance of the model when varying hidden layer sizes are considered. When the hidden layer size increases from 64 to 256, the model capacity increases while the validation loss gradually decreases. Our model demonstrates the best performance when $d = 256$, thereby suggesting that the dimension of embeddings can be neither too small nor too large.

6   Conclusion

In this paper, we propose an attentional meta-path-based RNN that effectively utilizes auxiliary information in HINs for POI recommendation. We first use the multi-modal RNN to capture the complex transition relationship. Afterward, we use the meta-path attention embedding module to capture the mutual influence between the user meta-path-based global information in HIN and the users' current mobility status. The user global meta-path-based context embedding then interacts with the users' dynamic mobility state to generate the most related context. By combining this context with the users' current mobility status, we predict the mobility based on not only the sequential relation but also the meta-path-based global information. We also employ a recurrent layer to capture the dynamic state changes of users. The experiment performed on real-world datasets demonstrate the effectiveness of our proposed model.

References

1. Chen, M., Liu, Y., Yu, X.: NLPMM: a next location predictor with Markov modeling. In: Tseng, V.S., Ho, T.B., Zhou, Z.-H., Chen, A.L.P., Kao, H.-Y. (eds.) PAKDD 2014. LNCS (LNAI), vol. 8444, pp. 186–197. Springer, Cham (2014). https://doi.org/10.1007/978-3-319-06605-9_16
2. Cheng, C., Yang, H., King, I., Lyu, M.R.: Fused matrix factorization with geographical and social influence in location-based social networks. In: AAAI Conference on Artificial Intelligence, pp. 17–23 (2012)
3. Cheng, C., Yang, H., Lyu, M.R., King, I.: Where you like to go next: Successive point-of-interest recommendation. In: International Joint Conference on Artificial Intelligence, pp. 2605–2611 (2013)
4. Dong, X., Yu, L., Wu, Z., Sun, Y., Yuan, L., Zhang, F.: A hybrid collaborative filtering model with deep structure for recommender systems. In: AAAI Conference on Artificial Intelligence, pp. 1309–1315 (2017)
5. Feng, S., Li, X., Zeng, Y., Cong, G., Chee, Y.M., Yuan, Q.: Personalized ranking metric embedding for next new poi recommendation. In: International Joint Conference on Artificial Intelligence, pp. 2069–2075 (2015)
6. Feng, W., Wang, J.: Incorporating heterogeneous information for personalized tag recommendation in social tagging systems. In: SIGKDD International Conference on Knowledge Discovery and Data Mining, pp. 1276–1284 (2012)
7. Grover, A., Leskovec, J.: node2vec: scalable feature learning for networks. In: KDD, pp. 855–864 (2016)
8. He, X., Liao, L., Zhang, H., Nie, L., Hu, X., Chua, T.-S.: Neural collaborative filtering. In: International World Wide Web Conference, pp. 173–182 (2017)
9. Hu, B., Shi, C., Zhao, W.X., Yang, T.: Local and global information fusion for top-n recommendation in heterogeneous information network. In: ACM International Conference on Information and Knowledge Management, pp. 1683–1686 (2018)
10. Koren, Y., Bell, R., Volinsky, C.: Matrix factorization techniques for recommender systems. Computer **8**, 30–37 (2009)
11. Li, X., Cong, G., Li, X.-L., Pham, T.-A.N., Krishnaswamy, S.: Rank-GeoFM: a ranking based geographical factorization method for point of interest recommendation. In: SIGIR Conference on Research & Development in Information Retrieval, pp. 433–442 (2015)

12. Lian, D., Zhao, C., Xie, X., Sun, G., Chen, E., Rui, Y.: GeoMF: joint geographical modeling and matrix factorization for point-of-interest recommendation. In: SIGKDD Conference on Knowledge Discovery and Data Mining, pp. 831–840 (2014)

13. Liang, D., Altosaar, J., Charlin, L., Blei, D.M.: Factorization meets the item embedding: regularizing matrix factorization with item co-occurrence. In: ACM Conference on Recommender Systems, pp. 59–66 (2016)

14. Liao, D., Liu, W., Zhong, Y., Li, J., Wang, G.: Predicting activity and location with multi-task context aware recurrent neural network. In: International Joint Conference on Artificial Intelligence, pp. 3435–3441 (2018)

15. Liao, D., Zhong, Y., Li, J.: Location prediction through activity purpose: integrating temporal and sequential models. In: Kim, J., Shim, K., Cao, L., Lee, J.-G., Lin, X., Moon, Y.-S. (eds.) PAKDD 2017. LNCS (LNAI), vol. 10234, pp. 711–723. Springer, Cham (2017). https://doi.org/10.1007/978-3-319-57454-7_55

16. Liu, Q., Wu, S., Wang, D., Li, Z., Wang, L.: Context-aware sequential recommendation. In: IEEE International Conference on Data Mining, pp. 1053–1058 (2016)

17. Liu, Q., Wu, S., Wang, L., Tan, T.: Predicting the next location: a recurrent model with spatial and temporal contexts. In: AAAI Conference on Artificial Intelligence, pp. 194–200 (2016)

18. Mnih, A., Salakhutdinov, R.R.: Probabilistic matrix factorization. In: Annual Conference on Neural Information Processing Systems, pp. 1257–1264 (2008)

19. Perozzi, B., Alrfou, R., Skiena, S.: DeepWalk: online learning of social representations. In: ACM SIGKDD International Conference on Knowledge Discovery & Data Mining (2014)

20. Pham, T.-A.N., Li, X., Cong, G.: A general model for out-of-town region recommendation. In: International World Wide Web Conference, pp. 401–410 (2017)

21. Rendle, S., Freudenthaler, C., Gantner, Z., Schmidt-Thieme, L.: BPR: Bayesian personalized ranking from implicit feedback. In: International Conference on Uncertainty in Artificial Intelligence, pp. 452–461 (2009)

22. Rendle, S., Freudenthaler, C., Schmidt-Thieme, L.: Factorizing personalized Markov chains for next-basket recommendation. In: International World Wide Web Conference, pp. 811–820 (2010)

23. Shi, C., Li, Y., Zhang, J., Sun, Y., Philip, S.Y.: A survey of heterogeneous information network analysis. IEEE Trans. Knowl. Data Eng. **29**(1), 17–37 (2017)

24. Shi, C., Zhang, Z., Luo, P., Yu, P.S., Yue, Y., Wu, B.: Semantic path based personalized recommendation on weighted heterogeneous information networks. In: ACM International on Conference on Information and Knowledge Management, pp. 453–462 (2015)

25. Sun, Y., Han, J., Yan, X., Yu, P.S., Wu, T.: PathSim: meta path-based top-k similarity search in heterogeneous information networks. VLDB Endow. **4**(11), 992–1003 (2011)

26. Wang, H., Wang, N., Yeung, D.-Y.: Collaborative deep learning for recommender systems. In: SIGKDD Conference on Knowledge Discovery and Data Mining, pp. 1235–1244 (2015)

27. Wang, Y., et al.: Regularity and conformity: location prediction using heterogeneous mobility data. In: SIGKDD Conference on Knowledge Discovery and Data Mining, pp. 1275–1284 (2015)

28. Wu, C.-Y., Ahmed, A., Beutel, A., Smola, A.J., Jing, H.: Recurrent recommender networks. In: ACM International Conference on Web Search and Data Mining, pp. 495–503 (2017)

29. Xingjian, S., Chen, Z., Wang, H., Yeung, D.-Y., Wong, W.-K., Woo, W.-C.: Convolutional LSTM network: a machine learning approach for precipitation nowcasting. In: Annual Conference on Neural Information Processing Systems, pp. 802–810 (2015)

30. Yang, D., Zhang, D., Zheng, V.W., Yu, Z.: Modeling user activity preference by leveraging user spatial temporal characteristics in LBSNs. IEEE Trans. Syst. Man Cybern. **45**(1), 129–142 (2015)

31. Yao, D., Zhang, C., Huang, J., Bi, J.: SERM: a recurrent model for next location prediction in semantic trajectories. In: ACM International Conference on Information and Knowledge Management, pp. 2411–2414 (2017)

32. Yu, X., et al.: Personalized entity recommendation: a heterogeneous information network approach. In: ACM International Conference on Web Search and Data Mining, pp. 283–292 (2014)

33. Zhang, J.-D., Chow, C.-Y.: iGSLR: personalized geo-social location recommendation: a kernel density estimation approach. In: ACM International Conference on Advances in Geographic Information Systems, pp. 334–343 (2013)

34. Zhao, S., Zhao, T., Yang, H., Lyu, M.R., King, I.: STELLAR: spatial-temporal latent ranking for successive point-of-interest recommendation. In: AAAI Conference on Artificial Intelligence, pp. 315–322 (2016)

Discovering Attractive Segments
in the User Generated Video Streams

Jie Zhou[1,2], Jiangbo Ai[2], Zheng Wang[2(✉)], Si Chen[3], and Qin Wei[1]

[1] Guizhou Provincial Key Laboratory of Public Big Data, GuiZhou University,
Guiyang 55002, Guizhou, China
`weiq@gzu.edu.cn`
[2] School of Computer Science and Engineering,
University of Electronic Science and Technology of China, Chengdu, China
`zhoujie.0714@gmail.com, jiangbom1@gmail.com, zh_wang@hotmail.com`
[3] Information Science Academy, China Electronics Technology Group Corporation,
Chengdu, China
`chensi@cetc.com.cn`

Abstract. With the rapid development of digital equipment and the continuous upgrading of online media, a growing number of people are willing to post videos on the web to share their daily lives [1,2]. Generally, not all video segments are popular with audiences, some of which may be boring. In recent years, crowd-sourced time-sync video comments have emerged worldwide, supporting further research on temporal video labelling. In this paper, we propose a novel framework to achieve the following goal: Predicting which segment in a newly generated video stream will be popular among the audiences. At last, experimental results on real-world data demonstrate the effectiveness of the proposed framework and justify the idea of predicting the popularities of segments in a video exploiting crowd-sourced time-sync comments as a bridge to analyse videos.

Keywords: Time-sync comment · User generated video stream · Segment popularity prediction · Video-to-text transfer

1 Introduction

Recently, the booming of on-line sharing media has provided widely popular channels for people to watch user generated video streams of pets, entertainment, sports, news, etc. And the researches about images and videos are much more than that in the past [3–8,33]. According to the statistics, videos uploaded in Youtube have exceeded 400 hours in a minute. No wonder that there is increasing demand for fast video digestion due to the prevalence of video sharing. Though a great deal of efforts have been made on the prediction for the popularities of videos [9,10], there is little work for discovering the interesting points in a newly generated video stream. In an user generated video stream with dozens of minutes long, attractive segments may just last two or three minutes. Predicting

© Springer Nature Switzerland AG 2019
J. Shao et al. (Eds.): APWeb-WAIM 2019, LNCS 11642, pp. 236–250, 2019.
https://doi.org/10.1007/978-3-030-26075-0_18

popular video segments in a new video will be of great help not only for the audiences to better enjoy this video stream and skip the boring parts, but also for this video to be spread. Analyzing which emotion would be produced by the audiences when they watch a video can also be very meaningful. Different videos inspire emotions of people when they watch a video.

In recent years, time-sync comments (TSCs) [11] (also named barrage in [12], danmaku in [13], bullet-screen comments in [14]) have emerged in many countries, are now available in niconico in Japan or Bilibili in China. They are called "bullet-screen" because the comments made by the viewers flying across the screen, which are just like a hail of bullets. With this form, viewers can share their feelings and comments about the video on the screen. Meanwhile, the bullet-screen comments sent by the users are according to the current video segment, thus this is a new opportunity for temporal video labeling, as video contents could now be accurately located with timestamps. Figure 1 shows an example of how time-sync comments roll on the screen.

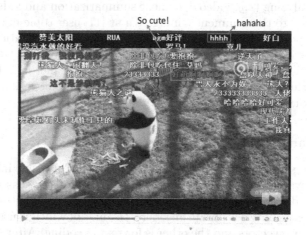

Fig. 1. A diagram of time-sync comments flowing across the screen.

According to the characteristics of TSCs, we build two tasks to analyze the videos: (1) Predicting which segment in a newly generated video stream among the audiences will be popular. (2) Predicting which emotion would be induced by the audiences when they watch a newly released video.

2   Related Work

Typically, time-sync comments based researches are for the videos with corresponding time-sync comments. The pop research directions include highlight detection, crowd-sourced time-sync comment mining and text transferring tasks.

2.1 Highlight Detection

Video highlight [17,18] is the task that to find the most the memorable shots in a video with high emotion intensity [15], it focuses on extracting the affective contents [19]. Before the rise of the time-sync comment research, some researchers utilize low-level features, including motion and vocal effects, to construct the event development story-lines [20,21]. These methods only concentrate on the video, ignoring the audiences' feelings. After the time-sync comments emerged. Qing at [15] proposed a highlight method, which uses the word-to-emotion mapping to tackle the issue of lag-calibration, emotion-topic concentration balance problems. Both of the two researches are based on the unsupervised methods including clustering and LDA.

2.2 Crowd-Sourced Time-Sync Comment Mining

Comment mining is to find the useful information about audiences. The quality of time-sync analyzing (*e.g.* video document summarization and video highlight) is directly related to the comment mining. Wu at [11] uses topic models, he considers not only semantic correlations, but also audiences' correlations. Another work about this is to use the pre-trained embedding model to get the semantic vectors. Lv at [14] uses this idea and proposed T-DSSM method. This method uses EM algorithm to train the deep semantic embedding network by harnessing the temporal correlation between comments.

2.3 Text Transferring

Text transferring methods are widely used in multi-modal tasks, including captioning or retrieval. Most existing text transferring methods are based on images. Kurach proposed Visually Enhanced Text Embeddings (VETE) model in [22]. This model consists of two separate encoders, the first of which is used for encoding the images into vectors and the other is for text encoding. After the encoding step, the cosine similarity of the image and text vectors is calculated. For the matched pair, the goal is to maximize the similarity, while the pair are not matched, the goal is to minimize the similarity. For the language Transfer(LT) sub-module we proposed, we modify the VETE model so that it can be used in video-to-text transferring task. And this work achieves promising performance.

3 Data Explanation and Problem Definition

In this section, we first introduce the methods for preparing the data in detail. Then we define our task of video segment popularity prediction in detail. Then we define our two problems of video segment popularity prediction and audiences' feeling prediction separately.

3.1 Videos Split into Segments

Given a video sequence $V = \{f_1, f_2, ..., f_{|V|}\}$, we use color histograms method to select the key frames $K(V) = \{f_{x1}, f_{x2}, ..., f_{xm-1}\}$ [16,23]. According to key frames $K(V)$, we can split the video V into m segments. And we would predict the popularity of each segment, this is detailed in the following sections. Note that all the datasets are organized according to playback time, including f in V, s in $S(V)$.

3.2 Time-Sync Comments Data Process

Given a set of time-sync comments $C = \{c_1, c_2, ..., c_{|C|}\}$ and a set of timestamps $T = \{t_1, t_2, ..., t_{|C|}\}$, where the set of comments C is corresponding to a video V, and each comment c_i in C is corresponding to V at timestamps t_i. Each t_i is a time point in V. After segmentation of video detailed in previous subsection, we get a segment $S(V)$ with m segments, so that each comment c_i belongs to a segment s_j. In other words, each segment s_j have a set of comments $s_j(C) = \{c_{j1}, c_{j2}, ..., c_{j|s|}\}$.

3.3 Video Segment Popularity Prediction

The problem of video segment popularity prediction in this paper can be formulated as follows. Given a video sequence V (we regard this video as newly released and hasn't been commented on), we split it into m segments $S(V)$ as described in Sect. 3.1. For each segment s_i, we predict the number $|s_i(C)|$ of comments, which would be sent in s_i by the audiences. For that the time-sync comments are audiences' emotion expression and discussion of video content, the number of comments can reflect the popularity of this video segment. The more comments receives, the more this segment is concerned by audiences. So we use the number of comments as popularity of the video segment.

3.4 Audiences' Feeling Prediction

In this subsection, we present the feeling prediction formally. We have a set of videos V. After splitting it into segments set $S(V)$ of size $|S|$, we carry out classification operation for each segment s_i in S. The classification labels are consists of human feelings including happy and angry. The ground-truth labels are obtained from LDA model detailed in Sect. 3.2.

4 Data Preparation and Proposed Model

In this section, we first introduce how we make the raw data into dataset we can use. Then we present our segment popularity prediction model.

4.1 Data Preparation

Time-sync comments are sent by audiences casually and leisurely. The characteristics of the comments are limited in length and confused in semantics. Besides, emoticons("ˆ _ ˆ" means "happy") and internet slangs ("233333..." means "ha ha ha") are widely used. So it is crucial to extract key information and remove the semantic noise. The text processing steps are listed as follows: We first use Chinese word segmentation tool 'Jieba' to tokenize Chinese sentences into words sequences according to certain specifications. Next, we deal with each word separately according to the predefined dictionary, which records many correspondence. We replace the emoticons into emotional words like "happy" and "sad". For Internet slangs like "2333...", we use regular expression matching to find and replace them to emotional words.

4.2 Emotion Topic Model Construction

A topic is a general description of clustering of points of interest, which can roughly distinguish different types of points of interest.

To construct emotional dataset, we only keep emotional words in the time-sync comments. In a segment, we combine all the emotional words in it as a piece of data. For all the emotional words sets of segments, we use LDA method to construct a topic model.

Specifically, for text to topic sampling matrix θ, we have

$$\theta = [\vec{\theta_1}, \vec{\theta_2}, ..., \vec{\theta_S}], \tag{1}$$

$$\theta_{s,k} = \frac{n_{s,k} + \alpha_k}{\sum_{i=1}^{K}(n_{s,i} + \alpha_i)} \tag{2}$$

where $\theta_{s,k}$ stands the sampling vector for kth topic in sth video segment emotional words set, α is the Latent Dirichlet Allocation, K is the number of topics we set. For topics to words sampling matrix ϕ, we have

$$\phi = [\vec{\phi_1}, \vec{\phi_2}, ..., \vec{\phi_M}], \tag{3}$$

$$\phi_{k,w} = \frac{n_{k,w} + \beta_w}{\sum_{i=1}^{K}(n_{k,i} + \beta_i)} \tag{4}$$

where $\phi_{k,w}$ stands the wth word in k topic, β is the Latent Dirichlet Allocation.

The determination of the distribution of topics includes the selection of the number of topics and the keywords derived from the implementation of the theme model. As previous work [15] does, we put the emotional words' sets into LDA model and make $K = 5$. And we get five emotional categories, including angry, fear, sad, happy and surprise, detailing in Sect. 5.5. Some segments have no emotional words, so we set six emotional labels, which are used in audiences' emotional prediction task, to each segment of videos.

4.3   Video Encoder Model

In the case of machine process, it is natural to use a recurrent neural network (RNN) for the encoder, since the input is a variable-length sequence of symbols [24,25]. And the performance of LSTM [26] can be improved if additional non-linearity is added. Applying stacked layers is a straight forward way for this objective [27]. In our proposed model, we change traditional stacked lstm structure [28,29] to fit our task. Our model is improved from HRNE model in [27], and our encoder structure process variable length of segments features and we apply bi-directional LSTM structure.

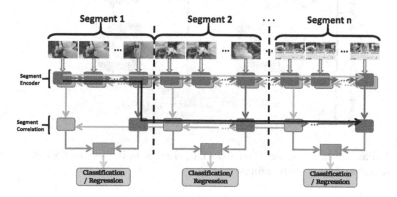

Fig. 2. A diagram of Video Encoder (VE) model. It consists of segment encoder and segment correlation sub-modules.

As is illustrated in Fig. 2, our proposed Video Encoder (VE) model has two main layers: segment encoder and segment correlation. First,we use LSTM to construct segment encoder layer to generate segments' representation with emphasis on temporal modelling. Then, we use a sparse LSTM layer to get information from the changes of scenes.

4.4   Language Transfer Model

The videos in the testing set are treated as newly released without comments for them. With the help of video-to-text transferring model, we can easily get what audiences' thinking when they watch the videos.

Figure 3 illustrates the Language Transfer (LT) Model that we proposed. It consists of two independent sub-modules, named encoder module and comparison.

For the paired of video segment and corresponding time-sync comment, we use our encoder module, consisting of two independent encoders, to encode the video content and text comment separately. For the video encoding part, we use LSTM structure to process the segments in videos. For each segment, we only keep the output of last step of LSTM. Next, we adopt fully connected network

242   J. Zhou et al.

to transfer the video vectors into fixed dimension. For the text encoding part, we first adopt Doc2Vec model to convert each comment into a vector, as we detailed in Sect. 4.1.

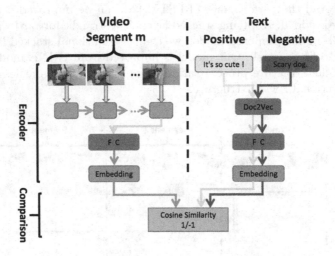

Fig. 3. A diagram of Language Transfer (LT) model. It is used to find effective and reasonable video-to-text embeddings.

After encoding operation, both the segment vectors and text vectors are sent to comparison part. Here, we adopt cosine distance to measure their similarity. We set v_s as encoded segment vector, and v_c as encoded comment vector. The cosine distance of v_s and v_c can be written as:

$$sim(v_s, v_c) = \frac{v_s \cdot v_c}{\|v_s\| \|v_c\|} \qquad (5)$$

where sim denotes the cosine calculation of two vectors, · denotes the inner product of two vectors, $\|\|$ denotes the l2 norm of a vector. If a comment is corresponding to the segment(this time-sync comment is sent in this segment), we would maximize the similarity of them. In other words, we set their cosine similarity ground-truth as 1. Otherwise, we set their cosine similarity training label as -1 (If two vectors are similar to each other, their cosine distance is around 1. If two vectors are not similar to each other, their cosine distance is around -1).

To fit the LT, we compare three different kinds of loss functions to test the effect of the model. To explain clearly, let us set $sim(v_s, v_c)$ as $y = \{y_1, y_2, ..., y_B\}$, and target label as $t = \{t_1, t_2, ..., t_B\}$. Both of y and t are batched with the size of B. Then the loss functions are listed as follows:

1. **Covariance:** In the theory of probability and statistics, covariance is used to measure the overall error of two variables. For the batched data of y and t,

covariance loss measures the relevance of them. The covariance can be written as:

$$Cov(y, t) = E[yt] - E[y]E[t] \tag{6}$$

where E is the expected value of a variable. And we adopt $1.0 - Cov(y, t)$ as our loss function.

2. **Surrogate Kendall:** Kendall correlation measures the strength of association of the cross tabulations. According to [30], we apply SKT_α, which is differentiable. It can be written as:

$$SKT\alpha(y, t) = \frac{\sum_{i,j} tanh(\alpha(y_i - y_j)(t_i - t_j))}{B(B-1)/2} \tag{7}$$

where $\alpha > 0$ is a hyper-parameter, B is the number of batch size. And we adopt $1.0 - SKT\alpha(y, t)$ as our loss function.

3. **Rank:** We also apply pairwise ranking loss proposed in [31]. The ranking loss can be written as:

$$rank(c_p, c_n, s) = \frac{1}{B} \sum_{i=1}^{B} max(0, \alpha - c_{pi} \cdot s + c_{ni} \cdot s_i) \tag{8}$$

where c_p c_n denote batch of the positive comment and negative samples respectively. s is the corresponding segment of a video. $\cdot$ denotes inner product. And α here is a hyper parameter.

4.5   Time-Sync Comments Based Popularity Prediction Model

After modeling both visual and text representation, we combine the proposed model two sub-modules to construct the Time-Sync Comments Based Popularity Prediction Model (T-BPPM). As illustrated in Fig. 4, we concatenate the corresponding segment vector and text vector, which are the outputs of VE and LT respectively. In this way we can comprehensively analyze the information of video segment and comment text. After some fully connected layers, we get the vector v_{st}.

In the task of segment popularity prediction, we apply both classification and regression methods to predict the number of time-sync comments would be sent to the video segment. The steps of classification is similar to that introduced in the last paragraph. For the regression problem, given a vector v_{st}, we use the regression equation:

$$y(v_{st}, \mathbf{w}) = w_0 \cdot v_{st}^0 + w_1 \cdot v_{st}^1 + ... + w_M \cdot v_{st}^M \tag{9}$$

where y is the regression polynomial function, and v_{st}^i is v_{st} raised to the power of i. The polynomial coefficients $w_0, w_1, ..., w_M$ are collectively denoted by $\mathbf{w}$. Note that the polynomial function $y(v_{st}, \mathbf{w})$ is a linear function of the coefficients $\mathbf{w}$, although y is a nonlinear function of v_{xt}.

Both the values of the coefficients of classification and regression methods are determined by minimizing the loss functions. Let us set the batch size of

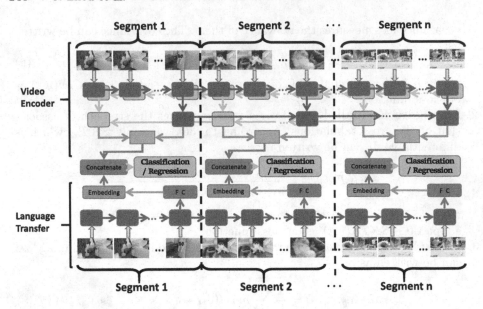

Fig. 4. A diagram of T-BPPM model. It combines the pre-trained VE and LT models.

training data as B, the class size as d. And we set y as the prediction results and t as the corresponding target labels, both of them are batched with the size of B. For the classification task, our choice of loss function is cross entropy loss, which can be written as:

$$L_c(y,t) = \frac{1}{B} \sum_{i=1}^{B} (- \sum_{j=1}^{d} y_{ij} \log t_{ij} + (1 - y_{ij}) \log(1 - t_{ij})) \tag{10}$$

where L_c is the loss function of classification. A piece of label have the dimension of d. While for regression task, we adopt the squares of the error. This loss function can be written as:

$$L_r(y,t) = \frac{1}{2} \frac{1}{B} \sum_{i=1}^{B} (y_i - t_i)^2 \tag{11}$$

where L_r is the loss function of regression. Because the predicting result of regression is the scalar, both y_i and t_i are numbers.

5   Experiment and Evaluation

In this section, we conduct experiments on large real datasets. We first introduce the dataset that we build. We then introduce our training process of the proposed T-BPPM. Next, we give the benchmarks and experiment results. At last, we give our analysis according to the results.

5.1 Dataset

In this section, we describe the datasets collected and constructed in our experiments. We have collected a large corpus of time-sync comment from Bilibli (https://www.bilibili.com/), a content sharing website in China with time-sync comments in China with time-sync comments.

We removed the videos which are less than 30 s, or have less than 10 time-sync comments, or less than the average of one comment every ten seconds. For the words which appear less than 5 times in our dataset, we just remove them from our dataset. The statistics of the data we collect is illustrated in Table 1.

Table 1. Statistical data of our dataset

Data source	Bilibili
Video number	5138
Segment number	57397
Comment number	810943
Vocabulary size	45721
Emotional vocabulary size	6800

After collecting the data we need, we uniformly process the data so that it can be used in our model. We take one frame every ten frames in each video. With the help of Caffe, we extract feature of each frame. We apply Resnet101 proposed in [32]. We use the output of the 2048-way *pool*5 layer from Resnet101 pre-trained on the ImageNet dataset. For the time-sync comments data, we let each comment text corresponds to the video segment according to the sending time of each comment. We find that only 20% of the segments have more than 10 comments. Only less than 5% of the segments have more than 15 comments. So we divide the segments into five classes: less than 2 comment, less than 3 comments, less than 4 comments, less than 10 comments and more than 10 comments. In this way, each class has approximately equal samples.

For the regression task, in order to prevent data imbalance, if a has more than 15 comments, we just set the number of comments is 15. Then we apply 0-1 normalization to map the number of comments $n_c \in [0, 1]$, so that the regression method can fit the results easier.

5.2 Models Pre-train

To get a better final result, before training our overall model T-BPPM, we first use our dataset to pre-train the two sub-modules, VE and LT.

For pre-training process of VE, we use the video features as the input. Each batch of input video is a three-dimensional tensor$V_B \in R^{B*(S*L)*2048}$, where B is batch size. S is the number of segments of videos. L is the length of a segment, we set it as 750 (max length of a segment). From this input, we got the prediction result, which is also a three-dimensional tensor $P_B \in R^{B*S*5}$. While for the regression task, the result is $P_B \in R^{B*S*1}$ because the result of the regression is a scalar.

For pre-training process of LT, we also use the video features as the input. During training process of LT, for a time-sync comment c_p, we select its paired segment s as the positive sample (c_p, s), and set their training label as 1; and we randomly choose a comment c_n which is not describing this segment, we set them as negative sample (c_n, s) and set their training label as -1. For the parameters of Doc2Vec, we set the vector size as 300 and the window size as 10.

5.3 Train the Integrated Model

After pre-training process, we integrate the VE and LT to the overall model $T-BPPM$. We remove the last fully connected layers in both VE and LT, and concatenate the output vectors of the two models for final prediction. During the training of the $T-BPPM$, we fixed the parameter of LT part, so that LT can keep the text information of comments.

We adopted the Adadelta optimizer to fit our model. In order to avoid overfitting, we set the dropout ratio to 0.5 for all fully connected layers. In addition, we also added the weight decay and set the value to 0.01. We set batch size as 32. All experiments were implemented in Theano, using a NVIDIA GTX1080 GPU with 8 GB memory.

5.4 Results of Segment Popularity Prediction

In this section, we show the result of our experimental results for segment popularity prediction task. Tables 2 and 3 are the results of classification and regression methods respectively. In order to compare the two methods more clearly, we map the results of regression method to the numerical range of classification method. So the classification and regression results can apply to the same metric.

The "one layer of LSTM" is our baseline model, which just applies one layer of LSTM to encode the video frames and directly uses the last vector of each segment to predict the popularity of the video segment.

We use both precision and recall to evaluate the proposed methods. We can conclude from the results that the Video Encoder(VE) outperforms one layer of LSTM model. The reason is that the VE model uses the improved stacked of two LSTM to extract more rigorous information from the videos, and it can better model the relevance between each segment at the second layer of LSTM. And after combining the LT, our T-BPPM gets further promotion. The reason lies in the LT models learn the effective transferring rules and reduce the semantic gap between the videos and comments. All the three LTs with different loss functions improve the results in different degrees. Covariance and Kendall loss functions extract more information from the comments while the remaining two methods extract less information.

From the results, we can find that the LT model gives less promotion of results than VE model. The reasons may lie in that: First, some comments are

Table 2. Results of segment popularity prediction for classification

Model	Precision	Recall
One layer of LSTM	0.355	0.267
Video Encoder	0.412	0.298
T-BPPM (Covariance)	**0.441**	0.312
T-BPPM (Kendall)	0.429	**0.313**
T-BPPM (Rank)	0.421	0.304

Table 3. Results of segment popularity prediction for regression

Model	Precision	Recall
One layer of LSTM	0.323	0.264
Video Encoder	0.384	0.287
T-BPPM (Covariance)	0.415	**0.313**
T-BPPM (Kendall)	0.411	0.296
T-BPPM (Rank)	0.408	0.307

not related to the video contents. For example, someone tell a joke in the time-sync comment, making other audiences laugh and send "hahaha" comments; or the audiences discuss the news, which happens soon after the video was released, by the time-sync comments. These are the noise data for our tasks. Second, the interesting points may lie in audio data, like a cat yelling sweet, or a fashion background music when some people dancing in the video. We don't use the audio data in our tasks. Third, it can be difficult to extract some interesting points from the videos, although these points are related to the video contents. For example, someone in the video may look like a super star, this can cause the discussion by the audiences; or the performer in the video did some actions and dress clothing styles which are fashionable in the period of that time. It needs massive excess video data and real time popular information to fit these factors. These factors make LT model give limited promotion.

5.5   Results of Audiences' Emotion Prediction

In this section, we show the result of our experimental results for audiences' emotion prediction task. Table 4 is the top words of LDA topics (some of the words are converted from the internet language like 'wordless' and 'oh my god'). And Table 5 is the result of our proposed model.

From Table 4, the words in different topics have certain discrimination. From our statistics, different types of videos have different effects on audiences emotions. For example, the segments in pets videos are likely to be popular if the audiences produce happy emotions (pets barks happily and lovely in the video), while if the audiences produce angry or fear emotions (someone does harm to animals in the video), these segments are more likely to be unpopular. For the game videos, audiences are more willing to see the segments which can make them produce surprise or fear emotions (the games containing brilliant thrilling fighting scenes). This may due to our dataset contains many and adventure games and horror games.

Table 4. The top words of LDA topics

Topic	Top words
Angry	Crazy, Angry
Fear	Horrible, Convulsions
Sad	Wordless, Doubt
Happy	Haha, Like
Surprise	Astonishing, Oh my god

Comparing to segment popularity prediction task, LT gives more promotion in this task. The reason is that audiences' emotion are the presentations of inner feeling of audiences. So emotion prediction task relies more on the content of comments than popularity prediction task.

Table 5. Accuracy of emotion prediction models

Model	Precision	Recall
One layer of LSTM	0.304	0.225
Video Encoder	0.378	0.246
T-BPPM (Covariance)	0.420	0.270
T-BPPM (Kendall)	0.413	0.266
T-BPPM (Rank)	0.411	0.258

6 Conclusion

In this paper, we propose a novel framework for segment popularity prediction task based on CNN and LSTM. This work is helpful for guiding the video makers to make more attractive videos. Our model takes use of the time-sync comment as the transcendental knowledge to assist the analysis of videos' contents. For the video-to-text transferring, we compare three different losses to find the best choice. And we construct dataset for these tasks. In an extensive experimental evaluation, we show our models fits the tasks well. We also show that we can dig effective information in the time-sync comments.

Acknowledgements. This work is supported by Major Scientific and Technological Special Project of Guizhou Province (20183002).

References

1. Jelodar, A.B., Paulius, D., Sun, Y.: Long activity video understanding using functional object-oriented network. IEEE Trans. Multimedia (2018)
2. Chen, Y., Hao, C., Liu, A.X., et al.: Multi-level model for video object segmentation based on supervision optimization. IEEE Trans. Multimedia (2019)
3. Liu, J.Y., Yang, Y.H., Jeng, S.K.: Weakly-supervised visual instrument-playing action detection in videos. IEEE Trans. Multimedia (2018)
4. Yang, Y., Zhou, J., Ai, J., et al.: Video captioning by adversarial LSTM. IEEE Trans. Image Process. **27**(11), 5600–5611 (2018)
5. Zhang, M., Yang, Y., Zhang, H., et al.: More is better: precise and detailed image captioning using online positive recall and missing concepts mining. IEEE Trans. Image Process. **28**(1), 32–44 (2019)
6. Qiu, Y., Liu, Y., Arteaga-Falconi, J., et al.: EVM-CNN: real-time contactless heart rate estimation from facial video. IEEE Trans. Multimedia (2018)
7. Bin, Y., Yang, Y., Shen, F., et al.: Describing video with attention-based bidirectional LSTM. IEEE Trans. Cybern. **99**, 1–11 (2018)
8. Hu, M., Yang, Y., Shen, F., et al.: Collective reconstructive embeddings for cross-modal hashing. IEEE Trans. Image Process. (2018)
9. Li, H., Ma, X., Wang, F., et al.: On popularity prediction of videos shared in online social networks. In: Proceedings of the 22nd ACM International Conference on Information & Knowledge Management, pp. 169–178. ACM (2013)
10. Yang, Y., Duan, Y., Wang, X., et al.: Hierarchical multi-clue modelling for poi popularity prediction with heterogeneous tourist information. IEEE Trans. Knowl. Data Eng. (2018)
11. Wu, B., Zhong, E., Tan, B., et al.: Crowdsourced time-sync video tagging using temporal and personalized topic modeling. In: Proceedings of the 20th ACM SIGKDD International Conference on Knowledge Discovery and Data Mining, pp. 721–730. ACM (2014)
12. Hamasaki, M., Takeda, H., Hope, T., et al.: Network analysis of an emergent massively collaborative creation community: how can people create videos collaboratively without collaboration?. In: Third International AAAI Conference on Weblogs and Social Media (2009)
13. Wu, Z., Ito, E.: Correlation analysis between user's emotional comments and popularity measures. In: 2014 IIAI 3rd International Conference on Advanced Applied Informatics, pp. 280–283. IEEE (2014)
14. Lv, G., Xu, T., Chen, E., et al.: Reading the videos: temporal labeling for crowd-sourced time-sync videos based on semantic embedding. In: Thirtieth AAAI Conference on Artificial Intelligence (2016)
15. Ping, Q., Chen, C.: Video highlights detection and summarization with lag-calibration based on concept-emotion mapping of crowd-sourced time-sync comments. arXiv preprint arXiv:1708.02210 (2017)
16. Girgensohn, A., Boreczky, J.: Time-constrained keyframe selection technique. Multimedia Tools Appl. **11**(3), 347–358 (2000)
17. Jiao, Y., Li, Z., Huang, S., et al.: Three-dimensional attention-based deep ranking model for video highlight detection. IEEE Trans. Multimedia **20**(10), 2693–2705 (2018)

18. Merler, M., Mac, K.N.C., Joshi, D., et al.: Automatic curation of sports highlights using multimodal excitement features. IEEE Trans. Multimedia (2018)
19. Lin, K.S., Lee, A., Yang, Y.H., et al.: Automatic highlights extraction for drama video using music emotion and human face features. Neurocomputing **119**, 111–117 (2013)
20. Hanjalic, A., Xu, L.Q.: Affective video content representation and modeling. IEEE Trans. Multimedia **7**(1), 143–154 (2005)
21. Ngo, C.W., Ma, Y.F., Zhang, H.J.: Video summarization and scene detection by graph modeling. IEEE Trans. Circuits Syst. Video Technol. **15**(2), 296–305 (2005)
22. Kurach, K., Gelly, S., Jastrzebski, M., et al.: Better text understanding through image-to-text transfer. arXiv preprint arXiv:1705.08386 (2017)
23. Ferman, A.M., Tekalp, A.M., Mehrotra, R.: Robust color histogram descriptors for video segment retrieval and identification. IEEE Trans. Image Process. **11**(5), 497–508 (2002)
24. Yao, L., Torabi, A., Cho, K., et al.: Describing videos by exploiting temporal structure. In: Proceedings of the IEEE International Conference on Computer Vision, pp. 4507–4515 (2015)
25. Sutskever, I., Vinyals, O., Le, Q.V.: Sequence to sequence learning with neural networks. In: Advances in Neural Information Processing Systems, pp. 3104–3112 (2014)
26. Hochreiter, S., Schmidhuber, J.: Long short-term memory. Neural Comput. **9**(8), 1735–1780 (1997)
27. Pan, P., Xu, Z., Yang, Y., et al.: Hierarchical recurrent neural encoder for video representation with application to captioning. In: Proceedings of the IEEE Conference on Computer Vision and Pattern Recognition, pp. 1029–1038 (2016)
28. Venugopalan, S., Rohrbach, M., Donahue, J., et al.: Sequence to sequence-video to text. In: Proceedings of the IEEE International Conference on Computer Vision, pp. 4534–4542 (2015)
29. Venugopalan, S., Hendricks, L.A., Mooney, R., et al.: Improving LSTM-based video description with linguistic knowledge mined from text. arXiv preprint arXiv:1604.01729 (2016)
30. Huang, W., Chan, K.L., Li, H., Lim, J.H., Liu, J., Wong, T.Y.: Content-based medical image retrieval with metric learning via rank correlation. In: Wang, F., Yan, P., Suzuki, K., Shen, D. (eds.) MLMI 2010. LNCS, vol. 6357, pp. 18–25. Springer, Heidelberg (2010). https://doi.org/10.1007/978-3-642-15948-0_3
31. Kiros, R., Salakhutdinov, R., Zemel, R.S.: Unifying visual-semantic embeddings with multimodal neural language models. arXiv preprint arXiv:1411.2539 (2014)
32. He, K., Zhang, X., Ren, S., et al.: Deep residual learning for image recognition. In: Proceedings of the IEEE Conference on Computer Vision and Pattern Recognition, pp. 770–778 (2016)
33. Hu, M., et al.: Hashing with angular reconstructive embeddings. IEEE Trans. Image Process. **27**(2), 545–555 (2018)

Spatial Temporal Trajectory Similarity Join

Tangpeng Dan[1,2], Changyin Luo[1,2(✉)], Yanhong Li[3], Bolong Zheng[4],
and Guohui Li[4]

[1] School of Computer, Central China Normal University, Wuhan, China
tangpengdan@mails.ccnu.edu.cn, changyinluo@mail.ccnu.edu.cn
[2] Hubei Provincial Key Laboratory of Artificial Intelligence and Smart Learning,
Central China Normal University, Wuhan, China
[3] College of Computer Science, South-Central University for Nationalities,
Wuhan, China
[4] School of Computer Science and Technology,
Huazhong University of Science and Technology, Wuhan, China

Abstract. Existing works only focus on spatial dimension without the consideration of combining spatial and temporal dimensions together when processing trajectory similarity join queries, to address this problem, this paper proposes a novel two-level grid index which takes both spatial and temporal information into account when processing spatial-temporal trajectory similarity join. A new similarity function MOGS is developed to measure the similarity in an efficient manner when our candidate trajectories have high coverage rate CR. Extensive experiments are conducted to verify the efficiency of our solution.

Keywords: Spatial-temporal database · Two-level grid index ·
Trajectory similarity join

1 Introduction

Trajectory similarity join, which, given a set of trajectories and a query trajectory Q, returns top-k similarity trajectories from trajectory database. Trajectory join can be recorded using in many applications, such as data cleaning, taxi recommending system, traffic condition analysis. For example, a database contain several similar trajectories, in order to reduce the redundancy, similarity join can be used to data cleaning. Given a query trajectory $\{q\}$, we may find two highest ranked similar trajectories $\{T_1, T_2\}$, and only keep the most similar T_1 as the representative trajectory. In the literatures, many studies have been proposed to address the problem of trajectory similarity join [3,6], and they have their own merits. However, they seldom consider how to take both spatial and temporal information into trajectory similarity. For example, trajectory pairs (T_1, T_3) and (T_2, T_3) are similarity on spatial domain, but the time period for T_1, T_2 and T_3 are $(13:00, 15:00)$, $(8:00, 9:00)$, $(7:30, 10:00)$, respectively. Hence, only (T_2, T_3) is a spatial-temporal similarity pair.

© Springer Nature Switzerland AG 2019
J. Shao et al. (Eds.): APWeb-WAIM 2019, LNCS 11642, pp. 251–259, 2019.
https://doi.org/10.1007/978-3-030-26075-0_19

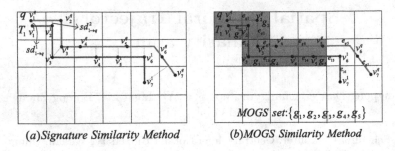

(a)Signature Similarity Method   (b)MOGS Similarity Method

Fig. 1. Trajectory similarity methods

Some works focus on trajectory similarity join, but they are inefficient. As shown in Fig. 1a, if adopting signature method [3], even T_1 and q are close to each other, we still need to evaluate their spatial similarity by computing spatial distance, which consumes much more memory and time. In order to improve efficiency, Maximum Overlapping Grid Segment (MOGS) method is proposed in Sect. 4.3, we can obtain the similarity of T_1 and q by adding their road segments instead of computing their spatial distance as in Fig. 1b, which helps us save more much computation cost. Coverage Rate (CR) is defined to measure how close two trajectories are. To summarize, our contributions can be summarized as follows.

- We propose a two-level grid index when processing spatial-temporal trajectory similarity join queries.
- We develop a time-first searching framework to prune unpromising trajectory pairs in an efficient way, and propose a novel MOGS method.
- In order to further improve efficiency of query processing, a dynamical pruning method based on triangle inequality is presented.

2 Related Works

A number of trajectory similarity measurement functions have been proposed, which can be roughly grouped into two types: (1) The spatial based metrics, such as the Closest-Pair Distance(CPD) [4] and the One Way Distance (OWD) [2], These metrics directly use the Euclidean distance for corresponding sample point pairs to define the similarity. (2) The spatio-temporal metrics, such as the Dynamic Time Warping (DTW) [1,5]. Specifically, the Closest-Pair Distance(CPD) [4] is a variation of Euclidean Distance which was introduced to find closest trajectories for given query in spatial networks. The One Way Distance (OWD) [2] focuses on shape similarity for trajectories in grid representations. For Dynamic Time Wrapping (DTW) [1,9] distance allows some sample points to repeat in order to achieve the best alignment, i.e., one point in one trajectory can match multiple points in another trajectory. DTW was claimed to be vulnerable to noises since some noise points can introduce large distance between trajectories. Other methods, such as the trajectory similarity join method in [7] uses point-to-point to compute the correlation between two trajectories, which the sample points on trajectories may not be well aligned. All these methods cannot be employed to solve our problem directly.

3   Problem Definition

Definition 1 *Trajectory.* *A trajectory T is defined as $T_i = \{v_1^i, v_2^i, v_3^i, \cdots, v_n^i\}$, where v_n^i is a sample point in T_i, $v_n^i = [p_n, (t_{ns}, t_{ne})]$, p_n is the spatial location, (t_{ns}, t_{ne}) indicates the earliest arrival time and the latest arrival time for p_n.*

Given two trajectories T_i and T_j, a sample point v_n^i on T_i, we define the minimum distance on a road network from v_n^i to T_j as $Sdis(v_n^i, T_j)$. $sd_{i \to j}^n$ denotes the spatial distance between a sample point v_n^i to a trajectory T_j, and **a threshold distance rd** indicates influence radius given by the user.

$$sd_{i \to j}^n = \begin{cases} Sdis(v_n^i, T_j) & if\ Sdis(v_n^i, T_j) \le rd \\ +\infty & if\ Sdis(v_n^i, T_j) > rd \end{cases} \tag{1}$$

Definition 2 *Trajectory-spatial Similarity Function.* *Given trajectories T_i and T_j, trajectory-spatial similarity function is defined as follows.*

$$S_{sim}(T_i, T_j) = \frac{\sum_{k=1}^{|T_i|} e^{-sd_{i \to j}^k}}{|T_i|} + \frac{\sum_{k=1}^{|T_j|} e^{-sd_{j \to i}^k}}{|T_j|} \tag{2}$$

Here, $|T|$ denotes the number of sample points in a trajectory. Similarly, **temporal distance** $td_{i \to j}^n$ denotes the minimum temporal distance between a sample point v_n^i to a trajectory T_j, which is defined as Eq. 3, where rt is the threshold time, and $\left| v_n^i.t_{ne} - v_n^j.t_{ns} \right| \le rt$.

$$td_{i \to j}^n = \begin{cases} \frac{\min\{|v_n^i.t_{ne}-v_n^j.t_{ns}|, |v_n^i.t_{ne}-v_n^i.t_{ns}|, |v_n^j.t_{ne}-v_n^j.t_{ns}|\}}{\left|\max\{v_n^i.t_{ne}, v_n^j.t_{ne}\}-\min\{v_n^i.t_{ns}, v_n^j.t_{ns}\}\right|} & if\ \left|v_n^i.t_{ne}-v_n^j.t_{ns}\right| \le rt \\ +\infty & if\ \left|v_n^i.t_{ne}-v_n^j.t_{ns}\right| > rt \end{cases} \tag{3}$$

Definition 3 *Trajectory-temporal Similarity Function.* *Given trajectories T_i and T_j, trajectory-temporal similarity function is defined as follows.*

$$T_{sim}(T_i, T_j) = \frac{\sum_{k=1}^{|T_i|} e^{-td_{i \to j}^k}}{|T_i|} + \frac{\sum_{k=1}^{|T_j|} e^{-td_{j \to i}^k}}{|T_j|} \tag{4}$$

Definition 4 *Spatial Temporal Similarity Score.*

$$ST_{sim}(T_i, T_j) = \lambda \cdot S_{sim}(T_i, T_j) + (1 - \lambda) \cdot T_{sim}(T_i, T_j) \tag{5}$$

$\lambda \subset [0, 1]$ controls the relative importance of the spatial and temporal similarities.

Definition 5 *Spatial Temporal Similarity Joins.* *Given a set of trajectories*
$P = \{T_1, T_2, \cdots, T_n\}$ *and a query trajectories set* $Q = \{q_1, q_2, \cdots, q_n\}$, *a top-*
k *spatial temporal similarity joins retrieves a set* $P_s \subseteq P$ *with* k *trajectories:*
$\forall T \in P_s, \forall T' \in P - P_s, ST_{sim}(Q, T) > ST_{sim}(Q, T')$

4 Solution

4.1 Two-Level Grid Index

In order to efficiently utilize temporal and spatial information to compute trajectory similarity, we build a two-level grid index. The first level of the index
mainly stores temporal information, and the second level stores spatial information. As shown in Fig. 2, grid index is employed to organize trajectory in the
second level.

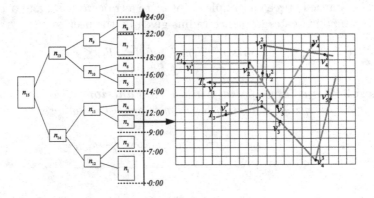

Fig. 2. Two-level grid index

4.2 Time First Searching Framework

Considering the inefficiency of pruning dissimilarity pairs in spatial domain, a
time-first search framework is proposed in Algorithm 1, which has two stages:
at first, we find all trajectories in a leaf node of the first level of our index,
second, if their time period difference is less than the threshold time rt, verify
the similarity between the trajectories in this node. Otherwise, we prune this
trajectory.

4.3 Maximum Overlapping Grid Segments

Coverage Rate (CR) is defined to measure whether two candidate trajectories
have close spatial distance. Based on point signature and trajectory signature
described in [3], its definition is:

$$CR(T_i, T_j) = \frac{1}{2}\left(\frac{\bigcup_{1 \leq n \leq |T_i|}(G^t(T_j) \cap G^r(v_n^i))}{G^t(T_j)} + \frac{\bigcup_{1 \leq n \leq |T_j|}(G^t(T_i) \cap G^r(v_n^j))}{G^t(T_i)}\right)$$

(6)

Algorithm 1. Time-First Searching Framework

Input: index T_r, trajectory set P, query set Q, rd, rt, λ, CR threshold θ
Output: $A = \{P_S \mid \forall T \in P_S, \forall T' \in P - P_S, ST_{sim}(Q,T) > ST_{sim}(Q,T')\}$

1 we adopt pre-order traversal to search leaf node in T_r;
2 **for** *each leaf node in T_r* **do**
3   **if** *n.time range $\leq rt$* **then**
4   ⌊ spatial similarity computation(T, θ, rd, λ);

5   **if** *The temporal distance between n and n.sibling $\leq rt$* **then**
6   merge n and n.sibling into n.parent;
7   find qualified trajectories in n.parent;
8   ⌊ spatial similarity computation(T, θ, rd, λ);

9   **if** *The temporal distance between n and n.parent $\leq rt$* **then**
10   find qualified trajectories in n.parent;
11   ⌊ spatial similarity computation(T, θ, rd, λ);

12 return A;

As shown in Fig. 3a, based on Eq. 6, brown grids depict a trajectory signature $G^t(T_i)$, blue grids represent points signature $G^r(v_n^j)$, and green grids are intersection for points and trajectory. When CR is more larger, the two trajectories are more closer, MOGS has better performance.

Inspired by [8], we propose the MOGS similarity function to measure the similarity for a trajectory pair. Given two candidate trajectories T_i and T_j, their edge segments are $T_i = \{e_{i1}, e_{i2}, \cdots, e_{in-1}\}$ and $T_j = \{e_{j1}, e_{j2}, \cdots, e_{jn-1}\}$ respectively. MOGS similarity function is defined as follows.

$$
S_{mogs}(T_i, T_j) = \begin{cases} 0, \ if \ T_i \ or \ T_j = \emptyset \\ \min(|e_{in}|, |e_{jm}|) + S_{mogs}(U(T_i), U(T_j)), \ if v_i^n, v_i^m \ in \ same \ grid \\ \max(S_{mogs}(U(T_i), T_j), S_{mogs}(T_i, U(T_j))), \ otherwise \end{cases}
\tag{7}
$$

Where $|e_{in}|$ is the travel length of trajectory edge e_{in}. $U(T_i) = \{e_{i1}, \cdots, e_{in-2}\}$ is the sub-trajectory of T_i minus the last point. Using MOGS, the length of segments is added to the overall similarity instead of computing their spatial distance in signature method, which is more discriminative when two trajectories have high coverage rate CR. As in Fig. 1b, given two trajectories q and T_1, we get $S_{mogs}(q, T_1) = |e_{11}| + |e_{q2}| + |e_{q3}| + |e_{14}|$.

The framework of MOGS is presented in Algorithm 2, which is composed of filtering (Line 2 to 8) and refinement (Line 19 to 22). For MOGS, after accessing grid index of all candidate trajectories, we can find the list of common edges $T \cap Q$. Therefore, **the upper similarity bound** is the sum of the travel length $|e|$ of all searched edges e, which is defined as follows.

$$
ub.S_{MOGS}(Q, T) = \sum\nolimits_{e \in T \cap Q} |e|
\tag{8}
$$

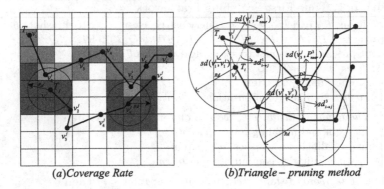

Fig. 3. Example of coverage rate & pruning method

Algorithm 2. Spatial Trajectory Similarity Search

Input: Q, k, T, index G, CR threshold θ and similarity measure S
Output: Top-k result set A

1 can$\leftarrow \emptyset$, A$\leftarrow \emptyset$, $UB \leftarrow 0$, $LB \leftarrow 0$
2 **for** *every* $q \in Q$ **do**
3 　|　**if** $CR > \theta$ **then**
4 　|　|　$S \leftarrow$ MOGS method;
5 　|　|_　can$\leftarrow$can$\cup G_e(q)$;
6 　|　**if** $CR < \theta$ **then**
7 　|　|　$S \leftarrow$ signature method;
8 　|　|_　can$\leftarrow$can$\cup \bigcup_{q' \in T} G_T(q')$;

9 sort all the trajectories $T_i \in can$ by ub.$S(Q, T_i)$;
10 **if** S *is signature method* **then**
11 　|　**for** *every point* v_n^i *in* T_i *and* Q **do**
12 　|　|　**if** $sd_n(Q, T).lb > LB$ **then**
13 　|　|　|_　$LB \leftarrow sd_n(Q, T).lb$;
14 　|　|　**if** $sd_n(Q, T).ub < UB$ **then**
15 　|　|　|_　$UB \leftarrow sd_n(Q, T).ub$;
16 　|　|　**if** $(LB > UB)$ *or* $(sd_n(Q, T).ub < LB)$ **then**
17 　|　|　|_　break;
18 　|　|_　choose top-k result and update A;

19 **while** $T_i \in can$ **do**
20 　|　A.add$(A, S(Q, T_i))$;
21 　|　**if** $S(Q, T_i) \geq$ ub.$S(Q, T_{i+1})$ **then**
22 　|　|_　break;

23 **return** A;

Lemma 1. $\forall T' \in can, S_{MOGS}(Q, T') = S_{MOGS}(Q, T)$

Proof. This lemma can be easily derived by Eq. 7. Any edge that do not intersect with the query, denotes as $T - T'$, cannot influence the similarity. Because we only add the length of an edge when two edges overlap.

Pruning for Signature Method. As shown in Fig. 3b, the triangle inequality in spatial networks is represented as $sd(v_1^i, v_1^j) + sd(v_1^j, P_{near}^n) > sd_{i \to j}^n$ and $sd(v_1^i, v_1^j) - sd(v_1^j, P_{near}^n) < sd_{i \to j}^n$. Here, sd means the spatial distance, and P_{near}^n is the closest point from T_j to T_i. LB and UB are global lower and upper bounds. The lower bound $sd_n(T_i, T_j).lb$ and upper bound $sd_n(T_i, T_j).ub$ are defined as follows.

$$sd_n(T_i, T_j).lb = \sum_{n \in |T_i|, m \in |T_j|} \left(sd(v_n^i, v_m^i) + sd(v_m^j, P_{near}^n) \right) \tag{9}$$

$$sd_n(T_i, T_j).ub = \sum_{n \in |T_i|, m \in |T_j|} \left(sd(v_n^i, v_m^i) - sd(v_m^j, P_{near}^n) \right) \tag{10}$$

Lemma 2. *Given two candidate trajectories T_i and T_j, if $LB > UB$ or $sd_n(T_i, T_j).ub < LB$, T_i and T_j cannot be similar.*

Proof. According to triangle inequality, the sum of any two sides of a triangle is greater than the third side. So, UB should be greater than LB. If $LB > UB$ or $sd_n(T_i, T_j).ub < LB$, it violates triangle inequality, T_i and T_j cannot be similar.

5   Experiments

5.1   Experimental Settings

We use real spatial network, namely New York Road Network (NRN)[1]. All the algorithms are implemented in C++, and run on a PC with 3.4 Ghz Intel Core I7-6700, 16 GB RAM memory. We mainly examine our proposed techniques in filtering step. The method in our paper is named **Two-level**. We also reproduce many classic methods. Specifically, the method adopting TF-matching [7] and R-tree index is named **TF-R-tree**, the other one employing signature method [3] and R-tree index is called **Sig-R-tree**, and the baseline method is denoted by **Bas-lin** which employs TF-matching and inverted index. Due to space limitation, only parts of experiment results are listed here.

---

[1] https://lab-work.github.io/data/.

5.2   Various Testing

As shown in Fig. 4a, as the threshold increases, the number of searched trajectories grows fewer. The reason is obvious, a lager threshold θ helps us to filter more dissimilarity trajectory pairs. In Fig. 4b, as rd increases, the number of searched trajectories is rising. This is mainly because: (i) a lager rd means more trajectories need to be computed and (ii) influence grid set depends on rd, with the increasing of rd, $G^r(v_n^i)$ covers more grids. As in Fig. 4c, the number of the searched trajectories keeps almost constant as w increases. A larger $|P|$ causes more trajectory pairs to be searched in Fig. 4d.

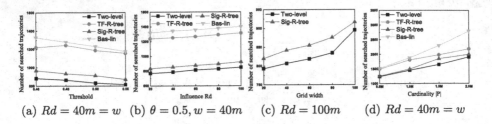

(a) $Rd = 40m = w$ (b) $\theta = 0.5, w = 40m$ (c) $Rd = 100m$ (d) $Rd = 40m = w$

Fig. 4. Evaluating filtering: number of searched trajectories on NRN

6   Conclusion

In this paper, we study the trajectory similarity join query in road networks. To process this query, a novel index, searching algorithms and pruning methods are developed. Experimental results show that our methods can gain a good performance. Our future work will study how to extend our methods to various distributed environments.

Acknowledgments. This work is supported in part by Hubei Natural Science Foundation under Grant No. 2017CFB135, NSFC Grant No. 61309002, and the Fundamental Research Funds for the Central Universities under Grants No. CCNU18QN017, CZZ17003, and Teaching Research Projects NO. JYX17032.

References

1. Assent, I., Wichterich, M., Krieger, R., Kremer, H., Seidl, T.: Anticipatory DTW for efficient similarity search in time series databases. Proc. VLDB **2**(1), 826–837 (2009)
2. Lin, B., Su, J.: Shapes based trajectory queries for moving objects, pp. 21–30 (2005)
3. Na, T., Li, G., Xie, Y., Li, C., Hao, S., Feng, J.: Signature-based trajectory similarity join. IEEE TKDE **29**(4), 870–883 (2017)
4. Papadias, D., Zhang, J., Mamoulis, N., Tao, Y.: Query processing in spatial network databases. Proc. VLDB **29**, 802–813 (2003)

5. Sakurai, Y., Yoshikawa, M., Faloutsos, C.: FTW: fast similarity search under the time warping distance. In: Twenty-Fourth ACM Sigmod-Sigact-Sigart Symposium on Principles of Database Systems (2005)
6. Shang, S., Chen, L., Jensen, C.S., Wen, J.R., Kalnis, P.: Searching trajectories by regions of interest. IEEE TKDE **29**(7), 1549–1562 (2017)
7. Shang, S., Chen, L., Wei, Z., Jensen, C.S., Zheng, K., Kalnis, P.: Trajectory similarity join in spatial networks. Proc. VLDB **10**(11), 1178–1189 (2017)
8. Wang, S., Bao, Z., Culpepper, J.S., Xie, Z., Liu, Q., Qin, X.: Torch: a search engine for trajectory data. In: SIGIR, pp. 535–544 (2018)
9. Yi, B.K., Jagadish, H.V., Faloutsos, C.: Efficient retrieval of similar time sequences under time warping. In: Fourteenth International Conference on Data Engineering, pp. 201–208 (1998)

Data Driven Charging Station Placement

Yudi Guo, Junjie Yao$^{(\boxtimes)}$, Jiaxiang Huang, and Yijun Chen

East China Normal University, Shanghai, China
guoyd21@gmail.com, junjie.yao@sei.ecnu.edu.cn, jiaxiang845@vip.qq.com,
benjaminchen2016@outlook.com

Abstract. With the rapid increasing availability of EV (electric vehicle) users, the demand for charging stations has also become vast. In the meanwhile, where to place the stations and what factors have major influence, remains unclear. These problems are bothering when EV companies tries to decide the locations for charging stations. Therefore, we tried to find an effective and interpretable approach to place them in more efficient locations. In common sense, a better location to place a station should relatively has a higher usage rate. Intuitively, we decided to predict usage rates of the candidate locations and tried to explain the result in the meantime, i.e. to find out how much important each feature is or what kind of influence they have. In this paper, we implement 2 models for the usage rate prediction. We also conduced experiments on real datasets, which contains the real charging records of anyo charging company in Shanghai. Further analysis is conducted as well for interpretation of the experiment result, including feature importance.

Keywords: Charging station · Location selection · Feature importance

1 Introduction

Nowadays, EVs can be seen everywhere in daily life and charging stations for EVs is also very common in parking areas. Instead of only recharging cars with private charging stations, the number of public charging stations keeps growing.

However, the cost of construction of charging stations is considerable and often very costly, not to mention reallocating. This made the location of first placement of charging stations very crucial. In a typical view, a 'good' placement is a charging station with a high usage rate. Traditional location selection methods are mainly for sharing bikes. They focus much more on bikes' or stations' spatial-temporal features. [1] makes use of sharing bikes' trajectory data for bike lane planning. [7] clusters stations into groups according to their status and used a reinforcement learning approach.

To simplify the problem, we divide the stations into three usage rate levels, which makes the regression into a classification. After the classification, we rank the features that is correlated with the results and . Our datasets is the real using records of charging stations in Shanghai, of which the time length is about a

© Springer Nature Switzerland AG 2019
J. Shao et al. (Eds.): APWeb-WAIM 2019, LNCS 11642, pp. 260–267, 2019.
https://doi.org/10.1007/978-3-030-26075-0_20

month. According to the real station locations, we also collected POI information around them. Furthermore, we do some detailed analysis on the features proved to have significant influence on the usage rate. At last, we evaluate our method on two districts subsets and different time periods subsets. Experiment results show that the significance of the chosen features, especially some of POI features do have great influence on prediction, which can hugely help planning the location selection.

In summary, the contributions of this work are listed as follows:

- We implement a random forests and a MLP to predict what level of usage rate a station is and which district a station belongs to, based on operator's charging station data and important features.
- We do detailed analysis on both stations data and features data to obtain basic information and find the relationships between station's usage rate and those features.
- We evaluate our method on datasets of the real charging stations in Shanghai, and it performs well in both classification and feature importance ranking task.

Design Overview. Inspired by [13], we think it is important that the features fed into a framework should be interpretable. In this paper, we not only focus on the prediction accuracy but also make attempts to have an interpretation of the features with feature importance. Figure 1 below gives an overview of our predicting pipeline. There are many factors that affect location selection for charging stations. In this paper, we consider a high usage rate as a 'success' sign for a station. Therefore, the original problem turns into how to get a higher usage rate and what are the factors behind it. The main objectives of our work is three-fold. First, we aim to distinguish some important features that have more influence on prediction. Second, we try to study the different 'behaviours' in different situations, such as urban and suburb, weekly and daily. Finally, we predict the level of usage rate and according to the results we rank the features.

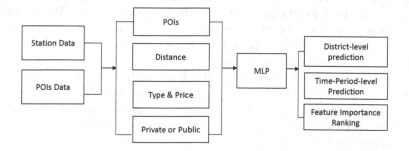

Fig. 1. Overview of the pipeline

2   Related Work

Existing similar works can be divided into 2 directions, with or without machine learning methods. The majority is to dig deeper into spatio-temporal information. [2,3,5,8] is based on sharing-bikes' trajectory data, which utilizes spatial-temporal information. [7] introduces a reinforcement learning approach to solve the problem of repositioning sharing-bikes. First of all, it uses an inner-balance clustering algorithm to cluster stations into groups, then the reinforcement learning is applied in each group to learn a reposition policy. It only used the spatial-temporal data, while the nearby information and raw descriptions of the stations are left out. [11] gives another insight of this problem. Its way of traffic prediction no longer focuses on the history data only. It also use the social media based on the location to collect a much larger range of the traffic information to help predicting traffic flows.

Other works on urban area utilize spatio-temporal data and solve the problem with some machine learning models, such as [4,6,9,11,14,16]. [16] makes use of users' geographical check-in information in Wechat and dig into the rich spatio temporal representations behind users' activity. Then the authors propose a latent Dirichlet allocation model to identify latent patterns of urban cultural interactions. [14] is another good example for spatio-temporal mobility event. It encodes each POI's spatio-temporal dependencies rather than neglect the correlations between POIs. [15] introduces a model for bicycle mobility prediction. It relies on historical bike-sharing data at a per-station basis with sub-hour granularity. It use a random forest model to implement their experiments and obtain a rather good result. However, neither of them tries to solve the problem with a more simple way, ignoring those simple but very important features.

Some other works try to carefully design the model for the problem, i.e. model the problem with mathematic approaches. [1,7,10,12,15] focus on a similar problem in the domain of bike-sharing. The objective is to find a proper strategy for bike lane setting or sharing-bikes reposition, in order to come up with a more reasonable and convenient plan. [1] provides a data-driven approach to deal with bike lane construction problem. There are some constraints used to formulate the problem, such as budget limitations, construction convenience and bike lane utilization. Furthermore, the problem is proved to be NP-hard so that they propose a greedy network expansion algorithm, which is scalable and an approximation solution. The approach works well in the given problem, however it does not contains any ML methods.

We also find one, [10], focuses on the features before fed into the model. It proposes a new method using weighted K-Nearest-Neighbor to predict bike-sharing stations' pick-up demand and establish another simulation model to generate(predict) the drop off demand, it also tries to simplify the problem with clustering the stations.

Tremendous efforts were made to solve the problem in the real complicated situations. While the current work of location selection is mainly based on the flow prediction of a single station and relies on the historical data. We insist our work on interpretation of features is essential and could also attain the goal of high accuracy.

3   Methodology

3.1   Feature Extraction

Point of Interest. In a big city like Shanghai, there are substantial POIs(points of interest) on the map, e.g. shopping malls, schools, estates, companies, etc. Understanding the main activity of the people in the area will help us to predict when there will be a high peak of charging or not. Therefore, we decide to extract the POI information around each existing charging station. There are too many POIs in Shanghai in fact and they are too close to each other, so we set a radius and then collect the POIs within the radius. Empirically, setting the radius as 300 meters is proper. In our work, we get 80 different types of POI totally. Some of the POIs are very similar to each other. Therefore, we aggregate the 80 POIs into 10 kinds at last.

Distance. The factor of distance should also be considered. People will not choose to park their electric cars for charging if the destination is too far. We assume that a station with less distance to metro stations, financial centers and major functional buildings is possibly to be occupied more often. We calculate the least distance to the following POIs: company, estate, hospital, metro station, shopping center and university.

Type and Price. By further digging into the data, we find that there is a slight correlation between price for charging and the usage rate. Since there are two types of charging ports: DC and AC. We would include the number of ports and the price of both types in a charging station as one of its feature.

Private or Public. Through statistics and observation, it turns out that most of the charging stations are private ones, which means they are mainly used by only some users, such as fixed ones for electric buses, company stations for employees only. It takes up 70% of the total stations. For the private ones are used by more regular users, its usage rate are about 5% higher compared to public ones.

3.2   Models

Random Forests. For the random forests model, we initially set the number of decision-making trees 'n_estimators' to 20. After several tests, we find the optimal value to be 8. As the random forests inherently calculate the feature importance, there's no extra work for ranking.

MLP. For the MLP model, we choose 'lbfgs' as solver to speed up the training and set the activation function to 'relu'. In order to avoid overfitting, we set the regular term alpha as 1e-4. We simply use an MLP with 2 hidden layers.

After several attempts, the hidden_layer_sizes is set to (5,3) to achieve the best performance. However, the MLP cannot directly generate the feature importance score. To solve this, after fine-tune of the MLP, we randomly generated some data and fed it to the model to have the data labeled. Then we use the generated data to train a new random forests model to get the feature importance. As the random forests is trained to perform the same as the MLP do, it should have learned the feature importance information that the MLP implicitly contains.

4   Experiments

We compare a classic Random Forests with a MLP model in classification and then provides the feature importance ranking of our model's result to find out the correlation between the features and the usage rate.

4.1   Districts Prediction

The district prediction aims to classify station usage level into high, medium and low. As the usage rate of charging stations ranges in [0,1) as float number, we do the simplification as mentioned above. According to the statistics of the usage rate, we set 0 to 20% as low, 20% to 50% as medium and above 50% as high. We divide our dataset into two subsets, urban and suburb. About 30% of the data is the urban ones and the rest is the suburb ones. For each subset, we pick 80% of the data as training data and the left of it as test data. We did a 3-fold cross-validation and take the MAP as evaluation metric.

Table 1 shows the prediction result of the two models on urban and suburb datas. From the results we can observe that the MLP does not outperform the classic random forests in both subsets. which indicates though the DNN has stronger ability of modeling a complicated problem, a naive DNN without well design could have worse performance than classic methods.

Table 1. Evaluation results on urban/suburb prediction

Model	Accuracy	
	Urban	Suburb
MLP	74.35%	**80.72%**
Random forest	**79.52%**	78.31%

Then we conduct the feature ranking. Figure 2(a) and (b) are the results in urban prediction and suburb prediction. The higher score represents the higher importance. For both subsets, we can see that the POI 'metro_stations' plays the most significant role in prediction. In urban area, usage rate is influenced more by 'hospitals' than 'shopping_centers', while in suburb area, these two features' ranking are reversed.

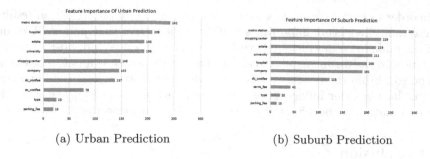

(a) Urban Prediction

(b) Suburb Prediction

Fig. 2. Feature importance of 2 types of districts

4.2 Time Periods Prediction

Usage rates in different time periods is a more concerned problem we want to explore. We divide the dataset into 4 types of time periods: weekday, weekend, morning, evening, while other features remain unchanged. The ratio of train and test sets is also 8:2.

Table 2 shows the accuracy of different models on the subsets.

Table 2. Evaluation results on time frames prediction

Model	Weekday	Weekend	Morning	Evening
MLP	**76.72%**	**92.13%**	**77.59%**	81.90%
Random forest	72.41%	90.27%	74.14%	**83.62%**

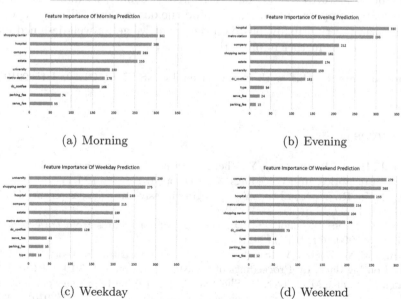

(a) Morning

(b) Evening

(c) Weekday

(d) Weekend

Fig. 3. Feature importance of morning & evening, weekday & weekend prediction

In order to gain a complete view of feature significance on prediction results, we also rank the feature importance at different length of time periods. We conduct the ranking on morning and evening, weekday and weekend. F0-F10 are the same meaning as we've introduced above. The results are shown in Fig. 3(a), (b), (c) and (d). From these results, it is clear that there exists some fixed important features have greater influence for prediction, such as some POI features. The POI information do benefits the prediction and is not neglectable.

5   Conclusion

In this paper, we implement a random forests and a MLP for usage rate prediction of charging stations and explain the feature importance correlated with prediction result. We make some explorations on features like station's surrounding POIs, price, charging types, etc. We believe that the usage rate varies in different districts and different length of time period, so we divide our dataset into urban and suburb areas and several time period granularity to do further analysis. In the experiments, the MLP seems to model the prediction better than the classic random forests, as it shows better accuracy in most of the time. Furthermore, we conduct feature importance ranking for each subset and find out the important POIs that have greater influence than the other features. In the mean time, the most influential POI may not be the same in different districts or different time period granularity, which indicates that when planning charging stations placement, spatio-temporal features should be considered as well. For the future work, we think, firstly, only four main types of features are considered. There could be other features we may have neglected. Secondly, we didn't fully utilize the rich spatio-temporal information behind the dataset, we will dig deeper into it in our future work. Finally, based on the result we get, a well-designed model can be proposed to further improve the accuracy.

Acknowledgement. This work is supported by NSFC 61502169, U1509219 and SHEITC.

References

1. Bao, J., He, T., Ruan, S., Li, Y., Zheng, Y.: Planning bike lanes based on sharing-bikes' trajectories. In: Proceedings of KDD, pp. 1377–1386 (2017)
2. Bao, J., Li, R., Yi, X., Zheng, Y.: Managing massive trajectories on the cloud. In: SIGSPATIAL GIS, p. 41. ACM (2016)
3. Chen, Z., Shen, H., Zhou, X.: Discovering popular routes from trajectories. In: ICDE, pp. 900–911. IEEE (2011)
4. Hoang, M.X., Zheng, Y., Singh, A.K.: FCCF: forecasting citywide crowd flows based on big data. In: Proceedings of SIGSPACIAL, pp. 6:1–6:10 (2016)
5. Jiang, Z., Evans, M., Oliver, D., Shekhar, S.: Identifying K primary corridors from urban bicycle GPS trajectories on a road network. Inf. Syst. **57**(2016), 142–159 (2016)

6. Li, Y., Fu, K., Wang, Z., Shahabi, C., Ye, J., Liu, Y.: Multi-task representation learning for travel time estimation. In: Proceedings of KDD, pp. 1695–1704 (2018)
7. Li, Y., Zheng, Y., Yang, Q.: Dynamic bike reposition: a spatio-temporal reinforcement learning approach. In: Proceedings of KDD, pp. 1724–1733 (2018)
8. Li, Y., Bao, J., Li, Y., Wu, Y., Gong, Z., Zheng, Y.: Mining the most influential k-location set from massive trajectories. In: SIGSPATIAL GIS, p. 51. ACM (2016)
9. Liao, B., et al.: Deep sequence learning with auxiliary information for traffic prediction. In: Proceedings of KDD, pp. 537–546 (2018)
10. Liu, J., Sun, L., Chen, W., Xiong, H.: Rebalancing bike sharing systems: a multi-source data smart optimization. In: Proceedings of KDD, pp. 1005–1014 (2016)
11. Liu, X., Kong, X., Li, Y.: Collective traffic prediction with partially observed traffic history using location-based social media. In: Proceedings of CIKM, pp. 2179–2184 (2016)
12. Liu, Z., Shen, Y., Zhu, Y.: Where will dockless shared bikes be stacked?: – parking hotspots detection in a new city. In: Proceedings of KDD, pp. 566–575 (2018)
13. Marco Tulio, R., Sameer, S., Carlos, G.: "why should I trust you?": explaining the predictions of any classifier. In: Proceedings of the 22nd ACM SIGKDD, San Francisco, CA, USA, 13–17 August 2016, pp. 1135–1144 (2016)
14. Shen, B., Liang, X., Ouyang, Y., Liu, M., Zheng, W., Carley, K.M.: Stepdeep: a novel spatial-temporal mobility event prediction framework based on deep neural network. In: Proceedings of KDD, pp. 724–733 (2018)
15. Yang, Z., Hu, J., Shu, Y., Cheng, P., Chen, J., Moscibroda, T.: Mobility modeling and prediction in bike-sharing systems. In: Proceedings of MobiSys, pp. 165–178 (2016)
16. Zhou, X., Noulas, A., Mascolo, C., Zhao, Z.: Discovering latent patterns of urban cultural interactions in wechat for modern city planning. In: Proceedings of KDD, pp. 1069–1078 (2018)

An Efficient Top-*k* Spatial Join Query Processing Algorithm on Big Spatial Data

Baiyou Qiao[✉], Bing Hu, Xiyu Qiao, Laigang Yao, Junhai Zhu,
and Gang Wu

School of Computer Science and Engineering, Northeastern University,
Shenyang, China
qiaobaiyou@mail.neu.edu.cn

Abstract. Based on Spark platform, we propose an efficient top-*k* spatial join query processing algorithm on big spatial data, in which, the whole data space is divided into same-sized cells by using a grid partitioning method. Then spatial objects in two data sets are projected and replicated to these cells by projection and replication operations respectively, meanwhile a filtering operation is used to speed up the processing. After that, an R-tree based local top-*k* spatial join algorithm is proposed to compute the top-*k* candidate results in each cell, which extends the traditional R-tree index and combines threshold filtering techniques to reduce the communication and computation costs, therefore speeding up the query processing. Experimental results on synthetic data sets show that the proposed algorithm is significantly better than the existing top-*k* spatial join query processing algorithms in performance.

Keywords: Big spatial data · Spark · Top-*k* spatial join query · R-tree

1 Introduction

Top-*k* spatial join query is a special type of complex spatial queries and is widely used in traffic monitoring systems, ultra large scale integrated circuit design and other fields. It has long been an important research topic in the field of spatial data management. In recent years, with the rapid development and wide application of the Internet of Things, earth observation technology, and location-based services technology, the size of spatial data has increased dramatically, bringing spatial data within the realm of big data. How to execute computationally expensive top-*k* spatial join queries efficiently on such big spatial data has become a major challenge. Centralized solutions have been proposed, for example based on R-trees [1], aggregation spatial query processing [2, 3], or probability spatial join query processing with spatial sweep [4], but they do not scale well. In this case, distributed parallel computing using shared-nothing clusters on extreme-scale data has become a dominating trend in the context of data processing and analysis, such as Hadoop-GIS [5], SpatialHadoop [6], SpatialSpark [7], GeoSpark [8], LocationSpark [9] and etc. These systems provide some basic query operations for big spatial data, and do not provide top-*k* spatial join operators. In top-*k* join query processing, distributed solutions mostly based on the MapReduce framework [10–13]. [10] proposed a top-*k* join algorithm on high-dimensional vector data, [11] studied top-*k* similarity join queries,

© Springer Nature Switzerland AG 2019
J. Shao et al. (Eds.): APWeb-WAIM 2019, LNCS 11642, pp. 268–275, 2019.
https://doi.org/10.1007/978-3-030-26075-0_21

Xu et al. proposed MUSK [12], a parallel top-*k* query processing algorithm for uncertain data streams. For top-*k* spatial join query processing, Liu et al. proposed a MapReduce-based algorithm TKSJMR [13]. TKSJMR performs partial aggregation operations in the spatial join phase, and merges the result aggregation and top-*k* result acquisition phases into a single MapReduce phase, which reduces the processing phase. However, TKSJMR uses a simple data projection and replication strategy in the data partition stage, resulting in a large number of data replications, this increases the computation cost and affects the performance of query processing.

To solve the above problem, an efficient top-*k* spatial join query processing algorithm based on Spark (ETKSJS) is proposed in this paper. ETKSJS first divides the data space into same-sized cells, and then uniquely projects each spatial object in one data set *R* onto a cell according to the position of the object's central point. For each cell, the MBR^r of all spatial objects projected onto it is computed, and the spatial objects in another data set *S* overlapping with the MBR^r are replicated to the cell. The spatial objects in *S* not overlapping with any MBR^r are filtered out. Similarly, the MBR^s of the spatial objects in *S* on each cell is also computed. The objects in *R* not overlapping with any MBR^s are also filtered out. As a result, the spatial objects that have no join results are filtered out, which reduces the cost of subsequent top-*k* spatial join processing. An R-tree based local top-*k* spatial join query algorithm is proposed to compute the local top-*k* results for each cell, which makes full use of the filtering ability of R-tree to speed up the query processing and threshold filtering is also applied to reduce the amount of the communication and computation costs of intermediate join results in local top-*k* spatial join query processing. Experimental results show that the proposed algorithm has better performance than the exiting top-*k* spatial join query processing algorithms.

2   Definition of Top-*k* Spatial Join Query

A top-*k* spatial join query is to find the *k* spatial objects that best satisfy some spatial predicate [1, 13]. Top-*k* spatial join queries are clearly more complex and more computationally intensive than general spatial queries.

Definition 1 (Spatial Join Query). Given two data sets *R* and *S*, the spatial join query *SJ(R,S,P)* returns the spatial object pairs (*r*, *s*), where *r* ∈ *R*, *s* ∈ *S*, and the geometric properties of *r* and *s* satisfy the spatial join predicate *P*. In what follows, *P* is assumed to be the intersection, or spatial overlap relationship.

Definition 2 (Top-*k* Spatial Join Query). Given two data sets *R* and *S*, the top-*k* spatial join query $SJ_{topk}(R,S)$ retrieves the set of *k* objects in data set *R* or *S* that has the greatest amount of overlap with objects in the other set.

3   An Efficient Top-*k* Spatial Join Query Processing Algorithm

Unlike prior approaches that rely on the MapReduce, our solution is based on Spark. In the following, we will describe the proposed efficient top-*k* spatial join query algorithm (ETKSJS) in detail from data partitioning, R-tree based local top-*k* spatial join processing algorithm, and overall top-*k* spatial join query processing flow.

3.1 Data Partitioning

To achieve large-scale parallel top-k spatial join query processing, the first thing to do is data partitioning. ETKSJS uses grid partition approach to partition the whole data space into non-overlapping equal-sized cells, projects spatial objects onto these cells, and a hashing function is used to map these cells to many data partitions, each data partition is processed by one executor in Spark system. Usually the number of cells should be much larger than the number of data partitions, which can help make the mapping more uniform. Each cell is then encoded using the Z-order curve space-filling method, as it is relatively simple and has been shown to exhibit good performance [14]. ETKSIS uses data projection, data replication and data filtering three operations to achieve data partitioning. Here are the operations.

Data Projection: The data projection operation uniquely maps the spatial objects into cells. We represent the data space's partition into n cells as $C = (c_1, c_2, \ldots, c_n)$, where c_i is the Z-order of cell i. A spatial data object is uniquely mapped onto a cell according to its center point, as follows. Let R be a spatial data set, and $u \in R$. If u's center point is located in the cell c_i, then u is projected onto cell c_i, and the corresponding key-value pair (c_i, u) is generated.

Data Replication: The data replication operation replicates the spatial objects in another data set to the corresponding cells according to the overlap of MBRs from the data set that has already been projected. Let $c_i.\mathrm{MBR}^R$ be the boundary MBR of cell c_i (i.e., the MBR of the all objects in R projected onto cell c_i), S be another spatial data set, and $s \in S$. If s overlaps with $c_i.\mathrm{MBR}^R$, then s is replicated onto cell c_i, and the corresponding key-value pair (c_i, s) is generated.

Data Filtering: The data filtering operation filters out the spatial objects in one data set not overlapping with the MBR formed by the data objects in another data set. Let $c_i.\mathrm{MBR}^S$ be the boundary MBR of cell c_i (i.e., the MBR of the objects in data set S replicated onto cell c_i), R_i be a data set consisting of the objects in R projected onto cell c_i, and $r \in R_i$. If r overlaps with $c_i.\mathrm{MBR}^S$, then the corresponding key-value pair (c_i, r) is reserved, otherwise (c_i, r) is filtered out.

3.2 R-tree Based Local Top-k Spatial Join Algorithm

The local top-k spatial join query algorithm mainly performs spatial join operations on two types of spatial objects partitioned into each cell, and generates candidate result sets consisting of the spatial objects may be top-k results. A key element of the process is plane sweeping, used to judge whether two spatial objects truly overlap. Traditional plane sweeping algorithms scan spatial objects along a specified dimension, usually the X-axis from left to right, find the span of each object in that dimension, scan the corresponding orthogonal region of space for spatial objects from the other data set, perform spatial join operation, and output candidate results for the top-k spatial join. To enhance the processing efficiency of top-k spatial join query, we propose an R-tree based local top-k spatial join query algorithm which makes full use of the powerful search and filtering ability of R-tree index to quickly filter out spatial objects in another spatial data set that cannot overlap with a given spatial object, thereby speeding up top-k spatial join query processing. We simple extend the node structure of an R-tree index by adding an attribute *Number* to each node of the R-tree, which is used to record the number of the spatial objects contained by the node's MBR. Based on the extended R-tree index, the local top-*k* spatial join algorithm is designed. In the algorithm, the extended R-tree index and the threshold are used to filter out objects which will not be the results, speed up the processing of the local top-*k* spatial join query, and finally output the local top-*k* join results. The detailed description, see Algorithm 1.

Algorithm 1. Local Top-k With Rtree
Input: $k, R_i, S_i (R_i, S_i$:data sets partitioned to cell i)
Output: pairs of (*object, Num*)

```
rtreeR = new Rtree()
rtreeS = new Rtree()
H = new Heap(k) // store Top-k results
Threshold = 0
For object in Si do
   rtreeS.insert(object)
Endfor
For object in Ri do
   rtreeR.insert(object)
   Num = topkSearch(rtreeS,object,Threshold)
   If Num != 0 Then
      Update H and Threshold
   Endif
Endfor
For object in Si do
   If object.token=0 then//object exists only in a cell
      Num = topkSearch(rtreeR,object,Threshold)
      if Num != 0 then
         Update H and Threshold
      Endif
   Else //object is replicated into multi cells
      Num = joinSearch(rtreeR,object)
      If Num>Threshold Then
         Update H and Threshold
      Else If Num>0 Then
            Output(object,Num)
         Endif
      Endif
   Endif
Endfor
Output(H)
```

In algorithm 1, a heap H of size k is used to store k local top-k join results. Each result can be represented as a pair (O_{id}, Num), where O_{id} is the ID of a spatial object, and Num is the overlap number between O_{id} and the objects in the other dataset. The results in H are sorted in descending order according to the attribute Num, and the results in H are updated with the local top-k join results. *Threshold* represents the top-k threshold, its value is equal to the attribute Num of the k-th element in H. During the processing, for an object r in data set R_i, if Num returned by the procedure *topkSearch* is not equal 0, that means the number of spatial join results between r and objects in S_i is greater than *Threshold*, the r is a local top-k result, then H and *Threshold* are updated. If Num is equal 0, that means the r will not be a local top-k result, and r will be filtered out directly without outputting the result. For an object s in data set S_i, if s is replicated onto only one cell, i.e., its attribute *token* is 0. If Num returned by the procedure *topkSearch* is not equal 0, that means the number of spatial join results between s and the objects in R_i is greater than *Threshold*, the s is a local top-k result, then H and *Threshold* are updated. If Num is equal 0, this means that s will not be a local top-k result and be filtered out directly without outputting the result. If s is projected onto multi cells, i.e., its attribute *token* is 1, that means s may be a top-k result and cannot be filtered out directly.

The procedure *joinSearch* (*node*, *object*) is a traditional R-tree based spatial join procedure, where *node* is the root node of an extended R-tree, *object* is a spatial object. It is used to return the number of spatial join results between *object* and the objects in R-tree *node*. Since the procedure is very simple, its detail description is omitted. Here *joinSearch* is used to compute the overlapping number Num between s and the objects in data set R_i. If Num is greater than *Threshold*, then H and *Threshold* are updated. If Num is less than *Threshold* and not equal to 0, then the result (s, Num) is outputted directly.

When the k-th object in H is updated, if it is an object in R_i or it is an object in S_i whose attribute *token* is 0, then it is directly updated without outputting the result. If it is an object in S_i whose attribute *token* is 1, then the result should be outputted, and it will participate in the next processing stage. The use of the heap H and parameter *Threshold* can improve memory usage and reduce the computational cost.

Procedure *topkSearch* (*root*, *object*, *Threshold*) is a threshold-based top-k spatial join algorithm, where *root* is the root node of an extended R-tree, *object* is a spatial object, *Threshold* is the current top-k threshold. This algorithm is used to determine whether *object* is a top-k candidate result according to *Threshold*, if *object* will not be a top-k candidate result, it outputs 0, otherwise it outputs the number of spatial join results between *object* and the objects in sub R-tree *root*. The algorithm makes full use of the fast search and filtering ability of the extended R-tree index, it also use threshold. *Threshold* to further perform filtering and pruning, thereby speeding up the processing speed of the algorithm. For paper size limitation, the detailed description is omitted.

3.3   The Overall Processing Flow of ETKSJS Algorithm

Having described its main elements, we are now in a position to present the complete ETKSJS algorithm. A high-level view of the overall processing flow of ETKSJS is depicted in Fig. 1. The algorithm consists of 3 main stages, namely data partitioning, local top-*k* spatial join processing, and global top-*k* aggregation processing, the detail descriptions are as follows.

Stage 1 handles the data partitioning, as described in Sect. 3.1. Cells are encoded using Z-order curve space filling. Spatial objects in *R* are projected by using data projection operation. The projection results are stored in a resilient distributed dataset, RDD_r. Spatial objects in *S* are replicated by using data replication operation, and the

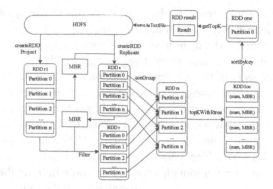

Fig. 1. Processing flow of ETKSJS

token information is added to identify whether the spatial object is replicated to multiple cells. If the object is replicated to more than one cells, the token is set to 1, otherwise the token is set to 0. The replication results of the objects in dataset *S* are stored in RDD_s.

Stage 2 performs local top-*k* spatial join processing. This stage first executes a Congroup operation on RDD_s and RDD_r, and generates the dataset RDD_{rs}. Then, the R-tree based local top-*k* spatial algorithm of Sect. 3.2 is used to perform the local top-*k* join query on each partition.

Stage 3 global top-*k* aggregation processing. Prepares the final top-*k* results. Merging each intermediate local top-*k* results on each partition, summing the overlapping counts of the same objects, and sorting them in descending order, the algorithm outputs the final top-*k* spatial join results, and save them as a file of HDFS.

4 Performance Evaluation

In order to verify the performance of ETKSJS, we run a series of experiments on synthetic data sets. We opt to ETKSJS against the TKSJMR [16]. TKSJMR's research content and target are the same as ETKSJS's. To be fair, we re-implemented TKSJMR using Scala on the Spark platform. The experimental environment consists of 10 servers with E5-2620 CPU (6 cores, 2.0 GHz), 32 GB memory and 1 TB SATA disk. Each machine is set up to run the Spark cluster software and the related algorithm modules. One acts as the management node, and the others are computing nodes. Synthetic data sets are generated by a script, with a data space size of 100 k × 100 k. We randomly choose the initial position of spatial objects using a Gaussian distribution, and randomly set the length and width of every spatial object, generating 6 groups of spatial data sets in 2 classes, with between 0.5 and 16 million spatial objects. We compared ETKSJS with TKSJMR on different grid partition granularity, execution time, degree of parallelism and value of k. The partial experimental results are as follows.

Figure 2 shows how execution time changes with the number of cells, when the number of tasks is 16, the value of k is 100, and the size of the two data sets is 4 million spatial objects. It can be seen that the execution time of two algorithms is also decrease to a point respectively, and then begins to rise again, the reason is that the grid partition granularity is small at the beginning, so that data skew creates an uneven data distribution, which, in turn, causes some tasks to take longer to run, and thus the overall execution time is relatively long. As the grid partition granularity increases, data objects in the cells can be allocated to the tasks more uniformly, and the running time thus decreases. But, as the number of cells continues to grow, there will be an increasing number of spatial objects across multiple cells, which causes unnecessary data replication and, with it, an increase in the computation and communication costs. Figure 2 also clearly shows that ETKSJS has consistently shorter execution times than TKSJMR. The main reason is that ETKSJS reduces replication operations: in the local top-k spatial join phase, every cell only outputs the local top-k results and intermediate results of some objects spanning multiple cells.

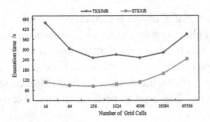

Fig. 2. Execution time vs. number of cells   **Fig. 3.** Execution time vs. data set size

Figure 3 shows how execution time changes with the number of spatial objects, when the number of cells is 4,096, the number of tasks in Spark is 16, and the value of k is 100. Figure 3 shows that, as the number of data objects increases, the execution time of both algorithms also increases, consistent with expectation. However, the execution time of ETKSJS is lower than that of TKSJMR, and the difference becomes increasingly significant with the number of data objects. The superiority of ETKSJS is due to its adoption of boundary MBR filtering, which reduces useless spatial objects, and its use of the top-k threshold filtering strategy in the subsequent local top-k spatial join phase, which leads to reduced transfer of intermediate results, thus limiting the amount of data communication and computation in the top-k aggregation phase. By contrast, TKSJMR needs to transmit all of the intermediate join results, with associated communication and computations costs that only get worse as the data sets get larger.

5   Conclusion

In this paper, we have focused on the problem of top-k spatial join query processing in cloud environments, and have proposed an efficient top-k spatial join query processing algorithm based on Spark (ETKSJS). ETKSJS uses grid partitioning method to divide the data space, applies Z-order curve space-filling to encode the cells, and adopts boundary MBR to replication and filter spatial objects, which reduces the cost of subsequent top-k spatial join processing. An R-tree based local top-k spatial join algorithm is also proposed to speed up the computation of intermediate results and reduce communication costs. Experiments show that the ETKSJS algorithm exhibits better performance overall than the TKSJMR algorithm in terms of computational cost, and it is also more scalable and more adaptable. Future work will focus on further experimentation, as well as investigating the use of new data partition and index technology to realize additional performance gains with ETKSJS.

Acknowledgements. This research was supported by the National Key R&D Program of China (NO. 2016YFC1401900 and 2018YFB1004402) and National Natural Science Foundation of China (No. 61872072 and 61073063).

References

1. Zhu, M., Papadias, D., Lun Lee, D., Zhang, J.: Top-k spatial joins. IEEE Trans. Knowl. Data Eng. **17**(4), 567–579 (2005)
2. Govindarajan, S., Agarwal, P.K., Arge, L.: CRB-tree: an efficient indexing scheme for range-aggregate queries. In: Calvanese, D., Lenzerini, M., Motwani, R. (eds.) ICDT 2003. LNCS, vol. 2572, pp. 143–157. Springer, Heidelberg (2003). https://doi.org/10.1007/3-540-36285-1_10
3. Tao, Y., Papadias, D.: Range aggregate processing in spatial databases. IEEE Trans. Knowl. Data Eng. **16**(12), 1555–1570 (2004)
4. Ljosa, V., Singh, A.K.: Top-k spatial joins of probabilistic objects. In: Proceedings of the 24th International Conference on Data Engineering, pp. 566–575 (2008)
5. Aji, A., et al.: Hadoop-GIS: a high performance spatial data warehousing system over MapReduce. PVLDB **6**(11), 1009–1020 (2013)
6. Eldawy, A., Mokbel, M.F.: Spatialhadoop: a mapreduce framework for spatial data. In: ICDE Conference, pp. 1352–1363 (2015)
7. You, S., Zhang, J., Gruenwald, L.: Large-scale spatial join query processing in cloud. In: ICDE Workshops, pp. 34–41 (2015)
8. Yu, J., Wu, J., Sarwat, M.: Geospark: a cluster computing framework for processing large-scale spatial data. In: SIGSPATIAL Conference, pp. 70:1–70:4 (2015)
9. Tang, M., Yu, Y., Malluhi, Q.M., Ouzzani, M., Aref, W.G.: Locationspark: a distributed in-memory data management system for big spatial data. PVLDB **9**(13), 1565–1568 (2016)
10. You-Zhong, M.A., Xiang, C.I., Meng, X.-F.: Parallel top-k join on massive high-dimensional vectors. Chin. J. Comput. **38**(1), 86–98 (2015). (in Chinese)
11. Kim, Y., Shim, K.: Parallel top-k similarity join algorithms using MapReduce. In: Proceedings of the 28th International Conference on Data Engineering, pp. 510–521 (2012)
12. Xu, H., Ding, X., Jin, H., Jiang, W.: Parallel top-k, query processing on uncertain strings using MapReduce. In: Proceedings of the 20th International Conference on Database Systems for Advanced Applications, pp. 89–103 (2015)
13. Liu, Y., Chen, L., Jing, N., Liu, L.: Parallel top-k spatial join query processing on massive spatial data. J. Comput. Res. Dev. **48**(1), 163–172 (2011). (in Chinese)
14. Zhang, S., Han, J., Liu, Z., Wang, K., Xu, Z.: SJMR: parallelizing spatial join with Mapreduce on clusters. In: Proceedings of the IEEE International Conference on Cluster Computing, pp. 1–8 (2009)

Multi-view Based Spatial-Keyword Query Processing for Real Estate

Xi Duan, Liping Wang$^{(\boxtimes)}$, and Shiyu Yang

School of Computer Science and Software Engineering,
East China Normal University, Shanghai, China
duanxi_15edu@126.com, {lipingwang,syyang}@sei.ecnu.edu.cn

Abstract. The real estate search web systems such as Zillow, Anjuke, and Lianjia have become very popular in daily life. Generally, the comprehensive query results combined with transportation, health care, education, POIs, etc. are expected, but those surrounding information are rarely utilized in traditional query methods, which thereby restricts the results of the query. In this paper, we address the above limitations and provide a novel multi-view based query method, named KBHR. We investigate feature extraction method and introduce multi-view to represent comprehensive real estate data. The proposed method, KBHR, is based on BHR-tree which is a hybrid indexing structure and a kernel based similarity function developed to rank the query results of multi-view data. We construct experiments and evaluate KBHR on real-world data sets. The experimental results demonstrate the efficiency and effectiveness of our method.

Keywords: Spatial-keyword query · Multi-view data ·
Hybrid indexing structure · Kernel function

1 Introduction

The real estate search web systems are popular in daily life [1,2]. Users who will buy or rent a house usually not only concern the house basic features such as the prices, the number of bedrooms, the location, the floor area, etc., but also survey the surrounding info such as traffic information, points of interests (POIs), health care and education etc. The web systems like Zillow, Anjuke, and Lianjia have provided the query method to help user to find the interested house, but the surrounding information is rarely utilized in those systems. As the query result is just based on the house basic features, user will spend much time to finally filter the result and find the house with satisfied surroundings. In this paper, we address the above limitations and aim to provide a more convenient query model, by which the various surrounding information is carefully introduced and the comprehensive query results are provided.

In the real world, the description of the same thing can often be obtained from many different ways or different perspectives [11]. These multiple descriptions

© Springer Nature Switzerland AG 2019
J. Shao et al. (Eds.): APWeb-WAIM 2019, LNCS 11642, pp. 276–291, 2019.
https://doi.org/10.1007/978-3-030-26075-0_22

can be regarded as multiple views of things. The combination of basic features and surroundings can describe housing data more clearly, which can match the user's diversified demand for housing better. Usually, the housing basic features such as the prices, the number of bedrooms, and the floor area etc. are specified, which can be collected easily. However, the description of surroundings is collected from different sources. Those textual data have different structures, it need more effort to extract features that describe multiple views of housing from complex real estate data. In this paper, we devise a series of preprocessing and feature extraction methods to construct the multi-view housing data.

Recently, multi-view often be utilized in machine learning and recent study have demonstrated the advantages of fusing information from multiple view for various machine learning applications [13]. Eaton et al. [12] has proved that multi-view learning can obtain better performance than single-view learning through the mutual promotion of information between views. At present, research methods for multi-view data have been widely used to solve various problems. For example, Zheng et al. proposes a co-training model based on multi-view data in [14,15], which can infer more fine-grained urban air quality based on a variety of city-related data. Wang et al. [16] proposes the multi-manifold ranking (MMR) method which utilizes multiple data structures of the images to provide a better ranking of the images. And Dhillon et al. [17] calculated the canonical correlation analysis (CCA) between different views of the data to estimate low-dimensional contextual representations of unlabeled data in the NLP questions. Our work is difference from the existing works for we investigate the effective query method on multi-view data, but existing works focused on the classification problems.

On the other hand, Real estate data contain both spatial and textual information, referred to as a kind of spatial-textual data. Spatial-keyword query for real estate aims to retrieve the relevant spatial-textual data for a given spatial-keyword. Recently, some practical and novel problems about spatial-keyword query are well studied, which include joint top-k spatial-keyword query [7], Boolean Range continuous queries over a stream of incoming geo-textual objects [6], collective spatial keyword query [5], and so on. But none of them is suitable for our multi-view based query problem. Generally, different indexing techniques and query algorithms [3,4,9] are used in spatial query and keyword search methods separately. For example, tree structures such as R-tree and quadtree are widely used during spatial queries, while inverted lists are generally used in keyword searches. For spatial-keyword query, the nomination of the different index is needed and the naive methods include spatial query first, or textual query first [8]. Obviously, the naive methods are inefficiency during query on large scaled data on web. Therefore, in order to improve the efficiency of querying large-scale spatial-textual data, many researchers combined the spatial index with the textual index, and propose a variety of hybrid indexing structures. R*-IF index [9] is an existing widely-used hybrid index, which is a kind of spatial-priority index that combines R*-tree structure and inverted files. This indexing structure adds inverted files to leaf nodes of the R*-tree, so that objects used for keyword search are largely reduced by spatial pruning in query. On the contrary, there is a textual-priority index IF-R* index [9], which establishes a separate R*-tree for objects associated with each keyword on the inverted file. Moreover, IR2-tree [10] is proposed as a hybrid indexing structure, which integrates signature files, describing the keyword state, into each node of the R-tree. Note that those hybrid indexing structures are only suit for the query on spatial textual data with single view, while our problem focus on the query on spatial textual data with multiple views. Indexing structure and rank function are both needed to be improved, so as to guarantee the efficiency and effectiveness of the query.

Contributions. The principle contributions of this paper are as follow.

- We devise a novel multi-view based spatial-keyword query framework for real estate data. Surrounding info and basic features of housing are carefully considered and extracted as multi-view in the framework, thus more comprehensive query result will be achieved.
- A multi-view based query method, named KBHR is proposed. KBHR is based on BHR-tree which can integrate the spatial and textual information of the objects seamlessly and present high time performance. Moreover, a kernel based similarity function developed to rank the query results of multi-view data.
- We construct extensive experiments and evaluate KBHR on real-world estate data sets. Comprehensive comparisons are made between KBHR and representative algorithms. The experimental results demonstrate the efficiency and effectiveness of our proposed method.

The rest of this paper is organized as follows: We briefly introduces the framework of multi-view based query processing for real estate in Sect. 2. Section 3 introduces the preprocessing and feature extraction methods for real estate data, and defines the model of the multi-view housing object. A novel multi-view based query method and a hybrid indexing structure are devised in Sect. 4. We compared our method with other baseline methods via some experiments, and given a performance evaluation of our method in Sect. 5. Finally, we conclude this paper in Sect. 6.

2   Framework Overview

Our framework for searching housing is shown in Fig. 1 which consists of two major stages, the multi-view housing object modeling and the multi-view based housing query.

Multi-view Housing Object Modeling. Given the real estate dataset, we first preprocess the dataset and transform the original data into an algorithm-readable format. The preprocessed data integrates the housing's basic information with its surrounding information. Then, we extract the corresponding characteristics of a housing object from three aspects: architectural feature, environmental feature and location feature. Finally, we generate feature vectors of

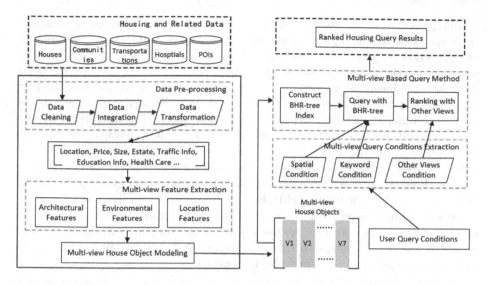

Fig. 1. The framework of multi-view based query processing for real estate.

multiple views for housing objects from the extracted features, and use these to construct multi-view housing objects.

Multi-view based Housing Query. After modeling the multi-view housing object, based on the spatial feature of housing objects and the textual information describing their architectural feature, we build a hybrid indexing structure proposed in this paper, named BHR-tree. Given a user's query, we first extract its spatial condition, keyword condition and conditions on other views. For its spatial and keyword conditions, we search all multi-view housing objects using multi-view based query method proposed in this paper. Meanwhile, we sort the query results according to other views' conditions with a multi-view based similarity function.

In the next chapter, we will introduce the steps of modeling the multi-view housing object and the processing of the multi-view based query for houseing object in detail.

3   Modeling the Multi-view House Object

In this section, we first introduce the pre-process to different formats of raw housing related data and the feature extraction process of the housing object. Then, we give the definition of the multi-view housing object and model the housing object to multiple views by rearranging the extracted features.

3.1   Data Pre-process and Feature Extraction

Data Pre-process. In this paper, we preprocess different raw data from real world. Absent info, redundant info and inconsistency info etc. are needed to be handled previously. In order to obtain structured and unified house samples, three methods that is data cleaning, data integration, and data transformation are proposed to preprocess real world data [21]. Firstly, in the data cleaning stage, we use the similarity value to fill in the missing value, and replace the noise data with the mean value. Secondly, in the data integration phrase, we integrate the basic features of estates with surrounding info. Finally, we discretize and normalize different types of data. For numerical data, it is discretized by the equal interval division method. For example, for the floor feature, we first use the floor of the housing and the total number of floors to calculate the ratio, which is a numerical value existed in the interval [0,1]. Then, we convert the ratio with labels such as *"low"*, *"medium"* and *"high"*, using the equal interval division method on the interval [0,1]. For non-numerical data, keyword-matching method is mainly used to find the keyword representing the category in the text information. For instance, we use keyword-matching for text information of hospitals and divide them into three categories: AH (hospital of grade A), GH (general hospital), and SH (specialized hospital).

Feature Extraction. The housing industry has mature housing related theory. In accordance with the theory proposed in [18], we divide the characteristics of the housing data into three aspects: architectural features, environmental features, and location features. The architectural features mainly include the basic features of estates, such as the size, price, height, type, orientation and area of the housing. The environmental features mainly come from the acquired community information data, such as the type of community, greening rate, plot ratio, and property management fees. The location features are mainly based on the geographical location of the housing, combined with the surrounding info. We extracted different features from the surroundings, including the characteristics of the traffic conditions, the educational environment, the medical environment and living facilities.

3.2 Multi-view Housing Object Modeling for Real Estate

The architectural features, environmental features and location features give an all-around description for a house. We model houses as *multi-view objects* according to the features property. More specifically, considering the features of the three aspects for real estate data, we sort out seven common descriptive views from the original data which are spatial view, keywords view, environment view, traffic view, education view, recreation view and healthcare view (refer to Table 1). Thus, the *multi-view housing object* is formally defined in the *Definition 1*.

Definition 1. *(Multi-view Housing Object.) A multi-view housing object is formalized as $o = (o.s, o.t, o.v)$, where $o.s$ is the spatial position of the house o, $o.t$ is a set of keywords used to describe basic features of the house o, and $o.v$ denotes a set of vectors to describe the surrounding info of the house o.*

Table 1. Example views for house data.

View	Contents description
Spatial view	A location of house with latitude and longitude
Keywords view	A set of keywords describing basic features of housing
Environment view	A feature vector describing the community environment
Traffic view	A feature vector contains counts and mean distances of surrounding subways and buses
Education view	A feature vector contains count and quality of surrounding schools
Recreation view	A feature vector contains counts of surrounding malls and parks
Healthcare view	A feature vector contains count and level of surrounding hospitals

4   Multi-view Based Spatial-Keyword Query

Problem Statement. In this paper we tackle the problem of spatial-keyword query on multi-view housing object. Specifically, given a query including geo-location, keywords and user preferred housing objects, we aim to rapidly return all matched housing objects and rank those objects by multi-view analysis.

Definition 2. *(Multi-view Housing Query.) Consider a multi-view housing query $q = (q.s, q.t, q.v)$, where $q.s$ is the query location represented by a longitude and a latitude in the two dimensional geographical space, $q.t$ is a group of words that describe user's query intention, and $q.v$ denotes preferred housing objects by user. The answer to query q is a list of k objects which are in descending order by the user preference and whose descriptions contain the set of query keywords $q.t$.*

Definition 3. *(Candidate Housing Object.) Given a multi-view housing query q, a multi-view housing object o is said to be a candidate house object, if its descriptive keywords contain all keywords from q, i.e. $q.t \subseteq o.t$.*

Definition 4. *(Multi-view Based Similarity Function.) Given a multi-view housing query q, a multi-view housing object o, their similarity on i^{th} view can be denoted as $sim(q.v_i, o.v_i)$, which is measured by the similarity metric. By combining the similarity from multiple views of object and query, we further define a multi-view based similarity function of q and o, denoted as $\mathcal{S}(q, o)$ in Eq. (1).*

$$\mathcal{S}(q, o) = \sum_{i=1}^{V} w_i^p sim (q.v_i, o.v_i), w_i \geq 0, \sum_{i=1}^{V} w_i = 1, p \geq 1. \tag{1}$$

where V is number of views of $o.v$, w_i are the view weights and p is an exponent.

For the housing query problem studied in this paper, we propose a novel method that combines multi-view data with spatial-keyword query. The hybrid indexing structure and multi-view based query method are introduced in Sects. 4.1 and 4.2 separately.

4.1   Hybrid Indexing Structure

In this section, we present an improved hybrid indexing structure, namely BHR-tree (**B**-tree & **H**ilbert **R**-tree), which can integrate the spatial and textual information of the housing objects seamlessly while avoiding large dead space. In designing BHR-tree, shown as Fig. 2, we use the Hilbert R-tree to maintain the spatial information of housing objects and use the B-tree to maintain the textual information of objects. The process of building the hybrid index structure is as follows.

Firstly, we apply the method proposed in [19] to build a Hilbert R-tree, which outperforms all the previous R-tree methods on spatial partition. Secondly, we construct a B-tree on all of the distinct keywords for housing objects. Thirdly, in order to use the spatial information and textual information of housing objects to prune the search space simultaneously in the query, we establish the connection between the above two kinds of index structure, and regard it as a hybrid index structure.

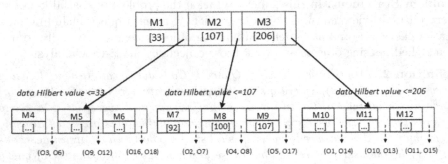

(a) The spatial component (The file structure for the Hilbert R-tree).

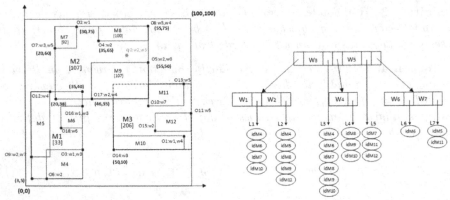

(b) The sample dataset organized in Hilbert R-tree.

(c) The textual component(The file structure for the B-tree).

Fig. 2. A sample dataset and the BHR-tree.

Algorithm 1. BHR-tree Building Algorithm

Input: dataset D
Output: a spatial-textual index I_{st}
1: Build a Hilbert R-tree with spatial view of dataset D
2: Build a B-tree with textual view of dataset D
3: **for** each key w in B-tree's node **do**
4:     Add a list $MBRList$ as it's value
5: Do breadth first traversal on R-tree
6: **for** each MBR m in R-tree's node **do**
7:     Sign it with an integer in order
8:     Get a keywords set contain all keywords of objects in m
9:     **if** m exist in R-tree's leaf node **then**
10:         **for** each keywords w in m's keywords set **do**
11:             **if** w exist in B-tree's node **then**
12:                 Add m's identifier to the $MBRList$ of key w
13: I_{st} = B-tree with $MBRLists$ + R-tree
14: return I_{st};

Algorithm 1 shows the construction process of the BHR-tree index, and present the details of the linkage between two indexes. In line 3–4, we generate a list structure for each keyword stored in B-tree, namely $MBRList$, which is used to record the identifiers of minimum bounding rectangles (MBRs) stored in the leaf nodes of the Hilbert R-tree. In order to efficiently record MBRs on the Hilbert R-tree, we assign MBRs with a string of sequential integers according to the breadth-first traversal result on the Hilbert R-tree (line 6–12). Meanwhile, we maintain a keywords set for each MBR, if the MBR is located in the leaf node, its keywords set is a union of the keywords from the contained objects. Otherwise, its keywords set combines all keywords sets from its child nodes. Finally, for the MBR on each leaf node, we add the MBR identifier to the $MBRList$ of the keyword in the B-tree, according to each keyword in the keywords set associated with the MBR.

Example 1. An example of BHR-tree is shown as Fig. 2, and Fig. 2(b) illustrates a sample data set and a query point q_0 organized in Hilbert R-tree. The Hilbert values of the rectangles' center are the numbers in the brackets. Figure 2(a) shows how the tree of Fig. 2(b) is stored on disk. As shown in 2(c), $L_1 - L_7$ are the seven $MBRLists$ corresponding to keywords $w_1 - w_7$, and each one contains at least one MBR identifier. For instance, when we traverse the MBR $M4$ on the leaf node, since $M4$ contains two objects o_3 and o_6, we can get its keywords set (w_1, w_2, w_3). Hence, we add $M4$'s identifier'id_{M4}' to $MBRList$ L_1, L_2, L_3 in the B-tree to connect the spatial and textual info. When we search keyword w_1 on B-tree, there is a $MBRList$ L_1 which contains $id_{M4}, id_{M6}, id_{M7}, id_{M10}$. Each of element in L_1 points to a MBR in Hilbert R-tree. By $MBRList$ L_1, we can rapidly filter the irrelevant objects and found the spatial info of targeted housing object.

4.2 Multi-view Based Query Method

Algorithm 2 illustrates the query precessing mechanism over the BHR-tree. Given a multi-view query q, the algorithm can provide effective spatial-textual pruning using the BHR-tree, and return objects which satisfies textual requirements and with maximum similarity from all views to q. Here, Algorithm 2 is named KBHR(**K**eneral funcion & **BHR**-Tree base query method).

The main idea of KBHR is that we can group the objects based on spatial information, and prune a group of them which do not contain all keywords using textual pruning. For each group containing all keywords, if their distance to the query point is larger than a threshold, we can prune the objects in the group using the spatial pruning. Thus we can do both spatial pruning and textual pruning in a combined way. The detail steps are as follows.

Firstly, we build a proposed BHR-tree among all house objects contained by dataset D, based on the spatial and textual views information of each house object o_i $(1 \le i \le N)$, denoted as $o_i.s$ and $o_i.t$ in *Definition* 1. Then we use each leaf-level MBR as a group. To do the textual pruning, for each query keyword in $q.t$, we first retrieve the list of leaf-level MBRs identifiers, which is the value of it on B-tree part. Then we intersect the MBRs identifiers for all query keywords. Each MBR in the intersection is a *candidate region*, all objects that are in any candidate region are saved, and the rest can be pruned.

For example, as shown in Fig. 2(b), we given a query point q_0 with keywords "w2" and "w3". We can easily retrieve the MBRs list for keyword "w2" is $L_2 = \{id_{M4}, id_{M5}, id_{M8}, id_{M9}, id_{M12}\}$, illustrated in Fig. 2(c). Similarly We retrieve the MBRs list for keyword "w3" is $L_3 = \{id_{M4}, id_{M6}, id_{M7}, id_{M8}, id_{M9}, id_{M10}\}$. By intersecting these two lists of entry MBRs identifiers, we get a new MBRs list $L' = \{id_{M4}, id_{M8}, id_{M9}\}$, each of it points to a candidate region which contains keywords "w2" and "w3".

Algorithm 2. Kernel function & BHR-based Query Algorithm

Input: dataset D, query q and user-specified k
Output: top-k result objects list L_{rs}
1: Use dataset D build a BHR-tree
2: Init candidate region priority queue $\mathcal{R}_{cand}$ is empty
3: **for** each keyword w in $q.t$ **do**
4:     **if** w exist in B-tree's node **then**
5:         Retrieve the MBRs list $L(w)$ for w
6:         **for** each MBR in $L(w)$ **do**
7:             Compute its distance to $q.s$
8:             Add it to $\mathcal{R}_{cand}$
9: Init candidate object priority queue $\mathcal{O}_{cand}$ is empty
10: **while** $\mathcal{R}_{cand} \ne \Phi \parallel \mathcal{O}_{cand} < k$ **do**
11:     Pop an element r from $\mathcal{R}_{cand}$
12:     **if** R is a candidate region **then**
13:         **for** each object o in r **do**
14:             **if** o is a candidate object **then**
15:                 Compute $S(q, o)$ using Eq.(2)
16:                 Add it to $\mathcal{O}_{cand}$
17: $L_{rs} = \mathcal{O}_{cand}$
18: return L_{rs};

And for each candidate region, we compute its minimum distance to the query point, and use it as an estimation of the distances of all objects in the candidate region to the query point. Then we add it to a priority queue sorted by their distances to the query point in an ascending order, and we define $\mathcal{R}_{cand}$ to denote this priority queue.

Next, we pop the element from the $\mathcal{R}_{cand}$ in order. We pop the one element r with the minimal distance, if the element is a candidate region noted by r_c then traverse all object o_c in r_c. If o_c is a candidate object defined by *Definition* 3, we add it to another priority queue $\mathcal{O}_{cand}$, otherwise, we drop it. The $\mathcal{O}_{cand}$ is sorted by their similarity to the query point on multiple views. As discussed in *Definition* 4, we utilize the *Radial basis function kernel* [22] (RBF kernel), which is a popular kernel function used in various kernel based learning algorithms, to compute the similarity between a query q and a candidate object on multiple views. Here, derived from the similarity function defined by Eq. (1), we rewrite Eq. (1) as

$$\mathcal{S}(q, o_c) = \sum_{v=1}^{V} w_i^p K\left(q.v_i, o.v_i\right), w_i \geq 0, \sum_{i=1}^{V} w_i = 1, p \geq 1. \qquad (2)$$

where

$$K\left(q.v_i, o.v_i\right) = \exp\left(-\frac{\|q.v_i - o.v_i\|^2}{2\sigma^2}\right). \qquad (3)$$

$\|q.v_i - o.v_i\|^2$ may be recognized as the squared Euclidean distance between the two feature vectors, σ is a free parameter. An equivalent, but simpler, definition involves a parameter $\gamma = \frac{1}{2\sigma^2}$:

$$K\left(q.v_i, o.v_i\right) = \exp\left(-\gamma\|q.v_i - o.v_i\|^2\right). \qquad (4)$$

According to the definition of the Boolean kNN query problem [4], we determine the number of objects in the $\mathcal{O}_{cand}$ each time, if the number greater than the integer k, we stop popping and retrieve all objects in the $\mathcal{O}_{cand}$ to list L_{rs} in order, which regarded as the query result; otherwise, we repeat the above steps until there are k objects in the $\mathcal{O}_{cand}$ or the $\mathcal{R}_{cand}$ gets empty.

5   Experiments and Results

In this section, we evaluation our proposed method on the real estate data and present experimental results on its effectiveness and efficiency.

5.1   Baselines

We select three representative spatial-keyword search methods as the baselines in our experiments. Note that we investigate a new query problem, there is no existing method to resolve our problem. Here we select the representative methods and improve them to suit for the multi-view object.

- keyword-search-first algorithm (KSF): It is a kind of typical textual-priority two-phase query algorithm. KSF first filter the objects according to the textual constraints of a query. Then, the candidate objects are sorted by the distance to the query point.
- kNN-first algorithm (kNN): It is a kind of typical spatial-priority two-phase query algorithm. Firstly, the algorithm filter the objects according to the spatial index(R-tree). Then, the candidate objects are filter by keywords one by one.
- R*-IF based algorithm: The R*-IF based algorithm [9] uses a spatial-priority index structure that combines R*-tree and inverted files, which is widely used spatial-keyword query algorithm.

5.2 Experimental Setups

Data Set. We crawled about 500,000 housing resources from the famous estate websites[1] in China, and collected other six datasets related to housing from other data platforms. These datasets include the data of housing communities, sites and lines information of subways and buses, the data of hospitals and the data of POIs. The statistical description about these datasets are shown in Table 2.

Table 2. Statistics of the experimental data.

Data source	Properties	Statistics
Housing	Number of real housing resources	500,000
	Size of maximal region (km)	133.6*95.7
	Time period of resources	01/2016-12/2016
Housing community	Number of housing community	14576
	Size of maximal region (km)	133.6*95.7
	Time period of resources	01/2016-12/2016
Subway info	Number of subway stations	365
	Number of subway lines	14
Bus info	Number of bus stops	15,000
	Number of bus lines	1400
Hospital info	Number of hospital	1021
	Level types of hospitals	9
POIs info	Number of POIs	100,000
	Number of categories POIs	10

We can see from Table 2 that the total number of multi-view housing objects is 500,000. To evaluate the performance of methods in different data size, we randomly select and generate four housing object datasets from the overall dataset,

[1] http://sh.fang.com/.

which include 50,000, 100,000, 250,000 and 500,000 multi-view housing objects separately. Besides, in order to evaluate the performance of methods in the case of different number of query keywords, we generate five query sets for each dataset. Each query set contains 100 multi-view housing queries cases. The number of query keywords ranges from 1 to 5 and five query sets correspond to different number of keywords.

Evaluation Metrics. In this paper, we focus on both the time performance of query methods and the effectiveness of query results. For time performance, we record the overall elapsed time for processing queries when varying the size of datasets and the number of keywords. For effectiveness of query results, we concern on the rank and correctness of each object in query result, so the precision and recall are not suitable and Normalized Discounted Cumulative Gain (NDCG) [23] is used to measure the quality of sorting. Here give a brief introduction of its application in our problem.

Let q be a multi-view housing query and L_{rs} be the list of returned multi-view housing objects for q. the DCG indicator is the basis of the NDCG indicator and can be caculated as follows:

$$DCG@\mathbb{K} = \sum_{r=1}^{\mathbb{K}} \frac{2^{rel(o_r,q)} - 1}{\log(r+1)}. \tag{5}$$

where $\mathbb{K}$ represents the maximum number of objects that need to be evaluated. And the NDCG indicator is actually a normalization of DCG indicator, its calculation formula as shows in Eq. (6), where $IDCG@\mathbb{K}$ represents the ideal DCG value.

$$NDCG@\mathbb{K} = \frac{DCG@\mathbb{K}}{IDCG@\mathbb{K}}. \tag{6}$$

$rel(o_r, q)$ calculates the correlation score between the r-th object in the sorted results list L_{rs} and the query q. We define the *correlation scoring function* between q and a housing multi-view object $o_r \in L_{rs}$, $1 \leq r \leq |L_{rs}|$, as follows:

$$rel(o_r, q) = \sum_{i=1}^{V} d\left(S\left(q.v_i, o_r.v_i\right),\ \alpha\right). \tag{7}$$

where V is the number of views in the object, $S\left(q.v_i, o_r.v_i\right)$ denotes the similarity between the query q and a object o_r on the i-th view, and α is determined parameter. Here, $d\left(S\left(q.v_i, o_r.v_i\right),\ \alpha\right)$ returns a boolean value. If $S(q.v_i, o_r.v_i) \geq \alpha$, it returns 1; otherwise, it returns 0.

In the above definition, the function for calculating the similarity between vectors is also implemented by the Gaussian kernel function proposed in Eq. (4). However, unlike the similarity function, which only considers views except the spatial view and keyword view of the housing object, in the query processing. The correlation scoring function considers all the views of the object. In the experiments, we compute the NDCG@10, NDCG@50, and NDCG@100 of 100 queries as the final results.

5.3   Results

In the following, we present the results of the evaluation. To get comprehensive result, we run 100 times of different query cases in each experiment and compute the average time as the final time consuming.

Effect of the Number of Query Keywords. We evaluate the performance of four algorithms against the datasets where the number of the keywords varies from 1 to 5. Figure 3(a) shows the experiment result when dataset includes 250,000 housing objects and k values is 100. We can see that KBHR has absolute advantage in time performance. This is due to the adopted BHR-tree index, which enables the algorithm to do spatial-textual pruning simultaneously, and less candidate objects can decrease calculation time for similarity. For the other three algorithms, since they are not good at housing object pruning by spatial and textual info, the query time is relatively long. When the number of keywords increased to 5, the *KSF* method start getting better, owing to the number matched objects reduced as the keyword increasing. However, the time consuming still worse than KBHR.

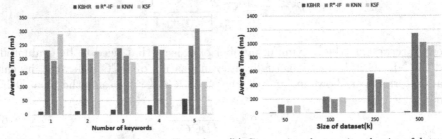

(a) Comparison by varying keyword numbers (dataset=250k, $k = 100$).
(b) Comparison by varying the size of dataset (keywords=3, $k = 100$).

Fig. 3. Performance comparison between methods on average elapsed time.

Effect of the Size of Dataset. Figure 3(b) presents the elapsed times of four methods under different size of dataset. We can see that, compared with baseline methods, KBHR's elapsed time increases proportionally when the size of dataset increasing. This is because the textual index of housing object is growth slowly in different data size. We can almost spend same time to get the *MBRList* by which the candidate objects can be retrieved directly. As a result, for KBHR, the pruning operation on objects is minor affected by the size of the dataset. The most affected algorithm is R*-IF algorithm, due to the increase of house objects, its spatial-priority index takes up a lot of memory, which affect the query efficiency.

Effectiveness of Multi-view Based Query. We use the experiment shown in Fig. 4 to evaluate the effectiveness of multi-view application in the housing query method. We modify each of previous method to simple method that does traditional spatial keyword query. Those methods noted by upper character S like KBHR(S) are applied in the experiment. In Table 3, we present the effectiveness comparison of nDCG between methods. As shown in Fig. 4, a more intuitive display can be seen in Table 3, we can see that the multi-view based method outperform the traditional spatial-keyword based method generally. The results demonstrate that the utilization of multi-view to housing object can return more satisfied query result. Moreover, the accuracy of our method KBHR is better than kNN and RIF which performed worst due to its independent two-phase manner. The KSF method is slightly better than KBHR for it traversed all house objects, but KSF presented low time performance. In general, the proposed method KBHR achieves the balance of efficiency and accuracy.

Table 3. Effectiveness comparison between multi-view and spatial-keyword.

Metric	Method					
	KBHR	KBHR(S)	KNN/RIF	KNN/RIF(S)	KSF	KSF(S)
nDCG@10	0.919	0.8519	0.7766	0.6434	0.9844	0.9241
nDCG@50	0.8584	0.7941	0.822	0.6785	0.9445	0.8459
nDCG@100	0.8724	0.8195	0.8366	0.7168	0.9486	0.8586

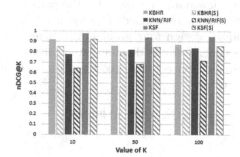 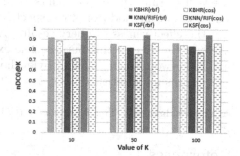

Fig. 4. nDCG@K of methods with multi-view and spatial-keyword.

Fig. 5. nDCG@K of methods with rbf kernel and cosine similarity.

Effect of Kernel Funcion for Multi-view Object. We use the experiment shown in Fig. 5 to evaluate the effectiveness of method with different similarity functions. The *RBF kernel* is utilized to compute the similarity on multiple views. *Cosine Similarity* [20] is commonly used in information retrieval to evaluate document similarity. We modify the kernel function in each previous method to cosine function. Figure 5 and Table 4 present the effectiveness comparison of nDCG between RBF kernel or cosine similarity, where parameter σ in kernel is set to 0.5. Both figures and table show that the methods with RBF kernel perform better than the methods with cosine similarity.

Table 4. Effectiveness comparison between different kernels.

Metric	Method					
	KBHR(rbf)	KBHR(cos)	KNN/RIF(rbf)	KNN/RIF(cos)	KSF(rbf)	KSF(cos)
nDCG@10	0.919	0.8914	0.7766	0.7207	0.9844	0.929
nDCG@50	0.8584	0.833	0.822	0.7572	0.9445	0.8666
nDCG@100	0.8724	0.8465	0.8366	0.7815	0.9486	0.8692

6 Conclusions

In this paper, we successfully investigate an usable new way to housing object query on web systems. A novel multi-view based spatial-keyword query framework for real estate data is devised. Based on this framework, we first propose the preprocessing method and the feature extraction method for real estate data, and give the definition of the multi-view housing object. Then, we design a hybrid indexing structure, named BHR-tree, and propose a multi-view based query method, named KBHR. Moreover, we propose a kernel based similarity function to rank the query results of multi-view data. We evaluate the performance of our method from two aspects: the time performance of query methods and the effectiveness of query results. And we design four groups of comparative experiments for this purpose. The experiment results demonstrate that our spatial-keywords query for multi-view housing object achieves good performance and returns more satisfied query result to custom.

Acknowledgment. This work was partially supported by NSFC 61401155.

References

1. Hartz, D.K., Gorman, M.T., Rossum, E.: Real-estate information search and retrieval system. In: US (2003)
2. Martinez, L., Contreras, J., Mendoza, R.: INMO: a web architecture for real estate search systems. IEEE Latin Am. Trans. **13**(4), 1148–1152 (2015)
3. Liu, X.P., Wan, C.X., Liu, D.X.: Survey on spatial keyword search. J. Softw. **27**(2), 329–347 (2016)
4. Chen, L., Cong, G., Jensen, C.S.: Spatial keyword query processing: an experimental evaluation. Proc. VLDB Endow. **6**(3), 217–228 (2013)
5. Cao, X., Cong, G., Jensen, C. S., Ooi, B.C.: Collective spatial keyword querying. In: SIGMOD Conference, pp. 373–384 (2011)

6. Chen, L., Cong, G., Cao, X.: An efficient query indexing mechanism for filtering geo-textual data. In: SIGMOD Conference, pp. 749–760 (2013)
7. Wu, D., Yiu, M.L., Cong, G., Jensen, C.S.: Joint top-k spatial keyword query processing. IEEE Trans. Knowl. Data Eng. **24**(10), 1889–1903 (2012)
8. Zhang, C., Zhang, Y., Zhang, W.: Inverted linear quadtree: efficient top k spatial keyword search. IEEE Trans. Knowl. Data Eng. **28**(7), 1706–1721 (2016)
9. Zhou, Y., Xie, X., Wang, C.: Hybrid index structures for location-based web search. In: International Conference on Information & Knowledge Management, pp. 155–162. ACM (2005)
10. Felipe, I.D., Hristidis, V., Rishe, N.: Keyword search on spatial databases. In: IEEE International Conference on Data Engineering, pp. 656–665 (2008)
11. Xu, C., Tao, D., Xu, C.: A survey on multi-view learning. Comput. Sci. (2013)
12. Eaton, E., Desjardins, M., Jacob, S.: Multi-view clustering with constraint propagation for learning with an incomplete mapping between views. In: ACM International Conference on Information & Knowledge Management, pp. 389–398 (2010)
13. Deng, C., Lv, Z., Liu, W.: Multi-view matrix decomposition: a new scheme for exploring discriminative information. In: International Conference on Artificial Intelligence, pp. 3438–3444. AAAI Press (2015)
14. Yuan, N.J., Zheng, Y., Xie, X.: Discovering urban functional zones using latent activity trajectories. IEEE Trans. Knowl. Data Eng. **27**(3), 712–725 (2015)
15. Zheng, Y., Liu, F., Hsieh, H.P.: U-Air: when urban air quality inference meets big data. In: ACM SIGKDD International Conference on Knowledge Discovery and Data Mining, pp. 1436–1444 (2013)
16. Wang, Y., Cheema, M.A., Lin, X., Zhang, Q.: Multi-manifold ranking: using multiple features for better image retrieval. In: Pei, J., Tseng, V.S., Cao, L., Motoda, H., Xu, G. (eds.) PAKDD 2013. LNCS (LNAI), vol. 7819, pp. 449–460. Springer, Heidelberg (2013). https://doi.org/10.1007/978-3-642-37456-2_38
17. Dhillon, P.S., Foster, D., Ungar, L.: Multi-view learning of word embeddings via CCA. In: Proceedings of Nips, pp. 199–207 (2011)
18. Krainer, J., Wei, C.: House prices and fundamental value. FRBSF Econ. Lett. (2004)
19. Kamel, I., Faloutsos, C.: Hilbert R-tree: an improved R-tree using fractals. In: International Conference on Very Large Data Bases, pp. 500–509 (1994)
20. Manning, C., Raghavan, P.: Introduction to Information Retrieval, pp. 824–825. Cambridge University Press, Cambridge (2010)
21. Yu, L.H., Du, Y.: Methods and technology of data preprocess in data mining. J. Anhui Vocat. College Electron. Inf. Technol. (2009)
22. Fu, K.S.: Pattern Recognition and Machine Learning, pp. 461–462. Springer, New York (2006)
23. Liu, L.: Normalized discounted cumulated gain (nDCG). Encyclopedia of Database Systems, p. 1920. Springer, Boston (2009). https://doi.org/10.1007/978-0-387-39940-9_3166

Text Analysis and Mining

PowerMonitor: Aspect Mining and Sentiment Analysis on Online Reviews

Zhibin Zhao, Lan Yao$^{(\boxtimes)}$, Siyuan Wang, and Ge Yu

College of Computer Science and Engineering, Northeastern University,
Shenyang 110819, Liaoning, China
{zhaozhibin,yaolan,yuge}@mail.neu.edu.cn

Abstract. Customer reviews on a product regard multi-aspect with emotional tendencies. Aspects in a review show what properties customers concern about and sentiment towards an aspect reveals how a customer evaluates it. The aspect mining and sentiment analysis provides a lot of valuable references and market feedback information to online commercial platforms. Due to the unpredictability of aspects appearing in a review, the method proposed in this paper is supposed to be dynamic and intelligent and to define the sentiment related to an aspect negative or positive polarity in semantic analysis. Based on the improved aspect dictionary and sentiment dictionary, this paper presents a framework for aspect mining and sentiment analysis for online customer reviews-PowerMonitor. The experimental results show that the framework performs well in aspect extraction and aspect emotion judgment. We evaluate the model using small, widely used sentiment and subjectivity corpora from JD.com and find it out-performs several previously introduced methods for sentiment classification. We also introduce future works to serve as a reference for efforts in this area.

Keywords: Text mining · Aspect extraction · Sentiment analysis

1 Introduction

Online commerce is under a rapid expansion in recent year. The transaction records and reviews are massive and rich of experiences, evaluation and recommendation. Especially the reviews are consequential to improve the online business with commercial values. Consumers refer to these reviews when they consciously purchase a product and obviously reviews therefore play an important role in online business. Manufacturers take these reviews into account to improve these products and they are valuable for the enrichment of service providers as well. Most upgrading on products and service and development are launched and designed base on review analysis. Therefore, online review mining has become a hot research issue for business industry and research.

This work is supported by the National Natural Science Foundation of China under Grant No. U1811261 and U1435216.

© Springer Nature Switzerland AG 2019
J. Shao et al. (Eds.): APWeb-WAIM 2019, LNCS 11642, pp. 295–309, 2019.
https://doi.org/10.1007/978-3-030-26075-0_23

When a customer posts a review, he always mentions multi-aspect of the purchase, and expresses his attitude to each aspect. This fact makes the research on review analysis consist of two parts: aspect mining (AM) [1] and aspect-level sentiment analysis (ASA) [2].

For AM, it generally has been converted to the problem of Multi-label Classification. The solutions include a label set provided by industrial experts to describe all potential aspects. Then a review text and labels are connected by running a multi-label algorithm over them [3]. To further aspect-level sentiment analysis, sentences related to a label are clarified while aspects are mined. As follows, the aspect-level sentiment analysis is aggregated as the issue of classic sentiment analysis. While, the methods mentioned above show weakness in: (1) the professional experts are subjected to provide the label set. This makes this set all come from the experiences of industrial experts. Moreover, new aspect may be mentioned by customers. Therefore, it is hard to ensure the correctness and integrity of the label set; (2) the voluntary reviews are unstructured and their aspects are unpredictable. Most algorithms are incapable to label these reviews with essential aspects accurately because of this uncertainty. This results in the low accuracy of aspect-level sentiment classification.

This paper proposes a solution to aspect mining and sentiment analysis for reviews with hybrid word vector model, word2vec+LDA. This solution embraces dynamic label set and aspect exaction, as well as predication on sentiment polarity. The clustering is applied to achieve a dynamic label set. We thus derive dictionary based pattern matching to fulfill the aspect extraction. We introduce word2vec+PMI to reveal the pattern of words collocation in reviews. This technique is sufficiently effective to accomplish the label dictionary with high coverage and low maintaining workload. After exacting aspects, we provide a method on recognizing central aspects and discovering the relation between the aspects and sentiment polarity words. Segmentation technology is applied to enhance the accuracy on sentiment words exaction. To confirm the polarity of sentiment words, sentiment word dictionary is developed. After presenting the model in detail, we provide illustrative examples of the patterns it learns, and then we systematically evaluate the performances of the approach involving a dataset of informal products consumers' reviews.

2   Related Works

Aspect extraction is essentially a multi-label classification and has received much attention from academic field. Generally, the solutions to this problem are within the following three scopes: machine learning, deep learning and rule marching based on lexicon. Zhang [3] has systematically concluded solutions in machine learning: (1) one-order algorithms. It assumes that labels are independent that multi-label can be converted to a serial of classic classification problems. The outstanding one order algorithms are BR (Binary Relevance) [4] ML-kNN (Multi-Label k-Nearest Neighbor) [5] and ML-DT (Multi-Label Decision Tree) [6]; (2) two-order algorithms. It involves the correlation of each label couple and is therefore qualified with much more complexity compared with the one order. Calibrated Label Ranking [7], Rank-SVM (Ranking Support Vector Machine) [8], and CML (Collective Multi-Label Classifier) [9] are outstanding algorithms out of the two-order; (3) high-order algorithms. It is so called due to the correlation of multiple labels, with which the operation of this algorithm is eventually most complex. Classifier Chains [10] and Random k-labelsets [11] are referred as to the well-known representations of this type. In Zhang's paper, he summarizes solutions on aspect extraction and presents a semi-supervised method on entity extraction. Recent years, taking the advantages of the success in deep learning, Read et al. [12] constructs a hidden layer with Restricted Boltzmann Machine to increase the precision and reduce the temporal consumption as well.

Despite the advantages that machine learning and deep learning have shown, there remain two crucial challenges on multi-label classification: (1) training data should be abundant and accurate for model training. However, data skew happens and gets worse while label amount is large, which means inadequate training data under some labels. Data skew essentially causes low precision in classifying with machine learning or deep learning. (2) classification results are unexplainable and not promising for debugging. The above challenges make either machine learning or deep learning fail to be applied for practical systems. Main solutions to sentiment analysis are embracing the following methods.

Sentiment dictionary based sentiment analysis applies precise and comprehensive sentiment dictionary as the foundation. Manek et al. extract professional terms from movie reviews and mark polarity [13] to derive the dictionary. Arababah et al. use labeled polarity and synonyms from WordNet as auxiliary to mark new words' polarity [14]. Wang derives an emotion dictionary for Weibo corpus [15] and this method achieves higher precision.

Approaches based on machine learning are perceived as Decision Tree, SVM or Naive Bayes. The core of these approaches is to model classifiers through training sets for further prediction on new words polarity. Works of Tripathy, Hampton, Kang et al. [16–18] involve DT, SVM, max entropy and supervised Markov Model. Their experimental results convince SVM or Naive Bayes more efficient in different scenario respectively and the best precision reaches 77%. [19] mines latent aspects, sentiment polarity and aspect weight while the overall sentiment is known and experiments with hotel reviews and MP3 player reviews. [20] conducts the same three mining through CARW framework.

3 Problem Description

When consumers express their attitudes towards merchandise through posting online reviews, they mention multi-aspect of it together with sentiment polarity and level.

We instantiate the reviews on detergent by sentiment polarity annotations of JD.com online documents. Table 1 shows the analysis on three reviews, c_1, c_2 and c_3. c_1 concerns the smells and shipping service. The sentiment polarities are both positive. c_2 describes three aspects as cleaning power, concentration and shipping service with the polarities of negative, mild and positive. c_3 mentions brand loyalty, cleaning power, price and shipping service, and the sentiment attitudes to these four aspects are positive, positive, negative and negative.

Table 1. An instance on aspect extraction and sentiment analysis on detergent reviews.

	Reviews	<aspect, sentiment polarity>
c_1	Good nature smell, shipment is awesome!!!	<smell, positive>, <shipping service, positive>
c_2	Awful cleaning effect! concentration is average, but we get the product on time	<cleaning power, negative>, <concentration, mild>, <shipping service, positive>
c_3	Have been doing laundry with this detergent for a long time. It cleans clothes very well. Not the best deal specially in this grand 11.11 festival. The shipment took too much time. Will buy more as a better deal is provided	<brand loyalty, positive>, <cleaning power, positive>, <price, negative>, <shipping service, negative>

We present a set of reviews as $C = \{c_1, c_2, c_3, ..., c_{|c|}\}$, $A = \{a_1, a_2, ..., a_m\}$ is a set of potential aspects, and that is the entire set of essential and extensive properties of products, where m is the number of aspects. A review concerns some or all of these m aspects. Hence the aspects mentioned in review c_i is represented as an m-dimensional vector $V_i = <v_i^{a_1}, v_i^{a_2}, ..., v_i^{a_m}>$, where

$$\begin{cases} v_i^{a_x} = 1, & iff \quad a_x \in c_i \\ v_i^{a_x} = 0, & iff \quad a_x \notin c_i \end{cases} \tag{1}$$

The sentiment polarity about aspect a_x $(a_x \in A)$ in review c_i is $s_i^{a_x}$. $s_i^{a_x}$ in this paper is defined as four levels: 1 - positive, 0 - mild, -1 - negative, and -2 - not mentioned. The sentiment polarity of c_i is a m-dimensional vector $S = <s_i^{a_1}, s_i^{a_2}, ..., s_i^{a_m}>$, where

$$\begin{cases} s_i^{a_x} \in \{-1, 0, +1\}, & iff \quad a_x \in c_i \\ s_i^{a_x} = -2, & iff \quad a_x \notin c_i \end{cases} \tag{2}$$

Based on the definition above, the issues researched in this paper is presented as follows:

- Aspect-mining: for a given set of reviews C, label set L is mined from C and the formal description is $H :: C \rightarrow L$;
- Aspect-mining from a single review: for any review c_i in C, capturing aspect vector for c_i, which is described as $F :: c_i \rightarrow V_i$ for formal.
- Sentiment polarity discovery: for any review c_i in C, we assume that the aspect vector V_i comes out with function F, then the corresponding sentiment vector S_i is defined as $G :: (c_i, V_i) \rightarrow S_i$.

4   Aspect-Mining and Sentiment Analysis on Online Customer Reviews

In this paper, we derive a word2vec+LDA model to mine label set. Aspect dictionary is initialized by applying PMI accomplishing rule-based aspect mining. The Distance measure is proposed for the association of aspects and sentiment words, and it is also a basis for the aspect-level sentiment analysis.

4.1   Label Set Mining

Label set mining is implemented by review clustering. Compared with manual label set, we launch segmentation and vectorization on reviews according to hybrid word vector model, which is the foundation for clustering on review corpus. The clustering turns out to be cluster tags composing the label set.

Professional Term Discovery. Reviews may contain particular professional terms, which makes professional term dictionary necessary for segmentation. 'oxygen rich-low foaming', 'aroma essence' and 'la mamma' are all terms for detergent for instance. N-gram statistic algorithm [21] derived by Roziewski et al. is efficient to weigh and conclude frequent string set. However, it is obvious that frequent string is not an inevitable term. A string quoted in a text frequently is alternative to be a word or a phrase [22]. Some of the words in a phrase, but not all, may have relation with aspects we target to extract and analyze. Therefore, we use the string cohesion to describe aggregation between words and exclude the words in low cohesion rate from the string set. After this filtering, the elements remaining in this string set turn out to be terms and they form the professional term set. In this paper, based on the professional term set, we leverage Jieba [23] as segmentation tool. The performance of the segmentation will be shown as a part of our method in the evaluation session.

Label Set Mining. The following step for segmentation is Text Vectorization, which fulfills the vector mathematic form for words. The combination of language based word2ved and statistic based LDA is involved in our model-PowerMonitor, which is a hybrid word vector (HWV) model. Word vector from word2vec reflects the context and semantic relation at sentence-level. Therefore it is a kind of precious description [24]. LDA (Latent Dirichlet Allocation) [25] models at two levels: document-topic and topic-word with the objective of providing probabilistic distribution of topics in each document, as well as the corresponding words to every topic. LDA involves polysemy more and reveals the relations between words at topic-level. We extend the model with the combination component of word2vec and LDA as HWV, which is coinstantaneous of context-level and document-level. We illustrate the exact construction of HWV in Fig. 1.

Word vectors from HWV are too dispersive to express the topic of a review text. We cluster these word vectors with k-means clustering algorithm applying

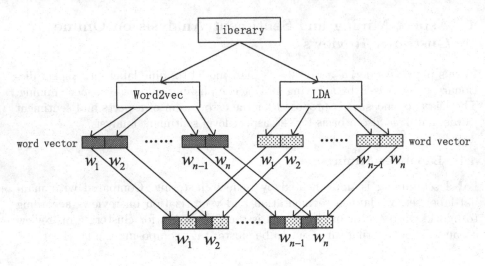

Fig. 1. Hybrid word vector model.

Cosine Similarity as the measurement to the distance between cluster centers [26,27]. For PowerMonitor, the results of the clustering are used as label-set.

4.2 Aspect Extraction

Aspect extraction on review is essentially a multi-label classification problem, which has attracted much research attention. The main solutions involve probabilistic based and knowledge rule matching based methods. The former one is further researched with machine learning and deep learning [28–30]. However, the probabilistic based method is found unfulfillable for these reasons: (1) the classification accuracy declines when clusters are alternating much and show overlapped properties; (2) quality and quantity of training data are constrained, which makes it unpractical; (3) it is incapable to definitize key words to classify texts, which results in failure of aspect-level sentiment analysis.

Thus, we use model matching based on dictionary to out-perform in aspect extraction through the most key issue, professional terms dictionary which reflects the characters of the corpora.

Professional terms dictionary contains aspects as items and their corresponding explanations. These items are stated from label-set in Sect. 4.1. When a customer's review concerns an aspect, the label of this aspect may not be mentioned in the text, while related words instead. For example, when a customer is commenting price, he may state "cheap", "reasonable" or "expensive", where "price", as a label, does not appear. The dictionary is defined to explain this corresponding relation. We draw inspiration from TFIDF to build a seed dictionary. TFIDF provides a set of single related words for each aspect. However, some phrases are correlatives as well. To extend the seed dictionary to be comprehensive with phrases, PMI (Pointwise Mutual Information) is introduced to measure the probability of some words being a phrase.

t_i and t_j are words in seed dictionary. The PMI of t_i, t_j is

$$PMI(t_i; t_j) = \log \frac{p(t_i, t_j)}{p(t_i)p(t_j)} = \log \frac{p(t_i|t_j)}{p(t_i)} = \log \frac{p(t_j|t_i)}{p(t_j)} \tag{3}$$

In Eq. (3), $p(t_i, t_j)$ is the probability of t_i and t_j appearing in a sentence. $p(t_i)$ is the probability of t_i appearing in a sentence. If t_i is not correlative with t_j, $p(t_i, t_j) = p(t_i) \times p(t_j)$; the more they are correlative, the greater the ratio of $p(t_i, t_j)$ to $p(t_i) \times p(t_j)$ is.

If $PMI(t_i; t_j) < PMI(t_i; t_k)$, t_i is more related to t_k than to t_j. We therefore do PMI for every two words in seed dictionary and select 2-word phrases with highest Top-k PMI values as supplementary.

To discern 3-word or 4-word phrases from annotations, we use the 2-word set above to collocate for 3-word in an enumeration method. We calculate PMI of each collocated 3-word to measure whether this 3-word phrase is appreciate to be appended to the dictionary. Figure 2 shows how PMI and enumeration work together for 3-word discovery.

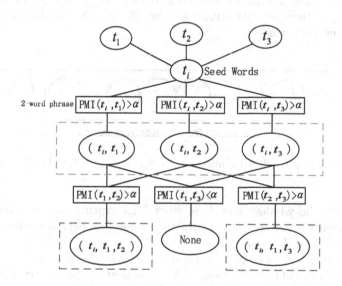

Fig. 2. Finding 3-word strings.

In Fig. 2, α is the customized threshold of PMI to describe how deeply the words link to each other. Theoretically, recognition of 3-word phrases increases the precise rate for aspect mining, while excessive phrases may cause over fitting and decline the recall rate.

The foundation of aspect mining - aspect dictionary is thus ready through the above method we propose with high expandability, compatibility and accuracy.

4.3   Aspect-Level Sentiment Analysis

It is not hard to discovery sentiment words in a text given existing methods on word mining. However, when a review text mentions multi-aspect, we have to category these sentiment words to their corresponding aspect. We build a two-layer model to link sentiment words to their aspect.

Firstly, we leverage the fact that some aspects and sentiment words are implicitly relevant. In this layer, when a sentiment word is mentioned, the customer is definitely referring to a certain aspect. Such as "clean" is related to washing efficiency and "unsealed" is describing the packing. Other sentiment words which are not patently and inherently regarding an aspect are connected to aspects accordingly by the approach of sliding window on layer two.

We assume that review c consists of n distinct words, which are denoted as an n-gram $<t_1, t_2, ..., t_n>$. An aspect in c is $a_x (a_x \in A)$. Through looking up in the dictionary we proposed in Sect. 4.2, if t_i in c is related to a_x, the location of t_i in c is remarked as $loc(t_i)$.

Generally, a sentiment is near to an aspect in term of location. Given this fact, we locate the related sentiment words in a certain distance. Assume the window size is L and we search sentiment words in $[loc(t_i) - L/2, loc(t_i) + L/2]$. Once the sentiment words are located and exacted, we use sentiment dictionary to analysis their polarity. Figure 3 shows the principle of sliding window on searching sentiment words.

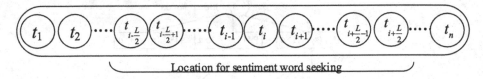

Fig. 3. Seeking t_i related sentiment words in $[loc(t_i) - L/2, loc(t_i) + L/2]$.

Obviously, the window size L is crucial for sentiment word discovery. A greater L results in redundant capture and wrong link between aspect and sentiment, while a less L causes a loss.

The sentiment dictionary is applied to analyze the polarity. For Chinese, the Hownet from cnki [31], commendatory-derogatory dictionary proposed by Li [32] and NTUSD from Taiwan University are outstanding works. However, a sentiment essentially expresses different polarity under varying aspects. "quick" is positive when is related to delivery service, while is negative in durability, for instance. Therefore, we derive a granularity based sentiment dictionary to increase the accuracy in sentiment analysis, as well as for the benefit of sharing aspect-level sentiment dictionary among diverse product categories.

5   Experiments and Evaluation

We evaluate our model with aspect-level sentiment analysis task in the domain of online skin care reviews from JD.com. We initialize the label set with 10 manually picked terms by professional experts at first-level and 65 terms at second-level. 32,800 reviews are used as test data set and labeled with these 65 labels and corresponding sentiment words by 20 volunteers. Table 2 shows the statistic of the test set.

Table 2. Statistic of test set.

Aspects in a review	Reviews	Words in a review
0	5897	10 ± 6
1	15955	15 ± 8
2	7634	24 ± 15
3	2511	32 ± 20
4	590	55 ± 28
5	160	76 ± 45
6	44	100 ± 78
≥ 7	9	233 ± 124

Table 2 shows that only 9 out of 32,800 reviews contains over 100 words and less than 1% regard 5 aspects or above. This fact illustrates short reviews are majority.

We conduct three experiments to verify the following performances: (1) HWV's efficiency on label mining; (2) the efficiency of PMI based aspect dictionary for aspect extraction; (3) the validity of sliding window and effect of window size L for aspect-level sentiment analysis.

5.1   Experiment and Evaluation on Label Mining

For label-set mining, we use the same clustering algorithm over HWV model and word2vec respectively to compare them.

When measuring experimental results, manual label based F-score is applied. The set $X = \{x_1, x_2, ..., x_n\}$ is clustered and the result is $H = \{H_1, H_2, ..., H_m\}$, where $H_i \neq \varnothing$ is a non-empty set consisting of elements from X and defined as a cluster here.

The manually labeled cluster set is $P = \{P_1, P_2, ..., P_s\}$, where P_i is a non-empty set with elements of X. We assume that for any P_j, there is a H_i matching it well, however this matching is unknown. For a given P_j, to find the corresponding H_i, we traverse H and calculate precision, recall and F-score for each couple of (P_j, H_i) respectively. We determine H_i is P_j's matching cluster when (P_j, H_i) is with the optimal values on these three parameters [33].

In this experiment, 2,500 skin care reviews are manually clustered and 8 clusters are yielded as results. Therefore, when we use k-means to cluster the word vectors, the target number of clusters is 8. The $Class\_F$ values of HWV and word2vec under different word2vec dimensionality are shown in Fig. 4.

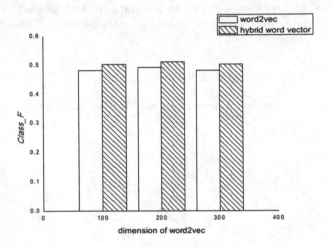

Fig. 4. Assessment on clustering.

Dimensionality of word2vec is given with three values as 100, 200 and 300 respectively. Under each dimension value, HWV outperforms word2vec, which shows the HWVs priority on $Class\_F$.

5.2 Experiments on Aspect Extraction

The essential aspect extraction consists of two parts: aspect dictionary and aspect mining. Aspect dictionary is the foundation of mining and crucial for performances. The approach we propose to derive aspect dictionary is based on PMI. We design the following experiments to evaluate the efficiency of aspect mining based on this aspect dictionary. As mentioned above, aspect mining is defined as multi-label categorization and property of multi-label makes the very popular evaluation indexes for supervised single label approach inapplicable. Therefore, we evaluate our model through two multi-label evaluation indexes [3]: sample-based assessment and category-based assessment.

Sample-Based Assessment. Two sample-based indexes are used to in this section for performance assessment.

- Subset accuracy. It is an index to measure how aspects we extract based on aspect dictionary map the real aspects. The value of this index is the proportion of aspects both in extracted aspect set and real aspect set to the total real aspect set. A greater Subset accuracy reflects a better performance in label extraction.

– Hamming loss. It is a fault rate to describe the inconsistency between extracted aspects and real aspects. It is the proportion of fault aspects in extracted aspect set to real aspect set. A less Hamming loss is expected for a better performance.

The experimental results are shown in Table 3.

Table 3. Hamming loss and subset accuracy.

Training set ratio	Approaches	Hamming loss	Subset accuracy
20%	Single word dictionary	0.0572	0.3827
	2-word dictionary	0.0254	0.6263
	3-word dictionary	0.0092	0.8142
40%	Single word dictionary	0.0421	0.4151
	2-word dictionary	0.0209	0.6975
	3-word dictionary	0.0079	0.8309
60%	Single word dictionary	0.0398	0.4593
	2-word dictionary	0.0198	0.7359
	3-word dictionary	0.0098	0.8173
80%	Single word dictionary	0.0353	0.4725
	2-word dictionary	0.0159	0.7708
	3-word dictionary	0.0081	0.8236
100%	Single word dictionary	0.0361	0.4845
	2-word dictionary	0.0115	0.7901
	3-word dictionary	0.0085	0.8251

We conduct the aspect dictionary under diverse training set ratios, which means we use different data scale as training set. In Table 3, when training set is given, the single-word dictionary based on TFIDF is inferior to PMI based 2-word dictionary on both Hamming loss and Subset accuracy. When we increase the scale of training set, the Subset accuracy declines on 3-word dictionary, however, its overall performance much precedes over 2-word and single word. It is concluded that the size of training set effects PMI based dictionaries and a larger size makes the dictionaries more comprehensive. It definitely results in a better performance in aspect extraction as well.

Category-Based Assessment. Macro-averaging and Micro-averaging are two indexes on aspect extraction for category-based algorithms.

Macro-Precision, Macro-Recall, and Macro-F are three parameters for Macro-averaging by averaging all sub-categories' indexes. This index inclines the sub-category with more samples.

Micro-averaging is arithmetic average on performances of each review with no consideration of categories. This index regards Micro-Precision, Micro-Recall and Micro-F.

We conduct experiments with respect to our aspect dictionary and aspect mining on our data set and calculate the above two indexes accordingly. The results are in Table 4 which verifies a better performance with a higher index value.

Table 4. Using category-based multi-label classifier assessment indexes for evaluation.

Training set ratio	Approaches	Macro-averaging			Micro-averaging		
		P	R	F	P	R	F
20%	Single word dictionary	0.369	0.383	0.375	0.392	0.417	0.404
	2-word dictionary	0.573	0.558	0.565	0.614	0.607	0.610
	3-word dictionary	0.791	0.782	0.786	0.807	0.793	0.800
40%	Single word dictionary	0.427	0.435	0.431	0.453	0.468	0.460
	2-word dictionary	0.629	0.603	0.616	0.651	0.634	0.642
	3-word dictionary	0.825	0.819	0.822	0.833	0.824	0.828
60%	Single word dictionary	0.459	0.473	0.466	0.491	0.480	0.485
	2-word dictionary	0.685	0.667	0.676	0.706	0.681	0.693
	3-word dictionary	0.814	0.832	0.823	0.829	0.848	0.839
80%	Single word dictionary	0.482	0.501	0.491	0.513	0.522	0.517
	2-word dictionary	0.726	0.714	0.720	0.745	0.738	0.741
	3-word dictionary	0.821	0.830	0.826	0.835	0.839	0.837
100%	Single word dictionary	0.527	0.544	0.535	0.547	0.541	0.544
	2-word dictionary	0.753	0.742	0.747	0.769	0.750	0.759
	3-word dictionary	0.832	0.826	0.829	0.841	0.846	0.843

In Table 4, 2-word dictionary seems better in aspect extraction than single-word dictionary. Although, 3-word dictionary which is formed from 2-word preforms well in general, it contains noise items and therefore turns out a higher recall. Our alternative testing sets vary a lot in categories. This is the reason for the higher Micro-averaging over Macro-averaging. From the perspective of systematical comparison of Micro-F and Macro-F, PMI based dictionary is highlighted for its performances.

Evaluation on Aspect-Level Sentiment Analysis. We remain the reviews on skin cares from JD.com as the data set to assess our sentiment analysis model which is based on sliding windows. The aspect extraction method introduced and experimented in the previous section is used as the foundation for aspect extraction. For comparison, we implement several alternative window sizes that conceptually affect the accuracy on sentiment analysis.

The implementation includes: locating aspect strings and marking the start and end location (if the aspect string is a single word, the start and end location overlaps); locating sentiment words based on window sizes and start-end locations; sentiment analysis based on sentiment word dictionary. Especially, when the window size is beyond the length of the review text, it will be adjusted to the less one.

We conduct 9 experiments with distinct window sizes. Considering that customers usually express one polarity for one aspect, sentiment analysis is single-labeled multi-category problem. The assessment indexes for this kind of problem involve Precision, Recall and F1-score.

Table 5 shows the indexes values when we vary window sizes.

Table 5. Indexes values for sentiment analysis when window size s are adjusted.

Window size	Precision	Recall	F1-score
2	0.513	0.537	0.525
4	0.636	0.614	0.652
6	0.78	0.773	0.776
8	0.869	0.854	0.861
10	0.857	0.862	0.859
12	0.845	0.86	0.852
14	0.841	0.859	0.85
16	0.839	0.86	0.849
18	0.832	0.855	0.843

The experimental results illustrate that when we choose a small window size as 3 or less, the precision is low for few informational sentiment words in windows. When window sizes are switched to 5 and up, our method performs well and tends to stay stable. However, we discover the overmatching may be caused by a large window size for introduced noise words and this results in an increasing recall. Besides the definition of a window size, the approach of sliding windows on sentiment analysis performs well in both precision and comprehensiveness.

6   Conclusions

We propose a model - PowerMonitor for aspect extraction on online reviews and further sentiment analysis. The model's probabilistic foundation gives a justified technique for dynamic labeling instead of subjective labels from experts. Based on these labels, we launch an aspect dictionary by TFIDF and PMI to involve latent 2-word and 3-word phrases. This dictionary is a magnificent improvement in aspect mining with high performance. The sentiment analysis leverages this aspect dictionary as well and PMI model to improve general sentiment dictionary to aspect-level sentiment dictionary, which is highly flexible and applicable in this regard. Experiments are conducted to compare PowerMonitor to key-word based method with initially labeled data set in aspect capture and sentiment analysis. The results highlight PowerMonitor outperforming other method in precision, recall and F value.

We apply and implement PowerMonitor for custom reviewing corpus in skin care products and it turns out an efficient method. For the future work, we will extend it to capture subjectivity from other annotations, such as movie reviews, serving as a more robust breakthrough for work in this area. Following the success in syntax analysis, the extension will overcome the inconvenience from the diversity of customers expression and show better performances.

References

1. Marstawi, A., Sharef, N.M., Aris, T.N.M., et al.: Ontology-based aspect extraction for an improved sentiment analysis in summarization of product reviews. In: International Conference on Computer Modeling and Simulation, Australia, pp. 100–104. ACM (2017)
2. Schouten, K., Frasincar, F.: Survey on aspect-level sentiment analysis. IEEE Trans. Knowl. Data Eng. **28**(3), 813–830 (2016)
3. Zhang, M., Zhou, Z.: A review on multi-label learning algorithms. IEEE Trans. Knowl. Data Eng. **26**(8), 1819–1837 (2014)
4. Tanaka, E.A., Nozawa, S.R., et al.: A multi-label approach using binary relevance and decision trees applied to functional genomics. J. Biomed. Inform. **54**, 85–95 (2015)
5. Kanj, S., Abdallah, F., Denoeux, T., Tout, K.: Editing training data for multi-label classification with the k-nearest neighbor rule. Pattern Anal. Appl. **19**(1), 145–161 (2016)
6. Si, S., Zhang, H., Sathiya Keerthi, S., Mahajan, D., Dhillon, I.S., Hsieh, C.-J.: Gradient boosted decision trees for high dimensional sparse output. In: Proceedings of the 34th International Conference on Machine Learning, vol. 70, pp. 3182–3190 (2017). JMLR.org
7. Furnkranz, J., Hullermeier, E., Mencia, E.L., et al.: Multilabel classification via calibrated label ranking. Mach. Learn. **73**(2), 133–153 (2008)
8. Chen, W.-J., Shao, Y.-H., Li, C.-N., Deng, N.-Y.: MLTSVM: a novel twin support vector machine to multi-label learning. Pattern Recogn. **52**, 61–74 (2016)
9. Wu, Q., Chen, J., Ho, S.-S., Li, X., Min, H., Han, C.: Multi-label regularized generative model for semi-supervised collective classification in large-scale networks. Big Data Res. **2**(4), 187–201 (2015)
10. Read, J., Pfahringer, B., Holmes, G., et al.: Classifier chains for multi-label classification. Mach. Learn. **85**(3), 333–359 (2011)
11. Kimura, K., Kudo, M., Sun, L., Koujaku, S.: Fast random k-labelsets for large-scale multi-label classification. In: 2016 23rd International Conference on Pattern Recognition (ICPR), pp. 438–443. IEEE (2016)
12. Read, J., Perez-Cruz, F.: Deep learning for multi-label classification. Mach. Learn. **85**(3), 333–359 (2014)
13. Manek, A.S., Deepa Shenoy, P., Chandra Mohan, M., Venugopal, K.R.: Aspect term extraction for sentiment analysis in large movie reviews using Gini Index feature selection method and SVM classifier. World Wide Web **20**(2), 135–154 (2017)

14. Alrababah, S.A.A., Gan, K.H., Tan, T.-P.: Mining opinionated product features using WordNet lexicographer files. J. Inf. Sci. **43**(6), 769–785 (2017)
15. Wang, H., Xu, H., Liu, L., Song, W., Du, C.: An unsupervised microblog emotion dictionary construction method and its application on sentiment analysis. J. Inf. Comput. Sci. **12**(7), 2729–2739 (2015)
16. Tripathy, A., Agrawal, A., Rath, S.K.: Classification of sentimental reviews using machine learning techniques. Procedia Comput. Sci. **57**, 821–829 (2015)
17. Hampton, K.N., Shin, I., Weixu, L.: Social media and political discussion: when online presence silences offline conversation. Inf. Commun. Soc. **20**(7), 1090–1107 (2017)
18. Kang, M., Ahn, J., Lee, K.: Opinion mining using ensemble text hidden Markov models for text classification. Expert Syst. Appl. **94**, 218–227 (2018)
19. Li, H., Lin, R., Hong, R., Ge, Y.: Generative models for mining latent aspects and their ratings from short reviews. In: 2015 IEEE International Conference on Data Mining, pp. 241–250. IEEE (2015)
20. Wang, F., Chen, L.: Review mining for estimating users' ratings and weights for product aspects. Web Intell. **13**(3), 137–152 (2015)
21. Roziewski, S., Stokowiec, W., Sobkowicz, A.: N-gram collection from a large-scale corpus of polish internet. In: Ryżko, D., Gawrysiak, P., Kryszkiewicz, M., Rybiński, H. (eds.) Machine Intelligence and Big Data in Industry. SBD, vol. 19, pp. 23–34. Springer, Cham (2016). https://doi.org/10.1007/978-3-319-30315-4_3
22. Society language in Internet age: text mining based on SNS. http://www.matrix67.com/blog/archives/5044. Accessed 30 July 2018
23. Jieba phrasing for Chinese. https://github.com/fxsjy/jieba. Accessed 27 June 2018
24. Research on short text classification based on word vector. http://cdmd.cnki.com.cn/Article/CDMD-10335-1015635339.htm. Accessed 10 Feb 2018
25. Blei, D.M., Ng, A.Y., Jordan, M.I.: Latent Dirichlet allocation. J. Mach. Learn. Res. **3**(1), 993–1022 (2003)
26. Chen, K.: Research on k-means text clustering with variety distance measurement. Software **2015**(1), 56–61 (2015)
27. Dhillon, I.S., Modha, D.S.: Concept decompositions for large sparse text data using clustering. Mach. Learn. **42**(1), 143–175 (2001)
28. Berger, M.J.: Large scale multi-label text classification with semantic word vectors. Technical report, Stanford University (2014)
29. Gakuto, K., Xiang, B., Zhou, B.: Improved neural network-based multi-label classification with better initialization leveraging label co-occurrence. In: Conference of the North American Chapter of the Association for Computational Linguistics: Human Language Technologies, San Diego, pp. 521–526. Association for Computational Linguistics (2016)
30. Chen, G., Ye, D., Xing, Z., et al.: Ensemble application of convolutional and recurrent neural networks for multi-label text categorization. In: International Joint Conference on Neural Networks, Anchorage, pp. 2377–2383. IEEE (2017)
31. Hownet. http://www.keenage.com/html/index.html. Accessed 18 Oct 2018
32. Li, J., Sun, M.: Experimental study on sentiment classification of Chinese review using machine learning techniques. In: IEEE International Conference on Natural Language Processing and Knowledge Engineering, Beijing, pp. 393–400. IEEE (2007)
33. Zhou, S.: Evaluation on Text Clustering Analysis and Research on Text Expression. Chinese Academy of Sciences, Beijing (2005)

Transformer and Multi-scale Convolution for Target-Oriented Sentiment Analysis

Yinxu Pan[1,2,3]($\boxtimes$), Binheng Song[1,2], Ningqi Luo[1,2], Xiaojun Chen[3], and Hengbin Cui[3]

[1] Department of Computer Science and Technology,
Tsinghua University, Beijing, China
{pyx16,lnq16}@mails.tsinghua.edu.cn
[2] Graduate School at ShenZhen, Tsinghua University, Beijing, China
songbinheng@sz.tsinghua.edu.cn
[3] Ant Financial Services Group, Xihu, China
{tiandan.cxj,alexcui.chb}@antfin.com

Abstract. Target-oriented sentiment analysis aims to extract the sentiment polarity of a specific target in a sentence. In this paper, we propose a model based on transformers and multi-scale convolutions. The transformer which is based solely on attention mechanisms generalizes well in many natural language processing tasks. Convolution layers with multiple filters can efficiently extract n-gram features at many granularities on each receptive field. We conduct extensive experiments on three datasets: SemEval ABSA challenge Restaurant and Laptop dataset, Twitter dataset. Our framework achieves state-of-the-art results, including improving the accuracy of Restaurant dataset to 84.20% (5.81% absolute improvement), improving the accuracy of the Laptop dataset to 78.21% (4.23% absolute improvement), and improving the accuracy of the Twitter dataset to 72.98% (0.87% absolute improvement).

Keywords: Target-oriented sentiment analysis ·
Multi-scale convolution · Transformer

1 Introduction

Target-oriented sentiment analysis is also known as aspect-term sentiment analysis, which is a central concern of the semantic web and the computational linguistics in recent years [3,8]. The goal of target-oriented sentiment analysis is to identify the sentiment polarity (i.e., negative, neutral, or positive) of a specific opinion target expressed in a comment or review by a reviewer. For example, in the sentence *"great food but the service was dreadful!"*, the polarity of target *"food"* is positive while the polarity of target *"service"* is negative.

Recent years have witnessed the significant advances in sentiment analysis. For the task of target-oriented sentiment analysis, most of the previous models focus on three methods: attention mechanism, gate mechanism, and memory network.

© Springer Nature Switzerland AG 2019
J. Shao et al. (Eds.): APWeb-WAIM 2019, LNCS 11642, pp. 310–321, 2019.
https://doi.org/10.1007/978-3-030-26075-0_24

RNN with attention mechanism is becoming the most popular technique for this task. For example, ATAE-LSTM [16] is an LSTM model taking both the target embedding and sentence embedding as input and using an attention mechanism to calculate the representation of the sentence; IAN [7] calculates the target representation and the sentence representation in an interactive way using attention.

There are two categories of gate mechanism: the first separates the sentence using the target words, and uses gates to control the importance of each part, the second uses gates to control the importance of each word. In the first category, BILSTM-ATT-G [6] splits a sentence into three sections including the target, its left contexts and its right contexts, and then represents words in the input using a bidirectional gated recurrent neural network, and then uses three-way gated neural network structure to model the interaction between the target and its left and right contexts. In the second category, ACGE [17] is a model based on convolution neural networks and gating mechanism, which is more accurate and efficient. The gating mechanism can selectively output the sentiment features according to the given target.

Memory networks make use of multiple computational layers to capture the importance of each word. MemNet [12] takes the embedding of sentence words as memories, each layer of the MemNet is a typical attention layer. To overcome the shortcoming of attention mechanism that it cannot capture position information, MemNet employs a position weight. Based on MemNet, RAM [14] uses BiLSTM output as memories. A GRU cell is used to process the representation of each layer in RAM. TNet [5] can also be viewed as a variant of MemNet. It proposes a component to generate a target-specific representation of words in the sentence as well as incorporates a mechanism for preserving the original contextual information from the RNN layer.

These models use LSTM or CNN to process the sentence. LSTM is a sequential model, which is hard to be parallelized. And a single CNN layer does not connect all pairs of input and output positions. To tackle this problem, we propose a model based on transformer and multi-scale convolution. Transformer [15] is solely based on attention mechanisms. Previous works show that language model which is pre-trained on large corpus can generalize well in many different natural language processing tasks. Based on the transformers, OpenAI GPT [10] is one of the best pre-trained language models. We use OpenAI GPT [10] to get the representation of each word. Instead of using the representation of the start token for classification and ignoring the representations of the other tokens, we use a multi-scale convolution to extract n-gram features at many granularities. We conduct extensive experiments on SemEval 2014 Restaurants and Laptops dataset [3] and Twitter dataset, and our framework achieves state-of-the-art results, including improving the accuracy of restaurant dataset to 84.20% (5.81% absolute improvement), improving the accuracy of laptop dataset to 78.21% (4.23% absolute improvement), and improving the accuracy of twitter dataset to 72.98% (0.87% absolute improvement).

Here are our main contributions:

First, we use transformer encoders instead of LSTM or CNN encoders to improve the generalization ability of the model.

Second, multi-scale convolution can learn variable n-gram features flexibly.

Third, our model gets state-of-the-art performance on widely used datasets.

2   Transformer and Multi-scale Convolution for Target-Oriented Sentiment Analysis

In this section, we will introduce our model which combines transformer and multi-scale convolution. Figure 1 shows the structure of our model. We concatenate the sentence and the target. A multi-layer transformer is used the process the input. The multi-scale convolution learns variable n-gram features flexibly. We begin this section by presenting the problem formulation, and then describe the structure of the transformer. At last, we talk about the multi-scale convolution structure.

2.1   Problem Formulation

The input of this task is a target-sentence pair (w^τ, w), where target $w^\tau = \{w_1^\tau, w_2^\tau, ...w_m^\tau\}$ is a subsequence of sentence $w = \{w_1, w_2, ...w_n\}$. The aim of target-oriented sentiment analysis is to predict the sentiment polarity y of the sentence w over the target w^τ, where $y \in \{P, N, O\}$, P, N, O denotes "*positive*", "*negative*" and "*neutral*", respectively. For example, the sentiment polarity of sentence "*great food but the service was dreadful!*" towards target "*food*" is positive, while the sentiment polarity towards target "*service*" is negative.

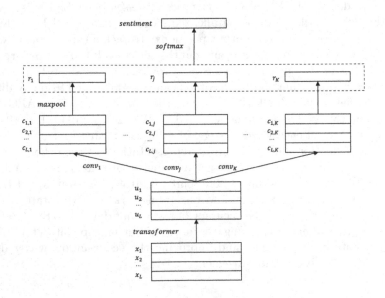

Fig. 1. Model structure

2.2   Transformer

Recurrent and convolution layers are commonly used for mapping one variable-length sequence of symbol representations to another sequence of equal length. Recurrent layers typically factor computation along the symbol positions of the input and the output sequences. Aligning the positions to steps in computation time, they generate a sequence of hidden states. This inherently sequential nature precludes parallelization within training examples, which becomes critical at longer sequence lengths, as memory constraints limit batching across examples. A single convolution layer does not connect all pairs of input and output positions, which makes the path length between long-range dependencies in convolution layer much longer.

Transformer [15] is the first transduction model relying entirely on self-attention to compute representations of its input and output without using sequence aligned RNN or convolution. In this part, we will give a brief introduction to the transformer.

Transformer follows an overall architecture using stacked self-attention and point-wise, fully connected layers, shown in Fig. 2.

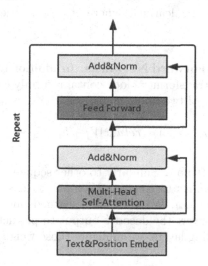

Fig. 2. Structure of transformer

Dot-Product Attention. The scaled dot-product attention is different from the conventional attention mechanisms as its attention weights are computed by a dot-product operation. Given queries $Q \in R^{T_q \times d_k}$, keys $K \in R^{T_v \times d_k}$ and values $V \in R^{T_v \times d_v}$, the attention output is

$$Attention(Q, K, V) = softmax(\frac{QK^T}{\sqrt{d_k}})V \qquad (1)$$

where T_q is the sequence length of queries and T_v is the sequence length of queries and T_v is the sequence length of keys and values. d_k is the vector dimension of queries and keys, and d_v is the vector dimension of values. The sequence length of keys T_v and the sequence length of values T_v are equal. The vector dimension of queries d_k and the vector dimension of keys d_k are equal. $\sqrt{d_k}$ is used for scaling here, which guarantees the numerical stability.

Multi-head Attention. Instead of performing a single attention function with keys, values, and queries, we linearly project the queries, keys, and values h times with different, learned linear projections. Multi-head attention allows the model to jointly attend to information from different representation subspaces at different positions. With a single attention head, averaging inhibits this.

$$MultiHead(Q, K, V) = Concat(head_1, ..., head_h)W^O$$
$$where\ head_i = Attention(QW_i^Q, KW_i^K, VW_i^V) \tag{2}$$

where the projections are fully connected layers without biases. $W_i^Q \in R^{d_{model} \times d_k}$, $W_i^K \in R^{d_{model} \times d_k}$, $W_i^V \in R^{d_{model} \times d_v}$ and $W_O \in R^{hd_v \times d_{model}}$ are the parameters to be learned, where d_{model} is the dimension of token embeddings.

Position-Wise Feed-Forward Networks. In addition to attention sub-layers, each of the layers in a transformer block contains a fully connected feed-forward network, which consists of two linear transformations with a ReLU activation in between.

$$FFN(x) = relu(xW_1 + b_1)W_2 + b_2 \tag{3}$$

Embeddings and Softmax. Similarly to other sequence transduction models, we use learned embeddings to convert the input tokens and output tokens to vectors of dimension d_{model}. We also use a learned linear transformation and softmax function to convert the decoder output to predicted next-token probabilities. In the embedding layers, we multiply those weights by $\sqrt{d_{model}}$.

Positional Encoding. Since the multi-head attention and feed-forward network contain no convolution layers or recurrent cells, positional encoding is essential for leveraging the relative position information in sequence. We use learned position embedding instead of the sinusoidal version proposed in the original work [10].

In this paper, we use a language model which is based on transformers, and the language model is pre-trained on large corpus without supervision. The output of the language model is used as auxiliary features, and then we fine-tune it on target-oriented sentiment analysis task with supervision [10].

2.3   Multi-scale Convolution

We regard the target-oriented sentiment analysis task as a sequence pair classification problem. We concatenate the sentence $w = (w_1, w_2, ..., w_n)$ and the
target $w^\tau = (w_1^\tau, w_2^\tau, ..., w_m^\tau)$, and then add a start token $start$ at the beginning, add an end token end at the end, add a delimiter token del between the
sentence and the target. The concatenated sequence is denoted as X, where
$X = (start, w_1, w_2, ..., w_n, del, w_1^\tau, w_2^\tau, ..., w_m^\tau, end) = (x_1, x_2, ..., x_L)$. X is fed
into a multi-layer transformer to get the representations of each token, where
$L = m + n + 3$. For simplicity, the multi-layer transformer can be denoted as
follows.

$$u_1, u_2, ..., u_L = transformer(x_1, x_2, ..., x_L) \tag{4}$$

Typically, the representation of the start token u_1 is used to represent the
sentence and the target. This method ignores the representations of the other
tokens, which may be helpful to predict the correct sentiment polarity. To tackle
this problem, we use a multi-scale convolution to make use of the representations
of all the tokens. Instead of using a single convolution layer, we use a multi-scale
convolution. In the sentence, there are phrases of different lengths. To extract
the representation of phrases in different length, we use convolution layers with
different filter sizes. We pad the input sequence to keep the length of the output
sequence same as the input sequence. K is the number of different filter sizes.

$$c_{i,j} = tanh(u_{i:i+k_j} * W_j + b_j) \tag{5}$$

where W_j and b_j are the parameters of the j-th convolution, k_j is the filter
size of the j-th convolution. A max pooling layer is then used to get the most
important feature.

$$r_j = max(c_{1,j}, ..., c_{i,j}, ..., c_{L,j}) \tag{6}$$

We concatenate all the max pooling outputs and get the final representation of
the input.

$$r = concat(r_1, ..., r_j, ..., r_K) \tag{7}$$

At last, a fully connected layer with softmax activation is used to predict the
sentiment polarity of this sentence.

$$\hat{y} = softmax(Wr + b) \tag{8}$$

where W and b are the parameters of the fully connected layer.

2.4   Loss Function

The model is trained by minimizing the sum of the language model loss and
classification loss.

$$Loss = Loss_{lm} + Loss_{clf} \tag{9}$$

$\hat{x}_i$ is the i-th output of the language model, where $i \in [1, L]$. The language model
loss is

$$Loss_{lm} = \sum_i \sum_n \hat{x}_{i,n} log(x_{i,n}) \tag{10}$$

where n is the index of a data sample, i is the index of word. The classification loss is a cross-entropy loss between the ground-truth y and the predicted value $\hat{y}$ for all data samples.

$$Loss_{clf} = \sum_i \sum_j \hat{y}_{i,j} log(y_{i,j}) \tag{11}$$

where i is the index of a data sample, j is the index of a sentiment class.

3   Experiments

We describe the experimental setting and report experimental results in this section.

3.1   Experimental Setting

We conduct experiments on three datasets: Restaurant and Laptop are from SemEval ABSA challenge [3]; Twitter is a target-oriented sentiment analysis dataset [2] which contains twitter posts. Table 1 shows the statistics of these datasets. These datasets are the most widely used datasets in target-oriented sentiment analysis. Following other previous work [5,11], we remove some examples having the "conflict" label. All tokens are lowercased, and we do not remove any stop words, symbols or digits. All the sentences are padded to the max length using token "PAD". Accuracy and macro-averaged F1 score are used as the main evaluation metric. For each class, precision is defined as $P = \frac{TP}{TP+FN}$, recall is defined as $R = \frac{TP}{TP+FP}$ and the F1 score is computed by $\frac{2PR}{P+R}$. TP, TN, FN and FP are the number of true positives, true negatives, false negatives, and false positives, respectively. The macro-averaged F1 score is the average F1 score across all classes [13].

Table 1. Statistics of the datasets.

Dataset	Positive	Negative	Neutral
Laptop-Train	994	870	464
Laptop-Test	341	128	169
Restaurant-Train	2164	807	637
Restaurant-Test	728	196	196
Twitter-Train	1567	1563	3127
Twitter-Test	174	174	346

Our model is compared with the following models:

- Majority is a fundamental method which assigns the majority sentiment label in training set to each instance in the test set.

- SVM uses a traditional support vector machine using n-gram features, parse features and lexicon features [4].
- AE-LSTM is a simple LSTM model that takes the target embedding and sentence embedding as input [16].
- ATAE-LSTM extends AE-LSTM with attention mechanism [16].
- IAN calculates the target representation and sentence representation in an interactively way [7].
- BILSTM-ATT-G uses gates to measure the importance of the left context and the right context, which is separated by the target [6].
- ACSA-GCAE is a model based on convolution neural networks and gating mechanisms, which is more accurate and efficient [17].
- MemNet takes the word embeddings as memory and uses a multi-layer attention mechanism to get the final representation of the sentence. Attention mechanism cannot capture position information, MemNet also uses position weights to overcome this shortcoming [12].
- RAM is an extension of the MemNet model. Different from MemNet, it uses BiLSTM hidden states as memory. A GRU cell is used to process the sentence representation of each layer. A different position weight is used for RAM [14].
- TNet propose a component to generate target-specific representations of words in the sentence, meanwhile incorporate a mechanism for preserving the original contextual information from the RNN layer [5].

We re-implemented most of these baseline models using pytorch[1] to make their results as similar as possible to those in the original papers. Each model is optimized independently. For these models, we use pre-trained GloVe vectors [9] to initialize the word embeddings and the embedding dimension is 300. We follow the parameter settings in the original paper of the baselines. The implementation of these models are available[2].

We use a 12-layer transformer with self-attention heads (768 dimensional states and 12 attention heads). We first load the pre-trained weights from OpenAI GPT, and then we fine-tune the parameters with the follow-up structures. We use five different filter sizes (from 1 to 5) for the multi-scale convolution layer. And the convolution channel is set to 100. We use Adam optimizer, and the learning rate is set to 6.25e-5. The model gets the best result within 20 epochs. The source code of our model is open and available[3].

3.2 Main Result

Table 2 shows the main results of our experiments. As the table shows, our model gets the best performance on Restaurant, Laptop, and Twitter dataset. We get 84.20% accuracy (5.81% absolute improvement) on restaurant dataset, 78.21% accuracy (4.23% absolute improvement) on laptop dataset, and 72.98% accuracy (0.87% absolute improvement) on twitter dataset.

---

[1] https://pytorch.org/.

[2] https://github.com/Cppowboy/ABSC_APWEBWAIM.git.

[3] https://github.com/Cppowboy/APWEB-WAIM.git.

LSTM has the worst performance of all neural networks. ATAE-LSTM improves its performance by taking the target into account and using the attention mechanism. IAN works better because it uses two attention layers. For the twitter dataset, BILSTM-ATT-G and RAM cannot perform as efficiently as they do in restaurant and laptop dataset, because they are heavily rooted in LSTM, which is not good at processing ungrammatical sentences. TNet is a model based on LSTM and CNN, which makes it works well on all the three datasets. Different from previous models, our model is based on transformers, which can solve long term dependencies and can be easily parallelized. The multi-scale convolution layer in our model can extract multi-grained features. The transformer and multi-scale convolution structure help our model get the best performance on all the three datasets.

Table 2. Experiment results (%). The result with symbol "*" is retrieved from the original paper.

Models	Restaurant		Laptop		Twitter	
	ACC	Macro-F1	ACC	Macro-F1	ACC	Macro-F1
Majority	65.00	-	53.45	-	50.00	22.22
SVM	80.89	-	72.10	-	63.40	63.30
LSTM	76.70	63.57	69.28	63.30	66.04	63.46
ATAE-LSTM	77.23	63.73	69.44	63.46	71.24	69.19
IAN	78.60*	-	72.10*	-	-	-
BILSTM-ATT-G	79.20	67.07	71.32	64.88	71.68	70.37
GCAE	78.12	62.50	70.38	64.02	72.40	70.89
MemNet	77.86	64.47	68.18	62.46	69.80	66.86
RAM	78.30	65.42	71.63	66.73	71.24	68.75
TNet	78.39	65.37	73.98	68.64	72.11	70.01
Ours	84.20	76.35	78.21	73.31	72.98	71.40

3.3 Effectiveness of Pretraining

To show the effectiveness of the pre-training procedure, we train our model twice: the first time we use pre-trained parameters from the OpenAI GPT and then fine-tune the parameters, the second time we train the model from scratch. The experiments are conducted on the restaurant and laptop dataset. Table 3 shows the result of the experiments.

As the table shows, training from scratch works poorly, and the pre-trained work has a significant performance gain. We observe that the lack of pre-training hurts performances, resulting in a considerable performance decrease compared to our full model.

Table 3. Effectiveness of pre-training

Models	Restaurant		Laptop	
	ACC	Marco-F1	ACC	Marco-F1
w/o pre-training	69.20	48.16	64.89	59.25
w/ pre-training	84.20	76.35	78.21	73.31

3.4 Effectiveness of Multi-scale Convolution

In this part, we design a simple model without multi-scale convolution. The simplified model uses the representation of the first token as the representation of the input and uses a fully connected layer for classification. Another model we used is our full model. The experiments are conducted on the restaurant and laptop dataset. Table 4 shows the result of the experiments. As the table shows, the multi-scale convolution layer improves the performance of our model (including 0.81% improvement for the restaurant dataset and 0.78% improvement for the laptop dataset).

Table 4. Effectiveness of multi-scale CNN

Models	Restaurant		Laptop	
	ACC	Marco-F1	ACC	Marco-F1
w/o cnn	83.39	74.40	77.43	72.42
w/ cnn	84.20	76.35	78.21	73.31

3.5 Case Study

Table 5 shows some sample cases. The input targets are wrapped in the brackets with the correct labels given as subscripts. The notations P, N and O in the table represent positive, negative and neutral respectively. For example, for the target "coffee" in the first sentence, the sentiment polarity is positive.

Our model can predict target sentiment more accurately than ATAE-LSTM and GCAE. ATAE-LSTM is an LSTM based model, which relies on sequential information. It can perform well for formal sentences. For the first two sentences, ATAE-LSTM gets the correct prediction, while GCAE fails to get the correct prediction. GCAE is a CNN based model, which is good at processing ungrammatical text. For the third and the fourth sentence, GCAE get the correct prediction, while ATAE-LSTM fails to get the correct prediction. Our model is a transformer based model, which can process both grammatical and ungrammatical sentences. And our model can solve some difficult cases. For the fifth and the sixth sentence, our model can extract the sentimental relation between context words such as negation and comparison. For the last sentence, because of the multi-scale convolution layer, our model can deal with the noncompositional sentiment expression "what I go for" and make the correct prediction.

Table 5. Example predictions. The input targets are wrapped in brackets with the true labels given as subscripts. ✗ indicates incorrect prediction.

Sentence	ATAE-LSTM	GCAE	Ours
[Coffee]$_P$ is a better deal than overpriced sandwiches	P	$O^{\text{✗}}$	P
But make sure you have enough room on your credit card as the [bill]$_P$ will leave a big dent in your wallet	P	$O^{\text{✗}}$	P
Aww, it's okay... You have a [PSP]$_P$. :D That's good already	$O^{\text{✗}}$	P	P
I hate my [iPod]$_N$! It's dead! dead dead dead! ! ! Someone wanna fix it for me?	$O^{\text{✗}}$	N	N
I have never had a bad [meal]$_P$ (or bad service) at pigalle	$N^{\text{✗}}$	$N^{\text{✗}}$	P
The [staff]$_N$ should be a bit more friendly	$P^{\text{✗}}$	$P^{\text{✗}}$	N
It's a basic pizza joint, not much to look at, but the [pizza]$_P$ is what I go for	$N^{\text{✗}}$	$O^{\text{✗}}$	P

4 Conclusion

In this paper, we proposed a model, which combines transformer and multi-scale convolution. The transformer can solve long term dependencies and can be easily parallelized. The multi-scale convolution can extract multi-grained features. The performance of our model consistently dominates previous state-of-the-art methods on different types of data. The experiments show the efficacy of different modules of our model.

References

1. Chollet, F.: Xception: deep learning with depthwise separable convolutions. In: Proceedings of the IEEE Conference on Computer Vision and Pattern Recognition, pp. 1251–1258 (2017)
2. Dong, L., Wei, F., Tan, C., Tang, D., Zhou, M., Xu, K.: Adaptive recursive neural network for target-dependent twitter sentiment classification. In: Proceedings of the 52nd Annual Meeting of the Association for Computational Linguistics (Volume 2: Short Papers), vol. 2, pp. 49–54 (2014)
3. Kirange, D., Deshmukh, R.R.: Emotion classification of restaurant and laptop review dataset: SemEval 2014 task 4. Int. J. Comput. Appl. **113**(6) (2015)
4. Kiritchenko, S., Zhu, X., Cherry, C., Mohammad, S.: NRC-Canada-2014: detecting aspects and sentiment in customer reviews. In: Proceedings of the 8th International Workshop on Semantic Evaluation (SemEval 2014), pp. 437–442 (2014)
5. Li, X., Bing, L., Lam, W., Shi, B.: Transformation networks for target-oriented sentiment classification. arXiv preprint arXiv:1805.01086 (2018)

6. Liu, J., Zhang, Y.: Attention modeling for targeted sentiment. In: Proceedings of the 15th Conference of the European Chapter of the Association for Computational Linguistics: Volume 2, Short Papers, vol. 2, pp. 572–577 (2017)
7. Ma, D., Li, S., Zhang, X., Wang, H.: Interactive attention networks for aspect-level sentiment classification. arXiv preprint arXiv:1709.00893 (2017)
8. Nakov, P., Ritter, A., Rosenthal, S., Sebastiani, F., Stoyanov, V.: SemEval-2016 task 4: sentiment analysis in twitter. In: Proceedings of the 10th International Workshop on Semantic Evaluation (SemEval-2016), pp. 1–18 (2016)
9. Pennington, J., Socher, R., Manning, C.: Glove: global vectors for word representation. In: Proceedings of the 2014 Conference on Empirical Methods in Natural Language Processing (EMNLP), pp. 1532–1543 (2014)
10. Radford, A., Narasimhan, K., Salimans, T., Sutskever, I.: Improving language understanding by generative pre-training (2018). https://s3-us-west-2.amazonaws.com/openai-assets/research-covers/language-unsupervised/language_understanding_paper.pdf
11. Tang, D., Qin, B., Feng, X., Liu, T.: Effective LSTMs for target-dependent sentiment classification. arXiv preprint arXiv:1512.01100 (2015)
12. Tang, D., Qin, B., Liu, T.: Aspect level sentiment classification with deep memory network. arXiv preprint arXiv:1605.08900 (2016)
13. Tay, Y., Tuan, L.A., Hui, S.C.: Dyadic memory networks for aspect-based sentiment analysis. In: Proceedings of the 2017 ACM on Conference on Information and Knowledge Management, pp. 107–116. ACM (2017)
14. Tran, K., Bisazza, A., Monz, C.: Recurrent memory networks for language modeling. arXiv preprint arXiv:1601.01272 (2016)
15. Vaswani, A., et al.: Attention is all you need. In: Advances in Neural Information Processing Systems, pp. 5998–6008 (2017)
16. Wang, Y., Huang, M., Zhao, L., et al.: Attention-based LSTM for aspect-level sentiment classification. In: Proceedings of the 2016 Conference on Empirical Methods in Natural Language Processing, pp. 606–615 (2016)
17. Zhang, M., Zhang, Y., Vo, D.T.: Gated neural networks for targeted sentiment analysis. In: AAAI, pp. 3087–3093 (2016)

A New Feature Selection Algorithm Based on Category Difference for Text Categorization

Wang Zhang[1,2], Chanjuan Chen[3], Lei Jiang[1], and Xu Bai[1(✉)]

[1] Institute of Information Engineering, Chinese Academy of Sciences, Beijing, China
{zhangwang,baixu}@iie.ac.cn
[2] School of Cyber Security, University of Chinese Academy of Sciences, Beijing, China
[3] China National Machinery Industry Corporation, Beijing, China

Abstract. The feature selection is an important step which can reduce the dimensionality and improve the performance of the classifiers in text categorization. Many popular feature selection methods do not consider the difference in the distribution of different categories on a feature. In this paper, we propose a new filter based feature selection algorithm, namely fused distance feature selection (FDFS), which evaluates the significance of a feature by taking account of the difference in the distribution of different categories and selects more discriminative features with the minimal number. The proposed algorithm is investigated both inside and outside perspectives on four benchmark document datasets, 20-Newsgroups, WebKB, CSDMC2010 and Ohsumed, using Linear Support Vector Machine (LSVM) and Multinomial Naïve Bayes (MNB) classifiers. The experimental results indicate that our proposed method provides a competitive result, where its average ranking is 1.25 on LSVM and 1 on MNB.

Keywords: Feature selection · Text classification · Text mining

1 Introduction

The number of digital documents available on the Internet has been growing significantly in recent years. In every minute of 2018, Google receives 3,877,140 search queries, Twitter users send 473,400 tweets and people send 159,362,760 emails [6]. It is necessary to develop more efficient techniques to process such a large amount of text data. Text classification is described as a construction problem of models which can classify new documents into pre-defined classes [8] and it finds applications in a wide variety of domains in text mining such as document retrieval, opinion mining and spam filtering [4]. Text classification contains three stage processes: feature preprocessing, feature selection/projection and classification [11]. Many text mining methods use the bag-of-words representation where the frequency of each word is used as a feature due to its simplicity in feature

© Springer Nature Switzerland AG 2019
J. Shao et al. (Eds.): APWeb-WAIM 2019, LNCS 11642, pp. 322–336, 2019.
https://doi.org/10.1007/978-3-030-26075-0_25

preprocessing. However, the feature vector of every document using the bag-of-words model is sparse and high dimensional. Therefore, feature selection is a very important task for text classification and it ensures that the features which are most relevant to particular class labels can be picked out for model training.

Feature selection techniques are generally divided into three categories: filter, wrapper, and embedded. The filter methods first use an evaluation function to compute the score of every feature. Then all features are sorted according to the score, and top-k features are selected to form a feature subset for model training. Thus, it only relies on the data itself and is independent of any classification algorithm. The wrapper methods use the performance of the classifier as the evaluation criterion to select a feature subset. It selects the feature subset that yields the best performance for the learning algorithm. Thus, it may significantly increase computation time and overfitting risk. The embedded methods combine feature selection steps with the learning algorithm. It becomes an implicit part of their learning algorithm. The wrappers and embedded methods require a frequent classifier interaction in their flow, thus, filter-based methods are preferred more in comparison to wrappers and embedded methods [5].

Many classical feature selection methods such as Information Gain, improved Gini Index and Chi-square, usually consider the probability of class c_i when term t_k is present or absent, and select the representative terms of a class. However, they may ignore the difference in the distribution of different categories on a term. For example, both class c_a and class c_b contain term t_1. Word frequency of term t_1 of all samples in class c_a is 1 and word frequency of term t_1 of all samples in class c_b is 5. If we use Information Gain method to select features, the information gain on term t_1 is zero because both class c_a and class c_b contain term t_1. It is difficult to distinguish the instances of the class c_a and class c_b in this case. While term t_1 is also a discriminative feature due to the enormous difference between class c_a and class c_b on term t_1. Our proposed method focuses on two kinds of difference in the distribution of categories and avoid the above situation. Besides, we also adopt two-stage greedy strategy to take full advantage of the two kinds of category difference.

Our main contributions are listed as follows:

- we present a new metric, fused distance, using two kinds of difference on a term, to measure the representation of every feature more accurately.
- we present a new filter based feature selection algorithm, FDFS, using the proposed evaluation function and two-stage greedy strategy, to pick out more discriminative features with the minimal number.

The rest of this paper is organized as follows. The related work is discussed in Sect. 2. The details of our approach are described in Sect. 3. The experimental results and discussion are presented in Sect. 4. Finally, the paper is concluded in Sect. 5.

2   Related Work

There are some commonly used feature selection methods such as Information Gain [10], Improved Gini Index [12], Chi-square [19], Orthogonal Centroid Feature Selection [15] and Distinguishing Feature Selector [14]. Information Gain and Chi-square are the two most effective feature selection methods [19]. Improved Gini index is an improved feature selection based on Gini index and it is reported that Improved Gini Index performs more effective than Information Gain and Chi-square [12]. Orthogonal Centroid Feature Selection optimizes the objective function in a discrete solution space and outperforms Information Gain and Chi-square in terms of classification accuracy and computation [15]. Distinguishing Feature Selector selects distinctive features which frequently occur in a single class or occur in some of the classes and rarely occur in the other classes [14].

There are also many significant works about feature selection for text categorization. Pinheiro et al. [9] proposed a feature selection method called ALOFT, which ensures every document is represented by at least one feature. Yang et al. [17] proposed a feature selection method called CMFS that measures the score of a term both in inter-category and intra-category. Rehman et al. [11] improved the feature selection method ACC2 by taking account of the relative document frequencies and proposed a new feature selection method named NDM. Zhang et al. [20] proposed a combined feature selection method with inter-category and intra-category divergence. Labani et al. [7] took advantage of minimal-redundancy and maximal-relevancy concepts to reduce redundant features and select relevancy ones. Variable Global Feature Selection Scheme (VGFSS) selects a variable number of features from each class to introduce more important features in the final feature set [5]. Meaning Based Feature Selection (MBFS) selects the meaningful features based on the Helmholtz principle from the Gestalt theory of human perception [13]. However, many classical feature selection methods ignore the difference in the distribution of different categories on a feature. These methods may miss some important features. Different from previous work, our method utilizes two kinds of category difference and selects more representative features.

3   Feature Selection Method

In this section, we firstly describe three basic distance methods in Sects. 3.1, 3.2 and 3.3, respectively. We then present our fused distance metric and FDFS algorithm in Sect. 3.4.

3.1   Global Distance Method

To improve the above predicament, centroid u_{ik} and standard deviation sd_{ik} are used as the representative of the distribution of class c_i on a feature (term) t_k. More exactly, centroid u_{ik} is used to measure the difference between categories and standard deviation sd_{ik} is used to find out clusters on a feature. For example, as seen in Fig. 1(a), the difference of centroid on feature 2 is the same as on feature 1. However, the clustering effect of class a and b on feature 2 is more obvious, in other words, the sum of standard deviation on feature 1 is larger than on feature 2. Thus, feature 2 is more valuable than feature 1.

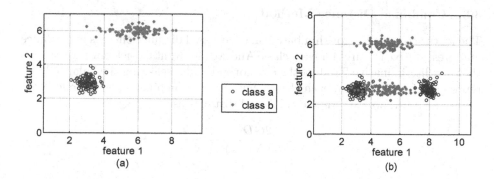

Fig. 1. Two examples for distance method

Mathematically, global distance is defined as:

$$GD_k = \frac{1}{\sum_{i=1}^{N} sd_{ik}} \sum_{i=1}^{N} \sum_{j=i+1}^{N} |u_{ik} - u_{jk}| \tag{1}$$

where N is the number of categories, u_{ik} and sd_{ik} is the centroid and standard deviation of class c_i on a feature (term) t_k.

Global distance algorithm firstly obtains centroid u_{ik} and standard deviation sd_{ik} for each class, then calculates the sum of the distance between different category pairs (Eq. (1)), and finally selects top-K features (terms) based on the score of the metric method.

3.2   Type-Based Distance Method

The global distance method may have a problem that sometimes a class is lack of their representative features and is difficult for the classifier to distinguish it. The global distance method may neglect the distance between a specific category and others, and cause an imbalance problem in text categorization [18]. Thus, it is necessary to ensure the balance of representative features for each class. To solve this problem, type-based distance is defined as:

$$TD_{ik} = \frac{1}{\sum_{i=1}^{N} sd_{ik}} \sum_{j=1}^{N} |u_{ik} - u_{jk}| \tag{2}$$

For each class c_i, we calculate the distance TD_{ik} between this class and others, then average the requested number of features to each class to ensure

326 W. Zhang et al.

the balance of their representative features. In other words, we just select K/N (K is the total requested number of features and N is the total number of categories.) features for each class based on their TD_{ik} scores. It ensures that every class obtains equal and enough representative features.

3.3 Combined Distance Method

The feature selection algorithm based on type-based distance ensures the balance of representative features for each class. And we also want to pick out the features that are discriminative for all of the categories besides selecting the balanced and representative features for each class. Thus, we can combine global distance with type-based distance, and define combined distance as:

$$CD_{ik} = \frac{2GD_k}{N(N-1)} + \frac{TD_{ik}}{N-1} \tag{3}$$

3.4 Fused Distance Method

Sometimes, it's not accurate to find out the main difference in the distribution of different categories on a feature by using the above distance method. The distribution of different categories may be very complicated. For example, as seen in Fig. 1(b), although global distance on feature 2 is more larger, there is less overlap between class a and b on feature 1. Thus, feature 1 is more valuable than feature 2. This is due to the deviation of centroid. We should pick out the features that contain unique and enough representative difference for every category especially when the number of selected features is small. Thus, we define type-based difference rate as:

$$DR_{ik} = \frac{1}{N-1} \sum_{j=1}^{N} \frac{1}{2} \sum_{x \in X_k} |p_{ik}(x) - p_{jk}(x)| \tag{4}$$

where X_k is a set of all values on feature k, $p_{ik}(x)$ is the probability of class i having value x on feature k. By fusing difference rate, we define fused distance as:

$$FD_{ik} = CD_{ik} * DR_{ik} \tag{5}$$

However, we can't just select features based on their FD_{ik} scores due to the inherent characteristics of probability. Type-based difference rate can find the difference in probability, thus, we introduce it into combined distance and pick out the features that contain unique and enough representative for every category. We utilize type-based difference rate to compensate for the deviation of centroid. However, fused distance scores are of little value when difference rate is small.

Thus, we introduce two-stage greedy strategy to make up for the above faults. The two-stage greedy strategy is introduced as shown in Fig. 2. The motivation is to take advantage of the fused distance containing the difference information in probability and clustering effect information to find the main representative characteristics of each category, then use combined distance to find the remaining bits and pieces of representative characteristics of each category. Fused distance method not only introduces the difference information in probability, but also fuses another distance information. We present the fused distance feature selection algorithm as follows (see Algorithm 1).

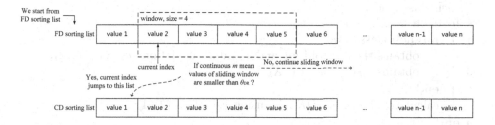

Fig. 2. Two-stage greedy strategy

The fused distance feature selection algorithm first select features from FD_{ik} list. At the same time, we calculate the mean value of original DR_{ik} values in current sliding window. If continuous m mean values are smaller than θ_{DR}, we consider that the remaining features in FD_{ik} list are of little value. We present the relationships of four distance methods in Fig. 3.

The computational complexity of FDFS consists of two parts. The calculation of four distance methods requires $O(|\overline{D}_i|NM)$, where $|\overline{D}_i|$ is the average size of each class c_i, where N is the total number of categories, M is the total number of features. And the selecting features costs $O(NM^2)$. Thus, the total time complexity is $O(|\overline{D}_i|NM + NM^2)$.

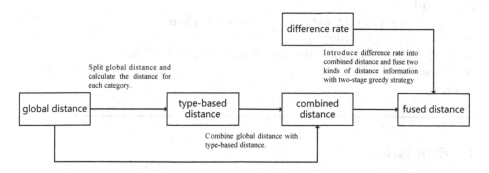

Fig. 3. The relationships of four distance methods

Algorithm 1. fused distance feature selection algorithm

Input: D - the preprocessed data set, K - the requested number of features, θ_{DR} - minimum threshold for difference rate, Δ_{win} - the size of sliding window, m - the number of continuous mean values of difference rate in sliding window

Output: S - the selected feature subset

1 $S=\{\}$;
2 averages the requested number of features and sets the selected number of each class c_i as n_i;
3 **foreach** *term* t_k **do**
4   **foreach** *class* c_i **do**
5   obtains the centroid u_{ik} and standard deviation sd_{ik} of class c_i;
6   obtains $p_{ik}(x)$ for $\forall x \in X_k$;
7   **end**
8   calculates the TD_{ik}, DR_{ik} by using Equation (2)(4);
9 **end**
10 calculates the GD_k, CD_{ik} and FD_{ik};
11 **foreach** *class* c_i **do**
12   arranges all terms in descending order based on their FD_{ik} and CD_{ik}, respectively, then get FD_i and CD_i list;
13      $num_{FD} = 0$;
14   **while** $num_{FD} < n_i$ **do**
15   select current feature from FD_i list into S;
16          $num_{FD} + +$;
17   calculates the mean value of original DR_{ik} values in current sliding window (from *current index* to *current index*$+\Delta_{win}$);
18   **if** *continuous* m *mean values are smaller than* θ_{DR} **then**
19   convert to CD_i list;
20   break;
21   **end**
22   **end**
23   **if** *convert to* CD_i *list* **and** $n_i > num_{FD}$ **then**
24          $rest = n_i - num_{FD}$;
25   selects top-*rest* terms into S according to CD_i list;
26   **end**
27 **end**
28 **return** S;

---

4   Evaluation

In this section, we use four datasets to fully verify the presented feature selection algorithm, and show the experimental results on 20-Newsgroups, WebKB, CSDMC2010 and Ohsumed datasets in Sects. 4.1, 4.2, 4.3 and 4.4, respectively. Finally, we discuss the above experiments in Sect. 4.5.

We employ two famous different classification algorithms, Linear Support Vector Machine (LSVM) and Multinomial Naïve Bayes (MNB), to prove the efficacy of the proposed method. The above classification methods have been widely used in text classification research and proved to be very successful [4].

In all experiments, two well known F1 measures, Macro-F1 and Micro-F1 [14], were used to evaluate the performance. Mathematically, Macro-F1 and Micro-F1 can be formulated as:

$$Macro\text{-}F1 = \frac{\sum_{k=1}^{N} \frac{2*p_k*r_k}{p_k+r_k}}{N} \qquad (6)$$

$$Micro\text{-}F1 = \frac{2*p*r}{p+r} \qquad (7)$$

where N is the total number of categories. p_k and r_k correspond to precision and recall values of class c_k, respectively. p and r correspond to the accuracy and recall values of all classification decisions within the entire data set, respectively.

We set $m = 2$ and $\Delta_{win} = 10$ in all experiments. We suggest the value of θ_{DR} ranges from 0.01 to 0.2. We removed stop words and used bag-of-words model to preprocess the datasets.

4.1 20-Newsgroups

The 20-Newsgroups [3] dataset collects about 20,000 newsgroup documents and is evenly divided into 20 different categories. In this experiment, we used by date version of the dataset, which contains 18846 documents and is sorted by date into training (60%) and test (40%) sets. After preprocessing, the dimension of the features is 129326. We set $\theta_{DR} = 0.1$ in this experiment.

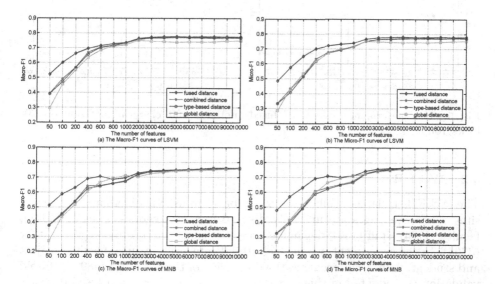

Fig. 4. The performance curves of four distance methods on 20-Newsgroups

The performance curves of four distance methods on 20-Newsgroups are drawn in Fig. 4. It shows that fused, combined and type-based distance methods are always superior to global distance method with 6 exceptions on MNB classifier. Fused method is significantly superior to combined method when the number of selected features is small, combined method is a bit superior to type-based method, and there is no obvious difference between the above three methods when the number of selected features is large.

The performance curves of fused distance methods and five classical methods (Information Gain, Improved Gini Index, Chi-square, Orthogonal Centroid Feature Selection and Distinguishing Feature Selector) on 20-Newsgroups are drawn in Fig. 5. The curve of fused method approaches unselected curve first. Specifically, fused distance method using LSVM classifier produces the highest macro-F1 values in 15 out of 16 cases and the highest micro-F1 values in 16 out of 16 cases. And it also produces the highest macro-F1 values in 12 out of 16 cases and the highest micro-F1 values in 13 out of 16 cases on MNB classifier.

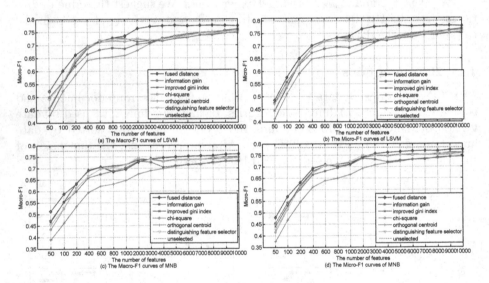

Fig. 5. The performance curves of fused methods and classical methods on 20-Newsgroups

4.2   WebKB

The WebKB [1] dataset collects 8282 webpages from four different college websites. These webpages are unevenly divided into 7 categories: student (1641), faculty (1124), staff (137), department (182), course (930), project (504), other (3764). In the experiment, we just selected 4 categories: course, faculty, project and student. After preprocessing, the dimension of the features is 48909. 10-fold validation was adopted in this experiment. We set $\theta_{DR} = 0.2$ in fused distance method.

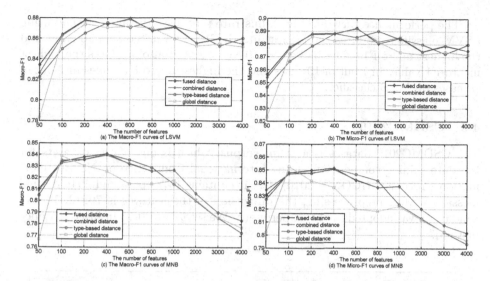

Fig. 6. The performance curves of four distance methods on WebKB

As seen in Fig. 6, fused, combined and type-based distance methods are always superior to global distance method. Fused distance method is also superior to combined distance method when the number of selected features is small. As for combined and type-based distance methods, their curves are indented and intertwined. However, averaged Macro-F1 and Micro-F1 values of combined method are higher than type-based method.

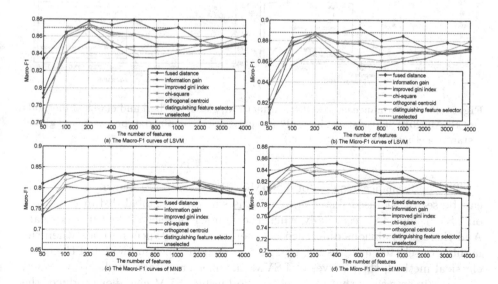

Fig. 7. The performance curves of fused methods and classical methods on WebKB

The performance curves in Fig. 7 illustrate that fused distance method using LSVM classifier produces the highest macro-F1 values in 8 out of 10 cases and the highest micro-F1 values in 8 out of 10 cases. And it also produces the highest macro-F1 values in 7 out of 10 cases and the highest micro-F1 values in 7 out of 10 cases on MNB classifier.

4.3 CSDMC2010

The CSDMC2010 dataset is a spam corpus, which is one of the datasets for the data mining competition at the International Conference on Neural Information Processing (ICONIP 2010) [16]. It contains 1378 spam and 2949 normal messages. After preprocessing, the dimension of the features is 79212. 10-fold validation was adopted in this experiment. We set $\theta_{DR} = 0.15$ in fused distance method.

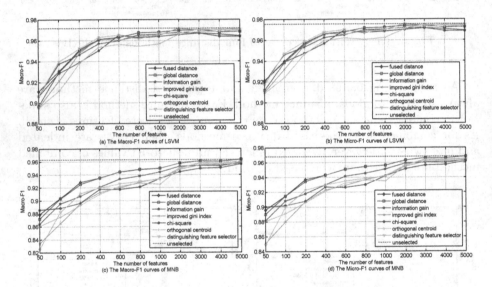

Fig. 8. The performance curves of fused method, global method and classical methods on CSDMC2010 (This dataset has only two categories, combined, type-based and global distance methods are the same ones.)

The performance results for CSDMC2010 dataset are shown in Fig. 8. It can be seen that fused distance method is superior to global distance method on LSVM and MNB especially when the number of selected features is small. And there is no obvious difference between the two distance methods when the number of selected features is large. As for fused distance method and the other classical method, their curves of LSVM classifier are intertwined. To be exact, the experiments show that distance method using LSVM classifier produces the highest macro-F1 values in 3 out of 11 cases and the highest micro-F1 values in

3 out of 11 cases. And it also produces the highest macro-F1 values in 10 out of 11 cases and the highest micro-F1 values in 10 out of 11 cases on MNB classifier.

4.4   Ohsumed

Ohsumed [2] includes medical abstracts from the MeSH categories. We use the first 20,000 documents and remove duplicate documents. It remains 13929 (6286 for training and 7643 for testing) abstracts. After preprocessing, the dimension of the features is 29809. We set $\theta_{DR} = 0.08$ in this experiment.

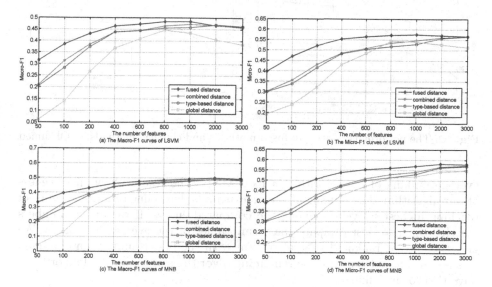

Fig. 9. The performance curves of four distance methods on Ohsumed

The performance curves in Fig. 9 illustrate that fused distance method outperforms the other methods with 2 exceptions on LSVM classifier. Fused distance method is significantly superior to three distance method especially when the number of selected features is small. And combined distance method is a bit superior to type-based distance method. Global distance method is not good enough in most cases.

As seen in Fig. 10, the experiments show that fused distance method using LSVM classifier produces the highest macro-F1 values in 9 out of 9 cases and the highest micro-F1 values in 6 out of 9 cases. And it also produces the highest macro-F1 values in 9 out of 9 cases and the highest micro-F1 values in 6 out of 9 cases on MNB classifier.

4.5   Discussion

In order to compare the performance of the proposed method with the previous approaches, the rankings of the six algorithms are shown in Table 1. The average ranking of our algorithm is 1.25 when using the LSVM classifier. And the

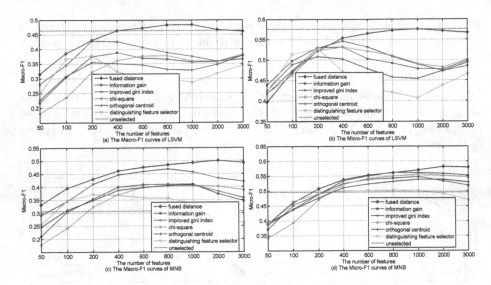

Fig. 10. The performance curves of fused methods and classical methods on Ohsumed

average ranking of our algorithm is 1 on MNB. The results show effectiveness of our algorithm. The ranking of the algorithm is determined by the number of reaching highest F1 values among the compared curves. If the above numbers are the same, we just compare the mean values of the average-F1 curves. We give the current ranking to the algorithm with the best results, then eliminate this algorithm and compare the remaining algorithms again until all algorithms have their own rankings.

Table 1. Algorithm ranking table

	LSVM						MNB					
	FD	IG	IGINI	CHI2	OCFS	DFS	FD	IG	IGINI	CHI2	OCFS	DFS
20-ng	1	2	5	4	6	3	1	5	2	4	6	3
WebKB	1	3	5	2	6	4	1	4	5	3	6	2
CSDMC	2	4	3	5	6	1	1	2	5	6	4	3
Ohsumed	1	4	2	3	5	6	1	4	2	3	5	6
Average ranking	1.25	3.25	3.75	3.5	5.75	3.5	1	3.75	3.5	4	5.25	3.5

In general, the results of 20-Newsgroups, WebKB, CSDMC2010 and Ohsumed show that our method, FDFS, outperforms the other classical metrics in 87.50%, 75.00%, 59.09% and 83.33% cases, respectively. This result also shows effectiveness of our algorithm. Among the four distance methods, we observe that fused, combined and type-based methods are superior to global distance method in most cases. This demonstrates the importance of picking out balanced features for different categories. We also observe that combined method is a little better than type-based method. This reveals that it is beneficial to introduce global information not just based on local information. As seen in above experiments, fused method outperforms the other three distance methods especially when the number of selected features is small. It shows the significance of firstly picking out the features that contain the main distinguishing information.

5   Conclusion

In this paper, we present a new filter based feature selection algorithm, which focuses on fusing the difference in the distribution of different categories, to improve the performance of text classification. The experimental results show that FDFS, that fuses two kinds of distance between categories, outperforms five classical methods (Information Gain, Improved Gini Index, Chi-square, Orthogonal Centroid Feature Selection and Distinguishing Feature Selector) on 20 newsgroups, WebKB, CSDMC2010 and Ohsumed datasets in 87.50%, 75.00%, 59.09% and 83.33% of the classification cases, respectively. And the average ranking of our proposed method is 1.25 on LSVM and 1 on MNB. The above experimental results also show the effectiveness of our algorithm. In the future, we will continue to optimize the performance and computational efficiency of the algorithm.

Acknowledgement. This paper is Supported by National Science Foundation for Young Scientists of China (Grant No. 61702507).

References

1. The 4 universities data set (1998). http://www.cs.cmu.edu/afs/cs.cmu.edu/project/theo-20/www/data/. Accessed 4 June 2018
2. Text categorization corpora (2004). http://disi.unitn.it/moschitti/corpora.htm. Accessed 4 June 2018
3. Home page for 20 newsgroups data set (2008). http://www.qwone.com/~jason/20Newsgroups/. Accessed 4 June 2018
4. Aggarwal, C.C., Zhai, C.: A survey of text classification algorithms. In: Aggarwal, C., Zhai, C. (eds.) Mining Text Data, pp. 163–222. Springer, Boston (2012). https://doi.org/10.1007/978-1-4614-3223-4_6
5. Agnihotri, D., Verma, K., Tripathi, P.: Variable global feature selection scheme for automatic classification of text documents. Expert Syst. Appl. **81**, 268–281 (2017)
6. James, J.: Data never sleeps 6.0 (2018). https://www.domo.com/blog/data-never-sleeps-6/. Accessed 4 July 2018
7. Labani, M., Moradi, P., Ahmadizar, F., Jalili, M.: A novel multivariate filter method for feature selection in text classification problems. Eng. Appl. Artif. Intell. **70**, 25–37 (2018)
8. Mirończuk, M.M., Protasiewicz, J.: A recent overview of the state-of-the-art elements of text classification. Expert Syst. Appl. **106**, 36–54 (2018)

9. Pinheiro, R.H., Cavalcanti, G.D., Correa, R.F., Ren, T.I.: A global-ranking local feature selection method for text categorization. Expert Syst. Appl. **39**(17), 12851–12857 (2012)
10. Quinlan, J.R.: Induction of decision trees. Mach. Learn. **1**(1), 81–106 (1986)
11. Rehman, A., Javed, K., Babri, H.A.: Feature selection based on a normalized difference measure for text classification. Inf. Process. Manag. **53**(2), 473–489 (2017)
12. Shang, W., Huang, H., Zhu, H., Lin, Y., Qu, Y., Wang, Z.: A novel feature selection algorithm for text categorization. Expert Syst. Appl. **33**(1), 1–5 (2007)
13. Tutkan, M., Ganiz, M.C., Akyokuş, S.: Helmholtz principle based supervised and unsupervised feature selection methods for text mining. Inf. Process. Manag. **52**(5), 885–910 (2016)
14. Uysal, A.K., Gunal, S.: A novel probabilistic feature selection method for text classification. Knowl.-Based Syst. **36**, 226–235 (2012)
15. Yan, J., et al.: OCFS: optimal orthogonal centroid feature selection for text categorization. In: Proceedings of the 28th Annual International ACM SIGIR Conference on Research and Development in Information Retrieval, pp. 122–129. ACM (2005)
16. Yang, J., Liu, Y., Liu, Z., Zhu, X., Zhang, X.: A new feature selection algorithm based on binomial hypothesis testing for spam filtering. Knowl.-Based Syst. **24**(6), 904–914 (2011)
17. Yang, J., Liu, Y., Zhu, X., Liu, Z., Zhang, X.: A new feature selection based on comprehensive measurement both in inter-category and intra-category for text categorization. Inf. Process. Manag. **48**(4), 741–754 (2012)
18. Yang, J., Qu, Z., Liu, Z.: Improved feature-selection method considering the imbalance problem in text categorization. Sci. World J. **2014**(3), 17 (2014)
19. Yang, Y., Pedersen, J.O.: A comparative study on feature selection in text categorization. In: ICML 1997, pp. 412–420 (1997)
20. Zhang, W., Bai, X., Chen, C., Chen, Z.: Booter blacklist generation based on content characteristics. In: Gao, H., Wang, X., Yin, Y., Iqbal, M. (eds.) CollaborateCom 2018. LNICST, vol. 268, pp. 529–542. Springer, Cham (2019). https://doi.org/10.1007/978-3-030-12981-1_37

Opinion-Aware Knowledge Embedding
for Stance Detection

Zhenhui Xu[1], Qiang Li[2], Wei Chen[3]([✉]), Yingbao Cui[2], Zhen Qiu[2],
and Tengjiao Wang[1,3]

[1] Center for Data Science, Peking University, Beijing, China
{xuzhenhui,tjwang}@pku.edu.cn
[2] State Grid Information and Telecommunication Group, Beijing, China
{liqiang,cyb,qiuzhen}@sgitg.sgcc.com.cn
[3] Key Lab of High Confidence Software Technologies (MOE), School of EECS,
Peking University, Beijing, China
pekingchenwei@pku.edu.cn

Abstract. As an emerging text classification task, stance detection is
much helpful in reviewing subjective text and mining expressed attitudes
of a person or organization towards an object. Due to the similarity
with other text classification tasks, stance detection is always tackled
by conventional classification methods. However, there is a big difference between stance detection and others, since stance detection depends
much on human background knowledge while others do not. Therefore,
to address such a unique problem, we propose a novel method, which
leverages knowledge graph and incorporates text-mentioned knowledge
with a deep classifier, by a key component named Opinion-aware Knowledge Embedding (OKE). The proposed OKE can integrate the objective knowledge facts and subjective text opinion well by a customized
and effective attention mechanism. Our experiments also show that the
proposed method comprehensively outperforms all the baselines on real
datasets.

1 Introduction

In text mining area, stance detection, as a variant derived from sentiment analysis, is to identify the attitude instead of sentiment expressed by a person or
organization in written text, towards a target object or topic. Intuitively, the
big difference between the sentiment and attitude is that they are not always
consistent, when with some ironical or implicit expressions in the text. Therefore, In many real applications like opinion poll, product review, social survey,
etc., stance detection plays a more vital role in automatically processing massive
data and therefore saving much human effort [1,11].

Although stance detection is one of the text classification tasks, we claim that
there is a great difference when handling it. Specifically, as we can notice, most of
the similar tasks can be tackled by textual features well, e.g., sentiment analysis
by the emotional polarity of words, while stance detection cannot do because of

© Springer Nature Switzerland AG 2019
J. Shao et al. (Eds.): APWeb-WAIM 2019, LNCS 11642, pp. 337–348, 2019.
https://doi.org/10.1007/978-3-030-26075-0_26

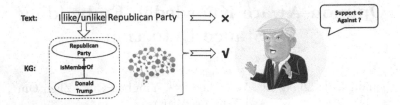

Fig. 1. The difference of stance detection. When meeting a task to detect the stance towards "Donald Trump", the machine cannot identify it by the single text, but can do it with good use of both the text opinion and knowledge graph (KG).

its high dependency on background knowledge. For example in Fig. 1, it is relatively easy to know the sentiment of *"I like/unlike Republican Party."*, but the implicit attitude towards *"Donald Trump"* in it will never be detected without any background knowledge about the connection between *"Donald Trump"* and *"Republican Party"*. Additionally, one's attitudes towards the typical entities are always closely related to his stance, such as the opinion towards *"Republican Party"* is critical to detect his stance towards *"Donald Trump"*. To conclude, the knowledge behind the entities and the opinions targeting the entities are much important when dealing with stance detection.

Therefore, most of the existing methods, which only treat stance detection as a common classification task, can hardly achieve good performance. Among these methods, some [11] try the SVM, LR, or some other traditional models for this task while the others [1,8,20] employ deep models such like CNN, LSTM or combination of them to detect the stance. Generally, both traditional models and deep models only use statistical textual information to identify the classification labels but without any background knowledge incorporated. And essentially, regardless of the statistical features (e.g., TF-IDF) used in traditional models or the well-known word embedding in deep models, neither of them can contain much enough knowledge. Individually, even for the more powerful word embedding, it is primarily driven by co-occurrence frequency of the words, but it is not frequent enough in lexicons to leverage specific knowledge to word vectors accurately.

To address such a challenging problem, in this paper, we propose a novel stance detection method to incorporate background knowledge from the knowledge graph into deep classification models. The key component of our method is *opinion-aware knowledge embedding (OKE)*. The proposed OKE realize the integration of external knowledge and internal opinion by a customized attention mechanism. Specifically, OKE takes the pre-trained knowledge graph embeddings (for entities) and trainable opinion embeddings into a multi-head attention mechanism, and get the weights of neighbor opinions towards each target entity. After that, OKE produces distributed representations for all corresponding entities by the weighted sum of opinion embeddings and their own entity embeddings. Finally, the output of OKE can be utilized in various deep models for the classification task. For the example as mentioned earlier, with the help of

OKE, it is much easier to capture both the opinion towards *"Republican Party"* (from the internal text) and its relation to *"Donald Trump"* (from the external knowledge graph). As the experiments show, equipping with OKE, many classification models achieve apparent improvement over all the benchmarks.

In conclusion, the main contributions of this paper are threefold:

- We first propose a novel method named OKE to leverage both the external knowledge graph and internal opinion information, which can address the lack of background knowledge for stance detection.
- We customize an effective attention mechanism in OKE for opinion-aware knowledge integration, with well-decoupled neural structures, while giving new insight into knowledge graph application.
- Experimental results show our proposed method obviously and efficiently outperforms the baselines on multiple stance detection datasets.

2   Related Work

2.1   Background on NLP Tasks

Stance Detection Methods. Regarding stance detection, as long as a certain classification model can be used for text, it may also be tried for this task. Therefore, there are mainly two kinds of models applied, containing traditional models and deep models.

Concerning traditional models, [11] tackles this task with the SVM model and focuses much on feature combining, where the main contribution is in feature engineering. As for the deep models, [20] proposes the most advanced method at the time with a Convolutional Neural Network (CNN) model on the stance detection competition. Also in this competition, [1] achieve a bidirectional conditional encoder for this task. After that, [8] makes use of both CNN and Long Short-Term Memory Network (LSTM) for further improving, where one is good at feature extraction when the other benefit long sequence modeling.

To our best knowledge, there is no knowledge-based classification applied for stance detection currently. Although in some similar area like sentiment analysis, previous works [10,13] are more concentrate on making good use of semantics, but not take background facts and opinions into careful consideration.

Attention Mechanism. Currently, Attention Mechanism plays a vital role in Natural Language Processing (NLP) area, containing machine translation, language modeling, text classification, *etc.* In [15], given queries' matrix Q, keys' matrix K and values' matrix V, the typical attention function is defined as

$$\text{Attention}(Q, K, V) = \text{softmax}(\frac{QK^T}{\sqrt{d_k}})V. \tag{1}$$

Based on it, state-of-art Transformer and its variants (e.g. BERT) [5,12] achieve good performance on many tasks and also generate some pre-trained powerful models which can be applied to other tasks.

Besides, attention mechanism has also applied into deep classifier for sentiment analysis in some previous works. For aspect-level sentiment analysis, [13] also employ attention mechanism to capture the context information around the specific aspect in the text and lead to improved performance. However, it still cannot capture any background knowledge if applied for stance detection.

2.2 Knowledge Graph and Its Application

Current Knowledge Graph (KG) is constructed typically by triplets, i.e. (head entity, relation, tail entity), which demonstrates the relation between two entities. Therefore, the facts in the knowledge graph are high dimensional, which is hard for application into current main classification models. So there are many works dedicated to manipulating the knowledge graph for some NLP tasks, which is introduced below.

Knowledge Graph Embedding. Knowledge Graph Embedding (KGE) aims at projecting the aforementioned high-dimensional knowledge in KG to distributed representation, containing all of the entities and relations, while retaining the structure information at the same time. To tackle this issue, most of the existing available methods adopt the translational distance models beginning with the most representative one, TransE [2].

In terms of TransE and its extensions, Given a fact (h, r, t), the relation is interpreted as a translation vector r so that the embedded entities h and t can be connected by r with low error, i.e., $h + r \approx t$ when (h, r, t) holds [18]. Specially, the basic scoring function of TransE is defined as,

$$f_r(h, t) = -||h + r - t||_{1/2}. \tag{2}$$

Improved from it, TransH [19] and TransR [9] try to overcome the disadvantages of TransE in dealing with complex relations by optimizing the scoring function; DKRL [22] and SSP [21] tend to add semantic information into the embedding vectors.

Knowledge Graph Application. With the advancement of KGE, its related applications for some NLP tasks have also gradually emerged. For example, DKN [16] incorporates knowledge graph representation into News recommendation and [23] applies it into topic models and makes the topics more interpretable.

Besides representing the facts into low-dimensional vectors, [4] propose opinion-aware knowledge graph, which constructs more powerful opinion-aware entities according to different stances, to identify the stances by matching the trained entities and mentioned entities opinion in text.

In terms of some other types of knowledge embedding, also in aspect-based sentiment analysis area, [10] proposed an LSTM-based hybrid network to leverage commonsense knowledge for the task, but the knowledge is from SenticNet semantic network [3] containing less real facts but focus more on the semantics in natural language. On the other hand, the knowledge used in Sentic-LSTM depends much on its customized structure and is different from the knowledge graph embedding we adopted here.

3   Opinion-Aware Knowledge Embedding

In this section, we will introduce the details of the key method, Opinion-aware Knowledge Embedding (OKE) and its application into deep models. With OKE equipped on classifiers, the problem above can be addressed effectively.

3.1   Preliminaries

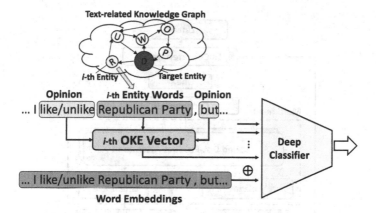

Fig. 2. Overview of OKE-based stance detection method. The brown circle "D" in knowledge graph denotes "Donald Trump", the target object of stance to detect, and the circle "R" denotes "Republican Party". (Color figure online)

The primary purpose of OKE we proposed here is to integrate the external knowledge graph and the internal text opinions. So the first step of OKE-based method is extracting the entities words and opinion words from the text, where the former are recognized from knowledge graph and the latter are always some subjective words from the text. Then, given entities and opinions, OKE is used to blend them together and produces distributed representations. Finally, the representations are input into deep classifier models with the normal word embeddings. The overview of OKE-based method is shown in Fig. 2.

Importantly, we can notice that each one-dimensional vector of OKE is assigned to each specific entity, which means that OKE focuses on catching the context opinions towards each entity. Based on it, the representation produced by OKE contains rich opinion information. Moreover, we use static pre-trained knowledge embeddings, which are trained according to the triplets in the given knowledge graph, as the input of OKE. So it promises the external knowledge can be contained continuously during the process.

To conclude, with the help of the above design, OKE can well address the aforementioned challenges for stance detection task. And the details of OKE is demonstrated in the next subsection, containing the detailed algorithm and formulas.

3.2   Method

As shown overall architecture in Fig. 3, the bottom layers of OKE are the entity embeddings and opinion embeddings, whose input words are both recognized from the text. The entity embeddings are pre-trained by KGE models, which is TransE in our implementation, while the opinion embeddings is a new individual word embeddings input with objective words.

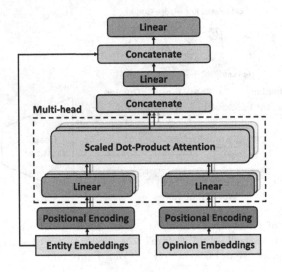

Fig. 3. Overall architecture of OKE.

The key process of OKE is a customized attention mechanism. Before this, the embedded vectors are processed by positional encoding, which benefits the opinion integration around the target entity. The positional encoding function is defined as the sine or cosine functions of different frequencies. Consulting the description in [15], given the entities' matrix E, objective words' matrix O, they are first projected by a linear layer respectively, which is defined as

$$E_p = \sigma(W_E^T E + b_E),$$
$$O_p = \sigma(W_O^T O + b_O),$$

(3)

where $\sigma(\cdot)$ denotes applying activation function, W and b mean the weights and biases in linear layer. Then, let $Q = E_p$, $K = V = O_p$ in Eq. 1, the scaled dot-product attention mechanism is

$$H = \text{softmax}(\frac{E_p O_p^T}{\sqrt{d_o}})O_p. \tag{4}$$

Attention mechanism here aims to catch the relation between one target entity and its neighbor opinion semantics. To make it more powerful, we also adopt multi-head attention in OKE, the multiple outputs of multi-head attention are concatenated first and projected into a new representation with the given dimension, which is

$$H_c = \sigma(W_c^T(\overset{n}{\underset{i=1}{\|}} H_i) + \boldsymbol{b}_c), \tag{5}$$

where $\|$ denote the concatenate operation. The output of multi-head attention is treated as the opinion integration for one target entity. Next, we combine the opinion embedding together with the original entity embedding and put them into the last linear projection. Then the final opinion-aware knowledge embedding outputs are defined as

$$E_O = W^T(E_p \| H_c) + \boldsymbol{b}. \tag{6}$$

Finally, under the above architecture, we get the target representation E_O (called entity vectors below) for each entity, a vector containing both knowledge from KG and opinion from the text. Therefore, on the one hand, OKE can give optimized models the capacity to recognize the relations between different entities; On the other hand, the models can also easily capture the opinion towards one target entity from OKE, which is input as a good feature to identify stance.

3.3 Application and Discussion

Given OKE, it is relatively easy to combine it with multiple deep models. Intuitively, a direct way is concatenation, that we can append the entity vectors into the word vector matrix, which means

$$V_{we} = V_w \| E_O, \tag{7}$$

where V_w is the original word vectors and V_{we} is a new input for downstream deep models containing CNN, LSTM, Transformer, *etc.* And undoubtedly, we can also customize different method to add OKE according to structure difference of models. For example, we can add a special channel for CNN, which is composed of entity vectors and fix them to corresponding positions.

Since the process of OKE is differentiable, all of the parameters could be updated by backpropagation. For the two embedding layers, the one for entities is static which is initialized by external pre-trained knowledge graph embedding, and the other one for opinions is trained dynamically by backpropagation. Therefore, the trainable parameters of OKE mainly contain the weights and biases in linear layers and opinion embedding layer.

4   Experiment

We apply OKE to multiple models on various real datasets, which is demonstrated below.

4.1   Experimental Setting

Datasets. We utilize three real datasets for stance detection to evaluate the performance gaining from OKE. (1) Convote is the Congressional debates data [14] that has annotation ("liberal" vs. "conservative") on the author level. (2) IBC is the Ideological Books Corpus which contains a million sentences written by authors with well-known political leanings, whose annotated version [6] ("liberal", "conservative" and "neutral") is adopted in our experiment. (3) Stock is a 3-classes stock short reviews data from several stock forums, containing 14 thousand training samples and 3 thousands of test samples. It is a typical stance detection dataset because the emotions of text are always inconsistent with the stance of the reviewer on the stock. Some other details of the above datasets are listed in Table 1.

Table 1. Statistics of datasets used in experiments.

Data	#avgLength	#Class	#Train	#Test
Convote	25.5	2	3.3K	0.8K
IBC	41.4	3	3.5K	0.9K
Stock	53.5	2	14K	3K

Models. To evaluate the effectiveness of OKE, we first benchmark multiple baseline models for this task. Then, we applied OKE into these models and evaluate their performance.

- SVM and OKG [4]. They are not deep neural models, and SVM is a basic classification model for text, OKG is a state-of-art model for political ideology detection, which is a special case of stance detection.
- TextCNN [7]. It is the first CNN model applied for text classification. Our implementation contains three filters with different sizes, [3–5] exactly, then the feature maps are flattened to a vector and input to the last hidden layer and softmax layer.
- CB-LSTM [8]. It is a combination of CNN and Bi-directional LSTM. The target-related representations are first extracted by CNN and then be fed to LSTM. It was claimed as the state-of-art deep models at the time.

Besides, to evaluate the ablations effectiveness in OKE, we also try to apply only entities vectors without opinion-aware component (denoted "+KGE") into the baseline models. Especially, the "TextCNN+KGE" is essentially a more powerful KCNN [17], or the component applied in DKN [16]. Additionally, to compare the strength of OKE with the vanilla context attention, we add "+Attention" methods to each model, which means the entities embedding layer in OKE is initialized randomly instead of the pre-trained KGE.

Note on Preprocessing. With the help of DBpedia[1] and its annotation tool[2], we first recognize and extract a text-related sub-KG from DBPedia. Besides, after that, TransE [2] is adopted to project the entities in KG to vector spaces. In terms of subjective words, they are recognized by NLTK[3].

Table 2. Test accuracy results. Notably, the symbol * denotes that the results of OKG are reported by the authors, where IBC is simplified and used for binary classification.

Model	Convote	IBC	Stock
SVM	68.1%	64.5%	69.5%
OKG* [4]	81.5%	**81.4%**	-
TextCNN [7]	85.7%	66.7%	72.9%
TextCNN+KGE [16,17]	86.8%	69.7%	74.2%
TextCNN+Attention [13]	86.7%	68.2%	73.5%
TextCNN+OKE	**88.1%**	**73.1%**	**76.4%**
CB-LSTM [8]	86.1%	68.2%	73.3%
CB-LSTM+KGE	87.6%	69.8%	74.2%
CB-LSTM+Attention [13]	87.2%	69.2%	74.0%
CB-LSTM+OKE	**89.1%**	**70.9%**	**76.1%**

4.2   Experimental Result and Analysis

Overall Performance. The experimental result is shown in Table 2. Generally, after applying OKE, all of the models are improved by about 3%. And compared with the model only applied KGE, it can also increase by about 2%. Moreover, we can find the attention mechanism exactly improve the performance, but its performances are also below OKE. Therefore, the knowledge embedding from KG benefits the performance much, and at the same time, the opinion integration is also important (Table 3).

Additionally, as the example curve shown in Fig. 4, we can find that OKE converges much faster than the normal one or the one with KGE. Moreover, the convergence points of OKE are also much better.

[1] https://wiki.dbpedia.org/.
[2] https://github.com/dbpedia-spotlight/dbpedia-spotlight.
[3] http://www.nltk.org/.

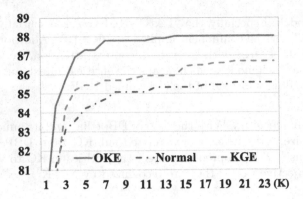

Fig. 4. The iteration-accuracy curve over test set of convote, with TextCNN model.

Table 3. Some cases from IBC with TextCNN. Intuitively, the first sentence is against "Bush", who is a Republican member, so the normal model cannot detect it well; Similarly, the second sentence is against a democratic member. Therefore, knowledge is exactly much essential for stance detection.

Content	Normal	With OKE
As his job approval ratings dropped in 2005, White House aides peddled the idea that, rather than being a caretaker president, Bush is a revolutionary leader who suffers low ratings only because he is unafraid to fight for radical ideas like private Social Security accounts or sweeping tax changes	Neutral	Liberal
As the Democratic Grinches prepared to vote on their version of the widely despised, destructive, and chaotic health care bill, they tried to spice up their fruitcake with distortions, distractions, and flat-out lies	Neutral	Conservative

Case Study. To intuitively observe the effectiveness of OKE in real data, we give two cases where the normal classifier cannot identify the correct stance, but the one with OKE gives the right label. These given cases are from IBC, the 3-classes dataset. We can notice that the normal classifier always give the sentence "Neutral" label because of its ability lack to deal with many strange entities, though they are much critical to the detection. On the Contrary, with the help of knowledge graph, the connections between the entities are captured well by OKE, which leads to good performance as the cases show.

5   Conclusion and Future Work

To conclude, in this paper, we find that the stance detection needs more background knowledge compared with other text classification tasks, so the OKE is proposed to integrate the external information from knowledge graph (KG) and internal opinion information. And our method can improve all of the models effectively and efficiently in experiments as expected.

Moreover, we think incorporating the external knowledge from KG can also benefit some other similar tasks, and the interaction of external and original information can make big differences. Especially, with the appearance of pre-trained models for NLP, there is a good insight to design effective and efficient component to embed more external features so that enriching the inputs, especially when the textual features pre-modeling is becoming more and more powerful.

Acknowledgements. This work is supported by State Grid Technical Project (No. 52110418002W).

References

1. Augenstein, I., Rocktäschel, T., Vlachos, A., Bontcheva, K.: Stance detection with bidirectional conditional encoding. arXiv preprint arXiv:1606.05464. Version 1 (2016)
2. Bordes, A., Usunier, N., Garcia-Duran, A., Weston, J., Yakhnenko, O.: Translating embeddings for modeling multi-relational data. In: Advances in Neural Information Processing Systems, pp. 2787–2795 (2013)
3. Cambria, E., Speer, R., Havasi, C., Hussain, A.: SenticNet: a publicly available semantic resource for opinion mining. In: 2010 AAAI Fall Symposium Series (2010)
4. Chen, W., Zhang, X., Wang, T., Yang, B., Li, Y.: Opinion-aware knowledge graph for political ideology detection. In: Proceedings of the 26th International Joint Conference on Artificial Intelligence, pp. 3647–3653. AAAI Press (2017)
5. Devlin, J., Chang, M.W., Lee, K., Toutanova, K.: Bert: pre-training of deep bidirectional transformers for language understanding. arXiv preprint arXiv:1810.04805. Version 1 (2018)
6. Iyyer, M., Enns, P., Boyd-Graber, J., Resnik, P.: Political ideology detection using recursive neural networks. In: Proceedings of the 52nd Annual Meeting of the Association for Computational Linguistics (Volume 1: Long Papers), vol. 1, pp. 1113–1122 (2014)
7. Kim, Y.: Convolutional neural networks for sentence classification. arXiv preprint arXiv:1408.5882. Version 1 (2014)
8. Li, X., Chen, W., Wang, T., Huang, W.: Target-specific convolutional bi-directional LSTM neural network for political ideology analysis. In: Chen, L., Jensen, C.S., Shahabi, C., Yang, X., Lian, X. (eds.) APWeb-WAIM 2017. LNCS, vol. 10367, pp. 64–72. Springer, Cham (2017). https://doi.org/10.1007/978-3-319-63564-4_5
9. Lin, Y., Liu, Z., Sun, M., Liu, Y., Zhu, X.: Learning entity and relation embeddings for knowledge graph completion. In: Twenty-Ninth AAAI Conference on Artificial Intelligence (2015)
10. Ma, Y., Peng, H., Cambria, E.: Targeted aspect-based sentiment analysis via embedding commonsense knowledge into an attentive LSTM. In: Thirty-Second AAAI Conference on Artificial Intelligence (2018)
11. Mohammad, S., Kiritchenko, S., Sobhani, P., Zhu, X., Cherry, C.: SemEval-2016 task 6: detecting stance in tweets. In: Proceedings of the 10th International Workshop on Semantic Evaluation (SemEval-2016), pp. 31–41 (2016)

12. Radford, A., Narasimhan, K., Salimans, T., Sutskever, I.: Improving Language Understanding by Generative Pre-training. Technical report, OpenAI (2018)
13. Tang, D., Qin, B., Liu, T.: Aspect level sentiment classification with deep memory network. arXiv preprint arXiv:1605.08900 (2016)
14. Thomas, M., Pang, B., Lee, L.: Get out the vote: determining support or opposition from congressional floor-debate transcripts. In: Proceedings of the 2006 Conference on Empirical Methods in Natural Language Processing, pp. 327–335. Association for Computational Linguistics (2006)
15. Vaswani, A., et al.: Attention is all you need. In: Advances in Neural Information Processing Systems, pp. 5998–6008 (2017)
16. Wang, H., Zhang, F., Xie, X., Guo, M.: DKN: deep knowledge-aware network for news recommendation. arXiv preprint arXiv:1801.08284. Version 1 (2018)
17. Wang, J., Wang, Z., Zhang, D., Yan, J.: Combining knowledge with deep convolutional neural networks for short text classification. In: Proceedings of International Joint Conferences on Artificial Intelligence Organization, pp. 2915–2921 (2017)
18. Wang, Q., Mao, Z., Wang, B., Guo, L.: Knowledge graph embedding: a survey of approaches and applications. IEEE Trans. Knowl. Data Eng. **29**(12), 2724–2743 (2017)
19. Wang, Z., Zhang, J., Feng, J., Chen, Z.: Knowledge graph embedding by translating on hyperplanes. In: Twenty-Eighth AAAI Conference on Artificial Intelligence (2014)
20. Wei, W., Zhang, X., Liu, X., Chen, W., Wang, T.: pkudblab at SemEval-2016 task 6: a specific convolutional neural network system for effective stance detection. In: Proceedings of the 10th International Workshop on Semantic Evaluation (SemEval-2016), pp. 384–388 (2016)
21. Xiao, H., Huang, M., Meng, L., Zhu, X.: SSP: semantic space projection for knowledge graph embedding with text descriptions. In: Thirty-First AAAI Conference on Artificial Intelligence (2017)
22. Xie, R., Liu, Z., Jia, J., Luan, H., Sun, M.: Representation learning of knowledge graphs with entity descriptions. In: Thirtieth AAAI Conference on Artificial Intelligence (2016)
23. Yao, L., et al.: Incorporating knowledge graph embeddings into topic modeling. In: Thirty-First AAAI Conference on Artificial Intelligence (2017)

History-Driven Entity Categorization

Yijun Duan$^{(\boxtimes)}$, Adam Jatowt, and Katsumi Tanaka

Graduate School of Informatics, Kyoto University, Kyoto, Japan
{yijun,adam}@dl.kuis.kyoto-u.ac.jp, tanaka.katsumi.85e@st.kyoto-u.ac.jp

Abstract. Knowledge of entity histories is often necessary for comprehensive understanding and characterization of entities. In this paper we
introduce a novel task of *history-based entity categorization*. Taking a
set of entity-related documents as an input we detect latent entity categories whose members share similar histories, effectively, grouping entities based on the similarities of their historical developments. Next, we
generate comparative timelines for each generated group allowing users
to spot similarities and differences in entity histories. We evaluate our
approach on several datasets of different entity types demonstrating its
effectiveness against competitive baselines.

Keywords: Entity categorization · Entity comparison · Digital history

1 Introduction

Grouping is a common technique used for organizing and understanding entities.
For example, Wikipedia, which is considered to be the most comprehensive encyclopedia, contains over 1.13 million categories [2] consisting of multiple members
that share some common traits (e.g., list of cities in China, list of American Noble
Prize winners, etc.). However few such groups are explicitly constructed around
the common or similar histories of their included members. Yet, historical aspects
are often quite important as, in many cases, the history shapes and defines the
present characteristics of entities. Moreover, for certain kinds of entities, their
histories determine their perceived values (e.g., historical buildings in touristic
cities). We thus think that constructing history-centered entity groupings can
provide novel and useful ways of entity understanding and comparison.

*How could Chinese cities be grouped according to their historical similarities?
What are the different types of biographies of American scientists in the* 20th
century? Questions of this type are not easy to be answered because studying
the histories of all the members belonging to a given entity group is quite an
arduous task, not to say anything about its structuring. Note that currently
entities are usually not grouped based on their common histories. For example,
there are no dedicated list pages in Wikipedia for sub-groups of Chinese cities
or American scientists that would share similar historical developments.

© Springer Nature Switzerland AG 2019
J. Shao et al. (Eds.): APWeb-WAIM 2019, LNCS 11642, pp. 349–364, 2019.
https://doi.org/10.1007/978-3-030-26075-0_27

To enable history-based entity grouping, we formulate the *latent history-based category* hypothesis, which states that *entities can be categorized based on the similarity of their histories, such that entities included in the same category have more similar histories to each other than to ones in other categories*. In order to group entities based on their histories, we propose a concise optimization model inspired by the popular Affinity Propagation (AP) algorithm for exemplar-based clustering. To the best of our knowledge, this is the first optimization formulation presented aiming at history-driven entity-centric tasks.

Since history-based categories can be too large to allow users easily understand common aspects of its members, we additionally propose to describe each generated category. Cognitive science studies suggest two modes in which people can effectively understand and memorize categories: *exemplar theory* [5] and *prototype theory* [20]. Both modes embody the idea of *graded structure* of a category, according to which some members of a category are more central than others. *Exemplar theory* posits usage of real member entities as exemplars to represent the category, while *prototype theory* is its alternative that proposes describing category by constructing the "average" of all members as an abstract prototype. Entities closer to the exemplar or to the prototype are considered better examples of the category.

Inspired by this, in this study we first propose to represent each generated latent category by the *exemplar* towards a more efficient understanding. The advantage of using *exemplars* for category explanation is that they represent the actual member of the category and are easy to be remembered [13]. What is more, good exemplars are often more effective to describe shared aspects in history than the descriptions of separate features (in our case events) because of the high coherence of the former. Still however, the full comprehension of category's history cannot be done using only a single selected entity, and without the comparison to the histories of other related categories. We then also generate a summarized timeline (i.e., *prototype*) for each category indicating the similarities of its members and dissimilarities to other categories for enabling effective characterization and comparison. With such a dual representation of each latent category we think that users should be able to more easily understand the common and distinguishing historical aspects of the derived history-based categories, and could benefit from the constructed historical knowledge for supporting various kinds of analyses including evolution and causality analysis, finding historical explanations, provenance investigation, and for answering history-related questions.

To sum up, we make the following contributions in this paper:

1. We introduce a new research problem of *automatically discovering history-based latent categories*.
2. We propose to represent the constructed categories by two means, by *exemplar* which is the most representative entity belonging to each category, and by *prototype* which is an informative timeline summarizing category history.
3. We develop an unsupervised approach for these tasks based on a concise optimization formulation.

4. The effectiveness of our methods is proved by experiments on 7 datasets and by comparison with competitive baselines.

2   Problem Definition

2.1   Input

The input in our task are documents containing descriptions of entity histories. Each such document "spans" over a certain range of time and each sentence is assumed to refer to a historical event. The dates of events can be either explicitly mentioned in the sentence or could be estimated based on nearby sentences.

2.2   Research Problem

Given a set of history-related documents $[d_1, d_2, ..., d_n]$, each about a particular entity and a pre-set time window $[t_{begin}, t_{end}]$, the first task is to detect latent categories $[c_1, c_2, ..., c_k]$ and their corresponding exemplars $[d_e^1, d_e^2, ..., d_e^k]$ where entities within each category share similar histories. Moreover, for a set of history-related documents $[d_1^j, d_2^j, ..., d_i^j]$, each about a particular entity within the same category j ($j \in [1, ..., k]$), the second task is to select m most important events $[e_1, e_2, ..., e_m]$ to form a concise timeline reflecting typical history of the category.

3   Event Importance Calculation

Each category is going to be represented by its exemplar. The characteristics of a category will be thus embodied in the history of its exemplar. Naturally, those entities which have many important events in their histories are more representative and should be chosen as exemplars.

The task of estimating historical significance of events is usually done by historians. During this process several criteria are adopted to help them make judgments. For instance, *remarkable* (the event was remarked on by people at its time or after), *remembered* (the event is important within the collective memory of a group or groups), *resulting in change* (the event had significant consequences for the future) and so on. Manually estimating significance of any historical events under the above-listed criteria is of course labour intensive, time consuming and may require special expertise, hence, we attempt to estimate the importance automatically. As it is relatively easy to obtain publicly available datasets of historical events marked as important (e.g., the list of important events in 1990s), we propose a method to compute event importance in a semi-supervised way.

Given a set of historical events $P = \{p_1, p_2, ..., p_k\}$ where each event is marked as important, and a set of unlabeled events $U = \{u_1, u_2, ..., u_i\}$, the task is to estimate the degree of importance of each event in U. We use $I(u_i)$ to denote the importance of ith event in U. The key feature of this problem is that there is no negative example set (i.e., labeled unimportant events), which is needed for accurate learning of features of important events. In the recent years, PU-learning [15] studies the problem of building classifiers using positive and unlabeled examples. A few algorithms [16,26] based on a two-step strategy were proposed for solving the problem as follows.

Step 1: Identifying a set of reliable negative examples from the unlabeled set.

Step 2: Iteratively applying a classification algorithm for generating a set of classifiers and then selecting the best classifier.

In this study, we adopt the 1-DNF technique [26] to identify a set of reliable unimportant events from the unlabeled set U in step 1, and we use the EM algorithm with a NB classifier for constructing the final estimator in step 2.

1-DNF. 1-DNF technique first constructs a set of positive features containing words that occur more frequently in the labeled important event set P than in the unlabeled set U. Then an event in U that does not contain any positive feature is regarded as a strongly unimportant event, and is included in the reliable negative set RN.

Naive Bayesian classifier. Let $C = \{c_1, c_2\}$ be the two pre-defined classes which are important events and unimportant events, respectively. Given a set of training events E, we use $x_{e_i,m}$ to denote the word x_t in position m of event e_i, where x_t is a word in the vocabulary $V = \{x_1, ..., x_{|v|}\}$. The posterior probability $Pr(c_j|e_i)$ is computed to perform classification. We have:

$$Pr(c_j) = \frac{\sum_{i=1}^{|E|} Pr(c_j|e_i)}{|E|} \tag{1}$$

$$Pr(x_t|c_j) = \frac{\lambda + \sum_{i=1}^{|E|} N(x_t, e_i)Pr(c_j|e_i)}{\lambda|V| + \sum_{s=1}^{|V|} \sum_{i=1}^{|E|} N(x_s, e_i)Pr(c_j|e_i)} \tag{2}$$

where λ is the smoothing factor (typically set as 0.1), $N(x_t, e_i)$ is the number of times that word x_t occurs in event e_i. Finally, we obtain the NB classifier:

$$Pr(c_j|e_i) = \frac{Pr(c_j) \prod_{m=1}^{|e_i|} Pr(x_{e_i,m}|c_j)}{\sum_{r=1}^{|C|} Pr(c_r) \prod_{m=1}^{|e_i|} Pr(x_{e_i,m}|c_r)} \tag{3}$$

EM. Each event in P and RN is assigned the initial label 1 and -1, respectively. Each event $e \in U - RN$ will not be assigned to any label initially but it will got assigned a probability $Pr(1|e)$ at the end of the first iteration of EM. Then the set $U - RN$ will participate in EM with its assigned probabilistic labeles in subsequent iterations. The EM algorithm consists of the *Expectation* step and the *Maximization* step. In the *Expectation* step the probabilistic labels of each event $e \in U - RN$ are produced and revised based on Eq. (3), and then the parameters of classifiers are re-estimated in the *Maximization* step using Eqs. (1) and (2). This leads to the next iteration of the algorithm. When EM converges, the degree of importance of each event u in the unlabeled set U takes the value in [0,1], which is equal to the probability of event to belong to the class P (i.e., the class of important events). Table 1 shows several examples of events with their estimated importance scores.

Table 1. A sample of 4 historical events with their estimated importance scores from the histories of Japanese cities.

Original sentence	Importance
The tower of Karatsu Castle was built in 1966	0.015
1949 also saw the opening of Fukushima University	0.363
January 17, 1995: Great Hanshin earthquake causes more than 100 casualties	0.786
During World War II, the July 19, 1945 Bombing of Okazaki killed over 200 people and destroyed most of the city center	0.937

4 History-Based Entity Categorization

4.1 Event Representation

We assume a historical event to be represented by a sentence and be associated with a date of its occurrence. Each sentence is first normalized by pre-processing steps such as removing stopwords, stemming and retaining the most frequent 5,000 unigrams and bigrams. In this study, we use word2vec [17] to represent terms and events. We obtain the distributed vector representations of each word by training the Skip-gram model on the entire English Wikipedia from 2016 using the gensim Python library [19]. The vector representation of an event in our case is a weighted combination of the vectors of terms contained in the normalized sentence that describes the event, where the weight of a term is its TF-IDF value calculated based on the input histories of entities.

4.2 Entity Similarity Calculation

We now introduce the computation of similarity s_{ij} between entities d_i and d_j. Since cosine similarity is not a proper similarity measure for sequences such as sequences of events, we propose a weighted dynamic time warping model for measuring distances between entities' histories. Dynamic time warping is one technique utilized for computing similarity between two temporal sequences which may vary in speed, by calculating an optimal match between them. Hence, entities' histories can be "warped" non-linearly in the time dimension so as their similar events become aligned. Furthermore, when computing this similarity in our case, events closer to each other and with higher importance score will be more heavily weighted. Given the importance and the date of an event e denoted by $I(e)$ and $T(e)$, respectively, the process is shown in Algorithm 1.

```
input  : Two sequences of events d_i = {e_1^i, e_2^i, ..., e_n^i} and d_j = {e_1^j, e_2^j, ..., e_m^j}
output: Simlarity(d_i, d_j)
1  M ← array[0..n, 0..m];
2  for i ← 0 to n do
3  |   M[i, 0] ← infinity;
4  end
5  for j ← 1 to m do
6  |   M[0, j] ← infinity;
7  end
8  for u ← 1 to n do
9  |   for v ← 1 to m do
10 |   |   cost ← I(d_i[u]) · I(d_j[v]) · (2 / (e^{|T(d_i[u])-T(d_j[v])|}+1)) · Distance_cosine(d_i[u], d_j[v]);
11 |   |   M[u, v] ← cost + minimum(M[u − 1, v], M[u, v − 1], M[u − 1, v − 1]);
12 |   end
13 end
14 Simlarity(d_i, d_j) ← −M[n, m];
```
Algorithm 1: Weighted Dynamic Time Warping

4.3 Optimization Model for Exemplar Detection

In this section, we describe the method proposed for categories generation and exemplar detection. The goal is to select a subset of entities as exemplars and assign every non-exemplar entity to exactly one exemplar, so as to maximize the overall sum of similarities between entities and their exemplars and the exemplar importance. Then the objective can be expressed as follows:

$$Obj_1 = \lambda \cdot \sum_{i,j} s_{ij}h_{ij} + (1-\lambda) \cdot \sum_i p_iq_i \tag{4}$$

where s_{ij} is the similarity of entity d_i to entity d_j, and p_i denotes the average importance of events contained in the histories of entity d_i. Furthermore, let h_{ij} and q_i be binary hidden variables where $h_{ij} = 1$ indicates entity d_i has chosen entity d_j as its exemplar, and $q_i = 1$ indicates entity d_i is chosen as an exemplar. λ is a trade-off parameter weighting the exemplar importance and the similarities between non-exemplars to examplars[1]. Solving Obj_1 is essentially a hard combinational optimization problem, it can be transformed into a more feasible optimization problem by introducing the following constraint functions:

$$C^1(h_{i:}) = \begin{cases} 0 & \sum_j h_{ij} = 1, \\ -\infty & otherwise \end{cases} \tag{5}$$

$$C^2(h_{:j}) = \begin{cases} 0 & q_j = h_{jj} = max_ih_{ij}, \\ -\infty & otherwise \end{cases} \tag{6}$$

where $h_{i:} = h_{i1}, ..., h_{in}$ and $h_{:j} = h_{1j}, ..., h_{nj}$. The constraint function (5) forces each entity to be assigned to exactly one exemplar (which can be itself), while (6) enforces that an entity must be an exemplar if other entities choose it as an exemplar. Thus the goal is to maximize

$$Obj_2 = \lambda \cdot \sum_{i,j} s_{ij}h_{ij} + (1-\lambda) \cdot \sum_i p_iq_i + \sum_i (C^1(h_{i:}) + C^2(h_{:i})) \tag{7}$$

[1] We experimentally set the value of λ to be 0.4.

By running the *max-sum algorithm* [14], an approximate solution for the above problem can be efficiently achieved. More explicitly, after normalizing all similarities and importance to $[-1, 0]$ range, two sets of messages are calculated iteratively until convergence:

$$\alpha_{ij} = \begin{cases} \frac{p_j \cdot (1-\lambda)}{\lambda} + \sum_{k \neq j} max(0, \rho_{kj}) & i = j, \\ min[0, \frac{p_j \cdot (1-\lambda)}{\lambda} + \rho_{jj} + \sum_{k \notin \{i,j\}} max(0, \rho_{kj})] & i \neq j \end{cases} \qquad (8)$$

$$\rho_{ij} = s_{ij} - max_{k \neq j}(\alpha_{ik} + s_{ik}) \qquad (9)$$

where $\alpha_{ij} = 0$ and $\rho_{ij} = 0$ initially. Intuitively, message α_{ij} corresponds to how willing entity d_j is to serve as the exemplar for entity d_i, while message ρ_{ij} conveys to which extent entity d_i wants entity d_j to be its exemplar. Finally the exemplar d_j for entity d_i can be obtained by

$$d_j = argmax_j\{\alpha_{ij} + \rho_{ij}\} \qquad (10)$$

4.4 Prototype Timeline Generation

Previously we explained the process of splitting entities into latent categories from history viewpoint, where each category is represented by its *exemplar*. We then generate a summarized timeline (effectively, a *prototype*) for each discovered latent category using a mutually-reinforced random walk model [8] (Table 4 will show examples of generated summary). Such summary includes not only events similar between the category members but also considering differences from the timelines of other categories.

5 Experiments

5.1 Datasets

We test our methods on entities of different types from different time periods and locations. In particular, we perform experiments on 7 Wikipedia categories including 3 city categories and 4 person categories. The city categories are Japanese cities, Chinese cities and English cities (denoted by D_1, D_2, D_3, respectively), while for the person categories we use American scientists, French scientists, Japanese Prime Ministers until the end of WW2 (1945) and Japanese Prime Ministers after WW2 (denoted by D_4, D_5, D_6, D_7, respectively). Note that, in general, our methods are not bound to Wikipedia categories as any listing of entities can form an input, provided the historical description of each entity is available. We use Wikipedia categories in this work as a convenient data source.

Historical event extraction has some new research works recently [9]. For preparing the city categories, each city history is extracted from the "History" section in the corresponding Wikipedia article. To capture historical events, we collect all sentences with dates using SUTime [7]. As further preprocessing, we reduce inflected words to their word stems and retain only the terms that are among the most frequent 5,000 unigrams and bigrams, excluding stopwords and numbers. Each historical event is then represented by the bag of unigrams extracted from its sentence along with the corresponding date.

For the person categories, we utilize a dataset of 242,970 biographies publicly released by Bamman *et al.* [3]. Every biography consists of several life events, each represented by bag of unigrams and a date. Unlike in the city datasets, the date here is a relative number when counting from a person's birth year. The basic statistics of all the datasets are shown in Table 2.

As for the set of labeled important historical events necessary for event importance calculation, we have collected brief descriptions of key events from Wikipedia year pages[2] for each year from AD1 to the present. The total number of the captured event descriptions is 39,881.

Table 2. Summary of datasets.

Dataset	Wikipedia category	# Entities	Time range
D1	Japanese Cities	532	40–2016
D2	Chinese Cities	357	12–2016
D3	UK Cities	68	1–2016
D4	American Scientists	141	0–103
D5	French Scientists	41	0–101
D6	Japanese PMs (pre WW2)	32	0–98
D7	Japanese PMs (post WW2)	30	0–93

5.2 Analyzed Methods

To compare with our proposed optimization formulation, 4 competitive models including *AP, MMR, DFP* and *K-Means* clustering are set up as baseline methods. All the analyzed methods are briefly discussed below:

(1) *Affinity Propagation (AP)* [11] views the clustering as identifying a subset of representative exemplars. In particular, it assigns each non-exemplar entity to an exemplar entity under the objective of maximizing the sum of similarities between non-exemplar entities and their assigned exemplar entities.

(2) *Maximal Marginal Relevance (MMR)* [6] is a typical instance of implicit search result diversification techniques. To obtain the optimal list of exemplar entities, it applies greedy strategy that follows a heuristic criterion of making the locally optimal choice at each round.

---

[2] For example, https://en.wikipedia.org/wiki/1939.

(3) *Desirable Facility Placement (DFP)* [27] uses greedy best k strategy for generating the desired exemplars' list L based on a two-step process. It initializes L with an arbitrary solution, and then iteratively refines L by swapping an entity in L with another one outside L.

(4) *K-Means Clustering (K-Means)* [12] is a popular method used for cluster detection. It partitions all entities into k clusters in which each event belongs to the cluster that has the nearest mean (given k as the size of exemplars).

5.3   Evaluation Criteria

Quantitative Evaluation Criteria. For a given Wikipedia category composed of n entities that become partitioned into k groups $[C_1, C_2, ..., C_k]$, we use d_i^t and d_e^t to denote the ith entity in the tth group and the exemplar in the tth group, respectively. We then evaluate the representativeness of the identified set of exemplars D_e in terms of the following metrics:

Intra-Similarity (IntraSim) which measures how similar an exemplar is to the entities in its category. The *higher* IntraSim, the more effective the adopted algorithm is.

$$IntraSim(D_e) = \frac{\sum_{t=1}^{k} \sum_{d_i^t \in C_t, d_i^t \neq d_e^t} Sim_{cosine}(d_i^t, d_e^t)}{n - k} \qquad (11)$$

Inter-Similarity (InterSim) which describes how similar an exemplar is to the other exemplars. The *lower* InterSim, the better the performance is.

$$InterSim(D_e) = \frac{\sum_{t=1}^{k} \sum_{s=1, s \neq t}^{k} Sim_{cosine}(d_e^s, d_e^t)}{k * (k - 1)} \qquad (12)$$

Ratio of intra-similarity to inter-similarity (Ratio) which takes into account both *IntraSim* and *InterSim*, thus reflecting the degree of representativeness of an exemplar.

$$Ratio(D_e) = \frac{IntraSim(D_e)}{InterSim(D_e)} \qquad (13)$$

Saliency (AveImp) which measures how important the events in the histories of exemplars are.

$$Sailency(D_e) = \frac{\sum_{t=1}^{k} \sum_{i=1}^{|d_e^t|} I(e_{d_e^t, i})}{k} \qquad (14)$$

where we use $e_{d_e^t, i}$ to denote the ith event of entity d_e^t.

Qualitative Evaluation Criteria. We also ask users to evaluate the quality of identified categories and corresponding exemplars. Each category in the summary is graded in terms of:

– *Saliency* which measures how sound and important each exemplar is.

- *Comprehensibility* which measures how easily the generated category can be understood.
- *Novelty* which measures how varying and diverse information the annotators could acquire after viewing the result.

We have 5 methods here to be tested (1 proposed method and 4 baseline methods). 5 annotators (4 males, 1 female) who have significant interest in history were asked to evaluate the generated categories. Each category was ensured to be evaluated by 3 annotators. During the assessment, the annotators were allowed to utilize any external resources including the Wikipedia, Web search engines, books, etc. All of the scores were given in the range from 1 to 5 (1: not at all, 2: rather not, 3: so, 4: rather yes, 5: definitely yes). Lastly, we averaged all the individual scores given by the annotators to obtain the final scores per each category.

5.4   Evaluation Results

Evaluation Results for Quantitative Metrics. Table 3 shows the performance in terms of *InterSim*, *IntraSim*, *Ratio* and *AveImp*. We can observe that the proposed optimization framework has better performance than all the baseline methods in terms of two main evaluation metrics, *Ratio* and *AveImp*. Besides, we can also notice that two search result diversification models *MMR* and *DFP* outperform two clustering models *K-Means* and *AP* in terms of *AveImp*.

Table 3. Performance of different models on the city and person datasets w.r.t. quantitative metrics. The best result of each setting is in bold.

Model	Data	IntraSim	InterSim	Ratio	AveImp
K-Means	Cities	**0.888**	0.780	1.139	0.697
	Persons	0.535	0.462	1.190	0.722
AP	Cities	0.884	0.770	1.148	0.732
	Persons	0.619	0.476	1.330	0.779
MMR	Cities	0.820	0.563	1.490	0.898
	Persons	0.572	**0.344**	2.084	0.879
DFP	Cities	0.874	0.809	1.080	0.912
	Persons	**0.770**	0.738	1.044	0.879
Our model	Cities	0.859	**0.543**	**1.620**	**0.939**
	Persons	0.758	0.478	**2.152**	**0.914**

Now we investigate the possible reasons for the above findings. *MMR* relies on the best first strategy, making it simple and computationally efficient. However at a particular round, the heuristic criterion may incur *error propagation*.

DFP can alleviate such problem, but it is based on hill climbing algorithm. A potential problem is that hill climbing may converge to a local maximum. On the other hand, though AP shares many similar characteristics with our model, it does not guarantee to globally identify the optimal subset of important exemplars, hence its lower performance. As for K-$Means$, it suffers from strong sensitivity to outliers and noise, which leads to varying performance.

Both MMR and DFP models take importance of entities into consideration during the process of identifying exemplars, which can explain why they have better performance in terms of $AveImp$ than the two clustering methods. The last finding is that cities may have larger homogeneity than persons, as supported by the observation that generally all methods achieve larger scores in terms of $IntraSim$ on city datasets than on person datasets.

Evaluation Results for Qualitative Metrics Figure 1 shows the average scores of summaries in 3 criteria by all the methods generated on all the city and person datasets, respectively. We first note that our optimization model outperforms the baselines based on almost all the criteria (the only exception is that our method achieves worse results than AP and MMR in terms of comprehensibility by 4% on person datasets). On average, our model outperforms all baselines by 16.9% and 11.9% across all the metrics on the city and person datasets, respectively. In particular, it achieves better results than all the baselines by 8.1%, 10.0%, 22.7% in terms of saliency, comprehensibility and novelty, respectively.

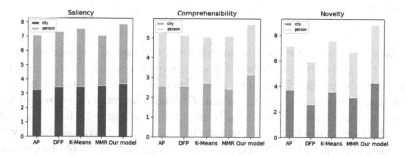

Fig. 1. Performance of different models on city and person datasets w.r.t. qualitative metrics.

5.5   Example Categorization

We present in Fig. 2 and Table 4 the summary of three identified latent history-based categories of Japanese cities (dataset D1) using our approach. The summary of each category consists of a timeline containing 10 events ordered chronologically (see Fig. 2), followed by a table (see Table 4) which includes up to 10 top scored words representing each event. For every event in Fig. 2, we display its manually created label based on the extracted terms that are shown in Table 4. In addition, each summary event is associated with two numbers indicating, respectively, the median date and the standard deviation of the occurrence years of the event instances it covers.

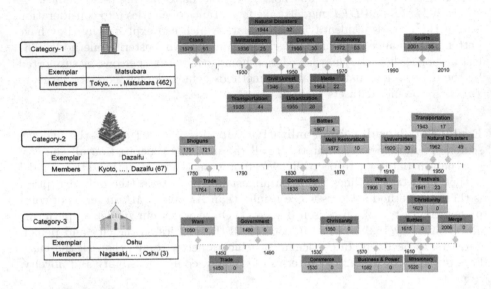

Fig. 2. Typical histories of 3 latent history-based categories of Japanese cities learned from 532 instances.

As we can notice, cities in category-1 form the largest number of Japanese cities. Most of these cities had their key events quite recently as shown in Fig. 2. In the past, the cities within this group tended to be dominated by powerful local clans, as reflected by the event *Clans*. The modern *transportation* infrastructure in Japan started to advance from the early 20th century. After WW2 (*Militarization*), these Japanese cities were largely transformed by rapid *Urbanization*, and were affected by rapid social development and economic growth, embodied in the events of *Media*, *Autonomy* and *Sports*. During such process, the society once had occasional political protests and violent oppositions, as reflected by *Civil Unrest*. Besides, it can be observed that these Japanese cities often suffered from *Natural Disasters* such as earthquakes, typhoons and tsunamis. *Matsubara* and *Tokyo* serve as good examples of the group.

Histories of cities in category-2 express more features of ethnic culture of Japan. These traditional cities have typical regional characters and local culture and, generally, they are not as modern as cities in the first category. For example, *Shoguns* was the type of military dictator and dominator of Japan for around 700 years until *Meiji Restoration*, which began Japan's transformation from

Table 4. Events in the summary of 3 identified latent history-based categories of Japanese cities. For each event we show up to top 10 words due to space limit.

	Event	Terms
1	District	matsubara, village, district, amami, area, part, incorporated, city, tannan, prefectures
	Civil Unrest	occurred, end, widely violent, strike protest, opposed, matsukawa, incident, demonstration
	Transportation	sapporo, route, completed, megumino, built, meter, main, linking, highway, bypass building
	Natural Disasters	killed, earthquake, suffered, damage, light, left, tsunami, mikawa, february, dead, typhoon
	Urbanization	renamed, irino, neighborhood, hall, split, respectively, mura, elevated, status new, incorporated
	Militarization	japanese, industry, navy, military, imperial, center area, works, warehouse, training, support
	Media	continued, television, spring largescale, included, firebombing, expo, broadcasts, bombing, nhk
	Sports	shizuoka, held, sport, park, national, garden university, pacific, international, high, competition
	Clans	clan, shimazu, province, local, vassal takada samurai, ruled, powerful, perished, lord, unified
	Autonomy	core, autonomy, system prefectural, government, city, establishment designation, structure
2	Meiji Restoration	abolition, period kuroda dazaifu, uetsu, reppan part, meiji, joined, edo, dispossessed, daimyo
	Battles	navy, japanese, satsuma, royal, refusal, punish previous, pay, indemnity, compensation, charles
	Wars	japanese, navy, imperial, base, air, togos, russojapanese, orient nickname, nelson naval, military
	Festivals	festival, first, took, snow, place, maple, lantern, held, chrysanthemum cherry blossom, castle
	Construction	warehouse, stone, torn, stonework, reconstructed original, form, date, constructed, builder
	Transportation	railway, development, increase, via, scale, sagami rapid, railroad, rail, connected, led
	Universities	university, taught, matsue lafcadio, learn, author, hirosaki, established
	Commerce	much, fire, consumes, area, replanned, maritime, ginza, commerce, canal, accommodate, city
	Natural Disasters	earthquake, volcano, throughout, spread, relatively, outages, numerous, morioka, hit, extensive
	Shoguns	daimyo tokugawa, shogun shigeharu, sakamoto, rule, position, newly, metsuke, income
3	Wars	war, zenkunen, yoriyoshi, takenori, reinforced, dewa, defeated, abe, province, minamoto
	Government	city, suggests, reliable, publicly, point, notices, legal, issued, governing, council
	Battles	summer, battle, ground, burned, osaka, sakai
	Commerce	wealthiest, residents, population, people, living, enterprise, earned, commercial, almost, japan
	Christianity	went, outlawed, hiding, escape, christianity, capture
	Merge	isawa, city, village, modern, merger, maesawa, koromogawa, established, district, town
	Christianity	xavier, prosperity, priests, including, francis, documented, christian, sengoku, period, visited
	Missionary	stand, sent, sendai reach, portugal, padre, new, missionary, many, jesuit hour, diogo
	Trade	trade, using, richest, muromachi, mouth, location, inland connect, became, foreign, sengoku
	Business & Power	weaken toyotomi, stronghold, seized, reportedly, power, nobunaga, move, merchant, central

a feudal society to a modern industrialized state, and is regarded as the most significant turning point in the history of Japan. Many cities in this group were involved in continuous **Battles** in the middle and late 19th century. Hundreds of Japanese castles were constructed throughout the whole country, as reflected by the event **Construction**. **Festivals** relates to major traditional cultural activities in lives of city residents, such as viewing the cherry blossom and autumn colors. Cities such *Dazaifu* and *Kyoto* represent this category well.

Histories of cities in the third category embody the multi-ethnic side of the Japanese society, by showing the pattern of assimilating foreign culture. As evidence, the corresponding summary includes events such as **Christianity**, **Missionary** and **Trade**[3]. Cities in this category played a vital role in enhancing the international exchange of Japan in the past, such as *Oshu* and *Nagasaki*.

Finally, some events appear in more than one category, e.g., **Natural Disasters**, **Transportation** and **Wars**. Such events can be regarded as a common characteristic shared by all the categories.

6   Discussions

We discuss here several relevant aspects to the task of history-driven entity categorization and characterization as well as the limitations of our approach.

- Latent groups can be detected for different time periods (e.g., histories of cities during Renaissance or histories of famous persons during their early careers).

---

[3] Note that the standard deviations of event occurrence times are 0 here as the total number of used events is quite small.

Different input time periods will usually result in different discovered latent groups.

- Currently, the exemplars are selected on the basis of the similarities of their histories to histories of other entities. However, other attributes could be also considered in the process of exemplar selection - for instance, popularity or familiarity among users (e.g., while *Dazaifu* may be a good exemplar for its latent group, *Kyoto* which belongs to the same group is more known and recognized by potential users). Hence, entity popularity or importance could serve as an additional component for the exemplar selection.
- We would like to emphasize that the proposed task is a novel kind of historical knowledge generation and organization. This could offer interesting insights to historians, especially, as they can provide more complete data as an input. Furthermore, based on history-based entity grouping, a history of any given entity could be now seen not independently but rather in relation to the typical history of an underlying latent group it belongs to.

7   Related Work

To the best of our knowledge, the research problem of forming history-based entity groups has not been proposed neither approached so far. Our work is nevertheless connected to the research area: *exemplar detection for entity categorization* that is surveyed below.

Cognitive science studies suggest that people tend to understand and memorize categories through the *exemplar theory* [5], which argues that individuals make category judgments by comparing new stimuli with *exemplars* already stored in their memory. There are several determinants of exemplars, such as central tendency [4] and stimulus similarity [18]. The *exemplar theory* was widely adopted in many research fields, such as conceptual modeling [1] and entity summarization [10].

The work of exemplar detection is closely related to two different areas: *affinity propagation for clustering* and *cluster-based information retrieval*. Under the Affinity Propagation (AP) algorithm [11], clustering is viewed as the process of identifying a subset of representative exemplars. The AP algorithm is widely deployed in many research fields such as image categorization [23], image segmentation [24] and so on. A large body of work on cluster-based approach for IR aims for returning a ranked list of a set of exemplar documents representing the clusters of documents relevant to a given query. The research problem here can also be considered as *search result diversification (SRD)*. The MMR model [6] applies the *greedy best first strategy* to obtain the ranked list of exemplars. Later on, the Modern Portfolio Theory (MPT) [22] model and the Exp-1-$call@k$ [21] model were proposed for improving implicit SRD. The well-known Desirable Facility Placement (DFP) [27] model uses the *greedy best k strategy* for ranking the exemplars in a more general way. Recently, an integer linear programming model [25] formulates implicit SRD as a process of ranking k exemplar documents from the top-m documents of an initial retrieval.

8 Conclusions

It is natural for humans to categorize entities based on their common traits. Given the importance of history on shaping the characteristics of many entities, a useful way to form categories is by considering similarities in the entity historical developments. In this paper we introduce for the first time a novel research problem of categorizing entities into history-based categories for category characterization and understanding. To solve this problem we propose an unsupervised approach based on a concise optimization framework. The effectiveness of our methods is demonstrated in experiments on 7 Wikipedia category datasets through both qualitative and quantitative analysis.

In future, we plan to design more problem-specific optimization model (e.g., integer linear programming model) with better scalability based on its intrinsic flexibility for the purpose of entity summarization and understanding.

Acknowledgements. This research has been supported by JSPS KAKENHI grants (#17H01828, #18K19841, #18H03243).

References

1. Au Yeung, C.M., Leung, H.F.: A formal model of ontology for handling fuzzy membership and typicality of instances. Comput. J. **53**(3), 316–341 (2008)
2. Bairi, R.B., Carman, M., Ramakrishnan, G.: On the evolution of Wikipedia: dynamics of categories and articles. In: AAAI (2015)
3. Bamman, D., Smith, N.A.: Unsupervised discovery of biographical structure from text. TACL **2**, 363–376 (2014)
4. Barsalou, L.W.: The instability of graded structure: implications for the nature of concepts. In: Concepts and Conceptual Development: Ecological and Intellectual Factors in Categorization, pp. 10139 (1987)
5. Brooks, L.R.: Nonanalytic concept formation and memory for instances (1978)
6. Carbonell, J., Goldstein, J.: The use of MMR, diversity-based reranking for reordering documents and producing summaries. In: SIGIR, pp. 335–336. ACM (1998)
7. Chang, A.X., Manning, C.D.: SUTime: a library for recognizing and normalizing time expressions. In: LREC 2012, pp. 3735–3740 (2012)
8. Chen, Y.N., Metze, F.: Two-layer mutually reinforced random walk for improved multi-party meeting summarization. In: 2012 IEEE SLT, pp. 461–466 (2012)
9. Li, C., Cheng, H., Xiao, Y., Xie, C., Jiang, H., Feng, S.: Timeline: a Chinese event extraction and exploration system. In: SoMeT 2018 (2018)
10. Duan, Y., Jatowt, A., Tanaka, K.: Discovering typical histories of entities by multi-timeline summarization. In: Proceedings of the 28th ACM HT, pp. 105–114 (2017)
11. Frey, B.J., Dueck, D.: Clustering by passing messages between data points. Science **315**(5814), 972–976 (2007)
12. Hartigan, J.A., Wong, M.A.: A k-means clustering algorithm. JSTOR: Appl. Stat. **28**(1), 100–108 (1979)
13. Hintzman, D.L., Ludlam, G.: Differential forgetting of prototypes and old instances: simulation by an exemplar-based classification model. Mem. Cogn. **8**(4), 378–382 (1980)

14. Kschischang, F.R., Frey, B.J., Loeliger, H.A., et al.: Factor graphs and the sum-product algorithm. IEEE Trans. Inf. Theory **47**(2), 498–519 (2001)
15. Liu, B., Dai, Y., Li, X., Lee, W.S., Yu, P.S.: Building text classifiers using positive and unlabeled examples. In: ICDM 2003, pp. 179–186. IEEE (2003)
16. Liu, B., Lee, W.S., Yu, P.S., Li, X.: Partially supervised classification of text documents. In: ICML, vol. 2, 387–394 (2002)
17. Mikolov, T., Chen, K., Corrado, G., Dean, J.: Efficient estimation of word representations in vector space. arXiv preprint arXiv:1301.3781 (2013)
18. Nosofsky, R.M.: Similarity, frequency, and category representations. J. Exp. Psychol.: Learn. Mem. Cogn. **14**(1), 54 (1988)
19. Řehůřek, R., Sojka, P.: Software framework for topic modelling with large corpora. In: LREC 2010, pp. 45–50 (2010)
20. Rosch, E.: Cognitive representations of semantic categories. J. Exp. Psychol. Gen. **104**(3), 192 (1975)
21. Sanner, S., Guo, S., Graepel, T., Kharazmi, S., Karimi, S.: Diverse retrieval via greedy optimization of expected 1-call@ k in a latent subtopic relevance model. In: CIKM, pp. 1977–1980. ACM (2011)
22. Wang, J., Zhu, J.: Portfolio theory of information retrieval. In: SIGIR, pp. 115–122. ACM (2009)
23. Wang, Y., Chen, L.: K-MEAP: multiple exemplars affinity propagation with specified k clusters. IEEE Trans. Neural Netw. Learn. Syst. **27**(12), 2670–2682 (2016)
24. Xiao, J., Wang, J., Tan, P., Quan, L.: Joint affinity propagation for multiple view segmentation. In: ICCV 2007, pp. 1–7. IEEE (2007)
25. Yu, H.T., et al.: A concise integer linear programming formulation for implicit search result diversification. In: WSDM, pp. 191–200. ACM (2017)
26. Yu, H., Han, J., Chang, K.C.C.: PEBL: positive example based learning for web page classification using SVM. In: SIGKDD, pp. 239–248. ACM (2002)
27. Zuccon, G., Azzopardi, L., Zhang, D., Wang, J.: Top-k retrieval using facility location analysis. In: Baeza-Yates, R., et al. (eds.) ECIR 2012. LNCS, vol. 7224, pp. 305–316. Springer, Heidelberg (2012). https://doi.org/10.1007/978-3-642-28997-2_26

MBMN: Multivariate Bernoulli Mixture Network for News Emotion Analysis

Xue Zhao, Ying Zhang$^{(\boxtimes)}$, Wenya Guo, and Xiaojie Yuan

College of Computer Science, Nankai Univeristy, Tianjin, China
{zhaoxue,zhangying,guowenya,yuanxiaojie}@dbis.nankai.edu.cn

Abstract. In the text classification task, besides the text features, labels are also crucial to the final classification performance, which have not been considered in most existing works. In the context of emotions, labels are correlated and some of them can coexist. Such label features and label dependencies as auxiliary text information can be helpful for text classification.

In this paper, we propose a Multivariate Bernoulli Mixture Network (MBMN) to learn a text representation as well as a label representation. Specifically, it generates the text representation with a simple convolutional neural network, and learns a mixture of multivariate Bernoulli distribution which can model the label distribution as well as label dependencies. The labels can be sampled from the distribution and further used to generate a label representation. With both text representation and label representation, MBMN can achieve better classification performance.

Experiments show the effectiveness of the proposed method against competitive alternatives on two public datasets.

Keywords: Mixture density networks · Sentiment analysis ·
Label emebedding

1 Introduction

The promise of AI is to make work and life more productive, which requires AI to better understand humans. However, a significant limitation, to date, is to understand human emotions. Fortunately, abundant user-generated emotion-labeled data has been available thanks to the active development of web applications. Mining such data is of great help in modeling emotions and developing the intelligence of machines.

Extensive research has been conducted to identify the emotions expressed in tweets [1], blogs [2] and stories [3]. However, in many scenarios where the context is less subjective and emotional words are rare, it is difficult to extract affective information for emotion prediction, which motivates us to explore emotions on the less subjective text, such as news articles. There are various news websites providing 'mood meter', as shown in Fig. 1, with which readers can express how

© Springer Nature Switzerland AG 2019
J. Shao et al. (Eds.): APWeb-WAIM 2019, LNCS 11642, pp. 365–379, 2019.
https://doi.org/10.1007/978-3-030-26075-0_28

they feel after reading the news by clicking one of the emotion buttons. Existing research on emotion analysis mainly focuses on identifying emotional words [4,5] or extracting emotion-related features [6–8]. However, these models neglect the useful knowledge contained in emotion labels, which can directly influence the final emotion prediction. Emotions are intrinsically correlated and can coexist. The emotion dependencies thus can be useful as a type of auxiliary information to the text. Recent work [9,10] on label embeddings built text representations by projecting the labels and words into the same embedding space. However, the correlation between labels has not been discussed.

Fig. 1. The emotion votes for a *Rappler* news article.

In light of the above, we model the label distribution by a mixture of Bernoulli distribution which can automatically take care of the label dependencies by its covariance matrix. We propose a Multivariate Bernoulli Mixture Network to generate both **label representation** as well as **text representation** for a better emotion classification result. The main contributions are two folds:

- propose a novel mixture density network structure based on multivariate Bernoulli distribution, which can specifically encode the label dependencies by its covariance.
- given the text, sample labels from label distribution and use label embedding as well as neural network to generate a label representation. We utilize both label representation and text representation to do text classification.

It is worth noting that our task is a multi-class classification problem instead of a multi-label one because the data is not multi-labelled. We evaluate our method by not only measuring the accuracy of top-one emotion prediction but also the error of distribution prediction. The experiment results prove that the proposed model outperforms other text/sentiment classification baselines on two public online news datasets.

2 Preliminaries

Different from the existing work, we learn a label distribution where label dependencies can be encoded. This can be achieved by using mixture of Bernoulli distribution which learns binary variables and their dependencies with its nondiagonal covariance matrix. Therefore, we propose MBMN which incorporates the mixture of multivariate Bernoulli and the mixture density networks. In this section, we briefly introduce the distribution and the network.

2.1 Mixture of Multivariate Bernoulli

Observations of multiple discrete binaries are usually assumed to be generated from a mixture of Multivariate Bernoulli distribution [11]. Consider a binary label set $Y = \{\mathbf{y_1}, \ldots, \mathbf{y_N}\}$ with N observations and the number of label (emotion) classes C, where $\mathbf{y} = \{y_1, \ldots, y_C\}^T$, y is governed by a Bernoulli distribution with parameter μ_c, so that

$$p(\mathbf{y}|\boldsymbol{\mu}) = \prod_{c=1}^{C} \mu_c^{y_c}(1-\mu_c)^{1-y_c} \tag{1}$$

where $\boldsymbol{\mu} = (\mu_1, \ldots, \mu_C)^T$. Noted that we use characters in bold to represent vectors in the paper. A mixture model is a probability function having K components. Each component is a multivariate Bernoulli distribution, which is weighted by π_k, where $\sum_{k=1}^{K} \pi_k = 1$. The probability function for each observation can be formed as:

$$p(\mathbf{y}|\boldsymbol{\mu}, \boldsymbol{\pi}) = \sum_{k=1}^{K} \pi_k p(\mathbf{y}|\boldsymbol{\mu_k}) \tag{2}$$

where $\boldsymbol{\pi} = \{\pi_1, \ldots, \pi_K\}$, $\boldsymbol{\mu} = \{\boldsymbol{\mu_1}, \ldots, \boldsymbol{\mu_K}\}$. For each observation, although C classes (emotions) are assumed to be independent in each component, the dependencies can be captured by the mixture in general by the covariance matrix cov $[\mathbf{y}]$ which is no longer diagonal. In particular, the number of components can be viewed as the number of types of dependencies.

$$\text{cov}[\mathbf{y}] = \sum_{k=1}^{K} \pi_k \{\boldsymbol{\Sigma}_k + \boldsymbol{\mu_k}\boldsymbol{\mu_k}^T\} - \mathbb{E}[\mathbf{y}]\mathbb{E}[\mathbf{y}]^T \tag{3}$$

where $\boldsymbol{\Sigma}_k = \text{diag}\{\mu_{ki}(1-\mu_{ki})\}$, and mean of the mixture distribution $\mathbb{E}[\mathbf{y}] = \sum_{k=1}^{K} \pi_k \boldsymbol{\mu_k}$.

2.2 Mixture Density Networks

Mixture Density Network (MDN) [12] trains a neural network as well as a mixture of Gaussian distribution. The parameters of Gaussian mixture are generated by the neural network. An MDN $\mathcal{M}$ first takes a set of input features $\mathbf{x}$ and outputs a set of parameters for the Gaussian mixture, including the weight of components w_m, mean μ_m and variance σ_m^2. The full probability density function of an output y, conditioned on the input features, $p(y|\mathbf{x}, \mathcal{M})^1$ is given as:

$$p(y|\mathbf{x}, \mathcal{M}) = \sum_{m=1}^{M} w_m(\mathbf{x}) \cdot \mathcal{N}(y; \mu_m(\mathbf{x}), \sigma_m^2(\mathbf{x})) \qquad (4)$$

where M is the number of mixture components and $w_m(\mathbf{x})$, $\mu_m(\mathbf{x})$ and $\sigma_m^2(\mathbf{x})$ correspond to the component weights, mean and variance of the m-th Gaussian component, given $\mathbf{x}$. The GMM parameters can be derived from the MDN as

$$w_m(\mathbf{x}) = \frac{\exp\left(z_m^{(w)}(\mathbf{x}, \mathcal{M})\right)}{\sum_{l=1}^{M} \exp\left(z_l^{(w)}(\mathbf{x}, \mathcal{M})\right)} \qquad (5)$$

$$\sigma_m(\mathbf{x}) = \exp\left(z_m^{(\sigma)}(\mathbf{x}, \mathcal{M})\right) \qquad (6)$$

$$\mu_m(x) = z_m^{(\mu)}(\mathbf{x}, \mathcal{M}) \qquad (7)$$

where $z_m^{(w)}(\mathbf{x}, \mathcal{M})$, $z_m^{(\sigma)}(\mathbf{x}, \mathcal{M})$, and $z_m^{\mu}(\mathbf{x}, \mathcal{M})$ are the activations of the output layer of the MDN corresponding to the mixture weight, variance, mean for the m-th Gaussian component, given $\mathbf{x}$ and $\mathcal{M}$, respectively. The use of the softmax function in Eq. 5 constraints the mixture weights to be positive and sum to 1. Similarly, Eq. 6 constraints the standard deviations to be positive. Training of the MDN aims to maximize the log-likelihood of $\mathcal{M}$ given the data as

$$\hat{\mathcal{M}} = \operatorname*{argmax}_{\mathcal{M}} \sum_{n=1}^{N} \sum_{t=1}^{T^{(n)}} \log p(y_t^{(n)}|x_t^{(n)}, \mathcal{M}) \qquad (8)$$

where N is the number of instances and T is the size of output features y. Once the MDN has been trained, we can predict conditional density function of the target data for a given value of input vector.

Bernoulli mixture can depict the correlation among labels with its non-diagonal covariance matrix, while Gaussian mixture cannot as its covariance is diagonal. Therefore, in this paper, we use mixture of Bernoulli to build a mixture density network, so that the emotion dependencies can be better captured. Accordingly, we describe emotions with binary variables (1 if the emotion with the highest probability, 0 otherwise) which can be better modeled by Bernoulli distribution.

3   Approach

In this section, we present the proposed network MBMN, as shown in Fig. 2. MBMN is to build a neural network which generates the parameters for a mixture

---

[1] For simplicity of notation, here the output feature is assumed to be a scalar value. The extension to a vector is straightforward.

of multivariate Bernoulli distribution, which is represented in Eq. 2. It has a word embedding layer and an emotion embedding layer. Convolutional neural network (CNN) is used to extract features from words and labels. In particular, the text representation is generated by a CNN layer. With the same CNN and a fully connected layer, the parameters are generated and the Bernoulli mixture can thus be initialized. The emotions are sampled from the Bernoulli mixture and vectorized by the emotion embedding layer. Another CNN will be used to generate a label representation. The final representation is the concatenation of text representation and label representation.

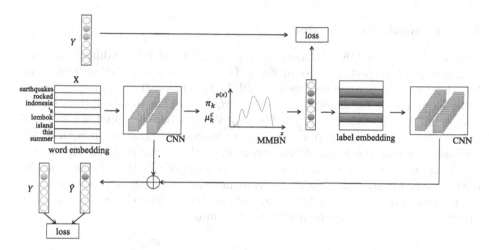

Fig. 2. Architecture of the proposed MBMN. Y represents the ground truth and $\hat{Y}$ is the prediction. The data X starts to flow from the left. The first CNN is to generate a text representation, and is followed by a fully connected layer which outputs parameters π and μ. With parameters, the mixture of multivariate Bernoulli distribution can be set up so that emotions can be sampled. The labels can be transformed into a label representation by label embedding and the second CNN module. The concatenated text and label representation will be fed to a softmax layer for final prediction.

3.1 CNN Feature Extraction

We design a feature extraction module based on CNN structure proposed in [13]. The input word sequence of news article will be projected into a low-level representation by a d-dimensional word embedding layer into $\mathbf{S}$. Then we extract feature maps for $n$grams with a 2-dimension convolution operation with filter $\mathbf{W_1}$, where f is the number of filters and (n, d) is kernel size.

$$\mathbf{U} = \text{ELU}(\mathbf{W_1} \cdot \mathbf{S}_{i:i-n+1} + \mathbf{b})$$
$$\mathbf{V} = \text{Maxpooling}(\mathbf{U}) \tag{9}$$

$\mathbf{b}$ is the bias item. We use the exponential linear unit (ELU) as activation to reduce the bias shift effect. Then we apply the Maxpooling operation to maintain the most salient features. Noted that we use the same CNN structure to extract label features but with different kernel size.

A fully connection layer is used in order to generate parameters π and μ. It takes $\mathbf{V}$ as input, and output $\mathbf{X}$ through $(K+K \times C)$ units which are activated by a non-linear function ($tanh$ is used in the experiment). K parameters are mixture component weight π, and $K \times C$ parameters are used in Bernoulli distribution $p(\mathbf{y}|\mu)$.

$$\mathbf{X} = \mathbf{W_2} \cdot \mathbf{V} + \mathbf{b} \tag{10}$$

where the weight matrix $\mathbf{W_2}$ and bias $\mathbf{b}$ are trainable parameters.

3.2 Bernoulli Mixture Module

The obtained K and $K \times C$ outputs are transformed by non-linear function $\mathbf{f}(\mathbf{x})$ and $\mathbf{g}(\mathbf{x})$, respectively. As in Eq. 5, $\mathbf{f}(\mathbf{x})$ can be formulated as a softmax function so that the component weights will be larger than 0 and sum to 1. On the other hand, the $K \times C$ binary units are parameters of the Bernoulli distribution $p(\mathbf{y}|\mu)$ in Eq. 2. We define $p(\mathbf{g}|x) = \mathcal{B}(p = g(\mathbf{Wx}))$, where each unit $\mathbf{g}$ is sampled independently with rate $g(\mathbf{Wx})$ set by the non-linear activation function g. We implement g with the Sigmoid function $\sigma(\mathbf{Wx} + \mathbf{b})$ as the rate of sampling 1.

With the sampling operations $\mathbf{g} \sim \mathcal{B}(p = g(\mathbf{Wx}))$, the binaries can be obtained. However, it is difficult to train networks with these binary stochastic neurons. Here we use a lower variance estimator introduced by [14]. The approach decomposes the stochastic neurons into

$$\mathbf{g} = g(\mathbf{Wx}) + \epsilon, \quad \text{with} \quad \epsilon = \begin{cases} 1 - g(\mathbf{Wx}) \\ -g(\mathbf{Wx}) \end{cases} \tag{11}$$

which expresses Bernoulli unit as the sum of the deterministic term $g(\mathbf{Wx})$ and the stochastic term ϵ. The strategy propagates the gradient only through the deterministic term which is the output of the gating function and ignores the gradient coming from ϵ. The term ϵ has zero mean, as $E[\mathbf{g}] = g(\mathbf{Wx})$. Therefore, training stochastic binary units can be simple when the forward pass accumulates the training loss with sampled binaries while the backporpogation will only go through the Sigmoid activation functions as if there was no sampling. The method has been proved to be effective in practice and incurs only a small bias.

The sampling process is straightforward. We sample from each multivariate Bernoulli in K components to obtain $K \times C$ binaries, weight them by the component weights π and sum up the weighted binaries. The weighted and summed results contain 1s and decimals, where only the 1s are kept. As 1 can only be derived when all the components generate 1 after weighted by π. In this scenario, all the components 'agreed' upon the decision of sampling 1. All the other conditions will derive a decimal, or 0 when all the components give 0. This sampling procedure obeys the Bernoulli mixture because the sample from a Bernoulli mixture also satisfies all its components, as Eqs. 1 and 2. Therefore, in the forward pass, the binary samples are derived by

$$\mathbf{E} = \begin{cases} 1, & \text{if } \sum_{k=1}^{K} \pi_k \mathbf{g}_k = 1 \\ 0, & \text{else} \end{cases} \tag{12}$$

where $\mathbf{E}$ denotes the emotion multivariate binary samples, and $\mathbf{g}_k$ denotes the multivariate Bernoulli in ith component. The sampled emotion labels $\mathbf{E}$ will be projected into vectors by an emotion embedding layer. Another CNN feature extraction module will be used to generate a label representation. Finally, the text representation and label representation will be concatenated and fed to a label-size fully connected layer with Softmax activation. Then the output will be the predicted distribution over emotions.

3.3   Training MBMN

During the training phase, the samples are governed by Bernoulli mixture with parameter $\boldsymbol{\pi}$ and $\boldsymbol{\mu}$. The raw sample is represented by $\sum_{k=1}^{K} \pi_k \mathbf{g}_k$, which should be close to 1 for the true labels and close to 0 for the false labels. This prediction loss can be calculated by the binary cross entropy. On the other hand, the final prediction is a distribution over emotions, the prediction error is a typical cross entropy loss.

Therefore, we optimize our network with two objectives, loss from the final predictions and the closeness between μ and true labels. The first part is a binary cross entropy loss and the second is a cross entropy loss. Assuming θ contains all the parameters of the network, the training loss is computed as follows:

$$\mathcal{L}(\theta) = -\frac{1}{N} \sum_{i=1}^{N} \mathcal{B}\left(\boldsymbol{y}_i, \sum_{k=1}^{K} \pi_{ik} \boldsymbol{g}_{ik}\right) - \frac{1}{N} \sum_{i=1}^{N} \mathcal{H}(\boldsymbol{y}_i, \hat{\boldsymbol{y}}_i) \tag{13}$$

where $\mathcal{B}$ is the binary cross entropy loss and $\mathcal{H}$ is the cross entropy loss between the gold one-hot labels $\boldsymbol{y}_i$ and the rates $\sum_{k=1}^{K} \pi_{ik} \boldsymbol{g}_{ik}$ or predicted labels $\hat{\boldsymbol{y}}_i$ for document i. N is the number of news articles in training dataset.

4   Experiment

In this section, we introduce two public online news datasets, baseline models, model configurations and experiment results.

4.1   Datasets

We conduct experiments and evaluate the proposed approach on two datasets: *Rappler*[2] and *Yahoo*[3], both datasets are publicly accessible. *Rappler* is developed by [15] with English news articles over 8 emotion categories, and *Yahoo* is

Table 1. Datasets statistics: number of articles that the emotion has the highest number of votes.

Rappler	# of articles	Yahoo	# of articles
Happy	12,304	Happy	17,023
Sad	4,571	Sad	1,545
Angry	3,003	Angry	12,884
Amused	3,449	Surprised	3,001
Afraid	2,576	Bored	2,429
Annoyed	1,311	Warm	521
Inspired	2,729	Awesome	2,123
Don't care	1,164	–	–
Total	31,107	Total	49,000

a Chinese Yahoo Kimo news dataset with 7 emotions (originally 8 emotion categories, but we excluded label "informative" as it is not related to an emotional state). Table 1 summaries the statistic of the datasets.

We split the data into training, development, testing by 7/1/2. Because the data is highly imbalanced, stratified sampling is applied to keep the proportion of each category the same in training, development, testing.

4.2   Baselines

The main contribution of our work lies in the way of feature extraction. In particular, we use a Bernoulli mixture to model label distribution to obtain a better representation for classification. Hence, we compare our method with popular and effective feature extraction methods for text classification. We also compare MBMN with a state-of-the-art text classification work using label features [10]. We organized these baselines into four groups. The first group is based on traditional machine learning models.

- **LG + BoW**, Logistic Regression with 50,000 most frequent words weighted by tf-idf.
- **SVM + ngrams**, SVM multi-class classifier is applied to unigram and bigram features.

Group 2 has RNN-based neural networks.

- **GRNN**, a Gated RNN structure proposed in [16].
- **SelfATTN**, a structured self-attentive sentence embedding for text classification proposed in [17].
- **BLSTM-ATTN**, Bidirectional LSTM with an attention layer over the hidden outputs.

- **HAN**, a hierarchical attention structure proposed in [18] for modeling words and sentences with GRU.

Group 3 contains CNN-based neural networks.

- **CNN**, a CNN model for sentence classification, proposed in [13].
- **CNN-ATTN**, an attention-based CNN model with label embedding technique for sentiment classification, proposed by [10].
- **Inception**, proposed in [20] with a deeper architecture of convolutions.

Group 4 has neural networks without RNN/CNN structures for text classification.

- **Transformer** an attention-only model proposed in [19].
- **FastText**, a simple neural network to learn task-specific embedding for text classification, proposed in [21].

4.3 Model Configuration

All the neural networks including the proposed one are using 200-dimension word embedding initialized with Glove [22] pre-trained word vectors. The label embedding size is 200. The number of the hidden layers existing in the models is set as 256. Dropout is set as 0.3. All the models are optimized by Adam optimizer with a proper learning rate of 0.001. The kernel size in CNN-based structures, including the proposed MBMN, is set as $3, 4, 5$, as [13] suggested. The kernel size for filters used in label feature extraction is chosen among $\{2, 3\}$ and we only report the best result. The number of components is set as $2, 3$, or 4.

Some uncommon parameters, such as the number of attention heads, are set properly according to the original papers.

4.4 Measures

We use Accuracy and RMSE to evaluate the performance of models. Accuracy is a standard metric to measure the overall emotion classification performance. T denotes the number of news articles that are correctly classified and D is the total number of news in the test dataset. RMSE measures the divergences between predicted and the ground truth emotions, where $\hat{y}_i$, y_{id} are vectors representing the predicted output and gold emotion distribution, respectively. N is the number of news articles in training dataset. The Accuracy and RMSE are defined as:

$$\text{Accuracy} = \frac{T}{D} \tag{14}$$

$$\text{RMSE} = \sqrt{\frac{\sum_{i=1}^{N}(\hat{y}_i - y_{id})^2}{N}} \tag{15}$$

Table 2. Emotion classification on different models.

Models	Rappler		Yahoo	
	Accy%	RMSE	Acc%	RMSE
LR	57.93	0.234	70.04	0.187
SVM	72.99	0.234	78.43	0.234
GRNN	75.07	0.232	83.04	0.203
SelfATTN	75.01	0.229	83.86	0.223
BLSTM-ATTN	78.37	0.215	84.67	0.193
HAN	75.08	0.221	82.16	0.214
CNN	78.23	0.191	85.09	0.189
CNN-ATTN	78.18	0.214	85.27	0.225
Inception	75.38	0.222	80.45	0.227
Transformer	77.98	0.183	84.72	0.277
FastText	75.99	0.226	84.23	0.227
MBMN-2	**80.24**	**0.181**	85.50	**0.165**
MBMN-3	79.22	0.204	83.70	0.236
MBMN-4	79.14	0.210	**85.70**	0.228

4.5   Results

We summarize the experiment results in Table 2, from which we can observe that the machine learning models are comparably weaker than deep learning models.

By in-group comparison, BLSTM-ATTN performs the best among all the RNN-based models, owing to the strengths of bidirectional encoding and attention mechanism. HAN is proposed by introducing sentence-word structure information, however, it does not improve the prediction results. This indicates that the information conveyed in the sentence-word structure is not really helpful in differentiating the emotions in news articles. MBMN, without bidirectional encoding, attention mechanism, or sentence structure information, still outperforms BLSTM-ATTN and HAN.

From the third group, we can observe that simple CNN structure outperforms all the other CNN models. The evaluation of accuracy and RMSE shows that our model can achieve better performance in all scenarios. In particular, CNN-ATTN also builds a representation with label embedding. However, because MBMN not only encodes the label information to interact with text features but also encodes the label-label dependencies, it receives a better result than CNN-ATTN in the experiment.

As for the models in group 4, MBMN outperforms these baselines that have no CNN/RNN structure. This indicates that CNN based density network with Bernoulli mixture is more effective in extracting text features and label features than CNN/RNN-free neural networks, so that the prediction is more accurate.

We also experiment with different settings for the proposed MBMN by using a different number of components K. As shown in Table 2, when $K = 2$, MBMN performs the best on *Rapper*. When $K = 4$, MBMN shows to be the best on *Yahoo* with regards to the accuracy. When $K = 2$, it has the smallest RMSE on *Yahoo*. Generally, when $K = 2$ the model performs better on two datasets. This implies that the emotions or their dependencies can be roughly grouped into two categories.

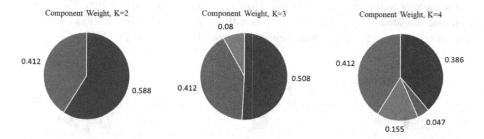

Fig. 3. π given the number of components K as 2, 3, 4. Best viewed in color.

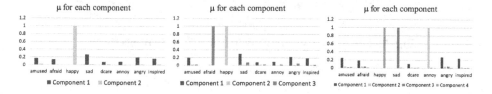

Fig. 4. μ given the number of components K as 2, 3, 4. Best viewed in color.

5 Discussion

5.1 Influence of K on μ and π

We have applied different $K = 2, 3, 4$ in the experiment. In Figs. 3 and 4 we show the different weights of components π and the expectation μ of multivariate Bernoulli distribution in each component. The result is based on *Rappler* dataset.

In Fig. 3, it can be observed that there are two major proportions in all three pie charts. When K increases, the newly created proportion is fairly small. Especially when $K = 4$, the smallest weight is only 0.047 while the two major components have around 0.4 proportion of the pie chart. This indicates that the 8 emotions can be roughly grouped into two categories, which also explains the experiment result on *Rappler* dataset where MBMN-2 achieves the best results compared to results given $K = 3, 4$.

Figure 4 shows the parameter of multivariate Bernoulli distribution in each component. The probability of an emotion being sampled depends on both component weights (pie charts) and the Bernoulli distribution. In all three bar charts, *happy* always obtains a spike in one of the components and the corresponding component has a large weight which can be observed in Fig. 3. This means *happy* has a higher probability to be sampled in the mixture distribution. When $K = 3$, because the smallest component (in grey) only contributes 0.08 proportion of pie chart, although its Bernoulli distribution has a spike on category *afraid*, the probability of sampling *afraid* is still small. This also happens when $K = 4$, the spikes of *sad* and *annoyed* will not be as influential as the spike of *happy* because their corresponding component weights are small, as shown in Fig. 3.

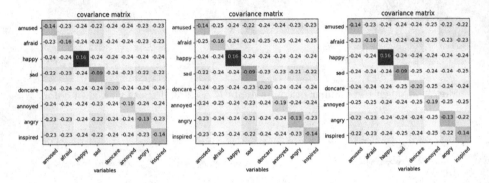

Fig. 5. The covariance matrix when $K = 3$, 4, 5, respectively.

5.2   Influence of K on Emotion Correlations

The mixture structure assigns different weights to the multivariate Bernoulli distribution, by which the correlations of variables can also be captured by its covariance matrix. We calculate the covariance by Eq. 3 and the matrices are displayed in Fig. 5. Surprisingly, the covariance has no significant change with a varying K. It is worth mentioning that as long as the covariance in the matrix is non-zero, the matrix can capture certain correlations between variables.

6   Related Work

6.1   Emotion Analysis

Emotion analysis aims to identifying the emotions from the text, which requires the ability to extract features from the text. Traditional machine learning methods, such as Logistic Regression and SVM, use word units as features to do classification, which serve as strong baselines for text analysis task. On the other hand, there are many effective neural-based methods for text feature extraction.

For example, RNN-based methods can model the word sequence features [16–18], CNN-based methods [10,13,20] are able to extract local and global features in the text. Specifically, a RNN-based method [18] is to build attention layers not only on word level, but also on sentence level. The hierarchical attention mechanism can better capture important words as well as important sentences. Differently, a CNN-based approach [10] builds an attention layer on both text representation and label representation, by first projecting text and labels into same vector space with word embedding and label embedding, then applying attention mechanism on the word-label representation. The proposed MBMN shares the same idea of building a word-label joint representation. More importantly, with the mixture of Bernoulli distribution, the proposed model can also encode latent label-label dependencies into the final representation.

6.2   Mixture Density Networks

Mixture density networks (MDN) can give full probability density functions over real-valued output features conditioned on the corresponding input features. This is achieved by modeling the conditional probability distribution of output features given input features with a Gaussian mixture model, where its parameters are generated using a neural network trained with a log likelihood-based loss function.

MDN has been widely used in voice conversion [23] and speech synthesis [24, 25] tasks. WaveNet [26], as a neural network-based waveform generation model, is popular in voice conversion areas [27,28]. However, MDN has not been applied to text classification tasks. In our work, we apply a Bernoulli-based mixture density network to model the label distribution, then use a label embedding and a neural network to further extract the features of labels.

7   Conclusion

In this paper, we predict emotional responses evoked by news articles by proposing a new density network, which takes advantage of the rich information embedded in the labels. We combine the CNN networks and a multivariate Bernoulli mixture distribution to generate a label representation and a text representation. Specifically, the network first extracts text features with CNN and output text representation as well as the parameters for the Bernoulli mixture model. The emotion labels can be sampled from the Bernoulli mixture distribution and will be further vectorized by a label embedding layer. Another CNN will be used to generate a label representation. The text representation and label representation will be concatenated and further fed into a classification Softmax layer.

However, the number of labels in our case is small, which can be a limit to our proposed method. In the future, we will work on data with more labels where labels can be much more important and helpful.

Acknowledgement. We thank the reviewers for their constructive comments. This research is supported by National Natural Science Foundation of China (No. U1836109) and the Fundamental Research Funds for the Central Universities, Nankai University (No. 63191709 and No. 63191705).

References

1. Mohammad, S.M., Kiritchenko, S.: Using hashtags to capture fine emotion categories from tweets. Comput. Intell. **31**(2), 301–326 (2015)
2. Tang, Y.J., Chen, H.H.: Emotion modeling from writer/reader perspectives using a microblog dataset. In: Proceedings of the Workshop on Sentiment Analysis Where AI Meets Psychology (SAAIP 2011), pp. 11–19 (2011)
3. Mohammad, S.: From once upon a time to happily ever after: tracking emotions in novels and fairy tales. In: Proceedings of the 5th ACL-HLT Workshop on Language Technology for Cultural Heritage, Social Sciences, and Humanities, pp. 105–114. Association for Computational Linguistics, June 2011
4. Rao, Y., Lei, J., Wenyin, L., Li, Q., Chen, M.: Building emotional dictionary for sentiment analysis of online news. World Wide Web **17**(4), 723–742 (2014)
5. Staiano, J., Guerini, M.: Depeche mood: a lexicon for emotion analysis from crowd annotated news. In: Proceedings of the 52nd Annual Meeting of the Association for Computational Linguistics (Volume 2: Short Papers), vol. 2, pp. 427–433 (2014)
6. Bhowmick, P.K., Basu, A., Mitra, P., Prasad, A.: Multi-label text classification approach for sentence level news emotion analysis. In: Chaudhury, S., Mitra, S., Murthy, C.A., Sastry, P.S., Pal, S.K. (eds.) PReMI 2009. LNCS, vol. 5909, pp. 261–266. Springer, Heidelberg (2009). https://doi.org/10.1007/978-3-642-11164-8_42
7. Lin, K.H.Y., Yang, C., Chen, H.H.: Emotion classification of online news articles from the reader's perspective. In: Proceedings of the 2008 IEEE/WIC/ACM International Conference on Web Intelligence and Intelligent Agent Technology-Volume 01, pp. 220–226. IEEE Computer Society, December 2008
8. Deyu, Z.H., Zhang, X., Zhou, Y., Zhao, Q., Geng, X.: Emotion distribution learning from texts. In: Proceedings of the 2016 Conference on EMNLP (2016)
9. Tang, J., Qu, M., Mei, Q.: PTE: predictive text embedding through large-scale heterogeneous text networks. In: Proceedings of the 21th ACM SIGKDD, August 2015
10. Wang, G., et al.: Joint embedding of words and labels for text classification. In: ACL (2018)
11. Dai, B., Ding, S., Wahba, G.: Multivariate bernoulli distribution. Bernoulli **19**(4), 1465–1483 (2013)
12. Bishop, C.M.: Mixture density networks, p. 7. Technical report NCRG/4288, Aston University, Birmingham, UK (1994)
13. Kim, Y.: Convolutional neural networks for sentence classification. In: Proceedings of the 2014 Conference on Empirical Methods in Natural Language Processing (EMNLP), pp. 1746–1751 (2014)
14. Raiko, T., Berglund, M., Alain, G., Dinh, L.: Techniques for learning binary stochastic feedforward neural networks. arXiv preprint arXiv:1406.2989 (2014)
15. Song, K., Gao, W., Chen, L., Feng, S., Wang, D., Zhang, C.: Build emotion lexicon from the mood of crowd via topic-assisted joint non-negative matrix factorization. In: Proceedings of the 39th International ACM SIGIR Conference on Research and Development in Information Retrieval, pp. 773–776. ACM, July 2016

16. Tang, D., Qin, B., Liu, T.: Document modeling with gated recurrent neural network for sentiment classification. In: EMNLP (2015)
17. Lin, Z., et al.: A structured self-attentive sentence embedding. In: ICLR (2017)
18. Yang, Z., Yang, D., Dyer, C., He, X., Smola, A., Hovy, E.: Hierarchical attention networks for document classification. In: NAACL (2016)
19. Vaswani, A., et al.: Attention is all you need. In: NIPS (2017)
20. Szegedy, C., et al.: Going deeper with convolutions. In: ICLR (2015)
21. Joulin, A,, Grave, E., Bojanowski, P., Mikolov, T.: Bag of tricks for efficient text classification. In: Proceedings of the European Chapter of the (2017)
22. Pennington, J., Socher, R., Manning, C.: Glove: global vectors for word representation. In: EMNLP (2014)
23. Ahangar, M., Ghorbandoost, M., Sharma, S., Smith, M.J.: Voice conversion based on a mixture density network. In: 2017 IEEE Workshop on Applications of Signal Processing to Audio and Acoustics (WASPAA), pp. 329–333. IEEE, October 2017
24. Richmond, K.: Trajectory mixture density networks with multiple mixtures for acoustic-articulatory inversion. In: Chetouani, M., Hussain, A., Gas, B., Milgram, M., Zarader, J.-L. (eds.) NOLISP 2007. LNCS (LNAI), vol. 4885, pp. 263–272. Springer, Heidelberg (2007). https://doi.org/10.1007/978-3-540-77347-4_23
25. Uria, B., Murray, I., Renals, S., Richmond, K.: Deep architectures for articulatory inversion. In: Proceedings of Interspeech, pp. 867–870 (2012)
26. Den Oord, A.V., et al.: WaveNet: a generative model for raw audio. In: 9th ISCA Speech Synthesis Workshop (SSW9), pp. 125–125 (2016)
27. Kobayashi, K., Hayashi, T., Tamamori, A., Toda, T.: Statistical voice conversion with WaveNet-based waveform generation. In: INTERSPEECH, pp. 1138–1142, August 2017
28. Niwa, J., Yoshimura, T., Hashimoto, K., Oura, K., Nankaku, Y., Tokuda, K.: Statistical voice conversion based on WaveNet. In: 2018 IEEE International Conference on Acoustics, Speech and Signal Processing (ICASSP), pp. 5289–5293. IEEE, April 2018

Multi-label Text Classification: Select Distinct Semantic Understanding for Different Labels

Wei Sun[✉], Xiangying Ran, Xiangyang Luo, Yunlai Xu, and Chongjun Wang

National Key Laboratory for Novel Software Technology, Department of Computer
Science and Technology, Nanjing University, Nanjing, China
weisun_@outlook.com, lebronran@gmail.com, lxypaul2016@gmail.com,
yunlaixu@gmail.com, chjwang@nju.edu.cn

Abstract. Multi-label classification is a challenging task in natural language processing. Most of existing methods tend to ignore the semantic
information of the text. Besides, different parts of the text contribute
differently to each label, which is not considered by most of existing
methods. In this paper, we propose a novel model for multi-label text
classification. This model generates high-level semantic understanding
representations with a multi-level dilated convolution. The multi-level
dilated convolution effectively reduces dimension and expands the receptive fields without loss of information. Moreover, a hybrid attention
mechanism is designed to capture most relevant information of the text
based on trainable label embeddings and semantic understanding. Experimental results on the dataset AAPD and RCV1-V2 show that our model
has significant advantages over baseline methods.

1 Introduction

Multi-label classification (MLC) refers to assigning multiple labels for a given
text, which can be applied in a number of real-word scenarios, such as text
categorization [21], tag recommendation [10], information retrieval [6], and so
on. As a significant task of natural language processing (NLP), many methods
have been proposed and achieved satisfactory performance.

Binary relevance (BR) [1] is one of the earliest attempts to solve the MLC
task by transforming the MLC problem into multiple single-label classification
problems. However, BR ignores the correlations among labels. Classifier chains
(CC) [19] converts the MLC problem into a chain of binary classification problems to capture the correlations among labels. However, it is computationally
expensive for large datasets. Other methods such as MLKNN [30], Rank-SVM
[4] and Adaboost. MR [21] can only used to model first-order or second-order
label correlations or are computationally intractable when high-order label correlations are considered.

With the development of deep learning, neural networks have achieved amazing success in the field of NLP. Some neural network models have been applied

© Springer Nature Switzerland AG 2019
J. Shao et al. (Eds.): APWeb-WAIM 2019, LNCS 11642, pp. 380–393, 2019.
https://doi.org/10.1007/978-3-030-26075-0_29

in the MLC task. For example, [29] utilizes fully connected neural network with pairwise ranking loss function.Convolutional neural network (CNN) [13] and recurrent neural network (RNN) [2] are proposed to perform classification. Recently, [27] regards the multi-label text classification as a sequence generation model (SGM) to capture the correlations among labels, while the performance of SGM can be affected by the order of label easily. In these models, they either only learn a shared and medial representation for all labels instead of considering the distinctness in the contributions of textual contents for different labels or neglects the high-level semantic information of textual contents.

For text classification, human does not assign labels to textual contents simply based on the word-level information but usually based on their understanding of the salient meanings in textual contents. For example, regarding the text "The beautiful girls are dancing with great excitement and obviously they enjoy the fun of feast", it can be found that there are two salient ideas, which are "the girls are beautiful" and "feast is full of happiness". We call the two salient ideas as "semantic understanding" of the text. The semantic understanding along with word-level information can be better for classifying the text into the target categories "beauty" and "sociality". In order to capture semantic understanding in the text, we find that these high-level semantic information are often wrapped in phrases or sentences, connecting with other semantic understanding with the help of contexts. Inspired by the application of convolution in NLP [8], therefore, we design a multi-level dilated convolution for textual contents to capture these semantic understanding without loss of coverage as we do not apply any form of pooling or strided convolution.

Meanwhile, for all labels, most of neural network models only learn a shared presentation, with the purpose of multi-label text classification. However, as the above, the label "beauty" should pay more attention to "the beautiful girls" and the label "sociality" should pay more attention to "the fun of feast". Inspired by [27], it is significantly important to select the most relevant information of textual contents automatically for different labels. Therefore, we implement a hybrid attention mechanism for all labels based on trainable label embeddings with the purpose of capturing the relevant information each label itself have to attends to. Furthermore, different labels can extract distinct word-level information and high-level semantic understanding representations from textual contents.

In brief, our contributions are illustrated below:

- We propose a multi-level dilated convolution to capture high-level semantic understanding representations of textual contents.
- We design a hybrid attention mechanism to extract the most distinct word-level information based on label embeddings and semantic understanding for different labels.
- Experiments results demonstrate that our model outperforms the baseline methods and achieve the state-of-the-art performance on the dataset AAPD and RCV1-V2.

The whole paper is organized as follows. We describe our model in Sect. 2. In Sect. 3, we present the experiments and make analysis. Section 4 introduces the

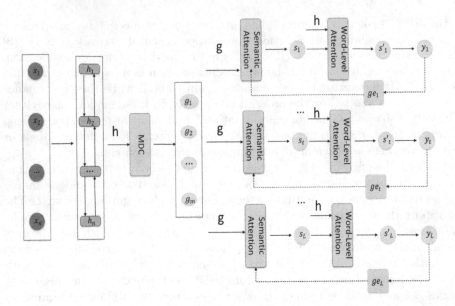

Fig. 1. The Overview of Our Proposed Model. ge_t denotes the global embedding of the t-th label. The inputs of our model are word embeddings imported into the bidirectional LSTM and h is hidden states of the bidirectional LSTM. MDC denotes the multi-level dilation convolution for capturing semantic understanding and g is the output of the MDC. The hybrid attention mechansim is composed of two parts: s_t is the most relevant semantic understanding of the t-th label and s'_t is the most relevant word-level information based on semantic understanding s_t.

related work. Finally, in Sect. 5, we conclude this paper and explore the future work.

2   Proposed Method

In the following, we introduce our proposed method to improve the conventional neural network models for multi-label text classification. First, we give an overview of our model. Second, we explain the details of the proposed model, consisting of two components: multi-level dilated convolution (MDC) as well as hybrid attention mechanism.

2.1   Overview

Multi-label text classification can be formulated as below. Given the label space with L labels $\zeta = \{l_1, l_2, \ldots, l_L\}$, a text sequence $\mathbf{x}$ containing n words, the task is to assign a subset $\mathbf{y}$ in the label space ζ to $\mathbf{x}$.

An overview of our proposed model is shown in Fig. 1. First, all labels will be initialized into global embeddings, which can be trainable. Then, a text sequence $\mathbf{x}$ is encoded to the hidden states using a bidirectional LSTM. After capturing the semantic understanding of the text by the MDC layer, we design a hybrid attention mechanism with the purpose of extracting the most distinct information for different labels. Finally, results can be predicted based on semantic understanding representations and word-level information.

2.2 Multi-level Dilated Convolution

Let $(w_1, w_2, \ldots, w_n)$ be a sentence with n words and w_i is the index of the i-th word in vocabulary. We first embeded w_i to an embedding vector x_i by an embedding matrix $E \in \mathbb{R}^{k \times |V|}$. Here, V is the size of the vocabulary and k is the dimension of the embedding vector.

We use a bidirectional LSTM [7] to read the text sequence $\mathbf{x}$ from both directions and compute the hidden states for each word,

$$\overrightarrow{h_i} = \overrightarrow{LSTM}(\overrightarrow{h_{i-1}}, x_i) \tag{1}$$

$$\overleftarrow{h_i} = \overleftarrow{LSTM}(\overleftarrow{h_{i-1}}, x_i) \tag{2}$$

We obtain the final hidden representation of the i-th word by concatenating the hidden states from both directions, $h_i = [\overrightarrow{h_i}; \overleftarrow{h_i}]$, which embodies the information of the sequence centered around the i-th word.

On top of the representations generated by the bidirectional LSTM, we apply a multi-layer convolutional neural network to generate semantic understanding representations. To be specific, our CNN is a three-layer one-dimensional CNN without any form of pooling or strided convolution. Following the previous work [9], we use one-dimensional convolution with the number of channels equal to the number of units of the hidden layer, so that the information at each dimension of one representation will not be disconnected.

A special design for the CNN is the implementation of dilated convolution. Dilation has achieved great developments in semantic segmentation in computer vision in recent years [25,28] and it has been applied in NLP [8]. Dilated convolution refers to convolution inserted with "holes" so that it can remove the negative effects such as information loss and expand the receptive fields at the exponential level without the increasing number of parameters. Thus, the dilated convolution can capture the long-term dependency. Therefore, we implement a multi-level dilated convolution with different dilation rates at different levels.

Since the same dilation rates with common factor, which can cause gridding effects, we apply MDC with different dilation rates. Following the work in [25], which has given the relationship of dilation rates in each layer, we set the dilation rates to $[1, 2, 3]$ and the number of convolution layers to 3 in our experiments. Thus, the gridding effects can be avoided and the top layer to process information between longer distance can also be allowed without loss of coverage. Therefore, our MDC can generate semantic understanding representations at phrase level with small dilation rates and those at sentence level with large rates.

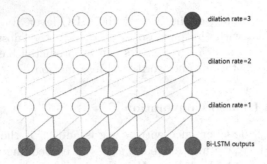

Fig. 2. The Structure of Multi-level Dilated Convolution. The kernel size is 2 and dilation rates is [1, 2, 3].

As Fig. 2 shows, on top of the word-level information from the bidirectional LSTM, the semantic understanding representations g can be formulated as follows.

$$g = MDC(h) \tag{3}$$

Here, MDC is a three-layer dilated convolution and dilation rates are set to $[1,2,3]$. The final output of semantic understanding by MDC is set to $g = \{g_1, g_2, \ldots, g_j, \ldots, g_m\}$ and the word-level information is hidden states from the bidirectional LSTM, where $h = \{h_1, h_2, \ldots, h_i, \ldots, h_n\}$. Besides, the dimension of semantic understanding g_j is equal to the one of h_i.

2.3   Hybrid Attention Mechanism

As we have obtained the word-level information from the bidirectional LSTM and semantic understanding representations from MDC, we design a type of attention mechanism to capture distinct word-level and high-level semantic information for different labels. Different from most of multi-label neural network models, which only obtain a shared representation, we initialize global embeddings for each label, helping capture the most relevant textual information corresponding to the label itself.

Motivated by multi-step attention [5] (i.e., a type of multi-hop attention mechanism), we design two hops attention. The first hop attends to the high-level information from MDC and the second hop attends to the word-level information based on the first attention. Details of this process can be described as follows.

For each label embedding, it not only attends to the word-level information from the bidirectional LSTM but also attends to the semantic understanding representations from MDC. In our model, each label first pays attention to semantic understanding representations from MDC to obtain the most relevant semantic information with itself and generate a new representation based on the attention. Then, the new representation from the global embedding of label and the semantic understanding attends to the word-level information from the bidirectional LSTM with the guidance of the semantic understandings, mitigating the irrelevance and redundancy of textual contents.

To be specific, the global label embedding matrix can be initialized randomly as a trainable matrix GE, where $GE \in \mathbb{R}^{k \times L}$. For each label embedding ge_t, it first attends to the semantic understanding g and generates a new representation s_t, where $t \in \{1, 2, \ldots, L\}$.

$$s_t = \sum_{j=1}^{m} \alpha_{tj} g_j \tag{4}$$

$$\alpha_{tj} = \frac{exp(e_{tj})}{\sum_{k=1}^{m} exp(e_{tk})} \tag{5}$$

$$e_{tj} = v_a^{\mathsf{T}} tanh(W_a[ge_t; g_j]) \tag{6}$$

Then the new representation s_t attends to the word-level information h from the bidirectional LSTM and generates another representation s_t', which is below.

$$s_t' = \sum_{i=1}^{n} \alpha_{ti} h_i \tag{7}$$

$$\alpha_{ti} = \frac{exp(e_{ti})}{\sum_{k=1}^{n} exp(e_{tk})} \tag{8}$$

$$e_{ti} = v_a^{\mathsf{T}} tanh(W_a[s_t; h_i]) \tag{9}$$

In the final, we obtain the distinct representation s_t' for each label t, containing word-level information and high-level semantic understanding representations.

2.4   Output Layer

we use a fully connected layer to get a new representation r_t for each label. Thereafter, we use the sigmoid cross entropy loss as the loss function for the model, which is formulated as:

$$\varepsilon = \sum_{t=1}^{L} [y^t log \hat{y}^t + (1 - y^t) log(1 - \hat{y}^t)] \tag{10}$$

where

$$\hat{y}^t = 1/(1 + exp(-r^t)), \hat{y}^t \in [0, 1] \tag{11}$$

where ε is the loss, $\hat{y}^t$ is the probability of that r belongs to the t-th label, y^t is the target probability.

3   Experiments

In this section, we evaluate our proposed methods on two datasets. We first introduce the datasets, evaluation metrics, experimental details, and all baselines. Then, we compare our model with those baseline methods. Finally, we give the analysis and discussion of experimental results.

3.1 Datasets

Arxiv Academic Paper Dataset (AAPD)[1]: This dataset is provided by [27]. It contains the abstract and corresponding subjects of 55,840 papers in the computer science field from Arxiv [2]. An academic paper may have multiple subjects and there are 54 subjects in total. To be specific, the training set contains around 53,840 samples, while the validation and test set contain 1000 samples.
Reuters Corpus Volume I (RCV1-V2)[3]: This dataset is provided by [14]. It consists of over 800,000 manually categorized newswire stories available by Reuter LTd for research purpose. Multiple topics can be assigned to each newswire and there are 103 topics in total. To be specific, the training set contains around 802,414 samples, while the validation and test set contain 1000 samples.

This statistical characters of the two datasets are shown in Table 1.

Table 1. Statistical characters of dataset AAPD and dataset RCV1-V2.

Dataset	Total samples	Label sets	Words/Sample	Labels/Samples
AAPD	55,840	54	163.42	2.41
RCV1-V2	804,414	103	123.94	3.24

3.2 Evaluation Metrics

Following the previous work [2,30], we choose hamming loss and micro-F1 to evaluate the performance of our model. Micro-precision and micro-recall are also reported in experimental results. Hamming loss [20] evaluates the fraction of misclassified instance-label pairs, where a relevant label is missed or an irrelevant is predicted. Micro-F1 [16] refers to the weighted average of the precision and recall, which is calculated by counting the total true positives, false negatives, and false positives.

3.3 Experimental Details

The word vectors are initialized using 300 dimensional Glove vectors [18]. Meanwhile, the trainable label embeddings are initialized randomly as 300 dimension vectors. We extract the vocabularies from the training sets. For the AAPD dataset, the size of the vocabulary is 30,000 and the unfound words in word vectors are replaced with *unk*. Each text is truncated at the length of 250. Besides, the hidden sizes of the LSTM are 150 and the number of LSTM layers is 2. For the RCV1-V2 dataset, the size of vocabulary is 50,000 and the unfound words

---

[1] https://github.com/lancopku/SGM/.

[2] https://arxiv.org/.

[3] http://www.ai.mit.edu/projects/jmlr/papers/volume5/lewis04a/lyrl2004_rcv1v2_README.htm.

are replaced with *unk*. Each text is truncated at the length of 250. There are two LSTM layers and its size is 150.

We implement our experiments in Tensorflow on an NVIDIA 1080Ti GPU. In the experiments, we use Adam [12] optimization method to minimize the cross entropy loss on the training data. For the hyper parameters of the Adam, we set the learning rate $\alpha = 0.0001$, two momentum parameters $\beta_1 = 0.9$ and $\beta_2 = 0.999$ respectively, and $\epsilon = 1 \times 10^{-8}$. In addition, we utilize the dropout regularization [22] to avoid overfitting problems and clip the gradients [17] to the maximum norm of 10.0. During the training process, we train the model for fixed epochs and monitor its performance on the validation set. Once the training is finished, we will select the model with the best micro-F1 score on the validation set as our final model, which can be saved in the training process, and evaluate its performance on the test set.

Table 2. Comparison between our model and baseline methods on two datasets. HL, P, R and F1 denote hamming loss, micro-precision, micro-recall, micro-F1. The symbol "↑" indicates that the higher the value is, the better the model performs. The symbol "↓" is the opposite.

Method	HL (↓)	P (↑)	R (↑)	F1 (↑)
(a) Performance on the dataset AAPD.				
BR	0.0316	0.644	0.648	0.646
CC	0.0306	0.657	0.651	0.654
LP	0.0312	0.662	0.608	0.634
CNN	0.0256	**0.849**	0.545	0.664
CNN-RNN	0.0278	0.718	0.618	0.664
SGM	0.0245	0.748	0.675	0.710
Our Model	**0.0233**	0.741	**0.730**	**0.736**
(b) Performance on the dataset RCV1-V2.				
BR	0.0086	0.904	0.816	0.858
CC	0.0087	0.887	0.828	0.857
LP	0.0087	0.896	0.824	0.858
CNN	0.0089	**0.922**	0.798	0.855
CNN-RNN	0.0085	0.889	0.825	0.856
SGM	0.0075	0.897	0.860	0.878
Our Model	**0.0073**	0.881	**0.887**	**0.884**

3.4 Baseline Methods

In the following, we introduce the baseline methods for comparison for both datasets.

- **Binary Relevance (BR)** [1] transforms the MLC tak into multiple single-label classification.
- **Classifier Chains (CC)** [19] transforms the MLC task into a chain of binary classification problems to model the correlations between labels.
- **Label Powerset (LP)** [24] creates one binary classifier for every label combination attested in the training set.
- **CNN** [11] uses multiple convolution kernels to extract text feature, which then input to the linear transformation layer followed by a sigmoid function to output the probability distribution over the label space.
- **CNN-RNN** [2] utilizes CNN and RNN to capture both global and local textual semantics and model label correlations.
- **Sequence Generation Model (SGM)** [27] is a sequence-to-sequence model with the attention mechanism for multi-label classification respectively.

Following the previous work [2], we adopt the linear SVM as the base classifier in BR, CC and LP, which are implemented by Scikit-Multilearn [23], an open source library for the MLC task. Additionally, We tune hyper parameters of all baseline methods on the validation set based on the micro-F1 score.

3.5   Experimental Results

In this section, we report the results of our model and all baseline methods on the test sets. The experimental results of our model and baseline methods on the dataset AAPD are shown in Table 2. Results show that our proposed model give the best performance in the hamming loss and micro-F1. Our model achieve a reduction of 26.26% hamming loss and an improvement of 13.9% micro-F1 score over the most ordinarily used baseline method BR. Besides, our model outperforms other traditional deep learning models by a large margin. For example, the proposed model achieves a reduction of 8.98% hamming loss and an improvement of 10.8% micro-F1 score over traditional CNN model.

Table 2 shows the results and the baselines on the RCV1-V2 test set. Similar to the experimental results on the AAPD test set, our model still performs all baseline methods by a large margin in main evaluation metrics. This further confirms that our model can have significant advantages over previous work on large datasets.

3.6   Ablation Test

To evaluate the effectiveness of our proposed model, we propose an ablation test for our model. We remove some certain modules so that their effects can be obviously compared. To be specific, we evaluate the performance of five models on the dataset RCV1-V2, which are model **without** attention, one with only

Table 3. Performance of the models with different modules on the dataset RCV1-V2 test set. HL, P, R, F1 denote hamming loss, micro-precision, micro-recall, micro-F1.

Method	HL($\downarrow$)	P($\uparrow$)	R($\uparrow$)	F1($\uparrow$)
Without	0.0087	**0.914**	0.821	0.865
Word-level	0.0086	0.889	0.847	0.867
Semantic	0.0078	0.881	0.875	0.878
Conventional	0.0077	0.884	0.870	0.877
Our Model	**0.0073**	0.881	**0.887**	**0.884**

attention to **word-level** information from LSTM, one with only attention to high-level **semantic** understanding from MDC, one with **conventional** attention based on MDC and our model. Thus, each module of our model, including MDC and hybrid attention, can be evaluated well without the influences of the other modules.

The results in Table 3 report that our model still performs the best. We can find that the high-level semantic understanding from MDC contributes much to the performance of our model for multi-label text classification, which achieves an improvement 1.50% micor-F1 score over the model without attention. Moreover, the model with a conventional attention mechanism based on MDC, which learns a shared representation for each label, only achieves similar performance with the model based on MDC. Therefore, the conventional attention mechanism makes little contributions in multi-label text classification. Our proposed model, consisting of MDC and the hybrid attention mechanism, can improve the performance of multi-label text classification based on the word-level information and high-level semantic understanding of textual contents.

3.7 Attention Visualization

When our model predicts different labels, there are distinctness in the contributions of different words. Our model can select the most relevant words for each label by utilizing the hybrid attention mechanism. The visualization of the word-level attention mechanism is shown in Table 4. According to Table 4, when our model predicts label "CL". It can automatically assign larger weights to more relevant words are like "sentence", "memory", "recurrent", and so on. For the label "CV", Table 4 shows that the selected words are "image", "visual", "videos", etc. This shows that our proposed model is able to consider the differences in the contributions of word-level contents and select relevant words automatically based on semantic understanding and label embedding when predicting different labels.

Table 4. An example abstract in the dataset AAPD. We extract three informative sentences. This abstract is assigned two labels: "CL" and "CV", which are denoted as computational language and computer vision.

(a) Visual analysis when predicting label "CL".

• generating descriptions for videos has many applications including assisting blind people and human robot interaction
•many of the proposed methods for image captioning rely on pre trained object classifier cnns and long short term memory recurrent networks
• we show how to learn robust visual classifiers from the weak annotations of the sentence descriptions

(b) Visual analysis when predicting label "CV".

•generating descriptions for videos has many applications including assisting blind people and human robot interaction
•many of the proposed methods for image captioning rely on pre trained object classifier cnns and long short term memory recurrent networks
• we show how to learn robust visual classifiers from the weak annotations of the sentence descriptions

4   Related Work

The current methods for the MLC task can be categorized into three types: problem transformation, algorithm adaptation, and neural network models.

Problem transformation methods regard the MLC task into multiple single-label learning tasks. BR [1] algorithm is a straightforward method to decompose a multi-label learning problem into independent binary classification problems. In order to model label correlations, CC [19] transforms the MLC task into a chain of binary classification problems, where subsequent binary classifiers in the chain are build upon the predictions of preceding ones. LP [24] transforms the MLC task into a multi-class problem with a classifier trained on all unique label combinations. However, the computational efficiency and performance of these methods are challenged by applications with massive labels and samples.

Algorithm adaptation methods extend specific learning algorithms to handle multi-label data directly. Multi-Label Decision Tree [3] adopts decision tree technology to deal with multi-label problems by utilizing an information gain criterion. Ranking Support Vector Machine [4] minimizes the empirical ranking loss and enables to handle nonlinear cases with kernel tricks to adapt maximum margin. Multi-Label k-Nearest-Neighborhood [30] is the first lazy learning approach, which utilizes maximum a posteriori to determine the label sets for the unseen instances instead of considering label correlations. Adaboost. MR [21] is an improved boosting algorithm to tackle the MLC task on text and speech categorization tasks. [15] propose a novel joint learning algorithm that allows the feedbacks to be propagated from the classifier for the current label.

In recent years, some neural networks models have been used for the MLC task. [29] utilizes fully connected neural network with pairwise ranking loss function. [13] utilizes word embeddings based on CNN to capture label correlations. CNN and RNN are combined to perform classification in [2]. Recently, [27] regards the multi-label text classification as a sequence generation problem to capture the correlations among labels. For reducing the dependence on the label order in [26, 27] proposes a sequence-to-set framework utilizing deep reinforcement learning.

5 Conclusion

In this paper, we propose our model based on the multi-level dilated convolution and the hybrid attention mechanism, which can extract the word-level information and high-level semantic understanding representations. Experimental results show that our model can significantly outperform the baseline methods. Further analysis of experimental results demonstrate that our model not only can capture the semantic understanding from MDC but also can select the most distinct words automatically for different label. In the future work, we plan to conduct more experiments on other multi-label datasets to fully prove the usefulness of our model.

Acknowledgment. This paper is supported by the National Key Research and Development Program of China (Grant No. 2016YFB1001102), the National Natural Science Foundation of China (Grant Nos. 61876080), the Collaborative Innovation Center of Novel Software Technology and Industrialization at Nanjing University.

References

1. Boutell, M.R., Luo, J., Shen, X., Brown, C.M.: Learning multi-label scene classification. Pattern Recogn. **37**(9), 1757–1771 (2004)
2. Chen, G., Ye, D., Xing, Z., Chen, J., Cambria, E.: Ensemble application of convolutional and recurrent neural networks for multi-label text categorization. In: 2017 International Joint Conference on Neural Networks (IJCNN), pp. 2377–2383. IEEE (2017)
3. Clare, A., King, R.D.: Knowledge discovery in multi-label phenotype data. In: De Raedt, L., Siebes, A. (eds.) PKDD 2001. LNCS (LNAI), vol. 2168, pp. 42–53. Springer, Heidelberg (2001). https://doi.org/10.1007/3-540-44794-6_4
4. Elisseeff, A., Weston, J.: A kernel method for multi-labelled classification. In: Advances in Neural Information Processing Systems, pp. 681–687 (2002)
5. Gehring, J., Auli, M., Grangier, D., Yarats, D., Dauphin, Y.N.: Convolutional sequence to sequence learning. arXiv preprint arXiv:1705.03122 (2017)
6. Gopal, S., Yang, Y.: Multilabel classification with meta-level features. In: Proceedings of the 33rd International ACM SIGIR Conference on Research and Development in Information Retrieval, pp. 315–322. ACM (2010)

7. Hochreiter, S., Schmidhuber, J.: Long short-term memory. Neural Comput. **9**(8), 1735–1780 (1997)
8. Kalchbrenner, N., Espeholt, L., Simonyan, K., Oord, A.V.D., Graves, A., Kavukcuoglu, K.: Neural machine translation in linear time. arXiv preprint arXiv:1610.10099 (2016)
9. Kalchbrenner, N., Grefenstette, E., Blunsom, P.: A convolutional neural network for modelling sentences. arXiv preprint arXiv:1404.2188 (2014)
10. Katakis, I., Tsoumakas, G., Vlahavas, I.: Multilabel text classification for automated tag suggestion. In: Proceedings of the ECML/PKDD, vol. 18 (2008)
11. Kim, Y.: Convolutional neural networks for sentence classification. arXiv preprint arXiv:1408.5882 (2014)
12. Kingma, D.P., Ba, J.: Adam: a method for stochastic optimization. arXiv preprint arXiv:1412.6980 (2014)
13. Kurata, G., Xiang, B., Zhou, B.: Improved neural network-based multi-label classification with better initialization leveraging label co-occurrence. In: Proceedings of the 2016 Conference of the North American Chapter of the Association for Computational Linguistics: Human Language Technologies, pp. 521–526 (2016)
14. Lewis, D.D., Yang, Y., Rose, T.G., Li, F.: RCV1: a new benchmark collection for text categorization research. J. Mach. Learn. Res. **5**(Apr), 361–397 (2004)
15. Li, L., Wang, H., Sun, X., Chang, B., Zhao, S., Sha, L.: Multi-label text categorization with joint learning predictions-as-features method. In: Proceedings of the 2015 Conference on Empirical Methods in Natural Language Processing, pp. 835–839 (2015)
16. Manning, C., Prabhakar, R., Hinrich, S.: Introduction to Information Retrieval, vol. 1. Cambridge University Press, Cambridge (2008)
17. Pascanu, R., Mikolov, T., Bengio, Y.: On the difficulty of training recurrent neural networks. In: International Conference on Machine Learning, pp. 1310–1318 (2013)
18. Pennington, J., Socher, R., Manning, C.: GloVe: Global vectors for word representation. In: Proceedings of the 2014 Conference on Empirical Methods in Natural Language Processing (EMNLP), pp. 1532–1543 (2014)
19. Read, J., Pfahringer, B., Holmes, G., Frank, E.: Classifier chains for multi-label classification. Mach. Learn. **85**(3), 333 (2011)
20. Schapire, R.E., Singer, Y.: Improved boosting algorithms using confidence-rated predictions. Mach. Learn. **37**(3), 297–336 (1999)
21. Schapire, R.E., Singer, Y.: BoosTexter: a boosting-based system for text categorization. Mach. Learn. **39**(2), 135–168 (2000)
22. Srivastava, N., Hinton, G., Krizhevsky, A., Sutskever, I., Salakhutdinov, R.: Dropout: a simple way to prevent neural networks from overfitting. J. Mach. Learn. Res. **15**(1), 1929–1958 (2014)
23. Szymański, P., Kajdanowicz, T.: A scikit-based Python environment for performing multi-label classification. arXiv preprint arXiv:1702.01460 (2017)
24. Tsoumakas, G., Katakis, I.: Multi-label classification: an overview. Int. J. Data Warehous. Min. (IJDWM) **3**(3), 1–13 (2007)
25. Wang, P., et al.: Understanding convolution for semantic segmentation. In: IEEE Winter Conference on Applications of Computer Vision (2018)
26. Yang, P., Ma, S., Zhang, Y., Lin, J., Su, Q., Sun, X.: A deep reinforced sequence-to-set model for multi-label text classification. arXiv preprint arXiv:1809.03118 (2018)
27. Yang, P., Sun, X., Li, W., Ma, S., Wu, W., Wang, H.: SGM: sequence generation model for multi-label classification. In: Proceedings of the 27th International Conference on Computational Linguistics, pp. 3915–3926 (2018)

28. Yu, F., Koltun, V.: Multi-scale context aggregation by dilated convolutions. arXiv preprint arXiv:1511.07122 (2015)
29. Zhang, M.L., Zhou, Z.H.: Multilabel neural networks with applications to functional genomics and text categorization. IEEE Trans. Knowl. Data Eng. **18**(10), 1338–1351 (2006)
30. Zhang, M.L., Zhou, Z.H.: ML-KNN: a lazy learning approach to multi-label learning. Pattern Recogn. **40**(7), 2038–2048 (2007)

Demos

FMQO: A Federated RDF System Supporting Multi-query Optimization

Qi Ge[1], Peng Peng[1(✉)], Zhiwei Xu[1], Lei Zou[2], and Zheng Qin[1]

[1] Hunan University, Changsha, China
{kathy_gq,hnu16pp,zhiweixu,zqin}@hnu.edu.cn
[2] Peking University, Beijing, China
zoulei@pku.edu.cn

Abstract. This demo designs and implements a system called FMQO that can support multiple query optimization in federated RDF systems. Given a set of queries posed simultaneously, we propose a heuristic query rewriting-based approach to share the common computation during evaluation of multiple queries. Furthermore, we propose an efficient method to use the interconnection topology between SPARQL endpoints to filter out irrelevant sources and join intermediate results during multiple query evaluation. The experimental studies over both real federated RDF datasets show that the demo is effective, efficient and scalable.

1 Introduction

Many data providers publish their datasets using open standards such as RDF [1]. RDF is a self-describing data model that represents data as triples of the form ⟨subject, property, object⟩ for modelling information in the Web, while SPARQL is a query language to retrieve and manipulate data stored in RDF format. Many data providers publish and store their RDF dataset at their own *autonomous* sites some of which are *SPARQL endpoints* that can execute SPARQL queries.

To integrate and provide transparent access over many SPARQL queries, federated RDF systems have been proposed [2–4,6], in which, a control site is introduced to provide a common interface for users to issue SPARQL queries. A popular federated RDF benchmark—FedBench [5]—is often used to evaluate the performance of the federated RDF systems.

However, existing federated RDF systems only consider query evaluation for a single query and miss the opportunity for multiple query optimization. In real application, many SPARQL queries are often posed simultaneously, and there is room for sharing computation when executing these queries. Thus, it is desirable to design a system that can support multiple SPARQL query optimization.

In this demo, we design and implement a system called FMQO that can rewrite a set of SPARQL queries posed simultaneously into a smaller set of rewritten query and then send it to relevant SPARQL endpoints, which can save both the number of remote accesses and query response time. As we rewrite

© Springer Nature Switzerland AG 2019
J. Shao et al. (Eds.): APWeb-WAIM 2019, LNCS 11642, pp. 397–401, 2019.
https://doi.org/10.1007/978-3-030-26075-0_30

multiple queries with commonalities, we consider both "OPTIONAL" and "FIL-
TER" clauses of SPARQL. This allows us significant rewrite opportunities.

In addition, FMQO optimizes source selection and partial match joins in
federated RDF systems. FMQO utilizes the topology structures of SPARQL
endpoints for source selection, and merges partial match joins during multiple
query processing to avoid duplicate computation in federated RDF systems.

Technical details of FMQO have been published in our previous paper [2] and
are summarized in Sect. 2 of this paper. In this demonstration paper we present
the prototype system architecture and functionality.

2   System Architecture

FMQO consists of a control site as well as some SPARQL endpoints. The control
site is amenable to receive a SPARQL query Q and decomposes it into several
subqueries that are sent to relevant SPARQL endpoints. Assume that several
subqueries that are sent to the same SPARQL endpoint share common sub-
structures. To improve the query performance, the control site rewrites them
into fewer rewritten queries. Results of decomposed subqueries are returned to
the control site and joined together to form complete results presented to users.

There are five components in FMQO: *query decomposition and source selection, query rewriting, local evaluation, postprocessing* and *partial match join* (see
Fig. 1). Note that only *local evaluation* is conducted over the remote SPARQL
endpoints and the other four steps work at the control site.

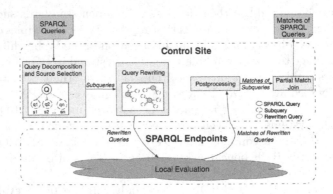

Fig. 1. Scheme for federated SPARQL query processing

Query Decomposition and Source Selection. FMQO first decomposes a
query Q into a set of subqueries expressed over relevant SPARQL endpoints.
FMQO utilizes the interconnection structure among different SPARQL endpoints to filter out irrelevant SPARQL endpoints. Given a query Q and the topology graph of SPARQL endpoints, the system find all homomorphism matches.

If a subquery of Q does not map to a SPARQL endpoint s in any match, s is not a relevant endpoint of the subquery.

Then, given a batch of SPARQL queries $\{Q_1, ..., Q_n\}$, the system obtain subqueries $\mathcal{Q} = \{q_1^1 @S(q_1^1), ..., q_1^{m_1} @S(q_1^{m_1}); \quad q_2^1 @S(q_2^1), ..., q_2^{m_2} @S(q_2^{m_2}); \quad ...; q_n^1 @S(q_n^1), ..., q_n^{m_n} @S(q_n^{m_n})\}$, where $\{q_i^1 @S(q_i^1), ..., q_i^{m_i} @S(q_i^{m_i})\}$ come from original SPARQL query Q_i and $S(q_i^j)$ is the set of relevant SPARQL endpoints for q_i^j.

Query Rewriting. After the first step, there are multiple subqueries. The set of subqueries that are planned to be sent to the same SPARQL endpoint provides an opportunity for multiple query optimization. The control site uses FILTER and OPTIONAL operators to rewrite these subqueries as a single query. Figure 2 illustrates our rewiring strategy, using OPTIONAL followed by FILTER.

Given subqueries $q_1^1 @\{GeoNames\}$, $q_2^1 @\{GeoNames\}$ and $q_3^1 @\{GeoNames\}$ in Fig. 2, the triple pattern "?l g:name "Canada"" is selected in the first step. It hits the three subqueries. The system divide them into two equivalence classes $\{q_1^1\}$, $\{q_2^1, q_3^1\}$ according to the query structure. Then, q_2^1 and q_3^1 are rewritten by using FILTER operator. Finally, the system rewrites the three queries using OPTIONAL operator using "?l g:name "Canada"".

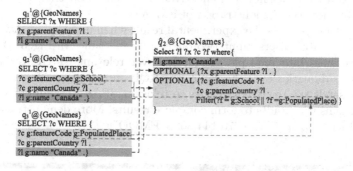

Fig. 2. Rewriting queries using OPTIONAL and FILTER operators

Assume that the SPARQL endpoint s is assigned a set of subqueries $\mathcal{Q}_s = \{q_s^1, ..., q_s^n\}$. After query rewriting, the system obtains a set of rewritten queries $\hat{\mathcal{Q}}_s$ ($|\hat{\mathcal{Q}}_s| \leq |\mathcal{Q}_s|$) that will be sent to the SPARQL endpoint s. Each rewritten query comes from a subset of $\mathcal{Q}_s$.

Local Evaluation. After query rewriting, the system rewrites subqueries into a set of rewritten queries $\hat{\mathcal{Q}}_s$. The system send the set of rewritten queries to their relevant SPARQL endpoints and evaluate them there. Local evaluation results will be return back to the control site.

Postprocessing. The local evaluation results from evaluating $\hat{Q}_s$ over the SPARQL endpoints are a superset of evaluating the original subqueries Q_s. Therefore, the control site necessitates a postprocessing step to check each local evaluation result against each query in Q_s. In this demo, FMQO propose a postprocessing method which only requires a linear scan on the local evaluation results of the rewritten queries.

Partial Match Join. For each subquery q_i^j in Q, collecting the matches at each relevant SPARQL endpoint in $S(q_i^j)$, we can obtain all its matches. Assume that an original query Q_i ($i = 1, ..., n$) is decomposed into a set of subqueries $\{q_i^1@S(q_i^1), ..., q_i^{m_i}@S(q_i^{m_i})\}$, we obtain query results of Q_i by joining the results of q_i^1, ..., and $q_i^{m_i}$. Considering the context of multiple SPARQL queries over a federated RDF system, we can merge some joins to avoid duplicate computation in join processing.

3   Demonstration

In this demo, we use a famous comprehensive benchmark suite for testing and analyzing both the efficiency and effectiveness of federated RDF systems, Fed-Bench [5], to show the demonstration of FMQO.

Figure 3 demonstrates the experimental result when users submit two queries at once. In Fig. 3(a), users input two queries at one time. In Fig. 3(b), FMQO decomposes them into multiple subqueries over relevant SPARQL endpoints, rewrites the subqueries over the same SPARQL endpoint into fewer rewritten subqueries, sends the rewritten queries to relevant SPARQL endpoints for evaluation and joins the results to form complete results. More demonstration could be referred with "http://39.98.70.144:8088/FMQO".

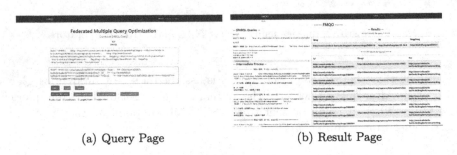

(a) Query Page   (b) Result Page

Fig. 3. Demonstration of FMQO

4   Conclusion

In this demo, we design and implement a federated RDF system called FMQO that can support multiple query optimization. FMQO rewrites queries into equivalent queries that are more efficient to evaluate while optimizing source selection and partial match joins in federated RDF systems.

Acknowledgment. This work was supported by The National Key Research and Development Program of China under grant 2018YFB1003504, NSFC under grant 61702171, 61772191, 61622201, 61472131 and 61532010, Hunan Provincial Natural Science Foundation of China under grant 2018JJ3065, the Fundamental Research Funds for the Central Universities, Science and Technology Key Projects of Hunan Province (Grant No. 2015TP1004, 2016JC2012), and Changsha science and technology project kq1804008.

References

1. Berners-Lee, T.: Linked Data? Design Issues. W3C (2010)
2. Peng, P., Zou, L., Özsu, M.T., Zhao, D.: Multi-query optimization in federated RDF systems. In: Pei, J., Manolopoulos, Y., Sadiq, S., Li, J. (eds.) DASFAA 2018. LNCS, vol. 10827, pp. 745–765. Springer, Cham (2018). https://doi.org/10.1007/978-3-319-91452-7_48
3. Quilitz, B., Leser, U.: Querying distributed RDF data sources with SPARQL. In: Bechhofer, S., Hauswirth, M., Hoffmann, J., Koubarakis, M. (eds.) ESWC 2008. LNCS, vol. 5021, pp. 524–538. Springer, Heidelberg (2008). https://doi.org/10.1007/978-3-540-68234-9_39
4. Saleem, M., Potocki, A., Soru, T., Hartig, O., Ngomo, A.N.: CostFed: cost-based query optimization for SPARQL endpoint federation. In: ISWC, pp. 163–174 (2018)
5. Schmidt, M., Görlitz, O., Haase, P., Ladwig, G., Schwarte, A., Tran, T.: FedBench: a benchmark suite for federated semantic data query processing. In: Aroyo, L., et al. (eds.) ISWC 2011. LNCS, vol. 7031, pp. 585–600. Springer, Heidelberg (2011). https://doi.org/10.1007/978-3-642-25073-6_37
6. Schwarte, A., Haase, P., Hose, K., Schenkel, R., Schmidt, M.: FedX: optimization techniques for federated query processing on linked data. In: Aroyo, L., et al. (eds.) ISWC 2011. LNCS, vol. 7031, pp. 601–616. Springer, Heidelberg (2011). https://doi.org/10.1007/978-3-642-25073-6_38

DataServiceHatch: Generating and Composing Continuous Data Services

Guiling Wang[1,2]([✉]), Tongtong Cui[1], Xiaojiang Zuo[1], Yao Xu[2], and Yanbo Han[1]

[1] Beijing Key Laboratory on Integration and Analysis of Large-Scale Stream Data, North China University of Technology, No. 5 Jinyuanzhuang Road, Shijingshan District, Beijing 100144, China
wangguiling@ict.ac.cn
[2] Ocean Information Technology Company, China Electronics Technology Group Corporation (CETC Ocean Corp.), No. 11 Shuangyuan Road, Badachu Hi-Tech Park, Shijingshan District, Beijing 100041, China

Abstract. In this paper, we present DataServiceHatch, a Web-based system that semi-automatically converts relational databases and stream data sources into Web Services and answers continuous queries on both traditional database tables and data streams by composing Web Services, rather than accesses databases or big data stream infrastructures directly. This can help organizations to unify the access entrance of all their data sources with just a few simple configurations and avoid exposing their data directly. DataServiceHatch also provides mechanisms to remove the need for manually writing a complex *SQL*-like query expression or service composition plan to answer a continuous query on data streams.

Keywords: Data stream · Big data · Data service · Service composition · Continuous query

1 Introduction

Modern business organizations often have multiple application systems, and they need to share data across various systems. Data services [1] provide a flexible, controlled and standardized approach to access or query an organization's data sources without exposing its databases directly. There are some earlier research work and tools on encapsulating data from relational databases based on Web Services technologies [1,2], and on integrating the database tables based on Web Services [3]. Recently, with the development of IoT (Internet of Things) systems and the emergency of distributed stream processing systems like [4–6], data stream becomes a kind of important data source. However, the existing work doesn't support automatic encapsulation and integration of data streams, especially the data streams generated from distributed stream processing systems. As a step towards automatically access and integration of any types of data sources based on data services, in this paper, we demonstrate DataServiceHatch,

© Springer Nature Switzerland AG 2019
J. Shao et al. (Eds.): APWeb-WAIM 2019, LNCS 11642, pp. 402–406, 2019.
https://doi.org/10.1007/978-3-030-26075-0_31

a Web-based system that supports semi-automatic service generation and composition for continuous query on data streams. DataServiceHatch is designed to be used by developers to reduce their burden of manually writing code to encapsulate data sources into data services and manually compose the data services to answer a continuous query on multiple data streams.

2   System Overview

DataServiceHatch abstracts "continuous data services" as views over streams. Being the same as a table view in a database, a view over streams can be seen as a function that maps a set of input data streams into an output data stream. In Fig. 1, this is represented as that the continuous data service subscribes the input streams and publishes the output stream. Each service has service operations and data and/or time constraints description on the input/output streams. User queries can be transformed into *SQL*-like query over data streams with time constraints. The mediator selects the services that can be combined to answer the submitted query using our continuous data service composition algorithm, which is mainly based on the techniques of query rewriting on views over streams. Then, it generates a composite service as an execution plan for the query, execute the composite service and push results to the users continuously.

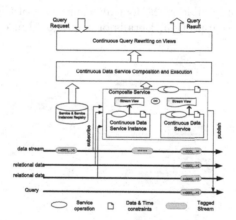

Fig. 1. Overview of the proposed approach

Implementation of the data service composition algorithm is available on Github[1]. Different from the traditional data service model, data services for queries on data streams need to continuously update service responses and consider temporal constraints (and this is why we call it "continuous data service"). In our approach, every service is implemented as a Spark Streaming [4] job. The underlying data streams are subscribed (represented as "sub" in Fig. 1) by

---

[1] https://github.com/declouddataservice/servicecomposition.

continuous data services based on Kafka [6]. And the outputs of a service are published (represented as "pub" in Fig. 1) to Kafka, which can be subscribed by other services. For those Web based clients, we expose continuous data service as REST-like APIs over HTTP protocol based on Web-based push technology. It allows continuous data services to push query results to clients continuously.

Continuous Data Services Composition. In order to answer queries over multiple data sources, one feasible solution is to model services as parameterized views over data sources, and compose the services using a query rewriting approach based on the service model. Every view has two components: data part and time constraints part. So that We can find the containment relationship by checking the containment relationship of both the data part and time constraints part between the query and the rewriting. This method extends the existing Bucket or MiniCon algorithm [7] for "answering queries using views" on finite data that only checks the containment relationship of the data part. In our algorithm, we determine input and output parameters and parameter values of service operations and add new attribute constrains to the view of a service when the service is instantiated.

Finding and composing the relevant services for answering queries is a NP-complete problem. For efficiency, we not only make use of the methods from Bucket or MiniCon algorithm to prune efficiently the set of data sources using the source description, but also firstly prune those data services whose time constrains are not compatible with the time constraint of the query, which can often avoid a lot of computation. Details of the algorithm can be found in our papers [8].

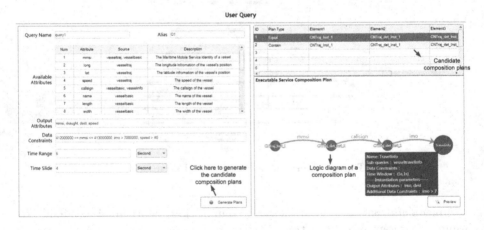

Fig. 2. User query interface

3   Demonstration Overview

The demonstration (demo. video is presented at[2]) shows how a continuous query can be answered by using the public services shared by other developers. In the demonstration, we present a user "orgA" as a service producer and "orgB" as a service consumer for simplicity. The user "orgA" registers several data sources like *vesselinfo, vesseltraj, vesseltravelinfo* etc. as stream source services. Then "orgA" creates several services and service instances and publishes them to "service hall" to share with other applications. The user "orgB" submits a query Q, asking every four seconds for vessels information (e.g. *mmsi, draught, destination*, etc.) with speed greater than 40 km/h within the last five seconds. Using DataServiceHatch, "orgB" can submit the query by selecting the output attributes, data constraints and time constraints as shown in the left part of Fig. 2, reducing the tedious work of editing a complicated *SQL* sentence (the advantage is especially apparent when it involves multiple data sources in a query). The candidate service composition plans can be generated automatically and presented to users. Then the user "orgB" can select one from the candidate plans, review the detailed services and service instances in this plan and execute it. Results can be previewed and the composition plan can be published as a new service for sharing.

Acknowledgments. This work is supported by Beijing Natural Science Foundation No. 4172018 and National Natural Science Foundation of China No. 61672042 and University Cooperation Projects Foundation of CETC Ocean Corp.

References

1. Carey, M.J., Onose, N., Petropoulos, M.: Data services. Commun. ACM **55**(6), 86–97 (2012)
2. Microsoft Inc.: WCF data services (2017). https://docs.microsoft.com/en-us/dotnet/framework/data/wcf/. Accessed 30 Mar 2017
3. Oracle Inc.: Oracle data service integrator. https://www.oracle.com/technetwork/middleware/data-service-integrator/overview/index.html. Accessed Dec 2018
4. Zaharia, M., Das, T., Li, H., Hunter, T., Shenker, S., Stoica, I.: Discretized streams: fault-tolerant streaming computation at scale. In: Proceedings of the Twenty-Fourth ACM Symposium on Operating Systems Principles SOSP 2013, pp. 423–438. ACM, New York (2013)
5. Carbone, P., Katsifodimos, A., Ewen, S., Markl, V., Haridi, S., Tzoumas, K.: Apache flink: stream and batch processing in a single engine. Bull. IEEE Comput. Soc. Tech. Comm. Data Eng. **36**(4) (2015)
6. Wang, G., et al.: Building a replicated logging system with Apache Kafka. Proc. VLDB Endow. **8**(12), 1654–1655 (2015)
7. Pottinger, R., Halevy, A.: Minicon: a scalable algorithm for answering queries using views. Int. J. Very Large Data Bases **10**(2–3), 182–198 (2001)

---

[2] https://www.youtube.com/watch?v=8j0YoIWTKEo.

8. Wang, G., Zuo, X., Hesenius, M., Xu, Y., Han, Y., Volker, G.: A data services composition approach for continuous query on data streams. In: Cai, Y., Ishikawa, Y., Xu, J. (eds.) APWeb-WAIM 2018. LNCS, vol. 10988, pp. 106–120. Springer, Cham (2018). https://doi.org/10.1007/978-3-319-96893-3_9

A Mobile Phone Data Visualization Tool for People Flow Analysis

Liangjian Chen[1], Siyu Chen[1], Shengnan Guo[1], Yue Yang[2], and Jianqiu Xu[1(✉)]

[1] Nanjing University of Aeronautics and Astronautics, Nanjing, China
{chenljian,siyu,gsn,jianqiu}@nuaa.edu.cn
[2] Jiangsu Academy of Architectural Sciences, Nanjing, China
yangyue78@qq.com

Abstract. Mobile phone data contain the information of each interaction between mobile phones and telecommunication infrastructures. These data provide a wealth of information about urban dynamics and human activities since each mobile phone can be seen as a sensor that senses the geographic position of the subscriber holder in real time. In this paper, we introduce an open-source and web-based data visualization tool for analyzing and displaying people flow information using mobile phone data. The developed tool provides users a user-friendly interface for data visualization. We demonstrate how to install and display this tool by using real mobile phone data.

Keywords: Data visualization · Mobile phone data · People flow

1 Introduction

Due to the increasing popularity of mobile phones, telecom companies have collected a large amount of mobile phone data recording when people enter and leave a specific area. That is, a mobile phone will interact with a base station when the mobile user enters the base station range until the user leaves. Actually, mobile phone data are better than the social media communication data for human mobility analysis because they reflect a larger set of users' mobility information at a high rate [1]. Therefore, how to visualize such large amounts of mobile phone data effectively and efficiently becomes an essential challenge for people who want to utilize these data. For example, urban managers can forecast emergent events with the help of people flow visualization technology [2], if the system detects that the population overgrows around a specific area, something special will be likely to occur, e.g. an illegal gathering or a soccer match. Then the government should take emergency measures for safety guarantee.

In the prior literature, there already exist some tools for visualizing mobile phone data. The on-line visualization application BDP [3] can be used to display spatio-temporal data. However, users need to upload their data to the server when they use this application to perform a data presentation task. That may infringe mobile phone users' privacy potentially since this information reveals the

(c) Springer Nature Switzerland AG 2019
J. Shao et al. (Eds.): APWeb-WAIM 2019, LNCS 11642, pp. 407–411, 2019.
https://doi.org/10.1007/978-3-030-26075-0_32

traces of mobile phone users. In addition, the on-line tool always has a limit on the data volume. Displaying millions of tuples on the on-line data visualization tool is not an easy task. Other visualization software such as [4,5] is designed for a specific task and not applicable to general people flow analysis.

In this paper, we process the raw mobile phone data on the Spark platform. In order to provide users a free and general mobile phone data presentation solution for people flow analysis, we develop a visualization tool named People Flow Analysis Visualization Tool (PFAVT for short) for people flow analysis and result presentation. PFAVT is an open-source software that is available publicly on this program's GitHub homepage (https://github.com/godisfair/PFAVT). Users can deploy PFAVT on Linux or Windows operation system since this tool is a cross-platform software. With PFAVT, users are able to display millions of data and no programming required anymore.

The rest of this paper is organized as follows: we introduce the system design of PFAVT in Sect. 2, and the demonstration process will be covered in Sect. 3.

2   System Design

The PFAVT system follows the client-server architecture and is composed of three components: *data process*, *client* and *server*, as shown in Fig. 1. *Data process* pre-processes raw mobile phone data on Apache Spark. *Client* mainly contains a browser and storage medium for storing data. *Server* consists of an HTTP server and the Back-end. We present the main components as follows:

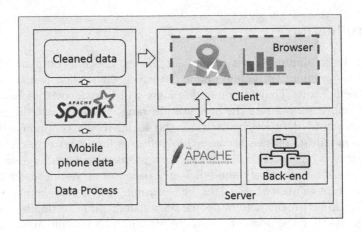

Fig. 1. PFAVT architecture

Data Process. Raw mobile phone data need to undergo a series of process steps before being displayed on PFAVT. We use Apache Spark which is a unified analytics engine for large-scale data processing as our data process platform because raw mobile phone data size always reaches TB even PB level. For people flow analysis, the data process generally consists of two steps: aggregation and sorting. Those operations can be accomplished with the help of spark RDD and DataFrame mechanism.

Client. PFAVT provides a user-friendly web interface for users to interact with the server. We use web languages (HTML, CSS, JavaScript) to develop its interface which provides useful visual feedback. We adopt a JavaScript library – *Echarts* to display heatmap and statistical charts. In order to address low data transmission rate problem between client and server, big data sets are usually stored on the client side.

Server. To address cross-platform compatibility issues, we use Apache which is an open-source HTTP server for modern operating systems including UNIX and Windows as PFAVT's HTTP server, whereas the Back-end is managed by Hypertext Preprocessor–PHP. In the data access layer, we program on thinkphp framework to control presentation logic and data flow.

3   Demonstration

In this paper, we use Windows 7 as our experiment platform. Our tool runs on Apache 2.4.37, PHP 7.2.12 and MySQL 5.7.17. Users can also deploy PFAVT on Linux or Windows since PFAVT is a cross-platform software. Our experimental data are the mobile station data of Yancheng between September 1 and 30, 2018.

3.1   Installation and Deployment

Users need to install Apache to the server host the same as the installation and deployment processes of other web-based applications. Then download our program from PFAVT's GitHub page, set its */public* directory as Apache's web page directory. After that, users can access PFAVT on the same host through a browser.

3.2   Processing Data

Mobile phone data is collected from thousands of base stations by China Mobile Jiangsu (CMJC). The original mobile phone data set is not aggregated and out-of-order. Hence it is essential to aggregate these data every hour and arrange these data in chronological order. That work is done on the CMJS's data center. We process raw data on Spark using Python language, the processed data are organized as a form of (lng, lat, $time$, num), which lng and lat are the longitude and latitude coordinates of each base station, $time$ represents the time interval of every hour, num is the number of mobile phones connected to the base station during that time interval.

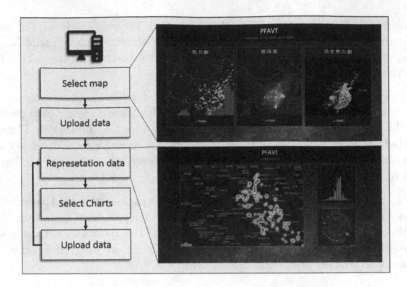

Fig. 2. The demonstration of effects

3.3 Data Visualization

Generally, the presentation process is divided into five steps as illustrated in Fig. 2. First, PFAVT provides three choices for users to select the main map: *route map*, *heatmap*, and *dynamic heatmap*. Then users need to select a map type and upload corresponding formatted data. After that, we provide some additional charts for users to choose from. Users can add some additional charts to express their results by clicking on the button and upload corresponding data once again. The presentation effect is shown in Fig. 2. Experiments show that PFAVT is able to effectively display data up to millions of levels.

Acknowledgments. The paper is partially supported by National Key R&D Program of China (2018YFB1003900) and the Fundamental Research Funds for the Central Universities, No. NS2017073.

References

1. Mota, T., Munjal, A., et al.: Large-scale human mobility analysis based on mobile phone and social media communication: a case-study in Africa. In: 2015 16th IEEE International Conference on Mobile Data Management, Pittsburgh, PA, USA, pp. 86–91. IEEE (2015)
2. Wang, D., Guo, D., et al.: Spatial temporal data visualization in emergency management: a view from data-driven decision. In: Proceedings of the 3rd ACM SIGSPA-TIAL Workshop on Emergency Management Using (EM-GIS 2017), Redondo Beach, CA, USA, pp. 1–7. ACM (2017)
3. BDP Online Personal Edition. https://me.bdp.cn/home.html. Accessed 14 Mar 2019

4. Sharmin, A., Bashir, I.M., et al.: Web visualization of temporal and spatial health data from smartphone app in smart and connected community. In: 2018 IEEE International Smart Cities Conference, Kansas City, MO, USA, pp. 1–6. IEEE (2018)
5. Manoranjan, D., Kee, K, et al.: Visualize people's mobility - both individually and collectively - using mobile phone cellular data. In: 2016 17th IEEE International Conference on Mobile Data Management, Porto, Portugal, pp. 341–344. IEEE (2016)

NativeHelper: A Bilingual Sentence Search and Recommendation Engine for Academic Writing

Weijian Ni[1], Yujian Sun[1], Tong Liu[1(✉)], Qingtian Zeng[1], and Nengfu Xie[2]

[1] College of Computer Science and Engineering,
Shandong University of Science and Technology, Qingdao, China
niweijian@gmail.com, sunyj1994@gmail.com, liu_tongtong@foxmail.com,
qtzeng@163.com
[2] Agricultural Information Institute, Chinese Academy of Agricultural Sciences,
Beijing, China
xienengfu@caas.cn

Abstract. This demo presents NativeHelper, a bilingual Chinese-English sentence search engine that aims to provide assistance for non-English academic writers. As opposed to most existing bilingual sentence search engines that rely heavily on parallel corpora, our system is built on monolingual sentence corpus and bilingual dictionaries which are more readily available. The system is implemented based on a large-scale English sentence database and a simple yet practically efficient bilingual language model. A screen cast is available at https://www.youtube.com/watch?v=oNYOYPDeTyM.

Keywords: Sentence retrieval · Bilingual search engine ·
Academic writing · Bilingual language model

1 Introduction

As most high-quality academic papers are written in English, English writing becomes a critical skill for researchers. However, for most researchers from non-English speaking backgrounds, how to express ideas in English correctly and natively is often a challenge. Recently, bilingual sentence search engines, e.g., Youdao and JuKuu, have become popular tools that provide assistance for non-native English writers. The results of bilingual sentence search engines, which is typically retrieved from parallel corpus provided by human annotators, is of higher quality than that of automatic machine translation. However, constructing a large scale parallel corpus is a labor-intensive and time-consuming work, making parallel corpus generally of limited size. Therefore, most bilingual sentence search engines may suffer from low coverage and insufficient diversity.

To address this problem, we introduce a novel bilingual Chinese-English sentence search engine named NativeHelper. The proposed system reduces the need

© Springer Nature Switzerland AG 2019
J. Shao et al. (Eds.): APWeb-WAIM 2019, LNCS 11642, pp. 412–416, 2019.
https://doi.org/10.1007/978-3-030-26075-0_33

for bilingual resources by using monolingual sentence corpus combined with a dictionary-based mapping technique. Because of the high quality and the large scale of the monolingual corpus, the proposed system tends to provide more precious and diverse results than existing bilingual sentence research engines. Further, it supports interactive exploration of search results to provide comprehensive guidance for the usage of the target language.

2   System and Main Components

The architecture of the NativeHelper system is depicted in Fig. 1, in which two major components are highlighted. The *Sentence Database* component aims to construct a large number of high-quality English sentence database. The *Sentence Retrieval Engine* component, is composed of two parts: *Query Processing* and *Sentence Matching*, which are responsible for transforming the query in the source language (Chinese) into the target language (English) and calculating the relevance of each candidate sentence, respectively.

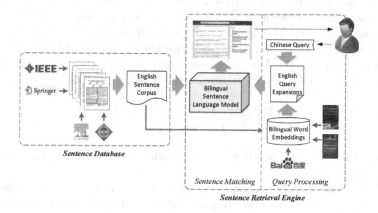

Fig. 1. The system architecture of NativeHelper

2.1   Sentence Database

To ensure the quality of the English sentence corpus, several well-known online academic digital libraries, i.e., ScienceDirect and Springer Link, are selected as the data resources. We develop targeted crawler to download academic papers from these websites and convert all the PDFs to text. The raw text generated is often noisy as the layout information of PDFs cannot be always well recognized, thus we apply sentence boundary detection techniques [1] combined with handcrafted rules to identify the whole sentences.

2.2   Sentence Retrieval Engine

The key task of sentence retrieval engine is to evaluate the relevance of English sentences w.r.t. user's Chinese queries. To this end, we propose a simple yet practically effective bilingual language model.

Formally, given a query Q in the source language (Chinese) and a sentence S' in the target language (English), the bilingual language model is defined as:

$$p(Q|S') = \max_{Q'\in\mathcal{Q}'} p(Q|Q') \cdot p(Q') \cdot p(Q'|S') \tag{1}$$

where $\mathcal{Q}'$ is the set of all possible translations of Q in the target language.

Query Processing. This part aims to estimate the translation model $p(Q|Q')$ and the translation prior $p(Q')$, which evaluate the reliability of a translation of the query.

We implement query translation with bilingual dictionaries $\mathcal{D}$. Suppose a word w in the source language is associated with several translations, denoted as $T_w = \{w'|(w,w') \in \mathcal{D}\}$. Given a query $Q = \{w_1, \cdots, w_n\}$, the possible translations can be written as $\mathcal{Q}' = T_{w_1} \times \cdots \times T_{w_n}$. Then, we estimate the translation model and the translation prior based on the distributed representation of queries, which is learned on the sentence corpus constructed in the first component. Based on the distributed representation, the translation prior $p(Q')$ is calculated by the average similarity between pairs of words in the translation:

$$p(Q') \propto \sum_{w_1'\in Q', w_2'\in Q'} 1 - \langle \mathbf{v}_{w_1'}, \mathbf{v}_{w_2'} \rangle \tag{2}$$

where $\mathbf{v}_w$ denotes the embedding vector of word w, and $\langle \cdot, \cdot \rangle$ the dot product of two vectors.

Similarly, the translation model $p(Q|Q')$ is calculated based on the Earth Mover's Distance (EMD) [2] between the distributed representations of the query and the translation:

$$p(Q|Q') \propto \sum_{w'\in Q'} \sum_{w\in Q} \text{cost}(\mathbf{v}_w, \mathbf{v}_{w'}) \cdot \langle \mathbf{v}_w, \mathbf{v}_{w'} \rangle \tag{3}$$

where $\text{cost}(\mathbf{v}_w, \mathbf{v}_{w'})$ is the transportation cost from the target word w' to the source word w, and can be obtained by solving a linear optimization problem.

Sentence Matching. This part aims to estimate the monolingual language model $p(Q'|S')$, which evaluates the relevance of a candidate sentence w.r.t. the translation of the query.

For the task of sentence retrieval, positions of matched query words is an important factor in measuring the relevance of sentences. Thus we design a positional monolingual language model that takes matching positions into account.

Given a query translation $Q' = \{w'_1, \cdots, w'_n\}$, the monolingual language model can be estimated as:

$$p(Q'|S) = p(w'_1|S) \cdot \prod_{i=2}^{n} p(w'_i|S, \text{pos}(w'_{i-1}, S)) \qquad (4)$$

where $\text{pos}(w'_{i-1}, S)$ is the matching position of w'_{i-1} in S. $p(w'_1|S)$ is traditional unigram language model and $p(w'_i|S, \text{pos}(w'_{i-1}, S))$ is positional bigram language model, which are estimated as follows:

$$p(w'_1|S) = \text{tf}(w'_1, S)$$

$$p(w'_i|S, \text{pos}(w'_{i-1}, S)) \propto \text{tf}(w'_1, S) \cdot \exp\left(\frac{-(\text{pos}(w'_{i-1}, S) - \text{pos}(w'_i, S) - 1)^2}{2\sigma^2}\right)$$

$$\qquad (5)$$

where $\text{tf}(w', S)$ is the term frequency of the translated query word w' in S. σ is the parameter that controls the scope of rewarding.

3   Demonstration

We present the demo using an example query "数据挖掘广泛应用" (*data mining wide application*). The intent of the user is to find some example sentences that states the wide applications of data mining. Figure 2 shows the web interface of NativeHelper.

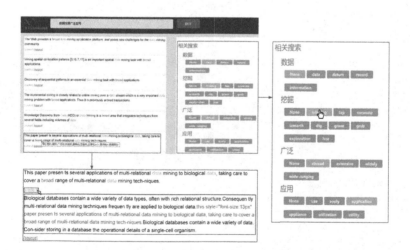

Fig. 2. The web interface of NativeHelper

The retrieved sentences are listed on the left side, with the translated query words shown in different colors. The full translation will appear as a tooltip when the mouse moves over the words. Each sentence is attached with two hyperlinks – *context* and *source*, which aims to provide users with context information and meta information about the sentence. By clicking on *context*, the user will be displayed with the paragraph of the original paper in which the sentence appears. By clicking on *source*, the user can navigate to the paper's publication page in the online academic digital library.

Apart from the sentence list, the system provides a query refinement interface on the right side. The possible translations of each query words are displayed by tags. Users can specify the translation of a query word by clicking on the corresponding tag. The search results will be updated after clicking or unclicking the translation tags.

Acknowledgement. This work is partially supported by Natural Science Foundation of China (61602278, 71704096 and 31671588).

References

1. Read, J., Dridan, R., Oepen, S., Solberg, L.J.: Sentence boundary detection: a long solved problem? In: Proceedings of CICLing, pp. 985–994 (2012)
2. Zhang, M., Liu, Y., et al.: Building earth mover's distance on bilingual word embeddings for machine translation. In: Proceedings of the 30th AAAI (2016)

PKRS: A Product Knowledge Retrieve System

Taoyi Huang[1], Yuming Lin[1(✉)], Haibo Tang[1], You Li[2], and Huibing Zhang[1]

[1] Guangxi Key Laboratory of Trusted Software, Guilin University of Electronic Technology, Guilin, China
ymlin@guet.edu.cn
[2] Guangxi Key Laboratory of Automatic Detecting Technology and Instruments, Guilin University of Electronic Technology, Guilin, China

Abstract. In this demo paper, we present the Product Knowledge Retrieve System (PKRS), which can retrieve the large-scale product knowledge efficiently. The PKRS has three features. Firstly, PKRS can retrieve not only the objective knowledge (e.g. categories) but also the subjective knowledge (e.g. users' opinion). Secondly, a learned mapping dictionary (LMD) is devised to accelerate the query parsing. Thirdly, PKRS adopts optimized join strategy to improve the retrieval effectiveness. For demonstration, we compare the performance of our PKRS with a state-of-the-art knowledge management system. The experimental results show that the PKRS can process the queries on product knowledge more effectively.

1 Introduction

Online reviews have great reference value to both product/service providers and potential customers, since they include rich users' opinion. However, it is difficult for users to retrieve the desired information due to the vast amount of reviews. One of the most effective way to tackle this problem is to extract such information from massive reviews and manage them with a structured manner like knowledge graph. Many systems have been proposed to retrieve knowledge such as SW-store [1], RDF-3x [3], Hexastore [4] and gStore [5]. The gStore is a state-of-the-art graph based knowledge retrieve system, which keeps the original structure of data and has good performance. However, gStore does not perform well in retrieving product knowledge, because both the organization of product knowledge data and queries on product knowledge have respective distinctiveness.

In this demo paper, we present a Product Knowledge Retrieve System (PKRS) for users to retrieve the product knowledge efficiently. The PKRS can retrieval the objective product category knowledge as well as the subjective users' opinion knowledge. In order to reduce the query cost, a learned mapping dictionary (LMD) is devised to convert literals to digital IDs. Moreover, we utilize an optimized join order and strategy to speed up the query execution.

© Springer Nature Switzerland AG 2019
J. Shao et al. (Eds.): APWeb-WAIM 2019, LNCS 11642, pp. 417–421, 2019.
https://doi.org/10.1007/978-3-030-26075-0_34

2   System Overview

The overall of product knowledge graph is shown in Fig. 1(a). The data is organized by RDF triples which is recommended by W3C. The objective knowledge is about categories and products, which is at the top two layers of the knowledge graph. The subjective knowledge is about the user's opinion on product aspect. Figure 1(b) shows a simple example in which Tony bought an iPhone and wrote a review on it. The review reflects that *Tony thinks the iPhone has a good size and a bright screen.*

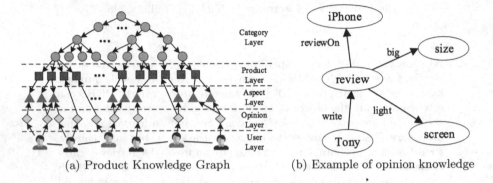

(a) Product Knowledge Graph   (b) Example of opinion knowledge

Fig. 1. Overview of the product knowledge graph

The product knowledge can be retrieved by PKRS. Figure 2 shows the architecture of PKRS, which is divided into two stage of online stage and offline stage. In the online stage, the system provides users with retrieval function. In the offline stage, the system stores and updates the product knowledge.

- **RDF Parser**. The RDF parser loads the RDF data file and decomposed it into a large collection of triples. Then we convert all literals in triples into digital IDs, because the length of literal is long and not fixed. We preserve the mapping between literal and ID through the LMD (see Fig. 3), which integrates the state-of-the-art learned index [2] to reduce the conversion cost. The first level of the LMD is shallow neural network model which is trained through the data distribution. In the second level, the data are fragmented according to the position predicted by the model in the first level and threshold value s. The data of each fragment is stored in B^+ tree separately.
- **RDF Graph Builder**. This module builds an RDF graph based on parsed triples. As the graph is directed graphs, we store the graph through adjacency list table and inverse adjacency list table. This can deal with different types of query statements.
- **Dictionary Maintenance**. This module is used to train or retrain the model in the first level of the LMD to maintain the performance. The training model takes on the order of minutes. However, when storing the knowledge graph,

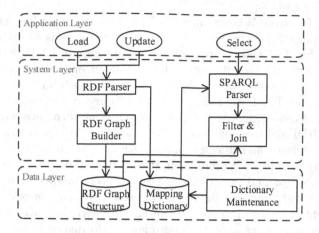

Fig. 2. The architecture of PKRS

the RDF graph builder take much more time than training, so we can train the model in parallel. Also, the knowledge graph is not real-time, and the new data can be updated in batches periodically. So, the LMD is updated infrequently. And the model in the LMD need to be retrain only when the amount of data in each fragment of the second level is unbalanced. Otherwise, the model does not need to be trained.

- **SPARQL Parser.** The SPARQL parser loads SPARQL query and generate into query statements. All literals in query statement is converted into IDs by using LMD. Then the system builds the ID-based query graph.
- **Fetcher and Join.** Firstly, each variable vertex obtains candidate set based on the adjacent vertices. Secondly, variable vertices are joined according to the structure of the query graph. We apply optimized join order and strategy when querying opinion.

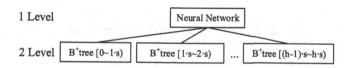

Fig. 3. The structure of learned mapping dictionary

3   Demonstration

In the demonstration part, there are two scenarios to be discussed. The PKRS runs on a machine with an Intel i5 CPU and a memory of 8 GB without GPU. We use the product knowledge graph mined from Amazon, which contains 211 million triples and 12 million literals. Literals are mainly the URI corresponding to entities such as categories, products and users.

- **SPARQL Parsing**. When a amount of queries are sent to the system, queries should be parsed quickly. We focus on converting literals to digital IDs here because it has I/O and comparison cost. We compare LMD with the traditional one with B^+ tree through a large number of random access. Table 2 shows that the LMD is more effective than the traditional one in both hot and cold cache. The LMD can reduce the I/O and comparison cost.
- **SPARQL Answering**. We compare the query performance with the state-of-the-art RDF database system - gStore. Three SPARQL queries used commonly to retrieve the subjective knowledge are shown in Table 1. The first one is used to query all opinion and aspects of the specific product. The second is used to find out which product aspects of specific user are more concerned about. And the third query is used to looking for relevant user not only bought the same product as the specific user, but also had the same preferences in product aspects. The query performance is show in Table 3, our system has good performance on the queries. With the increase of query complexity, query performance improvement is more obvious, since the join strategy reduces the intermediate result set and avoid the I/O cost greatly.

Table 1. SPARQL query samples

Q1	SELECT ?f ?o WHERE {?r rdf:type Review. ?r reviewOn P1. ?r ?o ?f.}
Q2	SELECT ?f (count(?o) AS ?count) WHERE {?p rdf:type Product. ?p productOf C1. ?r rdf:type Review. ?r reviewOn P1. ?r ?o ?f.} GROUP BY ?f
Q3	SELECT ?u ?f ?o WHERE {?r1 rdf:type Review. U1 write ?r1. ?p rdf:type Product. ?r1 reviewOn ?p. ?f rdf:type Aspect. ?r1 ?o ?f. ?u rdf:type User. ?r2 rdf:type Review. ?u write ?2. ?r2 reviewOn ?p. ?r2 ?o ?f.}

Table 2. LMD vs B^+Tree(Cost per Access)

Random access times	Cold cache (μs)		Hot cache (μs)	
	LMD	B^+Tree	LMD	B^+Tree
1K	60.42	98.83	6.51	7.09
10K	45.12	64.82	3.31	4.04
100K	27.99	43.68	3.03	3.75
1M	10.23	10.97	2.99	3.73

Table 3. Performance of query samples

Query	PKRS	gStore
Q1	269 ms	913 ms
Q2	2290 ms	>30 min
Q3	2389 ms	>30 min

Acknowledgment. The work is supported by National Natural Science Foundation of China (61562014, U1711263), the Project of Guangxi Natural Science Foundation (2018GXNSFDA281049), the Research Project of Guangxi Key Laboratory of Trusted Software (KX201916), the Innovation Project of GUET Graduate Education (2018YJCX48).

References

1. Abadi, D.J., Marcus, A., Madden, S., Hollenbach, K.: SW-Store: a vertically partitioned DBMS for semantic web data management. VLDB J. **18**(2), 385–406 (2009)
2. Kraska, T., Beutel, A., Chi, E.H., Dean, J., Polyzotis, N.: The case for learned index structures. In: SIGMOD 2018, pp. 489–504. ACM (2018)
3. Neumann, T., Weikum, G.: RDF-3X: a risc-style engine for RDF. PVLDB **1**(1), 647–659 (2008)
4. Weiss, C., Karras, P., Bernstein, A.: Hexastore: sextuple indexing for semantic web data management. PVLDB **1**(1), 1008–1019 (2008)
5. Zou, L., Özsu, M.T., Chen, L., Shen, X., Huang, R., Zhao, D.: gStore: a graph-based SPARQL query engine. VLDB J. **23**(4), 565–590 (2014)

DataSESec: Security Monitoring for Data Share and Exchange Platform

Guowei Shen[1,2,3]($\boxtimes$), Lu Liu[1,2]($\boxtimes$), Qin Wei[1]($\boxtimes$), Jicheng Lei[3]($\boxtimes$),
and Chun Guo[1,2]($\boxtimes$)

[1] College of Computer Science and Technology, Guizhou University,
Guiyang 550025, China
{gwshen,qwei}@gzu.edu.cn
[2] Guizhou Provincial Key Laboratory of Public Big Data, Guiyang 550025, China
gzuliulu@163.com, gc_gzedu@163.com
[3] CETC Big Data Research Institute Co. Ltd., Chengdu, China
leijicheng@cetcbigdata.com

Abstract. Data share and exchange platform is an infrastructure of data open and share. How to ensure the security of government data in the exchange and sharing platform is a key problem. To solve this problem, we developed a security monitoring system for data share and exchange platform - DataSESec. A multi-layer graph model is provided to realize multi-source heterogeneous security monitoring metadata organization, data tracking and forensics, and multi-dimensional security monitoring data analysis. The system extracts network traffic data without authorization, which can achieve early security warning. The deployment of the security monitoring system is very flexible, the interface that interacts with the existing platform is very flexible, and the impact on the existing data share and exchange platform is very small.

Keywords: Data share and exchange · Security monitoring ·
Data provenance

1 Introduction

Government data share and exchange platform supports cross-level, cross-regional, cross-system, cross-department, and cross-business data share and business collaboration, it is the basic interconnection platform for government data share and exchange.

Government data resource catalogue is the basis for the realization of government data resource share, business collaboration and data openness, it is also the basis for sharing data between government departments and the opening of government affairs data to the society. Government data resource metadata refers to the description of data, including: identifier, data class number, data class name, data type, presentation format, value range, providing department code, providing department name, providing department abbreviation, share class type, open

© Springer Nature Switzerland AG 2019
J. Shao et al. (Eds.): APWeb-WAIM 2019, LNCS 11642, pp. 422–427, 2019.
https://doi.org/10.1007/978-3-030-26075-0_35

type, delivery method, and remarks. In the government data resource catalogs, data can be classified into three types according to the type of data share, i.e., unconditional share data, conditional share data and non-share data.

Regarding to government data exchange share platform, the core security issues include: (1) whether the user exchanges or shares data according to the share and exchange regulation. (2) how to track data lineage [1,2] when data is exchanged or shared in platform. Therefore, how to effectively and safely monitor the data share and exchange platform is a key issue to ensure government data security during government data share and exchange platform.

To solve the above problems, a government data share and exchange security monitoring system – DataSESec based on open source implementations was provided. DataSESec have three major functions:

1. Without requiring authorization from data share and exchange platform, this monitoring system is able to collect monitoring metadata efficiently and passively, at the same time, have no effect the online services of sharing and exchanging government data.
2. A multi-layer model is provided to organize multi-source heterogeneous monitoring metadata, which supports multi-dimensional monitoring metadata analysis.
3. The security monitoring platform is very adaptable and does not require modification to the deployment of the online share and exchange platform.

2   System Overview

DataSESec adopts a hierarchical system architecture. The design of DataSESec is shown in Fig. 1. In this system, multisource heterogeneous data are efficiently collected and integrated during the integration layer. The analysis layer is the core layer of the system, mainly to achieve the goal of monitoring and analysing the security monitoring data. The application layer mainly implements business logic and visualization, the results are displayed in the web.

Data Source. The data processed by the system mainly includes three types: network traffic, data share and exchange system logs, and data resource catalogue. Network traffic refers to network mirror data generated by the shared switching platform. Data resource catalogue contains share class type, open type, and delivery method. The data must be shared or exchanged according to open type, sharing type, and delivery method in the data resource catalogue [3].

Integration Layer. Multi-source data integration primarily implement Kafka-based integration for the data from different sources. The main integrated message sources include: (1) Share or exchange logs generated by the share and exchange platform are pulled from FTP; (2) Unauthorized passively obtain the user behaviors and data contents extracted from the network traffic, and receiving data through the Socket interface; (3) The resource catalogue is pushed by the HTTP API, which is updated real time in DataSESec. How can integrate the

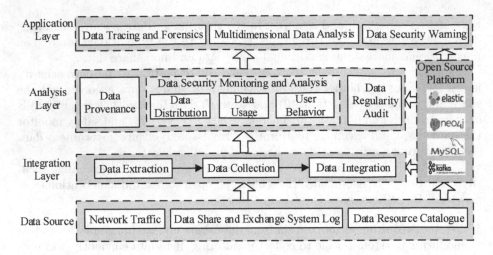

Fig. 1. System architecture.

data with other datasets? The platform is inspired by Data Lakes in realizing data fusion between multi-source security monitoring metadata [4]. Multi-source data enters data into Kafka cluster through multiple themes of Kafka cluster and consumes data of Kafka cluster into ElasticSearch database at the back end of the system. Kafka message transmission system can effectively analyze the back end and front end of the system and keep the internal interface of the system relatively simple.

Analysis Layer. At the analysis level, driven by the security monitoring metadata model, data provenance, security monitoring analysis and data regularity audit are implemented. The data of the system is stored in MySQL database, Neo4j, and ElasticSearch. In the exchange and share platform, the record information of the whole life cycle can be tracked and forensic. Data regularity audit performs regularity check based on metadata such as open type, shared type, and delivery protocol in the data resource catalogue, and generates early warnings and alarms.

Application Layer. The application layer implements functions such as data tracking and forensics, multi-dimensional statistical analysis, and data security alarms through Rest APIs.

2.1   Multilevel Graph Data Model

A multilevel graph data model shown in Fig. 2 is provided to organize the multi-source heterogeneous security monitoring metadata. The model contains three layers: data lineage graph, data version graph, data exchange and share model graph. The data lineage graph records the data flow spanning across the departments or regions in the government data share and exchange platform.

The data version graph records the version changes of the data. The data share and exchange model graph records protocols or tools used for data exchange or share. In this paper, HTTP and FTP protocols are considered in the platform.

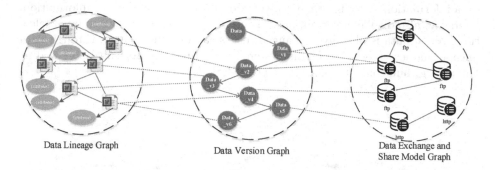

Data Lineage Graph   Data Version Graph   Data Exchange and
Share Model Graph

Fig. 2. A multilevel graph data model for organizing the multi-source heterogenous security monitoring metadata.

3 Demonstration Overview

We demonstrate a fully operational implementation of DataSESec through its web-based user interface. The demo is targeted for Data Share and Exchange Platform manager, they are interested in real-time data security risk warning or alarm and querying data provenance graphs.

The user interface of DataSESec is shown in Fig. 3. Users can know warning and alarm information, and as well as security statistical analysis results in

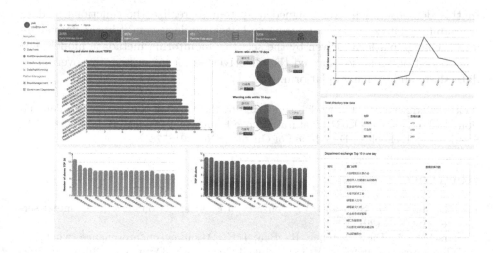

Fig. 3. The user interface of DataSESec.

real time through the web interface. Moreover, users can also perform query and interaction operations for specific warnings and alarms according to the interface.

An example showing data lineage query result is given in Fig. 4. Users can query historical lineage changes of the data object, including the change of metadata information, basic information, version information, and usage information. Users can also display a certain part of the information according to label selection. When data is illegally exchanged, users can obtain forensics through data lineage queries. The demo of the system's core functionality can be viewed at "https://github.com/DearDeer4869/DataSESec".

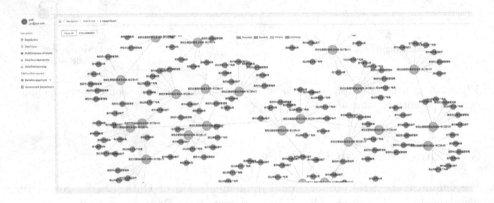

Fig. 4. An example showing data lineage query result.

4   Conclusions

In this demonstration, we designed a system to realize the functions of data traceability, data security monitoring and data regularity audit in the data share and exchange platform driven by the security monitoring metadata model. The demonstration scenarios showed the effectiveness of our system in government data share and exchange platform.

Acknowledgement. The work is supported by the National Natural Science Foundation of China (No. 61802081), Natural Science Foundation of Guizhou (No. 20161052), Science and Technology Foundation of Guizhou (No. 20185781).

References

1. Hellerstein, J.M., Sreekanti, V., Gonzalez, J.E., et al.: Ground: a data context service. In: CIDR (2017)
2. Herschel, M., Diestelkämper, R., Ben, L.H.: A survey on provenance: what for? What form? What from? VLDB J.-Int. J. Very Large Data Bases **26**(6), 881–906 (2017)

3. DB 52/T 1123–2016, Guizhou bureau of quality and technical supervision. Governmental Data Guidelines for Categorization and Classification of Data (2016)
4. Quix, C.: Data lakes: a solution or a new challenge for big data integration? In: DATA, p. 7 (2016)

Author Index

Ai, Jiangbo II-236

Bai, Wen I-255
Bai, Xu II-322
Bin, Yi II-42

Chai, Lele I-398
Chen, Chanjuan II-322
Chen, Hong II-103
Chen, Jianzong II-121
Chen, Liangjian II-407
Chen, Qian I-207
Chen, Runyuan I-255
Chen, Si II-12, II-42, II-236
Chen, Siyu II-407
Chen, Wei II-111, II-337
Chen, Xiansheng II-111
Chen, Xiaojun II-310
Chen, Yadi I-255
Chen, Yijun II-260
Chen, Zhigang I-45, I-329
Cheng, Lin I-19
Cheng, Yijian II-207
Chi, Renjun I-314
Conway, Michael I-196
Cui, Bin II-27
Cui, Hengbin II-310
Cui, Tongtong II-402
Cui, Yingbao II-337

Dan, Tangpeng II-251
Ding, Pengjie II-207
Du, Jiabing II-88
Du, Xiaoyong II-163, II-207
Duan, Xi II-276
Duan, Yijun II-349

Fu, Xiyao II-42

Gao, Guanglai I-345
Gao, Hong II-175
Ge, Liang I-171

Ge, Qi II-397
Gharibshah, Zhabiz I-196
Gu, Yu I-273
Guan, Yongming I-35
Gui, Fei I-110
Guo, Chun II-422
Guo, Shengnan II-407
Guo, Wenya II-365
Guo, Yudi II-260

Hainline, Arthur I-196
Han, Kai I-110
Han, Yanbo II-402
He, Fuzhen I-329
He, Jun II-163
He, Linzi I-365
Hu, Bing II-268
Hu, Gang II-152
Hu, Linmei I-95, I-314
Hu, Nan I-141
Huang, Hao II-207
Huang, Jiaxiang II-260
Huang, Taoyi II-417
Huang, Zhichuan I-255

Iwaihara, Mizuho I-299

Jatowt, Adam II-349
Jiang, Jiawei II-27
Jiang, Lei II-322

Lei, Jicheng II-422
Li, Cuiping II-103
Li, Guohui II-251
Li, Hang I-171
Li, Hanlu II-121
Li, Hongyan I-240
Li, Jianzhong I-61, II-175
Li, Junhao I-299
Li, Lin II-3, II-121
Li, Maolong I-329
Li, Mingdao I-223

Li, Qiang II-337
Li, Xiaokun I-264
Li, Yanhong II-251
Li, You II-417
Li, Yuming II-191
Li, Zhixu I-45, I-329
Lin, Haoyang II-152
Lin, Yuming II-417
Liu, An I-45
Liu, Baozhu I-398
Liu, Hongyan II-163
Liu, Jiamou I-207
Liu, Junling I-171
Liu, Lu II-422
Liu, Tong I-187, II-412
Liu, Yifei I-3, I-289
Liu, Yifeng I-382
Liu, Yong I-264
Liu, Yongjian II-121
Liu, Yongnan I-61
Liu, Yu I-3, I-289
Liu, Yuecan I-35
Liu, Zitu I-264
Lu, Wei II-207
Luo, Changyin II-251
Luo, Huanrui II-137
Luo, Jizhou II-175
Luo, Ningqi II-310
Luo, Xiangyang II-380

Ma, Xiao II-73
Ma, Zeyu II-12
Mei, Lang II-163
Mo, Songsong I-125

Na, Cai II-12
Ni, Weijian I-187, II-412

Pan, Yinxu II-310
Peng, Peng I-223, II-397
Peng, Zhiyong I-125

Qiang, Yang I-45
Qiao, Baiyou II-268
Qiao, Xiyu II-268
Qin, Zheng I-223, II-397
Qiu, Zhen II-337

Ran, Xiangying II-380
Ren, Yongjian I-19, I-156

Shan, Shuangli I-45
Shao, Yingxia II-27
Shen, Guowei II-422
Shen, Yanyan II-57
Sheng, Yongpan I-414
Shi, Chuan I-95
Shi, Shengfei II-175
Shi, Yuliang I-19, I-35, I-156
Song, Binheng II-310
Song, Jingkuan I-3
Song, Lingyun II-12
Song, Pingping I-110
Song, Zhen I-273
Su, Hongyi I-207
Sun, Jiayu II-152
Sun, Wei II-380
Sun, Yongyue I-240
Sun, Yujian II-412

Tanaka, Katsumi II-349
Tang, Haibo II-417
Tang, Yong II-88
Tian, Shan I-125
Tong, Peihao I-365

Wan, Xiaojun I-141
Wang, Chongjun II-380
Wang, Guiling II-402
Wang, Jun II-219
Wang, Liping II-276
Wang, Liwei I-125
Wang, Qingyun I-240
Wang, Siyuan II-295
Wang, Tengjiao II-111, II-337
Wang, Xiaochen II-152
Wang, Xin I-398
Wang, Yangtao I-3, I-289, II-73
Wang, Yashen I-382
Wang, Zheng II-12, II-42, II-236
Wang, Zihao I-77
Wei, Jinmao II-219
Wei, Qin II-42, II-236, II-422
Wu, Bin I-314
Wu, Di I-255

Wu, Gang   II-268
Wu, Peizhi   II-219
Wu, Yi   II-137

Xia, Hao   I-223
Xiao, Ding   I-95
Xiao, Zhili   I-3, I-289, II-73
Xie, Haiyong   I-382
Xie, Nengfu   I-187, II-412
Xie, Qing   II-3, II-121
Xie, Shengnan   I-264
Xing, Chunxiao   I-77
Xiu, Yeliang   II-103
Xu, Chaoting   I-110
Xu, Hengpeng   II-219
Xu, Jiajie   I-45
Xu, Jianqiu   II-407
Xu, Jingxin   I-110
Xu, Liang   I-365
Xu, Longlong   II-111
Xu, Xiaodong   I-289, II-73
Xu, Yang   I-223
Xu, Yao   II-402
Xu, Yue   II-111
Xu, Yunlai   II-380
Xu, Zenglin   I-414
Xu, Zhenhui   II-337
Xu, Zhiwei   II-397
Xue, Huanran   II-27

Yan, Bo   I-207
Yan, Rong   I-345
Yang, Ming   II-73
Yang, Ning   I-281, II-137
Yang, Qiang   I-329
Yang, Shiyu   II-276
Yang, Yajun   I-398
Yang, Yang   II-12
Yang, Yue   II-407
Yang, Yujuan   I-3, I-289
Yang, Zhenglu   II-219
Yao, Junjie   I-365, II-260
Yao, Laigang   II-268
Yao, Lan   II-295
Yao, Shuo   I-273
Ye, Guoqiao   I-255
Yu, Ge   I-273, II-295

Yu, Kaiqiang   I-273
Yu, Philip S.   I-281
Yuan, Xiaojie   II-365

Zeng, Jiangfeng   I-289, II-73
Zeng, Qingtian   I-187, II-412
Zhang, Chunxi   II-191
Zhang, Huanhuan   I-382
Zhang, Huibing   II-417
Zhang, Jianwei   II-3
Zhang, Kun   I-19, I-35, I-156
Zhang, Ping   I-125
Zhang, Rong   II-191
Zhang, Tao   II-175
Zhang, Wang   II-322
Zhang, Wei   II-175
Zhang, Xiaolei   II-191
Zhang, Ying   II-365
Zhang, Yong   I-77
Zhang, Yunlei   I-314
Zhang, Zhaokun   I-281
Zhao, He   I-207
Zhao, Jianan   I-95
Zhao, Lei   I-329
Zhao, Pengpeng   I-329
Zhao, Suyun   II-103
Zhao, Xue   II-365
Zhao, Zhibin   II-295
Zhen, Shuai   I-35
Zheng, Bolong   II-251
Zheng, Hong   I-207
Zheng, Yunpei   II-3
Zheng, Zetao   II-88
Zhong, Luo   II-3
Zhou, Aoli   I-171
Zhou, Aoying   II-191
Zhou, Jianyun   I-141
Zhou, Jie   II-236
Zhou, Ke   I-3, I-289, II-73
Zhou, Xian   II-57
Zhou, Zening   II-175
Zhu, Haozhe   II-57
Zhu, Jia   II-88
Zhu, Junhai   II-268
Zhu, Xingquan   I-196
Zou, Lei   II-397
Zuo, Xiaojiang   II-402

Printed in the United States
By Bookmasters

Printed in the United States
By Bookmasters